159174

Dennis & Sarah Bao

The Journey
from Texts
to Translations

In both the domains of nature and faith,
you will find the most excellent
things are the deepest
hidden.

Erasmus, *The Sages*, 1515
Erasmus of Rotterdam (c. 1466–1536)

Abraham Lincoln: "I believe the Bible is the best gift God has ever given to man. All the good from the Savior of the world is communicated to us through this book."

The Journey from Texts to Translations

The Origin and Development of the Bible

Paul D. Wegner

Baker Academic
A Division of Baker Book House Co
Grand Rapids, Michigan 49516

©1999 by Paul D. Wegner

Published by Baker Academic,
an imprint of Baker Books
a division of Baker Book House Company
P.O. Box 6287, Grand Rapids, Michigan 49516-6287

Corrected printing, December 2000

Printed in the United States of America

Library of Congress Cataloging-in-Publication Data
Wegner, Paul D.
    The journey from texts to translations : the origin and development of the Bible /
Paul D. Wegner.
        p.   cm.
    "A BridgePoint book."
    Includes bibliographical references and indexes.
    ISBN 0-8010-2169-3
    1. Bible—History. 2. Bible. English—Versions—History. I. Title.
BS445.W38   1999
220'.09—dc21
                                                          99-11224

For information about academic books, resources for Christian leaders, and all new releases available from Baker Book House, visit our web site:
                     http://www.bakerbooks.com

To my wife, Cathy, and my boys, Matthew and Scott

Contents ································

Illustrations

Figures

Maps ▲▲▲▲▲▲▲▲▲▲▲▲▲▲▲▲▲▲▲▲▲▲▲▲▲

Tables ▪▪▪▪▪▪▪▪▪▪▪▪▪▪▪▪▪▪▪▪▪▪▪▪▪

Preface ....

The Bible is a fascinating book that continues to have relevance in a world that is constantly changing, even though it was written millennia ago. The Bible encompasses the whole of history, from the beginning of creation (Gen. 1–2) to the destruction of the world and the creation of a new heaven and earth (Rev. 21–22). It claims to be the very Word of God (Jer. 1:1–2; Hos. 1:1; 2 Tim. 3:16), written so that we can know what God expects from us. And yet many people have little understanding of even the rudiments of the Bible, such as where it came from or the differences between various Bible versions.

How does the Bible differ from other ancient Near Eastern literature? How were the books of the Bible recognized as authoritative and by whom? Why do Jews consider only the Old Testament as authoritative whereas Christians hold that both Old and New Testaments are? Why do some religious traditions believe that the Apocrypha is part of Scripture while others do not? How accurate is the Bible, and how do present translations compare with the oldest manuscripts of the Bible? What are the differences between modern-day translations? These are just some of the important questions that we will investigate.

The purpose of this book is to provide a general survey of how the Bible we use came to be in its present form, but it will not delve into the authorship, dating, and purpose of individual books. The latter topics are discussed in general introductions to the Old[1] and New[2] Testaments. The discussions in this book are directed primarily toward the undergraduate student or layperson, but bibliographies and footnotes for more advanced research are also included, as well as brief summaries of scholarly debates in various areas.

Recently there have been several major attacks upon the truthfulness and accuracy of our modern translations, many of which would probably never have been given a hearing if the origin and translation principles of various translations were more generally known. This work will enable those in the church to determine the validity of charges leveled against modern versions, as well as to instill an appreciation of the difficulties of producing new translations of the Bible.

The book is divided into five parts. Part 1 looks at such introductory issues as what the Bible is and how it is arranged. Part 2 describes the canonization of the Bible, or how the books came to form one book called the Bible. Part 3 examines the transmission of the text—how the Bible has been passed on from generation to generation. Part 4 introduces the reader to early Bible versions, particularly how and why they were produced. Part 5 discusses English translations, including a history of the English Bible, differences between modern translations, and principles to help the reader choose a Bible translation.

This book is dedicated to my invaluable wife, Cathy, and my enthusiastic boys, Matthew and Scott, all of whom have enriched my life greatly. A special thanks also goes to the Trustees of the Moody Bible Institute for allowing me to have a sabbatical leave to work on this book, to Trinity International University for allowing the use of accommodations in England, to Tyndale House, Cambridge, which provided an excellent atmosphere to pursue my studies, and to Scott Karow and Rebekah Smith for helping prepare some of the illustrations.

It is my hope that this work will help create a strong desire in the hearts of its readers to know more about this wonderful book and the God who inspired it.

Abbreviations ....

Biblical Books ....

Old Testament

Gen.	Genesis
Exod.	Exodus
Lev.	Leviticus
Num.	Numbers
Deut.	Deuteronomy
Josh.	Joshua
Judg.	Judges
Ruth	Ruth
1–2 Sam.	1–2 Samuel
1–2 Kings	1–2 Kings
1–2 Chron.	1–2 Chronicles
Ezra	Ezra
Neh.	Nehemiah
Est.	Esther
Job	Job
Ps.	Psalms
Prov.	Proverbs
Eccles.	Ecclesiastes
Song	Song of Songs
Isa.	Isaiah
Jer.	Jeremiah
Lam.	Lamentations
Ezek.	Ezekiel
Dan.	Daniel
Hos.	Hosea
Joel	Joel
Amos	Amos
Obad.	Obadiah
Jon.	Jonah
Mic.	Micah
Nah.	Nahum
Hab.	Habakkuk
Zeph.	Zephaniah
Hag.	Haggai
Zech.	Zechariah
Mal.	Malachi

New Testament

Matt.	Matthew
Mark	Mark
Luke	Luke
John	John
Acts	Acts
Rom.	Romans
1–2 Cor.	1–2 Corinthians
Gal.	Galatians
Eph.	Ephesians
Phil.	Philippians
Col.	Colossians
1–2 Thess.	1–2 Thessalonians
1–2 Tim.	1–2 Timothy
Titus	Titus
Philem.	Philemon
Heb.	Hebrews
James	James
1–2 Pet.	1–2 Peter
1–3 John	1–3 John
Jude	Jude
Rev.	Revelation

Old Testament Apocrypha

Bar.	Baruch
1 Esd.	1 Esdras
2 Esd.	2 Esdras
Est. Add.	Esther Additions
Jth.	Judith
1 Macc.	1 Maccabees
2 Macc.	2 Maccabees
Pr. of Man.	Prayer of Manasseh
Sir.	Sirach/Ecclesiasticus
Sus.	Susanna
Tob.	Tobit
Wis. of Sol.	Wisdom of Solomon

General Abbreviations ▲▲▲

א	Codex Sinaiticus
A	Codex Alexandrinus
AB	Anchor Bible
ABD '	*Anchor Bible Dictionary*, ed. D. N. Freedman et al., 6 vols. (New York: Doubleday, 1992)
Abr.	Philo, *De Abrahamo* (*On the Life of Abraham*)
ABRL	Anchor Bible Reference Library
ACW	Ancient Christian Writers
add.	additional manuscripts
ANET	*Ancient Near Eastern Texts Relating to the Old Testament*, ed. J. B. Pritchard, 3d ed. with suppl. (Princeton: Princeton University Press, 1969)
Ant.	Josephus, *Antiquitates judaicae* (*Jewish Antiquities*)
AOS	American Oriental Series
ASV	American Standard Version
AV	Authorized Version
B	Codex Vaticanus
BA	*Biblical Archaeologist*
BANE	*The Bible and the Ancient Near East*, ed. G. E. Wright (Garden City, NY: Doubleday, 1961; repr. Winona Lake, IN: Eisenbrauns, 1979)
BAR	*Biblical Archaeology Review*
BASOR	*Bulletin of the American Schools of Oriental Research*
BETL	Bibliotheca ephemeridum theologicarum lovaniensium
BHS	*Biblia Hebraica Stuttgartensia*, ed. K. Elliger and W. Rudolph (Stuttgart: Deutsche Bibelstiftung, 1977)
Bib	*Biblica*
B.J.	Josephus, *Bellum judaicum* (*Jewish War*)
BJRL	*Bulletin of the John Rylands University Library of Manchester*
B.M.	British Museum
BST	Bible Study Today
BT	*The Bible Translator*
C	Codex Ephraemi Rescriptus
c.	*circa*, about
CAP	A. E. Cowley, *Aramaic Papyri of the Fifth Century* B.C. (Oxford: Clarendon, 1923)
CD	Cairo Genizah copy of the *Damascus Document*
CHB	*Cambridge History of the Bible*, ed. P. R. Ackroyd, C. F. Evans, G. W. H. Lampe, and S. L. Greenslade, 3 vols. (Cambridge: Cambridge University Press, 1963–70)
1 Clem.	*1 Clement*
cod.	codex
Comm. Matt.	Origen, *Commentarium in evangelium Matthaei* (*Commentary on Matthew* = *Scholia in Matthaeum*, Patrologiae cursus completus: Series graeca, ed. J.-P. Migne, 162 vols. [Paris, 1857–86], 17:290–310)
Congr.	Philo, *De congressu eruditionis gratia* (*On the Preliminary Studies*)
Contempl.	Philo, *De vita contemplativa* (*On the Contemplative Life*)
CRINT	Compendia rerum iudaicarum ad Novum Testamentum
D	Codex Bezae Cantabrigiensis
Decal.	Philo, *De decalogo* (*On the Decalogue*)
Dem. ev.	Eusebius, *Demonstratio evangelica* (*Demonstration of the Gospel*)

Det.	Philo, *Quod deterius potiori insidiari soleat* (*That the Worse Attacks the Better*)
Dial.	Justin Martyr, *Dialogus cum Tryphone* (*Dialogue with Trypho*)
DSS	Dead Sea Scrolls
EncBrit	*Encyclopaedia Britannica,* 24 vols. (London, 1945)
EncJud	*Encyclopaedia Judaica,* 16 vols. (Jerusalem, 1972)
ERV	Revised Version (English)
esp.	especially
ET	English translation
Exc. Ps.	Origen, *Excerpta in Psalmos,* Patrologiae cursus completus: Series graeca, ed. J.-P. Migne, 162 vols. (Paris, 1857–86), 17:106–50
fig(s).	figure(s)
GBS	Guides to Biblical Scholarship
Gk.	Greek
GNB	Good News Bible
GPT	Growing Points in Theology
Haer.	Irenaeus, *Adversus haereses* (*Against Heresies*)
Ḥag.	*Ḥagigah*
HE	*Historia ecclesiastica* (*Ecclesiastical History*)
Ḥev.	Naḥal Ḥever texts
Hom. Jer.	Origen, *Homiliae in Jeremiam*
HTR	*Harvard Theological Review*
HTS	Harvard Theological Studies
HUCA	*Hebrew Union College Annual*
IBD	*Illustrated Bible Dictionary,* ed. J. D. Douglas and N. Hillyer, 3 vols. (Leicester, England: Inter-Varsity; Wheaton, IL: Tyndale, 1980)
ICC	International Critical Commentary
IDBSup	*Interpreter's Dictionary of the Bible,* suppl. vol, ed. K. Crim et al. (Nashville: Abingdon, 1976)
IEJ	*Israel Exploration Journal*
Int	*Interpretation*
ISBE	*International Standard Bible Encyclopedia,* ed. G. W. Bromiley et al., rev. ed., 4 vols. (Grand Rapids: Eerdmans, 1979–88)
JAOS	*Journal of the American Oriental Society*
JB	Jerusalem Bible
JBL	*Journal of Biblical Literature*
JEA	*Journal of Egyptian Archaeology*
JETS	*Journal of the Evangelical Theological Society*
JNSL	*Journal of Northwest Semitic Languages*
JSNT	*Journal for the Study of the New Testament*
JSNTSup	Journal for the Study of the New Testament: Supplement Series
JSOT	*Journal for the Study of the Old Testament*
JSS	*Journal of Semitic Studies*
JTS	*Journal of Theological Studies*
KJII	King James II Version
KJV	King James Version
LB	Living Bible
LCL	Loeb Classical Library
lit.	literal, literally
LXX	Septuagint
M.	Midrash
Mas.	Masada texts
Meg.	*Megillah*
Message	E. H. Peterson, *The Message: The New Testament in Contemporary Language* (Colorado Springs: NavPress, 1993)

MS(S)	manuscript(s)
MT	Masoretic text of the Old Testament
Mur.	Murabbaʿat texts
NA	Nestle-Aland Greek New Testament (*Novum Testamentum Graece*)
NAC	New American Commentary
NASB	New American Standard Bible
NCB	New Century Bible
NCBC	New Century Bible Commentary
NEB	New English Bible
NHC	Nag Hammadi Codices
NIBCOT	New International Biblical Commentary on the Old Testament
NICNT	New International Commentary on the New Testament
NICOT	New International Commentary on the Old Testament
NIDCC	*New International Dictionary of the Christian Church*, ed. J. D. Douglas et al. (Exeter: Paternoster; Grand Rapids: Zondervan, 1974)
NIV	New International Version
NIVAC	New International Version Application Commentary
NKJV	New King James Version
NLT	New Living Translation
NRSV	New Revised Standard Version
n.s.	new series
NT	New Testament
NTC	New Testament Commentary
NTL	New Testament Library
NWT	New World Translation of the Holy Scriptures
OBS	Oxford Bible Studies
OBT	Overtures to Biblical Theology
Or.	Origen, *De oratione* (*On Prayer*)
OT	Old Testament
OTG	Old Testament Guides
OTL	Old Testament Library
OTS	Old Testament Studies
Pap. Nash	Nash Papyrus
PG	Patrologiae cursus completus: Series graeca, ed. J.-P. Migne, 162 vols. (Paris, 1857–86)
p(p).	page(s)
Praem.	Philo, *De praemiis et poenis* (*On Rewards and Punishments*)
Praep. ev.	Eusebius, *Praeparatio evangelica* (*Preparation for the Gospel*)
Q	Hypothetical source document of the Gospels
QHBT	*Qumran and the History of the Biblical Text*, ed. F. M. Cross and S. Talmon (Cambridge, MA: Harvard University Press, 1975)
Qidd.	*Qiddušin*
1QS	*Serek Hayyaḥad*, Rule of the Community (Manual of Discipline)
REB	Revised English Bible
RSV	Revised Standard Version
RV	Revised Version
Šabb.	*Šabbat*
Sanh.	*Sanhedrin*
SBAW	Sitzungsberichte der bayerischen Akademie der Wissenschaften
SBL	Society of Biblical Literature
SBLMasS	Society of Biblical Literature Masoretic Studies
SBT	Studies in Biblical Theology

Somn.	Philo, *De somniis* (*On Dreams*)
SP	Samaritan Pentateuch
SPB	Studia post-biblica
Spec.	Philo, *De specialibus legibus* (*On the Special Laws*)
T.B.	Babylonian Talmud
TNTC	Tyndale New Testament Commentaries
Tos.	Tosefta
T.P.	Palestinian Talmud
TWOT	*Theological Wordbook of the Old Testament*, ed. R. L. Harris, G. L. Archer Jr., and B. K. Waltke (Chicago: Moody, 1980)
TynBul	*Tyndale Bulletin*
UBS	United Bible Societies
VK	Van Kampen Collection, The Scriptorium, Grand Haven, MI
vol(s).	volume(s)
VT	*Vetus Testamentum*
VTSup	Vetus Testamentum Supplements
Vulg.	Vulgate
WBC	Word Biblical Commentary
ZAW	*Zeitschrift für die alttestamentliche Wissenschaft*

The Bible as the Word of God

In spite of its age the Bible remains the most popular and widely read book in the world with more than one hundred million new copies, in whole or in part, produced every year.[1] John Hayes of Emory University, Candler School of Theology, underscores its significance:

> The influence of the Bible permeates almost every aspect of life in the twentieth-century Western world—laws, literature, art, music, architecture, morals, and of course religion. Many of the Bible's words and phrases are a part of our current speech, and allusions to its stories are widely understood. It is a vital part of our total cultural heritage; indeed, many people would claim that it is, for a variety of reasons, the most important and influential collection of writings ever brought together and bound in a single volume. The Bible is a perennial best seller and has been translated into more than a thousand different languages and dialects.[2]

Importance of the Bible

Why has the Bible retained its relevance to people from the time it was first written until today? And why throughout history have people been willing to risk their lives to obtain a copy of the Bible or to translate it into their own language? On October 6, 1536, William Tyndale was burned at the stake because he dared to translate the Bible into English so that the common person could read it. As John Foxe records:

> At last after much reasoning, when no reason would serve, although he de-

served no death, he was condemned by virtue of the Emperor's decree made in the Assembly at Ausbrough, and upon the same brought forth to the place of execution, was tied to the stake, and then strangled first by the hangman, and afterwards consumed by fire, in the morning at the town of Filford, an. 1536; crying at the stake with a fervent zeal and a loud voice, "Lord, open the King of England's eyes."[3]

Figure 1.1. The martyrdom of William Tyndale, as depicted in an antique woodcut. (John Foxe, *Actes and Monuments of the Christian Faith* [London: Peter Short, 1596]). [Grand Haven, Mich., The Scriptorium, VK 772, p. 985]

Why would people like Tyndale and others translate the Scriptures even at the cost of their lives? Or why would generations of Hebrew scribes meticulously copy the Old Testament Scriptures, repeatedly checking their work letter by letter, even counting the letters to ensure their accuracy? The answer lies in the belief that the Bible is the very Word of God, thus necessitating its accurate transmission and its availability to people of any language.

But why is the Bible considered to be the Word of God? Early Jews believed that the Old Testament had been given to them directly from God as a faithful witness of the nation's past and the hope of a glorious future. Many early Christians were Jewish, and therefore Old Testament Scriptures were already sacred to them. Yet they also held the teachings of Christ to be authoritative, a dilemma described well by H. G. Wood:

> Their national sacred writings were to them the oracles of God, though they could no longer be regarded as containing the whole truth of God. The coming of the Messiah had revealed God with a completeness that could not be discovered in the Old Testament. The word of the Lord was authoritative as even Moses and the prophets were not. Yet since all the hopes of the Old Testament seemed to these Jewish Christians to be fulfilled in Jesus Christ, they more than ever were convinced that their national sacred books were divinely inspired. From this source they drew, if not the articles of their creed, at least the proofs and supports of their doctrines. Christ died and rose again, according to the scriptures. All the writings of the Old Testament spoke of Christ to them.[4]

Thus from the beginning early Christians viewed the Old Testament as their sacred Scriptures and the books of the New Testament as the fulfillment of them, thereby taking on the same authority (2 Pet. 3:15–16). The intrinsic unity of the two Testaments is reflected in the maxim of Augustine, a church father from the fourth century: "The New Testament lies hidden in the Old, and the Old Testament is manifest in the New."[5]

It is understandable that early Christians viewed the Scriptures as divinely inspired, but the Gentile world was also strangely attracted to this amazing book, as Wood further notes:

> It is more remarkable that the Old Testament in its Greek dress appealed to the Gentile world and became a valued weapon in the armoury of the Christian evangelist. It was not on account of any literary charm of the Greek version. Educated readers were offended by the poor

style of the Septuagint. But a passage from Tatian, a second century Apologist, may serve to show how this very poverty of style sometimes proved arresting. "When I was giving my most earnest attention to discover the truth, I happened to meet with certain barbaric writings, too old to be compared with the opinions of the Greeks, and too divine to be compared with their errors and I was led to put faith in these by the unpretending cast of the language, the inartificial character of the writers, the foreknowledge displayed of future events, the excellent quality of the precepts and the declaration of the government of the Universe as centred in one Being." (Tatian, *Address to the Greeks* 29)[6]

Others in the Roman Empire apparently were amazed at the antiquity and authoritative nature of the Old Testament Scriptures. Their simple yet profound answers to moral dilemmas proved convincing to the Gentiles, winning many to Christianity. The New Testament Scriptures emerged by the end of the first century and were composed in common Greek. The Gospel of Mark and the letters of Paul may not have been on a par with the high style of argumentation prevalent among Greek scholars, but their simplicity and use of Koine, or common, Greek was attractive to Gentiles.

Historically the Christian church has affirmed that the Bible is more than a collection of ancient documents; it tells us about God and how we are to live our lives to be pleasing to him. Traditionally the Bible is thought to have originated through human authors who were inspired by the Holy Spirit to compose God's truth for humankind.[7] Second Timothy 3:16–17 sets forth the importance of Scripture: "All Scripture is God-breathed and is useful for teaching, rebuking, correcting and training in righteousness, so that the man of God may be thoroughly equipped for every good work."

The Bible contains sixty-six books that are held to be canonical by a significant portion of the Christian church, but all or parts of the Bible are also held to be sacred by other major religions. Judaism holds that only the Old Testament contains the sacred words of God, but the Samaritans, who broke away from the Jews, believe that only the Pentateuch (i.e., the first five books of the Old Testament) constitute authoritative Scripture. Islam[8] acknowledges that the Old Testament (*taurat*, from the Hebrew *tôrâ*, "law") and the New Testament (*injīl*, from the Greek *euangelion*, "good news") are earlier divine revelations (Quran, Sura 3) though they would argue that they do not contain the full revelation of God.

Purpose of the Bible

The Bible explains that from the beginning God longed to have a relationship with humankind; we see this specifically in the garden of Eden (Gen. 1–2). But humanity rebelled and corrupted this relationship; the rest of Scripture teaches how God restores this relationship through Christ, which is the central theme of the Bible. The Old Testament looks forward to Christ and his work, explaining why we need his perfect sacrifice. The New Testament, then, reveals Christ as the fulfillment of the Old Testament promises and the one who heals the broken relationship between God and man.

One of the most significant differences between the God of Israel and other ancient Near Eastern gods was that Yahweh chose to reveal himself to his people—both who he is and how to please him. Some people have difficulty believing that God would reveal himself to human beings, an issue Peter Hicks addresses: "They feel that an infinite God is too great to limit himself to words or to any means of communication that human beings can grasp. But this is a wrong understanding of God's greatness. If he is so great, then he is able to do things that might seem impossible to us including communicating in a way that we can grasp."[9]

Divine revelation as recorded in the Bible brought with it both a further knowledge of the Creator God as well as a greater responsibility to obey his laws and stipulations. In the Old Testament this revelation was spread out over many centuries and came through various modes (e.g., dreams, visions, prophecies), but the ultimate and final form of revelation came in the incarnation of the God-man, Jesus Christ. Hebrews 1:1–2 says: "In the past God spoke to our forefathers through the prophets at many times and in various ways, but in these last days he has spoken to us *in* his son, whom he appointed heir of all things, and through whom he made the universe" (modified from the NIV). Verse 2 clearly states that God has spoken to us "in his son" and not simply "by his son,"[10] the implication being that Jesus was sent to earth as God's final revelation. God also ensured that the life and teachings of Jesus were written down in order to preserve them accurately and consistently. This revelation, recorded in the Bible, has now been translated into hundreds of languages—more than any other book.

The Bible can be read as great literature, as a history of the nation of Israel and the early church, or as a theological treatise, but it is intended to be more than any of these. It is God's revelation and is intended to change lives. The Book of Deuteronomy emphasizes a strong connection between obeying the Law recorded in Scriptures and having a proper attitude toward God: "The LORD will again delight in you and make you prosperous, just as he delighted in your fathers, if you obey the LORD your God and keep his commands and decrees that are written in this Book of the Law and turn to the LORD your God with all your heart and with all your soul" (Deut. 30:9b–10).

Total commitment, as evidenced by a person's desire to be obedient, was demanded by God. During the time of Nehemiah in the fifth century B.C., when Ezra read aloud the law, the priests explained it in Aramaic, and the people wept as they comprehended their disobedience to God's law (see Neh. 8:9b). God's word was living, arousing emotions that would motivate people to action. The Scriptures are still very much alive, a fact to which J. B. Phillips gave testimony when, in the mid-twentieth century, he translated them into modern English: "Without holding fundamentalist views on 'inspiration,' he [Phillips] is continually struck by the living quality of the material on which he is working. Some will, no doubt, consider it merely superstitious reverence for 'Holy Writ,' yet again and again the writer felt rather like an electrician re-wiring an ancient house without being able to 'turn the mains off.'"[11]

It is no accident that the Bible came down to us through so many centuries with such accuracy and power. God intended us to live our lives by this book, and many people dedicated themselves to the preservation of its sacred text. Its history will be described in the chapters that follow.

For Further Reading

Carson, D. A. *The Gagging of God: Christianity Confronts Pluralism*. Grand Rapids: Zondervan, 1996.

Carson, D. A., and J. D. Woodbridge, eds. *Scripture and Truth*. Grand Rapids: Zondervan, 1983.

———, eds. *Hermeneutics, Authority, and Canon*. Grand Rapids: Zondervan, 1986.

Fee, G. D., and D. Stuart. *How to Read the Bible for All Its Worth*. 2d ed. Grand Rapids: Zondervan, 1993.

Geisler, N. L., ed. *Inerrancy*. Grand Rapids: Zondervan, 1980.

Marshall, I. H. *Biblical Inspiration*. Grand Rapids: Eerdmans, 1982.

Radmacher, E. D., and R. D. Preus, eds. *Hermeneutics, Inerrancy, and the Bible*. Grand Rapids: Zondervan, 1984.

Woodbridge, J. D. *Biblical Authority. A Critique of the Rogers/McKim Proposal*. Grand Rapids: Zondervan, 1982.

Part 1

Preliminary Matters regarding the Bible

Description of the Bible

This chapter focuses on several general questions concerning the Bible. Some of the questions are complicated by the fact that the Bible was compiled over a long period of time and experienced various modifications, but an endeavor will be made to clarify its history.

What Is the Bible?

The Bible is a collection of books that have been considered authoritative by the Christian church and have been used to determine its beliefs and doctrines. The Bible, comprised of sixty-six books from more than forty authors, was called "the divine library" *(bibliotheca divina)* by Jerome, the translator of the Latin Vulgate in the late fourth century.[1] The authors of Scripture came from a variety of backgrounds, including a farmer (Amos), priests (Jeremiah and Ezekiel), a statesman (Daniel), fishermen (Peter and John), prophets (Isaiah, Micah), a physician (Luke), and a former tax collector (Matthew). The books were written in various countries (e.g., Israel, Babylon, Greece, Italy) and follow a variety of literary styles and genres (e.g., narrative, law codes, poetry, parables, Gospels, letters). The Bible, however, is not merely an anthology (i.e., a collection of diverse writings from various places); it has a unique unity and purpose. In addition, its authors claim to have been directed by God in their writings (e.g., 2 Pet. 1:20–21).

The Westminster Confession of Faith, produced in England in 1643–1646 by the Westminster Assembly composed of English divines and Scottish representatives, is a classic statement of Reformed theology. Concerning the Scriptures, it states:

> Although the light of nature, and the works of creation and providence, do so far manifest the goodness, wisdom, and power of God, as to leave men inexcusable [Rom. 1:17–20; 2:14]; yet they are not sufficient to give that knowledge of God, and of His will, which is necessary unto salvation [John 17:3; 1 Cor. 1:21; 2:13–14]: therefore it pleased the Lord, at sundry times, and in divers manners, to reveal Himself, and to declare that His will unto His Church [Heb. 1:1–2]; and afterwards, for the better preserving and propagating of the truth, and for the more sure establishment and comfort of the Church against the corruption of the flesh, and the malice of Satan and of the world, to commit the same wholly unto writing; which maketh the Holy Scripture to be most necessary; those former ways of God's revealing His will unto His people being now ceased.[2]

LAW	HISTORY	WISDOM & POETRY	PROPHETS	GOSPELS	HISTORY	LETTERS	APOCALYPSE
5 books Genesis– Deut.	12 books Josh.– Esther	5 books Job–Song of Songs	17 books Isaiah– Malachi	4 books Matthew– John	1 book Acts	21 books Romans– Jude	1 book Revelation
Old Testament (39 books)				**New Testament (27 books)**			

The Bible is primarily God's revelation to mankind concerning that which he expects us to know about himself and his actions. Revelation is the process by which God makes this truth about himself known to man and has two classifications.

General Revelation

General revelation is that which can be known about God through natural elements, human processes, or intuition. (See Ps. 19:1–6; Rom. 1). In classic Christian thought two arguments for the existence of God fall within the category of general revelation.

The cosmological argument builds a case for the existence of God upon the majesty and beauty of creation. Romans 1:18–20 says that creation reveals God's greatness: "The wrath of God is being revealed from heaven against all the godlessness and wickedness of men who suppress the truth by their wickedness, since what may be known about God is plain to them, because God has made it plain to them. For since the creation of the world God's invisible qualities—his eternal power and divine nature—have been clearly seen, being understood from what has been made, so that men are without excuse."

The teleological argument also looks to nature, but argues for the existence of God based upon the design and order evidenced in the natural world. The French Enlightenment philosopher Voltaire (1694–1778) states it simplistically: "If a watch proves the existence of a watchmaker but the universe does not prove the existence of a great Architect, then I consent to be called a fool."[3] Even Immanuel Kant (1724–1804), a great critic of natural theology, says approvingly: "This proof will always deserve to be treated with respect. It is the oldest, the clearest and most in conformity with human reason. . . . We have nothing to say against the reasonableness and utility of this line of argument, but wish, on the contrary, to commend and encourage it."[4]

General revelation can point to more than the mere existence of God; from it his creativity, his appreciation of beauty, and the massive proportions of his thoughts are demonstrated. Nevertheless general revelation can provide only a very limited picture of the God behind creation; this fact necessitates further revelation.

Special Revelation

Special revelation is that which can be known about God through some means of direct communication from him (e.g., the Bible, prophetic utterances, visions; see Ps. 19:7–14; Heb. 1:1–3).

There are things we could never know about God by merely observing creation; it is necessary that he reveal them to us (e.g., God desires to have a relationship with us; salvation comes through Jesus Christ). The Bible is the primary source of special revelation, beginning with topics such as how the universe came into being (Gen. 1–2) and the fall of man (Gen. 3), and looking toward future events and what the last days of the world will be like (Rev.). The controlling influence that God exerted over the human authors who wrote Scripture is called inspiration. Some scholars have suggested that the authors were merely instruments used by God, not unlike a pipeline or a conduit, through which information could pass without corruption; this is sometimes called the dictation theory. The assumption is that Scripture would be subject to human inadequacies and errors if this were not the case. The difficulty with this view is that each of the books of Scripture conveys the personality of its author. For instance, probably due to his training as a physician, Luke uses sophisticated and precise Greek when describing the life of Christ. John's Greek, however, was heavily colored by Hebraisms (i.e., phrases and grammar that are generally found in the Hebrew language) and expressions that are not usually employed in standard Greek grammar (e.g., Rev. 1:4, ἀπὸ ὁ ὤν [*apo ho ōn*, roughly equivalent to, "from *he* who is"] instead of grammatically regular Greek ἀπὸ τοῦ ὄντος [*apo tou ontos*, "from *him* who is"]). Paul was occasionally gripped by an enthusiasm that resulted in run-on sentences or other grammatical irregularities in some of his letters (see esp. Eph. 1:1–14; Col. 1:26; 2:2).[5] It would seem reasonable that if God authored all of Scripture and the human authors were mere scribes by whom the revelation was recorded, each of the books would have similar styles and faultless grammar.

A better understanding of how Scripture was communicated through its authors without losing divine purport is derived from two passages.

2 Timothy 3:16–17

All Scripture is God-breathed [Gk. *theopneustos*] and is useful for teaching, rebuking, correcting and training in righteousness, so that the man of God may be thoroughly equipped for every good work.

Verse 16 states that all Scripture is "breathed out" or "exhaled" by God. The process should not be viewed as one in which God breathed life into the words of an author after he had written them; if this were the case, they would be primarily man's words. The recording of Scripture was an innately complex process. God appears to have been so intimately involved in the lives of its writers that he knew what they would say and even how they would say it. Their individual personalities were thus combined with the indwelling, guiding work of the Holy Spirit to create Scripture. At the time Paul wrote to Timothy only the Old Testament existed and thus was considered Scripture, but later Peter equates Paul's letters with Scripture (2 Pet. 3:16).

2 Peter 1:20–21

Above all, you must understand that no prophecy of Scripture came about by the prophet's own interpretation. For prophecy never had its origin in the will of man, but men spoke from God as they were carried along by the Holy Spirit.

These verses emphasize that the message spoken by the authors of Scripture originated not with them but rather through the Holy Spirit. Scripture differs

---

2 Timothy 3:16

"All Scripture is God-breathed and is useful . . ."
There has been significant debate regarding the translation of this verse, which has been rendered in two ways:

"All Scripture is God-breathed and useful . . ."
(NIV, NASB, KJV, JB)
"Every inspired scripture has its use . . ." (NEB, REB)

The latter translation could be construed to suggest that only the "God-breathed" parts of Scripture are useful. The Greek text reads:

πᾶσα γραφὴ θεόπνευστος καὶ ὠφέλιμος . . .
All Scripture [is] God-breathed and useful . . .

Most scholars argue that the first rendering is the most plausible for the following reasons: (1) It is the most natural reading; the phrase does not have a verb and therefore both adjectives should be dealt with similarly. (2) A similar Greek structure found in 1 Timothy 4:4 strongly supports the first translation. (3) The usual order in Greek for the second translation would have the word *God-breathed* before the word *Scripture*. (4) The second translation runs counter to the argument in the rest of the passage if only parts of Scripture are God-breathed.

Bibliography
Fee, G. D. *1 and 2 Timothy, Titus,* 279–80. NIBC. Peabody, MA: Hendrickson, 1988. Guthrie, D. *The Pastoral Epistles,* 175–77. 2d ed. TNTC. Grand Rapids: Eerdmans, 1990. Hanson, A. T. *The Pastoral Epistles,* 151–52. NCBC. Grand Rapids: Eerdmans, 1982. Kelly, J. N. D. *A Commentary on the Pastoral Epistles,* 202–3. HNTC. New York: Harper & Row, 1963; reprint, Grand Rapids: Baker, 1981. Lea, T. D. *1, 2, Timothy, Titus,* 234–37. Nashville: Broadman, 1992. Stott, J. R. W. *Guard the Gospel: The Message of 2 Timothy,* 100–104. BST. Downers Grove, IL: InterVarsity, 1973.

---

from the messages of false prophets, which came from their own imagination (Jer. 23:25–26; Ezek. 13:3). Instead, the personalities and life experiences of the authors combined with the indwelling, guiding work of the Holy Spirit to create Scripture. Michael Green, director of evangelism for the Anglican church, likens the process to the effect of wind in sails: "The prophets raised their sails, so to speak (they were obedient and receptive) and the Holy Spirit filled them and carried their craft along in the direction He wished. Men spoke: God spoke. Any proper doctrine of Scripture will not neglect either part of this truth."[6]

Inspiration applies specifically to the process of writing God's revelation. Not all revelation can be classified as inspired since a certain degree of general revelation derives from nature, but all inspired writings record revelation. Scripture, therefore, has authority because it comes from God, who has the prerogative to tell us how to live our lives. Scripture's claim that it is the very Word of God has impelled the church to follow and cherish it. J. Daane, former professor of theology and ministry at Fuller Seminary, asserts: "Belief in an infallible, authoritative, reliable Scripture has always been part of the faith of the Church. Faith, by biblical definition, requires a sure Word of God. The very reality of faith is a sure knowledge and hearty confidence that depends upon a Scripture whose truth is certain and unfailing."[7]

What Does the Word *Bible* Mean?

Origin of the Word *Bible*

The most common English term used to refer to Scripture is the word *Bible*. It derives from the Latin translation of the Greek word *biblion* ("book"),[8] itself a derivation of the word *byblos*, one of the names of papyrus. Papyrus, produced from a reed plant that grew along the banks and marshes of the Nile River in ancient Egypt, was used as a writing material (see chap. 6, "Papyrus"). Multiple sheets of papyrus spliced together to form rolls (scrolls) were wound around wooden dowels called navels. A reader used one hand to unroll the text on one navel and the other hand to roll it up on another. This type of scroll was called a *biblos* in Greek, and thus during New Testament times the word *biblion* simply referred to a roll or book. Once a scroll reached a certain size, however, it became awkward to use, as was the case with several of the larger biblical books. For example, the Isaiah Scroll found at Qumran (1QIsa[a]) measured approximately twenty-three feet, about the limit for a scroll. Thus a new format was necessary to conveniently handle a book as large as the Old or New Testament.

As time passed it was discovered that sheets of papyrus could be placed on top of each other, folded in the middle, and bound, resulting in an easy-to-use book called a "codex." David Ewert, former president of Mennonite Bible College in Winnipeg, Manitoba, explains: "The Latin word *codex* originally meant the trunk of a tree, and then a block of wood split up into tablets or leaves. Such wooden tablets (perhaps coated with wax) were bound together to make a book. The same was done with leaves or sheets of papyrus. A codex, then, is a leaf book."[9] The codex was a significant improvement over scrolls, being easier to manage and easier to use in locating passages,[10] but scrolls continued to be used in synagogues even after the second century A.D.,[11] when the codex was introduced for private use. Christians quickly adopted the codex for its convenience, allowing multiple books in one codex. Initially codices were made of papyrus, but it was soon found that parchment (scraped animal skin that was soaked in lime) could be inscribed on both sides, producing books even less bulky and more durable. As a result, the term *biblia* evolved again, referring more broadly to codices or books.

The Septuagint, a Greek translation of the Old Testament produced probably between 250 and 100 B.C., uses the word *biblia*[12] in Daniel 9:2 to refer to Jeremiah's words, which may have been in the form of letters[13] or a collection of prophets.[14] Early Greek-speaking Christians employed the plural form *biblia* (τὰ βιβλία [*ta biblia*, "the books"]) to refer to the entire collection of Old and New Testament books, as explained by F. F. Bruce, former professor of New Testament at the University of Manchester: "Latin-speaking Christians then borrowed the word *biblia* but treated it as a singular noun, and from its Latin use the English word 'Bible' and similar forms in many other languages have been derived."[15]

The earliest recorded instance of the term *biblia* applied to the documents of the Christian church is found in 2 *Clement* 14.2 (dated to about A.D. 150), which states: "the books (*biblia*) and the Apostles declare that the Church . . . has existed from the beginning."[16]

Other Words for the Bible

The New Testament employs two other Greek synonyms to refer to the Bible; the first word is "writings" and the other is "Scriptures" (see table 2.1). Both words refer to the Old Testament writings in whole or in part. It is also possible that the Greek word μεμβράνα (*membrana*), usually translated "parchments" and used by Paul in 2 Timothy 4:13, may refer to the Scriptures, since parchment became the preferred writing material for Scripture.[17]

What Are the Testaments?

Change in Usage of the Word *Testament*

The Bible is a unity of two unequal parts called the Old and New Testaments; however, common usage of the English word *testament* today calls to mind a last will and testament, which can be defined as "an act by which a person determines the deposition of his property after his death."[18] In one sense the New Testament tells about the inheritance that believers receive because of Christ's death, but most scholars agree that it is an inadequate term for the two parts of Scripture since they encompass far more than this concept.

Probably a better term to refer to the parts of Scripture would be the word *covenant*, which is the word used in Jeremiah 31:31–34 to refer to God's relationship to his people:

> "The time is coming," declares the LORD, "when I will make a new *covenant* with the house of Israel and with the house of Judah. It will not be like the *covenant* I made with their forefathers when I took them by the hand to lead them out of Egypt, because they broke my covenant, though I was a husband to them." . . . "This is the *covenant* I will make with the house of Israel after that time." . . . "I will put my law in their minds and write it on their hearts. I will be their God, and they will be my people. No longer will a man teach his neighbor, or a man his brother, saying, 'Know the LORD,' because they

will all know me, from the least of them to the greatest." . . . "For I will forgive their wickedness and will remember their sins no more." (italics added)

In this passage the Hebrew word בְּרִית (*bᵉrît*, an agreement, covenant, contract, or alliance)[19] is used to make a distinction between God's previous relationship with his people under the old covenant and the new relationship he will have with them

Table 2.1 Greek Synonyms for "Bible"

Term	References
Writings	"the writings" (αἱ γραφαί [*hai graphai*] or some form of it): Matthew 21:42; Mark 14:49; Luke 24:32; John 5:39; 2 Timothy 3:16; 2 Peter 3:16 "the holy Scriptures" (γραφαῖς ἁγίαις [*graphais hagiais*]): Romans 1:2
Scriptures	"the sacred Scriptures" ([τὰ] ἱερὰ γράμματα [*ta hiera grammata*]): 2 Timothy 3:15

under the new covenant. The Septuagint and the New Testament translated this word as διαθήκη (*diathēkē*, which commonly means covenant);[20] the Greek versions, then, termed the two sections of the Bible "the old covenant" (ἡ παλαιὰ διαθήκη [*hē palaia diathēkē*]) and "the new covenant" (ἡ καινὴ διαθήκη [*hē kainē diathēkē*]). Later the Latin Vulgate accurately translated διαθήκη (*diathēkē*) as *testamentum*, so that the two portions of the Bible were known as the *Vetus Testamentum* ("Old Testament") and the *Novum Testamentum* ("New Testament"). The English language merely transferred the Latin word *testamentum*, which has subsequently acquired other meanings quite different from its initial usage. The English word *testament* is a poor translation of the word *bᵉrît*;[21] "covenant" better pictures the relationship God longs to have with his people.

The Concept of Covenant

In the Old Testament, God's redemptive relationship with humanity was mediated through a covenant with his people. God chose to make a covenant with Abraham in the second millennium B.C., thereby initiating a lasting relationship with the human race. Abraham is often mistakenly thought to be Hebrew or Israelite, but in reality he preceded the Jewish nation, which emanated from Jacob (Gen. 35:10–11); this covenant, therefore, was initiated before the Jewish nation ever existed, as Paul points out in Romans 4. The concept of a covenant was widespread throughout the ancient Near East, so Abraham would have been familiar with it. Covenants were generally secured by oaths made before each party's gods, the idea being that neither party would dare risk the wrath of their god(s) by breaking the covenant. Curses that the offending party would suffer were carefully enumerated, no doubt increasing the fear of breaking the covenant—thus an effective means of causing both sides to adhere to covenant stipulations.

The Abrahamic covenant described in Genesis 12–22 summarizes God's dealings with mankind and includes the following elements:

1. Covenant promise (12:1–3)
2. Covenant enactment (15:9–21)
3. Covenant sign (17:9–14)
4. Covenant oath (22:16–18)

The Abrahamic covenant is unconditional in that Yahweh holds himself responsible for seeing it through to fulfillment. This is most clearly portrayed in Genesis 15:9–21 in the covenant enactment ceremony wherein God tells Abraham to take five animals (a heifer, goat, ram, turtledove, and pigeon), split them apart, and place the pieces opposite each other (the birds were not divided). God then passed through the animal pieces, signifying that he was taking the covenant curses upon himself; that is, if God did not keep the covenant, he would make himself like the split-open animals (see Jer. 34:18–20).

The Abrahamic covenant is the overarching plan that unites God's dealings with his people and bridges the Old and New Testaments. This was God's unconditional plan for his people that he would see through to the end. Not everyone was required to participate; however, individual enjoyment of its benefits was conditional upon a person's obedience. During the Old Testament period, adherence to strict guidelines, as set forth in the Law, was required for a person to be included in the Abrahamic covenant. Thus in the Old Testament people like Rahab (Josh. 6:25) or Ruth (Ruth 1:16–17), who were not Israelites, needed to be incorporated into Israel by obeying the Law in order to receive the benefits of the Abrahamic covenant. These laws revealed the righteous standards that God demanded but that the Israelites could not or would not maintain. God had every right to annul the covenant, but instead he initiated a new covenant that would be fulfilled by putting one's trust in Christ and his atoning work on the cross. In the New Testament obedience is still necessary, but the Holy Spirit living within helps a person to obey God's requirements.

The Fulfillment of the New Covenant

The Old Testament depicts the history of Israel under the old covenant as a set

Abrahamic Covenant

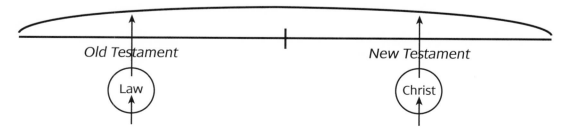

of external laws or rules that the nation failed to follow. By contrast the New Testament focuses on the new covenant, whose laws are written upon the hearts of God's people (Jer. 31:33). This was foretold in John 14:16–17 (emphasis added), when Jesus said that he would send the Holy Spirit to live within his disciples: "I will ask the Father, and he will give you another Counselor to be with you forever—the Spirit of truth. The world cannot accept him, because it neither sees him nor knows him. But you know him, for he lives *with* you and *will be in* you."

During the Last Supper, Jesus referred to the new covenant: "This cup is the new covenant in my blood, which is poured out for you" (Luke 22:20). Jesus was explaining that the new covenant would be inaugurated by the shedding of his own blood (Matt. 26:28; Mark 14:24; Luke 22:20; 1 Cor. 11:24–25), similar to Moses' instituting the old covenant with the sprinkling of blood (Exod. 24:8). Christ became the new mediator between God and humanity and fulfilled what was promised in the new covenant (Jer. 31). Two unique elements, absent from the old covenant, were added to the new: God, by means of the indwelling Holy Spirit, would put his law within the hearts of believers (John 14:17); and their sins would be remembered no more. Sacrifices in the Old Testament looked forward to the ultimate and final sacrifice accomplished by Christ. The sacrifice that Christ offered atoned for sins for all time (Heb. 10:11–12) and is able to cleanse the conscience from works that lead to death (Heb. 9:14). The prophets and righteous people of Old Testament times longed for God's promise to be accomplished, but Hebrews 11:13 declares that "All these people were still living by faith when they died. They did not receive the things promised; they only saw them and welcomed them from a distance." The promise these people longed for was realized in Christ.

The Relationship between the Old and New Covenants

Some people have argued that the Old Testament has been superseded by the New Testament and is thereby rendered unnecessary. One of the earliest to do so was Marcion, a native of Sinope in Asia Minor, who came to Rome about A.D. 140 and founded a sect contending that the Old Testament had been made obsolete by the New Testament. He argued that the Creator God, who manifested himself as Yahweh in the Old Testament, was inferior to the good and loving God in the New Testament who revealed himself as Father. Marcion further argued that the Old Testament ought not to be regarded as part of the Christian canon. He limited the canon of the New Testament to one Gospel and ten Pauline Epistles, primarily because he considered that Paul was the only apostle to remain true to Christ's teachings and that the other apostles had become Judaizers. The early church, however, rightly condemned Marcion as a heretic.

In the nineteenth century it was common to draw a contrast between the good, loving God of the New Testament and the harsh, legalistic God of the Old Testament. Although few people went as far as Marcion, some, like the great German historian Adolf von Harnack, came remarkably close: "The rejection of the Old Testament in the second century was a mistake which the great church rightly avoided; to maintain it in the sixteenth century was a fate which the Reformation was not yet able to escape; but still to preserve it in Protestantism as a canonical document since the nineteenth century is the consequence of a religious and ecclesiastical crippling."[22] The fact that books are still published attempting to work out the moral difficulties of the Old Testament is indicative of the tension there is in harmonizing the guidelines of the Old Testament with those of the New.[23] It is essential to remember that the Old Testament was the Bible for Jesus and his followers, from which, as Bruce notes, Jesus regularly taught fundamental principles: "That some of its provisions were of the nature of a temporary accommodation was recognised; Jesus, for example, said that the provision which the Mosaic law made for divorce and remarriage was introduced because of the men's 'hardness of heart'; but it was from the Old Testament that he took the fundamental and abiding principle in the light of which the Mosaic provision was seen in its true character."[24]

The word *old*, when it refers to the Old Testament, is not derogatory, nor does it mean the Old Testament is obsolete. Jesus himself said, "Do not think that I have come to abolish the Law or the Prophets; I have not come to abolish them but to fulfill them" (Matt. 5:17). Jesus was the fulfillment of the Old Testament Law, since his sacrificial death paid the righteous requirements that the Law demanded; in that sense he is the ultimate goal that the Old Testament anticipated.[25] Because the Old Testament prepares a foundation for the New Testament, both Testaments are closely related. Just as a foundation remains vital to a building once it is erected, so the Old Testament provides structure and stability for the New. The titles *Old Testament* and *New Testament* are a chronological reference—the Old Testament being written before the time of Christ and the New Testament books after. Many of the promises or prophecies in the Old Testament are fulfilled in the New Testament; both the initial statement and its fulfillment are equally important. When Jesus spoke to the two apostles on the road to Emmaus, he chided them: "'How foolish you are, and how slow of heart to believe all that the prophets have spoken! Did not the Christ have to suffer these things and then enter his glory?' And beginning with Moses and all the Prophets, he explained to them what was said in all the Scriptures concerning himself" (Luke 24:25–27). Jesus clearly saw himself as the fulfillment of the Old Testament promises. (The unity of the Bible will be further discussed in chapter 5.)

Jewish and Christian Views of the Authority of Scripture

Initially, early Christians and Jews worshiped together in the temple and in synagogues (Acts 3:1; 4:1; 5:42; 6:9–10; 13:14–15, 42; 14:1; 17:1–2), using the same books of Scripture, namely, the Old Testament, which they viewed as authoritative. However, they had significantly different vantage points, since Christians understood the Old Testament to be fulfilled in Jesus whereas Jews still awaited the Messiah. Christians later recorded the teachings of Jesus and the apostles, incorporating them into their sacred writings, which became known as the New Testament. While the two collections maintained their distinctiveness, there remained an organic unity between the two Testaments.

The Jewish View

Jews view the Old Testament as their Scriptures. L. I. Rabinowitz, deputy editor-in-chief of *Encyclopaedia Judaica,* states that "the Bible became for centuries the main, and for a long time the sole, intellectual preoccupation of the Jewish people."[26] This is why Jews are often labeled "the people of the book" (i.e., the Old Testament). They have gone to great lengths to meticulously preserve their Scriptures,

Jewish Literature

Halakhah: (lit., "the way of life") that part of Jewish literature containing rules for daily life

Haggadah: (lit., "narrative") that part of rabbinic literature that seeks to illustrate the Law

which they believe to be authoritative revelation given to them by God. A distinction is often made between the Pentateuch, the first five books of the Old Testament, from which their *halakhah* mainly derives, and the rest of the Old Testament.

Rabinowitz further clarifies the distinction:

> The Pentateuch was regarded as the main authoritative source for the *halakhah,* and verses from the prophets and the Hagiographa [the third section of the Old Testament, sometimes called Writings] were regarded merely as giving secondary support to it. They were called "Kabbalah" (tradition) and it was laid down that "no inference may be drawn concerning statements of the Pentateuch from statements found in the Kabbalah" (*Ḥag.* 10b). As a result, for the purpose of *halakhah* the entire weight was laid on the Pentateuch, and from the time of Ezra until the compilation of the Mishnah, the Pentateuch was practically the sole textbook for study.[27]

Gradually the whole of the Old Testament was subjected to intensive study and Midrashim (lit. "interpretations"; i.e., commentaries on the Scriptures) were developed for all portions of sacred Scripture.

Since following the Law was paramount in Jewish life, much time and effort was expended determining what the laws meant and spelling out exactly what they required. These explanations, known as the oral law, were recorded in the Mishnah and Talmud and in time became almost as authoritative as Scripture. G. F. Moore, former professor of the history of religion at Harvard University, states:

> The whole revelation from God was not comprised in the sacred books. By the side of Scripture there had always gone an unwritten tradition, in part interpreting and applying the written Torah, in part supplementing it. . . . Thus in every sphere there always existed beside the written law a much more extensive and comprehensive body of unwritten law more or less exactly and permanently formulated. . . . And since religion with all its duties and observances was revealed by God, the revelation necessarily

included the unwritten as well as the written law. The written law, again, was all revealed to Moses, and it was a very natural inference that its inseparable complement the unwritten law, which shared the immutability of all revelation, was revealed to him at the same time.[28]

Thus for the Jewish nation the written and oral laws were authoritative revelation from God and the foundation upon which they built their lives. Oral law surfaces in the New Testament in Matthew 15:1–3, when the Pharisees rebuked Jesus because his disciples did not wash their hands before eating: "Why do your disciples break the traditions of the elders?" (Matt. 15:2). The reference is to oral laws as recorded later in the Babylonian Talmud (e.g., *Ḥag.* 18b; *Šabb.* 13b–14a; *Yoma* 87b), and Jesus' response was to cite an instance when the Pharisees routinely broke the written law of God (Exod. 20:12; Deut. 5:16).

Following A.D. 70, when the temple was destroyed, the Jews could no longer follow explicit regulations concerning sacrifices, the Jewish nation had to rethink its religion. In time they decided that doing good works was an adequate sacrifice to God, and the basis of Judaism shifted to offering sacrifices of "good works."

The Christian View

The Christian church broke away from the Jewish synagogue in the latter half of the first century, but the Old Testament remained an integral part of its canon. Traditionally the church has held that both the Old and New Testaments are direct revelation from God and are equally part of God's redemptive plan for mankind. Hebrews 1:1–2 makes it clear that both the Old and New Testaments are considered God's revelation, but in the last days God chose to convey his revelation in the form of Jesus his Son. The New Testament builds upon ideas and concepts developed in the Old Testament and regularly quotes or alludes to passages from it. According to A. E. Hill, approximately 32 percent (nearly one-third) of the New Testament

Table 2.2 Contents of the Mishnah

The sixty-three tractates of the Mishnah are arranged in six main divisions (or orders). Both of the Talmuds contain the entire Mishnah along with additional comments on many of its tractates. The Palestinian Talmud expounds most of the tractates in *Zeraʿim, Moʿed, Našim,* and *Neziqin* (39 of the Mishnah's 63 tractates); the Babylonian Talmud expounds most of the tractates in *Moʿed, Našim, Neziqin,* and *Qodašim* (37 of 63).

1. *Zeraʿim* (Seeds)
Berakot (Benedictions)
Peʾah (Gleanings)
Demai (Produce Not Certainly Tithed)
Kilʾayim (Diverse Kinds)
Šebiʿit (Seventh Year)
Terumot (Heave Offerings)
Maʿaśerot (Tithes)
Maʿaśer Šeni (Second Tithe)
Ḥallah (Dough Offering)
ʿOrlah (Fruit of Young Trees)
Bikkurim (First Fruits)

2. *Moʿed* (Set Feasts)
Šabbat (Sabbath)
ʿErubin (Fusion of Sabbath Limits)
Pesaḥim (Feast of Passover)
Šeqalim (Shekel Dues)
Yoma (Day of Atonement)
Sukkah (Feast of Tabernacles)
Beṣah (Egg) or *Yom Ṭob* (Festival Days)
Roš Haššanah (Feast of the New Year)
Taʿanit (Days of Fasting)
Megillah (Scroll of Esther)
Moʿed Qaṭan (Mid-Festival Days)
Ḥagigah (Festival Offering)

3. *Našim* (Women)
Yebamot (Sisters-in-Law)
Ketubbot (Marriage Deeds)
Nedarim (Vows)
Nazir (Nazirite Vow)
Sotah (Suspected Adultress)
Giṭṭin (Bills of Divorce)
Qiddušin (Betrothals)

4. *Neziqin* (Damages)
Baba Qamma (First Gate)
Baba Meṣiʿa (Middle Gate)
Baba Batra (Last Gate)
Sanhedrin (Sanhedrin)
Makkot (Stripes/Punishments)
Šebuʿot (Oaths)
ʿEduyyot (Testimonies)
ʿAbodah Zarah (Idolatrous Worship)
ʾAbot (Fathers)
Horayot (Instructions)

5. *Qodašim* (Holy Things)
Zebaḥim (Animal Offerings)
Menaḥot (Meal Offerings)
Ḥullin (Animals Killed for Food)
Bekorot (Firstborn)
ʿArakin (Vows of Valuation)
Temurah (Substitute Offering)
Kerithot (Exterminations)
Meʿilah (Trespass)
Tamid (Daily Morning and Evening Offerings)
Middot (Measurements)
Qinnim (Bird Offerings)

6. *Ṭeharot* (Cleannesses)
Kelim (Vessels)
ʾOhalot (Dwellings)
Negaʿim (Leprosy Signs)
Parah (Red Heifer)
Ṭeharot (Cleannesses)
Miqwaʾot (Wells/Water Reservoirs)
Niddah (Menstrual Uncleanness)
Makširin (Liquids)
Zabim (Running Sores)
Ṭebul Yom (Day of Impurity)
Yadayim (Hands)
ʿUqṣin (Shells and Stalks)

is composed of Old Testament quotations and allusions.[29] Also 2 Peter 3:15–16 equates Paul's letters with the rest of Scripture, indicating that Peter believed that these New Testament letters are on a par with the Old Testament.

In summary, the significant difference between Jewish and Christian views of Scripture is that the latter considers the Old and New Testaments to be divine revelation and thus authoritative, whereas the former believes that the written law (i.e., the Old Testament) as well as the oral law (i.e., Jewish traditions of the rabbis, including the Midrash, Talmuds, and Tosefta) are authoritative.

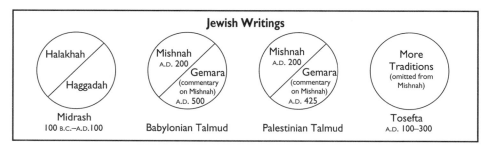

Jewish Writings

Halakhah / Haggadah — Midrash 100 B.C.–A.D. 100

Mishnah A.D. 200 / Gemara (commentary on Mishnah) A.D. 500 — Babylonian Talmud

Mishnah A.D. 200 / Gemara (commentary on Mishnah) A.D. 425 — Palestinian Talmud

More Traditions (omitted from Mishnah) — Tosefta A.D. 100–300

For Further Reading

Bruce, F. F. *The New Testament Development of the Old Testament Themes.* Grand Rapids: Eerdmans, 1968.

———. *The Books and the Parchments.* 5th ed. London: Marshall Pickering, 1991.

Ewert, D. *From Ancient Tablets to Modern Translations: A General Introduction to the Bible,* esp. 19–27. Grand Rapids: Zondervan, 1983.

Gaebelein, F. E. "The Unity of the Bible." In *Revelation and the Bible,* ed. C. F. H. Henry, 387–401. Grand Rapids: Baker, 1958.

Hillers, D. R. *Covenant: The History of a Biblical Idea.* Baltimore: Johns Hopkins University Press, 1969.

Kaiser, W. C. *Toward an Old Testament Theology.* Grand Rapids: Zondervan, 1978.

McCarthy, D. J. *Old Testament Covenant: A Survey of Current Opinions.* GPT. Richmond: John Knox, 1972.

McComiskey, T. E. *The Covenants of Promise: A Theology of the Old Testament Covenants.* Grand Rapids: Baker, 1985.

Martens, E. A. *God's Design: A Focus on Old Testament Theology.* Grand Rapids: Baker, 1981.

Robertson, O. P. *The Christ of the Covenants.* Grand Rapids: Baker, 1980.

Tasker, R. V. G. *The Old Testament in the New Testament.* Grand Rapids: Eerdmans, 1963.

Wiseman, D. J. "Books in the Ancient Near East and in the Old Testament." In *CHB,* 1:30–48.

The Old Testament

We have already seen that the Bible is divided into two unequal parts, the Old and New Testaments, with thirty-nine books and twenty-seven books respectively.

Historical Background of the Old Testament

The Old Testament forms roughly three-fourths of the entire Bible; it was written by about forty different authors and covers more than two thousand years of Israel's history. The world of the Old Testament differed significantly from that of the New. At the beginning of the Old Testament period, many people were nomadic, tending herds of goats and sheep. Caravans were the primary method of transport for goods and communication from other countries. Raiding parties would sweep across parts of the Fertile Crescent to pillage food and other goods. Major city centers were generally city-states that controlled the surrounding locality and provided safety for the inhabitants. The Assyrians assembled a major empire, rising to a formidable power in the eighth century under Tiglath-pileser III (744–727 B.C.; see fig. 3.1). They controlled much of the Fertile Crescent from Israel to Babylon for about a century and a half (750–612 B.C.).

The Babylonians, under Nebuchadrezzar II (605–562 B.C.), rose to power next, dominating the world scene until succumbing to the Persians in 539 B.C. The Medo-Persian Empire, founded by Cyrus the Great (539–530 B.C.), lasted until the entire Near Eastern area was overwhelmed by Alexander the Great (336–323 B.C.). Against this historical background the books of the Old Testament were written.

Divisions of the Old Testament

The Old Testament records the history of God's dealings primarily with the nation of Israel, beginning with the creation of the universe (Gen. 1–2) until about 400 B.C. (1 Chron. 3:24; Mal.).[1] Its literature varies considerably and is arranged in sections.

Divisions of the Old Testament in English

English translations of the Old Testament mainly follow the order and divisions of the Septuagint and the Latin Vulgate:

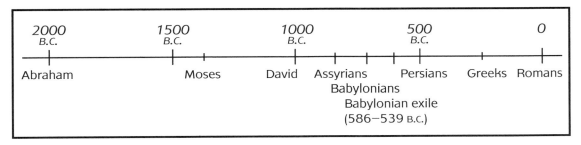

2000 B.C.	1500 B.C.	1000 B.C.	500 B.C.	0
Abraham	Moses	David	Assyrians	Persians Greeks Romans

Babylonians
Babylonian exile
(586–539 B.C.)

Figure 3.1.
Tiglath-pileser III, king of Assyria (744–727 B.C.), as portrayed on a rock relief from Nimrud. [British Museum]

1. Pentateuch (Genesis–Deuteronomy; 5 books)
2. Historical Books (Joshua–Esther; 12 books)
3. Poetic and Wisdom Literature (Job–Song of Songs; 5 books)
4. Prophets (Isaiah–Malachi; 17 books)

The first two sections of the Old Testament provide a chronological framework for the nation of Israel from the creation of the universe to the Persian Empire (539–330 B.C.). The two books of Chronicles detail much of this same period from another perspective, emphasizing that Israel prospered when the people obeyed God's word but met with certain disaster when they neglected it (e.g., 1 Chron. 10:13; 2 Chron. 14:5–6). G. F. Hasel underscores this theme in Chronicles: "The fact that of 822 verses in 2 Chronicles, 480 deal with four pious kings (Solomon, chs. 1–9;

Jehoshaphat, chs. 17–21; Hezekiah, chs. 29–32; Josiah, chs. 34f.) and 342 with seventeen others, shows that the emphasis is placed on those characteristics that bring God's blessing."[2] Strong emphasis on history in the Old Testament is not surprising given the fact that God continued to reveal himself throughout history and that he is portrayed as the God of history.

The third section, which comprises Poetic and Wisdom Literature, is a part of the Old Testament that teaches precepts and guiding principles. Poetry uses all of our senses to communicate concepts, create interest, and cause the reader to reflect.

The fourth section contains the writings of the prophets arranged in order of Major Prophets (Isa., Jer., Ezek., Dan.) and Minor Prophets (Hos., Joel, Amos, Obad., Jon., Mic., Nah., Hab., Zeph., Hag., Zech., Mal.; sometimes called the Book of the Twelve). The terms *major* and *minor* refer only to length, not content or importance.

Hebrew Old Testament Divisions

Initially the Old Testament books were written and circulated separately, but fairly early on their divine inspiration was recognized and they were treated with utmost care. Apparently some of the earliest books were kept near the ark (Deut. 31:25–26), but it is not clear how or when the books were compiled. Table 3.1 represents the standard structure of the Hebrew Old Testament: the Law, the Prophets, and the Writings. This threefold division of the Old Testament can be traced as far back as the prologue to Sirach, dated to about 132 B.C., which makes reference three times to "the Law and the Prophets and the others that followed them" (or similar wording, NRSV). Jesus also used similar terminology for the Old Testament when addressing his disciples: "This is what I told you while I was still with you: Everything must be fulfilled that is written about me in the Law of Moses, the Prophets and the Psalms" (Luke 24:44). In this verse, the designation *Psalms* most likely refers to the entire third section of the Old Testament since it is the first and largest book of that part.[3]

Sometimes Jews refer to their Scriptures as the Tanak (תנ״ך), which is an acrostic using the first letter from each of the three sections of the Old Testament—the *Torah* (תּוֹרָה [tôrâ, "Law"]), the *Nebiʾim* (נְבִיאִים [nᵉbîʾîm, "Prophets"]), and the *Kethubim* (כְּתוּבִים [kᵉṯûḇîm, "Writings"])—joined by the letter *a*. It is not clear exactly how this threefold division developed, but each of these sections contains specific types of material.

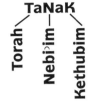

Table 3.1
Structure of the Hebrew Bible

Law (Torah)	Prophets (Nebiʾim)	Writings (Kethubim)
Genesis	**The Former Prophets**	**Poetic Books**
Exodus	Joshua	Psalms
Leviticus	Judges	Job
Numbers	Samuel	Proverbs
Deuteronomy	Kings	**Five Scrolls** (*Megillot*)
	The Latter Prophets	Ruth
	Isaiah	Song of Songs
	Jeremiah	Ecclesiastes
	Ezekiel	Lamentations
	The Book of the Twelve	Esther
		Historical Books
		Daniel
		Ezra–Nehemiah
		Chronicles

The Law (*tôrâ*)

The *Torah*, in Hebrew meaning "instruction" or "teaching," is often referred to as the Law and is comprised of Genesis, Exodus, Leviticus, Numbers, and Deuteronomy. Origen is credited as the first to refer to it as the Pentateuch, meaning "five books" (πέντε, *pente*, "five"; τεῦχος, *teuchos*, "scrolls or books")[4] though he may have acquired the name from the Alexandrian Jews. It is probable that the Pentateuch was originally viewed as one book that was divided into five portions due to limitations of scroll size, leading to Talmudic references to the Torah as five-fifths of the Law.[5] It is better, then, to regard the Pentateuch as a single work of five volumes rather than five separate books.

The Torah sets forth the requirements for becoming the people of God. However, it is much more than legal instruction, as E. E. Carpenter notes: "The Torah comprises not only ancient legislation given through God's spokesman Moses, but also an equally impressive amount of historical narrative that forms the context for the legal material. Thus the Torah is the most important section of the Jewish canon."[6] The Pentateuch begins in Genesis with the creation of the world and concludes in Deuteronomy when the Israelites are about to enter the promised land.

The Prophets (*nᵉḇîʾîm*)

The Prophets are divided into the Former Prophets—Joshua, Judges, Samuel, and Kings—and the Latter, or writing, Prophets—Isaiah, Jeremiah, Ezekiel, and the Book of the Twelve. While we may prefer to label these as historical books, the Israelites thought of them as prophetic works intended to serve as a guide for future generations. The terms *former* and *latter* are to some extent misnomers since chronologically parts of the Latter Prophets precede the Former Prophets. The Former Prophets are anonymous works that describe the history of Israel from the entrance into the promised land (c. 1400 /1240 B.C.) to the Babylonian exile (586 B.C.), while the Latter Prophets record God's messages given through the prophets to the nation of Israel during much of this same period. Usually the prophets furnish a historical context at the beginning of the book by recording the kings who ruled at the time of their messages (e.g., Isa., Jer., Hos.), though some of the books do not (e.g., Joel, Obad.). A prophet served as a mouthpiece to convey God's opinions, decisions, reactions, or other communication to his people. Often God graciously sent prophets at particularly difficult times in Israel's history to warn and/or encourage the people to obey his commands. Amos was sent to the northern kingdom during the reign of Jeroboam II (c. 782–753 B.C.), a period of intense idolatry and corrupt social behavior, to warn them of punishment if they did not change their actions. God sent several prophets, most notably Jeremiah and Ezekiel, to the Israelites during the difficult time immediately prior to the Babylonian exile (586 B.C.). Jeremiah was called to prophesy in Jerusalem and Ezekiel in Babylon. Both gave stern warnings to the people to turn from their sins and trust God or suffer severe punishment. However, both also spoke messages of hope and restoration that would follow punishment.

The Writings (*kᵉṯûḇîm*)

The term *Writings* derives from the Hebrew word *kāṯaḇ*, meaning "to write," and these works are also sometimes called *hagiographa* (holy writings). They are generally subdivided according to their various types of material. Jewish scholars consider Job, Psalms, and Proverbs especially poetic;[7] these are sometimes called the books of truth[8] (originating in a mnemonic device in which the first letter of each

Job אִיּוֹב (*ʾiyôḇ*) = א
Proverbs מִשְׁלֵי (*mišlê*) = מ
Psalms תְּהִלִּים (*tᵉhillîm*) = ת

אֱמֶת (*ʾᵉmet*) = truth

book's name together spells the Hebrew word for truth).

According to N. H. Ridderbos and H. M. Wolf, more than one-third of the Old Testament is written in poetic form, including some of the best loved passages in all of Scripture.[9] Undoubtedly one reason why there is so much poetry is that it moves the heart and emotions more than does prose.

Another section of the Writings is called the five scrolls, or *megillot* (Hebrew for "scrolls"). Later Jewish tradition indicates that each of these books was read in the synagogue on certain days (see table 3.2). Song of Songs was read as part of the Passover feast in early spring (about the end of March), because it was believed to picture God's love for Israel. At the feast of Pentecost in early summer (near the end of May), the Book of Ruth was read since its climax appropriately occurs during the wheat harvest. Lamentations was read on the ninth of Ab in late July to remember the destruction of Solomon's temple on that date in 586 B.C. The feast of Tabernacles occurred in early fall (in the first part of October) to commemorate the wilderness wanderings. For a week the people lived outside in booths made of branches to remind them of the difficulties their forefathers endured in the wilderness. The Book of Ecclesiastes, which highlights the futility of life, was read during this feast. The Book of Esther was read during the feast of Purim, celebrated on the fourteenth and fifteenth of Adar (the beginning of March). Purim is a postexilic festival in remembrance of the day that God delivered their forefathers from the hand of Haman (Est. 8–9).

The final section of the Writings features the historical works, Daniel, Chronicles, and Ezra–Nehemiah. The Book of Daniel primarily recounts the life of its main character, Daniel, who was taken to Babylon by Nebuchadrezzar in the first deportation, about 605 B.C. It is an apocalyptic book that provides a historical framework from the time of Nebuchadrezzar to possibly as late as the time of Christ. The Book of Chronicles records the history of the Jewish nation from the time of David until after the Babylonian exile with the decree of Cyrus allowing the Jews to return to Judah (539 B.C.). Ezra–Nehemiah picks up where Chronicles ends, from the return of Jewish exiles from Babylon to Nehemiah's arrival in Jerusalem as governor (c. 445 B.C.).

Significant questions have been raised as to why certain books are placed within the various sections. For example, why is Ezra–Nehemiah in the third section instead of the Prophets? Or why is Daniel in the Writings instead of among the Prophets? Scholars suggest that the books have been categorized into three divisions either

Table 3.2
The Five Scrolls (Megillot)

Book	Time of Reading
Song of Songs	Passover
Ruth	The feast of Pentecost
Lamentations	The ninth of Ab
Ecclesiastes	The feast of Tabernacles
Esther	The feast of Purim

according to: (1) their degree of canonicity; (2) their content and nature; or (3) the stage at which they were accepted into the canon of Scripture. Suggestion 2 is favored when one looks at the Book of Daniel, whose namesake was not technically a prophet but rather a statesman. Suggestion 3 may explain why the books of Chronicles and Ezra–Nehemiah, which record later material, were placed among the Writings.

Number and Order of the Old Testament Books

Since the number and order of Old Testament books are related topics, they will be discussed together.

Number of Old Testament Books

An apocryphal book 2 Esdras (also called 4 Ezra) states that there are twenty-four books in the Old Testament canon (2 Esd. 14:44–48), but Josephus clearly indicates that there were twenty-two (Josephus *Contra Apion* 1.7–8 §§ 37–39). The problem is further compounded by the fact that the modern Hebrew Bible contains thirty-six books whereas most English translations include thirty-nine. So how many Old Testament books are there? In reality each of these sources includes the same Old Testament books but divides them differently (see table 3.3).

In contrast to the list of thirty-nine books, the list of thirty-six groups Samuel, Kings, and Chronicles as each being one book with two parts. To arrive at twenty-four books, the Book of the Twelve (the Minor Prophets) is considered one book; and the list of twenty-two books joins Ruth with the Book of Judges and Lamentations with Jeremiah.

Table 3.3
Number of Old Testament Books

39 BOOKS (English OT Translations)	**36 BOOKS** (Modern Hebrew Bible)	**24 BOOKS** (Jerome)	**22 BOOKS** (Josephus)
Law 5 Genesis Exodus Leviticus Numbers Deuteronomy	**Law 5** Genesis Exodus Leviticus Numbers Deuteronomy	**Law 5** Genesis Exodus Leviticus Numbers Deuteronomy	**Law 5** Genesis Exodus Leviticus Numbers Deuteronomy

Historical 12
Joshua
Judges
Ruth
1 Samuel
2 Samuel
1 Kings
2 Kings
1 Chronicles
2 Chronicles
Ezra
Nehemiah
Esther
	Prophets
	Former Prophets 4
	Joshua
	Judges
	Samuel a, b
	Kings a, b
	Latter Prophets 15
	Isaiah
	Jeremiah
	Ezekiel
	Book of the Twelve
	  Hos. Nahum
	  Joel Hab.
	  Amos Zeph.
	  Obad. Hag.
	  Jonah Zech.
	  Micah Malachi
		Prophets
		Former Prophets 4
		Joshua
		Judges
		Samuel a, b
		Kings a, b
		Latter Prophets 4
		Isaiah
		Jeremiah
		Ezekiel
		Book of the Twelve
		(Hos., Joel, Amos,
		Obad., Jonah, Micah,
		Nahum, Hab., Zeph.,
		Hag., Zech., Malachi)
			Prophets
			Former Prophets 4
			Joshua
			Judges + Ruth
			Samuel a, b
			Kings a, b
			Latter Prophets 4
			Isaiah
			Jeremiah + Lamentations
			Ezekiel
			Book of the Twelve
			(Hos., Joel, Amos,
			Obad., Jonah, Micah,
			Nahum, Hab., Zeph.,
			Hag., Zech., Malachi)

Poetry 5 Job Psalms Proverbs Ecclesiastes Song of Songs		**Writings 11** Psalms Job Proverbs Ruth Song of Songs Ecclesiastes Lamentations Esther Daniel Ezra–Nehemiah Chronicles a, b	**Writings 9** Psalms Job Proverbs Song of Songs Ecclesiastes Esther Daniel Ezra–Nehemiah Chronicles a, b

Prophets 17
Isaiah
Jeremiah
Lamentations
Ezekiel
Daniel
Book of the Twelve
  Hos.   Nahum
  Joel   Hab.
  Amos   Zeph.
  Obad.   Hag.
  Jonah   Zech.
  Micah   Malachi
	Writings 12
	Psalms
	Job
	Proverbs
	Ruth
	Song of Songs
	Ecclesiastes
	Lamentations
	Esther
	Daniel
	Ezra
	Nehemiah
	Chronicles a, b		

It is not surprising that there are varying book divisions, since the combinations emerged over a long period of time by different people. As R. K. Harrison, former professor of Old Testament at Wycliffe College, University of Toronto, notes, even among early Jewish teachers there were differing opinions as to how the books should be arranged: "In his preface to Samuel and Kings, Jerome mentions twenty-two books, but he finally arrived at a total of twenty-four, whereas Origen adhered to the num-

Table 3.4
Order of Old Testament Books

Hebrew	Septuagint	Latin Vulgate	English
Torah	**Torah**	**Torah**	**Torah**
Genesis	Genesis	Genesis	Genesis
Exodus	Exodus	Exodus	Exodus
Leviticus	Leviticus	Leviticus	Leviticus
Numbers	Numbers	Numbers	Numbers
Deuteronomy	Deuteronomy	Deuteronomy	Deuteronomy
Prophets	**History**	**History**	**History**
Joshua	Joshua	Joshua	Joshua
Judges	Judges	Judges	Judges
Samuel a	Ruth	Ruth	Ruth
Samuel b	1 Samuel	1 Samuel	1 Samuel
Kings a	2 Samuel	2 Samuel	2 Samuel
Kings b	1 Kings	1 Kings	1 Kings
Isaiah	2 Kings	2 Kings	2 Kings
Jeremiah	1 Chronicles	1 Chronicles	1 Chronicles
Ezekiel	2 Chronicles	2 Chronicles	2 Chronicles
Hosea	Ezra	Ezra	Ezra
Joel	Nehemiah	Nehemiah	Nehemiah
Amos	Esther	Esther	Esther
Obadiah			
Jonah	**Poetry**	**Poetry**	**Poetry**
Micah	Psalms	Job	Job
Nahum	Proverbs	Psalms	Psalms
Habakkuk	Ecclesiastes	Proverbs	Proverbs
Zephaniah	Song of Songs	Ecclesiastes	Ecclesiastes
Haggai	Job	Song of Songs	Song of Songs
Zechariah			
Malachi	**Prophets**	**Prophets**	**Prophets**
	Hosea	Isaiah	Isaiah
Writings	Amos	Jeremiah	Jeremiah
Psalms	Micah	Lamentations	Lamentations
Job	Joel	Ezekiel	Ezekiel
Proverbs	Obadiah	Daniel	Daniel
Ruth	Jonah	Hosea	Hosea
Song of Songs	Nahum	Joel	Joel
Ecclesiastes	Habakkuk	Amos	Amos
Lamentations	Zephaniah	Obadiah	Obadiah
Esther	Haggai	Jonah	Jonah
Daniel	Zechariah	Micah	Micah
Ezra	Malachi	Nahum	Nahum
Nehemiah	Isaiah	Habakkuk	Habakkuk
Chronicles a	Jeremiah	Zephaniah	Zephaniah
Chronicles b	Lamentations	Haggai	Haggai
	Ezekiel	Zechariah	Zechariah
	Daniel	Malachi	Malachi

ber suggested by Josephus [twenty-two] (In Eusebius *HE* 6.25.1–2). Since both Origen and Jerome studied under Jewish teachers, it appears probable that the synagogue authorities themselves were somewhat undecided on the matter."[10]

The Jewish people have consistently maintained the same books in their canon, though during the first century debates flared up over certain books. Initially Christians accepted the Jewish Old Testament, but by at least the fourth century there was more variation concerning the number of books, a topic to be discussed later in this book.

Order of the Old Testament Books

The order of the books appearing in modern Bibles has come to be considered almost inviolable, but this was not the case in earlier times. Roger Beckwith, who has written a classic work on the Old Testament canon, states:

> This stability of order is a relatively modern phenomenon, and owes a good deal to the invention of printing. It was preceded by an era of fluidity, both among Jews (the chief guardians of the Hebrew Bible) and among Christians (the chief guardians of the Greek). In Jewish and Hebrew sources, it is true, the five books of the Law always appear in their natural, chronological order, and likewise the first four books of the Prophets; these are invariably the historical books Joshua, Judges, Samuel and Kings, which continue the historical sequence from the point where the Law leaves it. But the remaining books of the Prophets—the oracular books— have in the Jewish and Hebrew sources no settled order; which is likewise the case with the Hagiographa.[11]

When the books of the Bible were written on scrolls, order was not an issue. With the rising use of the codex by Christians by the early second century, arrangement became more of a consideration. The order of several texts of the Old Testament is shown in table 3.4. The order of the English

Bible derives from the Latin Vulgate, which is probably dependent upon the Septuagint. However, there is significant variation in the order of the Septuagint among different manuscripts (see appendix 1). How was one order chosen? To answer this let us take one step further back to see where the order of the Hebrew Bible originated.

The Hebrew Bible

The order of the Hebrew Bible follows the tripartite divisions of the Old Testament, with some variations among the translations and manuscripts. There is little difference in order of the books of the Law, presumably because they successively record historical events. This is also true of the Former Prophets (Josh.–Kings), though the Syriac Peshitta places Job between the Pentateuch and Joshua because of its presumed authorship by Moses.[12] More differences surface in the order of the Latter Prophets; in some instances Isaiah appears first (Codex Leningradensis [1008] and another Leningrad Codex [1009]), whereas Jeremiah sometimes is placed first (T.B. *Baba Batra* 14b, Madrid National Library Codex Ms. 1 [1280]). The oldest rabbinical order, *Baba Batra* 14b, arranges the Latter Prophets at least partially in descending order according to their length:

> Our Rabbis taught: The order of the Prophets is, Joshua, Judges, Samuel, Kings, Jeremiah, Ezekiel, Isaiah, and the Twelve Minor Prophets. Let us examine this. Hosea came first, as it is written, *God spake first to Hosea.* But did God speak first to Hosea? Were there not many prophets between Moses and Hosea? R. Johanan, however, has explained [what it means is that] he was the first of the four prophets who prophesied at that period, namely, Hosea, Isaiah, Amos and Micah. Should not then Hosea come first?—Since his prophecy is written along with those of Haggai, Zechariah and Malachi, and Haggai, Zechariah and Malachi came at the end of the prophets, he is reckoned with them. But why should he not be written separately and placed first?—Since his book is so small, it might be lost [if copied separately].[13]

It has also been argued that the Book of the Twelve was arranged chronologically, beginning with Hosea in the eighth century B.C. and ending with Malachi in the fifth century B.C. However, the dates of several of these books have been strongly debated (e.g., Joel, Obad., Jon.).

The Writings are the most divergent in their groupings. Sometimes they are separated into Former Writings (Ps., Job, Prov.), Latter Writings (Dan., Ezra–Neh., Chron.), and the five *megillot*. Other times they are divided into Major Writings (Ps., Job, Prov.), Minor Writings (Song, Eccles., Lam.), and Latter Writings (Est., Dan., Ezra–Neh., Chron.).[14] The books of this section have few links with each other; they have diverse literary forms and many cannot be dated precisely.

The Septuagint

The order of books in the Septuagint differs significantly from that of the Hebrew Bible. Modern publications of the Septuagint generally follow the order of the Codex Vaticanus:

tion: "The Septuagint arrangement may not have been new; it was possibly one of the arrangements current among the Jews at the time, but it was not the arrangement which prevailed among the Jews of Palestine and Babylonia, where the Hebrew Bible was preserved and edited."[15]

It is possible that in the Septuagint the books were arranged more chronologically than in the Hebrew order (cf. placement of Ruth; Chron.–Ezra–Neh.). Another major difference between the Septuagint and the Hebrew Bible arises in the Book of Jeremiah—in the Septuagint this book is about one-eighth shorter and follows a significantly different order after 25:13. There are no clear reasons for these differences, and scholars can only speculate concerning them.[16]

The English Bible

English Bibles derive their order of the Old Testament from the Latin Vulgate, which became the standard translation of the church for more than a thousand years. The Latin Vulgate drew mainly from the

Genesis	(1–2 Chron.)	Esther	Zephaniah	of Azariah and Song
Exodus	1 Esdras*	Judith*	Haggai	of the Three Young
Leviticus	2 Esdras (Ezra–Neh.)	Tobit*	Zechariah	Men,* Susanna,*
Numbers	Psalms [with Ps. 151*]	Hosea	Malachi	and Bel and the
Deuteronomy	Proverbs	Amos	Isaiah	Dragon*]
Joshua	Ecclesiastes	Micah	Jeremiah	
Judges	Song of Songs	Joel	Baruch*	
Ruth	Job	Obadiah	Lamentations	
1–4 Kingdoms (1–2	Wisdom of Solomon*	Jonah	Epistle of Jeremiah*	
Sam., 1–2 Kings)	[Wisdom of] Sirach/	Nahum	Ezekiel	
1–2 Paralipomenon	Ecclesiasticus*	Habakkuk	Daniel [with Prayer	*Apocrypha

But several other Septuagint codices have different arrangements: the Prophets appear after the historical books and before the poetical books in Codex Sinaiticus (fourth century) and Codex Alexandrinus (fifth century); and the Prophets are placed last in Codex Vaticanus (fourth century; see appendix 1). Though the order may vary, the main fourfold division of the books (i.e., the Pentateuch, Historical Books, Poetic Books, and Prophetic Books) remains intact. F. F. Bruce suggests that the order of the Septuagint may reflect earlier tradi-

Septuagint, though the books of Samuel and Kings are collectively called the Books of Kingdoms in the Septuagint (i.e., 1–2 Sam. + 1–2 Kings = 1–4 Kingdoms).

Titles of the Old Testament Books

It is interesting that a good number of books of the Old and New Testaments are anonymous, which suggests that knowing who the original authors were was apparently not as important to the first recipients as it is to us (see table 3.5). More important was that their message originated from God and demanded a response.

Hebrew Titles

Originally scrolls did not bear a title at the beginning of the book, although an identifying notation of some kind was probably made on the outside of the scroll.

The titles of the books appear to have been added later (the Qumran manuscripts, for instance, do not bear titles) and gained importance when they were used to distinguish the various books gathered into one canon. In the Hebrew Bible the Pentateuch book titles derive from the first important word or words in the book. The majority of Old Testament books, however, are named after their main characters (Josh., Ruth), supposed authors (Isa., Mic., Joel), or contents (Judg., Kings, Chron.).

Table 3.5
Names of Old Testament Books

Hebrew	Septuagint	Latin Vulgate	English
Bᵉrēʾšît In the beginning	Γενεσις Genesis	Genesis	Genesis
Wᵉʾēlleh šᵉmôt These are the names	Εξοδος Exodus	Exodus	Exodus
Wayyiqrāʾ And he called	Λευιτικον Leviticus	Leviticus	Leviticus
Bᵉmidbar In the wilderness	Αριθμοι Numbers	Numeri	Numbers
ʾElleh haddᵉbārîm These are the words	Δευτερονομιον Deuteronomy	Deuteronomium	Deuteronomy
Yᵉhôšuaᶜ Joshua	Ιησους Joshua	Iesu Nave/Iosue	Joshua
Šōpᵉṭîm Judges	Κριται Judges	Iudices	Judges
Rût Ruth	Ρουθ Ruth	Ruth	Ruth
Šᵉmûʾēl א 1 Samuel	Βασιλειων Α 1 Samuel	1 Reges/1 Samuhel	1 Samuel
Šᵉmûʾēl ב 2 Samuel	Βασιλειων Β 2 Samuel	2 Reges/2 Samuhel	2 Samuel
Mᵉlākîm א 1 Kings	Βασιλειων Γ 1 Kings	3 Reges/1 Malachim	1 Kings
Mᵉlākîm ב 2 Kings	Βασιλειων Δ 2 Kings	4 Reges/2 Malachim	2 Kings
Dibrê hayyāmîm א 1 Chronicles	Παραλειπομενων Α 1 Chronicles	1–2 Paralipomenon/Verba	1 Chronicles
Dibrê hayyāmîm ב 2 Chronicles	Παραλειπομενων Β 2 Chronicles	Dierum	2 Chronicles
ᶜEzrēʾ Ezra	Εσδρας Β Ezra– Nehemiah	1 Esdras (= Ezra)	Ezra
Nᵉhemyâ Nehemiah		2 Esdras (= Nehemiah)	Nehemiah
ʾEstēr Esther	Εσθηρ Esther	Esther/Hester	Esther
ʾÎyôb Job	Ιωβ Job	Iob	Job
Tᵉhillîm Psalms	Ψαλμοι Psalms	Psalmi	Psalms
Mišlê Proverbs	Παροιμιαι Proverbs	Proverbia Salomonis	Proverbs
Qōhelet Preacher	Εκκλησιαστης Ecclesiastes	Ecclesiastes	Ecclesiastes
Šîr haššîrîm The Song of Songs	Ασμα Song of Songs	Canticum Canticorum	Song of Songs
Yᵉšaᶜᵉyāhû Isaiah	Ησαιας Isaiah	Isaias	Isaiah
Yirmᵉyāhû Jeremiah	Ιερεμιας Jeremiah	Ieremias/Hieremias	Jeremiah
ʾÊkâ Lamentations	Θρηνοι Lamentations	Lamentationes	Lamentations
Yᵉhezqēʾl Ezekiel	Ιεζεκιηλ Ezekiel	Ezechiel/Hiezechiel	Ezekiel
Dānîyēʾl Daniel	Δανιηλ Daniel	Daniel/Danihel	Daniel
Hôšēaᶜ Hosea	Ωσηε Hosea	Osee	Hosea
Yôʾēl Joel	Ιωηλ Joel	Ioel/Iohel	Joel
ᶜĀmôs Amos	Αμως Amos	Amos	Amos
ᶜŌbadyâ Obadiah	Αβδιου Obadiah	Abdias	Obadiah
Yônâ Jonah	Ιωνας Jonah	Iona	Jonah
Mîkâ Micah	Μιχαιας Micah	Michaeas/Micha	Micah
Naḥûm Nahum	Ναουμ Nahum	Nahum/Naum	Nahum
Hᵉbaqqûq Habakkuk	Αβακουμ Habakkuk	Habacuc/Abacuc	Habakkuk
Ṣᵉpanyâ Zephaniah	Σοφονιας Zephaniah	Sophonias/Sofonias	Zephaniah
Ḥaggay Haggai	Αγγαιος Haggai	Aggaeus/Aggeus	Haggai
Zᵉkaryâ Zechariah	Ζαχαριας Zechariah	Zacharias/Zaccharias	Zechariah
Malʾākî Malachi	Μαλαχιας Malachi	Malachias/Malachi	Malachi

English Titles

The titles of the Old Testament books in our English versions come from the Latin Vulgate, which were translated from the Septuagint. These names reflect the content or main character as opposed to the first words of the books. The following list indicates the meanings of their names:

Genesis (origin, generation)

Exodus (departure)

Leviticus (pertaining to the tribe of Levi)

Numbers (numbers—two census records in book)

Deuteronomy (second law)

Joshua (main character)

Judges (main content)

1, 2 Samuel (history beginning with Samuel)

1, 2 Kings (main content)

1, 2 Chronicles (records)

Ezra (main character)

Nehemiah (main character)

Esther (main character)

Job (main character)

Psalms (songs)

Proverbs (wise sayings)

Ecclesiastes (preacher)

Song of Songs (songs)

Isaiah (main character)

Jeremiah (main character)

Lamentations (laments)

Ezekiel (main character)

Daniel (main character)

Hosea (main character)

Joel (main character)

Amos (main character)

Obadiah (main character)

Jonah (main character)

Micah (main character)

Nahum (main character)

Habakkuk (main character)

Zephaniah (main character)

Haggai (main character)

Zechariah (main character)

Malachi (main character)

For Further Reading

Anderson, B. W. *Understanding the Old Testament*. Abridged 4th ed. Upper Saddle River, NJ: Prentice-Hall, 1998.

Beckwith, R. *The Old Testament Canon of the New Testament Church and Its Background in Early Judaism*. Grand Rapids: Eerdmans, 1985.

Craigie, P. C. *The Old Testament: Its Background, Growth, and Content*. Nashville: Abingdon, 1986.

Dillard, R. B., and T. Longman. *An Introduction to the Old Testament*. Grand Rapids: Zondervan, 1994.

Harrison, R. K. *Introduction to the Old Testament*. Grand Rapids: Eerdmans, 1969.

Hill, A. E., and J. H. Walton. *A Survey of the Old Testament*. Grand Rapids: Zondervan, 1991.

LaSor, W. S., D. A. Hubbard, and F. W. Bush. *Old Testament Survey: The Message, Form, and Background of the Old Testament*. 2d ed. Grand Rapids: Eerdmans, 1996.

Rogerson, J., and P. Davies. *The Old Testament World*. Cambridge; New York: Cambridge University Press, 1989.

Van der Woude, A. S., ed. *The World of the Bible*. Vol. 1 of *Bible Handbook*. Translated by S. Woudstra. Grand Rapids: Eerdmans, 1986.

Appendix 1
Septuagint Manuscripts: Old Testament

Codex Vaticanus (fourth century A.D.)	**Codex Sinaiticus** (fourth century A.D.)	**Codex Alexandrinus** (fifth century A.D.)
Pentateuch	**Pentateuch**	**Pentateuch**
Genesis	Genesis	Genesis
Exodus	(missing Exodus and Leviticus)	Exodus
Leviticus	Numbers	Leviticus
Numbers	(missing Deuteronomy)	Numbers
Deuteronomy		Deuteronomy
	History	
History	(missing Joshua, Judges, Ruth,	**History**
Joshua	and 1–4 Kingdoms [1–2 Sam.,	Joshua
Judges	1–2 Kings])	Judges
Ruth	1–[2] Paralipomenon (1–2 Chron.)	Ruth
1–4 Kingdoms (1–2 Sam., 1–2	[1 Esdras*]	1–4 Kingdoms (1–2 Sam.,
Kings)	2 Esdras (Ezra–Neh.)	1–2 Kings)
1–2 Paralipomenon (1–2 Chron.)	Esther	1–2 Paralipomenon (1–2 Chron.)
1 Esdras*	Tobit*	
2 Esdras (Ezra–Neh.)	Judith*	**Prophets**
	1, 4 Maccabees*	Hosea
Poetic		Amos
Psalms [with Ps. 151*]	**Prophets**	Micah
Proverbs	Isaiah	Joel
Ecclesiastes	Jeremiah	Obadiah
Song of Songs	Lamentations	Jonah
Job	(missing Ezekiel, Daniel, Hosea,	Nahum
Wisdom of Solomon*	Amos, and Micah)	Habakkuk
[Wisdom of] Sirach/	Joel	Zephaniah
Ecclesiasticus*	Obadiah	Haggai
	Jonah	Zechariah
More History	Nahum	Malachi
Esther	Habakkuk	Isaiah
Judith*	Zephaniah	Jeremiah
Tobit*	Haggai	Baruch*
	Zechariah	Lamentations
Prophets	Malachi	Epistle of Jeremiah*
Hosea		Ezekiel
Amos	**Poetic**	Daniel [with Prayer of Azariah
Micah	Psalms [with Ps. 151*]	and Song of the Three Young
Joel	Proverbs	Men,* Susanna,* and Bel and the
Obadiah	Ecclesiastes	Dragon*]
Jonah	Song of Songs	
Nahum	Wisdom of Solomon*	**More History**
Habakkuk	[Wisdom of] Sirach/	Esther
Zephaniah	Ecclesiasticus*	Tobit*
Haggai	Job	Judith*
Zechariah		1 Esdras*
Malachi		2 Esdras (Ezra–Neh.)
Isaiah		1–4 Maccabees*
Jeremiah		
Baruch*		**Poetic**
Lamentations		Psalms [with Ps. 151*]
Epistle of Jeremiah*		Job
Ezekiel		Proverbs
Daniel [with Prayer of Azariah and		Ecclesiastes
Song of the Three Young Men,*		Song of Songs
Susanna,* and Bel and the		Wisdom of Solomon*
Dragon*]		[Wisdom of] Sirach/
		Ecclesiasticus*
*Apocrypha		Psalms of Solomon**
**Pseudepigrapha		

The New Testament

Like the Old Testament, the New Testament is a collection of books written by different authors in a variety of literary genres. It contains twenty-seven books from about ten authors, and records the history of Jesus from his life on earth to his future return when he will establish a new heaven and a new earth. The New Testament books were written between about A.D. 49 (Galatians)[1] and 95 (Revelation), but it was many years (possibly as late as the fifth century) before a unified canon was agreed upon by both divisions of the church (i.e., East and West).[2] The books are not arranged in chronological order; the Gospels, which begin the New Testament, were probably some of the latest books written. Most of the books are letters (twenty-one out of twenty-seven) written as simple communication from one person or persons to others. Paul Beasley-Murray observes, "The chief difference between first-century letters and those we send to each other today is that the sender's name came at the beginning. There usually followed a few lines of formal greeting, often mentioning the gods. Greetings and love to others were listed at the end."[3]

The New Testament letters are more formal than letters today and read more often like sermons written to a fairly wide audience.[4] Most claim to be written by Paul, a Jew who was converted to Christianity while traveling to Damascus in order to persecute the growing Christian church there (Acts 9). After his conversion Paul traveled widely throughout the Gentile world, and during three major missionary journeys he evangelized much of the Roman world.

Historical Background of the New Testament

The world of the New Testament differed significantly from that of the Old Testament. The Greeks, led by Alexander the Great, conquered vast areas to their

Figure 4.1. A coin of Alexander the Great (336–323 B.C.). [Paul Wegner]

Alexander portrayed as Herakles in a lion skin.

Zeus seated on a throne. The Greek inscription reads ΒΑΣΙΛΕΩΣ ΑΛΕΞΑΝΔΡΟΥ, "of [belonging to] King Alexander."

east and commanded an empire larger than any up to that time (fig. 4.1). They immediately set to work to unify each part of the empire by imposing upon it the Greek language and culture. Greek styles of dress and culture differed significantly from those of the Jews, as William Ramsay, former professor at Bethel College in McKenzie, Tennessee, notes:

> Almost all stylish women of the time wore lipstick. Dyed hair (especially red or blond) and permanent waves were in fashion, sometimes even for men. One famous glamour girl kept a herd of three thousand asses to provide milk for her daily bath, to give her a lovely complexion all over. . . . Country folks loved to go to fairs, where they would see sideshows featuring marionettes, acrobats, rope-walkers, jugglers, and fortune-tellers.

Figure 4.2.
A coin of Antiochus Epiphanes (reigned from c. 175–164 B.C.). [Paul Wegner]

Portrait of Antiochus

Zeus seated on a throne

ΘΕΟΥ
[ΕΠΙ]ΦΑΝΟΥΣ
"God Manifest"
[ΝΙΚΗ]ΦΟΡΟΥ
"Victory Bringer"

ΒΑΣΙΛΕΩΣ
ΑΝΤΙΟΧΟΥ
"King Antiochus"

Beach resorts were crowded each summer. Astronomers not only knew that the earth was round but had calculated the distance around it as being twenty-four thousand miles and the distance to the sun as ninety-two million miles.[5]

Because the Jewish nation strove to retain its heritage, the Jews became a thorn in the flesh to many Greek leaders. This reached a breaking point in the mid-second century B.C. when Antiochus IV (who called himself Epiphanes, meaning "God manifest") attempted to stamp out Judaism (fig. 4.2).

Josephus, a Jewish historian at the end of the first century, cites some of the events of 168 B.C. that incited the Jews:

> And so he [Antiochus Epiphanes] stripped the temple, carrying off the vessels of God, the golden lampstands and the golden altar and table and the other altars, and not even forbearing to take the curtains, which were made of fine linen and scarlet, and he also emptied the temple of its hidden treasures, and left nothing at all behind, thereby throwing the Jews into deep mourning. Moreover he forbade them to offer the daily sacrifices which they used to offer to God in accordance with their law, and after plundering the entire city, he killed some of the people, and some he took captive together with their wives and children, so that the number of those taken alive came to some ten thousand. And he burnt the finest parts of the city. . . . The king also built a pagan altar upon the temple-altar, and slaughtered swine thereon, thereby practising a form of sacrifice neither lawful nor native to the religion of the Jews. (Josephus *Ant.* 12.5.4 §§ 249–53)[6]

Some scholars have suggested that this was the "abomination of desolation" foretold in Daniel 9:27.[7] Shortly after this, Mattathias, a Jew from the village of Modin, refused to sacrifice to the king's gods; in his place another Jewish man came forward to make the sacrifice. Mattathias was so enraged that he killed this man and the king's officer who demanded the sacrifices. He and his sons that day launched what is commonly known as the Maccabean rebellion. The Maccabees were extremely successful in guerrilla warfare and won several significant victories against Antiochus. They set up the Maccabean dynasty and ruled over Judea for about a century; however, Hellenization (the spread of Greek culture) continued, and the Maccabean dynasty grew increasingly corrupt. The dynasty met its end in 63 B.C. when two brothers, Aristobulus II and Hyrcanus II, fought over the throne, and Pompey, a Roman general, stepped in to settle the conflict. He reestablished Roman order, and Judea became a province of the everexpanding Roman Empire.

The Romans ruled the Jews harshly, showing little tolerance toward their national laws or their God. About the time of Jesus' birth, Herod the Great (c. 37–4 B.C.; Matt. 2:1–19; Luke 1:5) sat upon the throne of Judea (fig. 4.3). Herod was an able military commander, builder, and political leader. Most of all he understood the ways of the Jews, as he was from Idumea, an area that had been conquered in war and converted to Judaism. Herod brought a great deal of stability to the land so that it was in the people's best interest to support him. However, he furthered the Hellenization of Judea by building a theater and amphitheater that housed the Roman athletic games. These games greatly offended the Jews, partly because they were closely associated with pagan gods but also because athletes competed in the nude.[8] Some Jewish athletes, wanting to compete in the Roman games, even had their circumcision reversed.[9]

Any threat to his throne infuriated Herod, who assiduously guarded the title King of the Jews. Ramsay describes his paranoia:

> Terrified by the slightest hint of threat to his throne, he murdered even his wife and two of his own sons on charges of plotting rebellion. Punning on two similar words, the emperor Augustus is said to have quipped, "I would rather be Herod's *hog* than Herod's *son*." Even during his final illness, Herod gave orders for the execution of forty protest demonstrators and another of his own children. His known cruelty is reflected in the story of Matthew's Gospel that

Herod ordered all male babies in Bethlehem to be killed because one of them was reported to be claimant to his own title, "King of the Jews."[10]

With the death of Herod stability in Judea also died. Herod had decreed that Archelaus should rule over Judea and

Figure 4.3. A coin of Herod the Great (c. 37–4 B.C.). [Paul Wegner]

Tripod table flanked by two branches

Samaria, but the Jews preferred to be under direct Roman rule, as Lester Grabbe, from the University of Hull, notes: "When Herod the Great died, a delegation of Jews appeared before Augustus to ask for direct Roman rule for Judea. A few years later they got their wish, and most of them doubtless lived to regret it. Through much of the first century of the Common Era Judea was a Roman province, and the consequences for most Jews were negative."[11]

Herod's son, Archelaus (4 B.C.–A.D. 6; see fig. 4.4), angered so many Jews that they formed guerrilla bands similar to those of the Maccabean revolt. During the last year of his rule, Archelaus attempted to crush the rising revolt:

> Probably in A.D. 6, stirred up in part by a major taxation comparable to the one Luke relates to the birth of Jesus, armed rebels seized the Roman arsenal at Sepphoris, a town in Galilee (northern Palestine) only four miles from Jesus' home in Nazareth. In punishment, the Romans crucified two thousand Jews. It is possible that Jesus as a child walked a road lined with crosses on which hung the

Figure 4.4.
A coin of
Archelaus
(4 B.C.–A.D. 6).
[Paul Wegner]

Cluster
of grapes

Roman helmet

Figure 4.5.
A coin of Nero
(A.D. 54–68).
[Paul Wegner]

Portrait of Nero.
The Latin
inscription reads
IMP[ERATOR]
NERO CAESAR,
"Emperor Nero
Caesar."

bodies of these nationalists. It is also possible that Jesus, as a young carpenter, helped rebuild Sepphoris after it was destroyed by the vengeful Romans.[12]

Archelaus was finally removed from office, but there was little improvement for the Jews. Roman governors over the Jews were often insensitive and, even worse, incompetent. Conditions deteriorated to such an extent that the Jews revolted again in 66–70, during the reign of Nero (fig. 4.5). Nero had been blamed for the great fire in Rome during the summer of 64, and the taxes levied afterward to help rebuild the city further eroded his popularity. It is believed that he blamed the Christians for the fire in an attempt to find a scapegoat; whether or not this is true, Christians were severely persecuted. Things were no better for the Jews, who were ready for rebellion but were greatly outnumbered and disorganized in the face of the massive and well-organized Roman armies. Grabbe explains:

> The Jews had no chance of success. This quickly became clear when they were confronted by the well-planned campaign of Vespasian. In some areas opposition collapsed immediately, and the resistance in others—brave as it was on occasion—was still not particularly effective. Jerusalem would probably have fallen in 68 except that the political situation in Rome made Vespasian delay the final assault on the city. When the siege of Jerusalem finally came under Titus's command in 70, the fanatical defense by the fighters was no match for the experienced, systematic siege of the Romans. The suicide defence at Masada has gone down in history, but it was equally futile—the war had been over for several years.[13]

In the forum in Rome tourists can still see the Arch of Titus (fig. 4.6), which commemorates this victory over the Jews in 70. The rock reliefs of the arch depict the Romans carrying off captives and a menorah, a seven-branched candlestick, from Herod's temple. These turbulent events of the first century formed the backdrop of the New Testament.

Divisions of the New Testament

The New Testament, although not as easily divisible as the Old Testament, can be arranged in the groupings indicated in table 4.1.

The Gospels

The four Gospels (lit., "good news") primarily record the events of Jesus' life, not as strict biographical accounts but rather as collections of Christ's teachings and ministry, each exhibiting a slightly different viewpoint. The good news of the New Testament is that God, in the person of Jesus Christ, visited mankind; the Gospels serve as valuable eyewitness accounts enabling succeeding generations of Christians to learn firsthand about Jesus' life and ministry. Neither are the Gospels merely historical books, since they have a clear theological intent; yet they are closer to historical writings than myths, as some have suggested them to be. Martin Hengel, professor of New Testament at the University of Tübingen, encapsulates this distinction: "We owe our thorough knowledge of the origins of Christianity above all to the fact that Luke and similarly the authors of the other two synoptic gospels, and indeed to some extent even the author of the Fourth Gospel, were not simply preachers of an abstract message, but at the same time quite deliberate 'history writers' . . . they did have a theological interest which was at the same time a historical one."[14]

Apparently many eyewitness accounts, or gospels, were written in the early first century (Luke 1:1), but only four remain. The first three Gospels are sometimes called the Synoptic Gospels, owing to the similarity of their content; it is helpful to align them in parallel columns (synoptically) in order to compare their similarities and differences. The Fourth Gospel was written significantly later by "the disciple whom Jesus loved"—most likely John, the son of Zebedee, the last surviving apostle, in the latter years of his life.

Matthew

The major emphasis of the Book of Matthew appears to be "the way of righteousness" (e.g., Jesus' baptism [Matt. 3:15]; righteousness is a key theme in the Sermon on the Mount [Matt. 5–7]), as G. N. Stanton, professor of New Testament at Cambridge, explains: "The noun 'right-

Figure 4.6. The Arch of Titus commemorates the fall of Jerusalem. The inset shows soldiers carrying off the table, trumpets, and gold lampstand from the temple. [Paul Wegner]

eous' is not found in Mark and it occurs only once in Luke (1:75). But in Matthew it is used seven times, and in every case the evangelist has almost certainly introduced the word himself. This is one of the [*sic*] Matthew's most important and distinctive themes."[15]

The Book of Matthew was written mainly to a Jewish audience and addresses questions of importance to that audience, such as tracing Jesus' lineage back to David (1:1–16) and how various Old Testament passages were fulfilled by Jesus (e.g., 1:22–23; 2:5–6; 2:16, 23). Yet it has a clear emphasis on the universality of the gospel and ends with Jesus' words, commonly called the Great Commission, a challenge to proclaim the gospel to the ends of the earth.

submitting to his Father. Jesus' own claim is "Whoever does God's will is my brother and sister and mother" (3:35). A servant must be ready at any time to do what his master requests; thus the word *immediately* is used frequently (e.g., 1:10, 12, 18, 20–21, 28–30, 42).

Paul Achtemeier believes that the author of Mark was born outside Aramaic-speaking Palestine, since he is fluent in Greek and knows that Sidon was south of Tyre (7:31). The author desired to reach a broader audience by translating Aramaic

Table 4.1
Books of the New Testament

Gospels	History	Letters		Apocalypse
Matthew	Acts	*Paul's Letters*	*General Letters*	Revelation
Mark		6 uncategorized letters (Romans;	Hebrews; James;	
Luke		1, 2 Corinthians; Galatians; 1, 2 Thessalonians)	1, 2 Peter;	
John		4 prison epistles (Ephesians, Philippians,	1, 2, 3 John; Jude	
		Colossians, Philemon)		
		3 pastoral epistles (1, 2 Timothy; Titus)		

Mark

Mark is the shortest Gospel, omitting much from the life of Jesus;[16] at the same time Mark's accounts are often more detailed or vivid than are parallel accounts in the other Gospels. With 90 percent of this book also recorded in either Matthew or Luke, R. A. Cole distinguishes its purpose:

> The scope of Mark's Gospel is . . . identical with that of the primitive apostolic preaching, beginning with John the Baptist and ending with the resurrection (cf. Acts 10:36–43; 13:24–37). . . . It bears, more clearly than any other Gospel, the marks of being a virtual 1st-century Teacher's Handbook, a summary of facts, with all save what was deemed significant ruthlessly pruned.[17]

The Gospel of Mark emphasizes true discipleship and willingness to suffer humility and rejection, that is, the way of the cross (see specifically Mark 8:31–33; 9:33–37; 10:28–34). While there is no doubt that Jesus is the "Son of God" (1:1), he vindicates his claim to that title by perfectly

words into Greek (*talitha koum* in 5:41; *ephphatha* in 7:34; *Eloi, Eloi, lama sabachthani* in 15:34) and by explaining certain Jewish customs (e.g., 7:2–4).[18]

Luke

The Book of Luke highlights Jesus' human side (e.g., John the Baptist's relationship to Jesus, 1:36–45; emphasis on Jesus' birth and childhood, 2:1–52; Jesus' genealogy traced through Joseph, 3:23) and develops the theme that despite temporary setbacks, God's way of salvation triumphs so that the gospel reaches to the very heart of the Roman Empire (see Acts 28:31).[19] Luke addressed both his writings (Luke and Acts) to Theophilus (meaning "God-lover"), and in Luke 1:1–4 he claims to have thoroughly investigated all the evidence in an attempt to present an accurate account of Jesus' life. The style of both books suggests that he was a well-educated (in Col. 4:14 Luke is called "our dear friend Luke, the doctor"), Greek-speaking Gentile.

Luke portrays the rejection of Jesus by his own people at the outset of his ministry and develops the theme that deliverance would be opened to the Gentiles (Simeon states that Jesus was to be "a light for revelation to the Gentiles" in 2:32; Luke traces Jesus' genealogy to Adam, the father of all races, in 3:23–38; in Matthew's account of Jesus sending out his disciples they are told not to go among the Gentiles [Matt. 10:5], but this phrase is omitted in Luke 9:1–6).

John

Although the Gospel of John includes many of the same stories, often with similar wording to the Gospel of Mark, it is not considered a Synoptic Gospel. The intent of this Gospel is significantly different, as exemplified in the following contrasts.[20] The Synoptic Gospels focus mainly on Jesus' Galilean ministry, whereas the Gospel of John centers on Jesus' ministry in Jerusalem and Judea. The Synoptics emphasize Jesus' parables—Matthew goes so far as to state that Jesus "did not say anything to them without using a parable" (Matt. 13:34). John, however, records no parables; instead Jesus often speaks in long monologues or engaging debates. The Synoptics emphasize Jesus' message that "the kingdom of God is near," whereas John refers to the kingdom of God only twice (John 3:3, 5). The Synoptics mention one Passover during Jesus' ministry; John records at least three, suggesting that Jesus' ministry extended three or three-and-one-half years.[21] The Synoptics' revelation of Jesus as the Son of God is a gradual process; from the outset in John, however, it is a foregone conclusion.

Map 1. Paul's first and second missionary journeys. [Moody Bible Institute]

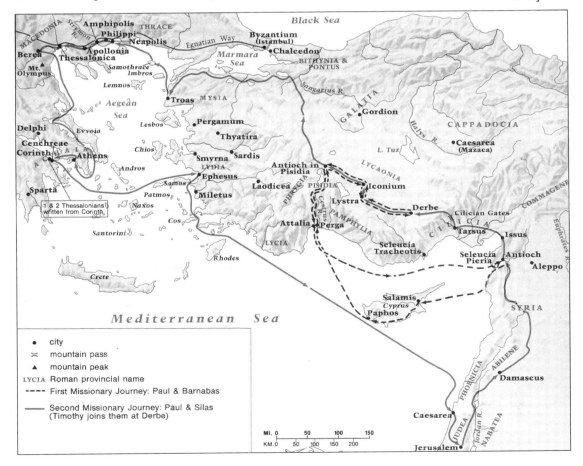

57

It is better to view the Gospel of John as a supplement to the other Gospels in which he presents Jesus as the only way to God ("the Lamb of God, who takes away the sin of the world" [1:29]; "I am the way and the truth and the life" [14:6]) with the following purpose as summarized in John 20:30–31:

> Jesus did many other miraculous signs in the presence of his disciples, which are not recorded in this book. But these are written that you may believe that Jesus is the Christ, the Son of God, and that by believing you may have life in his name.

Acts

Historically there has been little question that Paul's physician and fellow traveler, Luke (Col. 4:14; 2 Tim. 4:11; Philem.

Table 4.2
Paul's Letters

Letter	Date
Galatians	? early 49
1 Thessalonians	50
2 Thessalonians	51
1 Corinthians	55
2 Corinthians	56
Romans	57
Prison Epistles	Imprisonments
Ephesians	Caesarea (57–59), Acts 23–26
Philippians	Rome (60–62), Acts 28
Colossians	
Philemon	These letters were probably written during the latter imprisonment.
Pastoral Epistles	
1 Timothy	? 65
Titus	? 65
2 Timothy	? 65

24), wrote Acts to pick up the story where the Gospel of Luke ends. He records the history of the early church from the ascension of Christ to the preaching of the gospel throughout the Roman Empire and finally in Rome itself. The book pictures how, through the early church, the Great Com-

mission of Matthew 28:19–20 began to be fulfilled: "and you will be my witnesses in Jerusalem [1:12–6:7], and in all Judea and Samaria [6:8–12:25], and to the ends of the earth [13:1–28:31]" (Acts 1:8). While Luke shapes his historical narrative to highlight the Christian message, contemporary archaeological discoveries have supported Luke's historical accuracy.[22] Luke and Acts, then, form a two-volume work written in some of the most cultured Greek of the New Testament; their purpose is to provide a reliable account of Christianity to a Gentile audience.

Christianity is presented in a favorable light, not as a threat to established Roman law and order. In Luke, for example, Pilate proclaims three times that Jesus is not guilty of inciting insurrection (Luke 23:4, 14, 22); similarly in the Book of Acts political leaders freed Paul and his companions when charges against them could not be substantiated (Acts 16:19–40; 18:12–17; 19:31–41; 26:1–32). As Christianity progressed throughout the Roman Empire, the Book of Acts often depicts Jewish leaders as its bitterest enemies and the instigators of trouble (Acts 12:1–3; 13:45, 50; 14:2–6, 19; 17:5, 13). Acts ends abruptly; Paul had reached his goal of preaching the gospel in Rome (Acts 19:21), but no mention is made whether Paul was acquitted or condemned. The abrupt ending of the book suggests that the early church's task of worldwide evangelization was not yet finished and is left in the hands of the church today to help complete.

The Epistles

The twenty-one Epistles are divided between General Epistles, written by a variety of early church leaders (James, Peter, John, Jude), and those authored by Paul (thirteen or fourteen, depending on Hebrews). Except for Philemon, which claims to have been written by Paul himself (Philem. 19), most of his letters were probably dictated to a secretary, or amanuensis (e.g., Tertius inscribed Romans [16:22]), with closings added in Paul's own handwriting (1 Cor. 16:21; Gal. 6:11; Col.

4:18; 2 Thess. 3:17). Some of Paul's letters cannot be dated with certainty, but table 4.2 notes probable dates.[23]

Of the letters associated with Paul, three are considered Pastoral Epistles (i.e., 1, 2 Tim., Titus) sent to two of Paul's associates in order to exhort and encourage them in the face of difficult responsibilities. These letters are generally thought to have been written late in Paul's life in order to prepare others to carry on his ministry. Four others are termed Prison Epistles (i.e., Eph., Phil., Col., Philem.) since they were most likely written when Paul was imprisoned for two years in Rome (Acts 28:30–31);[24] each makes reference to imprisonment (Eph. 3:1; 4:1; 6:20–22; Phil. 1:7–17; Col. 4:3, 18; Philem. 1, 9–10, 13, 23). Six of Paul's letters cannot be grouped according to a single theme or event and remained unclassified though not insignificant (e.g., Rom.; 1 and 2 Cor.; Gal.; 1 and 2 Thess.).

Sometime during the formation of the New Testament canon, the seven General Epistles (i.e., James, 1, 2 Pet., 1, 2, 3 John, Jude) were grouped together. These books are sometimes called Catholic Epistles; the word *catholic* in this sense means general or universal, reflecting the fact that the letters are anonymous (with the exception of 2 and 3 John) and are not addressed to any specific person or church.[25] The author of 2 John and 3 John is termed the elder, a title indicating his advanced age and possibly that he was the sole survivor of those who had been Jesus' original disciples.

The Epistle to the Hebrews is also an anonymous work. The most we can be sure of is that its author had a masterful command of the Greek language and that it was directed to a group of Jews who had become Christians but were in danger of falling back into the legalism of Judaism. Beyond this, as Origen of Alexandria asserted, "But who wrote the epistle, in truth God [only] knows" (Eusebius *HE* 6.25.14).[26]

The Apocalypse (Revelation)

Revelation is the last New Testament book and records a vision given to John while he was exiled on the island of Patmos (Rev. 1:9) sometime during the late first century. This book belongs to a special class of literature known as apocalyptic, which employs symbolism and

Figure 4.7.
A coin of Domitian (A.D. 81–96). [Paul Wegner]

Portrait of Domitian. The partially legible, abbreviated Latin inscription reads [IMP. C]AES.DOMIT. AUG.GERM. P.M.TR.[ ], which expands to IMPERATOR CAESAR DOMITIANUS AUGUSTUS GERMANICUS PONTIFEX MAXIMUS TRIBUNUS [ ], "Emperor Caesar Domitian Augustus of Germany, Chief Priest [and] Tribune."

visions to convey a message. For this reason it is one of the most difficult books of the New Testament to decipher. Revelation was written during the reign of Domitian (81–96; fig. 4.7), another ruthless Caesar described by Eusebius as a persecutor of Christians:

> When Domitian had given many proofs of his great cruelty and had put to death without any reasonable trial no small number of men distinguished at Rome by family and career, and had punished without a cause myriads of other notable men by banishment and confiscation of their property, he finally showed himself the successor of Nero's campaign of hostility to God. He was the second to promote persecution against us, though his father, Vespasian, had planned no evil against us. (Eusebius *HE* 3.17.1)[27]

Most of the Book of Revelation reveals glimpses into the future, describing events which will take place before the great and terrible Day of the Lord. The book ends with a picture of the new heavens and new earth where God will dwell with his people.

Order of the New Testament Books

The Gospels, which center around the life and work of Christ, are logically placed at the beginning of the New Testament to provide a foundation for the books that follow. While the order of the Gospels does vary (see table 4.3), modern Bibles follow most Greek manuscripts—Matthew, Mark, Luke, John—with Matthew provid-

Table 4.3
Order of the Gospels

Common Order	Western Order	Coptic Order
Matthew	Matthew	John
Mark	John	Matthew
Luke	Luke	Mark
John	Mark	Luke

Table 4.4
Order of the New Testament Books

Vaticanus (4th century)	Sinaiticus (4th century)	Alexandrinus (5th century)	Latin Vulgate (5th century)	Bezae (5th–6th century)
Matthew	Matthew	Matthew (defective)	Matthew	Matthew
Mark	Mark	Mark	Mark	John
Luke	Luke	Luke	Luke	Luke
John	John	John (defective)	John	Mark
Acts	Romans	Acts	Acts	Acts
James	I Corinthians	James	Romans	3 John
I Peter	2 Corinthians	I Peter	I Corinthians	
2 Peter	Galatians	2 Peter	2 Corinthians	
I John	Ephesians	I John	Galatians	
2 John	Philippians	2 John	Ephesians	
3 John	Colossians	3 John	Philippians	
Jude	I Thessalonians	Jude	Colossians	
Romans	2 Thessalonians	Romans	I Thessalonians	
I Corinthians	Hebrews	I Corinthians	2 Thessalonians	
2 Corinthians	I Timothy	2 Corinthians	I Timothy	
Galatians	2 Timothy	(defective)	2 Timothy	
Ephesians	Titus	Galatians	Titus	
Philippians	Philemon	Ephesians	Philemon	
Colossians	Acts	Philippians	Hebrews	
I Thessalonians	James	Colossians	James	
2 Thessalonians	I Peter	I Thessalonians	I Peter	
Hebrews	2 Peter	2 Thessalonians	2 Peter	
I Timothy	I John	Hebrews	I John	
2 Timothy	2 John	I Timothy	2 John	
Titus	3 John	2 Timothy	3 John	
Philemon	Jude	Titus	Jude	
Revelation	Revelation	Philemon	Revelation	
	Epistle of Barnabas	Revelation		
	Shepherd of Hermas	I Clement (defective)		
		2 Clement (defective)		
		Psalms of Solomon?		

ing a transition between the Old and New Testaments. Two other orders are the Western (from the Western branch of the church)—Matthew, John, Luke, Mark (Codex Bezae from the fifth to sixth century); and Coptic (seen in the Sahidic and Bohairic versions from the third to fourth century)—John, Matthew, Mark, Luke.[28]

Historically the Book of Acts makes a transition between the Gospels and the rest of the New Testament; however, there is some variation among manuscripts (see Codex Sinaiticus; table 4.4). The Epistles are letters written to churches that Paul and his colleagues had established while on their missionary journeys (as recorded in Acts) in order to strengthen them in the gospel. The order of the Epistles varies greatly; for example, Codex Sinaiticus (fourth century) inserted Paul's letters before Acts, and Martin Luther (1483–1546) placed Hebrews, James, and Jude immediately before Revelation.

The present arrangement of the Epistles is primarily according to length. Romans, which is the longest letter addressed to a

Figure 4.8. The capitula to Mark from the Codex Alexandrinus. [British Library]

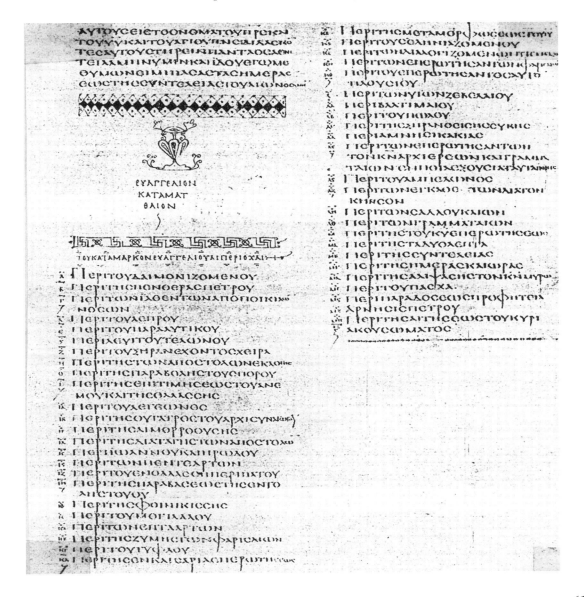

specific church, stands at the beginning of the Pauline Epistles, and 2 Thessalonians, the shortest, appears at the end. Similarly in the next series of letters addressed to individuals, 1 Timothy appears first as the longest, and Philemon, the shortest, is placed at the end.

Titles of the New Testament Books

The names of New Testament books are derived in a manner different from that of the Old Testament books. For example, the Pauline Epistles are generally named according to whom they were addressed (e.g., 1 and 2 Cor. were sent to the church at Corinth in Greece, and Eph. to the church at Ephesus in Asia Minor) and the General Epistles according to who wrote them (e.g., James, 1 and 2 Pet., Jude). The Book of Acts did not take on the title *The Acts of the Apostles* until the latter part of the second century; the adjective *all* was added at about the same time by an editor *(The Acts of All the Apostles).*[29] The Book of Revelation has borne a variety of titles, such as The Revelation of John; The Revelation of John the Divine; The Revelation of John the Evangelist; The Revelation of John the Apostle; and even The Revelation of the all-glorious Evangelist, bosom friend [of Jesus], virgin, beloved to Christ, John the theologian, son of Salome and Zebedee, but adopted son of Mary the Mother of God, and Son of Thunder.[30] The first version known to use titles was Codex Alexandrinus (fifth century).[31] These titles, continued by later manuscripts, are very simple and appear at the beginning and end of each book (e.g., ΕΥΑΓΓΕ-ΛΙΟΝ ΚΑΤΑ ΜΑΘΘΑΙΟΝ [*euaggelion kata maththaion*, Good news according to Matthew], or simply ΚΑΤΑ ΜΑΘΘΑΙΟΝ; ΠΡΟΣ ΕΦΕΣΙΟΥΣ [*pros ephesious*, to the Ephesians]). Some codices also include capitula, which summarize various sections and are often written in red ink beginning with the Greek word περί (*peri*, "about" or "concerning"; see fig. 4.8). For example, the first capitula for the Gospel of Mark in Codex Alexandrinus reads περὶ τοῦ δαιμο-νιζομένου (*peri tou diamonizomenou*, "concerning the one possessed by a demon"), which refers to the episode in Mark 1:21–28.

For Further Reading

Barrett, C. K. *The New Testament Background: Selected Documents*. San Francisco: Harper & Row, 1987.

Bouquet, A. C. *Everyday Life in New Testament Times*. New York: Scribner's Sons, 1954.

Bruce, F. F. *New Testament History*. Garden City, NY: Doubleday, 1972.

Carson, D. A., D. J. Moo, and L. Morris. *An Introduction to the New Testament*. Grand Rapids: Zondervan, 1992.

Gundry, R. H. *A Survey of the New Testament*. 3d ed. Grand Rapids: Zondervan, 1994.

Guthrie, D. *New Testament Introduction*. 4th ed. Downers Grove, IL: InterVarsity, 1990.

Harrison, E. F. *Introduction to the New Testament*. Rev. ed. Grand Rapids: Eerdmans, 1974.

Kümmel, W. G. *Introduction to the New Testament*. Translated by H. C. Kee. Rev. ed. Nashville: Abingdon, 1975.

Schürer, E. *The History of the Jewish People in the Age of Jesus Christ (175 B.C.–A.D. 135)*. Revised and edited by G. Vermes and F. Millar. Edinburgh: T & T Clark, 1973–87.

Appendix 2
The Synoptic Problem

Statement of the Problem

Many scholars have spent countless hours trying to determine the interrelationships of the Synoptic Gospels (Matt., Mark, Luke), an issue that has become known as the Synoptic Problem. In simple terms, it is an attempt to explain the remarkable similarities with which the Evangelists report the sayings of Jesus and the events of his life while still accounting for important differences. The significance of these similarities is compounded when we realize that Jesus probably spoke in Aramaic whereas the Evangelists recorded his sayings in Greek.

The following diagram indicates the similarities among the Synoptic Gospels.[32]

History of Interpretation

Until about 1790, it was commonly agreed that the Gospels were composed in canonical order (i.e., Matt., Mark, and Luke). From that point until about 1870 discussions continued, but the reigning hypothesis (especially in Germany and popularized by J. J. Griesbach) was that the Gospels were composed in the order Matthew, Luke, Mark, and John. It was

Table 4.5 Several Related Passages in the Synoptics

Matthew	Mark	Luke
Matthew 8:14–15	Mark 1:29–31	Luke 4:38–39
Matthew 19:13–15	Mark 10:13–16	Luke 18:15–17
Matthew 22:23–33	Mark 12:18–27	Luke 20:27–40

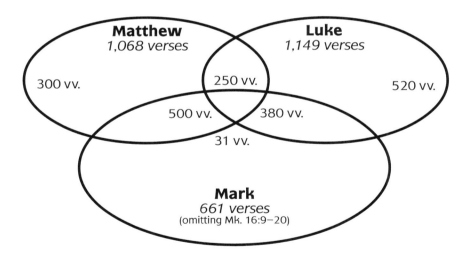

To state the similarities another way, there are only three pericopes (sections or units of Scripture) in Mark that are unique to this Gospel (i.e., Mark 3:19b–21; 4:26–29; 8:22–26). See table 4.5 for examples of overlap among the three Gospels.

largely agreed that Mark wrote his Gospel third with knowledge of the other two Gospels that preceded him (Farmer [1976]; Orchard [1976]). From about 1870 until 1970 Markan priority gained dominance. It was argued that Mark was written first and that both Matthew and Luke independently used this Gospel to compose their own. Since about 1970 the Synoptic Problem has increasingly become an open question, but Markan priority is still supported by the majority of Synoptic scholars (e.g., D. R. Catchpole [1993], G. N. Stanton [1992]; S. McKnight [1988]; C. M. Tuckett [1984], J. A. Fitzmyer [1981]).

Suggested Solutions

Markan Priority

In 1835 K. Lachmann argued for Markan priority based upon three principles: the order of the material found in the Gospels of Matthew and Mark sometimes agrees together against Luke; more often the sequence of material from Luke and Mark agrees against Matthew; and Matthew and Luke never agree together in their arrangement against Mark. From a detailed study of the Gospels Lachmann argued that the evidence could best be explained if the Gospel of Mark was used as a source by the other two Gospel writers. Even those who hold Markan priority are separated into two major schools of thought, the Farrer theory and the Oxford theory.

The Farrer Theory

This view suggests that the Gospel of Mark appeared first, which Matthew used to write his Gospel; Luke then used both Mark and Matthew to formulate his.

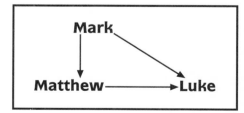

The Oxford Theory

This more complicated theory seems to better conform to the evidence. It argues that verbal agreement among the Synoptic Gospels suggests that similar material in both Matthew and Luke is based upon

Mark and a source known as Q. The following evidence is offered in support: the majority of material that is common to Mark and one or both of the other Synoptic Gospels is narrative (the principal exceptions are the parables of Mark 4 and the eschatological material of Mark 13); and the non-Markan material common both to Matthew and Luke (known as Q) consists mainly of sayings of Jesus. A further examination of Q indicates that it can be separated into the following categories: Jesus and John the Baptist; Jesus and the disciples; Jesus and his opponents; and Jesus and the future. Two other sources were available to the Gospel writers:

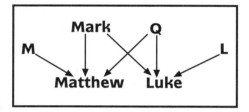

"M" A source used by Matthew that contained sayings of Jesus similar to Q.

"L" A source used by Luke especially in Luke 9–19 containing unique material, such as the parable of the good Samaritan (10:29–37), Jesus' visit to Mary's and Martha's home (10:38–42), the prodigal son (15:11–32), and the warnings about the deceitfulness of riches (12:13–15; 16:19–31).

However, one of the most difficult problems for Markan priority is when Matthew and Luke have "minor agreements" of wording against Mark (e.g., Matt. 16:21 and Luke 9:22 read "and on the third day be raised to life," whereas Mark 8:31 states "and after three days rise again"; Matt. 27:12 and Luke 23:9 record that "he [Jesus] gave [him] no answer" but in Mark 15:4 Pilate asks Jesus "Aren't you going to answer?"). These similarities suggest that Mark was not the only common factor.

Augustinian Theory

This view, which can be traced as far back as Augustine, proposes that in parallel accounts of Mark and Matthew, Mark abbreviates Matthew's material rather than Matthew amplifying Mark's. Luke then used both Matthew and Mark to compose his Gospel. However, there are significant problems with this view. Generally when Matthew and Mark have material in common, Mark's account is fuller than Matthew's, not abridged (e.g., Mark 2:1–12 // Matt. 9:1–8; Mark 9:14–29 // Matt. 17:14–21). It appears that Matthew more often abbreviates Mark rather than the other way around (e.g., Matt. 4:24–5:2 // Mark 3:7–13a; Matt. 8:28–34 // Mark 5:1–20).

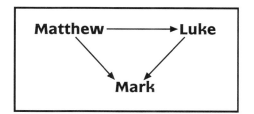

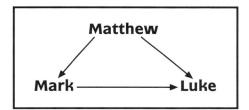

Griesbach Theory

This theory suggests that Matthew was the first Gospel written; Luke then used Matthew to compose his Gospel, and Mark used both Matthew and Luke to compose his. This theory dates as far back as H. Owen in 1764, but it was popularized by J. J. Griesbach in 1783. More recently it has been revived by W. R. Farmer (1976), J. B. Orchard (1976), and H.-H. Stoldt (1980). The strengths of this theory are that it adequately accounts for the similarities of the Gospels (e.g., Matt. and Mark against Luke; Mark and Luke against Matt.; Matt. and Luke against Mark) without reference to a Q source, and it explains what appear to be harmonizations in Mark (at least 213 of them, according to R. H. Stein),[33] as exemplified in table 4.6.

Griesbach's view, however, does not adequately account for differences among the Synoptics. For example, why would Luke agree with Mark against Matthew (e.g., "Gerasenes" in Mark 5:1 and Luke 8:26, but "Gadarenes" in Matt. 8:28; "Simon" in Mark 1:29 and Luke 4:38, but "Peter" in Matt. 8:14) or why would Matthew and Mark agree against Luke (e.g., "how they might kill Jesus" in Matt. 12:14 and Mark 3:6; but "what they might do to Jesus" in Luke 6:11)? There is also the problem of viewing Mark as an abridgment of Matthew when the former often has a fuller description of events (cf. Matt. 17:14–21 with Mark 9:14–29 and Luke 9:37–43a).

Table 4.6
Harmonizations in Mark

Matthew	Mark	Luke
Matthew 8:16 When evening came	Mark 1:32 That evening after sunset	Luke 4:40 When the sun was setting
Matthew 8:3 Immediately he was cured of his leprosy	Mark 1:42 Immediately the leprosy left him and he was cured	Luke 5:13 And immediately the leprosy left him
Matthew 5:15–16 Neither do people light a lamp and put it under a bowl. Instead they put it on its stand, and it gives light to everyone in the house.	Mark 4:21 Do you bring in a lamp to put it under a bowl, or a bed? Instead, don't you put it on its stand?	Luke 8:16 No one lights a lamp and hides it in a jar or puts it under a bed. Instead, he puts it on a stand, so that those who come in can see the light.

Oral Tradition

Proposed by J. G. von Herder in 1796 and further developed by J. K. L. Gieseler in 1818, this view argues that each of the Gospel writers had access to oral tradition that resulted in similarities among the Gospels. Most scholars today, however, believe that the similarities among the Gospels, especially in the order of material, go beyond what one would expect merely from oral tradition, as C. M. Tuckett explains: "For example, Matthew and Mark break their narrative of the ministry of Jesus to go back in time to give an account of the death of John the Baptist, and they do so at precisely the same relative point in the accounts (Mt. 14:3–12 = Mk. 6:17–29). Dependence on oral tradition can scarcely account for such a phenomenon of interruption of the story of Jesus' ministry at identical points in the two gospels."[34]

Conclusion

This difficult question raises important issues as to how the Synoptic Gospels were created and what sources the writers used. Even with its difficulties, the view of Markan priority remains strong, especially given the cumulative effect of the following evidence.

First, the order of the Synoptics suggests that both Matthew and Luke copied from Mark, based upon the following evidence: the arrangement of material in Matthew and Mark sometimes agrees together against Luke; there are even more passages in which Luke and Mark agree against Matthew; and the order of Matthew and Luke never agree together against Mark.

Second, a comparison of theological evidence from specific passages makes it more likely that Mark has been modified by Matthew and Luke rather than the other way around (see table 4.7). It is easy to see why Matthew (13:58) would omit part of Mark's (6:5–6) statement, for it gives the impression that Jesus is powerless. But it is not clear why Mark would add these details if he had begun with the information found in Matthew. Another example is Peter's confession. It is difficult to explain why Mark (8:29) would remove the statement of Matthew (16:16) and Luke (9:20) that Jesus is the Son of God; however, if Mark were the first Gospel to appear, the others would be reasonable expansions of it.

Third, occasionally the poor Greek of Mark is corrected in Matthew and Luke (see table 4.8). Mark also contains Aramaisms not found in Matthew and Luke, suggesting that they may have been omitted as unsuitable for proper Greek writing.

Table 4.7 Theological Evidence for Markan Priority

Matthew 13:58		Mark 6:5–6
And he did not do many miracles there because of their lack of faith.		He could not do any miracles there, except lay his hands on a few sick people and heal them. And he was amazed at their lack of faith.

Matthew 16:16	Mark 8:29	Luke 9:20
"You are the Christ, the Son of the living God."	"You are the Christ."	"The Christ of God."

Table 4.8 Linguistic Evidence for Markan Priority

Matthew	**Mark**	**Luke**
8:27	4:41	8:25
"What kind of man is this? Even the winds and the waves obey (ὑπακούουσιν, pl.) him!"	"Who is this? Even the wind and the waves obey (ὑπακούει, sing.) him!"	"Who is this? He commands even the winds and the water, and they obey (ὑπακούουσιν, pl.) him."
	5:9b–10	8:30b–31
	"for we are many." And *he* begged Jesus again and again not to send them out of the area.	because many demons had gone into him. And *they* begged him repeatedly not to order them to go into the Abyss.

Bibliography for Appendix 2: The Synoptic Problem

Catchpole, D. R. *The Quest for Q.* Edinburgh: T & T Clark, 1993.

Farmer, W. R. *The Synoptic Problem: A Critical Analysis.* Macon, GA: Mercer University Press, 1976.

Farrer, W. "On Dispensing with Q." In *Studies in the Gospels: Essays in Memory of R. H. Lightfoot,* ed. D. E. Nineham, 55–88. Oxford: Blackwell, 1955.

Fitzmyer, J. A. *The Gospel according to Luke I–IX. Introduction, Translation, and Notes.* AB 28. New York: Doubleday, 1981 (esp. pp. 63–106).

Lachmann, K. "De ordine narrationum in evangeliis synopticis." *Theologische Studien und Kritiken* 8 (1835): 570–90.

McKnight, S. *Interpreting the Synoptic Gospels.* Grand Rapids: Baker, 1988.

Orchard, J. B. *Matthew, Luke and Mark: Griesbach Solution to the Synoptic Question.* Manchester: Koinonia, 1976.

Stanton, G. N. *A Gospel for a New People: Studies in Matthew,* 23–40. Louisville, KY: Westminster/John Knox, 1993.

Stein, R. H. "Synoptic Problem." In *Dictionary of Jesus and the Gospels,* edited by J. B. Green and S. McKnight, 784–92. Downers Grove, IL: InterVarsity, 1992.

———. *The Synoptic Problem: An Introduction.* Grand Rapids: Baker, 1987.

Tuckett, C. M. *Synoptic Studies.* JSNTSup 7. Sheffield: Sheffield Academic Press, 1984.

The Unity of the Two Covenants

In spite of more than forty different authors writing during a span of possibly fifteen hundred years, the Bible has an amazingly consistent theme running through it: God chose to reveal himself to humanity and longed to establish a relationship with us. Initially the relationship between God and humanity in the garden of Eden was perfect, but when Adam and Eve rebelled against God, sin broke this fellowship. The rest of the Bible develops how God progressively revealed his plan to reestablish this relationship. Hebrews 1:1 says that God conveyed this plan "at many times and in various ways," but in the last days God spoke to man "*in* his son."[1] The message of the Bible comes to fulfillment in the New Testament through Jesus, the perfect God-man, who offered the perfect sacrifice to remove sin and effectively reopen communication and renew fellowship between God and his creation (Heb. 9:15–28). James Orr, former professor of apologetics and theology at Theological College of United Free Church, Glasgow, Scotland, summarizes God's plan in history:

> The Bible is the record of God's revelations of Himself to men in successive ages and dispensations (Eph. 1:8–10; 3:5–9; Col. 1:25f.), till the revelation culminates in the advent and work of the Son, and the mission of the Spirit. It is this aspect of the Bible that constitutes its grand distinction from all collections of sacred writings—the so-called "Bibles" of heathen religions—in the world. These, as the slightest inspection of them shows, have no unity. . . . The Bible, by contrast, is a single book because it embodies such a revelation and exhibits such a purpose. The unity of the book, made up of so many parts, is the attestation of the reality of the revelation it contains.[2]

Scholars have suggested many unifying themes that weave together the Old and New Testaments. John Bright, former professor of Hebrew and Old Testament interpretation at Union Theological Seminary (1940–1975), traces the concept of the kingdom of God through the two Testaments:

> For the concept of the Kingdom of God involves, in a real sense, the total message of the Bible. Not only does it loom large in the teachings of Jesus; it is to be found, in one form or another, through the length and breadth of the Bible—at least if we may view it through the eyes of the New Testament faith—from Abraham, who set out to seek "the city . . . whose builder and maker is God" (Heb. 11:10; cf. Gen. 12:1ff.), until the New Testament closes with "the holy city, new Jerusalem, coming down out of heaven from God" (Rev. 21:2). To grasp what is meant by the Kingdom of God is to come very close to the heart of the Bible's gospel of salvation.[3]

Gerhard von Rad, formerly Old Testament professor at the University of Heidelburg, bridges the gap between the Old and New Testaments by means of "salvation history," in which the confession of the saving acts of God is brought alive in each generation.[4] Oscar Cullmann, former New Testament professor at the Institute de France, nicely summarized von Rad's view: "the progressive reinterpretation of Israel's old traditions is continually awakened by new events in the present. This development of the traditions is itself salvation history and stands in continuity with the original event basis to the traditions."[5]

Von Rad's ideas were followed quite closely by G. Ernest Wright, former Old Testament professor at McCormick Seminary, who used the phrase "the Mighty Acts of God" to join the two Testaments and argued that the Bible's chief purpose is to proclaim the redemptive acts of God through history.[6] O. Palmer Robertson, former professor at Westminster Theological Seminary, and others have used the concept of covenant to demonstrate this unity,[7] while Walter C. Kaiser, president of Gordon-Conwell Theological Seminary, has chosen the idea of *promise*.[8] Each of these themes indicates a unity between the Old and New Testaments, an intrinsic solidarity that few scholars would deny.

Most scholars also agree that both parts of the Bible are equally important—in some sense the Old Testament prepares the foundation for the New Testament, and the New Testament is the fulfillment of the Old Testament. But if the New Testament is the fulfillment of the Old Testament, has the Old Testament any further value?

Challenges to the Importance of the Old Testament

Even in the middle of the second century, Marcion (d. c. 160) questioned the importance of the Old Testament. He established a sect arguing that the New Testament superseded the Old Testament, rendering the latter obsolete,[9] but the church rejected Marcion's heretical ideas. William Ramsay encapsulates the continued relevance of the Old Testament: "But Christians affirm that God speaks through the Old Testament as through the New. Few New Testament passages picture the care of God more beautifully than does the Old Testament's Twenty-third Psalm. What New Testament passage more forcefully presents God's demand for social justice than does the prophecy of Amos?"[10]

It is important to remember that for much of the New Testament period, the Old Testament was the main body of Scripture available to the church. Without it our understanding of many key doctrines would be greatly handicapped.

How Does the Old Testament Relate to the New Testament?

One of the most difficult issues arising from this question is what relevance the Old Testament has for the church today. In attempting to formulate a method for applying the Old Testament, the following approaches have been suggested.

Allegorical Approach

One of the earliest methods of determining the meaning of the Old Testament text is the allegorical approach to Scripture. The word *allegory* comes from the Greek ἀλληγορέω (*allēgoreō*, which is probably a combination of two words, ἄλλο [*allo*, another, other] and ἀγορεύω [*agoreuō*, to say], thus to say something other [than what the words normally imply]). An allegorical interpretation is one that assumes "the text to be interpreted says or intends to say something other than its literal wording suggests, that it contains hidden within it a deeper, mystical sense not derivable from the words themselves."[11] This type of interpretation is particularly associated with the Jews of Alexandria; one of the best known is Philo, a Jewish philosopher from about 20 B.C.–A.D. 50. But even he was following in the footsteps of pagan scholars who applied a similar methodology to the poems of Homer and other Greek mythology. Several of the early church fathers, especially those around Alexandria (i.e., Clement, Origen, Augustine), adopted the allegorical method of interpretation for the Old Testament in order to draw applications to their situations.[12] Augustine, an influential North African bishop, allegorized the story of the garden of Eden, arguing that the four rivers represented the four cardinal virtues, the fig leaves signified hypocrisy, and the skins with which Adam and Eve were clothed denoted their humanity. While this approach can be carried to absurd lengths, it is still held in various forms by scholars in spite of its arbitrariness and dependence upon imagination rather than exegesis.[13] As early as the third century, Nepos, an Egyptian bishop, wrote a work entitled a *Refutation of the Allegorists;* later a school arose near Antioch dedicated to refuting the Alexandrian school of allegorists.[14] Allegory is used in the biblical text, but only sparingly and with some indication in the context that this is the intent (e.g., Ps. 80:8–19; Eccles. 12:1–7; Ezek. 16–17; John 10:1–16; Gal. 4:21–23; Eph. 6:11–17).

Typological Approach

The English word *type* comes from the Greek τύπος (*typos,* meaning "pattern, example, model, or archetype"). Thus typology is a method of biblical exegesis or interpretation in which persons, events, or things from the Old Testament are interpreted as foreshadowings or prototypes of persons, events, or things in the New Testament.[15] Several times the New Testament utilizes the term *type* to indicate how the Old Testament prefigured a person or event in the New Testament (e.g., 1 Cor. 10:1–6; Heb. 8:5). Romans 5:14 explains that Adam was a type of Christ in that Adam was head of the race of sinners, and Christ the head of the redeemed.[16] The difference between an allegory and a type is that the former uses the original meaning of the Old Testament text as a symbol to refer to some hidden or unrelated meaning while the latter recognizes a revelatory connection between two historically distinct persons, things, or events. This method of interpretation has also been abused by those who, for instance, find references to the blood of Christ in every mention of blood, or baptism in every reference to water. A proper understanding of types does help to establish a unity between the Old and New Testaments but should be limited only to those types that are stated to be such in the New Testament.

Thematic Unity Approach

There is a consistent unity between the Old and New Testaments wherein themes and ideas that are first set forth in the Old Testament are further developed and advanced in the New Testament (e.g., the Old Testament idea of priesthood provides a context from which to understand Christ's eternal priesthood [Heb. 5–7]; Old Testament sacrifices are foundational to understanding the superiority of Christ's final sacrifice [Heb. 9–10]).[17] The similarities of themes in the two testaments do not appear to be random, but the purpose and object of their development suggests more than merely a thematic unity.

Promise and Fulfillment Approach

According to this approach the two testaments are linked by promises given by God in the Old Testament that have been fulfilled in the New Testament[18] (e.g., Isa. 9:1–2 is fulfilled by Jesus [Matt. 4:15–16]; the new covenant in Jer. 31:31–34 appears in the New Testament [Luke 22:20; 1 Cor. 11:25; Heb. 8:8–12]; Joel 2:28–32 foretells the arrival of the Spirit at Pentecost [Acts 2:17–21]). As Paul clearly states, "For no matter how many promises God has made, they are 'Yes' in Christ" (2 Cor. 1:20). However, not every Old Testament theme (e.g., the creation of the world, Gen. 1–2; Joseph's rise to power in the Egyptian government, Gen. 39–41) has a promise fulfilled later in the New Testament. Even for some New Testament passages that are said to fulfill Old Testament Scripture, it is not always clear how the fulfillment relates to the original statement (e.g., Hos. 11:1, "Out of Egypt I called my son," originally refers to Israel and not Jesus as in Matt. 2:15; Jesus went to Nazareth "so was fulfilled what was spoken through the prophets: 'He will be called a Nazarene'" [Matt. 2:23], though no known Old Testament passage makes such a claim).

Canonical Approach

In the 1970s Brevard S. Childs, professor emeritus of Old Testament at Yale University, argued that both the Old and New Testaments are Christian Scripture and witnesses to God's redemptive activity. Childs states:

> The Christian Church confesses to find
> a witness to Jesus Christ in both the Old

Testament and the New. Its Bible does not consist of the Hebrew scriptures plus an appendix called the New Testament. Rather, the form of the Christian Bible as an Old and New Testament lays claim upon the whole scripture as the authoritative witness to God's purpose in Jesus Christ for the church and the world. By reading the Old Testament along with the New as Christian scripture a new theological context is formed for understanding both parts which differs from hearing each Testament in isolation. The Old Testament is interpreted by the New, and the New is understood through the Old, but the unity of its witness is grounded in the One Lord.[19]

James Barr, emeritus professor of Hebrew Bible at Vanderbilt University, has sharply criticized Childs's view, contending that the Old Testament is Scripture, not Christian Scripture,[20] meaning that it may not be feasible to Christianize the Old Testament.

Progressive Development Approach

It is simplistic to attempt to encapsulate the unity between the Old and New Testaments with only one of the preceding approaches. Throughout history God progressively made known his revelation to his people. Certainly God had a clear structure and plan for his revelation and the more revelation God gave, the more clearly this plan emerges. God's revelation includes allegory (1 Cor. 10:1–4), typology (Rom. 5:14), even promise and fulfillment motifs (Gal. 3:16–22), but there is also an important element of progression and development as more revelation emerges. God's revelation progressed through history according to his foreordained plan as God interacted with people. According to this approach the Old Testament provided the foundation for the New Testament concepts, and the New Testament developed out of the Old.

For Further Reading

Anderson, B. W., ed. *The Old Testament and the Christian Faith: A Theological Discussion.* New York: Harper & Row, 1963.

Baker, D. L. *Two Testaments, One Bible.* 2d ed. Downers Grove, IL: InterVarsity, 1991.

Bright, J. *The Kingdom of God: The Biblical Concept and Its Meaning for the Church.* New York and Nashville: Abingdon, 1953.

Bruce, F. F. *The New Testament Development of Old Testament Themes.* Grand Rapids: Eerdmans, 1968.

Childs, B. S. *Introduction to the Old Testament as Scripture.* Philadelphia: Fortress, 1979.

France, R. T. *Jesus and the Old Testament.* London: Tyndale Press, 1971.

Fuller, D. P. *Gospel and Law: Contrast or Continuum?* Grand Rapids: Eerdmans, 1980.

Longenecker, R. N. *Biblical Exegesis in the Apostolic Period.* Grand Rapids: Eerdmans, 1975.

McComiskey, T. E. *The Covenants of Promise: A Theology of the Old Testament Covenants.* Grand Rapids: Baker, 1985.

Robertson, O. P. *The Christ of the Covenants.* Phillipsburg, NJ: Presbyterian & Reformed, 1980.

Rowley, H. H. *The Unity of the Bible.* New York: Meridian, 1957.

Wright, G. E. *God Who Acts: Biblical Theology as Recital.* SBT 8. London: SCM, 1952.

Zimmerli, W. "Promise and Fulfillment." *Int* 15 (1961): 310–38.

Part 2

Canonization of the Bible

Prerequisites to the Bible

efore there were written documents, information was transmitted orally so that accuracy depended upon the memory of the orator. Even Jesus' teachings were transmitted orally for several decades before being transcribed. The Pentateuch states that God commanded Moses several times to record specific information for the benefit of future generations (Exod. 17:14; 24:3–4, 7; 34:27; Num. 33:1–2; Deut. 31:9, 11, 22, 24). Not so long ago some biblical scholars argued that Moses could not possibly have written the Pentateuch because writing was believed to be unknown in Palestine at his time.[1] R. K. Harrison, however, correctly contests this assertion: "Contrary to the contentions of Wellhausen, who maintained, against archaeological evidence already available in his day, that writing did not appear among the Hebrews until the early monarchy, they had the means of producing written records at their disposal from very early times."[2] Since the invention of writing was prerequisite to recording the biblical books, it is important to understand its development.

Development of Writing

Drawings

Some of the earliest forms of writing are pictures and drawings that communicated a story or idea. The earliest of these are prehistoric rock carvings and paintings on the walls of caves (especially in Altamira, Spain; Lascaux, southern France; and the Vindhya Hills of the Miapur District, India); most of these works portray various kinds of animals or human beings engaged in some activity (see fig. 6.1) and may have been used for magical or religious purposes. Some scholars date them as far back as thirty thousand to sixty thou-

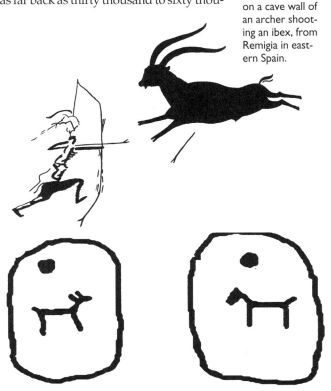

Figure 6.1. Early painting on a cave wall of an archer shooting an ibex, from Remigia in eastern Spain.

Figure 6.2. Two small, pictorial tablets (late fourth millennium B.C.) from Tell Brak in North Syria.

sand years. Pictures were also well known among the North American Indians and developed over time, as Keith Schoville, professor of Hebrew and Semitic studies at University of Wisconsin, Madison, observes: "The advantages of picture writing that was used by the North American Indians are that the simple drawings can be produced without much effort and that they do not offer too many difficulties to the 'reader.' At first the pictures bore much resemblance to reality; then they gradually became more stylized and more difficult to understand."[3]

Picture writing was also present in some of the earliest stages of both Sumerian and Egyptian writings. For example, in Mesopotamia, the land between the Tigris and Euphrates rivers, two small Sumerian tablets dated to about the late fourth millennium B.C. were discovered in 1984 at Tell Brak in northern Syria. One depicts a goat and the other a sheep, with the number 10 above each: apparently they were used as a record (fig. 6.2).

According to Christopher Walker, assistant keeper of the Western Asiatic Antiquities Department of the British Museum, record keeping appears to have been the first use of writing:

> Writing was invented in order to record business activities in the early Near East.

With the growth of centralised economies the officials of palaces and temples needed to be able to keep track of the amounts of grain and numbers of sheep and cattle which were entering or leaving their stores and farms. It was impossible to rely on a man's memory for every detail, and a new method was needed to keep reliable records.[4]

In early Egypt pictures were used to record history; for example, the palette of Narmer found at Herakleopolis in Upper Egypt records a historic victory dated to sometime before 3000 B.C. in which Narmer joined Upper and Lower Egypt into one country (fig. 6.3). One side of the palette pictures Narmer with mace in hand ready to strike an enemy; the other side depicts two animals with necks intertwined symbolizing the unity of Upper and Lower Egypt.

Picture writing has severe limitations—concepts such as love, hate, fear, or sorrow are difficult to portray; people can

Figure 6.3. The Palette of Narmer, found in 1898 at Herakleopolis in Upper Egypt; it is housed at the Egyptian Museum in Cairo. [Egyptian Museum]

interpret pictures differently; and once the meaning of the picture is forgotten, picture writing becomes merely art.

Pictograms

In a pictogram pictures of objects represent letters or sounds (e.g., a picture of a bull head represents an *ʾālep*); as time went on these pictures became more simplified and standardized. Walker describes the development from pictures to a sign representing a sound:

On the very earliest texts pictures (sometimes called pictographs) were drawn on damp clay using a pointed tool. But quite soon the scribes found it was quicker to produce a stylised representation of an object by making a few marks in the clay rather than attempt an artistic impression by naturalistic drawing in straight or curving lines. These stylised representations then had to be standardised so that everyone could recognise them. Since the scribes were no longer trying to be great artists the drawing instrument did not have to be finely pointed but could be blunt or flat. The

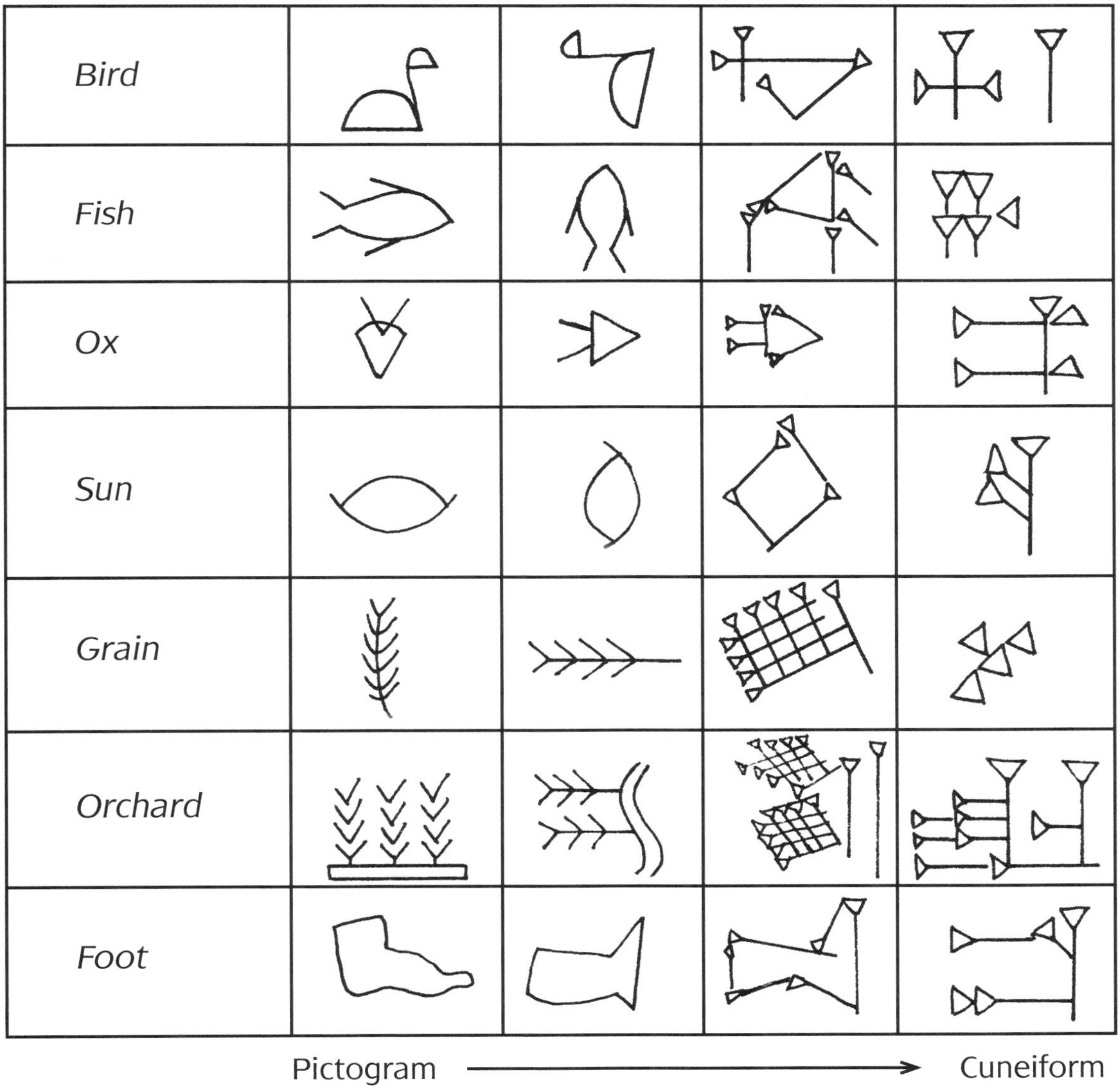

Figure 6.4.
This chart shows how several common words developed from pictograms to cuneiform writing.

Bird				
Fish				
Ox				
Sun				
Grain				
Orchard				
Foot				

Pictogram ⟶ Cuneiform

77

end of the wooden or reed stylus, which struck the clay first, made a wider mark than the shaft, and so came into being the typical wedge-shaped impression after which this writing system became known—cuneiform (from the Latin word *cuneus* meaning wedge). Many early tablets show a mixture of signs drawn and written in cuneiform.[5]

Initially scribes drew symbols or pictograms on tablets of soft clay that were either baked or left in the sun to harden. Cuneiform was first used to write Sumerian, an ancient language from about the third millennium B.C., then Akkadian and Ugaritic. Akkadian employed about six hundred different signs whereas Ugaritic had only thirty. An interesting development occurred at the end of this early period; the pictures rotated approximately 90° counterclockwise so that they appeared to rest on their backs. Figure 6.4 portrays the development of several words.

Walker also points out some of the problems encountered in interpreting pictograms:

Popular books on cuneiform have tended to give the impression that identifying the early signs is easy; in fact things are not so simple. Pictures of an ox or an ear of barley are identifiable, but there are many signs which we cannot yet explain as pictures even when by working back from the later lexical lists we are able to establish their meaning.

As soon as we are able to read the texts intelligibly, we are confronted by another difficulty. The early texts are not written in neat lines with every sign in the appropriate order—that came later—but with all the signs for each sense unit (or sentence) grouped together in a box.... The correct order in which to read the signs is thus a matter of interpretation.[6]

It was a natural transition from picture representation of an object to picture representation of a concept, the next stage of development.

Logograms

A logogram is a picture that represents a concept, and each picture may have sev-

eral different meanings. For instance, a picture of a bee might signify bee, or it may be the first unit in the word *business*. Schoville describes the changes that occurred at this stage of writing:

> In order to express abstract ideas, the meaning of the original sign was expanded to include other desired meanings. A picture could now stand for "sun," a symbol which can be labeled a pictogram, or it could express the ideas *day, time, bright, light,* and others. In this case the sign is an ideogram. The result was that one sign could acquire so many meanings that it was difficult, even in context, to decide what the scribe intended to express. To alleviate this difficulty the scribes invented a number of signs that were placed before the word to indicate the meaning which the writer intended to express. Thus a certain sign before a word could indicate plurality, another might designate that the word is a royal name. These signs are called determinatives.[7]

Both Sumerian in Mesopotamia and hieroglyphics in Egypt added determinatives, though in hieroglyphics they appear at the end, not at the beginning, of the word. Hieroglyphic writing was chiseled on stone or rock and preserved for thousands of years because the stone had been buried under sand (see fig. 6.5). Hieroglyphics retained their pictographic quality much longer than did Sumerian. Even though the determinatives helped somewhat, differentiating between the several meanings of signs remained difficult.

Syllabic Writing

In the next stage of writing, signs no longer represented a concept but a sound (usually a consonant and a vowel or vice versa). The wedge-shaped designs of Sumerian became highly stylized, laying the foundation for an alphabet, as described by Schoville:

> The syllabic writing systems of Mesopotamia and Egypt did not develop into a system of alphabetic writing, although the Egyptians had a number of signs for single consonants which were used pri-

marily for the transcription of foreign names. This potential alphabet was only an adjunct to the syllabic system of hieroglyphics, however, and in that system more than one symbol could be used to represent the same consonant. Until the development of the Canaanite alphabet nobody managed to invent a writing system in which one symbol stood for one consonantal sound.[8]

Once an alphabet was developed in the next stage of writing, there would be no limit to the possible word combinations that could be made.

Alphabet

In this stage a letter equals a sound so that words are formed by placing together

Figure 6.6.
A statue bearing graffiti, discovered in 1905 at Serbit el-Khadim in the Sinai Peninsula. The inset inscription reads [t] *nt l-b ꜥlt,* "gift for Baalat" (G. R. Driver, *Semitic Writing from Pictograph to Alphabet,* ed. S. A. Hopkins, rev. ed. [London: Oxford University Press, 1976], plate 40). [Egypt Exploration Society]

certain sounds.[9] The word *alphabet* comes from the first two letters of the Greek alphabet, *alpha* (ἄλφα) and *bēta* (βῆτα), which represent the Phoenician and the Hebrew words *ʾālep* and *bêt*, the first two letters of their alphabets. The alphabet, with its ability to reduce a language to between twenty and thirty signs, revolutionized communication—something we take for granted. But some modern languages, such as Chinese and Japanese, have retained numerous symbols and their accompanying encumbrances, as described by Professor Joseph Naveh of the Hebrew University, Jerusalem: "In 1946, in Japan, an attempt was made to reduce the number of writing symbols to 1850, of which 881 were to be taught in elementary schools. These numbers sound incredible to the Western mind, since English-speaking peoples are able to represent their language in 26 letters."[10] It is uncertain which language was the first to have an alphabetic script, but there are several possibilities.

One possibility is Proto-Sinaitic (Canaanite). Several inscriptions commonly classi-

fied as graffiti, discovered in 1905 at Serbit el-Khadim in the Sinai Peninsula less than fifty miles from the traditional site of Mt. Sinai, appear to be derived from an alphabet. They were initially dated by Sir Alan Gardiner, a pioneer in the deciphering of these inscriptions, to the period of the Twelfth Egyptian Dynasty (c. 1989–1776 B.C.; see fig. 6.6).[11]

Some inscriptions from Byblos (or ancient Gebal), dated to near the end of the Early Bronze Age (about 2000 B.C.), may exhibit an early form of alphabetic script (fig. 6.7). This town, located on the shores of the Mediterranean Sea, was known for its commercial activity and was an important link between the East and West. These inscriptions are written in a pseudohieroglyphic script that has yet to be translated.

A potsherd bearing three letters of a Sinaitic-type script dating between 1800 and 1650 B.C. (fig. 6.8A) was found at Gezer (Tell-el-Jazari). A plaque from Shechem (modern-day Nablus) bears eight signs on the front and three on the back (fig. 6.8B), and it is dated to about the same period as

Figure 6.7.
An inscription (dated to about 2000 B.C.), possibly in an early alphabetic script, from Byblos.

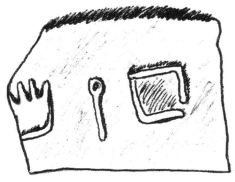

the potsherd from Gezer. A bronze dagger (fig. 6.8C) from a tomb at Lachish (Tell-ed-Duweir) is inscribed with four signs on the side of the blade and dates to about 1770–1550 B.C. All of these objects are early, undeciphered evidence of alphabetic script. Archaeological evidence to date points to the origin of the alphabet as either Canaanite or Phoenician from the first half of the second millennium B.C. The Phoenician alphabet had twenty-two letters and became the basis for subsequent alphabets[12]—Hebrew, Greek, and most other modern languages are based upon this stage in the development of writing.

Biblical Languages

The Old Testament was written in two related languages, Hebrew and Aramaic; the New Testament was written in Greek, a language that became the *lingua franca* of the Mediterranean area following its conquest by Alexander the Great (c. 332 B.C.).

Language by nature expresses a way of thinking in the wording of concepts and ideas and thus provides insights into culture. These three languages are not dead, as is sometimes thought, but are still used among some people groups. Hebrew has been the national language of Israel since 1948. Aramaic dialects are spoken by several small groups: certain inhabitants of villages in the Anti-Lebanon area; Christians or Jews from or near Azerbaijan and Kurdistan; and remnants of the gnostic sect of the Mandaeans.[13] Greek is spoken by

Figure 6.8.
Drawings of (A) a potsherd from Gezer and (B) a plaque from Shechem, and a photo of (C) a dagger from Lachish with inset of inscription.

81

Figure 6.9.
A drawing of the ʿIzbet Ṣarṭah Abecedary (alphabet), composed of two interlocking clay sherds, was found in 1976 at the excavation at ʿIzbet Ṣarṭah, a village in the vicinity of Aphek. These two ostraca preserve the oldest paleo-Hebrew alphabet yet discovered. The first four lines appear to be random letters, but the fifth is clearly the alphabet written from left to right. It is dated to the twelfth century B.C. [Tel Aviv University]

more than ten million Greeks and Cypriots.[14] These languages have changed and developed over the centuries, but the modern speaker would recognize much of their ancient counterparts, and there would be fewer differences between them than the English spoken today as compared with that spoken in the eleventh century.[15]

Hebrew

The majority of the Old Testament was written in what is commonly known as Classical Hebrew or Biblical Hebrew, as distinct from later forms of this language, such as Rabbinic Hebrew, Medieval Hebrew, and Modern Hebrew (Ivrit). It is difficult to know just how long Classical Hebrew was a spoken language, for the earliest extant texts come from about the twelfth (ʿIzbet Ṣarṭah Abecedary; fig. 6.9)[16] or tenth centuries B.C. (Gezer Calendar; fig. 6.10), and the latest known texts are letters found in the Murabbaʿat Caves

(dated to about A.D. 132–135); however, these texts probably do not indicate the complete range of usage.[17]

Hebrew experienced fairly wide usage—during the eighth century B.C., Isaiah calls it the language of Canaan (19:18), and even older documents written in the Phoenician language are very similar (e.g., the inscription on the sarcophagus of King Ahiram [Aḥīrâm] of Byblos; the inscriptions found at Kuntillet Ajrud in Sinai).

During the biblical period two different scripts were used for Hebrew, the earlier called paleo-Hebrew (or old Hebrew) and the later Square script (or Assyrian script after its origin; see table 6.1). The earliest recorded examples of Square script appear in the ʿAraq el-Emir inscription found in East Jordan from the fourth or third century B.C.[18] and in the earliest Qumran fragments (4QSam[b] and 4QJer[a]) from about 250 B.C.[19] Sometime after their return from the Babylonian exile (c. 538 B.C.) the Jews gradually adopted the Aramaic language and Square

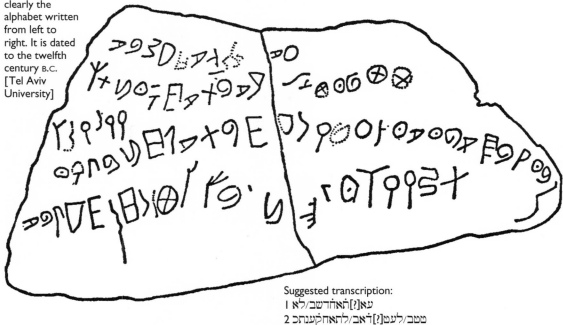

Suggested transcription:
1 עא[?]הֹאֹחֹדשב/לא
2 טטב/לעט[?]רֹאב/להאחקענתכ
3 קקשׁ[?]צ̇
4 שׁבערב/לחאל/בעאע[?]על/בקֹדהל/בתאגחנב/לפּֿקֹע
5 תשקקצעעפסנ]מ[?]לכיטוֹחוֹהדגבא

(M. Kochavi, "An Ostracon of the Period of the Judges from ʿIzbet Ṣarṭah," *Tel Aviv* 4 [1977]: 5)

1
2
3
4
5
6
7

Figure 6.10.
The Gezer Calendar (with line numbers added), from about the tenth century B.C., was discovered by an Irish archaeologist, R. A. S. Macalister, during the excavation at Gezer in 1908. [Archaeological Museum, Istanbul]

Transcription:
1 ‏ירחו אספ ירחו ז
2 ‏רע ירחו לקש
3 ‏ירח עצד פשת
4 ‏ירח קצר שערם
5 ‏ירח קצר וגל
6 ‏ירחו זמר
7 ‏ירח קץ

Translation:
1a His two months are (olive) harvest,
1b His two months are planting (grain),
2 His two months are late planting;
3 His month is hoeing up of flax,
4 His month is harvest of barley,
5 His month is harvest and *feasting*;
6 His two months are vine-tending,
7 His month is summer fruit.
(From W. F. Albright, in *ANET*, 320.)

Transliteration:
1 *yarḥêw ʾasîp yarḥêw ze*
2 *raʿ yarḥêw l-q-š*
3 *yarḥô ʿ-ṣ-d pišta*
4 *yarḥô qᵉṣîr śᵉʾorîm*
5 *yarḥô qᵉṣîr wa-gîl*
6 *yarḥîw zamîr*
7 *yarḥô qêṣ*
(Transcription and transliteration from W. F. Albright, "The Gezer Calendar," *BASOR* 92 [Dec. 1943]: 22–23.)

Table 6.1
Paleo-Hebrew and Square Scripts
Adapted from J. P. Lettinga, *Grammatica van het Bijbels Hebreeuws* (Leiden: Brill, 1962), 5.

Paleo-Hebrew Script	Square Script	Trans-literation	Paleo-Hebrew Script	Square Script	Trans-literation
	א	ʾ		ל	l
	ב	b		מ	m
	ג	g		נ	n
	ד	d		ס	s
	ה	h		ע	ʿ
	ו	w		פ	p
	ז	z		צ	ṣ
	ח	ḥ		ק	q
	ט	ṭ		ר	r
	י	y		ש/שׂ	ś/š
	כ	k		ת	t

script.[20] It is interesting to note that even after this change took place some later texts revert to paleo-Hebrew forms (e.g., Habakkuk Commentary [the name *Yahweh* is in paleo-Hebrew script; see fig. 6.11]; Bar Kochba's revolt coins [132–35]; see fig. 6.12).

The Hebrew alphabet has twenty-two letters, the order of which is found in several alphabetic acrostics in the Book of Psalms (Ps. 9–10, 25, 34, 37, 111, 112, 119, 145). Psalm 119 is the most well-known alphabetic acrostic psalm—the first eight

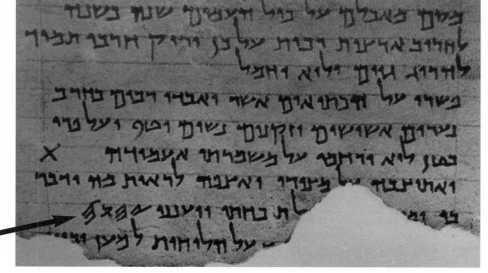

Figure 6.11. Photo of a page from the Habakkuk Commentary (1QpHab 10.9–15) from Qumran, written in Square script, but the divine name *Yahweh* appears in paleo-Hebrew script. [John C. Trever]

Figure 6.12. Coins from the Bar Kochba revolt. Followers of Bar Kochba may have used the paleo-Hebrew script to indicate that they, as opposed to those employing Assyrian (Square) script, were the legitimate continuation of the Jewish fathers. [Paul Wegner]

לחרות ירושלם, "For the freedom of Jerusalem"

שמעון, "Shimon"

verses each begin with the Hebrew letter א (*ʾālep*) then each of the second eight verses begin with the second Hebrew letter ב (*bêt*), and so forth through the rest of the alphabet. The total number of verses in this psalm is 176 (22 sections, each with 8 verses).

Originally the Old Testament was not written with vowel points because the points were not needed, but as the Jews began to rely on Aramaic as their spoken language, Hebrew became more and more neglected. During the Babylonian exile the conversion from Hebrew to Aramaic as the common language accelerated, so much so that Nehemiah was incensed to find that few people could speak or read Hebrew after their return from the exile (Neh. 13:24). It was considered the sacred language, however, and was kept alive by the rabbis. Eventually the Masoretes, scribes who helped to preserve the Hebrew text from about 500 to 1000, added vowel points to the text between the fifth to the eighth centuries in order to assist pronunciation.

Thomas Manson, former New Testament professor at University of Manchester (1936–1958), has suggested that Jesus usually spoke Aramaic but may have used Hebrew for his more formal disputes with the Pharisees.[21] Jesus was clearly aware that the Old Testament was written in Hebrew Square script when he said in Matthew 5:18, "I tell you the truth, until heaven and earth disappear, not one *iota*

or one *tittle*, will by any means disappear from the Law until everything is accomplished" (modified from the NIV). The word *iōta* is the Greek equivalent to the Hebrew letter *yôd* (י), which is the smallest Hebrew letter in Square script but not in paleo-Hebrew script. The *tittle* is a small penstroke that is used to help distinguish some letters (e.g., ד [*dālet*] and ר [*rēš*] are distinguished only by the small tittle on the top right side corner of the *dālet*) and is not the same in paleo-Hebrew.

Hebrew letters also signify numbers and at times may have been used as mnemonic devices to aid in remembering Scripture. For example, Matthew 1:1–17 makes it clear that Jesus was in the Davidic line and that there were fourteen generations from Abraham to David (vv. 2–6), from David to the deportation to Babylon (vv. 6–11), and from the Babylonian deportation to Jesus (vv. 12–17). When they are added up, the numbers of the name *David* equal fourteen.

דוד (*dwd*) = David
ד (= 4) + ו (= 6) + ד (= 4) = 14

Aramaic

The Aramaic language takes its name from the Arameans, or the people of Aram, who are mentioned in Old Akkadian writings from as early as the mid-

Figure 6.13. The Beth-David inscription, discovered at Tel Dan in 1994, is one of the oldest known Aramaic inscriptions. It contains the oldest extant reference to the "house of David." [Israel Antiquities Authority]

Line 8
מלך .ישראל .וקתל֯[ת .מל֯ן
"the king of Israel. And [I] slew [. . . the kin-]"

Line 9
ך . ביתדוד .ואשׂם֯. [.א֯].
"g of the *House of David.* And I put . . ."

(From "'David' Found at Dan," *BAR* 20.2 [March/April 1994]: 38–39.)

third millennium B.C.[22] Aram covered much of the upper Mesopotamian region and Aramaic became the international trade language, or *lingua franca*, of much of the ancient Near East. One of the earliest extant Aramaic documents comes from the early ninth century B.C. [see fig. 6.13];[23] while Aramaic is still in use, its peak was in the seventh and eighth centuries B.C. when the Assyrian Empire controlled much of the ancient Near Eastern area. According to 2 Kings 18:26 (cf. Isa. 36:11), the more educated person in Israel was able to speak both Aramaic and Hebrew. Five Old Testament passages are written in Aramaic (Gen. 31:47; Jer. 10:11; Dan. 2:4–7:28; Ezra 4:8–6:18; 7:12–26),[24] and the name אֲרָמִית (*ʾărāmît*), which refers to the Aramaic language, occurs twice (Ezra 4:7; Dan. 2:4). One of the rabbinical writings has the following injunction concerning Aramaic: "Let not the Aramaic be lightly esteemed by thee, seeing that the Holy One (blessed be He!) has given honor to it in the Law, the Prophets, and the Writings" (T.P. *Soṭah* 7.2). This refers to the three sections of the Old Testament—the Law, the Prophets, and the Writings—each of which has a passage written in Aramaic.[25]

When the Israelites were taken to captivity in Assyria and Babylon, they would have found it convenient to learn Aramaic to communicate with their neighbors. The problem came when they went back to Israel and found that a large number of children from mixed marriages were no longer able to speak Hebrew (Neh. 13:24). Aramaic almost died out with the spread of Hellenism and the effort to unify the Greek Empire under a common language.[26] However, it was still spoken during Jesus' time, for several of his statements are recorded in Aramaic (*talitha koum*, "little girl arise" [Mark 5:41]; *ephphatha*, "be opened" [Mark 7:34]; *Eloi, Eloi, lama sabachthani*, "My God, My God why have you forsaken me?" [Mark 15:34]). Several other common words derive from Aramaic (e.g., *Abba*, "father" [Mark 14:36]; *Marana tha*, "Come, O Lord," [1 Cor. 16:22]; *Golgotha*, "skull" [Mark 15:22]). Of the four Gospels, Mark records the most Aramaisms.

Greek

While Aramaic may have been the main language Jesus and the first Christians spoke, most of the New Testament is written in Greek with only a few Aramaic words recorded. Alexander the Great (356–323 B.C.) helped to unify his government by means of Greek, which became the trade language of the Mediterranean area and beyond. Even after the Romans acquired this region the vernacular continued to be Greek; Paul was therefore able to spread the gospel across the Roman Empire with virtually no language barriers. Latin, the official language of the Roman Empire, was relegated to use mainly in military and governmental documents. Greek is an expressive, concise, and flexible language, especially suited to record the New Testament.

Most scholars believe that the Greek alphabet was derived from the Phoenician alphabet, with at least five letters showing direct resemblance. The following evidence suggests that these two languages are related:

1. Nearly all the early Greek letters reflect a Semitic origin.
2. Phonetic values of the majority of early Greek letters are the same as Semitic values and their order is very similar.
3. Until about 500 B.C., Greek was written from right to left, similar to the Semitic languages.
4. Most Greek letter names are meaningless in Greek but mean something in Semitic languages. For example, *alpha* and *bēta* are simply

letter names in Greek but are almost identical to the names of the first two letters of the Hebrew alphabet, *ʾālep* and *bêt*, which can also denote objects that were probably originally represented by their shapes, namely, ox and house, respectively.[27]

The direction of Greek writing was at first from right to left; then it was written in alternating directions (one line from right to left, the next line from left to right), a practice called *boustrophēdon* (meaning "as the ox turns when plowing a field").[28] From about 500 B.C. onward, Greek was written from left to right, probably as a matter of convenience because a right-handed person would be less likely to smear the writing in this direction.[29]

The Greek language went through five stages of development (see table 6.2). One of the more important stages was Classical Greek, during which Homer wrote the *Iliad* and *Odyssey*. Modern Greek is fairly similar to Koine (except for vocabulary and some forms). As late as the nineteenth century, scholars still thought Koine [κοινή] Greek, the language of the New Testament, was a special language from God used specifically to write that body of literature.[30] This idea was finally overturned early in the twentieth century by Adolf Deissmann. While he was a pastor in Marburg, Germany, Deissmann examined a publication of some recently discovered Greek papyri and recognized the similarities between them and New Testament Greek.[31]

Another important work for biblical studies is the Septuagint (see also chap. 12), a Greek translation of the Old Testament written between 250–100 B.C. Approximately 80 percent of New Testa-

Table 6.2
Development of Greek

Stages of the Greek Language	Date
Pre-Homeric	1500–900 B.C.
Classical	900–330 B.C.
Koine	330 B.C.–A.D. 330
Byzantine	A.D. 330–1453
Modern	1453–onward

ment quotations of the Old Testament come from the Septuagint.[32] F. F. Bruce evaluates the quality of Septuagint Greek: "To one accustomed to reading good Greek, Septuagint Greek reads very oddly; but to a Greek reader acquainted with Hebrew idiom, Septuagint Greek is immediately intelligible. The words are Greek, but the construction is Hebrew."[33] The Septuagint's influence on early Christians can

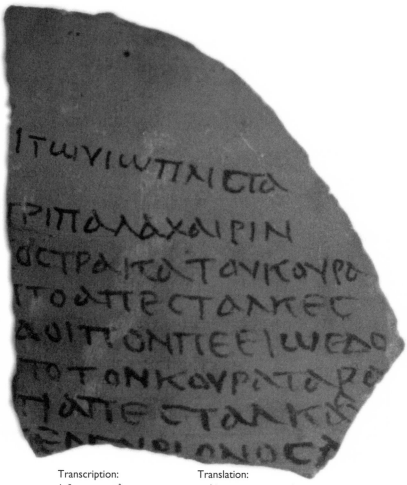

Figure 6.14.
A picture and translation of a Greek ostracon dated to approximately A.D. 160. It indicates that Greek at this time was written in uncials, with no punctuation or breaks between words. [Paul Wegner]

Transcription:
1.]ι τω υιω πλιστα
2.]τρι παλα χαιριν

3.] οστρακα του κουρα-
4. τοπος] πτο απεσταλκες
5.]δοι Πονπεειω εδο
6.]το τον κουραταρα
7.]τι απεσταλκας υ[
8.] κεντυριονος δ[

Translation:
to his son many greetings
(and to his) father/mother many greetings

You sent the curator's
ostraca [   ]
temple/tomb of Pompey
[you gave] the curator
[   ] you sent
[   ] centurion

Corrected spellings:
Line 1. πλειστα 2. πολλα; χαιρειν 4. απεσταλκας
6. κουρατορα

Translated by T. Pattie, British Museum

be seen in the number of Hebrew idioms and words found in the New Testament.

Greek is a precise language, perfect for theological discourses like Paul's letter to the Romans. It is an inflected language, which means that the nouns have case endings that signify the grammatical function of the word within a sentence. However, the complicated nature of Greek grammar often eludes the amateur, as Bruce warns: "It is nowhere more sadly true than in the acquisition of Greek that 'a little learning is a dangerous thing.'"[34] People have often erroneously tried to prove many things based on Greek grammar (e.g., denying the divinity of Christ in John 1:1, translating it as "the Word was a god").

During New Testament times Greek was written in capital letters, called uncials, with no divisions between words or punctuation marks (see fig. 6.14). Greek letters also served as numerals. To indicate this, a tick or a small horizontal line was written above the letter ($\bar{\alpha}$=1; $\bar{\beta}$=2; $\bar{\gamma}$=3; etc.). Since each Greek letter had a numerical value, the number of the beast in Revelation 13:18 is said to be 666, representing the combined values of the letters of his name (even so, the identity of the beast remains a mystery, with Caesar, Adolf Hitler, and Saddam Hussein suggested as possibilities).

Writing Materials

There was a great variety of writing materials in the Near East during the time of the transmission of the biblical texts. Generally the cheapest, most durable, and easiest-to-use materials were chosen for writing.

Stone

Stone was plentiful in much of the ancient Near East; it could be used for something as noble as a monumental inscription or as common as graffiti. It was, in fact, the earliest writing material mentioned in the Bible—Moses received the stone tablets with the Ten Commandments inscribed upon them by the finger of God (Exod. 24:12; 31:18; 32:15–19). Job 19:24

Figure 6.15. The Code of Hammurapi (found in 1901), showing Hammurapi (left) standing before a deity. Apparently the deity is validating the king's right to rule for another year. Underneath are listed 282 laws, some very similar to biblical laws. [Louvre]

Hieroglyphics

Demotic

Figure 6.16.
The Rosetta
Stone, discovered
in Rosetta, Egypt,
in 1799, and used
to decipher
hieroglyphics.
[British Museum]

Greek

Table 6.3
Comparison of Two Legal Codes

Code of Hammurapi	Biblical Laws
Law 22: "If a man committed robbery and has been caught, that man shall be put to death." (modified from *ANET*, 167)	Exodus 22:1 "If a man steals an ox or a sheep and slaughters it or sells it, he must pay back five head of cattle for the ox and four sheep for the sheep."
Law 23: "If the robber has not been caught, the robbed man shall set forth the particulars regarding his lost property in the presence of god, and the city and governor, in whose territory and district the robbery was committed, shall make good to him his lost property." (modified from *ANET*, 167)	Exodus 22:7–8 "If a man gives his neighbor silver or goods for safekeeping and they are stolen from the neighbor's house, the thief, if he is caught, must pay back double. But if the thief is not found, the owner of the house must appear before the judges to determine whether he has laid his hands on the other man's property."
Law 129: "If the wife of a man has been caught while lying with another man, they shall bind them and throw them into the water. If the husband of the woman wishes to spare his wife, then the king in turn may spare his subject." (modified from *ANET*, 171)	Deuteronomy 22:22 "If a man is found sleeping with another man's wife, both the man who slept with her and the woman must die. You must purge the evil from Israel."

Figure 6.17. Examples of clay tablets. [Paul Wegner]

refers to some type of rock engraving made with an iron stylus. Deuteronomy 27:2–3 states that stones were to be covered with lime and then the words of the law were to be written on them; perhaps the lime provided an easier surface to chisel, or more likely it provided a suitable background on which letters could be drawn.

Several important stone inscriptions have been discovered. One of these is the Code of Hammurapi (or Hammurabi; see fig. 6.15). This law code, which is housed at the Louvre in Paris, is inscribed on an eight-foot-high slab, or stela, of black basalt and probably dates to the beginning of the eighteenth century B.C. It was discovered in Suza, where it had been taken as booty by the Elamites from Babylon about six centuries after Hammurapi ruled. Originally 282 laws were inscribed on it, many of them very similar to biblical laws (see table 6.3). A significant number were later defaced by the Elamites.

The Rosetta Stone (see fig. 6.16), a slab of black basalt, was found in 1799 by a Frenchman named Bouchard, a lieutenant of Napoleon's expeditionary forces in Rosetta, Egypt, which is located in the western part of the Nile Delta. The stone, which measures 3 feet 9 inches long by 2 feet 4 and 1/2 inches wide and 11 inches thick, bears an inscription of a decree written in three languages: hieroglyphics (an early pictographic Egyptian language), Demotic (a cursive form of Egyptian derived from hieroglyphics), and Greek. This important record enabled scholars to decipher the two Egyptian languages, previously untranslatable, by the Greek. A French scholar, Jean-François Champollion, is given credit for finally deciphering the inscription in 1822. The Rosetta Stone is housed in the British Museum in London.

Clay Tablets

Another durable writing material common to the ancient Near East was clay tablets, which could be easily inscribed when wet but were virtually indestructible when dried or fired (fig. 6.17).

Figure 6.18.
The Cyrus cylinder, dated to about 539 B.C., records the victory of Cyrus over the Babylonians and is presently housed in the British Museum. [British Museum]

Many clay tablets were found throughout the Tigris-Euphrates river valley (e.g., about ten thousand at Bogazköy [Turkey], the Hittite capital; twenty thousand at Nuzi [Iraq]; twenty-two thousand at Mari [Syria]; twenty thousand at Ugarit [Syria]; and sixteen thousand at Ebla [Syria]). Among other things the tablets were often used to record temple offerings, personal possessions, and historical annals. Many were inscribed with a three-sided stylus made from a reed or wood; when the stylus was pressed into the soft clay, it created a wedge-shaped image. The tablet was often marked off with lines to ensure straight lettering. While they were cheap and durable, tablets were also heavy and bulky, so that very large works were not commonly produced upon clay tablets. Longer works appear on clay barrels or cylinders, some of which had a dowel through the middle to rotate the barrel, or cylinder, as it was read (e.g., the Cyrus cylinder, fig. 6.18).

Papyrus

Papyrus is a reed plant that grows in swamps along the Nile River (fig. 6.19). The pith of the reed was cut into strips about twelve to fifteen inches long and laid in two layers, alternating horizontally and vertically (fig. 6.20). The sheets were left to dry on a flat surface with a weight on top, causing the natural sugar in the plant to bond the layers together. The strips on the front *(recto)* of the papyrus ran horizontally, and those on the back *(verso)* ran vertically; the front was generally the only side written on because it was smoother.[35]

The Hebrew word for this marsh plant is most likely גֹּמֶא (*gōmeʾ*; Exod. 2:3; Job 8:11; Isa. 18:2; 35:7), which is sometimes translated in the Greek of the Septuagint as πάπυρος (*papyros*; the Latin spelling is *papyrus*) and is related to the English word *paper*. A single piece of papyrus in Greek is called χάρτης (*chartēs*), which is translated "paper" in 2 John 12 (NIV). It appears that as early as the third millennium B.C. papyrus was used for writing;[36] an Egyptian story from about 1090 B.C. records that a man named Wen Amon traded the Phoenicians papyrus for wood (see *ANET*,

Figure 6.19.
The papyrus plant with the bloom on top; the pulp, or pith, in the stalk is made into writing material.

28). Herodotus states that by the middle of the fifth century B.C. papyrus was such a common writing material that he could not conceive of civilized people using anything else (Herodotus *Historia* 5.58).[37] Pliny the Elder, a Roman historian (c. A.D. 100), gives one of the best descriptions of the preparation and uses of papyrus (Pliny *Naturalis Historia* 13.68–83).

Papyrus was significantly more convenient than clay tablets since it could be easily written upon, was very light, could be joined in scrolls or codices (books), and

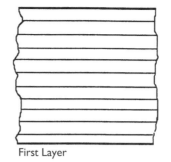

First Layer

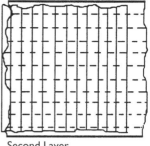

Second Layer

Figure 6.20. A diagram of how papyrus is made: the pith of the plant is cut into strips and laid out in two layers, horizontally (the first layer) and vertically (the second layer).

Figure 6.21. $\mathfrak{P}^{52}$ (P. Rylands 457), a papyrus fragment from the Gospel of John 18:31–33, dated to the early second century, possibly only about fifty years after it was written. This fragment was acquired in 1920 in Egypt and is located in the John Rylands Library in Manchester, England. [John Rylands University Library]

Figure 6.22.
A picture of the Isaiah Scroll (1QIsaᵃ), which was found at Qumran and is dated to the second century B.C. [John C. Trever]

was easily handled. However, there were some drawbacks to using papyrus: it was not nearly as durable as clay tablets; it was not readily available outside of Egypt; its surface was rough; it was susceptible to damage from water and light; and age caused it to become brittle and crumble into powder. The first modern discovery of ancient papyrus documents was in 1778, when some Egyptians found a jar containing forty to fifty documents. Since no one would buy them, they burned all but one.[38] Papyrus documents have been found only in dry climates, such as Egypt, the Sinai Desert, the Dead Sea area, and in the volcanic ash of Herculaneum. To date the oldest known New Testament papyrus document, called $\mathfrak{P}^{52}$, contains a few verses from John 18 and is generally dated to about A.D. 125 (fig. 6.21).

Concerning biblical papyrus documents versus clay records, Bruce observes: "So, while we can read the original inscriptions of the Assyrian and Babylonian kings and

the notes which common people wrote on pieces of pottery in eighth-century Samaria and sixth-century Lachish, the autographs of the Hebrew prophets who were their contemporaries have disappeared long ago, as also have the autographs of all the other Biblical writers, most—probably all—of whom wrote on papyrus."[39]

Leather

Leather was usually obtained from the hides of sheep, goats, antelope, and other similar animals; it was dried, shaved, and scraped clean for writing. Leather was more durable than papyrus and yet it still dries out, cracks and finally crumbles away. Prepared animal skins were used as writing materials from a very early date. F. G. Kenyon states:

In Egypt there are references to documents written on skins in the time of the IVth Dynasty (c. 2900–2750 B.C.), and the actual specimens are extant from the XIIth Dynasty (c. 2000–1788 B.C.). Ctesias, the Greek historian [of Persia], refers to the royal chronicles being written on leather, by the ancient Persians, but does not specify their precise dates. They may include those to which reference is made in Ezra vi. 1, 2 and Esther vi. 1. Herodotus records that once, when papyrus was scarce, the Ionian Greeks used sheepskins and goatskins in its place; and he adds that many of the "barbarians" still did so in his day. . . . More important for our present purpose is the traditional use of leather for the books of the Law in Hebrew. In the Talmud it is laid down that all copies of the Law used in public worship must be written on skins of clean animals, and in roll-form.[40]

A good share of the scrolls found at Qumran were made of leather and one of the most important was the Isaiah Scroll (1QIsaᵃ; fig. 6.22.).

If the *Letter of Aristeas* (second century B.C.) can be trusted, the original scrolls of the Hebrew Old Testament, which the translators of the Septuagint copied, were also made of leather (lines 176–178).[41]

Parchment

Parchment is also made from the skins of animals, such as sheep, calves, goats,

and antelope. The skins are soaked in lime water to make them white. Bruce Metzger notes: "The younger the animal, the finer was the quality of skin. Vellum was the finest quality of extra-thin parchment, sometimes obtained from animals not yet born."[42] Parchment was more expensive than papyrus, but it had several advantages: it is smooth and durable, both sides could be written on, the light color gave clarity to the writing, and parchment could be reused. But, according to Galen, a famous Greek physician of the second century, it had the drawback of being shiny and thus put more strain on the eyes than did papyrus.[43] The word *parchment* (περγαμηνή, *pergamēnē*) is derived from the name *Pergamum,* a city of Asia Minor that became important as a center of parchment production. Use of parchment in the production of books became widespread in the second century B.C.[44] and because of its durability parchment became the preferred writing material for the Scriptures. Often parchment was lined or scored before being used for writing, as samples from Qumran show.

Early Greeks wrote on parchment or papyrus with reeds that had been dried, sharpened to a point, and then split in the middle of the point to hold ink or frayed and used like a brush. Metzger claims that the first mention of a quill pen is in the

Figure 6.23.
A reconstructed ivory writing tablet.

Figure 6.24.
This seventh-century ostracon from Upper Egypt, containing Luke 22:70–71, is tenth in a series of ostraca covering Luke 22:40–71.
[IFAO Archives]

Transcription:
1 ειπαν δε παντες
2 συ ουν ει ο $\overline{υς}$ του $\overline{θυ}$
3 ο δε προς αυτους
4 εφη ὑμεις λεγετε
5 οτι εγω ειμι οι δε
6 ειπαν τι ετι χρειαν
7 :ο εχομεν μαρτυριαν
8 ι αυτοι γαρ ἡκουσαμε[ν]
9 απο του στοματος

Notes on the Greek text:
In line 2, the horizontal lines above the letters indicate that the words are abbreviated. The *omicron* and *iōta* beginning lines 7 and 8 respectively are written horizontally in the original. The purpose of the :ο is uncertain, but the ι is probably serving as the numeral ten and indicates the position of this ostracon in the series. In line 8, the omission of the final ν of ηκουσαμεν is a typical form of scribal shorthand.

Translation:
And they all said, "Are you then the Son of God?" And he said to them, "You say that I am." And they said, "What further need have we witness (*sic*)? For we ourselves have heard from . . . mouth."
(Adapted from A. Deissmann, *Light from the Ancient East,* trans. L. R. M. Strachan [reprinted, Grand Rapids: Baker, 1978], 58.)

Figure 6.25.
Ostracon no. 4 from Tell ed-Duweir (probably biblical Lachish) unearthed in 1935 during the excavations directed by British archaeologist J. L. Starkey. Ostraca from this find are dated to the Assyrian advance in 701 B.C. or the Babylonian conquest of 588 B.C. This ostracon tells that the people in Lachish can no longer see the signal fires of Azekah, suggesting its capture.

Translation, lines 13–14:
"And let him know that we ourselves are watching the smoke-signals from Lachish according to all the signals which my lord gives, for we cannot see Azekah."

fifth or sixth century, but quills were probably in use before this.[45]

Wooden or Ivory Tablets

A flat wood or ivory tablet covered with a thin, smooth layer of plaster (or later wax) was sometimes used for temporary messages (see fig. 6.23). A metal stylus or stiletto was used to scratch the message into the plaster, which could later be scraped off and coated with a new layer. This may be the "stick of wood" referred to in Ezekiel 37:15 (see also Isa. 30:8; Hab. 2:2). Wax tablets were an improvement in that a heated surface could be passed over the wax to ready it for the next message. Wooden tablets were known in Egypt at least as far back as the seventh century B.C., but the earliest found to date is from Nimrud, Assyria, dating to about 705 B.C.[46] These writing boards were generally hinged to form a diptych or polyptych that could easily be closed. They were commonly used in Greek and Roman times, but only one example has survived from Palestine—a letter from Bar Kochba discovered at Naḥal Ḥever.[47]

Potsherds (Ostraca)

Potsherds or ostraca are pieces of broken pottery (see Job 2:8; Isa. 30:14) used for jotting notes in the absence of better materials. Generally a pen or small reed brush was used for writing, but sometimes a name or a short note would be inscribed on the surface of a pot or a vessel. A few ostraca found in Egypt bear biblical texts (fig. 6.24), possibly the possession of a poor man.[48] Some of the most important ostraca from Israel are the Samarian Ostraca and the Lachish Ostraca (fig. 6.25).

Precious Metals

Several different types of precious metals were used as writing materials (e.g., gold, silver, copper, bronze, iron). A copper scroll found in cave 3 at Qumran (3Q15) bears a list of treasure and where it was supposedly hidden. Another, more significant find for the area of Bible intro-

Figure 6.26. This woodcut shows the process of making paper.

duction were two silver amulets found in 1985. These amulets (worn like a good-luck charm, generally with religious significance) were discovered in a grave about half a mile south of the Old City walls of Jerusalem (see fig. 12.1). Gabriel Barkay, the excavator in charge of this dig, dated the amulets to the mid-seventh century B.C., which would rank them the oldest biblical text found to date.[49]

Paper

Paper, the writing material with which we are most familiar, was introduced from central Asia to Egypt about A.D. 900. Paper was made by dipping a screen into a mixture of cotton fibers and water (fig. 6.26). The cotton mixture trapped on the screen was then turned out onto a mat, pressed to expunge excess water, and left to dry from one to four days. Paper, coupled with the emergence of movable print, enabled

Figure 6.27.
A bas-relief picturing Assyrian scribes.
[British Museum]

books to be printed cheaply and quickly. The first printed Bible, the Gutenberg Bible, was produced in 1452, using a combination of parchment and paper.

Ink

In 3 John 13 the Greek word for ink is μέλαν (*melan*, black); it was generally made from a mixture of charcoal, gum, and water. This type of ink, however, did not adhere well to parchment, which required a different recipe, as described by Metzger:

> One recipe for this second kind used nut-galls (oak-galls). These were pulverized and then water was poured over the powder. Sulfate of iron was afterwards added to it, as well as gum arabic. By the fourth century after Christ this type of ink tended to supersede carbon-based ink even for writing on papyrus. Nut-gall ink in the course of time takes on a rusty-brown color. The

chemical changes it undergoes may, in fact, liberate minute quantities of sulphuric acid that can eat through the writing material.[50]

Sometimes red or other colors of ink were used for titles. Red ink was made of iron-oxide or cinnabar gum; purple derived from the liquid secreted from sea animals (murex and purpura).[51]

The Writing Process

Scribes

It is difficult to know how widespread illiteracy was in the ancient Near East during the biblical period. The alphabetic script that probably developed by 1600 B.C. certainly made it easier for people to learn to read and write. André Lemaire states that "[w]ith the discovery of the alphabet any person of average intelligence could learn to read and probably write within a few weeks."[52] It appears that by the end of seventh century B.C. literacy was widespread, as Allen Millard, Reader in Hebrew and Ancient Semitic Languages from the University of Liverpool, observes: "Ancient Hebrew written documents, recovered by archaeology, demonstrate both that there were readers and writers in ancient Israel, and that they were by no means rare. Few places will have been without someone who could write, and few Israelites will have been unaware of writing."[53]

Many Israelites could probably perform only such rudimentary tasks as writing their own names. The more difficult tasks of composing letters or forming contracts were left to professional scribes (fig. 6.27). The training of a scribe was important and required great skill. This is particularly true in Mesopotamia, where the cuneiform language was extremely difficult; it took significant practice before a scribe was ready to write on tablets. First he learned to hold a tablet and stylus, then he gained practice by stringing cuneiform signs together as he copied various lists of names (fig. 6.28).

The next stage is described by Walker:

At this point the schoolboy was ready to go on to the next stage, which is marked by writing on a different kind of tablet, the round, bun-shaped tablet. On these the teacher would typically write out three lines on one side of a tablet, such as the names of gods, a list of technical terms, a short fragment of literature or a proverb; the schoolboy had to study these carefully, and then turn the tablet over and try to reproduce what the teacher had written. It is usually quite easy to see which side was written by the teacher and which by the schoolboy.[54]

By New Testament times, the job of a scribe had developed significantly; having gained knowledge in the workings of the law through copying and study, scribes became specialists in matters of the law.

Paleography

The word *paleography* derives from two Greek words (παλαιά [*palaia*, old], and γραφή [*graphē*, writing]); thus it is the study of ancient writing. This science is further broken into epigraphy, the study of ancient inscriptions on durable objects, such as stone, leather, or pottery, and numismatics, which examines coins and metals. The first book to systematically

Figure 6.28. Schoolboys' tablets: the first was a complete exercise ready to be inscribed on the back of the tablet; the second was used and discarded. [Paul Wegner]

deal with Greek paleography was published by a Benedictine monk, Bernard de Montfauçon (1655–1741), and was entitled *Palaeographia Graeca, sive de ortu et progressu literarum Graecarum . . .* (Paris, 1708). But it was not until the nineteenth century, with the studies of Constantin von Tischendorf (1815–1874), that major advances were made in Greek paleography. He made several trips to the Near East in search of Greek manuscripts and edited the Septuagint, the Greek New Testament, and many apocryphal books. Bruce Metzger states: "His knowledge of Greek uncial writing was unparalleled, being based upon an examination of some three hundred specimens."[55]

About the middle of the nineteenth century onward international scholarship in the area of Greek paleography virtually exploded, with the publication of many facsimile manuscripts, microfilms, and digitized computer reproductions. Today there are indexes, catalogs, and checklists of every major and many minor library collections. There are also several archives devoted entirely to the collection of biblical manuscripts (e.g., Ancient Biblical Manuscript Center at Claremont, California; Institute for New Testament Textual Research at Münster/Westphalia, Germany).

For Further Reading

Black, M. "The Biblical Languages." In *CHB*, 1:1–11.

Diringer, D. "The Biblical Scripts." In *CHB*, 1:11–29.

Driver, G. R. *Semitic Writing: From Pictograph to Alphabet.* Revised by S. A. Hopkins. London: Oxford University Press, 1976.

Gelb, I. J. *A Study of Writing.* 2d ed. Chicago: University of Chicago Press, 1963.

Metzger, B. M. *Manuscripts of the Greek Bible: An Introduction to Palaeography.* New York and Oxford: Oxford University Press, 1981.

Smelik, K. A. D. *Writings from Ancient Israel: A Handbook of Historical and Religious Documents.* Translated by G. I. Davies. Louisville, KY: Westminster/John Knox Press, 1991.

Walker, C. B. F. *Cuneiform.* Reading the Past. London: British Museum Publications, 1987.

Wiseman, D. J. "Books in the Ancient Near East and in the Old Testament." In *CHB*, 1:30–48.

Canonization of the Old Testament

The Jewish people preserved the writings of their prophets because they believed them to come directly from God. These works were considered authoritative and were the standard by which faith and practice were regulated and the history of the nation retained. R. K. Harrison notes that this is not unusual:

> The study of the Old Testament canon can properly commence with the observation that all the major world religions have as their legacy a collection of writings that the devout regard as the word of God to a greater or lesser extent, and therefore as containing authoritative norms for faith and practice. Not all adherents of the various religious faiths existing in the modern world maintain that their Scriptures are necessarily inspired, but in any event they normally regard them as enshrining the highest degree of religious authority.[1]

The books that were later placed into the Old Testament canon were of a self-authenticating nature and did not derive their authority from a person or an ecclesiastical decree. This point is crucial: the books did not receive their authority because they were placed into the canon; rather, they were recognized by the nation of Israel as having divine authority and were therefore included in the canon.[2] These books were used to determine beliefs and conduct long before ecclesiastical councils recognized their authority. A good share of them were viewed as authoritative almost immediately, such as the Law (Exod. 24:3–8).

Throughout church history there has been active discussion between the Roman Catholic, Eastern Orthodox, and Protestant churches regarding which books belong to the Old Testament canon (see table 7.1). This discussion dates back at least to Origen (A.D. 185–254), who included the Letter of Jeremiah (an apocryphal book) in his list of canonical works; the discussion about the canon continues to be a hotly debated topic in some circles.

It is sometimes difficult to realize that our Bible did not come to us as one book but rather as a collection of books written over a period of about fifteen hundred years. How did these books come into being? Why were particular books collected and determined to be canonical? These questions will be examined, but first we must begin by clarifying the meaning of canonization.

Definition of Canonization

The word *canon* today refers to a "collection or list of books accepted as an authoritative rule of faith and practice."[3] However, this word originally derives from a Semitic root, the Hebrew form being *qāneh* ("reed" or "stalk," 1 Kings 14:15; Job 40:21).[4] Certain reeds were also used as measuring sticks, and thus one of the derived meanings of the word became "rule." The Greeks incorporated this word into their language (κανών [*kanōn*]) with a somewhat broader meaning to refer to any type of standard or guideline. This is how Paul used it in Galatians 6:16: "Neither circumcision nor uncircumcision means anything; what counts is a new creation. Peace and mercy to all who follow this rule *(kanōn)*, even to the Israel of God" (Gal. 6:15–16). Origen also employed the word *kanōn* with this broader meaning:

We, on the other hand understand the phrase, "neither on this mountain [Jn. 4:21]," to mean the piety expressed by the

heterodox in their fantasy of Gnostic and supposedly lofty doctrines. And we take the words, "Nor will you worship the Father in Jerusalem," to refer to the Church's rule of faith [κανόνα *kanona*] so far as most people are concerned.[5]

Later the word came to mean a list of books which were held to be authoritative, as seen in the writings of the church father Athanasius (296–373), in the *Decrees of the Synod of Nicea* (5.18):

> For the blessed Paul in his Epistle to the Hebrews says, "By faith we understand that the ages were framed by the Word of God, so that that which is seen was not made of things which do appear." But nothing is common to the Word with the ages; for He it is who is in existence before the ages, by whom also the ages came to be. And in the Shepherd [of Hermas] it is written (since they allege this book also, though it is not of the *Canon*). . . .[6]

The basis for the concept of a canon containing authoritative information comes directly from Scripture itself (Deut. 4:2; 12:32; Jer. 26:2; 2 Pet. 3:15–16; Rev. 22:6–8, 18–19). G. C. Aalders points out three occasions in Israel's history when certain writings were recognized as having divine authority.[7] The first is when Moses came down from Mount Sinai with the book of the covenant and read it to the Israelites; their response was "We will do everything the LORD has said; we will obey" (Exod. 24:7). This verse indicates that the words Moses spoke were understood to come from God and should be obeyed. The second occasion was when King Josiah read the book of the covenant (2 Kings 23:3; cf. 2 Chron. 34:32) that was found in the temple by Hilkiah (622 B.C.); the people accepted the words of the covenant and were willing to put themselves under its authority. A third occasion was when Ezra read the law to the Babylonian exiles who had returned to Israel. The people wept as they listened and renewed their obedience to the law, implying that they believed the words to be authoritative (Neh. 8:9).

The prophets themselves claimed that their messages came from God (see table

Table 7.1
Various Forms of the Old Testament Canon

Protestant	Roman Catholic	Eastern Orthodox
Genesis	Genesis	Genesis
Exodus	Exodus	Exodus
Leviticus	Leviticus	Leviticus
Numbers	Numbers	Numbers
Deuteronomy	Deuteronomy	Deuteronomy
Joshua	Joshua	Joshua
Judges	Judges	Judges
Ruth	Ruth	Ruth
1–2 Samuel	1–2 Kings (1–2 Sam.)	1–2 Kingdoms (1–2 Sam.)
1–2 Kings	3–4 Kings (1–2 Kings)	3–4 Kingdoms (1–2 Kings)
1–2 Chronicles	1–2 Paralipomenon (1–2 Chron.)	1–2 Paralipomenon (1–2 Chron.)
Ezra	Ezra (1 Esdras)	1 Esdras (Ezra)
Nehemiah	Nehemiah (2 Esdras)	Nehemiah
Esther	Tobit	2–3 Esdras
Job	Judith	Esther [with six additions]
Psalms	Esther [with six additions]	Judith
Proverbs	1–2 Maccabees	Tobit
Ecclesiastes	Job	1–3 Maccabees
Song of Songs	Psalms	Job
Isaiah	Proverbs	Psalms [with Ps. 151]
Jeremiah	Ecclesiastes	Prayer of Manasseh
Lamentations	Canticle of Canticles (Song of Songs)	Proverbs
Ezekiel	Wisdom [of Solomon]	Ecclesiastes
Daniel	Ecclesiasticus (Sirach)	Song of Songs
Hosea	Isaiah	Wisdom [of Solomon]
Joel	Jeremiah	Wisdom of Sirach (Ecclesiasticus)
Amos	Lamentations	Hosea
Obadiah	Baruch [chap. 6 = Epistle of Jeremiah]	Joel
Jonah	Ezekiel	Amos
Micah	Daniel [with three additions]	Obadiah
Nahum	Hosea	Jonah
Habakkuk	Joel	Micah
Zephaniah	Amos	Nahum
Haggai	Obadiah	Habakkuk
Zechariah	Jonah	Zephaniah
Malachi	Micah	Haggai
	Nahum	Zechariah
	Habakkuk	Malachi
	Zephaniah	Isaiah
	Haggai	Jeremiah
	Zechariah	Baruch
	Malachi	Lamentations
		Epistle of Jeremiah
		Ezekiel
		Daniel [with three additions]

7.2, which cites several of them) and were therefore authoritative.

In the New Testament Paul recognizes that his words came with divine authority, for he states to the Corinthian Christians: "If anybody thinks that he is a prophet or spiritually gifted, let him acknowledge that what I am writing to you is the Lord's command. If he ignores this, he himself will be ignored" (1 Cor. 14:37–38). In the Book of Revelation, John states that the things that have been revealed in his book should not be added to or taken away from, for God will bring a curse upon anyone who would change them (Rev. 22:18–19).

The Scriptures, then, were written with a clear purpose that people should live according to them. Often the books were readily accepted into the canon based upon the authority of their author, but others may have taken some time. There appear to have been significantly different processes for the canonization of the Old and New Testaments, and therefore they will be discussed separately.

Designations of the Old Testament Canon

Evidence for a collection of sacred works comes from as early as Jesus ben Sirach's grandson, writing in about 132 B.C.,[8] who makes reference to biblical works and even calls them scriptures (γραφαί [*graphai*]):

Many great teachings have been given to us through the Law and the Prophets and the others that followed them, and for these we should praise Israel for instruction and wisdom. Now, those who read the *scriptures* must not only themselves understand them, but must also as lovers of learning be able through the spoken and written word to help the outsiders. So my grandfather Jesus, who had devoted himself especially to the reading of the Law and the Prophets and the other books of our ancestors, and had acquired considerable proficiency in them, was himself also led to write something pertaining to instruction and

wisdom, so that by becoming familiar also with his book those who love learning might make even greater progress in living according to the law. (prologue to Sirach NRSV, italics added)

The first reference to the Old Testament as "the (Most) Holy Scriptures or Writings" occurs in the works of Philo (c. 20 B.C.–A.D. 50).[9] Josephus, writing about A.D. 90–100, employs similar terms for these holy books (sacred [or holy] books, βιβλίων ἱερῶν [*biblīōn hierōn;* Josephus *Vita* 75 §418]; sacred books, ἱερῶν βίβλων [*hierōn biblōn;* Josephus *Contra Apion* 1.1 §1]). He describes the care taken in their preservation:

But that our forefathers took no less, not to say even greater, care than the nations I have mentioned in the keeping of their records—a task which they assigned to their chief priests and prophets—and that down to our own times these records have been, and if I may venture to say so, will continue to be, preserved with scrupulous accuracy, I will now endeavour briefly to demonstrate. (Josephus *Contra Apion* 1.6 §29)[10]

Table 7.2
Examples Portraying Scripture's Divine Authority

Prophet	Statement
Isaiah	"the Lord, the LORD Almighty, the Mighty One of Israel, declares"(Isa. 1:24) "declares the Lord, the LORD Almighty" (Isa. 3:15) "this is what the Sovereign LORD says" (Isa. 7:7) "this is the word the LORD has already spoken" (Isa. 16:13) "this is what the LORD says to me" (Isa. 18:4)
Jeremiah	"the word of the LORD came to him" (Jer. 1:2) "the word of the LORD came" (Jer. 1:4, 11, 13) "the LORD said to me" (Jer. 1:12, 14) "declares the LORD" (Jer. 1:15, 19) "this is what the LORD says" (Jer. 2:5)
Ezekiel	"the word of the LORD came to me" (Ezek. 6:1; 7:1; see also Ezek. 1:3) "he [the Lord] said to me" (Ezek. 2:1; 3:1, 4) "This is what the Sovereign LORD says" (Ezek. 3:11, 27) "the LORD said" (Ezek. 4:13)
Hosea	"the word of the LORD that came" (Hos. 1:1) "the LORD said" (Hos. 1:2, 4, 9) "declares the LORD" (Hos. 2:21)

It is clear that the Jews from this period revered their holy writings, especially the Torah, which was used as a guide for faith and practice, and that the early Christians took over these designations. The Old Testament is sometimes referred to in shorthand manner as either "the Law and the Prophets" or similar terminology (Zech. 7:12; 2 Macc. 15:9; 1QS 1.3; 8.15; 9.11 [DSS]; Matt. 5:17; 22:40; Luke 16:16, 29, 31; 24:27; Acts 13:15; 24:14; cf. Acts 26:22) or in a threefold division as "the Law, the Prophets, and the Writings" or similar terminology (prologue to Sirach ["The Law and the Prophets and other books of our fathers"]; Philo *Contempl.* 3.25 ["laws and oracles delivered through the mouth of the prophets, and psalms and anything else which fosters and perfects knowledge and piety"]; Josephus *Contra Apion* 1.8 §§38–41; T.B. *Baba Batra* 14b; Luke 24:44).

It is unclear how these distinctions were determined, though some scholars have suggested that they indicate different stages in the development of the canon. The first designation would describe an early stage when only the Pentateuch and the Prophets were acknowledged as authoritative material; the latter would designate a later stage when the writings were included. The most significant problem with this theory is that several of the prophetic books are as late as or later than books in the Writings. Also, many scholars argue that the Pentateuch did not reach its final form until the postexilic period. The formation of the canon, then, may not have been as clear-cut as some would suggest.

Table 7.3 lists titles used for the Old Testament Scriptures that suggest not only that they were highly regarded but also that they were viewed as a specific group of books.

Formation of the Old Testament Canon

There is still a great deal of uncertainty regarding when the Old Testament canon was formed. Scripture itself is almost silent

Table 7.3
Titles for the Old Testament

Titles	Passages
"The Law"	I Cor. 14:21; Philo *Contempl.* 10 §78; Eusebius *Praep. ev.* 13.12; Luke 16:17; John 10:34; 15:25
"The Law and the Prophets"	2 Macc. 15:9; 4 Macc. 18:10; Matt. 5:17; Luke 16:16; Rom. 3:21
"Moses and the Prophets" (or similar wording)	Luke 16:29, 31 (cf. 1QS 1.2–3); 24:27; John 1:45; Acts 26:22
"The Law of Moses, the Prophets and the Psalms"	Luke 24:44
"The Law and the Prophecies and the rest of the books" (or similar wording)	prologue to Sirach (three times)
"laws, and oracles delivered through the mouth of prophets, and psalms"	Philo *Contempl.* 3 §25
"The Scriptures"	Philo *Abr.* 61 §236; Matt. 21:42; Mark 12:24; 2 Pet. 3:16
"The Scriptures laid up in the Temple"	Josephus *Ant.* 5.1.17 §61
"The (Most) Holy Scriptures" (or similar wording)	Philo *Spec.* 2.28 §159; 2.43 §238; *Praem.* 14 §79; *Contempl.* 3 §28; 10 §§75, 78; Josephus *B.J.* 6.5.4 §311; *Ant.* 1.1.13 §13; 10.10.4 §210; *I Clem.* 45.2
"The Book of God"	Philo *Det.* 37 §139
"The (Most) Holy Books" (or similar wording)	I Macc. 12:9; Josephus *Vita* 75 §418; Eusebius *Praep. ev.* 9.24; Philo *Abr.* 30 §156; 33 §177; 64 §258
"The (Most) Holy Records" (or similar wording)	Philo *Somn.* 1.27 §172; *Congr.* 31 §175
"A very ancient and permanent record of the past"	Josephus *Contra Apion* 1.2 §8

regarding how or when the books were assembled and the process or stages of its growth. What can be pieced together of its history is gleaned from the few references found in Scripture and other literature.

Oral Transmission

It appears that the earliest transmission of biblical materials was oral. Moses commanded the people of Israel to teach their children God's laws and statutes and to make them known to their sons and their grandsons (Deut. 4:9). How long these traditions were transmitted orally is not known, but at some point they were committed to writing to better ensure accuracy.

The Initial Stages

Several biblical texts indicate that even at a very early period some books or parts of Scripture were treated with great reverence and were thought to be authoritative (Exod. 17:14–16; 24:3–4, 7). The stone tablets upon which the Lord inscribed the Ten Commandments were stored in the ark of the covenant (Exod. 25:16, 21; Deut. 10:2–5; 1 Kings 8:9; Heb. 9:4), a sacred place. The law of Moses was taught to the priests and commanded to be publicly read aloud every seven years so that the Israelites would not forget God's laws (Deut. 31:9–11); it was to be stored alongside the ark of the covenant (Deut. 31:24–26) and nothing was to be added to or deleted from its words (Deut. 4:2; 12:32). According to Joshua 8:35, the Israelites held the law of Moses in high regard: "there was not a word of all that Moses had commanded [them] that Joshua did not read to the whole assembly of Israel. . . ." The Book of Joshua claims that Joshua wrote the words of the covenant and put them in the book of the law of God, but it is not more explicit as to what this book was or where it was kept (Josh. 24:26). First Samuel 10:25 records that Samuel wrote down the ordinances of the kingdom in a book and placed it before the Lord, presumably in the sanctuary. Later in the seventh century B.C., during the reign of King Josiah, the law of Moses was found

in the temple and sparked a revival (2 Kings 22–23). Throughout the Old (Josh. 23:6; 1 Kings 2:3; 2 Kings 23:25; 1 Chron. 22:13; 2 Chron. 23:18) and New Testaments (Mark 10:5; 12:26; Luke 2:22 [v. 23 says "Law of the Lord"]; 16:29, 31; 20:28; 24:44) the law of Moses is referred to, suggesting that it was a distinct, authoritative source.

The Old Testament also mentions written forms of prophetic oracles (2 Chron. 21:12; Isa. 30:8; Jer. 25:13; 29:1; 30:2; 36:1–32; 51:60–64; Ezek. 43:11; Dan. 7:1; Hab. 2:2) and histories recorded by prophets (1 Chron. 29:29; 2 Chron. 9:29; 12:15; 13:22; 20:34; 26:22; 32:32; 33:18–19), but the first reference to a collection of biblical materials (בַּסְּפָרִים [bassᵉpārîm]) is in Daniel 9:2, which states: "in the first year of his reign [Darius], I, Daniel, understood from the Scriptures, according to the word of the Lord to Jeremiah the prophet, that the desolation of Jerusalem would last seventy years." Some scholars argue that the word בַּסְּפָרִים refers to letters from Jeremiah,[11] while others argue that by Daniel's time the Book of Jeremiah was part of a larger collection of books that he considered authoritative.[12]

Other biblical authors make reference to earlier biblical writings (2 Kings 14:6; 2 Chron. 25:4; 35:12; Ezra 5:1; 6:18; Neh. 8:1, 3, 5, 8, 18; 9:3; 13:1), and the prophets often rebuke Israel for not obeying the words of their predecessors (2 Chron. 24:19; 36:15–16; Ezra 9:11; Neh. 9:26, 30, 32; Jer. 7:25–26; 25:4; 29:19; 35:15; 44:4; Ezek. 38:17; Dan. 9:6, 10; Hos. 6:5; 12:10; Zech. 1:4–6; 7:7, 12; 8:9).

The Old Testament Canon

Evidence suggests that following the destruction of the temple there was a new emphasis on the collection and study of Scripture, as J. A. Sanders asserts: "It was because of the cataclysmic event of the destruction of the First Temple that what we now know as the Law and the Prophets first came to be collected and galvanized into the shape they now have."[13] Jewish traditions claimed that prophecy had ceased about 400 B.C. in Israel: "Since the death of the last prophets, Haggai, Zechariah and Malachi, the Holy Spirit [of prophetic inspiration] departed from Israel; yet they were still able to avail themselves of the *bath kol*."[14] (See also T.B. *Sanh.* 11a; Tos. *Soṭah* 13.2; baraita in T.B. *Yoma* 9b; T.B. *Soṭah* 48b.)

The phrase *bath kol* is literally translated as "daughter of a voice" (i.e., its sound or perhaps its echo),[15] connoting something that was not as reliable as the voice of prophets themselves. After direct revelation from God had ceased, the Jewish people were directed to listen to the words of the wise men—those who had been trained in the words of God.

> Until then [the coming of Alexander the Great and the end of the empire of the Persians] the prophets prophesied through the Holy Spirit. From then on, "incline thine ear and hear the words of the wise" (Seder Olam Rabbah 30, quoting Prov. 22.17).[16]

> Surely R. Samuel b. Inia said: . . . To indicate that in five things the first Sanctuary differed from the second: in the ark, the ark-cover, the Cherubim, the fire, the *Shechinah*, the Holy Spirit [of Prophecy], and the *Urim-we-Thummim* [the Oracle Plate]? (T.B. *Yoma* 21b; T.P. *Taʿanit* 2.1; T.P. *Makkot* 2.4–8)[17]

> R. Abdimi of Haifa said, Since the day when the Temple was destroyed, prophecy has been taken from the prophets and given to the wise. (T.B. *Baba Batra* 12a)[18]

These passages indicate that according to Jewish tradition the voice of God had ceased following the time of Malachi (about 400 B.C.), and thus new books were no longer being added to the sacred Scriptures. In the apocryphal Book of 1 Maccabees, Simon Maccabees speaks of the great sorrow in Israel such as there had not been since the prophets ceased to appear to them (1 Macc. 9:27). In the Pseudepigrapha, the author of *2 Baruch* (85.3) claims that the prophets had fallen asleep.

R. K. Harrison suggests that the Old Testament canon was probably completed about the third or fourth century B.C.: "In all its essentials the canon was most probably complete by about 300 B.C., and while discussion concerning certain component parts was continued well into the Christian era, the substance of the canon as it existed a century and a half after the time of Ezra and Nehemiah remained unaffected by these controversies."[19]

However, even at this early period there appear to have been at least two different canons—the Samaritan, which contained only the Pentateuch, and the Jewish, which contained the Hebrew canon. Later some uncertainty arose concerning the Old Testament canon since several pseudonymous works vied for canonical status. Noncanonical works found at Qumran (i.e., apocryphal works: Tobit, Ecclesiasticus, the Epistle of Jeremiah; pseudepigraphal works: *1 Enoch*; *Jubilees*) and the fact that they held in question the Book of Esther has caused some scholars to wonder whether this community had a set canon. However, F. F. Bruce cautions us to "bear in mind, of course, that not every book in a community's library reflects the community's ideas and behaviour."[20]

The Christian church, whose roots were in the Jewish nation, initially used the same canon (cf. Rom. 1:2), which it read in light of Christ's coming. Indeed, New Testament writers quote from almost every Old Testament book of the Protestant canon. Jesus seems clear about what constituted the Old Testament canon, stating in Luke 11:50–51 that it went from Genesis to Chronicles (see "Evidence from the New Testament" later in this chapter). Later the New Testament books were added to the Old Testament to constitute the Christian canon. Jesus recognized the authority of the Hebrew Old Testament, and in turn the disciples were taught to reverence it. Jesus often condemned the teachings of the Jewish scribes and Pharisees, but he never contradicted the clear teaching of the Old Testament Scriptures.

The Jewish nation did not accept New Testament teachings, and a split developed between Jews and Christians. Jews often persecuted the early church, thus causing it to spread widely across the Roman Empire. As time went on Christians had little contact or dealings with Jews and as a result grew uncertain as to which Old Testament books were canonical and which were not. The problem was compounded by the presence of heretics in the Christian church who claimed that certain Old Testament books were not canonical (e.g., Marcion in the mid-second century and Theodore of Mopsuestia at the end of the fourth). Among the early church fathers there appear to have been two traditions concerning the canon of the Old Testament. One canon tradition was broad, encompassing all of the Jewish works that were read in the church for purposes of edification, including apocryphal books as well as a few apocalyptic Pseudepigrapha. Augustine favored this broader canon, and probably due to his influence in the church, the copies of the Septuagint from the fourth and fifth centuries include some books of the Apocrypha. Several local synods in the Western church (e.g., Hippo, 393; Carthage, 397 and 419) authorized the use of apocryphal works as Scripture. The other canon tradition deemed only those books in the Jewish Bible to be canonical; scholars such as Melito, Origen, Cyril of Jerusalem, Athanasius, Epiphanius, and Jerome generally favored this position. Jerome made a clear distinction between *canonical* and *apocryphal* books. He was clearly convinced that there were twenty-two books in the Old Testament canon, corresponding to the twenty-two letters of the Hebrew alphabet.[21] However, others did not hold this view, leading to ambiguity regarding the canonical works.

This debate came to a head during the Reformation, when the Reformers (e.g., Martin Luther, John Calvin) saw that the church had become corrupt and needed to return to the ancient doctrines of the supremacy and sufficiency of Scripture. But this required knowing which books were Scripture and which were not. The Reformers aligned themselves with the canon identified by Jerome and others following him, but the Roman Catholic Church argued for the broader view of the canon, especially as they included teaching on prayers for the dead and purgatory (2 Macc. 12:40–45). At the Council of Trent

in 1546 the Roman Catholic Church determined that the Apocrypha as well as the Jewish Bible were authoritative Scriptures and firmly rejected anyone who did not agree (the "Decree Concerning the Canonical Scriptures"):

> And it has thought it meet that a list of the sacred books be inserted in this decree, lest a doubt may arise in any one's mind, which are the books that are received by this Synod. They are set down here below: of the Old Testament: the five books of Moses, to wit, Genesis, Exodus, Leviticus, Numbers, Deuteronomy; Josue [Josh.], Judges, Ruth, four books of Kings, two of Paralipomenon [Chron.], the first book of Esdras, and the second which is entitled Nehemias; Tobias, Judith, Esther, Job, the Davidical Psalter, consisting of a hundred and fifty psalms; the Proverbs, Ecclesiastes, the Canticle of Canticles, Wisdom, Ecclesiasticus, Isaias, Jeremias, with Baruch; Ezechiel, Daniel; the twelve minor prophets, to wit, Osee [Hos.], Joel, Amos, Abdias [Obad.], Jonas, Micheas, Nahum, Habacuc, Sophonias [Zeph.], Aggaeus [Hag.], Zacharias, Malachias; two books of the Machabees, the first and the second. . . .
>
> But if any one receive not, as sacred and canonical, the said books entire with all their parts, as they have been used to be read in the Catholic Church, and as they are contained in the old Latin vulgate edition; and knowingly and deliberately contemn the traditions aforesaid; let him be anathema.[22]

The Reformers fought back, using (ironically) Augustine's words: Jesus ordained the Jewish Scriptures, which did not include the Apocrypha.[23] Table 7.4 indicates the main differences between the two positions.

Discussions between the Reformers and the Roman Catholic Church continued unabated following the Council of Trent, and in 1719, Francis Lee argued that the Alexandrian Jews had a broader canon than did the Palestinian Jews. His idea was based on evidence from the earliest manuscripts of the Septuagint, which contained various apocryphal books. A Roman Catholic scholar named F. K. Movers later argued for an open canon even during the patris-

Table 7.4
Two Views of the Canon

Traditional Protestant	Traditional Roman Catholic
1. The church recognized the biblical books as inspired texts.	1. The church authorized the Bible.
2. The Bible and God's Word created the church.	2. The church created the Bible.
3. The Bible alone is inspired.	3. The Bible and church tradition are authoritative.
4. Revelation has ceased.	4. Revelation is continuing.
5. The Apocrypha is not accepted as inspired.	5. The Apocrypha is accepted.

tic period; he based this argument upon rabbinic discussions in the first century concerning the books of Ezekiel, Proverbs, Ecclesiastes, the Song of Songs, and Esther.[24] He even argued that the Old Testament canon was not closed until the Council of Trent. The idea of an open canon was appealing to scholars at this time, though few were convinced that the canon was open until the Council of Trent. The stage was therefore set in 1871 for a Jewish scholar named H. H. Graetz, who theorized that the Jewish canon remained open until the Council of Jamnia (or Jabneh) in 90, after the rise of Christianity.[25] This theory laid the groundwork for a book by H. E. Ryle, *The Canon of the Old Testament*,[26] which became the standard work on the subject for about a century and was modified only slightly by later scholars. Roger Beckwith, the librarian at Latimer House in Oxford, summarizes Ryle's view:

Ryle's theory is that the Old Testament was recognized as authoritative by the Jews in three main stages, corresponding to the three divisions of the Hebrew Bible. The Pentateuch was recognized as canonical in the fifth century BC, and hence was the only part of the Bible which the Samaritans took with them when their schism with the Jews occurred, during that century. The Prophets were recognized as canonical in the third century BC, too soon for late historical and oracular books like Chronicles and Daniel to be included. The Hagiographa, containing most of the books disputed by the rabbis, were not formally recognized as canonical until the synod of Jamnia, about AD 90.[27]

This critical consensus has more recently been challenged on several fronts. The late date of the Book of Daniel, which is crucial to their view of the development of the canon, has been questioned. The Samaritan schism, once thought to have occurred in the fifth century B.C., is now dated considerably later (even after the possible closing of the second part of the canon, the Prophets); thus the Samaritans willfully rejected part of the canon. The theory of the wider view (or Alexandrian canon) has been refuted by A. C. Sundberg.[28] J. P. Lewis challenges the existence of the Council of Jamnia, arguing instead that these debates were merely academic discussions.[29] Based upon this evidence, recent scholars, such as S. Z. Leiman and Beckwith, have argued that the closing of the Old Testament canon occurred in the mid-second century B.C. instead of in the late first century.[30]

Evidence for the Old Testament Canon

We have already seen that several modern scholars argue for an authoritative group of Old Testament books by the second century B.C. In support of this assertion, this section provides evidence ranging in date from the second century B.C. to the fifth century A.D.

The Septuagint

It would seem that the Septuagint (c. 250–100 B.C.)[31] would be an excellent, early witness to the existence of an Old Testament canon, for this Greek translation was based upon it. Unfortunately there has been great debate as to its date and to which books formed the Septuagint; the earliest extant copies from the fourth and fifth centuries (i.e., Vaticanus [fourth century], Sinaiticus [fourth century], and Alexandrinus [fifth century]) include some of the apocryphal books (see appendix 1), but which books the Septuagint contained before this is not clear. In all probability the Jews during the first and second centuries B.C. believed the Old Testament to contain only the typical Hebrew canon (see evidence presented in the sections about Josephus and Jesus); Philo, an Alexandrian Jew, shows no evidence that apocryphal books were included in the Hebrew canon.[32] Rather they were probably added later by Christians who were unfamiliar with the Hebrew canon.[33]

The Prologue to Ecclesiasticus

The prologue to the Book of Ecclesiasticus (sometimes called the Wisdom of Joshua ben [son of] Sirach; second century B.C.) was translated into Greek about 132 B.C. and refers to the Hebrew Bible several times using a three-part description, namely "the law, the prophets, and the others that followed them," thus suggesting that by this time the tripartite division had already been established (the last division later became known as the Writings). The prologue also indicates that by this time each of the three parts of the Hebrew Bible had been translated into another language (most likely the Greek Septuagint). Jesus son of Sirach states:

> You are invited therefore to read it with goodwill and attention, and to be indulgent in cases where, despite our diligent labor in translating, we may seem to have rendered some phrases imperfectly. For what was originally expressed in Hebrew does not have exactly the same sense when translated into another language. Not only this book, but even the Law itself, the Prophecies, and the rest of the books differ not a little when read in the original. (prologue to Sirach NRSV)

Evidence from the New Testament

Jesus describes the extent of the canon in Matthew 23:34–35 and Luke 11:49–51, about which Bruce observes: "No body of literature ever had its credentials confirmed by a higher authority."[34] Both passages state that the Jewish nation will be held responsible for the blood of the prophets from "the blood of Abel" (Gen. 4:8), the first recorded murder, "to the blood of Zechariah" (2 Chron. 24:20–22), the last recorded murder. The implication is that biblical history spans from Genesis to Chronicles (most likely the last book in the order of the Hebrew Bible), which is comparable to our saying from Genesis to Malachi. Jesus also uses the common tripartite division of the Hebrew Bible to refer to the canon in Luke 24:44: "This is what I told you while I was still with you: Everything must be fulfilled that is written about me in the Law of Moses, the Prophets and the Psalms." The last designation is evidently representative of the final group of Old Testament writings, of which Psalms was the first and largest book.[35] A similar designation for the Old Testament canon was in use from the time of Philo in the early first century ("[the] laws, and oracles delivered through the mouth of prophets, and psalms and anything else which fosters and perfects knowledge and piety" [*Contempl.* 3 §25])[36] until at least the tenth century (al-Masudi, an Arabian historian and geographer, describes the Hebrew canon as "the Law, the Prophets and the Psalms, which are the 24 books").[37] It is interesting to note that Jesus quotes from each of the three parts of Scripture as authoritative material (table 7.5).

Philo of Alexandria

Philo (c. 20 B.C.–A.D. 50) a well-educated Jew from Alexandria, appears to have accepted the Hebrew canon of Scripture as distinct from the Apocrypha. Beckwith observes: "though Philo quotes all the books of the Pentateuch, most of the books

Table 7.5
Jesus' Old Testament Quotations

Law	Prophets	Writings
Matt. 4:4; Luke 4:4/ Deut. 8:3	Matt. 10:35–36/ Mic. 7:6	Matt. 4:6; Luke 4:10–11/Ps. 91:11–12
Matt. 4:7; Luke 4:12/ Deut. 6:16	Matt. 11:10/ Mal. 3:1	Matt. 21:16/ Ps. 8:2
Matt. 4:10; Luke 4:8/ Deut. 6:13	Matt. 12:7/ Hos. 6:6	Matt. 22:44; Mark 12:36; Luke 20:42–43/
Matt. 5:27/ Exod. 20:14; Deut. 5:18	Matt. 13:14–15; Mark 4:12; Luke 8:10/	Ps. 110:1
Matt. 15:4; Mark 7:10/ Exod. 20:12;	Isa. 6:9–10	Matt. 23:39/ Ps. 118:26
21:17; Lev. 20:9; Deut. 5:16	Matt. 15:8–9; Mark 7:6–7/ Isa. 29:13	Matt. 24:15/ Dan. 9:27
Matt. 18:16/ Deut. 19:15	Matt. 21:13; Mark 11:17/ Isa. 56:7;	Matt. 27:46; Mark 15:34/ Ps. 22:1
Matt. 19:4/ Gen. 1:27	Jer.7:11	
Matt. 19:5/ Gen. 2:24	Matt. 24:29; Mark 13:24–26/ Joel 2:10, 31	
Matt. 22:32; Mark 12:26; Luke 20:37/	Mark 9:48/ Isa. 66:24	
Exod. 3:6	Mark 14:27/ Zech. 13:7	
Matt. 22:37; Mark 12:29–32; Luke	Luke 4:18–19/ Isa. 61:1–2	
10:27/ Deut. 6:4–5	Luke 22:37/ Isa. 53:12	
Luke 18:20/ Exod. 20:12–16;	Luke 23:30/ Hos. 10:8	
Deut. 5:16–20		

of the Prophets and several of the books of the Hagiographa, often with formulas recognizing their divine authority, he never once quotes a book of the Apocrypha."[38]

2 Esdras

The apocryphal Book of 2 Esdras (sometimes called 4 Esdras), written in the first century, contains a fictional account of Ezra rewriting the biblical books after they had been burned, most likely in the destruction of Jerusalem by Nebuchadrezzar (2 Esd. 14:21). In forty days Ezra was to proclaim to five scribes who were trained to inscribe quickly "everything that has happened in the world from the beginning, the things that were written in your law, so that people may be able to find the path, and that those who want to live in the last days may do so" (2 Esd. 14:22 NRSV). During those forty days Ezra wrote ninety-four books, and then God said to him:

"Make public the twenty-four books that you wrote first, and let the worthy and the unworthy read them; but keep the seventy that were written last, in order to give them to the wise among your

people. For in them is the spring of understanding, the fountain of wisdom, and the river of knowledge." And I did so. (14:45b–48 NRSV)

This passage clearly supports a canon of twenty-four Old Testament books.

Josephus

Josephus, a Jewish historian writing during the latter part of the first century (c. A.D. 37–100), states that the Jews had only twenty-two sacred books (he combines Ruth and Judges; Jeremiah and Lamentations):

It therefore naturally, or rather necessarily, follows (seeing that with us it is not open to everybody to write the records, and that there is no discrepancy in what is written; seeing that, on the contrary, the prophets alone had this privilege, obtaining their knowledge of the most remote and ancient history through the inspiration which they owed to God, and committing to writing a clear account of the events of their own time just as they occurred)—it follows, I say, that we do not possess myriads of inconsistent books, conflicting with each other. Our books, those which are justly accredited, are but two and twenty, and contain the record of all time. (Josephus *Contra Apion* 1.7–8 §§37–39)[39]

Melito, Bishop of Sardis

The first known list of Old Testament books from Christian circles was drawn up by Melito, bishop of Sardis (c. 170), who was said to have acquired the information while traveling in Syria (Eusebius *HE* 4.26.13–14). Melito writes to his friend Onesimus:

Melito to Onesimus his brother, greeting: Since you often desired, in your zeal for the true word, to have extracts from the Law and the Prophets concerning the Saviour, and concerning all our faith, and, moreover, since you wished to know the accurate facts about the ancient writings, how many they are in number, and what is their order, I have taken pains to do thus, for I know your zeal for the faith and interest in the word, and that in your struggle for eternal salvation you esteem these things more highly than all else in your love towards God. Accordingly when I came to the east and reached the place where these things were preached and done, and learnt accurately the books of the Old Testament, I set down the facts and sent them to you. These are their names: five books of Moses, Genesis, Exodus, Numbers, Leviticus, Deuteronomy, Joshua the son of Nun, Judges, Ruth, four books of Kingdoms, two books of Chronicles, the Psalms of David, the Proverbs of Solomon and his Wisdom, Ecclesiastes, the Song of Songs, Job, the prophets Isaiah, Jeremiah, the Twelve in a single book, Daniel, Ezekiel, Ezra. From these I have made extracts and compiled them in six books.[40]

The Book of Lamentations is probably included with Jeremiah and Nehemiah with Ezra, but it is unusual to find Ezra classified with the Prophets. The Book of Esther is missing, but Melito's list may derive from the Syriac church, which does not include Esther in its canon.[41]

A List in Jerusalem

Bruce cites a list of Old Testament books from about the same time or slightly later than Melito's list:

[it was] preserved in a manuscript in the Library of the Greek Patriarchate in Jerusalem, and reproduced in a somewhat later form in a treatise by the late fourth-century writer Epiphanius, bishop of Salamis in Cyprus. In this list the name of each Old Testament book is given twice, first in Hebrew or Aramaic transcribed into Greek characters, and then in the Greek Septuagint form. The total of the books listed is twenty-seven. . . . But these twenty-seven correspond to our thirty-nine, except that Lamentations is not included by name. The omission of Lamentations, however, may be only apparent; probably it was reckoned as an appendix to Jeremiah.[42]

Origen

Origen (c. 185–253), one of the greatest biblical scholars of the early church, states: "But it should be known that there are twenty-two canonical books, according to the Hebrew tradition; the same as the number of the letters of their alphabet." He then lists them according to their Hebrew and Greek names:

"These are the twenty-two books according to the Hebrews: That which is entitled with us Genesis, but with the Hebrews, from the beginning of the book, *Brēsith*, that is 'In the beginning.' Exodus, *Ouelle smōth*, that is, 'These are the names.' Leviticus, *Ouikra*, 'And he called.' Numbers, *Ammes phekōdeim*. Deuteronomy, *Elle addebareim*, 'These are the words.' Jesus the son of Nave, *Iōsoue ben noun*. Judges, Ruth, with them in one book, *Sōphteim*. Of Kingdoms i, ii, with them one, *Samuel*, 'The called of God.' Of Kingdoms iii, iv, in one, *Ouammelch david*, that is, 'The kingdom of David.' Chronicles i, ii, in one, *Dabrē iamein*, that is, 'Words of days.' Esdras i, ii, in one, *Ezra*, that is, 'Helper.' Book of Psalms, *Sphar thelleim*. Proverbs of Solomon, *Melōth*. Ecclesiastes, *Kōelth*. Song of Songs (not, as some suppose, Songs of Songs), *Sir assireim*.

111

Esaias, *Iessia*. Jeremiah with Lamentations and the Letter, in one, *Jeremia*. Daniel, *Daniēl*. Ezekiel, *Ezekiēl*. Job, *Jōb*. Esther, *Esthēr*. And outside these there are the Maccabees, which are entitled *Sar bēth sabanai el*." (Eusebius *HE* 6.25.1–2, italics added)[43]

The Book of the Twelve Prophets must also have been included in order to arrive at twenty-two books. The Book of Esther is here mentioned, and the Letter of Jeremiah was apparently included with the Book of Jeremiah.

Athanasius

In response to false teachers who claimed that other books were to be considered authoritative, Athanasius (c. 296–373), bishop of Alexandria, discussed the canon in his Easter letter to his parishioners in 367, delineating that the Old Testament canon contains twenty-two books (corresponding to our thirty-nine books, except that Esther is not mentioned and Jeremiah includes Lamentations, Baruch, and the Epistle of Jeremiah). The pertinent part of his letter says:

> "Forasmuch as some have taken in hand," to reduce into order for themselves the books termed apocryphal, and to mix them up with the divinely inspired Scripture, concerning which we have been fully persuaded, as they who from the beginning were eyewitnesses and ministers of the Word, delivered to the fathers; it seemed good to me also, having been urged thereto by true brethren, and having learned from the beginning, to set before you the books included in the Canon, and handed down, and accredited as Divine; to the end that any one who has fallen into error may condemn those who have led him astray; and that he who has continued stedfast in purity may again rejoice, having these things brought to his remembrance.
>
> There are, then, of the Old Testament, twenty-two books in number; for, as I have heard, it is handed down that this is the number of the letters among the Hebrews; their respective order and names being as follows. The first is Gen-

esis, then Exodus, then Leviticus, after that Numbers, and then Deuteronomy. Following these there is Joshua, the son of Nun, then Judges, then Ruth. And again, after these four books of Kings, the first and second being reckoned as one book, and so likewise the third and fourth as one book. And again, the first and second of the Chronicles are reckoned as one book. Again Ezra, the first and second are similarly one book. After these there is the book of Psalms, then the Proverbs, next Ecclesiastes, and the Song of Songs. Job follows, then the Prophets, the twelve being reckoned as one book. Then Isaiah, one book, then Jeremiah with Baruch, Lamentations and the epistle, one book; afterwards, Ezekiel and Daniel, each one book. Thus far constitutes the Old Testament. (*Letter* 39.3–4)[44]

He mentions the apocryphal books also (see chap. 8) but makes a clear distinction between canonical and noncanonical works; however, questions still arose as to which books were canonical.

Jerome

Jerome (c. 345–420) was one of the most qualified biblical scholars of the Latin church fathers. He clearly held that only the Jewish canon was authoritative, stating in the preface to his commentary on Daniel: "for all Scripture is by them divided into three parts: the law, the Prophets, and the Hagiographa [Writings], which have respectively five, eight, and eleven books. . . ."[45] These twenty-four books of the Hebrew canon correspond to the thirty-nine books of our present Old Testament. In the preface to the books of Samuel and Kings there is a long discussion concerning the number of Old Testament books as being twenty-two in number:

> That the Hebrews have twenty-two letters is testified by the Syrian and Chaldaean languages which are nearly related to the Hebrew, for they have twenty-two elementary sounds which are pronounced the same way, but are written differently. . . . And again, five are double letters, viz., *Caph, Mem, Nun, Phe, Sade*, for at the beginning and in the

middle of the words they are written one way, and at the end another way. Whence it happens that, by most people five of the books are reckoned as double, viz., Samuel, Kings, Chronicles, Ezra, Jeremiah, with *Kinoth, i.e.,* his Lamentations. As, then, there are twenty-two elementary characters by means of which we write in Hebrew all we say, and the compass of the human voice is contained within their limits, so we reckon twenty-two books, by which, as by the alphabet of the doctrine of God, a righteous man is instructed in tender infancy, and, as it were, while still at the breast.[46]

Jerome clearly limits the Old Testament canon to the Hebrew Old Testament, whether numbered at twenty-two, twenty-four, or twenty-seven books (by dividing into two books Samuel, Kings, Chronicles, Ezra-Nehemiah, and Jeremiah-Lamentations).

Tyrannius Rufinus

This church father (c. 345–411) lists the canonical books as follows:

Of the Old Testament, therefore, first of all there have been handed down five books of Moses, Genesis, Exodus, Leviticus, Numbers, Deuteronomy; then Jesus Nave, (Joshua the son of Nun), The Book of Judges together with Ruth; then four books of Kings (Reigns), which the Hebrews reckon two; the Book of Omissions, which is entitled the Book of Days (Chronicles), and two books of Ezra (Ezra and Nehemiah), which the Hebrews reckon one, and Esther; of the Prophets, Isaiah, Jeremiah, Ezekiel, and Daniel; moreover of the twelve (minor) Prophets, one book; Job also and the Psalms of David, each one book. Solomon gave three books to the Churches, Proverbs, Ecclesiastes, Canticles. These comprise the books of the Old Testament. (*Commentary on the Apostle's Creed* 37)[47]

Rufinus, who founded a monastery in Jerusalem, includes all the books of the Hebrew Old Testament, though they are divided into twenty-four, which was common among some Jews. Since Rufinus spent time in Palestine, he was probably familiar with both the Hebrew and early Christian Old Testament canons.

Table 7.6
Summary of Evidence for the Old Testament Canon

Source	Date	Evidence
1. Septuagint	c. 250–100 B.C.	Contains at least some books from each of the three parts of the Old Testament canon (Law, Prophets, and others)
2. Prologue to Sirach	c.132 B.C.	Tripartite division of the Old Testament (Law, Prophets, and others) and mentions a Greek translation of the Old Testament
3. Jesus	4 B.C.–A.D. 30	Matthew 23:34–35; Luke 11:50–51 "Genesis to Chronicles"; Luke 24:44 "Law of Moses, the Prophets and the Psalms"
4. Philo of Alexandria	c. 20 B.C.–A.D. 50	"Laws and oracles delivered through the mouth of prophets, and psalms"
5. 2 Esdras 14:45	1st century A.D.	Old Testament contains 24 books (same as our 39)
6. Josephus	c. A.D. 37–100	Old Testament contains 22 books (same as our 39; *Contra Apion* 1.7–8 §§37–39)
7. Melito, bishop of Sardis	c. A.D.170	List of all Old Testament books (except possibly Esther)
8. Jerusalem list	c. A.D. 170	All 39 Old Testament books
9. Origen	c. A.D.185–253	Old Testament contains 22 books (same as our 39)
10. Athanasius, bishop of Alexandria	c. A.D. 367	22 books (no mention of Esther; inclusion of Baruch and Epistle of Jeremiah)
11. Jerome	c. A.D. 345–420	22, 24, 27 but still referring to our 39 Old Testament books
12. Tyrannius Rufinus	A.D. 345–411	24 books (same as our 39 books, but different order)
13. Jewish tradition	3d–6th centuries A.D.	24 books (same as our 39 books, but different order)

Jewish Tradition

The Babylonian Talmud, which was compiled over a period from about the third to the sixth centuries, provides a thorough list of the books of Scripture and their order, although not in the same order as the modern Hebrew Old Testament. As the Pentateuch was not in question, it is not mentioned in this passage:

> Our Rabbis taught: The order of the Prophets is, Joshua, Judges, Samuel, Kings, Jeremiah, Ezekiel, Isaiah, and the Twelve Minor Prophets. Let us examine this. Hosea came first, as it is written, *God spake first to Hosea*. But did God speak first to Hosea? Were there not many prophets between Moses and Hosea? R. Johanan, however, has explained that [what it means is that] he was the first of the four prophets who prophesied at that period, namely, Hosea, Isaiah, Amos and Micah. Should not then Hosea come first?— Since his prophecy is written along with those of Haggai, Zechariah and Malachi, and Haggai, Zechariah and Malachi came at the end of the prophets, he is reckoned with them. But why should he not be written separately and placed first?— Since his book is so small, it might be lost [if copied separately]. Let us see again. Isaiah was prior to Jeremiah and Ezekiel. Then why should not Isaiah be placed first?—Because the Book of Kings ends with a record of destruction and Jeremiah speaks throughout of destruction and Ezekiel commences with destruction and ends with consolation and Isaiah is full of consolation; therefore we put the destruction next to destruction and consolation next to consolation.
>
> The order of the Hagiographa is Ruth, the Book of Psalms, Job, Prophets, Ecclesiastes, Song of Songs, Lamentations, Daniel and the Scroll of Esther, Ezra and Chronicles. Now on the view that Job lived in the days of Moses, should not the book of Job come first?—We do not begin with a record of suffering. But Ruth also is a record of suffering?—It is a suffering with a sequel [of happiness], as R. Johanan said: Why was her name called Ruth?—Because there issued from her David who replenished the Holy One, blessed be He, with hymns and praises. (T.B. *Baba Batra* 14b)[48]

Continuing Questions regarding the Old Testament Canon

Following the destruction of Jerusalem and the temple in A.D. 70, the nation of Israel was forced to rethink its religious practices. They could no longer offer sacrifices since the temple was now destroyed, but they still clung tightly to the words of their prophets as they had done during the Babylonian exile. During this period, questions arose regarding the canonicity of five Old Testament books (i.e., Ezek., Prov., Est., Eccles., and Song) which became known as *antilegomenoi* (lit., spoken against). These discussions, which took place at a rabbinic school in Jamnia (sometimes called Jabneh or Yavneh), have become commonly known as the Council of Jamnia.

The Council of Jamnia

Graetz, in his excursus to Qohelet (Ecclesiastes) in 1871,[49] was the first scholar to propose that formal pronouncements made by the Jewish authorities of the Council of Jamnia (A.D. 90) defined the limits of the canon, even though there is little evidence to support the existence of such a council. What is known about the discussions of the school at Jamnia is as follows. When the destruction of Jerusalem in A.D. 70 was imminent or shortly thereafter, R. Johanan ben Zakkai received permission to settle in Jamnia, near Jaffa, where he continued to carry on his study of Scripture. Eventually this city became an important center for the study of Scripture, and from time to time discussions must have occurred regarding the authority and legitimacy of certain books in the canon. H. H. Rowley correctly argues that these discussions "were informal, though none the less helping to crystallize and to fix more firmly the Jewish tradition."[50] J. P. Lewis observes that the Council of Jamnia is a misnomer:

> In short, the Council of Jamnia and its alleged date of about A.D. 90 is, in the absence of attestation in specific texts,

used in scholarship as a convenient symbol for the culmination of long processes in early Judaism. Sometimes used for any development between A.D. 70 and 135, the terminology has the disadvantage of inviting the uninformed to assume official action taken at specific meetings on specific dates.[51]

Questions concerning canonicity of the five books and their resolutions are as follows.

Ezekiel

Several charges were brought against the Book of Ezekiel. It contradicted the Law in several places (i.e., the ceremonial law in Ezek. 40–48 is hard to reconcile with the Pentateuch; see *Sipre* on Deuteronomy, 294; T.B. *Šabb.* 13b; T.B. *Menaḥot* 45a). The description of God's throne (or chariot) in Ezekiel 1 gave rise to speculative ideas later known as *Merᵉkābâ* (chariot) (T.B. *Ḥag.* 11b; see T.B. *Ḥag.* 13a); and Ezekiel 40–48 contained dimensions for a temple that do not coincide with any of the known temples erected in Israel (T.B. *Šabb.* 13b). Ḥananiah son of Hezekiah is generally given credit for working out these apparent contradictions. The Babylonian Talmud says:

> Rab Judah said in Rab's name: In truth, that man, Ḥananiah son of Hezekiah by name, is to be remembered for blessing: but for him, the book of Ezekiel would have been hidden, for its word contradicted the Torah. What did he do? Three hundred barrels of oil were taken up to him and he sat in an upper chamber and reconciled them. (*Šabb.* 13b)[52]

It was finally determined that these problems turned out to be matters of interpretation rather than inspiration.

This book, which was included in the second section of the Old Testament (i.e., the Prophets), proves to be a major problem for Ryle's view of Old Testament canon, for no one argues that this section remained open until the first century. There is also strong evidence for its canonicity; first, Ezekiel claims to be divinely commissioned (1:1, 3; 2:1–5; 3:1–9) and, second, both extracanonical and rabbinic

evidence indicates that the Jewish nation believed it to be authoritative.[53]

Proverbs

According to the Talmud, certain teachings of the Proverbs were contradictory: "The Book of Proverbs also they desired to hide, because its statements are self-contradictory" (T.B. *Šabb.* 30b).[54] For example, the Hebrew in Proverbs 26:4–5 appears even more contradictory than the English, which reads:

> Do not answer a fool according to
> his folly,
> or you will be like him yourself.
>
> Answer a fool according to his folly,
> or he will be wise in his own
> eyes.

The Babylonian Talmud explains why the Book of Proverbs was not withdrawn:

> Yet why did they not hide it? They said, Did we not examine the Book of Ecclesiastes and find a reconciliation? So here too let us make search. And how are its statements self-contradictory?—It is written, *Answer not a fool according to this folly;* yet it is also written, *Answer a fool according to his folly?* There is no difficulty: the one refers to matters of learning; the other to general matters. (*Šabb.* 30b)[55]

It is more likely that the verses imply that wisdom is often a matter of discernment—sometimes it is best to respond with silence since the fool will not listen anyway; other times a wise answer will catch a fool in his tracks and thereby teach him his mistake.

Esther

Apparently there was some question about the canonicity of Esther, for the Babylonian Talmud records, "Levi b. Samuel and R. Huna b. Ḥiyya were repairing the mantles of the Scrolls of R. Judah's college. On coming to the Scroll of Esther, they remarked, 'O, this Scroll of Esther does not require a mantle.' Thereupon he reproved them, 'This too savours of irreverence'" (*Sanh.* 100a; see also *Meg.* 7a).[56] This book may have been questioned on several grounds. It does not claim to be inspired; it appears to cover secular history; nowhere is the name *Yahweh* mentioned; it records the beginning of the celebration of the feast of Purim (a festival not mentioned in the Pentateuch) (*Meg.* 14a); and the Essenes questioned the calendar used in Esther since the second day of killing mentioned in Esther 9:15–22 would have been a Sabbath.[57]

Rabbis finally agreed to include Esther in the canon because God's presence was evident in the book—Esther exercised faith (Est. 4:16), and God delivered his people.

Ecclesiastes

Rabbi Simeon made the following distinction regarding the Book of Ecclesiastes: "The Song of Songs makes the hands unclean because it was spoken in the Holy Spirit. Ecclesiastes does not make the hands unclean because it is [merely] Solomon's wisdom" (Tos. *Yadayim* 2.14).[58] It is interesting that the question of Ecclesiastes' canonicity was one of the debates between the different Pharisaical schools in Israel. The Babylonian Talmud states: "R. Ishmael cites three instances of lenient ruling by Beth [house of] Shammai and rigorous rulings by Beth Hillel. The book of Ecclesiastes does not defile the hands according to the opinion of Beth Shammai; but Beth Hillel says: it defiles the hands (*'Eduyyot* 5.3; see also *Yadayim* 3.5)."[59] The complaint appears to have been that Ecclesiastes was too pessimistic or skeptical (Eccles. 1:2–18; 2:12, 14–16, 26), but the main purpose of the book is to demonstrate the futility of life apart from God (3:12; 12:13–14). Apparently a vote was taken at Jamnia to determine which school of thought would be favored. But as Beckwith points out, the decision was not binding since contrary opinions were still being expressed throughout the second century.[60]

Song of Songs

This work was questioned because of its explicitness regarding sexual love; Origen claims in his commentary on Song of Songs that Jewish custom forbade anyone to read it before reaching maturity.[61] After R. Akiba's staunch support for the book, however, there was little question as to its canonicity (M. *Yadayim* 3.5).[62] The targums interpreted this book as describing the history of Israel from the exodus to the messianic age and the building of the third temple.[63] Many early Christians also saw it as an allegory of Christ's love for the church (esp. Origen).[64]

Even though the canonicity of these books was questioned, it is doubtful that the scholars at Jamnia had the authority to modify the canon of Scripture; either way the Old Testament canon remained the same. Apparently some of the scholars questioned whether other books such as Ecclesiasticus, the *gilyonim* (Aramaic Gospel writings), and other books of the *minim* (heretics, including Jewish Christians) should be included, but the answer was overwhelmingly no.[65]

Alexandrian Canon

Some scholars have argued that there existed an Alexandrian canon, which was represented by the Septuagint and contained more books (some apocryphal ones), and a Palestinian canon containing only the Hebrew canon. The likelihood of a larger Alexandrian canon has been ruled out for the following reasons:

1. Two assumptions on which it was based have now been proven to be false—first, that Hellenistic Judaism was largely independent of Palestinian Judaism,[66] and second, that most of the Apocrypha was composed in Egypt in the Greek language.[67]
2. The prologue to Sirach specifically states that it was written in Egypt but mentions only the tripartite divisions of the Old Testament Scriptures, which probably did not include the Old Testament apocryphal books.
3. Jewish writers who commonly used the Septuagint (e.g., Josephus and Philo) did not consider the apocryphal books to be divinely inspired.[68]

It is becoming increasingly unlikely that there were differing canons in these two regions; thus the existence of certain apocryphal books in extant copies of the Septuagint must be accounted for by some other means.

Determination of Canonicity

While there is no record as to how the Jewish nation determined which works were canonical, some hints are found in Josephus's statement about the Jewish canon (*Contra Apion* 1.7–8 §§37–42, bold added):

> It therefore naturally, or rather necessarily, follows (seeing that with us it is not open to everybody to write the records, **and that there is no discrepancy in what is written**; seeing that, on the contrary, **the prophets alone had this privilege**, obtaining their knowledge of the most remote and ancient history **through the inspiration which they owed to God**, and committing to writing a clear account of the events of their own time just as they occurred)—it follows, I say, that we do not possess myriads of inconsistent books, conflicting with each other. Our books, those which are justly accredited, are but two and twenty, and contain the record of all time.
>
> Of these, five are the books of Moses, comprising the laws and the traditional history from the birth of man down to the death of the lawgiver. . . . The prophets subsequent to Moses wrote the history of the events of their own times in thirteen books. The remaining four books contain hymns to God and precepts for the conduct of human life.
>
> From Artaxerxes to our own time the complete history has been written, but has not been deemed worthy of equal credit with the earlier records, because of the failure of the exact succession of the prophets.
>
> We have given **practical proof of our reverence for our own Scriptures. For, although such long ages have now passed, no one has ventured either to add, or to remove, or to alter a syllable; and it is an instinct with every Jew, from the day of his birth, to regard them as the decrees of God, to abide by them, and, if need be, cheerfully to die for them.**[69]

The statements within this excerpt suggest some of the criteria that may have helped determine the Old Testament canon:

1. It does not contain contradictions.
2. It was written by a prophet or someone recognized as having divine authority.
3. It originated through inspiration from God.
4. It was accepted by the Jews as authoritative material.

When these criteria are used together they form a strong case as to how Scripture was recognized as authoritative. With regard to point 3, it is interesting to note that biblical books often claim to be from God by phrases such as "the word of the Lord came" (Jer. 1:2, 4; 2:1; Ezek. 6:1; 7:1) or "the Lord says" or similar wording (Isa. 37:22; 43:1; Jer. 13:1), whereas none of the apocryphal books include such statements. The Jews believed that prophecy ceased about 400 B.C., so that apocryphal works, written later, were necessarily attributed to prophets already recognized as authoritative.

Flavius Josephus (Roman name)/Joseph ben Mattathias (Jewish name), c. A.D. 37–100

A Jewish historian, politician, and soldier whose notable writings record the events and political atmosphere of the first century A.D., Josephus was a maternal descendant of the Hasmonean family that had ruled in Jerusalem a century earlier and was by birthright a priest. He was educated well in Jerusalem, and "at the early age of fourteen, so he boasted, he was so learned that the high priests and the leading men of the city of Jerusalem consulted him about matters of the law" (H. Schreckenberg, "Josephus, Flavius," *ISBE*, 2:1132). At age sixteen he received further training from the Pharisees, Sadducees, Essenes, and a hermit named Banus, an ascetic wilderness-dweller. At age nineteen Josephus became a Pharisee. In 64 he led a delegation from Jerusalem to the court of Nero in Rome and successfully secured the release of several pious priests who were his friends. While in Rome, Josephus was impressed by the wealth and power of the Roman empire. Shortly after his return from Rome, he assumed command of Jewish forces in Galilee and, even though he strongly opposed the rebellion against Rome, fought heroically to defend the city of Jatapata. The city was defeated, and Josephus fled with forty others to a cave. To avoid capture, the fugitives entered into a suicide pact. Josephus and one other survived, and he succeeded in convincing the other survivor to surrender to the Romans. Josephus later won the favor of the Roman commander Vespasian, at least in part by prophesying that Vespasian would become emperor. When the prediction came true, Josephus was set free, and he took the name Flavius (Vespasian's family name). Vespasian's son Titus took Josephus with him to Jerusalem to act as an interpreter. There Josephus witnessed firsthand the fall and capture of Jerusalem, after which he returned to Rome as a client and pensioner of the emperor. Because of his behavior during the war, Josephus was regarded as a traitor by the Jewish nation. He devoted much of his time to writing, addressing his works both to his fellow Jews in an effort to justify his conduct and his change of loyalties during the Roman War and to the wider Roman audience in order to gain sympathy for Jewish culture and religion.

For Further Reading

Anderson, G. W. "Canonical and Noncanonical." In *CHB*, 1:113–59.

Beckwith, R. *The Old Testament Canon of the New Testament Church and Its Background in Early Judaism.* Grand Rapids: Eerdmans, 1985.

Bruce, F. F. *The Books and the Parchments,* 86–95. 5th ed. London: Marshall Pickering, 1991.

Filson, F. V. *Which Books Belong in the Bible?* Philadelphia: Westminster, 1957.

Harrison, R. K. *Introduction to the Old Testament,* 1175–1278. Grand Rapids: Eerdmans, 1969.

Lewis, J. P. "What Do We Mean by Jabneh?" *The Journal of Bible and Religion* 32 (1964): 125–32.

Ryle, H. E. *The Canon of the Old Testament.* 2d ed. London: Macmillan, 1909.

Sundberg, A. C. *The Old Testament of the Early Church.* HTS 20. Cambridge, MA: Harvard University Press, 1964.

Old Testament Extracanonical Books

The Old Testament extracanonical books can be divided into three distinct groups: books mentioned in the Old Testament that appear to have been lost, the apocryphal books, and the pseudepigraphal books.

Noncanonical Works Mentioned in the Old Testament

Several works mentioned in the Old Testament did not become part of the Old Testament canon:

1. The Book of the Wars of Yahweh (Num. 21:14)
2. The Book of Jasher (Josh. 10:13; 2 Sam. 1:18; possibly the Septuagint of 1 Kings 8:12–13)
3. The Book of the Annals of Solomon (1 Kings 11:41)
4. The Book of the Annals of the Kings of Israel (1 Kings 14:19; 15:31; 16:5, 14, 20, 27; 2 Chron. 20:34)
5. The Book of the Annals of the Kings of Judah (1 Kings 14:29; 15:7, 23; 22:45; 2 Kings 8:23; 12:19)
6. The Book of the Annals of King David (1 Chron. 27:24)
7. The Annals of Samuel the Seer, the Annals of Nathan the Prophet, the Annals of Gad the Seer (1 Chron. 29:29)
8. The Annals of Nathan the prophet, the Prophecy of Ahijah the Shilonite, and the Visions of Iddo the Seer (2 Chron. 9:29)
9. The Annals of Shemaiah the Prophet and of Iddo the Seer (2 Chron. 12:15)
10. The Commentary of the Prophet Iddo (2 Chron. 13:22)
11. The Commentary of the Books of the Kings (2 Chron. 24:27)
12. The Acts of Uzziah (2 Chron. 26:22)
13. The Book of the Kings of Judah and Israel (2 Chron. 32:32)
14. The Annals of the Kings of Israel (2 Chron. 33:18)
15. The Book of the Annals (Neh. 12:23)
16. The Book of the Annals (Persian work; Est. 2:23; 6:1)
17. The Book of the Annals of the Kings of Media and Persia (Est. 10:2)

To date the works listed above are considered lost, but we know of their existence because the biblical authors make reference to them. The fact that they have not survived suggests that the Jewish nation placed more value on the canonical works than on noncanonical works like these.

Later Noncanonical Works

There is good evidence that none of the apocryphal or pseudepigraphal works were included in the Old Testament Hebrew canon used by Jews and early Christians. However, it is interesting that the earliest manuscripts of the Septuagint include several of them (with the exception of 2 [4] Esdras, which was never part of the Septuagint). There is no evidence that these books were ever accepted by Alexandrian Jews to form an Alexandrian canon in contrast to a Palestinian canon.[1] From where did they originate? Most likely these books developed from Jewish traditions or folklore arising from the biblical text during the Second Temple period (more specifically, from about 300 B.C. to A.D. 100), perhaps from a desire for further revelatory material after biblical revelation had ceased. It is possible that these noncanonical scrolls were stored together with canonical ones, and in time the distinctions between the two may have broken down.

The Old Testament Apocrypha

There are generally considered to be fifteen books in the Apocrypha; however, sometimes the Letter of Jeremiah is combined with Baruch. Many Protestants and Jews consider the Apocrypha to have some religious value but not on the same level as the canonical books, whereas Roman Catholics since at least the Council of Trent have viewed them as canonical. Many modern Roman Catholic scholars follow the practice introduced in 1566 by Sixtus of Sienna, in which the term *protocanonical* is used to refer to the books of Scripture originally accepted by the entire church as inspired and the term *deuterocanonical* to designate books whose inspiration was later recognized by the church (see table 8.1 for the latter).

These books are not always consistent in their names, and sometimes they are combined differently; for example, 3 and 4 Esdras are sometimes called 1 and 2 Esdras depending upon whether or not Ezra and Nehemiah are labeled as 1 and 2 Esdras. The Prayer of Manasseh and 1 and 2 Esdras were not accepted as canonical at the Council of Trent in 1546 and thus are generally placed in an appendix following the New Testament.

The apocryphal books contain a variety of material that can be grouped into four categories (see table 8.2). These books are generally located in the Septuagint among canonical books of the same class. First Esdras precedes Ezra and Nehemiah, while 1 and 2 Maccabees appear after the Prophets. Judith and Tobit follow Esther, and the additions of Esther and Daniel are included at various points within their respective books. Baruch appears after the Book of Jeremiah (Baruch was Jeremiah's scribe), and the Prayer of Manasseh is located in the collection of psalms and hymns at the end of the Septuagint. However, in Protestant English Bibles from the Coverdale Bible (1535) onward, the Apocrypha, if it is included at all, is placed as an appendix at the end of the Old Testament.

The Word *Apocrypha*

The word *apocrypha* (from the Greek word ἀπόκρυφος), used in a variety of ways

Table 8.1
Names of the Old Testament Apocryphal Books

Protestant Names	Traditional Roman Catholic Names
1. Tobit	1. Tobias
2. Judith	2. Judith
3. Wisdom of Solomon	3. Wisdom
4. Ecclesiasticus/Sirach	4. Ecclesiasticus
5. 1 Maccabees	5. 1 Machabees
6. 2 Maccabees	6. 2 Machabees
7. Baruch	7. Baruch 1–5
8. Epistle of Jeremiah	8. Baruch 6
9. Additions to Esther	9. Esther 10:4–16:24
10. Prayer of Azariah and Song of the Three Young Men	10. Daniel 3:24–90
11. Susanna	11. Daniel 13
12. Bel and the Dragon	12. Daniel 14
13. 1 Esdras	13. 3 Esdras (sometimes called 1 Esdras)
14. 2 Esdras	14. 4 Esdras (sometimes called 2 Esdras)
15. Prayer of Manasseh	15. Prayer of Manasseh

over time, generally refers to the collection of religious writings that are found in the Septuagint and the Latin Vulgate but not in the Hebrew Bible or most Protestant canons. These works are commonly known as the *Old Testament* Apocrypha since most of them were originally written in Hebrew or Aramaic and many refer to characters first found in the Old Testament. The word, however, did not always refer to a specific group of writings. In Classical,[2] Hellenistic,[3] and probably in New

make public so that both the worthy and the unworthy could read them. But seventy were to be kept only for "the wise among your people" (v. 46). The twenty-four books undoubtedly refer to the Hebrew Old Testament canon; the rest must be apocryphal books.

Apocrypha later came to refer to religious books considered to be of inferior quality to the Old and New Testaments. During the third century several church fathers (e.g., Origen [d. 253], Irenaeus [d. 202], Ter-

Table 8.2
Categories within the Apocrypha

Historical	Religious	Wisdom or Ethical Teaching	Apocalyptic
I Esdras	Tobit	Sirach	2 Esdras
I Maccabees	Judith	Wisdom of Solomon	
2 Maccabees	Susanna	Baruch	
	Additions to Esther	Prayer of Manasseh	
	Bel and the Dragon	Epistle of Jeremiah	
		Prayer of Azariah	

Testament Greek[4] the word *apokryphos* means "hidden" or "concealed," but how it came to refer to certain books is not clear.

In the patristic period, the word took on the meaning of "esoteric or secret knowledge" that was limited to a select few, a concept running counter to the gospel, which is open to everyone; for this reason a clear distinction was made between the books. However, as Christianity expanded it was easy for those in the Eastern church, who were converted out of Greek philosophy, to view their newfound faith esoterically. The early Jewish work entitled 2 Esdras, written in the first century, clearly teaches that some of Esdras's works were written only for the initiated and were not intended for everyone. Second Esdras 14 explains that Ezra was to write "everything that has happened in the world from the beginning, the things that were written in your law, so that people may be able to find the path, and that those who want to live in the last days may do so" (v. 22 NRSV). So he assembled five scribes trained to write rapidly and in forty days wrote ninety-four books—twenty-four of which he was to

tullian [d. 220]) used this term to distinguish these works from canonical works. Thus the word *apocryphal* was in contrast to the word *canonical*. This distinction was championed most strongly by church fathers, such as Irenaeus, Jerome, and Rufinus in the Western church.

History of the Apocryphal Books

Evidence from chapter 7 indicates that Jews and early Christians drew a distinction between the Hebrew Old Testament and noncanonical material. However, this distinction was not rigidly maintained, so that the two parts of the church dealt with apocryphal books differently. The Eastern church held to a threefold division of religious books: books that could be read in the church; books that could be read privately, and books that were not to be read at all. In the Western Church, however, this threefold division was never generally accepted; books were distinguished as either canonical or noncanonical, though the majority of church fathers in the West still included some apocryphal books in their lists (e.g.,

Eastern Church
Threefold Division:
1. Books to be read in church
2. Books to be read privately
3. Books not to be read at all

Western Church
Twofold Division:
1. Canonical books
2. Non-canonical books

Augustine). Jerome, the most qualified biblical scholar at the time, was an exception and was the first to use the term *apocryphal* for them (*Letter* 107.12).[5] The Latin Vulgate became the standard translation of the Bible for about a thousand years, and since it included the apocryphal books many people assumed that they were part of Scripture. (See table 8.3 for a description of the books in the Old Testament Apocrypha.)

Several early English Bibles include the Apocrypha (Coverdale Bible [1535]; Matthew's Bible [1537]; Taverner's Bible [1539]; the Great Bible [1539]; the Geneva Bible [1560]; the Bishops' Bible [1568]; the Authorized Version [1611]), but in the nine-

Table 8.3
Description of the Books in the Old Testament Apocrypha

Book	Date	Summary
Wisdom of Solomon	c. latter part of first century B.C.	Describes the benefits of wisdom and the joys that accompany righteous living, as well as punishments for the wicked.
Sirach	c. 180 B.C.	Very similar to the biblical Book of Proverbs, it includes moral and ethical maxims, proverbs, songs of praise, theological and philosophical reflections on life, and customs of the day.
Tobit	c. 180 B.C.	Tobit, a righteous Israelite living in Nineveh, is an example to the rest of the captives even in the midst of great adversities. Tobit becomes blind and prays to God to restore his sight. At the same time in Media, Sarah, Tobit's niece, prays to God for deliverance from the demon Asmodeus. God sends an angel named Raphael to deliver them both.
Judith	c. 150 B.C.	Nebuchadrezzar sends Holofernes to punish the people west of Babylon for their insubordination. The people of Judea pray to God for help; in answer Judith beguiles Holofernes, getting him thoroughly drunk, and then decapitates him.
I Esdras (3 Esdras)	c. second to first century B.C.	Begins abruptly by describing the reinstitution of passover by King Josiah in Jerusalem about 622/621 B.C. and continues to Ezra's reforms about 458 B.C., but the majority of the book emphasizes Ezra's reforms.
I Maccabees	c. latter part of second century B.C.	Covers Judean history from the accession of Antiochus IV (Epiphanes) in about 175 B.C. to the reign of John Hyrcanus I (134–104 B.C.).
2 Maccabees	c. end of second century to beginning of first century B.C.	Covers Jewish history from the time of the high priest Onias III and the Syrian King Seleucus IV (c. 180 B.C.) to the defeat of Nicanor's army (c. 161 B.C.).

teenth century it became more popular to publish the Bible without it. This practice was not without contention, as F. F. Bruce explains: "The fashion of printing Bibles without the Apocrypha received an impetus in the nineteenth century from the example of the British and Foreign Bible Society, which, in 1826, decided to print no more Bibles with the Apocrypha. It is recorded that this society offered to provide the official copy of the Bible for presentation to King Edward VII at his coronation in 1902, but the offer was declined by Archbishop Frederick Temple on the ground that a 'mutilated Bible' could not be accepted for the purpose."[6] This inci-

Table 8.3 (continued)
Description of the Books in the Old Testament Apocrypha

Baruch	c. second to first century B.C.	Claims to be a letter sent from Baruch to Jerusalem to be read on a feast day as a confession of their sin (1:14).
Epistle of Jeremiah	c. third to first century B.C.	Letter from Jeremiah to Jewish captives, soon to be taken to Babylon, describing the folly of idolatry.
2 Esdras (4 Esdras)	c. first century A.D.	Apocalyptic book dealing with the problem of why an all-powerful, loving God allows great evils to befall mankind. The reason is man's sinfulness.
Additions to the Book of Esther	c. latter part of second to first century B.C.	These six additions to the Greek text of Esther were apparently introduced to highlight the religious aspect of the story that the author thought was lacking.
Prayer of Azariah and Song of the Three Young Men	c. second to first century B.C.	Before being thrown into the fiery furnace (Dan. 3:23), Abednego (Azariah in Hebrew) prayed, asking God to bring glory to his name through this ordeal. It was followed by the song of the three young men who sang praise and glory to God.
Susanna	c. second to first century B.C.	Susanna is tried and found guilty because of the lies told by two elders of Israel. Daniel, however, has a vision from God and comes to the rescue.
Bel and the Dragon	c. second to first century B.C.	Daniel outwits the priests of Bel and shows that their great statue of Bel, the patron deity of Babylon, was a worthless idol. Next, Daniel kills a dragon that the Babylonians believed was a god. Daniel is thrown into the lions' den, but on the seventh day is removed and his enemies are thrown in.
Prayer of Manasseh	c. second to first century B.C.	2 Chronicles 33:10–13 says Manasseh prayed to God while in captivity and asked forgiveness for his many sins. This work supposedly records this prayer.

dent occurred almost eighty years after the British and Foreign Bible Society had determined to no longer print the Apocrypha in its Bibles.

Are These Books Canonical?

There has been significant disagreement among the various parts of the church as to what constitutes the true Old Testament canon. Six arguments have commonly been advanced for accepting the Apocrypha as canonical:

1. Some of the New Testament books possibly make allusions to apocryphal books (Heb. 11:35 may allude to 2 Macc. 7, 12) and pseudepigraphal books (Jude 9 may allude to the *Testament of Moses*; 2 Tim. 3:8 possibly makes reference to the *Testament of Moses*; and Jude 14, 15 quotes *1 Enoch* 1.9).
2. New Testament authors often quote from the Septuagint, the earliest manuscripts of which include the Apocrypha. Some scholars even argue that there was a broader Alexandrian canon that was preferred over the narrower Palestinian canon. A few of the early Greek manuscripts of the Bible that include apocryphal books interspersed among the Old Testament books are:

   א (Aleph) = Codex Sinaiticus (fourth century)

   A = Codex Alexandrinus (fifth century)

   B = Codex Vaticanus (fourth century)

3. Several apocryphal books were found among the Dead Sea Scrolls, suggesting that this community thought quite highly of them.
4. Early Christian art reflects some knowledge of the Apocrypha.
5. Certain early church fathers, particularly in the West, accepted the apocryphal books as authoritative; among the Eastern fathers, those who did so were:

Clement of Alexandria (Tobit, Sirach, Wisdom)[7]

Origen (Epistle of Jeremiah)[8]

Irenaeus (Wisdom)[9]

6. The Council of Trent (1546) proclaimed the Apocrypha canonical.

In response to the first argument regarding possible allusions to the apocryphal and pseudepigraphal books, neither is ever quoted as authoritative Scripture in any of the New Testament books. The fact that they contain truth that is recorded in Scripture does not demand that these sources are canonical. Jude 14 and 15 is by far the most difficult passage, but not for issues of canonicity.[10] Its difficulty lies in the fact that it suggests that Enoch, the seventh from Adam, spoke the words recorded in the book of *1 Enoch*, a work commonly dated between the second century B.C. and first century A.D.[11] Three possible resolutions to the problem can be put forth: Jude may simply refer to the book as a piece of literature with which his readers would have been familiar, just as a contemporary author might attribute a saying from John Bunyon's *Pilgrim's Progress* to Pilgrim, its main character;[12] the writer may be accommodating himself to his audience's high view of *1 Enoch*, whereas he himself may or may not endorse this view;[13] or *1 Enoch* draws upon an authentic tradition that derives from the historical Enoch, and Jude endorses the authority of those sayings but not all of *1 Enoch*.[14]

While the earliest manuscripts of the Septuagint include apocryphal works, as the second argument states, none dates earlier than the fourth century, by which time the influence of Augustine (c. 354–430) to accept apocryphal works was already being felt. Arguments against the third and fourth statements can be handled similarly since knowledge and usage of books does not necessitate their authority. As the fifth argument indicates, there was significant uncertainty concerning the extent of the Old Testament canon among some of the church fathers, though this uncertainty was not

Table 8.4
Inaccuracies in the Apocryphal Books

Book	Inaccuracy
I Esdras	**Chronology:** 5:56 (2d year of Cyrus should be 2d year of Darius); 5:73 (Cyrus [d. c. 530 B.C.] died more than 2 yrs. before reign of Darius [c. 522/521–486 B.C.]) **Simple Mistake:** 1:38 (cf. 2 Chron. 36:4) **Contradiction:** 5:5 (cf. Zerubbabel's genealogy in I Chron. 3:17–24)
2. Esdras	**Chronology:** 3:1 (Ezra lived a century later) **Simple Mistake:** 6:42 (water covers about 70% of earth's surface; *World Book Encycl.* [1996 ed.], s.v. "Water," 21:120) **Geography:** 1:11 (Tyre and Sidon are cities west of the Medes) **Theology:** 6:55 (Bible never says world was created for Israel); 8:4–5 (possibly suggests pre-existence of souls)
Tobit	**Chronology:** 1:1–4 (Tobit could not have lived through both the division of the Jewish kingdom [c. 931 B.C.] and the Assyrian deportation [c. 722/721 B.C.]; 1:15 (Shalmaneser died before the fall of Samaria, and Sennacherib was Sargon's son); 14:15 (Nineveh's conquerors were Nabopolassar and Cyaxares [612 B.C.]; cf. 1:4) **Geography:** 6:1 (Tigris River is west of Nineveh; Persia is east); 9:2 (Ecbatana to Rages is at least an 11-day trip but made to seem shorter)
Judith	**Chronology:** 1:1 (Nebuchadnezzar [c. 605–562 B.C.] ruled over Neo-Babylonia after Nineveh was destroyed [612 B.C.]; 2:1 (Nebuchadnezzar was king of the Babylonians, and Holofernes [v. 4] may be from a much later time); 4:3–4 and 5:19 (Nebuchadnezzar sent the Jews into exile, and they returned under Cyrus [c. 538 B.C.]) **Geography:** 1:6 (Hydaspes, a river of India, is erroneously placed in Mesopotamia); 2:21 (300 miles separating Nineveh and Bectileth makes a 3-day march impossible); 2:24 (normal route is south from Cilicia to Damascus, not following the Euphrates River)
Esther Additions	**Chronology:** 11:2–4 (the dates of Mordecai's captivity [597 B.C.] and dream [485/484 B.C.] would make him over 112 yrs. old)
Sirach	**Theology:** 3:3, 14–15 (kindness to parents atones for sins); 3:30 (almsgiving atones for sins)
Baruch	**Simple Mistake:** 1:11 (Belshazzar was the son of Nabonidus)
Epistle of Jeremiah	**Simple Mistake:** 6:1–3 (7 generations compared to 70 yrs.)
Bel and the Dragon	**Chronology:** v. 33 (Habakkuk wrote before 612 B.C. [cf. Hab. 1:6], making unlikely a visit to Daniel almost 75 yrs. later [c. 539 B.C.])
I Maccabees	**Geography:** 6:1 (contradicts 2 Macc. 9:2); 9:2 (Galilee, not Gilgal; cf. Josephus *Ant.* 12.11.1 §§420–21) **Contradictions:** 4:26–35 (contradicts 2 Macc. 10:37–11:12, which puts Lysias's defeat after the death of Timothy); 4:30–35 (contradicts 2 Macc. 11:6–15, which says it was a negotiated peace); 6:8–9 (contradicts 2 Macc. 9:5–12, which says that the king was struck with a repulsive physical disease)
2 Maccabees	**Chronology:** 1:19 (Persia should be Babylon [2 Kings 24:14]) **Theology:** 12:40–45 (praying for the dead); 15:14 (post-death visit by Jeremiah) **Contradictions:** 8:9 (contradicts I Macc. 3:38–4:25, which says that Gorgias, not Nicanor, was leader); 8:13 (contradicts I Macc. 3:56, which cites other reasons for the troop reduction); 10:3 (contradicts 1:19–2:1 on how altar fire was restarted; contradicts I Macc. 1:54 and 4:52, which say 3 yrs. instead of 2); 10:37 (contradicts 12:2, 18–25, where Timothy reappears; cf. I Macc. 5:11–40); 11:13–15 (contradicts I Macc. 4:35, which says that no peace was made); 13:16 (contradicts I Macc. 6:47, which says the Jews fled)

evident in the first century. Much later the Council of Trent appears to have authorized the apocryphal books for theological reasons in support of their views of purgatory and praying for the dead (2 Macc. 12:44–45); however, these doctrines are not confirmed elsewhere in Scripture.

The evidence for rejecting the canonicity of the Apocrypha is much stronger, as seen in the following arguments:

1. The New Testament never cites any apocryphal books as inspired; Jesus' usage of Scripture suggests that only the books in the Hebrew Bible were thought to be authoritative (Matt. 23:34–35; Luke 11:50–51).
2. None of the apocryphal books claim to be the word of the Lord as do many Old Testament books (Num. 35:1, 9; Josh. 1:1; Isa. 1:10, 18, 24; Jer. 1:2; Ezek. 1:3; Hos. 1:1; Joel 1:1).
3. The Old Testament canon is confirmed by many sources: 2 Esdras 14:45–48 (24 books); Josephus *Contra Apion* 1.7–8 §§37–42 (22 books); Melito (all Old Testament books except possibly Esther); Jerusalem List (all 39 books); Origen (22 books). Each of these sources list the same 39 Old Testament books as we have today (except possibly Melito, who omits Esther).
4. There is little evidence to suggest that two different canons originated in Palestine and in Egypt. In fact, Philo, a Jew from Alexandria, never quotes from an apocryphal book as authoritative.[15]
5. There are significant historical inaccuracies in the Apocrypha. For example, the events in the Book of Tobit (1:3–5) are chronologically incompatible—Tobit is said to live in Nineveh about 722 B.C., and yet he also saw the division of the united kingdom in 931 B.C.
6. There are theological inconsistencies; for example 2 Maccabees 12:43–45 espouses praying for the dead, but canonical books maintain that decisions about one's eternal destiny can only be made before death (Heb. 9:27).
7. Many early church fathers spoke against the canonicity of much or all of the Apocrypha (Melito, Origen, Cyril of Jerusalem, Athanasius, Jerome); no major church father accepted all of the apocryphal books until Augustine. The apocryphal books have never been universally accepted by the church.
8. The earliest list of the Old Testament canon by Melito (c. 170) does not include the Apocrypha.
9. Jerome, the most qualified Hebrew scholar in his time, argued against the canonicity of the Apocrypha.
10. During the Council of Trent, Martin Luther argued against the canonicity of the Book of Maccabees, citing the New Testament, early church fathers, and Jewish teachers in support. The Roman Catholic Church responded by canonizing the Apocrypha.

The above evidence weighs against placing the Apocrypha within the canon of the Old Testament, and Jesus himself appears to limit the Old Testament canon to the Hebrew Bible (Matt. 23:34–35; Luke 11:50–51). The early church adopted the canon of the Jews, which did not include the Apocrypha according to the evidence from Josephus, Philo, and the Talmud.

Inaccuracies in the Apocryphal Books

Several of the apocryphal books contain material that is contradictory to other parts of Scripture; others contain errors or mistakes (see table 8.4 for examples).

It is interesting that eleven out of fifteen apocryphal books have some type of inaccuracies in them. Those that do not are either very short (Prayer of Azariah and the Song of the Three Young Men; Prayer of Manasseh) or their content makes it difficult to determine whether they contain errors (Wisdom of Solomon; Susanna). Some scholars have suggested that problems of chronology within the apocryphal books are intentional so that people would know that it is fiction.[16]

Pseudonymity

Some of the apocryphal works are pseudonymous (lit., false name) or falsely claim to be written by well-known people in the Old Testament (e.g., Baruch, Epistle of Jeremiah, Prayer of Manasseh, Wisdom of Solomon). For example, Esdras (the Greek form of Ezra) lived about 450 B.C.; the title suggests that he was the author, but in reality the book dates to about A.D. 90, much later than Ezra. In view of this, it was either intentionally falsified in order to gain acceptance or written in a known literary genre common to the time and not intended to deceive. J. H. Charlesworth, a specialist in Christian origins at Princeton Theological Seminary, explains:

> Why did the authors of these writings attribute them falsely to other persons? These authors did not attempt to deceive the reader. They, like the authors of the Psalms of David, the Proverbs of Solomon, the Wisdom of Solomon, and the additions to Isaiah, attempted to write authoritatively in the name of an influential biblical person. Many religious Jews attributed their works to some biblical saint who lived before the cessation of prophecy and who had inspired them. Also, the principle of solidarity united early Jews with their predecessors who, in their eyes, had assuredly been guided by God himself. To place one's own name on a work was exceptional and ran against the tradition in the synagogue and temple: wisdom was the result of God's guidance and was often made possible through the devotion of a gifted teacher or rabbi. It is also conceivable that some of the apocalyptic writers had dreams or visions in which they experienced revelations given to Enoch, Abraham, Elijah, Ezra, Baruch, and others.[17]

Some of the points that Charlesworth makes here are good; for example, it is unusual for Jewish scribes to write their names on works, so possibly they felt somehow united with the message of the earlier

prophets. But Roger Beckwith refutes this, stating that some evidence (e.g., *1 Enoch* 82.1; *Jubilees* 45.16; *Assumption of Moses* 1.16–17; 2 Esdras 12:37–38) suggests that the intent was to convince the reader that the ancient personage authored the text:

> It therefore seems that, in Palestinian literature no less than Hellenistic, there was a class of pseudonymous writing which aimed to mislead the reader about its authorship, and often succeeded in doing so. The oldest works of the kind seem to be the apocalypses and other 'revelatory' books cherished and probably produced within the proto-Essene movement and the Essene party, such as 1 Enoch, the Testament of Levi, Jubilees and the Qumran Temple Scroll. They profess to reveal the true interpretation of the Pentateuch, and the secrets of nature, the unseen world and the future, and some of them indulge frequently in *vaticinia post eventum* [prophecy after the fact], doubtless designed to confirm their revelatory claims. Such works unmistakably involve pretence, and so do not come within the scope of any convention of pseudonymity which the Jews can be shown to have reckoned acceptable.[18]

Beckwith also argues that some of the works even explain why they were only then coming to light in the postbiblical period, suggesting that the authors were trying to deceive their readers to gain authoritativeness.[19]

The Old Testament Pseudepigrapha

Besides the biblical canon and the Apocrypha, a body of other works produced by Jewish authors is now generally known as the Pseudepigrapha. Scholars think that some of these works originally were written by Jewish authors but were expanded or rewritten by Christians. They were never seriously considered canonical, and their chief importance is to provide information concerning the thoughts and ideas circulating in the Jewish nation from about 200 B.C. to A.D. 200. The word *pseudepigra-*

Table 8.5
Description of the More Common Pseudepigraphal Books

Book	Date	Content
1 Enoch	second century B.C.– first century A.D.	Enoch was taken up by God and shown the mysteries of the universe, the future world, and the course of human history.
2 Enoch	late first century A.D.	Expansion of Genesis 5:21–32, covering the life of Enoch to the flood.
3 Enoch	fifth–sixth century A.D.	Purportedly an account by R. Ishmael describing how he ascended into heaven, saw God's throne and the wonders of the upper world, and then received revelations from the archangel Metatron.
Sibylline Oracles	second century B.C.–seventh century A.D.	Predictions of the prophetess concerning the woes and disasters to come upon mankind.
Treatise of Shem	first century B.C.	Shem, a son of Noah, describes what a year will be like depending on the sign of the zodiac upon which it begins.
Apocryphon of Ezekiel	first century B.C.– first century A.D.	A blind man and a lame man destroy the king's garden because they were not invited to a great feast. The king finds them out, and both are flogged. The moral drawn from the story is that in the resurrection both body and soul are reunited to receive their punishments.
Apocalypse of Zephaniah	first century B.C.– first century A.D.	Zephaniah glimpses the fifth heaven and is then escorted by the angel of the Lord to a broad plain where he receives more visions.
4 Ezra	late first century A.D.	Ezra sees several visions concerning the future and is told to write them down for future generations.
Greek Apocalypse of Ezra	second–ninth century A.D.	Ezra is taken into heaven to see the rewards for the righteous and then to Tartarus (hell) to view the punishment of the wicked.
Vision of Ezra	fourth–seventh century A.D.	Ezra is taken through hell, where he witnesses in great detail the punishments of the wicked; he is then taken to heaven.
2 Baruch	early second century A.D.	Baruch is told about future disasters for the Jews that will end with the coming of the Anointed One. He sees the final judgment and then asks about the righteous ones who will be saved.
3 Baruch	first–third century A.D.	God sends an angel to comfort Baruch after the destruction of Jerusalem by the Babylonians. He is then taken through the five heavens and shown their mysteries. Afterward he returns to tell these mysteries to mankind.
Apocalypse of Abraham	first–second century A.D.	Abraham determines that Yahweh is the true God and is then allowed to see heaven and the future for mankind where the Gentiles are punished and the righteous receive blessings.
Testaments of the Twelve Patriarchs	second century B.C.	Purportedly the utterances of the twelve sons of Jacob before their deaths; each son gathers his offspring around him, confesses his misdeeds, and exhorts his family to avoid his sins. Each son concludes with a prediction about Israel's future and instructions about his burial.
Testament of Job	first century B.C.– first century A.D.	At the end of his life Job calls together his family to bless them. Job continues to lament over the idolatry he sees and destroys an idol's shrine, which brings upon him Satan's attack. Job's three friends come to console him but are of little help. Job's three daughters ask about their inheritance and are given a magic cord. Finally, Job is buried with proper lamentations.

pha is derived from the plural form of the Greek word ψευδεπίγραφος (*pseudepigraphos*, false writing), denoting writings with false superscriptions; today it is applied to writings that are falsely attributed to ideal figures featured in the Old Testament.[20] Charlesworth describes the nature of these works:

> Almost always the Pseudepigrapha are influenced by the so-called OT: many supply revelations reputed to have been received by persons prominent in the OT; others are rewritten versions or expansions of biblical narratives; some are psalms that are occasionally modeled on the Davidic Psalter; and a few are compositions shaped by Jewish Wisdom Literature. Although these writings were composed long after Abraham, Moses, David, Solomon, Jeremiah, Isaiah, Ezra, and other famous men, they were often intentionally but incorrectly (pseudepigraphically) attributed to one of them.[21]

Copies of several pseudepigraphal works were found in the caves of Qumran—*Jubilees*, *1 Enoch*, and the *Testaments of the Twelve Patriarchs*—which for the first time provided evidence to date these and related works. *Jubilees* and the *Testaments of the Twelve Patriarchs* are generally dated to about the second century B.C., while *1 Enoch* must have been written before the destruction of the temple in A.D. 70.[22]

Introduction to the Pseudepigrapha

There is no set list of pseudepigraphal works, but the most recent collection contains sixty-three books.[23] Many of these works attempt to imitate Old Testament books or supply information not provided in the biblical books. Often they claim to be authored by or about famous Old Testament characters, and a good number belong to a type of literature known as apocalyptic (e.g., *1* and *2 Enoch*; *2* and *3 Baruch*; the *Testaments of the Twelve Patriarchs*; the *Sibylline Oracles*). Apocalyptic material appears to have arisen during periods of intense persecution and usually purports to reveal mysteries about the world or age to come in visions and symbolic language. Some works appear almost legendary in character (e.g., *Jubilees*; the *Letter of Aristeas*; the *Book of Adam and Eve*; the *Martyrdom of Isaiah*). There are didactic, or instructional, works (e.g., *Ahiqar*), poetry (e.g., *Psalms of Solomon*; *Odes of Solomon*), and historical books (e.g., *The Lives of the Prophets*; *History of Joseph*).

It is probable that these works gained considerable popularity among early Christians (e.g., Jude 14–15 quotes from *1 Enoch* 1.9). The reference to the archangel Michael fighting with Satan over the body of Moses in Jude 9 appears to be an allusion to the *Assumption of Moses*. Many new pseudepigraphal works were discovered among the Dead Sea Scrolls and are helpful to gain insight about the thoughts and ideas circulating at this time. (See table 8.5 for a description of some works.) The best and most recent collection of the pseudepigraphal books is *The Old Testament Pseudepigrapha*, edited by J. H. Charlesworth.

Reasons for Studying the Pseudepigrapha

One of the most important reasons to study pseudepigraphal works is the information they furnish concerning the social dimension of early Judaism. The postexilic Jews frequently struggled with internal divisions and sects, as well as foreign invaders who were often intent on destroying them. The apocalyptic materials appear to be at least one response to these pressures, for they portray God as sovereign over history and bringing it to its final climax, when he will punish those who have rebelled against him and set up a righteous kingdom for those who love him. The Pseudepigrapha includes many of these apocalyptic works. Second, the Pseudepigrapha shows how important the Old Testament was to the Jewish community. Third, pseudepigraphal books are helpful in showing how doctrines developed in relationship to the New Testament. Several concepts particularly developed and expanded are the Torah, the apocalyptic view of history, the kingdom of God, messianic expectations, the Son of man, this age versus the age to come, and sin and suffering versus righteousness and peace.

For Further Reading

Anderson, G. W. "Canonical and Non-canonical." In *CHB*, 1:113–59.

Charlesworth, J. H., ed. *The Old Testament Pseudepigrapha*. 2 vols. Garden City, NY: Doubleday, 1983–85.

Dentan, R. C. *The Apocrypha, Bridge of the Testaments*. New York: Seabury, 1964.

Goodspeed, E. J. *The Story of the Apocrypha*. Chicago: University of Chicago Press, 1939.

Harrison, R. K. *Introduction to the Old Testament*, 1175–1278. Grand Rapids: Eerdmans, 1969.

Metzger, B. M. *An Introduction to the Apocrypha*. New York: Oxford University Press, 1957.

Metzger, B. M., ed. *The Apocrypha of the Old Testament*. New York: Oxford University Press, 1965.

Nickelsburg, G. W. E. *Jewish Literature between the Bible and the Mishnah*. Philadelphia: Fortress, 1981.

Russell, D. S. *The Method and Message of Jewish Apocalyptic*. Philadelphia: Westminster, 1964.

Stone, M. E., ed. *Jewish Writings of the Second Temple Period: Apocrypha, Pseudepigrapha, Qumran, Sectarian Writings, Philo, Josephus*. CRINT 2.2. Assen, Netherlands: Van Gorcum; Philadelphia: Fortress, 1984.

Young, G. D. "The Apocrypha." In *Revelation and the Bible*, edited by C. F. H. Henry, 171–85. Grand Rapids: Baker, 1958.

Canonization of the New Testament

I t is important to remember at the beginning of our discussion of the New Testament canon that from its inception the early Christian church already had the Old Testament canon. C. F. Evans, former New Testament professor at the University of London, King's College, observes: "Christianity is unique among the world religions in being born with a Bible in its cradle."[1] The New Testament books came to be placed alongside the books that early Christians already believed to be authoritative Scriptures. New Testament books did not supplant the Old Testament, but rather the latter was interpreted by the apostles in the light of the New Testament books—many of the things that were expected and longed for in the Old Testament found their fulfilment in Christ. Thus the New Testament Scriptures were vital to complete God's revelation.

The issue of the New Testament canon is much more difficult to determine than that of the Old Testament canon since there is less definitive evidence. In a special way it fulfils Jesus' promise to send the Holy Spirit to teach us and bring to our remembrance what he had said (John 14:26). The Holy Spirit directed human authors to write the New Testament, and he helped confirm to the early church that these writings were also the Word of God, as David Ewert asserts: "The Christ who authenticated the OT [Old Testament] has also imparted his authority to the NT [New Testament]."[2]

Early History of the New Testament Books

It was crucial for the early church to have access to the very words of Christ and the apostles because this is the foundation upon which the church was built, as Floyd Filson, former New Testament professor at McCormick Theological Seminary, explains:

> In our study extending to A.D. 150, the church did not realize and protect its unity and continuity by agreement on a common creed. Nor did it do so by appeal to an unbroken line of episcopal control of its worship, life, and teaching. It was by continual attention to the apostolic witness that the church kept alive to what it was and what its task and privileges were. At first that witness was orally known and could be attested by those who had heard apostles or their personal assistants. As time went on, more emphasis inevitably was placed on the apostolic writings that continued that witness.[3]

Since the words of Jesus and the apostles were so important to the early church, these traditions needed to be guarded carefully; their accuracy was of utmost importance not only for early Christians but also for generations to follow. Much of the history of the early church and how the gospel began to spread throughout the Roman Empire is described in the Book of Acts. At first Christians worshiped in the temple and synagogues using the Old Testament for their Scriptures, as did their Jewish counterparts (Acts 3:1; 6:8–10; 9:20–21). Before long, however, Jewish leaders began to persecute Christians (Acts 8:1; 9:1–2; 12:11), forcing them to meet separately (Acts 12:12). The persecution grew worse, and in Philippi, Paul and Silas were thrown into prison (Acts 16:16–24). The Book of Acts records similar persecution in Thessalonica: "Some of the Jews were persuaded and joined Paul and Silas, as did a large number of God-fearing Greeks and not a few prominent women. But the Jews were jealous; so they rounded up some bad characters from the marketplace, formed a mob and started a riot in the city" (17:4–5a). Times worsened for Christians later in the first century, when the Romans also began to persecute the early church.

At the beginning of the church's history Christians could learn from eyewitnesses to Christ and the apostles and share the knowledge that they had accumulated, but as time went on fewer and fewer of those eyewitnesses remained. The need arose to record these sacred traditions to safeguard their accuracy. During the first century, the apostles began writing the New Testament books, some of which were copied almost immediately by early Christians and circulated among the other churches. These books were then collected by local congregations for use in their worship and teaching and were soon added to the Old Testament to form the canon of the Christian church. First Timothy 5:18 indicates that early Christians viewed both the Old Testament and Jesus' sayings as authoritative Scripture: "For the Scripture says, 'Do not muzzle the ox while it is treading out the grain [Deut. 25:4],' and 'The worker deserves his wages [Luke 10:7].'"

The public reading of the Christian sacred books became a central part of the early church's worship, since few individuals would have owned even a small portion of Scripture. Thus to learn what Jesus and the apostles had taught, Christians had to listen to the reading and instruction given in their local church. In several of Paul's letters he exhorts the church to read his letters (1 Thess. 5:27; 1 Tim. 4:13) or to pass them from church to church (Col. 4:16).

Period of Oral Transmission

If Jesus died about A.D. 30 and the earliest Gospel of his life was written about A.D. 60 then for approximately thirty years the events and teachings of Christ would have been transmitted orally. Some scholars propose that these oral accounts were corrupted in the telling, even to the extent that they became what the disciples wanted people to believe about Jesus instead of factual accounts. In response to this five checks and balances can be identified.

First, as is typical in oral transmission, accounts from Jesus' life would have taken on fixed forms in the telling; any embellishments or mistakes would have been easily detected by listeners, much as children can spot the slightest variation in their beloved stories. Since the foundation of the early church depended upon the transmission of accounts about Jesus' life and teachings, church leaders would have made every effort to ensure their accuracy. F. F. Bruce points out: "In fact, no body of literature has been subjected, over the past two centuries, to more intensive and critical analysis than the New Testament writings in general and the four Gospels in particular. It is on the basis of such scientific enquiry, not in despite of it, that such a credible account of Jesus as that given . . . by Professor C. H. Dodd in *The Founder of Christianity* is constructed."[4]

Second, it seems unlikely that the disciples and early Christians would have falsified accounts of Jesus' life and teachings when eyewitnesses were still alive to dispute those accounts. Paul reports that five hundred people saw Jesus alive after his resurrection, most of whom were still alive at the time of his writings (1 Cor. 15:6). Luke, in writing a Gospel account for the benefit of Theophilus (perhaps a pseudonym for any God-lover), states that he carefully examined the evidence from other eyewitness accounts in order to ensure the accuracy of his own writing. In the process he surely would have discovered discrepancies in the accounts if they had been altered.

Third, tradition maintains that all the disciples were martyred for their faith, something that seems unlikely if it were based on accounts that they themselves had falsified or fictionalized.

Fourth, extrabiblical records support scriptural accounts of Jesus' life and teaching.[5] Tacitus, a Roman historian, in his *Annals* (written between 115 and 117) states:

Therefore, to scotch the rumour, Nero substituted as culprits, and punished with the utmost refinements of cruelty, a class of men, loathed for their vices, whom the crowd styled Christians. Christus, the founder of the name, had undergone the death penalty in the reign of Tiberius, by sentence of the procurator Pontius Pilatus, and the pernicious superstition was checked for a moment, only to break out once more, not merely in Judaea, the home of the disease, but in the capital itself, where all things horrible or shameful in the world collect and find a vogue. (Tacitus *Annals* 15.44.)[6]

Tacitus was no lover of the Christians, yet he clearly states that Christ not only lived but also was crucified under Pontius Pilate.

Josephus, a Jewish historian who would have little reason to speak highly of Jesus, makes some interesting claims about him:

About this time there lived Jesus, a wise man, if indeed one ought to call him a man. For he was one who wrought surprising feats and was a teacher of such people as accept the truth gladly. He won over many Jews and many of the Greeks. He was the Messiah. When Pilate, upon hearing him accused by men of the highest standing amongst us, had condemned him to be crucified, those who had in the first place come to love him did not give up their affection for him. On the third day he appeared to them restored to life, for the prophets of God had prophesied these and countless other marvellous things about him. And the tribe of the Christians, so called after him, has still to this day not disappeared. (*Ant.* 18.3.3 §§63–64)[7]

Some scholars have questioned the authenticity of this passage (the so-called *Testimonium Flavianum*), particularly Josephus's claim that Jesus was the Messiah.[8] A case can be made, however, based on the evidence of Josephus's diction,[9] that we have here a core of authentic Josephan statements that were reworked by early Christians (preserved as early as the works of Eusebius about A.D. 325 [*HE* 1.11.7–8; *Dem. ev.* 3.5.105]).[10] While the nature of Josephus's original statement is conjectural, Bruce argues that it is plausible that

Josephus bears witness to Jesus' date, to his being the brother of James the Just, to his reputation as a miracle-worker, to his crucifixion under Pilate as a consequence of charges brought against him by the Jewish rulers, to his claim to be Messiah, and to his being the founder of the "tribe of Christians."[11]

In the Babylonian Talmud, a collection of Jewish oral traditions from about A.D. 200–500, we read:

On the eve of the Passover Yeshu [Jesus] was hanged. For forty days before the execution took place, a herald went forth and cried. 'He is going forth to be stoned because he has practised sorcery and enticed Israel to apostasy. Anyone who can say anything in his favour, let him come forward and plead on his behalf.' But since nothing was brought forward in his favour he was hanged on the eve of the Passover!—'Ulla retorted: Do you suppose that he was one for whom a defence could be made? Was he not a *Mesith* [enticer], concerning whom Scripture says, *Neither shalt thou spare, neither shalt thou conceal him?* With Yeshu [Jesus] however it was different, for he was connected with the government [or royalty, i.e., influential]. (*Sanh.* 43a)[12]

This passage confirms that Jesus was hung (the cross is assumed) and that he was somehow connected with royalty, the government, or simply was influential.

Fifth, biblical accounts include negative elements concerning the disciples, Paul, and the churches. These elements lend support to the accuracy of the accounts; fictionalized accounts fabricated by early Christians would probably not have included such unfavorable details (e.g., Matt. 26:47–52, 69–75; 27:3–5; Mark 16:8; Luke 24:11–12; John 20:24–29).

Why did it take so long for the New Testament traditions to be written? A variety of factors could have contributed to the delay. At this early stage firsthand witnesses and apostles were still alive; the term *apostle,* as used in the New Testament, appears to be limited to those who had personally heard Christ's teachings and seen the risen Lord (Acts 1:21–22).

Papias, a second-century bishop, often availed himself of eyewitnesses:

> but if ever anyone came who had followed the presbyters, I inquired into the words of the presbyters, what Andrew or Peter or Philip or Thomas or James or John or Matthew, or any other of the Lord's disciples, had said, and what Aristion and the presbyter John, the Lord's disciples, were saying. For I did not suppose that information from books would help me so much as the word of a living and surviving voice. (Eusebius *HE* 3.39.4)[13]

The early church had the Old Testament Scriptures, which could be read in light of Jesus' fulfilment of them. This was the only Bible that Jesus and the apostles had; thus the early church did have a Bible, though it was not God's total revelation.

In an age when many people were illiterate, oral tradition was common practice and may have been perceived as sufficient in the early years after Jesus' death. David Ewert notes that "when Jesus taught the multitudes, he would frequently say, 'You have heard!' (e.g., Matt. 5:27). They heard the Scriptures read in the synagogue, but there was little private reading. The matter was different, of course, among the scribes whom Jesus asked upon occasion, 'Have you not read?' (e.g., Mark 2:25)."[14]

We live in a culture that is saturated by the written word, but in an era when students were accustomed to memorizing their teacher's every word, it would be much more common to pass on information orally. Oral tradition surrounding the law (i.e., the Mishnah, Talmud, and other Jewish works) was massive (the Talmud alone occupies about ten volumes) yet was transmitted for generations. Students were well trained and accustomed to memorizing what their teachers passed on. Some teachers even boasted that their students were like well-plastered cisterns that did not lose a drop (cf. T.B. *ʾAbot* 2.8).[15]

The hope of Christ's imminent return (Rev. 22:20) may also have contributed to the delay in written accounts; there would have been little incentive to record events if Christ were coming so soon.

Reasons for Writing the New Testament Books

Over time several factors contributed to the need for written accounts of Jesus' life and teachings, as well as records of Christian doctrines and their application to the church.

Christian sacred traditions were recorded to ensure their accuracy after all firsthand witnesses died. Paul stressed the importance of holding on to the traditions that the early churches had been taught (1 Cor. 11:2; 2 Thess. 2:15).

As the church grew and spread to various parts of the world, it needed an accurate account of Jesus' and the apostles' teachings, since the latter could not physically be present at all locations. Concerning the extent of the early spread of Christianity, Bruce writes:

> By the end of the first century A.D. Christianity was well established in the Roman world. From its birthplace in Judaea it had spread west along the northern shore of the Mediterranean as far as Gaul, if not as far as Spain; it had spread along the North African coast to Cyrenaica, if it had not already reached the Roman province of Africa. Two hundred years were to elapse before the Roman state accepted the presence of the church; before that time intermittent attempts were made to repress and, if possible, extirpate Christianity, but the historian, looking back on the situation with all the advantages of hindsight, can see that by A.D. 100 Christianity had come to stay, that its abolition was no longer practicable.[16]

Written materials would help combat heresies that were beginning to penetrate the early church. False prophets claimed to have special insights into God's truth, and the church needed some standard to determine Scripture from error. One of the earliest heresies was Gnosticism, which maintained a radical cosmic dualism that the created world was evil and separate from the spirit world. According to this teaching the only hope of escaping this world was by possession of a divine spark *(pneuma)* that came through the enlightenment of a special knowledge *(gnōsis)*. Docetism, another early heresy, argued in a similar fashion to Gnosticism that matter was inherently evil and thus Jesus only seemed to be a man. Marcion of Sinope (c. 85–160), who has already been mentioned, was a heretic that the early church encountered. Montanus was a fanatic who believed that he was the promised Paraclete. He and two prophetesses, Prisca and Maximilla, prophesied "through the Spirit" of the imminent return of Christ. He claimed to be the mouthpiece of the Holy Spirit and that God was continuing to speak to the church through him. This forced the church to make some decisions concerning the limits of the authoritative canon.

Furthermore, the Greco-Roman world was a highly literary society, and thus a written Gospel would be much more appealing to it. E. A. Judge, professor of history at Macquarie University, New South Wales, Australia, describes the changes brought about by the Greek culture:

> The whole of the E[astern] Mediterranean and much beyond was raised to the common norm of civilization that Hellenism supplied. Both the opulence of the states and the degree of standardization are attested by the splendid ruins that indiscriminately litter these parts today.... Athens was still a home of learning, but Pergamum, Antioch and Alexandria, and many others in the new world, rivalled or eclipsed her.
> The states provided not only education but brilliant entertainment and a wider range of health and welfare services than most modern communities. It was membership in such a republic and use of the Greek language that marked a man as civilized (Acts 21:37–39).[17]

In 303, when the last great wave of persecution by the Roman Empire broke out, Scriptures were confiscated in an attempt to eradicate the sacred books of the Christians. The following edict (dated to 303) pronounced persecution for the Christians:

> It was the nineteenth year of the reign of Diocletian, and the month Dystrus, or March, as the Romans would call it, in which, as the festival of the Saviour's Passion was coming on, an imperial letter was everywhere promulgated, ordering the razing of the churches to the ground and the destruction by fire of the Scriptures, and proclaiming that those who held high positions would lose all civil rights, while those in households, if they persisted in their profession of Christianity, would be deprived of their liberty. Such was the first document against us. But not long afterwards we were further visited with other letters, and in them the order was given that the presidents of the churches should all, in every place, be first committed to prison, and then afterwards compelled by every kind of device to sacrifice. (Eusebius *HE* 8.2.4–5)[18]

It became an act of treason for Christians not to hand over copies of the sacred Scriptures to be destroyed. The temptation would be to hand over other Christian works in hopes that the Roman officials would not know the difference. Thus it was crucial for Christians to know which books were authoritative and needed to be guarded at all costs and those which were not.[19]

Evidence Supporting the Early Dates of New Testament Books

The New Testament works were written during a relatively short period of time between about 48 and 100; some of them would have circulated individually for a time. Scholars in the nineteenth century questioned the first-century dates of the New Testament books, as Ewert notes: "A century ago critics such as F. C. Baur of Tübingen, and his school, rejected the first-century dates of some of the NT books, thereby robbing them of their apostolic authority. With this came a loss of respect

Early Errors
Gnosticism (1st cent.)

Docetism (2d cent.)

Marcionism (2d cent.)

Montanism (late 2d cent.)

for the Bible, with disastrous spiritual consequences."[20] However, John claims to have been an eyewitness to Jesus, and Saul's persecution of the early church accords better with the first century than with the second, to note just some of the overwhelming evidence for a first-century date for the New Testament books. Thus, in contrast to the Old Testament, a relatively brief period exists between the actual writing of the New Testament texts and the extant copies.[21]

The Epistles

Some of the Epistles, or letters, are among the earliest New Testament books completed; a good share of them were written by the apostle Paul (c. 10–65) to encourage and exhort the various churches that he had started (1 and 2 Cor., Gal., Phil.) or people working with them (1 and 2 Tim., Titus). These letters were likely the first New Testament works to be accepted as canonical.

It is unclear whether Paul was aware that he was writing Scripture as he penned letters to the various churches; some letters apparently were lost (the first letter to the Corinthians [1 Cor. 5:9] and the letter to the Laodiceans [Col. 4:16]). But Paul recognized that some of his words carried divine authority and must be obeyed:

> Paul, an apostle—sent not from men nor by man, but by Jesus Christ and God the Father, who raised him from the dead. . . . (Gal. 1:1)

> So I tell you this, and insist on it in the Lord, that you must no longer live as the Gentiles do, in the futility of their thinking. (Eph. 4:17)

> I have become its [the church's] servant by the commission God gave me to present you the word of God in its fullness. . . . (Col. 1:25)

One of the strongest evidences is found in 2 Thessalonians 3:6–15, where Paul states:

> In the name of the Lord Jesus Christ, we command you, brothers, to keep away from every brother who is idle and does

not live according to the teaching you received from us. . . . Such people we command and urge in the Lord Jesus Christ, to settle down and earn the bread they eat. . . . If anyone does not obey our instruction in this letter, take special note of him. Do not associate with him, in order that he may feel ashamed. Yet do not regard him as an enemy, but warn him as a brother.

In 1 Corinthians 7:10–12 there is an interesting example of Paul clearly differentiating between his teaching and Christ's, but both teachings are seen as authoritative. In verses 10–11, Paul states: "To the married I give this command (not I, but the Lord): A wife must not separate from her husband. But if she does, she must remain unmarried or else be reconciled to her husband. And a husband must not divorce his wife." The phrase "not I, but the Lord" most likely means that Jesus had given specific teaching on this subject while he was on the earth and Paul was recounting this teaching. However, in verse 12 Paul proceeds to the next topic, upon which Christ had not given specific teaching, and thus Paul differentiates his inspired conclusions on the subject with "I, not the Lord." There is little doubt that by the end of the first century Paul's letters were seen as authoritative. In 2 Peter 3:16 Peter categorizes Paul's writings with the rest of Scripture, saying: "He [Paul] writes the same way in all his letters, speaking in them of these matters. His letters contain some things that are hard to understand, which the ignorant and unstable people distort, as they do *the other Scriptures*, to their own destruction" (italics added).

Evidence from early church fathers also shows that Paul's letters were widely known and accepted by the end of the first century.[22]

1. In a letter to the Corinthians (c. A.D. 95), Clement of Rome says: "Take up the epistle of the blessed Paul the Apostle" (*1 Clem.* 47.1),[23] implying that they had in their possession an authoritative letter from Paul.
2. Ignatius, bishop of Antioch (d. about the beginning of the first century) knew 1 Corinthians almost by

heart[24] and wrote to the Ephesians that Paul makes mention of them "in every Epistle,"[25] an exaggeration to be sure, but it still assumes that they are referred to in several letters.

3. Polycarp, bishop of Smyrna (c. A.D. 69–155), said to the church at Philippi that Paul had written to them "letters."[26] There is significant evidence that he knew of almost all the Pauline Epistles except for Colossians, 1 Thessalonians, Philemon, and Titus.[27] One of the most striking is when Polycarp quotes from both the Old and New Testaments, showing them to be equally authoritative: "It is declared then in these Scriptures; 'Be ye angry, and sin not,' [Ps. 4:5] and, 'Let not the sun go down upon your wrath' [Eph. 4:26]" (To the Philippians 12.1).[28]

4. By the middle of the second century Marcion had limited his canon to one Gospel (Luke) and ten of Paul's letters, thus confirming that most of Paul's epistles were collected and recognized by this date.

Everett Harrison, a former New Testament professor at Fuller Theological Seminary, explains that a Gnostic work entitled The Gospel of Truth contains significant evidence for the early date of many New Testament books:

This recently discovered work with observable Gnostic tendencies is probably attributable to Valentinus around A.D. 140. It has an important contribution to make to the study of the New Testament canon, since its use of the canonical writings is so comprehensive as to warrant the conclusion that in Rome at this period a New Testament was in existence that corresponded very closely with what we have today. Furthermore, what is utilized, whether from the Gospels, the Acts, the letters of Paul, Hebrews, or the Revelation, is regarded as authoritative.[29]

There is, then, adequate evidence to suggest that by at least the end of the first century most of Paul's writings were collected and viewed as authoritative material.

The Gospels

It would appear that Mark was the first Gospel, written about 60, but recording events that took place about a generation earlier. The other Gospels probably followed shortly thereafter. The earliest record of a "written" gospel is in the Didache, dated to about 100, which quotes the Lord's Prayer (Matt. 6:9–13) preceded by the words: "And do not pray as the hypocrites, but as the Lord commanded in his Gospel."[30] Similarly Ignatius, bishop of Antioch, who lived at about the same time, says: "For I heard some men saying, 'if I find it not in the chapters in the Gospel I do not believe'" (Ignatius To the Philadelphians 8.2).[31] William Schoedel, professor of religious studies at the University of Illinois, Urbana, states that Papias (probably living in the late first to early second centuries) "knew the Gospels of Mark, Matthew, and (probably) John, and the letters of 1 Peter and 1 John."[32] Further evidence suggests that several Gospels were in existence by the beginning of the second century and that all were written by at least the end of the second century:

1. A fragment of the Gospel of John from the John Rylands Library called $\mathfrak{P}^{52}$ may be dated as early as 130.

2. Papias, who wrote at the beginning of the second century, mentions the Gospels of Matthew and Mark by name (see Eusebius HE 3.39.14–16).

3. Justin Martyr wrote an apology (c. 150), which mentions the Gospels, suggesting that there were several.

4. Irenaeus defends the fourfold form of the Gospels in about 180 and specifically mentions the Gospel of Matthew.[33]

5. About 140, Marcion limited his canon to only the Gospel of Luke and ten Pauline Epistles, which suggests that he knew of more.

6. Tatian (c. 160) prepared a harmony of the Gospels called the Diatessaron which blended the four Gospels into one.

Luke claims that there were many Gospel accounts (Luke 1:1) and that he examined them carefully in preparing his record of these events. John mentions only the events that confirmed Jesus to be the Christ, the Son of God, and says that if he

Figure 9.1.
Coins from Felix, Festus, and King Agrippa II.

Felix (52–60)

Festus (59–62)

King Agrippa II (c. 49–93)

were to record all the things that Jesus had done "the whole world would not have room for the books that would be written" (John 21:25).

Acts

The Book of Acts is a history of the early church that claims to be written by Luke as a follow-up to his first book (Acts 1:1). It covers the events from Jesus' ascension (about 30) to Paul's imprisonment in Rome (about 60). The latter date is determined by the dates of the two procurators of Judea—Felix (52–60) and Festus (59–62)—and King Agrippa II (c. 49–93), before whom Paul was taken to decide his fate. It is difficult to know when the book was considered to be part of the canon of Scripture, but as it provides a necessary foundation for the Epistles it may have been added for that reason. Bruce explains:

> But Acts naturally shared the authority and prestige of the third Gospel, being the work of the same author; and besides, it was a very important book. Not only did it provide the sequel to the gospel story, but it was an indispensable companion to the Pauline collection. Who was this Paul? What were the grounds for the apostolic authority which he claimed for himself (as he was manifestly not one of the Twelve whom Jesus had appointed to be with him)? Such questions as these must have occurred to readers of the group of letters entitled *The Apostle*. But Acts made the source and quality of Paul's apostolic commission and service very plain. It therefore served as a link between the fourfold Gospel and the Pauline corpus. . . . [34]

Adolf von Harnack even goes so far as to say that this book is the "pivotal" book of the New Testament.[35]

Evidence indicates that Acts was known at least by the end of the second century:

1. The so-called Anti-Marcionite Prologue, probably dated to the end of the second century, says that Luke wrote a second volume entitled The Acts of All the Apostles.[36]

2. The Muratorian Fragment, dated to the end of the second century, contains the Book of Acts.[37]

3. Irenaeus mentions the Book of Acts and says that it was written by Luke (Irenaeus *Haer.* 3.14.1; 3.15.1).

The Apocalypse

The Book of Revelation was probably written by the apostle John (who also wrote the Gospel of John) during the reign of Domitian (81–96). However, significant debate has arisen on this point since the Greek of the Gospel of John is very smooth and idiomatic, whereas Revelation reads much less smoothly and is full of irregularities. It is possible that John used a scribe to write the Gospel of John whereas he could not do so while exiled on Patmos where he wrote Revelation;[38] it is more likely, however, that the irregular grammar is intentional, based upon the purpose of the writer.[39] It is classified as an apocalyptic work, and its purpose is to reveal God's plan for the future through visions and symbols. For some time there was debate whether to include Revelation in the canon, but at some unknown point there was ultimately a predominant readiness to include it. Concerning the importance of its message Filson observes: "It served to attest the Christian hope that following the period of the church, in which the apostolic witness is authoritative and the work of the Christian mission calls for the church's faithful dedication, God's plan will reach its full realization."[40]

By the end of the second century the Book of Revelation was known:

1. Melito, bishop of Sardis, about A.D. 170, wrote a commentary on the Book of Revelation (see Eusebius *HE* 4.26.2).

2. Justin Martyr, who lived in Ephesus about A.D. 135, declares that this book was written by John (Justin Martyr *Dial.* 81.15).[41]

3. The Muratorian Fragment, dated to the end of the second century, acknowledges the Book of Revelation.

Early Church Writers

Clement of Rome c. 60–100

Ignatius, Bishop of Antioch c. 60–117

Papias c. 60–130

Polycarp, Bishop of Smyrna c. 69–155

Marcion (heretic) c. 85–160

Justin Martyr c. 100–165

Tatian c. 110–172

Melito, Bishop of Sardis c. 110–190

Irenaeus c. 130–202

Clement of Alexandria c. 155–220

Tertullian c. 160–220

Hippolytus c. 170–235

Pseudo-Clementines c. 220

Origen c. 185–253

Eusebius of Caesarea c. 265–339

4. Irenaeus mentions the Book of Revelation and claims that it was written by John (Eusebius *HE* 5.18.14; Irenaeus *Haer.* 4.14.2; 4.17.6; 4.18.6; 4.21.3; 5.28.2).

The General Epistles (Hebrews; James; 1 and 2 Peter; 1, 2, and 3 John)

These more general letters were written to churches throughout Asia Minor (except for 2 and 3 John), but little else is known of their origin. They were challenged more than the others regarding their canonicity, partly due to questions of authorship. For instance, Eusebius of Caesarea, a third-century church father, said that the church of Rome questioned Hebrews because it was uncertain whether Paul wrote it.[42] The following list indicates evidence for the dating of the General Epistles:

1. The Book of Hebrews was used without explicit quotation in *1 Clement* (*1 Clem.* 17.1 // Heb. 11:37; *1 Clem.* 36.2–6 // Heb. 1:3–5, 7; etc.) as early as the end of the first century.[43]
2. Justin Martyr clearly knew of the Book of Hebrews (*Apology* 12:9 // Heb. 3:1; *Dial.* 13:1 // Heb. 9:13–14; etc.).
3. Irenaeus quotes from the Book of Hebrews (Eusebius *HE* 5.26.1).
4. This book was already known to Pantaenus (c. 180) and to his pupil Clement of Alexandria (Eusebius *HE* 6.14.1–4); it is found in the earliest extant manuscripts of the Pauline Letters (Chester Beatty Papyrus II [𝔓46]) dated about 200.[44]
5. Tertullian, a North African bishop, quotes from Hebrews 6:4–8 with the following introduction: "For there is extant withal an Epistle to the Hebrews under the name of Barnabas—a man sufficiently accredited by God" (*On Modesty* 20).
6. By the end of the second century, Jude was widely accepted as canonical (Tertullian; Clement of Rome; Origen; and the Muratorian Canon).[45]
7. The Muratorian Canon, dated to the end of the second century, mentions Jude and 1 and 2 John but does not mention James, 1 and 2 Peter, or Hebrews.
8. Polycarp made use of 1 Peter (cf. Eusebius *HE* 4.14.9).[46]
9. Clement of Alexandria comments on 1 Peter, Jude, and 1 and 2 John.
10. The earliest quotation from the Book of James arises in the third century in a passage by Pseudo-Clementine (*De Virginitate* 1.11.4). Origen (*Exc. Ps. 30* 12.129; *Exc. Ps. 65* 12.395) and Eusebius of Caesarea (*HE* 2.23.24–25) view James as canonical.
11. The earliest citations from 1 John come from Polycarp (*To the Philippians* 7) and Justin Martyr (*Dial.* 123.9). It was accepted as canonical by Irenaeus (*Haer.* 1.16.3; 3.16.5, 8; 3.17.3), Clement of Alexandria (*Paedagogus* 82, 98; *Stromateis* 3.32, 43, 44, 45), Origen (*Comm. Matt.* 13.26), Tertullian (*Adversus Praxean*), and Eusebius (*HE* 3.24.17–18; 3.25.2).
12. Irenaeus quotes from 2 John (*Haer.* 1.16.3 [2 John 11]; 3.16.8 [2 John 7–8]). Origen realized there were some doubts about the canonicity of the General Epistles (*In Johannem* 5.3), and Eusebius says that they are generally recognized by the church (*HE* 3.24.17–18; 3.25.2–3).

Formation of the New Testament Canon

During the time that the New Testament books were being collected many other Christian writings circulated among the various churches (cf. Luke 1:1–2). How then did these specific books come to be canonized among the plethora that existed?

The Canonization of the New Testament

Similarities in the process of canonization of the Old and New Testaments can be identified. Both were authored by respected and honored servants of God, called *prophets* in the Old Testament and *apostles* (or "sent ones") in the New; both were considered divine revelation and thus were retained and copied by those who cherished their traditions. But a gap of approximately four hundred years exists between the last writings of the Old Testament and the first writings of the New. Many of the New Testament books were probably collected into some form of a canon before the mid-second century.

Evidence for the New Testament Canon

Clement of Rome

An early Roman presbyter/bishop, who may have been mentioned in Philippians 4:3, Clement of Rome (c. 60–100) makes very loose and inexact quotations from Acts(?), Romans, 1 Corinthians, Ephesians, Titus, Hebrews, and 1 Peter.[47]

Ignatius

Ignatius (c. 60–117), bishop of Antioch, does not make any exact quotes from the New Testament books but probably alludes to Matthew, Luke, John, Romans, 1 and 2 Corinthians, Galatians, Ephesians, and 1 and 2 Timothy.[48] W. R. Inge believes that Ignatius must have known 1 Corinthians almost by heart.[49]

Polycarp, Bishop of Smyrna

Polycarp (c. 69–155), bishop of Smyrna, was martyred for his faith by Roman officials.[50] He recognized at least sixteen works as canonical.[51] He does not mention Matthew, Luke(?), Colossians, 1 Thessalonians, Titus, Philemon, James, 2 Peter, 1, 2 and 3 John, Jude, and Revelation.

Justin Martyr

Justin Martyr (c. 100–165) demonstrates awareness of at least the following biblical books: Matthew, Mark(?), Luke, John, Acts, Romans, 1 Corinthians, Galatians, Ephesians, Colossians, 2 Thessalonians, Hebrews, and 1 Peter.[52] However, it must be noted that he may have been aware of other canonical books even though he did not quote from them. He does not mention 2 Corinthians, Philippians, 1 Thessalonians, 1 and 2 Timothy, Titus, Philemon, James, 2 Peter, 1, 2 and 3 John, Jude, and Revelation.

Marcion

By about 140 the heretic Marcion rejected the Old Testament and chose only eleven New Testament books as canonical: Luke, Romans, 1 and 2 Corinthians, Galatians, Ephesians, Philippians, Colossians, 1 and 2 Thessalonians, and Philemon.[53] He does not mention Matthew, Mark, John, Acts, 1 and 2 Timothy, Titus, Hebrews, James, 1 and 2 Peter, 1, 2 and 3 John, Jude, and Revelation.

There were certainly more New Testament books than Marcion accepted, for Tertullian says of him:

> One man perverts the Scriptures with his hand, another their meaning by his exposition. For although Valentinus seems to use the entire volume, he has none the less laid violent hands on the truth only with a more cunning mind and skill than Marcion. Marcion expressly and openly used the knife, not the pen, since he made such an excision of the Scriptures as suited his own subject-matter. *(Prescription against Heretics 38)*[54]

Irenaeus

An early church father named Irenaeus (c. 130–202) became bishop of Lyon, Gaul (the Roman name for France), about 180. He was brought up in Asia Minor, trained by Polycarp, the disciple of John, and spent time in Rome, the center of the church, where he would have heard many prominent scholars preach. Irenaeus quotes

Evidence for the New Testament Canon

Clement of Rome (c. 60–100)
  Probably at least 6 bks.
Ignatius (c. 60–117)
  Probably alludes to 10 bks.
Polycarp (c. 69–155)
  Recognizes at least 16 bks.
Justin Martyr (c. 100–165)
  Aware of at least 12–13 bks.
Marcion (c. 85–160)
  11 bks.
Irenaeus (c. 130–202)
  Quotes from at least 24–25 bks.
Muratorian Canon (c. 190)
  At least 20 bks.
Clement of Alexandria (c. 155–220)
  At least 22 bks.
Tertullian (c. 160–220)
  At least 24 bks.
Hippolytus (c. 170–235)
  At least 25 bks.
Origen (c. 185–253)
  At least 22 bks.
Eusebius of Caesarea (c. 265–339)
  At least 22 bks.
Athanasius (c. 296–373)
  27 bks.

extensively from the New Testament and identifies in his writings the following books as canonical: Matthew, Mark, Luke, John, Acts, Romans, 1 and 2 Corinthians, Galatians, Ephesians, Philippians, Colossians, 1 and 2 Thessalonians, 1 and 2 Timothy, Titus, Hebrews, James, 1 and 2 Peter, 1 and 2 John, [Jude is questionable], and Revelation.[55] He does not mention Philemon, Jude(?), and 3 John; he also lists *Shepherd of Hermas*[56] and may have viewed *1 Clement* as authoritative.[57]

It is possible that Irenaeus was thinking specifically of Marcion when he emphasized the certainty of the fourfold Gospel in his treatise *Against Heresies* (3.11.8), written about 180. Although Irenaeus does not mention certain books, this does not mean he did not consider them canonical. Filson summarizes the status of the New Testament canon at this time: "It was to be many generations before the church reached final agreement on the exact number and the identity of the books that should be included in the New Testament. But by the middle of the second century the basic structure of the Christian canon of Scripture was emerging."[58]

The Muratorian Canon

Cardinal L. A. Muratori discovered in a library in Milan an eighth-century Latin manuscript including an early list of New Testament books (now called the Muratorian fragment; c. 190) drawn up in Rome, containing the following books:[59]

Luke
John
Acts
Romans
1 and 2 Corinthians
Galatians
Ephesians
Philippians
Colossians
1 and 2 Thessalonians
1 and 2 Timothy
Titus

Philemon
1 and 2 John
Jude
Revelation
Wisdom of Solomon
Apocalypse of Peter

The fragment is mutilated at the beginning but must have originally contained Matthew and Mark, for Luke is said to be the third Gospel. This fragment does not mention Hebrews, James, 1 and 2 Peter, and 3 John. Extra books that he includes are the Wisdom of Solomon and the *Apocalypse (Revelation) of Peter*, stating that some do not accept the latter.

The fragment makes very clear that the *Shepherd of Hermas* was not accepted as canonical, citing that it had been written only recently. B. F. Westcott makes the following observation about this fragment:

> The writer speaks throughout of a received and general opinion. He does not suggest a novel theory about the Apostolic books, but states what was held to be certainly known. He does not hazard an individual judgment, but appeals to the practice of "the Catholic [universal] Church." There was not indeed complete unanimity with regard to all the writings claiming to be apostolical, but the frank recognition of the divergence of opinion on the *Revelation of Peter* gives weight to the assumed agreement as to the authority and use of the other books.[60]

Clement of Alexandria

Clement (c. 155–220) was the first known Christian scholar and, according to Eusebius, he wrote commentaries on all the canonical Scriptures and even some of the disputed writings. Quotations in his writings imply that he considered at least the following books to be canonical: Matthew, Mark, Luke, John, Acts, Romans, 1 and 2 Corinthians, Galatians, Ephesians, Philippians, Colossians, 1 and 2 Thessalonians, 1 and 2 Timothy, Titus, Hebrews, 1 Peter, 1 John, Jude, and Revelation. He does not mention Philemon, James, 2 Peter, and 2 and 3 John. Among extra books, he includes the *Didache*, the *Epistle of Barnabas*, *1 Clement*, the *Apocalypse of Peter*, the *Shepherd of Hermas*, and possibly the *Acts of Peter* and the *Acts of Paul*.[61]

Clement makes a clear distinction between canonical and apocryphal works, as seen in an observation regarding one of the apocryphal Gospels: "We do not find this saying in our four traditional Gospels, but in the *Gospel according to the Egyptians*" (*Stromateis* 3.13.93.1).[62]

Tertullian

Tertullian (c. 160–220), a theologian from Carthage, quotes as widely as Irenaeus and includes at least the following books in his canon: Matthew, Mark, Luke, John, Acts, Romans, 1 and 2 Corinthians, Galatians, Ephesians, Philippians, Colossians, 1 and 2 Thessalonians, 1 and 2 Timothy, Titus, Hebrews, James, 1 Peter, 1 and 2 John, Jude, and Revelation (only Philemon, 2 Peter, and 3 John are not mentioned).[63] As extra books he includes Wisdom of Solomon and *Shepherd of Hermas*.[64]

Hippolytus

Hippolytus (c. 170–235), who was taught by Irenaeus, also quotes from most of the New Testament books: Matthew, Mark, Luke, John, Acts, Romans, 1 and 2 Corinthians, Galatians, Ephesians, Philippians, Colossians, 1 and 2 Thessalonians, 1 and 2 Timothy, Titus, Hebrews, James, 1 and 2 Peter, 1 and 2 John, Jude, and Revelation. He apparently had the same New Testament canon as his teacher, except that Jude is clearly mentioned. He does not mention Philemon or 3 John,[65] and he seems to believe that the *Acts of Paul* is authoritative.[66]

By the beginning of the third century onward the church fathers found themselves in the heart of a debate concerning the books of the New Testament canon. Several of the church fathers from this time prepared lists of the New Testament books, and their writings indicate that there were significant questions related to canonicity. The following lists were recorded.

Origen

Origen (c. 185–253) traveled widely throughout the Christian world (e.g., Rome, Athens, Syria, Cappadocia, and Arabia) and acquainted himself with the biblical material used at each location. About 230 he formulated a list of New Testament books accepted universally (*homologoumenoi*) by Christians: the four Gospels, Acts, Paul's thirteen epistles, 1 Peter, 1 John, and Revelation. He then cited those books held in dispute by some (*antilegomenoi*): Hebrews (he accepts), 2 Peter (he accepts), 2 and 3 John (he questions), James (he accepts), and Jude (he accepts). Noncanonical books included in his canon are the *Didache*, *Epistle of Barnabas*, *Shepherd of Hermas*, and possibly *1 Clement* and the *Acts of Paul*.[67]

Homologoumenoi
Books universally accepted as authoritative

Antilegomenoi
Books whose authority is disputed

Eusebius of Caesarea

Eusebius (c. 265–339), a church father from the early fourth century, inherited Origen's library and many of his traditions through his adoptive father, Pamphilus the martyr. He also had a fairly good awareness of the works used in the Christian church and mentions the following New Testament books:

> At this point it seems reasonable to summarize the writings of the New Testament which have been quoted. In the first place should be put the holy tetrad of the Gospels. To them follows the writing of the Acts of the Apostles. After this should be reckoned the Epistles of Paul. Following them the Epistle of John called the first, and in the same way should be recognized the Epistle of Peter. In addition to these should be put, if it seem desirable, the Revelation of John, the arguments concerning which we will expound at the proper time. These belong to the Recognized Books. Of the Disputed Books which are nevertheless known to most are the Epistle called of James, that of Jude, the second Epistle of Peter, and the so-called second and third Epistles of John which may be the work of the evangelist or of some other with the same name. Among the books which are not genuine must be reckoned the Acts of Paul, the work entitled the Shepherd, the Apocalypse

of Peter, and in addition to them the letter called of Barnabas and the so-called Teachings of the Apostles. And in addition, as I said, the Revelation of John, if this view prevail. For, as I said, some reject it, but others count it among the Recognized Books. Some have also counted the Gospel according to the Hebrews in which those of the Hebrews who have accepted Christ take a special pleasure. These would all belong to the disputed books. . . . (*HE* 3.25.1–6)[68]

His list includes all the New Testament books except James, Jude, 2 Peter, 2 and 3 John; these were questioned by some but accepted by the majority of Christians. He cites at the end as noncanonical books the *Acts of Paul*, the *Apocalypse of Peter*, the *Didache*, the *Epistle of Barnabas*, the *Shepherd of Hermas*, and the *Gospel of the Hebrews*.[69]

Athanasius

Athanasius (c. 296–373), the bishop of Alexandria, was the first to include all twenty-seven books of the New Testament in his canon. He enumerated them in an Easter letter to his parishioners in 367:

Again it is not tedious to speak of the [books] of the New Testament. These are, the four Gospels, according to Matthew, Mark, Luke, and John. Afterwards, the Acts of the Apostles and Epistles (called Catholic), seven viz. of James, one; of Peter, two; of John, three; after these, one of Jude. In addition, there are fourteen Epistles of Paul, written in this order. The first, to the Romans; then two to the Corinthians; after these, to the Galatians; next, to the Ephesians; then to the Philippians; then to the Colossians; after these, two to the Thessalonians, and that to the Hebrews; and again, two to Timothy; one to Titus; and lastly, that to Philemon. And besides, the Revelation of John. . . . But for greater exactness I add this also, writing of necessity; that there are other books besides these not indeed included in the Canon, but appointed by the Fathers to be read by those who newly join us, and who wish for instruction in the word of godliness. The Wisdom of Solomon, and the Wisdom of Sirach, and Esther, and Judith, and Tobit, and that which is called the Teaching of the Apostle, and the Shepherd. But the former, my brethren, are included in the Canon, the latter being [merely] read; nor is there in any place a mention of apocryphal writings. (*Letter* 39.5, 7)[70]

During the fourth and early fifth centuries, several synods and councils dealt with the issue of the New Testament canon, and a consensus began to emerge.

Table 9.1
Synodical and Conciliar Decisions on Canonicity

Name	Decision
Synod of Laodicea (363)	This synod met at Laodicea in Asia Minor and forbade the reading of noncanonical books. There is some uncertainty concerning which books were canonical, but it is most likely that all twenty-seven New Testament books (except possibly Revelation) were included.
Council of Hippo (393)	Convening at Hippo, North Africa, this council determined the same list of twenty-seven New Testament books.
Synod of Carthage (397)	Held in Carthage, North Africa, this synod determined that only canonical works should be viewed as authoritative and read in the churches as divinely inspired Scripture. The synod then listed the Old and New Testament books it believed were canonical; the New Testament included the same twenty-seven canonical books (the Book of Hebrews was listed apart from the rest of the Pauline epistles).
Council of Carthage (419)	This council reaffirmed the canon of Scripture and maintained that the Book of Hebrews was to be listed with the other Pauline epistles.

(See A. Souter, *The Text and Canon of the New Testament*, rev. C. S. C. Williams [London: Duckworth, 1965], 178–79.)

These councils did not determine the canonicity of the New Testament books but rather helped to confirm which books were accepted more widely throughout the early church. Synods were usually smaller and provide information as to what specific areas believed, whereas the councils were larger, reflecting views from major regions (see table 9.1).

While the majority of New Testament books were accepted as canonical by the middle of the second century, uncertainty regarding mainly the General Epistles remained well into the fourth century, as Harrison describes:

> Hebrews, questioned in the West because of uncertainty as to apostolic authorship, gained acceptance in the East under the plea of the Alexandrians that it was Pauline in some sense, and in due time it was classified as one of Paul's letters. In the case of James, several factors may have operated: uncertainty as to the identity of the James in question, the problem as to the meaning of the Twelve Tribes scattered abroad, and the scarcity of distinctive Christian teaching on the doctrinal side. Doubt arose respecting II Peter because it differs so greatly in vocabulary and somewhat in style from the First Epistle. It seems to have had limited circulation also. Failure to include II and III John is understandable in view of their brevity, personal nature, and the relative unimportance of their contents. Jude was plagued with uncertainty as to the apostolic standing of the writer, who seems to set himself apart from the apostles (v. 17).[71]

As these issues were resolved, the General Epistles were gradually added to the canon. However, other noncanonical books, some of which claimed to be written by apostles (e.g., the *Apocalypse of Peter*; the *Epistle of Barnabas*), were sometimes included in copies of the New Testament. Bruce offers a possible explanation: "In days when books were few and each copy had to be reproduced by hand, it was natural that some books would, for general convenience, be read at public gatherings of Christians which would nowadays be read at home. This may help to explain why early manuscript copies of the Scriptures have such books bound in with the canonical ones."[72]

This issue was compounded by the fact that the Eastern church had a different classification of Scripture than the Western church and therefore included more works in its canon.

Differences between Eastern and Western Canons

The Eastern church included in its classification of Christian books those that were helpful to be read in church but were not authoritative Scripture. No doubt because of this, people from the Eastern church were not as clear about which books were authoritative as were members of the Western church. A. Souter observes that it was not until "the middle of the fourth century that the Arian controversy brought East and West orthodox Christians together."[73]

The Western Church

By about 200, the Western church appears to have included at least twenty-

Table 9.2
Extracanonical Works in Major Codices

Greek Text	Date	Extra Books
Codex Vaticanus	4th century	End missing
Codex Sinaiticus	4th century	*Epistle of Barnabas*; *Shepherd of Hermas*
Codex Alexandrinus	5th century	*1* and *2 Clement*; (*Psalms of Solomon* [missing, but listed in the table of contents])

one books in its New Testament canon. However, the Book of Hebrews and some of the General Epistles (2 Peter, 2 and 3 John, James, and Jude) were usually questioned in these early lists of canonical works. The *Apocalypse of Peter* and the *Shepherd of Hermas* (who came from Rome) were very popular books in the West at this early period but were probably not considered canonical.

The Eastern Church

Origen, an early father from the Eastern church, believed that twenty-two books were agreed on by all, or what he called *homologoumenoi* ("confessed by all"), but the seven or eight still in question he called *amphiballomenoi* ("things thrown both ways"). He is uncertain concerning Pauline authorship of the Book of Hebrews but still ascribes it to Paul. By contrast, Eusebius of Caesarea (c. 303) made three distinct classifications of writings: *homologoumenoi* referring to books agreed upon by everyone; *antilegomenoi* ("spoken against"), referring to those that were questioned by some; and lastly "altogether absurd and impious writings"—books that few believed were canonical (*HE* 3.25.1–7). It is interesting that he placed the Book of Revelation in both the first and last groups, being well aware of significant opposition to it.[74]

Athanasius, the bishop of Alexandria, drew a firm line between canonical and noncanonical works and states the following about the Old and New Testaments:

> These are the fountains of salvation, that they who thirst may be satisfied with the living words they contain. In these alone is proclaimed the doctrine of godliness. Let no man add to these, neither let him take ought from these. For concerning these the Lord put to shame the Sadducees, and said, "Ye do err, not knowing the Scriptures." And He reproved the Jews, saying, "Search the Scriptures, for these are they that testify of Me." (*Letter* 39.6)[75]

Even though Athanasius had a definitive list of twenty-seven canonical books by the mid-fourth century, there was still a significant amount of variation in the number and makeup of New Testament canonical books well into the fifth century. Even the major Greek codices dated to the fourth and fifth centuries contained books outside the New Testament canon (see table 9.2).

It appears that interaction between the Eastern and Western churches helped to clarify which books were to be included in the canon. The Western church was more restrictive as to which books were included in their canon and the Eastern church more broad, but together they came to a satisfactory agreement. In the East the Book of Hebrews was recognized as canonical, and in the West the Revelation of John had a secure place; thus both were included. Some of the later books to be added to the canon were the General Epistles, but toward the end of the fourth century all seven had been accepted. By the fifth century, therefore, the church was in agreement as to what constituted Scripture.

This agreement continued up to the Middle Ages, but at the beginning of the Middle Ages scholars renewed questions about the New Testament canon. Thomas Aquinas (1225?–1274) and Nicholas of Lyra (c. 1265–1349) expressed doubts concerning the canonicity of Hebrews, though they were minor since Hebrews had retained a firm position in the canon for centuries.[76] Martin Luther (1483–1546) also raised questions about the canonicity of some New Testament books, arguing that the principle means of determining a book's authority was whether it promoted Christ or not. Luther's views concerning the New Testament canon made little noticeable difference in the church.

The Syriac Church

The Syriac church, located between the Tigris and Euphrates rivers (not to be confused with the Greek-speaking church of Syria), was part of the Eastern church. Syriac is a derivation of the Aramaic language, and the church originated possibly as early as the first century, when Jews at Pentecost brought the gospel back to their homelands. According to Ewert the Syriac church apparently had a limited New Testament canon:

> From the Teaching of Addai (A.D. 35) it appears that the Syriac church had, at the outset at least, a shorter canon than did the other churches. A Syriac canon of the Old and New Testaments from about A.D. 400 indicates that the four Gospels, the Acts, and fourteen letters of Paul (including Hebrews) were generally accepted. "This is all," adds the writer of the list.[77]

This canon, consisting of nineteen books, may have come to Syria from Tatian (c. 172) and included only those books commonly accepted in Rome.[78] Since the Syriac Christians had only limited interaction with the rest of the Christian church, they may have been unaware of the rest of the New Testament books. However, by about 425, the Syriac Peshitta, which became the standard form of the New Testament in Syriac, contained twenty-two books (adding James, 1 Peter, and 1 John). This version was revised in 508 to include all twenty-seven books of the New Testament, though it was never quite as popular as the Peshitta.

Determination of the New Testament Canon

It is important to remember that the Christian church did not canonize any book. Canonization was determined by God. But the early church needed to know how to recognize canonicity. The little we know regarding this process must be gleaned from the writings of the church fathers or other sources. Probably the most helpful resource is the Latin fragment called the Muratorian Canon. The fragment begins with the last words of a sentence that obviously refers to Mark's Gospel (relevant portions are set in bold):

> . . . but at some he was present, and so he set them down.
> The third book of the Gospel, **that according to Luke, was compiled in his**

own name on Paul's authority by Luke the Physician, when after Christ's ascension Paul had taken him to be with them like a legal expert. Yet neither did *he* **see the Lord in the flesh; and he too, as he was able to ascertain events, begins his story from the birth of John.**

The fourth of the Gospels was written by **John, one of the disciples.** When exhorted by his fellow-disciples and bishops, he said, "Fast with me this day for three days; and what may be revealed to any of us, let us relate it to one another." **The same night it was revealed to Andrew, one of the apostles, that John was to write all things in his own name, and they were all to certify.**

And therefore, though various ideas are taught in the several books of the Gospels, **yet it makes no difference to the faith of believers, since by one sovereign Spirit all things are declared in all of them concerning the Nativity, the Passion, the Resurrection, the conversation with his disciples and his two comings,** the first in lowliness and contempt, which has come to pass, the second glorious with royal power, which is to come.

What marvel therefore if John so firmly sets forth each statement in his Epistles too, saying of himself, *What we have seen with our eyes and heard with our ears and our hands have handled, these things we have written to you?* **[1 John 1:1, 3–4] For so he declares himself not an eyewitness and a hearer only, but a writer of all the marvels of the Lord in order.**

The Acts, however, of all the apostles are written in one book. Luke, *to the most excellent Theophilus* [Luke 1:3], includes events because **they were done in his own presence**, as he also plainly shows by leaving out the passion of Peter, and also the departure of Paul from the City on his journey to Spain.

The Epistles, however, of Paul themselves make plain to those who wish to understand it, what epistles were sent by him, and from what place or for what cause. . . . **For the blessed apostle Paul himself, following the rule of his predecessor John, writes only by name to seven churches in the following order**—to the Corinthians a first, to the Ephesians a second, to the Philippians a third, to the Colossians a fourth, to the Galatians a fifth, to the Thessalonians a sixth, to the Romans a seventh; although for the sake of admonition there is a second to the Corinthians, and to the Thessalonians, yet *one* Church is recognized as spread over the entire world. For John too in the Apocalypse, though he writes to seven churches, yet speaks to all. Howbeit to Philemon one, to Titus one, and to Timothy two **were put in writing from personal inclination and attachment, to be in honour however with the Catholic Church** [i.e., universal] **for the ordering of ecclesiastical discipline.** There is in circulation also one of the Laodicenes, another to the Alexandrians, **both forged in Paul's name to suit the heresy of Marcion, and several others, which cannot be received into the Catholic Church; for it is not fitting that gall be mixed with honey.**

The Epistle of Jude no doubt, and the couple bearing the name of John, are accepted in the Catholic Church; and the Wisdom written by the friends of Solomon in his honour. The Apocalypse also of John, and of Peter only we receive, which some of our friends will not have read in the Church. **But the Shepherd was written quite lately in our times in the city of Rome by Hermas, while his brother Pius, the bishop, was sitting in the chair of the church of the city of Rome; and therefore it ought indeed to be read, but it cannot to the end of time be publicly read in the church to the people, either among the prophets, who are complete in number, or among the Apostles.**[79]

Based primarily on the information set in boldface type in this quotation, the following principles have been derived for determining the New Testament canon:

1. Was the book written by an apostle, or at least someone of recognized authority?
2. Did it agree with the canon of truth?
3. Did it enjoy universal acceptance?
4. Does it have a self-authenticating divine nature?

Apostolic Authorship

Apostolic authorship appears to have been one of the chief means of determining canonicity, so that, for instance, works by the apostle Paul were readily accepted as canonical (see the Muratorian Canon). In the case of the Book of Hebrews, the Eastern church ascribed it to Paul and accepted it into the canon on that basis, but the Western church was reluctant to do so because Tertullian assigned authorship to Barnabas. Similarly, once the apostle Peter was determined to have authored 2 Peter, there was little difficulty in adding it to the canon. The apostles, being eyewitnesses to Jesus and his life, could speak authoritatively about that which they wrote (see 1 John 1:1, 3–4). They had heard Christ's teachings and were faithful to record and pass them on to others. Statements from the early church fathers indicate the importance of apostolic teaching:

> Clement of Rome: "The Apostles received the Gospel for us from the Lord Jesus Christ; Jesus the Christ was sent from God. The Christ therefore is from God and the Apostles from the Christ." (*1 Clem.* 42.1–2)[80]

> Irenaeus, speaking of Polycarp: ". . . having always taught the things which he had learned from the apostles, and which the Church has handed down, and which alone are true." (*Haer.* 3.3.4)[81]

> Ignatius of Antioch: "I do not order you as did Peter and Paul; they were Apostles, I am a convict; they were free, I am even until now a slave." (*To the Romans* 4.3)[82]

Some of the apocryphal works may have gained popularity on the basis that the author wrote in the name of one of the apostles (e.g., the *Apocalypse of Peter*).

However, this was not the only criterion for canonicity. Some works written by apostles did not form part of the New Testament canon (e.g., Paul's other letter to the Corinthians [1 Cor. 5:9] and the Laodiceans [Col. 4:16]), and other New Testament works are anonymous (e.g., the Gospels and Hebrews). Ewert states that: "anonymous books (such as the Gospels and several epistles) were accepted because they were apostolic in content. The apostolic content of books was known from the apostolic teaching that was well established in the churches—sometimes called the 'canon of truth.'"[83] He may be correct, but evidence from the Muratorian Canon argues that Luke was believed to be canonical based upon its author's relationship to Paul and not necessarily its apostolic content.

The Canon of Truth

The church fathers sometimes speak of the canon of faith (Latin: *regula fidei*) or the canon of truth (Latin: *regula veritatis*), a body of apostolic teaching by which the truth of other teaching could be evaluated until the written word was completed. Ewert relates the following illustration of this principle:

> We are told of a second-century bishop of Antioch, Serapion, who visited the Syrian town of Rhossos and found the church divided over the use of the Gospel of Peter. At first Serapion, not suspecting heresy, said a work of an apostle might be read. Then when he discovered its Docetic character (even though it claimed to be apostolic) he suppressed the book. Obviously this gospel did not measure up to the rule of faith.[84]

According to this principle, Scripture claims to have a divine origin and thus cannot contradict itself. Since certain books of Scripture were considered canonical almost immediately (e.g., the Gospels and Paul's Letters), their teaching could be used to evaluate that of other books. Luther used this principle to question the canonicity of the Book of James—he believed that James 2:17–18 and 24 contradicted Romans 3:28.

> In the same way, faith by itself, if it is not accompanied by action, is dead. But someone will say, "You have faith; I have deeds." Show me your faith without deeds, and I will show you my faith by what I do. . . . You see that a person is justified by what he does and not by faith alone. (James 2:17–18, 24)

> For we maintain that a man is justified by faith apart from the observing the law. (Rom. 3:28)

Both of these passages are true and in fact do not contradict each other, for James emphasizes the idea that a vibrant faith is one that wants to serve, whereas Paul emphasizes in Romans that no amount of works or keeping the law will ever earn salvation.[85] Each displays different aspects of salvation that are found elsewhere in Scripture.

Once again this principle cannot be the only criterion used to determine Scripture. Not all of the apocryphal works contain ideas contradictory to other parts of Scripture (e.g., the *Didache*, the *Shepherd of Hermas*). But the rule can be used to determine which books clearly go beyond the confines of the doctrine set forth in the rest of Scripture (e.g., the *Gospel of Thomas* contains Gnostic ideas).

Universal Acceptance

It was important that a book be accepted by both the Eastern and Western churches before it was recognized as canonical; in this way the church was not divided over specific books and doctrines. The interaction between the two branches of the church helped both the books of Hebrews and Revelation to become accepted. It also was at least part of the reason why the General Epistles were eventually added to the Syriac Peshitta. Initially some books experienced limited appeal, and thus it took longer for them to be recognized as authoritative, but in time the universal church agreed on the canonical books. It should be noted that only later did the Eastern Orthodox Church add other books to its canon and that during the Council of Trent in 1546 the Apocryphal books were included in the Roman Catholic canon.

Self-authenticating Divine Nature

Each book of Scripture has a divine element because it is God-breathed (2 Tim. 3:16). Even though the New Testament books do not specifically claim to bear a message from God, as do many Old Testament books, Hebrews 4:12 states that "the word of God is living and active. Sharper than any double-edged sword, it penetrates even to dividing soul and spirit, joints and marrow; it judges the thoughts and attitudes of the heart." Concerning the early church's recognition of the divine inspiration of New Testament books Bruce observes:

> We may well believe that those early Christians acted by a wisdom higher than their own in this matter, not only in what they accepted, but in what they rejected. Divine authority is by its very nature self-evidencing; and one of the profoundest doctrines recovered by the Reformers is the doctrine of the inward witness of the Holy Spirit, by which testimony is borne within the believer's heart to the divine character of Holy Scripture. This witness is not confined to the individual believer, but is also accessible to the believing community; and there is no better example of its operation than in the recognition by the members of the Early Church of the books which were given by inspiration of God to stand alongside the books of the Old Covenant, the Bible of Christ and his apostles, and with them to make up the written Word of God.[86]

Because this criterion is very subjective with the divine aspect being easier to identify in retrospect, it must be used in conjunction with other criteria for canonicity. H. E. W. Turner notes that there may be a level of conflict among these criteria:

> What happened when the principles of general utility and knowledge by the ancients come into conflict with a claim to apostolicity which could not be substantiated can be illustrated by the fate of Hermas. Here the Church was pulled in two directions and finally reached a compromise solution. The *Shepherd* was not apostolic and therefore could not be read publicly in Church, but proved useful as a book of ethical instruction and therefore could receive a less official circulation. Works of this useful but nonapostolic character make their appearance in some Biblical manuscripts and

even occupy the position of a New Testament Apocrypha in some lists of Canonical Books.[87]

When questions arose, there was probably a hierarchy of the criteria: apostolic authority was of prime importance, and contradictions to the canon of truth would probably be a very close second.

Is the New Testament Canon Closed?

By implication, the principle of apostolic authorship leads to the conclusion that once the apostles died, no more could be added to the collection of their writings. It is reasonable to say, then, that the canon was complete by the end of the first century, when all the apostles had died, though it took significantly longer for all of the books to be recognized. Later controversy over Montanus, who claimed to reveal new Scripture as the mouthpiece of the Holy Spirit, forced Christians to carefully examine the clear claims of Hebrews 1:1–2 that Christ was the final revelation of God. The Greek in verse 2 states, "but in these last days he has spoken to us *in his son*"; this means that Christ is God's final revelation and not simply that the final revelation came through him. Even Paul, who wrote many of the New Testament letters, did not claim to have new revelation but merely explained what God had already revealed in Christ. Bruce makes clear this differentiation:

> The earliest documents in the New Testament are letters written by apostles to their converts and other Christians imparting this teaching and applying it to the various situations that arose in the infant churches. As the apostles did this, we believe, they experienced the fulfilment of their Lord's promise that his Spirit would lead them into all the truth. But it is a remarkable fact that there is no teaching in the New Testament which is not already present in principle in the teaching of Jesus himself. The apostles did not add to his teach-

ing; under the guidance of the promised Spirit they interpreted and applied it.[88]

Since Paul did not claim to offer new revelation but saw himself as a witness to God's revelation in Christ (1 Tim. 2:7; 2 Tim. 1:10–11), so-called prophets like Muhammad (570?–632), Joseph Smith (1805–1844), or Sun Myung Moon (1920–), who claim further or new revelation for the church, are false prophets. Galatians 1:8 states: "But even though we or an angel from heaven should preach a gospel other than the one we preached to you, let him be eternally condemned!"

If another book was found, such as Paul's other letter to the Corinthian church or the letter to the Laodiceans, to gain canonicity it would have to agree with all the other books of the canon and be accepted by the entire Christian church, which at this point seems unlikely. It also seems unlikely that God would add another book to the New Testament canon now after so much church history has passed. Why would the church not have needed this book for almost two thousand years? Thus the evidence is fairly convincing that the New Testament canon is closed, though we cannot rule out in principle the possibility that a work could be found that would fit all the criteria given.

For Further Reading

Aland, K. *The Problem of the New Testament Canon.* London: Mowbray, 1962.

Bruce, F. F. "New Light on the Origins of the New Testament Canon." In *New Dimensions in New Testament Study*, edited by R. N. Longenecker and M. C. Tenney, 3–18. Grand Rapids: Zondervan, 1974.

Campenhausen, H. von. *The Formation of the Christian Bible.* Translated by J. A. Baker. Philadelphia: Fortress, 1977.

Filson, F. V. *Which Books Belong in the Bible?* Philadelphia: Westminster, 1957.

Goodspeed, E. J. *Formation of the New Testament Canon.* Chicago: University of Chicago Press, 1926.

Grant, R. M. "The New Testament Canon." In *CHB*, 1:284–307.

Guthrie, D. *New Testament Introduction*, 986–1000. Leicester, England: Apollos; Downers Grove, IL: InterVarsity, 1990.

Harrison, E. F. *Introduction to the New Testament*, 97–134. 2d ed. Grand Rapids: Eerdmans, 1971.

Kümmel, W. G. *Introduction to the New Testament.* Translated by H. C. Kee, 475–510. Rev. ed. Nashville: Abingdon, 1975.

Patzia, A. G. *The Making of the New Testament: Origin, Collection, Text, and Canon.* Downers Grove, IL: InterVarsity, 1995.

Ridderbos, H. "The Canon of the New Testament." In *Revelation and the Bible*, edited by C. F. H. Henry, 187–201. Grand Rapids: Baker, 1958.

Souter, A. *The Text and Canon of the New Testament.* Revised by C. S. C. Williams. London: Duckworth, 1965.

New Testament Extracanonical Literature

During the first to third centuries A.D. there arose a body of literature that circulated among early Christians but never became part of the New Testament canon. The number of extracanonical works should not surprise us, since the Greeks and Romans, who dominated much of the Mediterranean area, were quite literary and well educated. Many of the early church fathers were able to read and write and recorded many early traditions concerning Christ and the apostles, some of which are known as *agrapha* (not written; i.e., words that Jesus said but were not recorded), and others that are merely writings of the early church fathers. A distinction should be made between the New Testament apocrypha and the writings of the early church fathers. Certain writings of the early church fathers are occasionally included in collections of the New Testament (e.g., the *Epistle of Barnabas* and the *Shepherd of Hermas* in Codex Sinaiticus [fourth century]; *1* and *2 Clement* in Codex Alexandrinus [fifth century]), but to the best of our knowledge none of the so-called New Testament apocryphal books appeared in any list of New Testament books, even though a few are mentioned by early church fathers. It is reasonable to suppose that works from the church fathers were occasionally included in canonical collections of the Scriptures and read in public gatherings, being deemed useful for the early church. By the early fifth century, however, the New Testament canon was clearly established, so that these works were no longer included. The books of the New Testament apocrypha originated in various Christian communities over a wide period of time but never enjoyed the widespread acceptance of the New Testament books.

Scholars still disagree in their definition of the New Testament apocrypha. For our purposes, we will use the general definition from Stephen Patterson, assistant professor of New Testament at Eden Theological Seminary in St. Louis, Missouri: "various early Christian writings that are not included in the canonical NT,"[1] with an additional distinction between the writings of the church fathers (some of which were occasionally included in lists of the New Testament) and works that were intentionally written to supplement the existing New Testament canon but never became part of it. This distinction is not always easy to maintain, but the two types of works are significantly different.

The early church fathers had several different definitions for the word *apocrypha*, but it is unlikely that an established group of books was intended by the term (see chap. 8). The New Testament also makes it clear that there were a significant number of books available at the time of its writing (see table 10.1). It is our belief that these works were not intended to form part of the New Testament canon and thus were lost in the intervening generations. The following works also circulated at this time but are not mentioned in the New Testament.

The *Agrapha*

The word *agrapha* refers to sayings of Jesus that were not recorded in the New Testament. Jesus lived on earth for more than thirty years, and even though we have four different records of his life in the Gospels, they could not contain all the things Jesus did or said. John 21:25 says, "Jesus did many other things as well. If every one of them were written down, I suppose that the whole world would not have room for the books that would be written" (cf. Luke 1:1). While surely this is an exaggeration, it nevertheless indicates that much was not recorded in the Gospels and is now lost to us. However, some of Jesus' sayings were recorded elsewhere.

Mention of *Agrapha* in the New Testament

The apostle Paul records several *agrapha* of Jesus. In Acts 20:35 he states: "remembering the words the Lord Jesus himself said: 'It is more blessed to give than to receive.'" These words were never recorded in any of the Gospels, so Paul must have learned this saying from eyewitnesses. Several teachings in 1 Corinthians (e.g., 7:10; 9:14) may have as their basis *agrapha* of Jesus,[2] as well as the words Paul used to explain the Lord's Supper in 1 Corinthians 11:24–25. The words of 1 Thessalonians 4:15–17a are said to be Jesus' own:

> According to the Lord's own word, we tell you that we who are still alive, who are left till the coming of the Lord, will certainly not precede those who have fallen asleep. For the Lord himself will come down from heaven, with a loud command, with the voice of the archangel and with the trumpet call of God, and the dead in Christ will arise first. After that, we who are still alive and are left will be caught up together with them in the clouds to meet the Lord in the air. And so we will be with the Lord forever.

It is difficult to know where Jesus' words finish and Paul's resume, but at the very

least this passage is built upon Jesus' own words.

Agrapha in Variant Readings in New Testament Manuscripts

It is possible that the variant reading of Luke 6:5 found in Codex Bezae (dated from the fifth to sixth century) records a saying of Jesus, which states: "The same day, seeing a certain man working on the sabbath, he said to him, 'Man if indeed you know what you are doing, happy are you; but if not, you are accursed and a transgressor of the law.'"[3] The intent here is that if the man understood Jesus' teaching that the Sabbath is made for man, not man for the Sabbath, then the man would be blessed; however, if he was merely breaking the law he would be cursed.

Another addition appears in Codex Bezae after Matthew 20:28 and may include a saying of Jesus:

> But seek to increase from smallness and from the greater to become less. And when you go in and are invited to dine, do not recline in the prominent place lest one more illustrious than you come in, and he who invited you to dinner say to you, "Go even lower down; and you shall be put to shame." But if you recline in the lesser place and a lesser man come in, he who invited you to dinner will say to you, "Come up higher," and this will be profitable to you.[4]

This addition is very similar to Luke 14:8–10, perhaps a copyist included a version of it here, or it may be a separate tradition of one of Jesus' sayings.

In the Freer Gospels (also dated to the fifth century) in Washington, D.C., the following addition appears after Mark 16:14 and reflects a plausible saying of Jesus:

> And they excused themselves, saying, "This age of lawlessness and unbelief is under Satan, who by his unclean spirits does not allow the true power of God to be comprehended. Therefore now reveal your righteousness." So they spoke to

Table 10.1
Extracanonical Works Mentioned in the New Testament

Literary Work	Biblical Passage
Other Gospels	Luke 1:1; John 21:24–25
Paul's letter to Laodicea	Colossians 4:16
Paul's third letter to the Corinthians	1 Corinthians 5:9

Christ; and Christ addressed them thus, "The limit of the years of Satan's authority has been fulfilled, but other terrible things are drawing near, even to those sinners on whose behalf I was handed over to death, that they may turn to the truth and sin no more. In order that they may inherit the spiritual and incorruptible glory of righteousness in heaven [Mark 16:15 follows]."[5]

Agrapha Recorded by the Church Fathers

Several passages from the literature of the early church fathers (e.g., Papias, Eusebius, Justin Martyr, Tertullian, Clement of Alexandria, Origen, Jerome, Augustine, and others) claim to contain sayings of Jesus that may have formed part of the oral traditions passed down through generations. Some are significantly early, though this does not in itself guarantee their authenticity. Several examples of these purported *agrapha* follow. Papias, a bishop of Hierapolis in Phrygia (c. 60–130), is quoted in Irenaeus:

The Lord taught about those times and said, "The days will come in which vines will bear 10,000 branches, each branch 10,000 twigs, each twig 10,000 clusters, each cluster 10,000 grapes, and each grape when pressed will yield twenty-five measures of wine. When any saint takes hold of one such cluster, another cluster will exclaim, 'I am a better cluster; take me; bless the Lord through me!' Similarly a grain of wheat will produce 10,000 ears, each ear will have 10,000 grains, and each grain will yield ten pounds of fine flour, bright and pure; and the other fruit, seeds, and herbs will be proportionately productive according to their nature, while all the animals which feed on these products of the soil will live in peace and agreement one with another, yielding complete subjection to men." (Irenaeus *Haer.* 5.33.3)[6]

Origen, an Alexandrian theologian (c. 185–254), quoted other sayings:

I have read somewhere that the Saviour said—and I question whether someone has assumed the person of the Saviour, or called the words to memory, or

whether what is said is true—but at any rate the Saviour himself says, "He who is near me is near the fire. He who is far from me is far from the kingdom." (Origen *Hom. Jer.* 3.3)[7]

"Ask for the greater things, and the small shall be added to you; ask for the heavenly things, and the earthly shall be added to you." (Origen *Or.* 2)[8]

From Justin Martyr, an early Christian apologist (c. 100–65), comes this saying:

For he [Jesus] said, "Many shall come in my name clad outwardly with sheepskins, but within they are ravening wolves," and "There shall be divisions (schisms) and heresies." (Justin Martyr *Dial.* 35.3)[9]

Tertullian, an African apologist and theologian (c. 160–220) quoted this statement:

"No man can obtain the kingdom of heaven that hath not passed through temptation." (Tertullian *De baptismo* 20)[10]

Eusebius of Caesarea, sometimes called the father of church history (c. 265–339), says that the following authentic statement was found in the *Gospel of the Hebrews*:

"I will choose for myself the best which my Father in heaven has given me." (Eusebius *Theophania* 4.12)[11]

Some of these quotations bear the mark of Jesus' ideals and teachings, but their authenticity is difficult to determine.

Agrapha from Apocryphal New Testament Books

The apocryphal New Testament Gospels include many *agrapha;* the following three have significant claims to authenticity.

The *Gospel of the Hebrews*

The story of the rich young ruler also appears in the *Gospel of the Hebrews;* the first part of the story closely parallels the other Gospel records (Matt. 19:16–21; Mark 10:17–22; Luke 18:18–22):

155

Another rich man said to him, "Master, what good thing shall I do to live?" He said to him, "O man, fulfil the law and the prophets." He replied, "I have done that." He said to him, "Go, sell all that you possess and distribute it to the poor, and come, follow me."

The next portion that appears is a purported saying of Jesus:

But the rich man began to scratch his head and it did not please him. And the Lord said to him; "How can you say, 'I have fulfilled the law and the prophets,' since it is written in the law: You shall love your neighbour as yourself, and lo! many of your brethren, sons of Abraham, are clothed in filth, dying of hunger, and your house is full of many goods, and nothing at all goes out of it to them." (Origen *Comm. Matt.* 15.14)[12]

In evaluating the authenticity of this account of the rich young ruler, J. Jeremias weights the following factors:

When compared to the Gospel version, the text displays a curious combination of abbreviation and expansion. Despite this however, it does not look like an artificial compilation, for in itself it is remarkably compact and consistent and possesses a clearer unity than the Matthean version, which bears visible traces of being a revision of the Markan form. Most important, and to my mind conclusive, is the moral urgency which characterizes the new material. All these considerations suggest that we have here an independent version of the story of the Rich Young Man.[13]

Oxyrhynchus Papyrus 840 (P. Oxy. 840)

The Oxyrhynchus Papyri were discovered in 1897 by two British archaeologists, B. P. Grenfell and A. S. Hunt, at the ancient city of Oxyrhynchus, Egypt (modern Behnesa in central Egypt). P. Oxy. 840, found in December 1905, was described as a "seared, worm-eaten leaf measuring 8.8 X 7.4 cm. It comes from a parchment book, is written on both sides, and contains forty-five lines in Greek

characters. The script is microscopic, but clearly legible, and points to a date somewhere round 400."[14] This fragment is especially interesting because it uses the word *Savior* as a title for Jesus, something the canonical Gospels rarely, if ever, do (cf. Luke 2:11). It contains a story (with a possible saying of Jesus) about Jesus and a Pharisaic chief priest, though its translation is uncertain in some places:

. . . before he does wrong he makes all kinds of ingenious excuses. "But take care lest you also suffer the same things as they did, for those who do evil not only receive their chastisement from men but they await punishment and great torment." Then he took them with him and brought them into a place of purification itself, and was walking in the temple. A Pharisee, a chief priest named Levi, met them and said to the Saviour, "Who gave you permission to walk in this place of purification and look upon these holy vessels when you have not bathed and your disciples have not washed their feet? But you have walked in this temple in a state of defilement, whereas no one else comes in or dares to view these holy vessels without having bathed and changed his clothes." Thereupon the Saviour stood with his disciples and answered him. "Are you then clean, here in the temple as you are?" He said, "I am clean, for I have bathed in the pool of David and have gone down by one staircase and come up by the other, and I have put on clean white clothes. Then I came and viewed the holy vessels." "Alas," said the Saviour, "you blind men who cannot see! You have washed in this running water, in which dogs and pigs have wallowed night and day, and you have washed and scrubbed your outer skin, which harlots and flute-girls also anoint and wash and scrub, beautifying themselves for the lusts of men while inwardly they are filled with scorpions and unrighteousness of every kind. But my disciples and I, whom you charged with not having bathed, have bathed ourselves in the living water which comes down from heaven. But woe to those who. . . ."[15]

Initially this work was met with skepticism; however, several more recent scholars have argued for its authenticity.[16]

Oxyrhynchus Papyrus 1 (P. Oxy. 1)

This Greek fragment shows parallels with the Coptic *Gospel of Thomas* discussed below.

> 27. Jesus says, "If you do not fast as regards the world, you will not find the Kingdom of God, and if you do not keep the Sabbath as a Sabbath you will not see the Father." [Lines 4–11][17]

> 28. Jesus says, "I stood in the midst of the world and I was seen in the flesh by them and found all intoxicated and none among them did I find thirsting and my soul is afflicted for the sons of men because they are blind in their heart and do not see. . . ." [Lines 11–21][18]

> 30. Jesus says, "Wherever there are [three] they are without God and where there is one alone I say I am with him. Lift the stone and there you will find me: cleave the wood and I am there." [Lines 23–30][19]

Nag Hammadi Manuscripts

A group of twelve papyrus codices plus eight leaves written in Coptic (a language of the Egyptian Christians) were found at Nag Hammadi, located in Upper Egypt, in December 1945. They came from an ancient monastery at Chenoboskion; the vast majority contain Gnostic ideas (regarding Gnostic heresy, see chap. 9). One of the works that received the most publicity is entitled the *Gospel of Thomas*, a compilation of 114 sayings of Jesus. This work, not directly Gnostic but containing many sayings that have this flavor, begins with the words: "These are the secret words which the living Jesus spoke, and Didymus Judas Thomas wrote them down."[20] F. F. Bruce explains that this work may have a much earlier history:

> When scholars began to study it, they realised that portions of it had been known previously. About the end of the nineteenth century and beginning of the twentieth, much excitement was aroused

by the discovery in Egypt of papyrus fragments exhibiting utterances ascribed to Jesus, each of them introduced by the words "Jesus said." These fragments are commonly called the "Oxyrhynchus Sayings," from the ancient name of the place where they were found. They were written in Greek, whereas the recently-discovered "Gospel according to Thomas" is written in Coptic. But it is now clear that the "Oxyrhynchus Sayings" were fragments of a much larger Greek compilation, which was subsequently translated into Coptic for the benefit of the rank and file of the Egyptians who did not know Greek. And it is this Coptic translation that has now come to light as the "Gospel of Thomas." The Greek original of the compilation may be dated about the middle of the second century A.D., the Coptic translation is a century or two later.[21]

Some of the sayings in the *Gospel of Thomas* are not authentic, but others that are consistent with Jesus' character and teachings may be. A few appear verbatim in canonical or other Christian literature, but in some cases the original words of Jesus have been amplified, expanded, or conflated. Other sayings were unknown previous to this discovery—some are clearly spurious, conveying ideas that are Gnostic in character.

The following brief quotations are samples from the Nag Hammadi manuscripts.

Apocryphon of James (NHC I.2):

> "Do not let the kingdom of heaven wither away. For it is like a date-palm shoot whose fruit fell down around it. It put forth buds, and when they blossomed its productivity was caused to dry up. So it also is with the fruit that came from this singular root: when it was picked, fruit was gathered by many. Truly, this was good. Is it not possible to produce such new growth now? Cannot you (*sing.*) discover how?"[22]

Dialogue of the Savior (NHC III.5):

> [Judas] responded, saying, "Tell me, Lord, [how it is that . . .] . . . which shakes the earth moves." The Lord picked up a [stone and] held it in his hand, [saying,

"What] am I holding [in] my [hand]?" He said, "[It is] a stone." He [said] to them, "That which supports [the earth] is that which supports the heaven. When a Word comes forth from the Greatness, it will come on what supports the heaven and the earth. For the earth does not move. Were it to move, it would fall. But it neither moves nor falls, in order that the First Word might not fail. For it was that which established the cosmos and inhabited it and inhaled fragrance from it.[23]

The *Infancy Gospel of Thomas*

Here is an example of the legends that were created to supplement the scant information about Jesus' childhood.

2.1. When this boy Jesus was five years old he was playing at the crossing of a stream, and he gathered together into pools the running water, and instantly made it clean, and gave his command with a single word. 2. Having made soft clay he moulded from it twelve sparrows. And it was the sabbath when he did these things. And there were also many other children playing with him. 3. When a certain Jew saw what Jesus was doing while playing on the sabbath, he at once went and told his father Joseph, "See, your child is at the stream, and he took clay and moulded twelve birds and has profaned the sabbath." 4. And when Joseph came to the place and looked, he cried out to him, saying, "Why do you do on the sabbath things which it is not lawful to do?" But Jesus clapped his hands and cried out to the sparrows and said to them, "Be gone!" And the sparrows took flight and went away chirping. 5. The Jews were amazed when they saw this, and went away and told their leaders what they had seen Jesus do.[24]

There is significant disagreement as to how much credit to give to *agrapha*, especially since there has been a dramatic increase in their number in the past century. This debate is set forth nicely in two recent works, one by John Dominic Crossan, who relies heavily upon noncanonical materials as they relate to the Christ,[25] and another by John P. Meier, who considers these noncanonical materials to be of little value,[26] as he states in his conclusion:

Contrary to some scholars, I do not think that the . . . *agrapha*, the apocryphal gospels, and the Nag Hammadi codices (in particular the Gospel of Thomas) offer us reliable new information of authentic sayings that are independent of the NT. What we see in these later documents is rather . . . imaginative Christians reflecting upon popular piety and legend, and gnostic Christians developing a mystic speculative system . . . It is only natural for scholars—to say nothing of popularizers—to want more, to want other access roads to the historical Jesus. This understandable but not always critical desire is, I think, what has recently led to the high evaluation, in some quarters, of the apocryphal gospels and the Nag Hammadi codices as sources for the quest.[27]

According to Otfried Hofius, professor of New Testament in Tübingen, Germany, only a small number of *agrapha* are authentic: "The number of agrapha which can be put on a level with the sayings of Jesus in the synoptic Gospels is strikingly small: nine sayings, if one includes the texts which are doubtful from a tradition-historical point of view, and only four if one excludes them."[28] Hofius thinks the following four *agrapha* could be authentic words of Jesus:[29]

1. The addition to Codex Bezae in place of Luke 6:5 (see p. 154, col. b).
2. The *Gospel of Thomas* 82, which says "Whoever is near me is near the fire; whoever is far from me is far from the kingdom."
3. A phrase from the *Gospel of the Hebrews* quoted in Jerome, which says: "And never be joyful, save when you look upon your brother in love."
4. The fragment in the Oxyrhynchus Papyrus 1224, which states: "And pray for your [ene]mies (cf. Mt. 5:44), For he who is not [against yo]u is for you (cf. Lk. 9:50). [He that] stands far off [today] will tomorrow be [near you]."

The New Testament Apocrypha

While the New Testament records a great deal of important material about

Jesus' life, it also leaves many questions unanswered. The desire for more information about the life of Christ was, according to Everett Harrison, one factor leading to the writing of New Testament apocryphal books:

> Two factors are largely responsible for the creation of these writings. One was the desire for further information about the life of Jesus and the careers of the apostles. Scripture has little to say about our Lord prior to the opening of his ministry. This gap was an invitation and even a challenge to supply the deficiency by calling upon the resources of the imagination. . . .
>
> A second factor was the desire of those with heretical tendencies to foist their ideas on the church with the alleged endorsement of Christ or the apostles. By far the most common of these tendencies was the Gnostic. . . . It was rather easy to claim the authority of Jesus for teaching that went beyond that of the New Testament, since he himself had hinted that he had much to say that he was unable to impart to his disciples at the time (John 16:12). This was an open door for Gnostic propaganda, especially as it was put in the lips of the resurrected Saviour.[30]

The New Testament apocrypha are various writings produced from the second century, after the time of the apostles, up to the Middle Ages; these works were often written under the names of the apostles and associates of Christ. While some apocryphal writings were highly regarded by early Christians, most fall within the category of religious fiction, according to Bruce.[31] Many have a format similar to that of New Testament books—some, modeled after the Gospels, recount events from the life of Christ before he entered public ministry; others, similar to the Book of Acts, claim to record events from the lives of the apostles after Jesus' ministry. The apocalypses, like the Book of Revelation, describe a fiery destruction of this world (see especially the *Apocalypse of Peter*). Some of these works do not contradict the teaching of Scripture, but a significant num-ber were purposely written with the intent of lending support for various beliefs or practices (some heretical); for example, in the *Ebionite Gospel* John the Baptist is portrayed as a vegetarian, and the *Gospel of Thomas* claims Jesus spoke Gnostic ideas. The early church fathers were aware that some of these works contradicted Scripture, as Origen explains: "The church receives only four gospels; heretics have many, such as the gospel of the Egyptians, the gospel of Thomas, etc. These we read, that we may not seem to be ignorant to those who think they know something extraordinary, if they are acquainted with those things which are recorded in these books."[32]

The Most Common New Testament Apocryphal Books

Since the discovery of the large hoard of Gnostic writings from Nag Hammadi, there has been an ongoing increase in the number of the New Testament apocryphal works. Table 10.2 lists some of the more important works at present.[33]

Value of the New Testament Apocrypha

These works bear witness to customs, ideas, and philosophies of New Testament times as well as the diversity in thought that existed in early Christianity.[34] Some of the early New Testament apocryphal books may even contain early traditions about Christ and his teachings.[35] If nothing else, the apocryphal works serve to underscore the distinctiveness of the canonical books, as Harrison explains: "the student is able to compare this literature with the acknowledged books of the New Testament. If he has misgivings about the formation of the canon, feeling that perhaps the endorsement of the books was somewhat arbitrary, it is morally certain that he will be won to a position of complete confidence in the superiority of the New Testament books on the basis of comparison."[36]

Table 10.2
New Testament Apocrypha

I. Gospels and Related Forms
A. Narrative Gospels
  1. *Gospel of the Ebionites*
  2. *Gospel of the Hebrews*
  3. *Gospel of the Nazoreans*
  4. *Gospel of Nicodemus (Acts of Pilate)*
  5. *Gospel of Peter*
  6. *Infancy Gospel of Thomas*
  7. *P. Egerton 2* (a fragment of an unknown narrative Gospel)
  8. *P. Oxy. 840* (a fragment of an unknown narrative Gospel)
  9. *Protevangelium of James*
B. Revelation Dialogues and Discourses
  1. *(First) Apocalypse of James* (NHC V)
  2. *(Second) Apocalypse of James* (NHC V)
  3. *Apocryphon of James* (NHC I)
  4. *Apocryphon of John* (NHC II, III, IV, and BG 8502)
  5. *Book of Thomas the Contender* (NHC II)
  6. *Dialogue of the Savior* (NHC III)
  7. *Epistula Apostolorum*
  8. *Gospel of the Egyptians*
  9. *Gospel of Mary* (BG 8502)
  10. *Gospel of Philip* (NHC II)
  11. *Letter of Peter to Philip* (NHC VIII)
  12. *Pistis Sophia*
  13. *Questions of Mary*
  14. *Questions of Bartholomew*
  15. *Second Treatise of the Great Seth* (NHC VII)
  16. *Sophia of Jesus Christ* (NHC III and BG 8502)
  17. *Two Books of Jeu*
  18. *Bodlian Copt. MS d54* (a fragmentary dialogue between Jesus and John)
C. Sayings Gospels and Collections
  1. *Gospel of Thomas* (NHC II)
  2. *Teachings of Silvanus* (NHC VII)
II. Treatises
  1. *On the Origin of the World* (NHC II)
  2. *(Coptic) Gospel of the Egyptians* (NHC III and IV)
  3. *Gospel of Truth* (NHC I and XII)
  4. *Hypostasis of the Archons* (NHC II)
  5. *Treatise on Resurrection* (NHC I)
  6. *Tripartite Tractate* (NHC I)
III. Apocalypses
  1. *(Coptic) Apocalypse of Elijah*
  2. *(Arabic) Apocalypse of Peter*
  3. *(Coptic) Apocalypse of Peter* (NHC VII)
  4. *(Greek/Ethiopic) Apocalypse of Peter*
  5. *(Coptic) Apocalypse of Paul* (NHC V)
  6. *(Latin) Apocalypse of Paul*
  7. *Apocalypse of Sophonias*
  8. *Apocalypse of Thomas*
  9. *Ascension of Isaiah* (chaps. 6–11)
  10. *Christian Sibyllines*
  11. *Concept of Our Great Power* (NHC VI)
  12. *Book of Elchasai*
  13. *V and VI Ezra*
  14. *Melchizidek* (NHC IX)
  15. *Mysteries of St. John the Apostle and the Holy Virgin*

(continued on next page)

Table 10.2 (continued)
New Testament Apocrypha

IV. Acts
    1. *Acts of Andrew*
    2. *Acts of Andrew and Matthias*
    3. *Acts of John*
    4. *Acts of Paul (and Thecla)*
    5. *(Coptic) Act of Peter* (BG 8502)
    6. *(Greek) Acts of Peter*
    7. *Acts of Peter and the Twelve* (NHC VI)
    8. *Acts of Philip*
    9. *Acts of Thomas*
    10. *Kerygmata Petrou*

V. Letters
    1. *Abgar Legend*
    2. *Correspondence between Paul and Seneca*
    3. *Epistle of Pseudo-Titus*
    4. *Paul's Letter to the Laodiceans*

VI. Liturgical Materials
  A. Homilies
    1. *Interpretation of Knowledge* (NHC XI)
    2. *Kerygma of Peter*
    3. *Testimony of Truth* (NHC IX)
    4. *A Valentinian Exposition* (NHC XI)
  B. Psalms
    1. *Odes of Solomon*
  C. Prayers
    1. *On the Annointing* (NHC XI)
    2. *On Baptism A* (NHC XI)
    3. *On Baptism B* (NHC XI)
    4. *On the Eucharist A* (NHC XI)
    5. *On the Eucharist B* (NHC XI)
    6. *A Prayer of the Apostle Paul* (NHC I)

Key to abbreviations:
NHC = Nag Hammadi Codex
BG = Berlin Gnostic Papyrus

Adapted from S. J. Patterson, "Apocrypha:
New Testament Apocrypha," *ABD*, 1:295–96.

Writings of the Early Church Fathers

The earliest Christian writers apart from the New Testament, known as the Apostolic Fathers, lived between 80 and 180. During the early years of the church a wide variety of Christian literature circulated, much of which was read publicly in the church. The distinctiveness, however, of the writings of the Apostolic Fathers is described by Bruce: "Their works are not to be classed as 'New Testament Apocrypha'; they are simply what they profess to be, the writings of Christian men, designed for the edification of their fellow-Christians. But why are they not regarded as canonical? Because they do not bear the marks of canonicity. They themselves recognise the superior authority of the apostolic writings."[37]

Nonetheless some scholars still insist that these works should be included in any complete list of the New Testament apocrypha (e.g., Edgar Hennecke).[38] The more popular works that occasionally appeared in New Testament lists are set forth in table 10.3.

Other Christian writings extant during this period include hymns, sermons, and apologetic works. It is interesting that no major collection of hymns similar to the Psalms has been discovered, but most

Table 10.3
Early Christian Works Sometimes Considered Canonical

Book	Used as Canonical
Didache	Clement of Alexandria; Origen
Epistle of Barnabas	Clement of Alexandria; Origen
1 Clement	Irenaeus; Clement of Alexandria; Origen
Shepherd of Hermas	Irenaeus; Clement of Alexandria; Tertullian
Apocalypse of Peter	Clement of Alexandria
Acts of Paul	Clement of Alexandria (probably); Hippolytus; Origen (probably)

scholars agree that 1 Timothy 3:16 and perhaps Philippians 2:6–11 are early Christian hymns. The *Odes of Solomon* is a collection of Christian hymns from the late first- or second-century Syriac church. Several sermons have survived from early church fathers, such as *2 Clement* and those of Melito of Sardis, Clement of Alexandria, and Origen. There are also a signifi-cant number of Christian apologetic works: *Apology of Quadratus, Apology of Aristides, Apology of Athenagoras, Apology of Justin Martyr*, and the *Dialogue with Trypho* (Justin Martyr). These works were important to the early church and provided clear statements of the fundamental elements of Christianity with which to begin to fight heresy.

For Further Reading

Charlesworth, J. H., and C. A. Evans. "Jesus in the Agrapha and Apocryphal Gospels." In *Studying the Historical Jesus: Evaluations of the State of Current Research*, edited by B. Chilton and C. A. Evans, 479–533. New Testament Tools and Studies 19. Leiden: E. J. Brill, 1994.

Elliott, J. K., ed. *The Apocryphal New Testament: A Collection of Apocryphal Christian Literature in an English Translation*. Oxford: Clarendon, 1993.

Finegan, J. *Hidden Records of the Life of Jesus*. Philadelphia and Boston: Pilgrim, 1969.

Goodspeed, E. J. *A History of Early Christian Literature*. Chicago: University of Chicago Press, 1966.

Hofius, O. "Unknown Sayings of Jesus." In *The Gospel and the Gospels*, edited by P. Stuhlmacher, 336–60. Grand Rapids: Eerdmans, 1991.

Jeremias, J. *Unknown Sayings of Jesus*. Translated by R. H. Fuller. New York: Macmillan, 1957.

Patterson, S. J. "Apocrypha." In *ABD*, 1:294–97.

Robinson, J. M., ed. *The Nag Hammadi Library in English*. 3d rev. ed. San Francisco: Harper & Row, 1988.

Schneemelcher, W., ed. *New Testament Apocrypha*. Translated by R. M. Wilson. Rev. ed. 2 vols. Cambridge: James Clarke; Louisville, KY: Westminster/John Knox, 1991–92.

Stroker, W. D. *Extracanonical Sayings of Jesus*. SBL Resources for Biblical Study 18. Atlanta: Scholars Press, 1989.

Part 3

Transmission of the Bible

Transmission of the Old Testament

If Moses, living in the fifteenth (or even thirteenth) century B.C., wrote or collected any of the Pentateuch, then some Old Testament texts would have been transmitted for more than three thousand years before we received them in our modern translations. This naturally leads to such crucial questions as who copied these texts through the millennia and by what method, and whether the texts we have today are an accurate reflection of the original texts. Each of these questions will be examined.

Development of the Hebrew Text

No Original Manuscripts

It is important to note that there are no original manuscripts, or *autographa*, of either the Old Testament or the New. Any extant manuscript is a copy of an earlier one. The word *manuscript* derives from a Latin word meaning "that which is written by hand," and until the invention of the printing press in the fifteenth century all books were copied by hand. In an age of computers, laser printers, and photocopies, it is difficult for us to realize that for a long time the hand copying of each text was the only means of transmission.

Several factors have contributed to the disappearance of the original manuscripts.

Age and Decay

Original manuscripts of the Old Testament most likely would have been written on papyrus or leather, but because of the wear and tear of constant usage and the deterioration of most common writing materials,[1] it is very unlikely that any would survive. (The Silver Amulets upon which a small portion of the Old Testament is inscribed are a notable exception.)

Calamities That Befell the Jewish Nation

The land of Palestine suffered many wars and times of destruction. At least twice during the period in which the biblical texts were transmitted the city of Jerusalem was destroyed and much of it burned—the first in 586 B.C. at the hands of the Babylonians and the second in A.D. 70 by the Romans. Also the deportations of the Israelites that took place during the Assyrian exile of the northern kingdom in 722/721 B.C. and the Babylonian exile of the southern kingdom in 586 B.C. would have impeded the preservation of Israel's ancient manuscripts.

Reverence for the Text

When manuscripts began to show signs of wear, the Jewish scribes reverently disposed of them because they bore the sacred name of God. Disposing of the manuscripts avoided defilement by pagans. Since scribes were meticulous in copying biblical manuscripts, there was little reason to keep old manuscripts.[2] When the scrolls became worn, they were placed in a storage room called a *genizah* ("hidden") until there were enough to perform a ritual burial ceremony. In the late nineteenth century a *genizah*, now called the Cairo Genizah, was discovered in the Qaraʾite synagogue in Old Cairo.

People Who Sought to Destroy the Work

The prophets were not always well received, and sometimes their works were

Figure 11.1.
Written in paleo-Hebrew, this inscription at the end of Hezekiah's tunnel was discovered in 1880 by a schoolboy going to the tunnel to bathe. [Archaeological Museum, Istanbul]

destroyed (e.g., Jehoiakim; Jer. 36). During the medieval persecutions of the Jews, manuscripts were also destroyed. Sometimes manuscripts were hidden from invading armies and then never recovered (apparently the fate of the Dead Sea Scrolls).

The Old Testament Text prior to A.D. 100

Questions concerning the Early Texts

Until about fifty years ago very little was known about the Hebrew text of this time period. The only extant works that could shed light on it were the Samaritan Pentateuch, the Septuagint, and the Nash Papyrus. However, the discovery of the Dead Sea Scrolls provided a great number of manuscripts dated between about 250 B.C. and A.D. 50 (see chap. 12). Nevertheless significant questions remain.

First, in which language(s) were the earliest biblical manuscripts written? It is generally assumed that the earliest texts were first written in Proto-Canaanite or paleo- (early-) Hebrew script[3] and then later in square (or Aramaic) script. However, little is known about the earliest

Translation: [See] the boring. And this was the manner of the boring. While [the stonemasons were] still [striking with] the pick-axe, each man towards his comrade, and when there were still three ells *(1.35 m.)* to bore thro[ugh, there was hear]d the voice of a man shouting to his comrade, as there was a *resonance* in the rock, in the south and i[n the nor]th. And on the day of the boring the stonemasons had struck, each towards his own comrade, pick-axe against [pick]axe. Then the water ran from the spring to the pool for 1200 ells *(540 m.)*. And 100 ells was the height of the rock over the heads of the stonemasons. (K. A. D. Smelik, *Writings from Ancient Israel: A Handbook of Historical and Religious Documents,* trans. G. I. Davies [Louisville: Westminster/John Knox, 1991], 70)

Hebrew text since no manuscripts have surfaced from this early period. The earliest evidence of a biblical text appears on the Silver Amulets, which are generally

were written with spaces between the words to aid in the reading of the text, but at times these spaces are difficult to determine (see fig. 11.2).

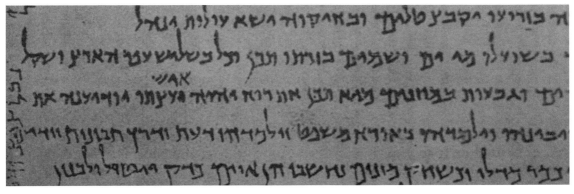

dated to the mid-seventh century B.C. and are written in paleo-Hebrew script. Manuscripts from Qumran dated many centuries later are written in Square script. The change from paleo-Hebrew to Square script probably took place between the fifth and third centuries B.C.[4] and would probably have been hastened by the Jews who returned from the exile, for their *lingua franca*, or trade language, in Babylon was Aramaic.

Second, did the Israelites originally use *scriptio continua* ("continuous writing") without spaces between words? Debate continues as to whether or not the Hebrews initially wrote with spaces between words. On the one hand we have early Aramaic correspondence that includes spaces and sometimes even markers between words; the paleo-Hebrew inscription at the end of Hezekiah's tunnel shows dots between words (see fig. 11.1). However, these are not biblical scrolls, and they date to a time significantly later than when the earliest biblical manuscripts would have appeared. On the other hand the earliest Proto-Canaanite or paleo-Hebrew inscriptions do not ordinarily indicate word divisions.

In the earliest biblical portion from the Silver Amulets, there are no spaces between letters, but amulets may not have been treated with the same reverence as biblical texts. Evidence indicates that at least from the time of the Qumran scrolls, biblical texts

Unclear or absent word divisions provide great potential for misreading the consonantal text, as the following English example illustrates:

Godisnowhere may be read as "God is now here" or "God is nowhere."[5]

While context and the translator's language ability can resolve many difficulties of word divisions, there are still potential problems. For example, Amos 6:12 is generally translated from the Hebrew as

Do horses run on the rocky crags?
Does one plow with oxen?
But you have turned justice into
   poison
and the fruit of righteousness into
   bitterness.

The second question seemingly does not fit the context, since the answer to the first question is clearly no, whereas the second question would usually be answered yes. This verse has been translated in several different ways, depending primarily on where one divides the words. The two most favored translations are

"Or does one plow (them) with oxen?"
(NASB, KJV)

אִם	יַחֲרוֹשׁ	בַּבְּקָרִים
(or)	(will one plow)	(with oxen)

Figure 11.2.
A portion of the Isaiah Scroll with unclear word divisions.
[John C. Trever]

167

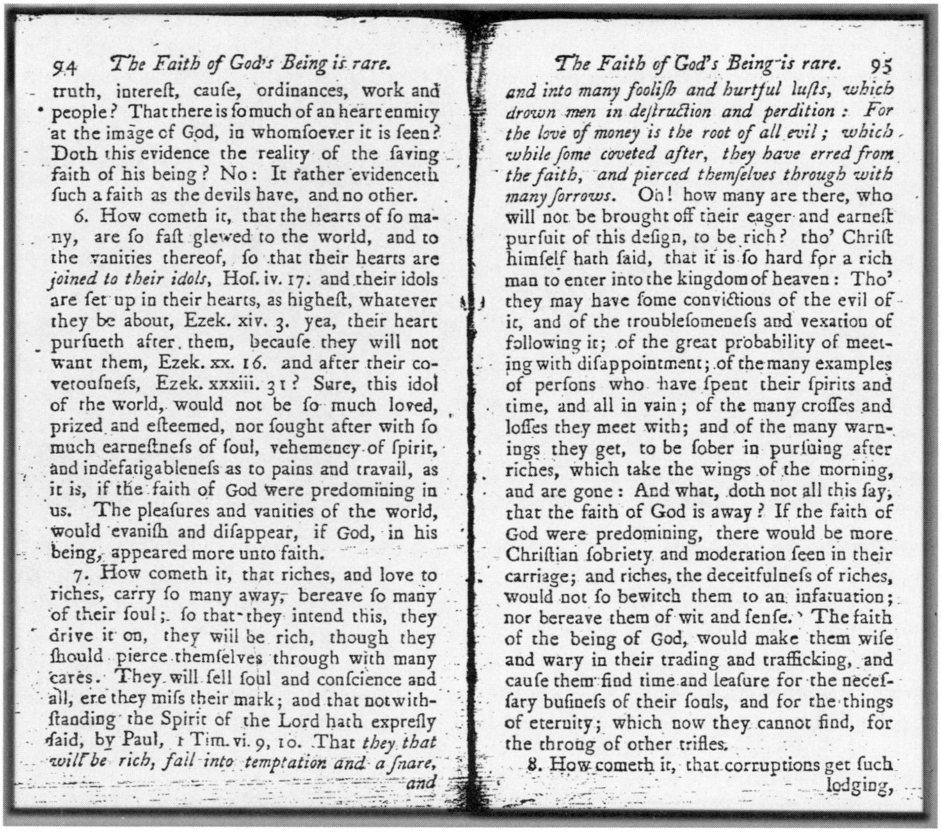

94 *The Faith of God's Being is rare.*

truth, intereſt, cauſe, ordinances, work and people? That there is ſo much of an heart enmity at the image of God, in whomſoever it is ſeen? Doth this evidence the reality of the ſaving faith of his being? No: It rather evidenceth ſuch a faith as the devils have, and no other.

6. How cometh it, that the hearts of ſo many, are ſo faſt glewed to the world, and to the vanities thereof, ſo that their hearts are *joined to their idols*, Hoſ. iv. 17. and their idols are ſet up in their hearts, as higheſt, whatever they be about, Ezek. xiv. 3. yea, their heart purſueth after them, becauſe they will not want them, Ezek. xx. 16. and after their covetouſneſs, Ezek. xxxiii. 31? Sure, this idol of the world, would not be ſo much loved, prized and eſteemed, nor ſought after with ſo much earneſtneſs of ſoul, vehemency of ſpirit, and indefatigableneſs as to pains and travail, as it is, if the faith of God were predomining in us. The pleaſures and vanities of the world, would evaniſh and diſappear, if God, in his being, appeared more unto faith.

7. How cometh it, that riches, and love to riches, carry ſo many away, bereave ſo many of their ſoul; ſo that they intend this, they drive it on, they will be rich, though they ſhould pierce themſelves through with many cares. They will ſell ſoul and conſcience and all, ere they miſs their mark; and that notwithſtanding the Spirit of the Lord hath expreſly ſaid, by Paul, 1 Tim. vi. 9, 10. That *they that will be rich, fall into temptation and a ſnare,*

and

The Faith of God's Being is rare. 95

and into many fooliſh and hurtful luſts, which drown men in deſtruction and perdition: For the love of money is the root of all evil; which while ſome coveted after, they have erred from the faith, and pierced themſelves through with many ſorrows. Oh! how many are there, who will not be brought off their eager and earneſt purſuit of this deſign, to be rich? tho' Chriſt himſelf hath ſaid, that it is ſo hard for a rich man to enter into the kingdom of heaven: Tho' they may have ſome convictions of the evil of it, and of the troubleſomeneſs and vexation of following it; of the great probability of meeting with diſappointment; of the many examples of perſons who have ſpent their ſpirits and time, and all in vain; of the many croſſes and loſſes they meet with; and of the many warnings they get, to be ſober in purſuing after riches, which take the wings of the morning, and are gone: And what, doth not all this ſay, that the faith of God is away? If the faith of God were predomining, there would be more Chriſtian ſobriety and moderation ſeen in their carriage; and riches, the deceitfulneſs of riches, would not ſo bewitch them to an infatuation; nor bereave them of wit and ſenſe. The faith of the being of God, would make them wiſe and wary in their trading and trafficking, and cauſe them find time and leaſure for the neceſſary buſineſs of their ſouls, and for the things of eternity; which now they cannot find, for the throng of other trifles.

8. How cometh it, that corruptions get ſuch

lodging,

Figure 11.3. Pages from an old book that shows how British publishers helped readers determine whether pages were missing: a word at the bottom of the page matches the word beginning the next page. These pages come from John Brown's *In a Practical Treatise upon Hebrews XI.5, 6* (Edinburgh: David Paterson, 1771), 94–95. [Tyndale House]

The translators of the NIV insert the word *there* (the NASB inserts "them") to refer to the rocks or cliffs mentioned in the earlier line and therefore translate the phrase "Or does one plow [there] with oxen?" While this translation makes good sense, the insertion of this word is questionable, since it would usually appear in the text if required by the context.[6]

"Does one plow the sea with oxen?" (RSV, LB, NRSV)

אִם יַחֲרוֹשׁ בַּבָּקָר | יָם

(the sea) (with oxen) (will one plow) (or)

The only difference between these translations is that the Hebrew word for oxen (בַּבְּקָרִים [*babbᵉqārîm*]), which was originally rendered as one word, has been divided in two and translated as "with oxen" (בַּבָּקָר [*babbāqār*]) and "sea" (יָם [*yām*]). This is probably the better translation because the Hebrew word בַּבָּקָר (*babbāqār*) is generally used as a collective noun; hence the plural would not be necessary. Also, the plural form בַּבְּקָרִים (*babbᵉqārîm*) occurs in only two other late biblical passages (2 Chron. 4:3 [cf. 1 Kings 7:24] and Neh. 10:37), both of which have been questioned on textual grounds in *Biblia Hebraica Stuttgartensia*. Lastly, the latter translation anticipates a negative answer like its parallel unit.[7]

Work of the Scribes

From about 500 B.C. to A.D. 100, an influential group of teachers and interpreters of the Law called *sopherim* (scribes) arose to preserve Israel's sacred traditions, the foundation of the nation.[8] The Babylonian Talmud (*Qidd.* 30a) says, "The early [scholars] were called *soferim* because they used to count [*sfr*] all the letters in the Torah."[9] It is likely that the biblical texts were written on papyrus or leather scrolls.

Jeremiah 36 gives some indication as to the writing process when in verse 2 God tells Jeremiah to "Take a scroll and write on it all the words I have spoken to you." In verse 23 it states: "Whenever Jehudi had read three or four columns of the scroll, the king cut them off with a scribe's knife and threw them into the firepot, until the entire scroll was burned in the fire." Scrolls were limited in length by their bulk and manageability. Since the Old Testament was very large it would necessitate the use of many scrolls and thus some system to provide the order for the scrolls was necessary. One method was to begin a new scroll with the final words of the previous scroll; this is the best explanation for the repetition of several verses at the end of Chronicles (2 Chron. 36:22–23) and the beginning of Ezra (Ezra 1:1–3a). A somewhat similar method was used for a time by British book publishers whereby the word that starts the next page appears at the bottom of the page in the margin so that the reader would know if a page had fallen out of the book (see fig. 11.3). Scrolls were still used in the synagogue even after the codex (a manuscript bound in book form) became popular for private use in the second century A.D.[10]

Scroll names and authors were also sometimes noted on a slip of papyrus or parchment attached to the outside of the scroll, a system F. F. Bruce describes:

When the roll was wound up, a slip containing the title of the work and the name of the author was usually pasted on the outside. This could easily fall off, leaving the work without a name. It may be that something like this happened to the Epistle to the Hebrews. This Epistle bears no writer's name, although it was not intended to be an anonymous letter; its recipients no doubt knew quite well who had sent it to them. A number of rolls would be kept together in a cylindrical box, which the Romans called a *capsa*. If an anonymous roll was kept in a box along with a number of other rolls by a known author, the nameless roll was apt to be credited to that author too. Thus, if the Epistle to the Hebrews was kept along with letters of Paul, it was not unnatural that Paul's name should come to be attached to it.[11]

Origin of the Scribes' Text

There is much disagreement as to the origin of the text that the scribes maintained. Paul de Lagarde (1827–1891, professor of Old Testament at Göttingen) argued that all the Hebrew texts revert to one original manuscript (a single copy [*ein einziges Exemplar*]); see fig. 11.4.[12] He reasoned that since all Masoretic manuscripts have some specific characteristics in common (e.g., the *puncta extraordinaria*, dots above letters considered questionable by scribes), they must be dependent on one

Figure 11.4. P. de Lagarde's and P. Kahle's understandings of the origin of the Masoretic Text.

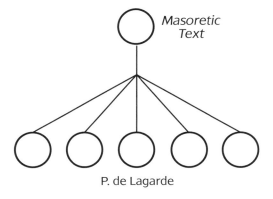

Begins with a single origin

Masoretic Text

P. de Lagarde

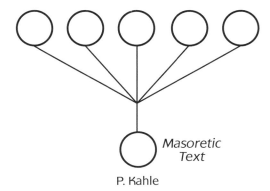

Begins with many "vulgar texts" that were then standardized

Masoretic Text

P. Kahle

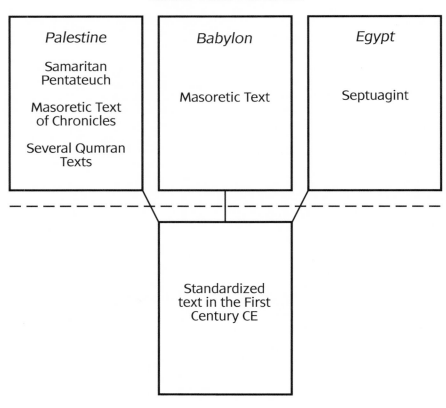

Local Text Families

Figure 11.5.
W. F. Albright's
and F. M. Cross's
view of the
origin of the
Masoretic Text.

Palestine	Babylon	Egypt
Samaritan Pentateuch	Masoretic Text	Septuagint
Masoretic Text of Chronicles		
Several Qumran Texts		

Standardized text in the First Century CE

another, and therefore it is possible to retrieve the original text.

By the time of Paul Kahle (1875–1964), an Old Testament professor from Oxford, several divergent text types had been identified. Kahle argued that there were many vulgar texts (*Vulgärtexte,* or "corrupted texts") that were then standardized into an official text (fig. 11.4).[13] In the mid-1950s, two other scholars, William F. Albright from Johns Hopkins University and Frank M. Cross from Harvard University, began to develop a third view, arguing for the possibility of local recensions/text types/families.[14] This theory reduced the textual witnesses to three text types from different areas: Palestine (Samaritan Pentateuch, Masoretic Text of Chronicles, several Qumran texts), Babylon (Masoretic Text), and Egypt (Septuagint; see fig. 11.5).[15]

Cross went on to argue that the Samaritan Pentateuch became a divergent sec-

tarian recension around 100 B.C., whereas the proto-Masoretic Text went on to become the standard text of the rabbis around A.D. 100. While the idea of local textual traditions is helpful in explaining the diversity among related manuscripts, the Qumran scrolls indicate greater similarities between some of these so-called text types than the concept allows. This model has been challenged by several scholars;[16] most recently Emanuel Tov, professor of Bible at Hebrew University, has questioned both the notion of an Ur-Text that gave rise to the divergent text types, as well as the grouping of Qumran texts into fixed text types. He has argued instead that the Qumran manuscripts are related to one another in an intricate web of agreements, differences, and exclusive readings.[17] Tov believes that the Qumran manuscripts reveal five different groups (four of which were unknown prior to the Qumran discoveries) distinguished on the basis of the content of their variants.[18]

Development of Hebrew Vowels

In the earliest phase of its development Hebrew was written only with consonants, but possibly as early as the time of the Hebrew monarchy (by the ninth century B.C.) the consonants ה *(hē)*, י *(yôḏ)*, and ו *(wāw)* were added to some words to indicate three classes of long vowels. These long vowels, used as case endings to signify the grammatical function of words, aided in the pronunciation of the text and were called *matres lectionis* (mothers of reading).[19] The use of *matres lectionis* did not affect the meaning or sound of the word but helped to clarify which form of the word the author intended. Words incorporating *matres lectionis* became known as *plene* (or full) writing;[20] the absence of *matres lectionis* was called defective (or partial) writing.

As the language continued to develop, scribes used more *matres lectionis*, which greatly reduced the translation possibilities of the text. D. N. Freedman has dated the present form of the Masoretic Text (usually denoted as MT) between the third and second century B.C. based on its orthography (primarily the number of *matres lectionis*).[21] Both the Samaritan Pentateuch and the Qumran materials use more *matres lectionis*. Once the Masoretic Text became an authoritative text, the further addition of *matres lectionis* was not permitted; another system to facilitate proper pronunciation was developed. Several different pointing systems appeared in various scribal schools, but the Tiberian pointing system gained general acceptance.[22]

The Old Testament Text (c. A.D. 100–500)

Standardized Text (c. A.D. 100)

It appears that during the first century a strong movement emerged in Judaism to establish a standardized text

| Plene: | כּוֹתֵב | *(kôṯēḇ)* (the long o vowel is represented by the consonant ו *wāw* plus *ḥōlem*) |
| Defective: | כֹּתֵב | *(kōṯēḇ)* (the long o vowel is represented merely by *ḥōlem*) |

of the Hebrew Bible. There is a significant difference between the varied textual traditions found at Qumran dating between the third and first centuries B.C. and the minimal deviations in the Hebrew texts from Masada (just prior to A.D. 73), the caves at Naḥal Ḥever (late first century), and Wadi Murabbaʿat (written before the Bar Kochba revolt of 132–35). Thus sometime between these periods the text must have been standardized. This standardized text was dependent upon the earlier traditions that were available to the Jewish scribes at that time, but variants and differences in the text were removed. Once this standardization of the text took place, scribes were meticulous to ensure that the Hebrew text did not become corrupted.

Tannaim

From about A.D. 20 to 200 a second group of scribes arose, called the Tannaim *(tannāʾîm, "to hand down orally, to study, to teach")*, who began copying their traditions shortly after the beginning of the Christian era. The Mishnah (Jewish oral traditions expounding the Old Testament laws), some of which may have originated in the early first century B.C., also began to take shape under the Tannaim, but the completion of these traditions took a long time. According to tradition, Rabbi Akiba (A.D. 55–137) established the structure of the Mishnah (six divisions with minor tractates), and Judah the Prince compiled it toward the end of the second century. Sometime during the talmudic period (100 B.C. to A.D. 400), which overlaps the periods of the Sopherim, Tannaim, and Amoraim, meticulous rules were developed to preserve the Old Testament text in synagogue scrolls:

171

1. Only parchments made from clean animals were allowed; these were to be joined together with thread from clean animals.
2. Each written column of the scroll was to have no fewer than forty-eight and no more than sixty lines whose breadth must consist of thirty letters.
3. The page was first to be lined, from which the letters were to be suspended.
4. The ink was to be black, prepared according to a specific recipe.
5. No word or letter was to be written from memory.
6. There was to be the space of a hair between each consonant and the space of a small consonant between each word, as well as several other spacing rules.
7. The scribe must wash himself entirely and be in full Jewish dress before beginning to copy the scroll.
8. He could not write the name *Yahweh* with a newly dipped brush, nor take notice of anyone, even a king, while writing this sacred name.[23]

Later an entire tractate was devoted to the proper procedure for preparing a sacred scroll; in addition to the preceding requirements, it stipulated that

1. No obsolete Hebrew characters or languages other than the Hebrew Square script were to be used.
2. The letters must not be written in gold.
3. A scroll written by a Sadducee, informer, proselyte, slave, woman, madman, or minor was not to be used for reading in the synagogue.
4. The following names could not be erased: אֵל (*ʾĒl*), אַד (*ʾad*, the first two letters of the name אֲדֹנָי [*ʾᵃdōnāy*, Lord]), יָה (*Yāh*, the first two letters of the name יהוה [*yhwh*, Yahweh]), שַׁדַּי (*Šadday*, Almighty), צבאות (*Sᵉbāʾôt*, short for [Lord of] hosts), אהיה אשר אהיה (*ʾEhyeh ʾᵃšer ʾEhyeh*, I am that I am, Exod. 3:14).[24]

Many more rules were developed, both to preserve the scrolls from mistakes and to remind the scribe that he was copying sacred material.

Amoraim

A third group of scribes who preserved the Hebrew texts from about A.D. 200 to 500 were called the *ʾāmôrāʾîm* (expositors). During this period, the Talmud (from לָמַד, *lāmad*, to study) began to be formed, containing further expositions on the stipulations included in the Mishnah and the Gemara (a commentary on the Mishnah). The Amoraim were centered in two areas, Babylonia and Palestine, giving rise to two Talmuds, the Babylonian and the Palestinian. Some type of verse divisions for the Hebrew text are known from this early period (even though Babylonian and Palestinian traditions differ),[25] as well as paragraph and liturgical divisions. Rabbinic tradition indicates that by this time scribes realized that the text was in need of some minor corrections, many of which are noted in *Biblia Hebraica Stuttgartensia*, either in the Masorah or in the text.

The Old Testament Text (c. A.D. 500–1000)

Masoretes

Around the end of the fifth century, a fourth group of scribes called the Masoretes inherited the scribal traditions and carried on the work of preserving the text. Their diligent labors from about A.D. 500 to 1000 helped to preserve the Hebrew text that we have, the Masoretic Text. These scribes were extremely careful and treated the text with great reverence. They made meticulous notes regarding the text, from recording the number of letters used in the book to indicating the middle letter of a book; as H. Wheeler Robinson of Oxford University observes: "Everything countable seems to be counted."[26]

There were two major venues of Jewish scholarship, one in Babylon and one in Palestine. Following the Islamic conquest of Palestine in A.D. 638, Tiberias once again revived and became the chief center for Jewish textual studies.[27] From about A.D. 500 to 800 the Masoretes added vowel points, accents, and the Masorahs (to help safeguard the text from error), as well as many scribal corrections.

In the early half of the tenth century two notable Masoretic families flourished in Tiberias, the Ben Asher and Ben Naphtali families. It was once thought that these two families maintained significantly different textual traditions, but more likely they represent only one textual tradition with minor variations.[28] There are only eight minor differences between the consonantal texts of these two families, though they also differ as to word division and vocalization.[29] Eventually the Ben Naphtali tradition died out, and the Ben Asher tradition was maintained as the superior text.

Masoretic Notations

After the standardization of the Hebrew Bible in the first century, scribes were reticent to change the text; the Masoretes created special notations to indicate a question in the text without actually changing the consonantal text. Examples of special notations used by the scribes are as follows.

Special points (*puncta extraordinaria*). The Masoretes added small diamonds over letters or words to indicate reservations (either textual or doctrinal) about the reading in fifteen places.[30] C. D. Ginsburg (1831–1914), a notable Hebrew Bible scholar, argues that they refer to letters or words that should be deleted; Saul Lieberman, formerly dean of the Institute for Talmudic Studies in Jerusalem, agrees, stating that similar signs are found in the Qumran materials and in some Hellenistic texts.[31] But a statement in ʾAbot de Rabbi Nathan (a minor tractate of the Babylonian Talmud) suggests that the textual tradition was merely in doubt: "Some say, 'why are the dots used?' Ezra said, 'If Elijah should come and ask me why I accept that reading, I can point out that I have dotted the letters in question (to show they are suspect), but if he should tell me

that the reading is correct, I can remove the dots (Version A, 34).'"[32]

Israel Yeivin, formerly Old Testament professor at Hebrew University, offers another explanation: "In most of the cases where a Rabbinic discussion of the dots is recorded, a midrashic explanation for their use is given, so it seems possible that even the Rabbis no longer knew the original meaning of these dots."[33]

In Numbers 3:39, וְאַהֲרֹן (wᵉʾahᵃrōn, and Aaron) is specially marked:

כָּל־פְּקוּדֵי הַלְוִיִּם אֲשֶׁר פָּקַד מֹשֶׁה וְאַהֲרֹן
עַל־פִּי יְהוָה לְמִשְׁפְּחֹתָם

All the numbered men of the Levites whom Moses *and Aaron* numbered according to the mouth of the Lord by their families. . . . (literal translation)

The Masoretes apparently questioned the originality of the phrase *and Aaron*, since both verses 16 and 42 state that Moses (no mention of Aaron) numbered the people. Since verse 38 mentions both "Moses and Aaron" serving in the tabernacle, it is possible that an unobservant scribe could have changed verse 39 to agree with verse 38.

Suspended letters (אותיות תלויות [ʾôtîyôṯ tᵉlûyôṯ or *litterae suspensae*]). Four letters are suspended above the normal line in the Masoretic Text, and all Masoretic Text manuscripts agree in marking them: נ (*n*) in Judges 18:30 and ע (ʿ) in Job 38:13, 15, and Psalm 80:14 (ET 80:13). As an example, note the suspended נ (*n*) in the second line of Judges 18:30:

וַיָּקִימוּ לָהֶם בְּנֵי־דָן אֶת־הַפָּסֶל
וִיהוֹנָתָן בֶּן־גֵּרְשֹׁם בֶּן־מְנַשֶּׁה הוּא וּבָנָיו הָיוּ
כֹהֲנִים לְשֵׁבֶט הַדָּנִי עַד־יוֹם גְּלוֹת הָאָרֶץ׃

The suspended *nûn* is generally thought to have been added to spare Moses (מֹשֶׁה [mōšeh]) the embarrassment of having a relative who set up graven images at Dan, an action more fitting of a relative of Manasseh (מְנַשֶּׁה [mᵉnaššeh]), a wicked king who was born several hundred years after the events in Judges 18.[34]

173

Table 11.1
Scripts of the Sacred Name *Yahweh* in Various Greek Manuscripts

Form	Source
𐤉𐤄𐤅𐤄	Fragment of the Twelve Minor Prophets written in Greek and found at Naḥal Ḥever (50 B.C.–A.D. 50)
יהוה	Papyrus Fouad Inv. 266
ΠΙΠΙ	Some Hexaplaric Fragments (S. Jellicoe, *The Septuagint and Modern Study* [Oxford: Clarendon, 1968], 131)

Perpetual *Qere*. The frequent notations[35] *kethib* (K) and *qere* (Q) indicate when the scribes felt the text to be unsatisfactory for some reason. Rather than change the consonantal text (the כְּתִיב [*kᵉtîḇ*] reading, meaning "what was written"), the Masoretes indicated their preferred reading (the קְרִי [*qᵉrê*] reading, meaning "what is to be read") in the margin (marked underneath with ק) and pointed the text (*kethib* reading) with the vowel points of the *qere* form. Words that consistently read differently than they are written in the Masoretic Text are called perpetual *qere*s. One of the most common perpetual *qere*s is the *tetragrammaton* (the Greek word *tetragrammaton* means "four letters" and refers to the four Hebrew letters יהוה [*yhwh* or Yahweh] that represent the name for God). When writing the sacred name for God, scribes at Qumran would sometimes use ancient Hebrew script (see fig. 6.11), a practice that was continued in some Greek manuscripts (e.g., the Greek fragment of the Twelve Minor Prophets found at Naḥal Ḥever and dated to 50 B.C.–A.D. 50; see fig. 12.8). Other Greek manuscripts would sometimes use Square Hebrew script יהוה (*yhwh*; e.g., P. Fouad Inv. 266) or the Greek letters ΠΙΠΙ (*pipi*), which are roughly similar in appearance to the Square Hebrew script characters (see table 11.1).[36]

By the fourth century the signification of the Greek letters ΠΙΠΙ (*pipi*) was lost to some, according to Jerome: "(the) tetragrammaton, which the Jews consider ἀνεκφώνητον, that is ineffable, and which is written with these letters: Iod, He, Vau, He; which, certain ignorant ones, because

of the similarity of the characters, when they would find them in Greek books, were accustomed to pronounce Pipi" (*Letter* 25).[37]

However, in the Old Testament other forms were used to distinguish the divine name (see table 11.2). These two words in Hebrew are names for God as they appear in the Masoretic Text, but in fact they represent the consonants of one word and the vowels of another. They have become perpetual *qere*s because the Jewish people did not want the name of their God to be taken lightly, as the third commandment states: "You shall not misuse the name of the LORD your God, for the LORD will not hold anyone guiltless who misuses his name" (Exod. 20:7). According to the Westminster Shorter Catechism, "The name of God only is that by which men ought to swear, and therein it is to be used with all holy fear and reverence; therefore to swear vainly or rashly by that glorious and dreadful name, or to swear at all by any other thing, is sinful, and to be abhorred."[38] The scribes reasoned that if they did not point the name *Yahweh* then it could never be treated lightly since his name would not really be known. Initially the real pointing was probably passed along by tradition, but in time it was lost. In Exodus 20:7 the name LORD is written in capital letters according to the convention of signifying the name *Yahweh*, but the name as it appears in the Hebrew text is יְהֹוָה (*yᵉhōwâ*), in which appear the consonants from the name *Yahweh* (יהוה [*yhwh*]) and

Table 11.2
Forms of the Sacred Name

Kethib	Perpetual Qere	Meaning	Examples
יְהֹוָה	אֲדֹנָי	the LORD	Gen. 2:4–5, 7–9, 15; etc.
יֱהֹוִה			Gen. 15:2, 8
יֱהֹוִה	אֱלֹהִים	God	Ps. 73:28
יֱהֹוִה			Isa. 22:5

the vowels from the word Lord (אֲדֹנָי [*ªdōnāy*]). Proof for the fabricated nature of this word are the two vowels which appear on the *wāw*, an impossibility in Hebrew:

$$\text{יהוה} \text{' + vowels from } \overset{\frown}{\text{אֲדֹנָי}} = \text{יְהֹוָה}$$

However, until the revival of the Hebrew language in western Europe scholars read the consonants YHWH (Germans would read them as JHVH) with the vowels of ᵓªdōnāy, thereby originating the incorrect form *Jehovah*. This word was then introduced into English by William Tyndale[39] and was continued by the King James Version.

Other notations in the Hebrew Bible. Table 11.3 indicates some of the other notations that can be found in the Hebrew text today.

The Hebrew Text after 1000

The Masoretic Text was hand copied until the invention of the printing press, and yet it has remained extremely accurate. Every copy of the Hebrew Scriptures was a monumental task, and the Masoretes prided themselves on retaining the accuracy of the Hebrew text. One of the Masoretic schools in Alcalá, Spain, was so well known for producing accurate manuscripts that for almost a century after the printing press was introduced the hand-printed manuscripts from this school still vied with those produced by the printing press. Some of these manuscripts from this period are still valuable to textual criticism

and are described later in this book. There are also about three thousand Hebrew manuscripts of the Tiberian tradition that date from the twelfth century on.[40] In 1488 the first complete Hebrew Bible was printed, and in 1516–1517 the first Rabbinic Bible appeared, which included rabbinic commentary. In 1524–1525 the second rabbinic edition was published; it was edited by a Hebrew Christian named Jacob ben Chayyim. This text included the rabbinic notes for the Hebrew text, which are the main reason the text retained such accuracy over centuries of copying.

Final Masorah

One example of these Masoretic notes appears in the final Masorah at the end of the Pentateuch (i.e., at the end of the Book of Deuteronomy). It indicates how meticulous the Masoretes were when copying the Hebrew texts.

סכום הפסוקים של ספר (the total of the verses which are in the book)

תשע מאות (900)

וחמשים וחמשה: (55)

הנ״ן (955)

וחציו ועשית על־פי (the middle of it [the book], namely ועשית על־פי is at Deut. 17:10)

וסדרים לא (the number of sᵉdārîm [divisions] in Deuteronomy are 31)

סכום הפסוקים של תורה (the total of the verses which are in the Torah [or Pentateuch])

חמשת אלפים (5,000)

ושמונה מאות (800)

וארבעים (40)

וחמשה: (5)
הוּ מֹה (5,845)
כל סדרי התורה (all the *sᵉdārîm* of the Torah)
מאה וששים ושבעה: (167)
קסֹז (167)
סכום התיבות של תורה (the total number of words in the Torah)
תשעה ושבעים אלף (97,000)
ושמונה מאות (800)
וחמשים (50)
וששה (6)
סכום האותיות של תורה (the total number of letters in the Torah)
ארבע מאות אלף (400,000)
ותשע מאות וארבעים (945)
וחמשה

This Masorah indicates the number of verses and the middle verse of the Book of Deuteronomy, as well as the number of verses, the number of words, and the number of letters in the Pentateuch. Although this required enormous effort, by counting words and letters in a manuscript inaccuracies would surface that could then be identified.

Chapter Divisions

Chapter divisions were not added until very late in this period; in fact, present-day chapter divisions were first added by Stephen Langton (1150–1228), archbishop of Canterbury, England, to a copy of the Latin Vulgate. They were later transferred to the Hebrew text by Salomon ben Ishmael (c. 1330).[41] Salomon must have adjusted them to some extent because chapter divisions in the English Bible sometimes differ from those in the Hebrew Bible. The Hebrew chapter divisions are generally preferred because several English chapter divisions separate literary units (Gen. 1:1–2:4; Exod. 21:37 [ET 22:1]; Isa. 8:23 [ET 9:1]; Ps. 42–43), sometimes hindering the meaning.

Table 11.3
Notations in the Hebrew Text

Notations	Examples*
1. Dots above doubtful letters	Gen. 16:5; 18:9; 19:33; 33:4; 37:12; Num. 3:39; 9:10; 21:30; 29:15; Deut. 29:28; 2 Sam. 19:20; Isa. 44:9; Ezek. 41:20; 46:22; Ps. 27:13
2. Letter resizings	
a. Enlarged letters	Gen. 1:1 (ב); 30:42 (ף); Exod. 34:14 (ר); Lev. 11:42 (ו); 13:33 (ג); Num. 13:30 (ס); 14:17 (י); 27:5 (נ); Deut. 6:4 (ע and ד); 29:27 (ל); 32:6 (ה)
b. Reduced letters	Gen. 2:4 (ב); 27:46 (ק); Lev. 1:1 (א); Deut. 32:18 (י); Isa. 44:14 (ו); Jer. 39:13 (ו); Prov. 16:28 (ו)
3. Inverted *nûn*	enclosing Num. 10:35–36; preceding Ps. 107:21, 22, 23, 24, 25, 26, 40
4. Suspended letters	Judg. 18:30 (נ); Ps. 80:14 (ע); Job 38:13, 15 (ע)
5. *Sebirin* (suggested emendations)	Gen. 19:23 (יָצְאָה for יָצָא); 49:13 (עַד for עַל)
6. *Kethib* (what is written) and *Qere* (what is to be read)	Gen. 49:10 (שִׁילֹה for שִׁילֹה)
7. Other minor notations	
a. Broken or reduced *wāw*	Num. 25:12 (שָׁלוֹם)
b. Broken *qôp*	Exod. 32:25; Num. 7:2
c. Final *mêm* in medial position	Isa. 9:6 (לְמַרְבֵּה)
d. Non-final *mêm* in final position	Neh. 2:13 (הֵם פְּרוּצִים)

*Not all of the scribal notations listed here are reproduced in modern printed editions of the Hebrew Bible. In *BHS* some notations appear in the text, others are mentioned in the apparatus and masorah (footnotes and marginal notes), and still others are not indicated.

Verse Divisions

Verse divisions were added very early, though there were significant variations according to various scribal centers. Standard verse divisions were set by the Ben Asher family (c. 900) and were indicated by a large colon called a *sôp pāsûq* (:), which means end of the verse. The Old Testament contains 23,100 verses. These end-verse indicators appear in Codex Cairensis (895), the Aleppo Codex (930), Or. 4445 (c. 920–950), and others. The Masoretes also added accents to the text that are generally either conjunctive (i.e., joining words) or disjunctive (i.e., separating words) and were used to denote syntactical relationships between words and clauses, as well as to assist reading the text in unison.

Recent Hebrew Bible

The most recent edition of the Hebrew Masoretic Text is the *Biblia Hebraica Stuttgartensia*, completed in 1977 by a committee of international scholars under the editorship of K. Elliger and W. Rudolph. This work is called a diplomatic edition because it follows the text of one Hebrew manuscript (i.e., the Codex Leningradensis, dated to 1008–9 and in the Ben Asher family, or tradition, which is thought to be the most accurate). We are extremely indebted to generations of scribes whose meticulous work and constant care maintained their sacred traditions and preserved an accurate text, but without any original autographs for comparison, how can the accuracy of these texts be determined? This is where the study of Old Testament textual criticism enters.

Old Testament Textual Criticism

The twentieth century has witnessed a great increase in the number of Hebrew sources available to the textual critic; in fact, many of the sources have been found within the last sixty years (e.g., the Dead Sea Scrolls, Masada manuscripts, Silver Amulets). This means that the Old Testament textual critic is better equipped to answer difficult questions regarding the original text than ever before. In general these manuscripts have revealed that there were three main stages in the development of the Old Testament biblical text:[42] (1) a rather fluid original text to which the scribes added explanations or elaborations at will; (2) a more fixed text to which minor additions and corrections were added for better understanding of the text (e.g., *matres lectionis* ["mothers of reading"]—were Hebrew consonants added to the text before the origination of vowel pointing to aid in pronunciation and understanding; see the discussion earlier in this chapter); and (3) a relatively stabilized text from which any variations were removed.

Even though we do not have any original autographs of the biblical authors, this does not mean there is no way to determine the accuracy of the biblical texts. The many biblical sources that have been discovered can be compared and evaluated to determine the most accurate reading of a text. This is the main goal of Old Testament textual criticism, which can be defined as *the science and art that seeks to determine the most reliable wording of the biblical text*.[43] It is a science because specific rules govern the evaluation of various types of copyist errors and readings, but it is also an art because these rules cannot be rigidly applied in every situation. Intuition and common sense must guide the critic in the process of determining the most plausible reading. Informed judgments about a text depend upon one's familiarity with the types of copyist errors, manuscripts, versions, and their authors.

The importance of Old Testament textual criticism is threefold. First and foremost, it attempts to establish the most reliable reading of the text. Second, in cases where a definitive reading is impossible to determine, it can help to avoid dogmatism. And third, it can help the reader better understand the significance of marginal readings that appear in various Bible translations. Thus the study of Old Testament textual criticism leads to increased confidence in the reliability of the text. Bruce Waltke, formerly Old Testament professor at Regent College in Vancouver, Canada, notes that in the *Biblia Hebraica Stuttgarten-*

sia approximately one textual note appears for every ten words; thus 90 percent of the text is without significant variation.[44] And Shemaryahu Talmon, from the Hebrew University in Jerusalem, asserts, "errors and textual divergences between the versions materially affect the intrinsic message only in relatively few instances."[45] Old Testament textual criticism, therefore, concerns mainly details and discrepancies in relatively insignificant matters.

Collecting the Evidence

In order to evaluate a variant reading, collect as much evidence concerning it as possible. A list of various sources with a description of each appears later in this book, but the following are the main sources:

1. The Masoretic Text (possibly contains very ancient traditions): Scribes maintained this Hebrew text tradition from about the first century until modern times. It derives its name from the Masoretes (c. 500–1000), but they received a tradition that goes back much earlier.
2. The Samaritan Pentateuch (third or second century B.C.): This work is helpful only for the Pentateuch.
3. Qumran manuscripts (250 B.C.–A.D. 50): Every book of the Old Testament except Esther (and possibly Nehemiah) had one or more manuscripts or fragments at Qumran.
4. Other Hebrew manuscripts (e.g., Nash Papyrus, Masada, Murabbaʿat, Cairo Genizah).
5. The Septuagint (250–100 B.C.): A Greek translation of the Old Testament.
6. Other Greek manuscripts (e.g., Aquila, Symmachus, Theodotion).
7. Syriac Peshitta (the traditions possibly date to the first century A.D.).
8. Jewish targums (third to fourth century A.D., but the traditions may go back much earlier).
9. Latin Vulgate (c. A.D. 390–405).

Because these sources are not of equal weight or value for textual criticism, they must be assessed carefully, which leads to the next step.

Evaluating the Evidence

The job of the text critic requires the perceptivity of a private detective in piecing together what steps led up to the present text. Every piece of evidence must be carefully examined before one draws a final conclusion.

Vowel Changes

The first step in resolving textual problems is to determine whether the vowel pointing has been corrupted. Vowel pointing was added late in the history of the text and thus has relatively little value for textual criticism. Identifying incorrect vowel pointing is one of the easiest ways to resolve an apparent corruption. It can be illustrated in English: The letters *b d* could be vocalized as bad, bade, bed, bid, bide, bode, bud, and so on. But in the sentence "John is a *b d* boy" we know that *bad* is most likely the correct word. A more difficult example in Hebrew is the word דבר in Jeremiah 9:21 (ET 9:22),[46] which can be read three ways equally well:

דִּבֶּר (*dibbēr*, "say" or "speak"; MT, NIV, NASB)
"*Say*, 'This is what the LORD declares, "The dead bodies of men will lie like refuse on the open field. . . .""

דָבָר (*dābār*, "word")
"*A word*, 'This is what the LORD declares. . . .'"

דֶּבֶר (*deḇer*, "plague" or "pestilence" [Origen, Lucian]; "death" [Theodotion])
"*Pestilence*, 'This is what the LORD declares. . . .'"

In this case the first choice seems to be most likely since Masoretic tradition, the Latin Vulgate, and the Aramaic targums support this reading.

Simple Copying Mistakes

Even though the scribes who copied the Old Testament were usually professionals who underwent rigorous training and followed strict rules when copying Scripture, there was still the possibility of errors creeping into the text each time that it was copied. Proofreading types of errors occur often enough and are fairly easy to spot, but miscopying a letter is perhaps the most frequent. For example, the Masoretic Text of Isaiah 9:8 (ET 9:9) reads וידעו (*wyd^cw*, and they will know), whereas the first Isaiah Scroll from Qumran (1QIsaª) reads וירעו (*wyr^cw*, and they will be friends). The latter reading makes little sense in context and is probably a mistake. Because of advancements in the area of epigraphy, it is now possible to determine when this change most likely could have occurred. Two or three different scripts were used during the transmission of the biblical text. Some letters of each script are similar and could lead to copyist mistakes, whereas other letters are significantly different and would not. In the example from Isaiah 9:8 (ET 9:9) the ד (*d, dālet*) and ר (*r, rēš*) look very similar in Square script but much less alike in the earlier paleo-Hebrew script (△ *dālet* and ٩ *rēš*); thus, it is most likely that the change occurred after the fourth century B.C., when the text was written in Square script. With the aid of table 6.1 one can examine variants to determine when they may have been incorporated into the text as a result of similar-looking letters.

Other types of mistakes are common to the transmission process, and a text critic should be well acquainted with them so as to be able to spot them more readily. Tables 11.4 and 11.5 describe and give examples of these common copyist errors.

Once we have an understanding of what types of mistakes can be made in the copying process we can better determine which reading is more likely.

Basic Principles for Old Testament Textual Criticism

The principles that must be used to determine which reading is more original are as follows:

1. Manuscripts must be weighed, not counted.
2. Determine which reading would most likely give rise to the others.
3. The more distinctive reading is usually preferable.
4. The shorter reading is generally favored.
5. Determine which reading is most appropriate to the context (examine literary structure, grammatical or spelling errors, historical context).

The first principle is important in that age, accuracy, and a manuscript's relationship to other manuscripts help determine its importance. P. Kyle McCarter of Johns Hopkins University believes that principle 2 is the primary basis for textual criticism and that all the other principles derive from it.[47] The third principle is built on the premise that when a scribe adds something to a text, he will more likely add something he is familiar with or makes sense to him. Thus a reading that at first glance seems hard to understand but after careful thought makes good sense is very possibly an original reading. The fourth principle suggests that a scribe is more likely to add to divine Scriptures (e.g., a clarifying note or explanation) than to remove something. The next step is to determine which reading is most likely the correct one.

Determining the Most Plausible Reading

External Evidence

External evidence (i.e., evidence from outside the text, such as other manuscripts or versions) is particularly important for determining the most plausible reading of a text. Since each of the sources is not of equal weight, however, some rules must be determined to help evaluate more important from the lesser important evidence. The following issues need to be considered, in order of their relative importance to textual criticism:

1. Language of the witness
2. Date of the witness
3. Reliability of the witness
4. Provenance (origin/source) and purpose of the witness
5. Interdependence of the witnesses

Language of the witness. Old Testament text critics are becoming more sophisticated in their evaluations, carefully examining each version to determine the standard deviations of an author in word usage (i.e., comparing how consistently an

Table 11.4
Unintentional Changes in the Hebrew Text

Error	Definition	Possible Examples
1. Mistaken letters	Confusion of similar letters.	Genesis 10:4 cites a race known as the "Dodanim" but 1 Chronicles 1:7 calls them the "Rodanim."
2. Homophony	Substitution of similar sounding words.	Isaiah 9:2 [ET 9:3]—the word לֹא (*lōʾ*, "not") was apparently incorrectly substituted for the word לוֹ (*lô*, "to him" or "to it"). Compare KJV "Thou hast multiplied the nation, and not increased the joy" to NIV "You have enlarged the nation and increased their joy [lit., joy to it]."
3. Haplography	Omission of a letter or word usually due to a similar letter or word in context.	In Judges 20:13 בְּנֵי־בִנְיָמִן (*bᵉnê ḇinyāmin*) is written as בִּנְיָמִן (*binyāmin*).
4. Dittography	A letter or word that has been written twice rather than once.	In Jeremiah 51:3a the word יִדְרֹךְ (*yidrōḵ*, he drew) appears twice.
5. Metathesis	Reversal in order of two letters or words.	In Deuteronomy 31:1 the Masoretic Text reads וַיֵּלֶךְ מֹשֶׁה (*wayyēleḵ mōšeh*, and Moses went), but a manuscript from Qumran (1Q5) has ויכל משה (*wayḵal mōšeh*, And Moses finished).
6. Fusion	Incorrect word division that results in two words joined as one.	Leviticus 16:8: לַעֲזָאזֵל (*laⁱᵃzāʾzēl*, "for Azazel," should be divided into two words לָעֵז אֹזֵל for the "goat of departure" [or "going away"]).
7. Fission	Incorrect word division that results in one word written as two.	Hosea 6:5c: the Masoretic Text reads וּמִשְׁפָּטֶיךָ אוֹר יֵצֵא (*ûmišpāṭeyḵā ʾōr yēṣēʾ*, "and your judgments, light goes forth"), but it should probably read וּמִשְׁפָּטִי כְאוֹר יֵצֵא (*ûmišpāṭî kᵉʾōr yēṣēʾ*, "and my judgment goes forth like light"; see Septuagint).
8. Homoioteleuton	An omission caused by two words or phrases that end similarly.	In 1 Samuel 14:41, a portion is missing from the Masoretic Text that appears in other versions. The Septuagint reads: And Saul said, "O Lord, God of *Israel,* why have you not answered your servant this day? If the iniquity is in me or in my son Jonathan, O Lord, God of Israel, give Urim(?); but if this iniquity is in thy people *Israel,* give Thummin(?)." The words between the two italicized words do not appear in the Masoretic Text, perhaps because the scribe jumped from the first occurrence of the word *Israel* to the third, omitting the words in between.
9. Homoioarchton	An omission caused by two words or phrases that begin similarly.	Genesis 31:18 in the Septuagint may be an example of this omission, for the Masoretic Text reads that Jacob "drove off all his livestock and all his possessions, which *he acquired,* [the cattle that he possessed, which *he acquired*] in Paddan Aram." The words in brackets are missing from the Septuagint.
10. Other omissions	Any other omissions.	The years that Saul reigned are omitted from 1 Samuel 13:1.

author translated a specific Hebrew word into another language), grammar, and sentence structure. Through this type of in-depth comparison they can determine specific translation characteristics and how close a given version is to its *Vorlage* (manuscript from which the scribe copied). Nevertheless, texts written in Hebrew should be given primary importance since translations do not always exactly convey the original.

Date of the witness. Generally the more times a text has been copied, the greater possibility there is for corruption. However, there are those rare exceptions when a copyist or a translator rendered so poor a copy that the texts that derive from it are even worse than older texts copied more often with greater care or skill. Also, because the Masoretic Text was standardized during the first century, texts before this date may contain variant readings that were removed during standardization. For example, some of the readings of the Septuagint or the Old Syriac may include early traditions that furnish important evidence concerning the original reading of the text. This is one reason why the Dead Sea Scrolls, many of which date from before the first century, are so important to textual criticism.

Reliability of the manuscript. Reliability of a manuscript is based on two factors: its textual tradition (most scholars consider the Masoretic Text the most reliable textual tradition to date); and the number of errors it contains. The Dead Sea Scrolls have shown how accurate the Masoretic Text has remained for more than one thousand years, but there are places where variant traditions of the Hebrew text are favored.

Provenance (origin/source) and purpose of the text. When weighing evidence, it is important to understand the background of a manuscript and why it was written. For example, the Samaritan Pentateuch was either written or emended to confirm doctrines sacred to the Samaritans (e.g., Deut. 12:5 identifies "the place the Lord your God will choose" as Gerizim instead of Jerusalem).

Interdependence of witnesses. Some witnesses are interdependent and should be considered a single witness where they agree. This principle comes into play with the Septuagint and the following versions that are in some way dependent on it: Peshitta (later intrusions of Septuagint readings); Old Latin; Vulgate; Sahidic; Bohairic; Ethiopic; Armenian; and Arabic. It is still important to consult these versions since they may be dependent on the Septuagint in general and yet disagree in specific readings. Where a version disagrees with the Septuagint, an original, independent reading may be reflected.[48]

Table 11.5
Intentional Changes in the Hebrew Text

Changes	Examples
1. Changes of rare or unusual usages of words	In Isaiah 39:1 the Masoretic Text uses the word חֲזַק (*ḥāzaq*) with the unusual meaning of "to get well, recuperate," but 1QIsaᵃ changes it to חָיָה (*ḥāyâ*) with the same meaning.
2. Euphemistic changes	"Shame" replaces the Hebrew word for "Baʿal" (cf. 2 Sam. 2:8 [Ishbosheth] with 1 Chron. 8:33 and 9:39 [Ishbaal]).
3. Additions and/or glosses	In Genesis 7:6b the word *flood* is explained by "water upon the earth."
4. Modernizations a. Grammatical b. Spelling c. Pronunciation	Masoretic Text of Psalm 11:1. Paragogic *nûn* (1 Kings 8:38). Masoretic Text of Numbers 11:11.
5. Suppression of incorrect readings	The incorrect reading of 1 Samuel 13:1 in the Masoretic Text is omitted in Codex Vaticanus.

Internal Evidence

Internal evidence (i.e., indications in the text itself that help determine which reading is correct) includes common scribal errors (e.g., haplography, dittography, metathesis), as well as common sentence structures, word usages, and literary structures (e.g., ellipsis [omission of an implied word or phrase]; alphabetic acrostic; chiasm [inverted sequence or crossover of parallel words or phrases—a b b' a' pattern]). Questions of spelling or word usage, for example, may be resolved by examining spelling or usage in the rest of the book or in similar parts of the Old Testament.

The most plausible reading of the text can be decided by weighing the internal and external evidence according to the principles listed above. The following examples demonstrate how the process works.

Genesis 4:8 reads as follows in the Hebrew Bible:

> And Cain told Abel his brother. And it came about when they were in the field, that Cain rose up against Abel his brother and killed him.

Internal evidence suggests that something is missing from this verse because we are not told what Cain said to Abel. The next step is to see whether any external evidence suggests what has dropped out. In this case there is a significant amount of external evidence—the Septuagint, Syriac Peshiṭta, Latin Vulgate, the Samaritan Pentateuch, and two targums (Targum Yerušalmi I and the Fragmentary Targum) include the phrase "Let us go into the field," resulting in the reading, "And Cain told Abel his brother, 'Let us go into the field.'" Adding this phrase goes against the fourth principle that the shorter reading is preferable, but in this case many witnesses and the logic of the passage suggest that something has fallen out.

Psalm 145 is an alphabetic acrostic psalm wherein each successive line begins with a new letter of the Hebrew alphabet. However, there is no line for the letter *nûn* (n) in the Hebrew Bible (Masoretic Text), so that internal evidence suggests a problem in this passage. External evidence indicates that several different versions and manuscripts (Dead Sea Scroll mss., Septuagint, and Syriac Peshiṭta) include the following line beginning with a *nûn*: "The Lord is faithful in all his promises and merciful towards all his works." This line may have been omitted due to *homoioarchton* (i.e., similarity between the beginning of two words or lines causing one of them to be left out). In this case verse 13 would have begun with the phrase "*the* LORD *is faithful*" and verse 14 with "*the* LORD *upholds all who are fallen*"; it is plausible that the copyist skipped verse 13 because the word LORD appeared in both phrases. The corrected reading is most likely:

> Your kingdom is an everlasting kingdom,
> and your dominion endures through all generations.
>
> *The* LORD *is faithful to all his promises and loving toward all he has made.*
>
> The LORD upholds all those who fall and lifts up all who are bowed down. (Ps. 145:13–14)

For Further Reading

Brotzman, E. R. *Old Testament Textual Criticism: A Practical Introduction.* Grand Rapids: Baker, 1994.

Klein, R. W. *Textual Criticism of the Old Testament: The Septuagint after Qumran.* GBS. Philadelphia: Fortress, 1974.

McCarter, P. K. *Textual Criticism: Recovering the Text of the Hebrew Bible.* GBS. Philadelphia: Fortress, 1986.

Orlinsky, H. M. "The Textual Criticism of the Old Testament." In *The Bible and the Ancient Near East*, edited by G. E. Wright, 113–32. Garden City, NY: Doubleday, 1961; reprint, Winona Lake, IN: Eisenbrauns, 1979.

Payne, D. F. "Old Testament Textual Criticism: Its Principles and Practice." *Tyn Bul* 25 (1974): 99–112.

Roberts, B. J. *The Old Testament Text and Version: The Hebrew Text in Transmission and the History of Ancient Versions*. Cardiff: University of Wales Press, 1951.

———. "The Textual Transmission of the Old Testament." In *Tradition and Interpretation*, edited by G. W. Anderson, 1–30. Oxford: Clarendon, 1979.

Talmon, S. "The Old Testament Text." In *CHB*, 1:159–99; reprinted in *Qumran and the History of the Biblical Text*, edited by F. M. Cross and S. Talmon, 1–41. Cambridge, MA: Harvard University Press, 1975.

Thompson, J. A. "Textual Criticism, OT." In *IDBSup*, 886–91.

Tov, E. *Textual Criticism of the Hebrew Bible*. Minneapolis: Fortress; Assen and Maastricht: Van Gorcum, 1992.

———. "The Text of the Old Testament." In *Bible Handbook*, vol. 1, *The World of the Bible*, edited by A. S. van der Woude, translated by S. Woudstra, 156–90. Grand Rapids: Eerdmans, 1986.

Waltke, B. K. "The Textual Criticism of the Old Testament." In *Biblical Criticism: Historical, Literary, and Textual*, by R. K. Harrison et al., 47–82. Grand Rapids: Zondervan, 1978. Also found in *The Expositor's Bible Commentary*, edited by F. E. Gaebelein, 1:211–28. 12 vols. Grand Rapids: Zondervan, 1979.

Yeivin, I. *Introduction to the Tiberian Masorah*. Translated and edited by E. J. Revell. SBLMasS 5. Missoula, MT: Scholars Press, 1980.

Sources for Old Testament Textual Criticism

Primary Sources: Hebrew Manuscripts

Silver Amulets

The oldest known Old Testament texts extant are the Silver Amulets (see fig. 12.1) dated by the excavator, Gabriel Barkay, to about the mid-seventh century B.C.[1] Amulets were worn as charms against evil or injury; the Silver Amulets were probably worn on a necklace or a bracelet. These amulets were found in 1985 in a grave near the St. Andrew's Church of Scotland, Jerusalem, about a mile south of the old city walls. They are made of thin, rolled-up silver sheets, the larger measuring about 4 inches long by 1 inch wide and the smaller only about 1 and 1/2 inches long by 1/2 inch wide. They bear a copy of the priestly benediction similar to Numbers 6:22–27 in the Masoretic Text, which says: "The LORD bless you and keep you; the LORD make his face shine upon you and be gracious unto you; the LORD turn his face toward you and give you peace."

The Samaritan Pentateuch (ﬡ)

Brief History of the Samaritans

The Samaritans claim to be the descendants of the northern tribes of Ephraim and Manasseh, following their destruction by the Assyrians in 722 B.C. When the northern kingdom fell, a relatively small number of Israelites (27,290) were exiled to Assyria, and those who remained probably considered themselves to be the true remnant of Israel. The Assyrians replaced the Israelite exiles with Assyrians from other parts of their kingdom, and these people intermarried with the Jews to become the race known as the Samaritans.[2] Initially the Samaritans worshiped their foreign gods, but later they renounced those gods and worshiped only Yahweh. The Judean kings Hezekiah and Josiah tried unsuccessfully to reunite the northern and southern kingdoms via a return to the worship of Yahweh in Jerusalem (2 Chron. 30:1–27; 35:17–18). Sometime following the return of the exiles from Babylon in 538 B.C., a schism developed between the Jews and the Samaritans. However, Samaritan history claims that this schism occurred more than 500 years earlier, when Eli moved the sanctuary from Shechem to Shiloh and established an illegitimate priesthood and place of worship, resulting in an era of disfavor that would last until the coming of the Taheb, or savior.[3] It is questionable whether the schism occurred this early, but signs of growing animosity between these two groups date from as early as the time of the return of the Israelites in the late sixth century B.C. (Ezra 4; Neh. 2:10, 19; 4:1–14) and are confirmed in the books of Maccabees (1 Macc. 3:10; 2 Macc. 6:1–2) and in Josephus (*Ant*. 12.4.1 §§154–57; 11.4.9 §§114–19; 20.6.1 §§118–24). By the New Testament period they were unquestionably separate groups (John 4:20–24).[4] When the Samaritans were not allowed to help the Israelites rebuild the temple after their return from Babylon, they finally decided to build their own temple on Gerizim about 400 B.C. This is what the woman at the well meant when she said "our fathers worshiped on this mountain"

1

2

Figure 12.1.
A picture of the Silver Amulets, which are dated to about the mid-seventh century B.C. [Israel Antiquities Authority]

185

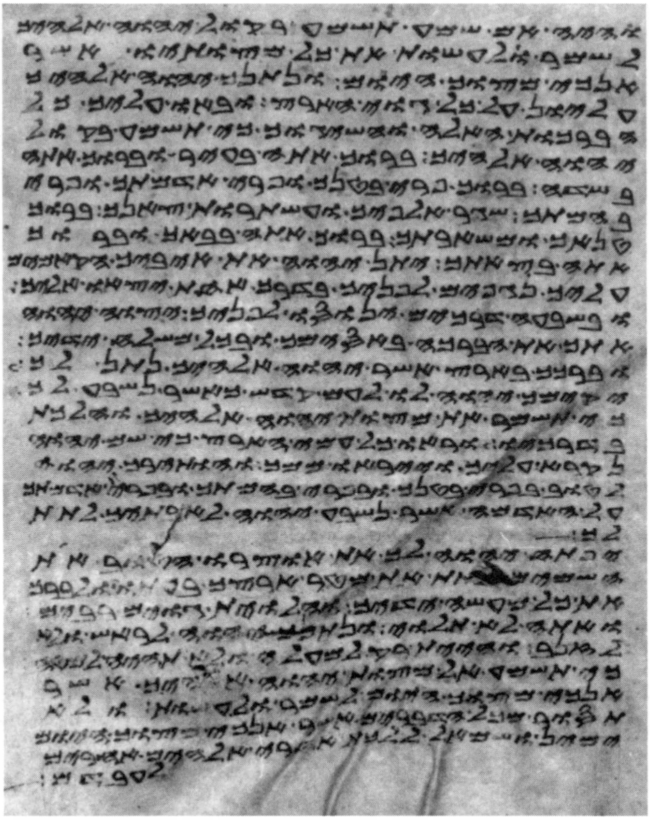

Figure 12.2.
A portion of
Deuteronomy
28 from the
Samaritan Penta-
teuch (Nablus?,
13th cent.).
[Grand Haven,
Mich., The Scrip-
torium, VK MS
540]

there are also several significant expansions of the text (e.g., in Exod. 14:12 after the Israelites complain to Moses that they would have been better off in Egypt, the question "Is this not what we said to you in Egypt?" appears in the Samaritan Pentateuch but not in the Masoretic Text). Sectarian differences color portions of the Samaritan Pentateuch. For example, in Genesis 22:2 Abraham builds an altar to offer up Isaac on Mount Moreh near Shechem, a chief place of worship for the Samaritans, instead of Mount Moriah as in the Masoretic Text. In the Samaritan Pentateuch of Deuteronomy 12:5, Moses says they are to worship at "the place where Yahweh has chosen" (meaning Mount Gerizim) instead of the future tense as in the Masoretic Text: "the place where the LORD your God will choose" (meaning Jerusalem). Copies of the Samaritan Pentateuch are written in a paleo-Hebrew script that appears to be older than the Aramaic or Square script used by the Hebrews. This script, somewhat similar to that found on the Moabite stone, the Siloam inscription, and the Lachish letters with the addition of a great deal of ornamentation, was probably retained to legitimate the Samaritans' claim of having preceded the Jewish nation (see fig. 12.2). The Samaritan Pentateuch is valuable for the study of Old Testament textual criticism since it is a separate tradition from an early period, but its sectarian tendencies must also be considered when dealing with a text that may be affected by those views.

whereas the Jews worship in Jerusalem (John 4:20).

During the second century B.C., the Hasmoneans attempted to expand their borders northward and under John Hyrcanus in 108 B.C. extended Jewish domination over the Samaritans, causing the Samaritans' hatred of the Jews to increase.

The Samaritan Pentateuch

The Samaritans accepted only the Pentateuch as authoritative Scripture and the Samaritan Pentateuch differs from the Masoretic Text in about six thousand places. However, most points of disagreement are minor spelling or grammatical changes, and a least sixteen hundred of them agree with the Septuagint.[5] The Samaritan Pentateuch tends toward harmonization (to bring into accord with the Masoretic Text) or conflation (to combine readings from two manuscripts),[6] but

The Dead Sea Scrolls (DSS)

In 1947 an Arab shepherd boy was looking for a lost goat in caves in the Judean desert on the west side of the Dead Sea when he chanced upon some of the first Dead Sea Scrolls (often called the Qumran scrolls). He was throwing rocks into the caves to see if the goat was there, and instead he heard the breaking of pottery. The sound frightened him and he ran away, but later he returned to examine the caves and found the broken pots containing manuscripts. The discovery of several other ancient manuscripts from Qumran shook the scholarly world: one was the Isaiah Scroll (1QIsaᵃ; fig. 12.3) and another the Habakkuk Commentary (1QpHab). The scholars at the American School of Oriental Research realized immediately that these scrolls were older than any Old Testament manuscripts to date. At least eleven caves in the vicinity of Qumran (about seven miles south of Jericho; see map 2) held manuscripts of all the biblical books (usually many copies) except Esther and Nehemiah. The dates of these manuscripts range from about 250 B.C. to A.D. 50.

Until 1947 the oldest complete Hebrew manuscript of the Old Testament was the text of Codex Leningradensis (Leningrad Public Library Ms. B 19ᴬ), dated to 1008–9, though there were portions of the Old Testament from possibly a century earlier. The Dead Sea Scrolls provided texts of the Old Testament approximately one thousand years earlier, and their impact was explo-

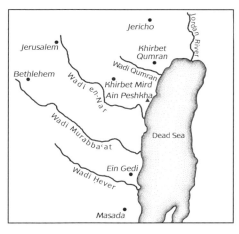

Map 2. The area around Qumran, where scrolls of the Old Testament were found.

sive on the field of textual criticism. Careful study of these manuscripts has helped to confirm that the Hebrew text we possess is very accurate; differences are minimal between a good number of the Dead Sea Scroll manuscripts and manuscripts from about A.D. 800 to 1000. However, even the Dead Sea Scrolls reveal a certain amount of diversity in the text of the Old

Figure 12.3. The Isaiah Scroll from Qumran. [John C. Trever]

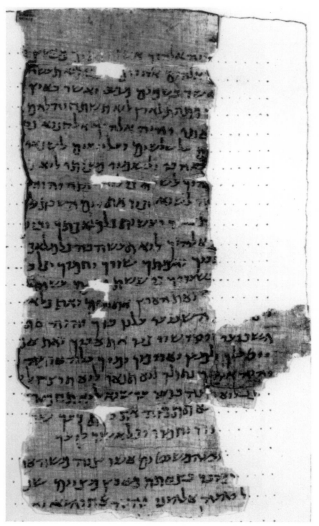

Figure 12.4.
A portion of the Nash Papyrus. [Cambridge University Library]

England, and donated by him to the Cambridge University library (fig. 12.4). This work was dated by paleographic evidence to the Maccabean period (169–37 B.C.) by William F. Albright;[7] Paul Kahle dates it before the destruction of the temple (i.e., A.D. 70) according to internal evidence.[8] It contains Exodus 20:2–17 (see also the parallel passage of Deut. 5:6–21, where some of the variants may have been derived) and the *Shema*ᶜ ("Hear, O Israel, the LORD our God, the LORD is one") from Deuteronomy 6:4. This combination of texts suggests that it was not part of a biblical scroll but rather a collection of texts used for another purpose, similar to the messianic anthology found in Cave 4 at Qumran (fig. 12.5). It is interesting that the sixth and seventh commandments are reversed and that the *Shema*ᶜ (שְׁמַע, *sᵉma*ᶜ, hear) begins with a word confirmed only by the Septuagint text.

Murabbaᶜat Manuscripts (Mur)

In the autumn of 1951, some bedouins from the Taamireh tribe came to Joseph Saad at the Palestine Archaeological (Rockefeller) Museum with a piece of a leather sandal and a scroll fragment that they had found in a cave located in the Wadi Murabbaᶜat (or Darajeh), about eleven miles south of Cave 1 at Qumran. Four caves are situated on a sheer vertical cliff about two hundred feet above the bottom of the wadi (fig. 12.6). The caves could not be excavated properly until January 1952 and even then proved to be one of the most difficult excavations in Israel due to the inaccessibility of the caves, fear of their collapse, and problems with lighting. The documents come almost exclusively from Cave 2. One of the more interesting finds was a letter from Simon bar Kochba, the leader of the second Jewish revolt (A.D. 132–135), to his official, Joshua ben Golgoula, in charge of the Murabbaᶜat outpost.

Several small fragments from the books of Genesis, Exodus, Numbers, Deuteronomy, and Isaiah were found in Cave 2, as well as the oldest papyrus document ever found in Israel. The most complete text

Testament in the centuries right before Christ. Some texts found near Qumran appear to follow more closely the Samaritan Pentateuch (4QpaleoExodᵐ; 4QNumᵇ), others tend toward the Septuagint (4QJerᵇ), and still others reflect the Masoretic Text.

The Nash Papyrus (Pap. Nash)

The Nash Papyrus is a damaged copy of the Decalogue (Ten Commandments) acquired in 1902 from a native Egyptian dealer by W. L. Nash, then the secretary of the Society of Biblical Archaeology in

from the Murabbaᶜat caves is a scroll of the Minor Prophets (Mur. 88, containing ten of the twelve Minor Prophets) that is written in Hebrew and is dated to the second century. This document was found by bedouins in a small cave on the other side of the wadi and was sold to the Palestinian Archaeological Museum for £2,200 (approximately $5,500). Because all the manuscripts found at Wadi Murabbaᶜat

Figure 12.5. A picture of Cave 4 at Qumran, which held fragments from about 600–800 scrolls. [Paul Wegner]

Figure 12.6. The Murabbaᶜat caves. [Israel Antiquities Authority]

are virtually identical to the Masoretic Text (e.g., only three meaningful variants in the scroll of the Minor Prophets), they help to confirm that by the second century the Masoretic Text was stabilized.[9]

Manuscripts at Masada (Mas)

Masada is located on a large plateau about two-thirds of the way down the western shore of the Dead Sea.[10] The site is a natural fortification whose sides are sheer cliffs measuring thirteen hundred feet in certain spots. Herod constructed a palace on Masada about 36–30 B.C. with a beautiful three-layered palace on its northern edge (fig. 12.7).

Later, during the first Jewish revolt (A.D. 66–73), a group of zealots captured Masada and held it until 73, three years after the fall of Jerusalem. The Jewish zealots used guerrilla warfare tactics to harass Roman troops and then fled to Masada for protection. In 72, Flavius Silva led the Tenth Legion against the zealots at Masada. He used Jewish prisoners to build a ramp up the side of Masada, since he knew that the zealots would not kill their own relatives. The Roman army breached the fortifications of the zealots in April 73, and Silva planned the final attack on Masada the following day. However, during the night the zealots committed suicide rather than give in to the Romans.

During the excavations on Masada in 1963–1965, the remains of fourteen scrolls, including biblical, sectarian, and apocryphal texts, were discovered. They are clearly dated before 73, when the fortress was stormed by the Romans. The biblical texts found at Masada come from Genesis, Leviticus, Deuteronomy, Psalms, and Ezekiel.

Manuscripts at Naḥal Ḥever [Wadi Habra] (Ḥev)

Naḥal Ḥever is located about one mile south of Ein Gedi on the western shore of the Dead Sea (see map 2) where in 1952 several fragmentary manuscripts of Genesis, Numbers, Deuteronomy, and Psalms were discovered. However, the most complete

Figure 12.7. A photograph of Masada with an inset of the palace on the northern end of the plateau. [Paul Wegner and Random House, Inc.]

Figure 12.8. A fragment of Zech. 1:1–4a in Greek from the scroll of the Minor Prophets found at Naḥal Ḥever. The fourth and the last lines (far left) show the divine name written in paleo-Hebrew script. [Israel Antiquities Authority]

discovery was a Greek manuscript of the Minor Prophets (8 HevXIIgr; fig. 12.8).

This Greek text is unusual in that the tetragrammaton (the name of the four Hebrew consonants YHWH) is written in ancient paleo-Hebrew script. These texts, along with two phylactery fragments of Exodus 13:2–16 from Naḥal Ṣeʾelim,[11] are dated to about 130 and are virtually identical to the Masoretic Text.

Genizah Fragments (ℭ)

The Cairo Genizah was a storage room located in the attic of the Ben-Ezra Synagogue, which was built in 1015 in Fostat, or Old Cairo.[12] It was a room of moderate dimensions without doors or windows; by climbing a ladder one could enter through a hole in the western wall.[13] This genizah was discovered sometime in the 1860s, though at first only small fragments were removed and found their way to Russia or England, their provenance being unknown. In 1890, when the Ben-Ezra Synagogue was renovated, many manuscripts and fragments were sold to travelers who then brought them to Europe. It has been estimated that about two hundred thousand fragments of a wide variety of mate-

rials were deposited in this hidden storeroom;[14] most fragments date from about 1000 to 1400, though some are centuries earlier. Several dozen of these manuscripts are palimpsests, about 15 percent of which are biblical texts found in Hebrew, Aramaic, and Arabic translations. Among the most important items discovered were the following:

1. An almost complete copy of the Wisdom of Jesus ben Sirach in Hebrew (previous to this discovery the work was only known from Greek texts)
2. The Zadokite Document (now generally known as the Damascus Document [CD])
3. Biblical documents, some of which date to the fifth century and shed new light upon the development of the pointing system

Two scholars took particular interest in these manuscripts. The first, Elkan Nathan Adler, son of the chief rabbi, visited Cairo and was allowed to remove a Torah cover full of fragments which he then took to England. The second scholar, Solomon Schechter, who at that time was reader of Rabbinics at Cambridge Uni-

Figure 12.9. Solomon Schechter examining the Cairo Genizah manuscripts in the Cambridge University library. [Cambridge University Library]

versity, went to Cairo in December of 1896 with a letter of introduction from the Cambridge University library; the head of the Ben-Ezra Synagogue allowed him to bring back whatever manuscripts he chose. He decided to take only handwritten, not printed, manuscripts, which he believed to be most important; however, even these amounted to well over one hundred thousand (fig. 12.9). Many of these fragments came to be housed at the Cambridge University library, but other institutions also have sizable collections, such as the Jewish Theological Seminary of New York, the Bodleian Library of Oxford, the British Museum in London, the John Rylands Library in Manchester, and the Saltykor-Shchedrin Public Library of Leningrad.

Several Early Ben Asher Manuscripts of the Old Testament

From the second half of the eighth century to the mid-tenth century, the ben Asher family played a leading role in recording and maintaining the Masoretic Text at Tiberias.[15] Several extant ben Asher manuscripts provide important examples of this tradition.

Codex Cairensis (C)

This manuscript, containing only the Former and Latter Prophets, appears to have been written and pointed by Moses ben Asher in Tiberias for a Karaite Jew, Yabes ben Shelomo, in 895. The codex is very well preserved, probably due to the fact that it was revered and protected by the Karaite Synagogue of Cairo (al-Kahira).

Aleppo Codex (A)

Dated to the first half of the tenth century this manuscript originally contained the complete Old Testament, but during anti-Jewish riots in Aleppo in 1947 and 1948, one quarter of it was destroyed (Gen. 1:1–Deut. 28:16; Song 3:12 to the end). Its colophon states that Aaron ben Moses ben Asher wrote the pointing and the Masorah about 930, but that Shelomo ben Buyaa copied the consonantal text. During the Crusades (July 15, 1099) it was taken as booty but about seven years later was returned to the Karaites, who then brought it to the Karaite community in Cairo. It is now being used in Jerusalem by the Hebrew University as the basis for another critical edition of the Old Testament.

Oriental 4445

This manuscript contains 186 folios (a folio is a folded sheet of paper yielding two pages of a book) of the Pentateuch, namely,

Genesis 39:20–Deuteronomy 1:33. However, 55 of these folios were added by a later hand and are dated about 1540. The remaining 129 folios reflect an early form of the ben Asher text dated about 950.[16] They are written in very large, bold handwriting, including the consonants, full Palestinian or Western vowel points, and accents but no verse dividers (sôp pāsûq [:]) at the end of sentences. Each page is divided into three columns with the left edge of each column differing in length. The Masorahs (textual remarks), both Magna (generally at the bottom of the page) and Parva (generally along the side), have been added later than the

Figure 12.10. Deut. 28:17–45 from Codex Leningradensis (c. A.D. 1008). [National Library of Russia]

original writing. This manuscript is currently housed at the British Museum.

Codex Leningradensis (Leningrad Ms. B 19ᴬ; L)

This text (see fig. 12.10), an important witness to the ben Asher family, is dated to about 1008 by a colophon.[17] Another colophon states:

> Samuel ben Jacob wrote and pointed and provided with Masora this codex of the Holy Scriptures from the corrected and annotated books prepared by Aaron ben Moses ben Asher the teacher, may he rest in the Garden of Eden! It has been corrected and properly annotated.[18]

This manuscript was the main source for the most recent critical Hebrew texts (*Biblia Hebraica*, edited by R. Kittel [1929–1937] and *Biblia Hebraica Stuttgartensia*, edited by K. Elliger and W. Rudolph [1967–1977]) and it was chosen because older manuscripts were unavailable at the time.

Secondary Sources: Languages Other Than Hebrew

Greek versions can be particularly helpful to the Old Testament text critic because some are very early; a large portion of the Jewish nation used them during a key period in the transmission of the Old Testament; and they are probably the *Vorlage* (manuscript from which the scribe copied) for many of the non-Greek versions. A few of the non-Greek versions also have significant importance (e.g., Aramaic targums, Syriac versions, and the Latin Vulgate) and may contain reliable readings. The Old Testament text critic needs to be aware of the relationship of some of these non-Greek versions to the Septuagint when determining the importance of certain readings.

Historically, secondary sources were considered of prime importance in determining the original text of the Old Testament, but with the discovery of many Hebrew manuscripts in the twentieth cen-

tury the value of secondary sources to Old Testament textual criticism has diminished. Also secondary sources must be used with great caution. A careful evaluation of each ancient source is important since they differ greatly in quality and purpose, factors described by B. K. Waltke:

> Just as the great variety of English Bibles reflects the philosophies and abilities of the translators, so also the variants in the ancient MSS reflect the philosophies and the abilities of the scribes who produced them. The scribes were further influenced in their attitudes toward the transmission of the text by their own time and place in history. Similar differences characterize the sources of information that are available to modern textual scholarship.[19]

Each copy of a manuscript is dependent upon the accuracy of the original manuscript being copied and the ability of the scribe to reproduce it. Knowledge about the author of a secondary translation is even more important, since he was not merely a copyist but produced the text. The more familiar one is with the secondary sources, the better one understands the philosophy, purpose, and plausible changes that each of the authors could have introduced.

The Septuagint (LXX)

The Septuagint is a Greek translation of the Old Testament from between 250–100 B.C. The name *Septuagint* comes from the Latin word *septuaginta*, meaning "seventy," and its abbreviation, LXX, is the Roman numeral for seventy. This abbreviation probably derives from the *Letter of Aristeas*, which states that 72 Jewish scholars wrote the Pentateuch in 72 days (the number is rounded off to seventy) on the island of Pharos, Egypt. This pseudepigraphal letter[20] purports to give the history of the Septuagint, though scholars have questioned some of its details. It is said to be written by Aristeas, a royal official, to his brother Philocrates and states that King Ptolemy Philadelphus of Egypt (285–246 B.C.) wanted to assemble a great library, collecting books from all over the known world. F. F. Bruce says that "Ptolemy was renowned as a patron of literature and it was under him that the great library of Alexandria, one of the world's cultural wonders for 900 years, was inaugurated."[21] Demetrius, his librarian, informed him that the Jewish law was indeed worthy to be placed in his library but first would have to be translated into Greek. An Egyptian delegation was sent to Jerusalem to inform the Jewish high priest, Eleazer, of the plan. When Eleazer heard of it, he was pleased to send to Egypt an accurate copy of the Hebrew law written in gold letters, along with seventy-two rabbis (six from each of the twelve tribes) for the translation project, whose work was accepted with joy by the Jewish community. R. W. Klein describes how these details were exaggerated over time:

> Later, as this story was retold in the early church, it got "better and better." According to Justin Martyr, the translation included the whole Old Testament. Later in the second century Irenaeus reports that the translators worked in isolation but came up with identical results, thanks to the inspiration of God. Finally, Epiphanius of Salamis (314–403) pushed the isolation idea to the limit. He had the translators do everything in pairs, even going by thirty-six boats each night to dine with the king. When the thirty-six independent translations were read before the king, they were found to be completely identical.[22]

Modern scholars usually consider the *Letter of Aristeas* a legendary account written about 100 B.C. to enhance the status of the Septuagint. Jesus ben Sirach, in his prologue to Ecclesiasticus (c. 132 B.C.), implies that a great deal of the Old Testament, if not all of it, was available in Greek.[23]

Historically the Septuagint had an important influence on both Jews and Christians. As the Greek language was disseminated throughout the ancient Near East by the conquests of Alexander the Great, it became more and more important to have the Scriptures in a language that the people could understand. Bruce notes that "[b]y the early years of the Christian era we are told that there were

almost a million Jews in Egypt, that two out of the five wards of Alexandria were known as Jewish districts, and that others were scattered throughout the remaining three wards."[24] Jewish immigrants living in the cosmopolitan city of Alexandria were forced by their situation to abandon their native language, but the translation of their laws into Greek was one way to help maintain their faith. The Septuagint became so popular that increasingly it was seen as the standard form of the Old Testament and subsequently was adopted by Christians. By the late fourth century, Augustine even demanded that Jerome use its order of books for his translation rather than the Hebrew.[25]

It is interesting that a work which the Jewish people originally esteemed so highly should eventually be rejected and condemned by them. This drastic change came about at least partly because the Septuagint increasingly became a sacred book for Christians, who used it to propagate Christian teaching. One example of a passage that supports the Christian teaching is Isaiah 7:14, where the word παρθένος (*parthenos*) is sometimes translated "virgin." It was used by Christians as strong evidence of their views about the virgin birth of Jesus (Matt. 1:23). Also, as the scribes began to accept the authoritative, standardized text of the Masoretic Text, the Septuagint, which was not based upon this text, was necessarily condemned.

Manuscripts of the Septuagint

Codex Vaticanus (B, 03; Vatican Library, Cod. Gr. 1209). This codex, probably from the fourth century, originally contained all the books of the Bible, but today portions are missing (Gen. 1:1–46:28a; 2 Sam. 2:5–7, 10–13; Ps. 105 [106]:27–137 [138]:6b; Maccabees; and in the New Testament from Heb. 9:14 on). There are 759 leaves (617, Old Testament; 142, New Testament), each page bearing three columns written in black ink on vellum (calfskin[26]). This codex is known to have existed in the Vatican library since 1475 or 1481,[27] thus its name, but initially the Vatican discouraged work on it. At the beginning of the nineteenth century

Napoleon carried off this codex to Paris with other manuscripts as a war prize, but upon his death in 1815 it was returned to the Vatican library. Constantin von Tischendorf (1815–1874) applied for permission to see the manuscript in order to collate difficult passages and was finally allowed to see it. He copied out or remembered enough of the text so as to be able to publish an edition of the Codex Vaticanus in 1867. Later in that century (1868–1881) the Vatican published a better copy of the codex, but in 1889/90 a complete photographic facsimile of this manuscript superseded any of the earlier attempts.

Codex Sinaiticus (ℵ or S, 01; B.M. Add. 43725). This codex, dated to the fourth century (fig. 12.11), includes part of the Old Testament and the Old Testament Apocrypha,[28] as well as all of the New Testament with two additions: part of the *Shepherd of Hermas* and the *Epistle of Barnabas*. It is written on vellum, four columns per page, with no breaks between words, no accents, and no breathing marks. This codex was discovered by Tischendorf in the middle of the nineteenth century at Saint Catherine's Monastery at the foot of Mount Sinai, hence the name Sinaiticus. Having been discovered after other Greek codices had been assigned letters of the English alphabet, it is designated by the first letter of the Hebrew alphabet, ℵ (*ʾālep*).

The history of Tischendorf's search for manuscripts is fascinating. In 1844 Tischendorf, a beginning lecturer at the University of Leipzig, was in the Near East looking for biblical manuscripts. While studying in the library of Saint Catherine's Monastery, he saw a basket of stray pages written in the oldest Greek he had ever seen. Upon further examination, they proved to be forty-three leaves of the Septuagint written in early Greek uncial script. The librarian said that the monks had already burned two baskets of similar material in the monastery furnace. Tischendorf was allowed to keep the forty-three leaves. In 1853 he revisited Saint Catherine's in hopes of finding more manuscripts, without success. Six years later, in 1859, he returned under the patronage of the czar of Russia, Alexander II, official protector of the Greek church, and by accident came across the manuscript later to be called Sinaiticus, a fourth-century uncial manuscript in perfect condition. F. G. Kenyon recounts the story:

> only a few days before he was to depart, in the course of conversation with the steward of the monastery, he showed him a copy of his recently published edition of the Septuagint. Thereupon the steward remarked that he too had a copy of the Septuagint, which he would like to show to his visitor. Accordingly he took him to his room, and produced a heap of loose leaves wrapped in a cloth; and there before the astonished scholar's eyes lay the identical manuscript for which he had been longing. Not only was part of the Old Testament there, but the New Testament, complete from beginning to end. Concealing his feelings, he asked to be allowed to keep it in his room that evening to examine it; leave was given, "and that night it seemed sacrilege to sleep."[29]

After an unsuccessful attempt to purchase the manuscript, Tischendorf returned to Cairo to speak with the abbot of Saint Catherine's monastery. After careful negotiations and the assistance of the czar, who as protector of the Greek church would help determine the next abbot of the monastery at Saint Catherine's, Tischendorf received the manuscript as a gift from the monks. In 1862, Codex Sinaiticus was published for the first time by its discoverer, and on Christmas Day 1933 the British Museum bought the manuscript from Russia for £100,000 (approximately half a million dollars). The Russian government was in need of money, not Bibles.

J. H. Ropes describes the quality of this codex: "Codex Sinaiticus is carelessly written, with many lapses of spelling due to the influence of dialectal and vulgar speech, and many plain errors and crude vagaries. Omissions by homoeoteleuton abound, and there are many other careless omissions. All these gave a large field for the work of correctors, and the manuscript does not stand by any means on the same level of workmanship as B."[30]

Codex Alexandrinus (A, 02; Royal MS 1 D V–VIII). This vellum codex of the Bible, generally dated to the middle of the fifth century, was the first great uncial made accessible to scholars (fig. 12.12). It includes the standard Old Testament books, as well as 3 and 4 Maccabees, Psalm 151, and the *Psalms of Solomon.* The order of the Old Testament is unusual in that the twelve Minor Prophets precede the Book of Isaiah. The New Testament books are followed by *1* and *2 Clement,* but once again the order is slightly unusual in that the Catholic Epis-

tles precede the Pauline Epistles. Now, however, most of Matthew (1:1–26:6), part of John (6:50–8:52), and 2 Corinthians 4:13–12:6 are missing. According to the table of contents, the *Psalms of Solomon* appeared at the end of this work but was lost along with the final portion of *2 Clement* (from 12.4 on). The text has two columns per page, written in large, square uncial writing without accents, breathing marks, or punctuation. The text has been corrected many times in the margin, sometimes by the original hand and sometimes

Figure 12.11.
John 21:1b–25
from Codex
Sinaiticus (fourth
century).
[British Library]

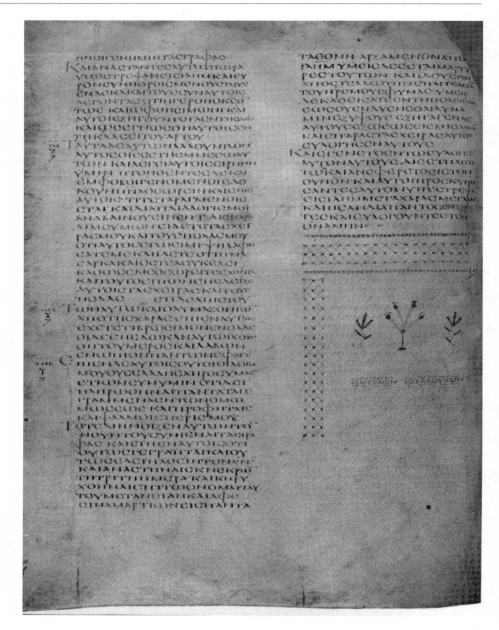

Figure 12.12.
Luke 24:33–47
from Codex
Alexandrinus
(fifth century).
[British Library]

by a later hand, which suggests that it was compared with other manuscripts.

In 1627 Cyril Lucar, patriarch of Constantinople (1621–1638), offered this manuscript to the English ambassador to Turkey, Sir Thomas Roe, as a gift to King James I. However, it came to England after King James had died and was instead presented to Charles I of England. Lucar probably obtained Codex Alexandrinus while he was patriarch of Alexandria (1602–1621), hence its name. The codex was housed first in the Royal Library, but in 1757 it was incorporated into the British Museum in London.

Importance of the Septuagint

Christians used this work extensively in their study of the Old Testament. Most

New Testament quotations of the Old Testament are taken from the Septuagint, especially in Luke and Hebrews. The Septuagint and other Greek translations of the Old Testament provide excellent sources of comparison with the Masoretic Text and occasionally offer significant improvements over it (see example of Ps. 145:13, end of chap. 11). Caution against emending too freely from the Septuagint (as was done in previous generations) should be exercised, since evidence from the Dead Sea Scrolls indicates that the Masoretic Text is highly reliable. The illustration from Psalm 145:13, however, suggests that it is possible to determine a form of the Hebrew text before its standardization.

Other Greek Translations

As Christians increasingly used the Septuagint for their Scriptures in defense of their faith, the Jews out of necessity began to distance themselves from it. Jewish leaders realized, however, that the people in the Dispersion needed Scriptures in a language that they could understand. As a result, in the second century several new Greek translations were rendered, accurately translating the Hebrew text so that they could be used in controversies with Christians.

Aquila (ἀ [Aqu])

Aquila was a Christian proselyte (a new convert) from Sinope in Pontus on the Black Sea. He was later converted to Judaism and became a disciple of Rabbi Akiba.[31] About 130 he produced a literal Greek translation that followed the Hebrew text so closely that the Greek often suffered. For instance, he used a single Greek word for each Hebrew root with all its nominal and verbal derivatives (forms of words related by similar roots). Even the Hebrew definite direct object marker (אֵת, ʾet), which is commonly left untranslated, is indicated by the article or the Greek word *syn* (σύν, with, together with) followed by the accusative case (grammatical case marking the direct object).[32]

S. Jellicoe classifies the work as essentially a teacher's book, aimed at giving an exact rendering of the Hebrew and usable only by one who already understood that language. Its function was interpretive rather than literary.[33] This literal rendering of the Hebrew text earned considerable authority among Aquila's Jewish contemporaries and also became valuable for Old Testament textual criticism. R. W. Klein describes Aquila's motivation in rendering his translation: "Aquila seems to have been motivated in part by a desire to expunge certain readings in the LXX which were being used by Christians for apologetic purposes. A classic example is his use of a word meaning 'young woman' instead of LXX's 'virgin' in Isa. 7:14."[34]

This work has been largely lost, but some of its readings can be determined from fragments of Origen's Hexapla, marginal readings in some codices, and patristic citations,[35] as well as from some sixth-century palimpsests discovered in the Cairo Genizah.[36]

Theodotion (θ [Theod])

According to early Christian tradition, Theodotion was a proselyte to Judaism who lived in Ephesus.[37] His translation of the Old Testament (second century) falls midway between the strictly literal translation of Aquila and the literary elegance of Symmachus and is based, according to Bruce, upon an earlier Greek translation: "This was not an original work; what Theodotion seems to have done is to have taken an older Greek translation belonging to the pre-Christian era—one, indeed, which appears to lie behind some of the Old Testament quotations in the New Testament, particularly in Revelation—and revised it in accordance with the standard Hebrew text."[38]

One peculiarity of this translation or revision is that Theodotion often transliterated words rather than translate them, even words that are fairly common.[39] He was perhaps preparing his translation for Jews who, even though they spoke Greek, were familiar with some Hebrew words,[40] an idea suggested by L. J. Greenspoon:

One of his goals, apparently, was to provide standard representations of key Hebrew works and phrases where the Old Greek he was revising preferred variety. He was also partial to transliteration of technical terms or of other unclear or obscure words. Many of the techniques used by Ur-Theodotion (and the *kaige* recensions in general) were perfected by Aquila, and it is for that reason that Barthélemy speaks of Theodotion-*kaige* as Aquila's precursor.[41]

Two other unusual characteristics of this work are that the Greek translation of Job is one-sixth longer than that of the Septuagint, and Daniel differs greatly—eventually it superseded the Septuagint's version.[42] Theodotion succeeded in producing a translation that retained much of its Semitic flavor and yet was readily understandable to his audience of Greek speakers.

Symmachus (σ´ [Symm])

It is generally agreed that Symmachus produced his Greek translation after Aquila and Theodotion had rendered theirs. References to him or his translation are noticeably absent from sources in the late second and early third centuries; thus he probably worked in the mid-third century shortly before Origen compiled the Hexapla.[43] Symmachus is said to have been an Ebionite by Eusebius and Jerome,[44] the latter of whom claims that Symmachus excelled at expressing the sense of the Hebrew text rather than merely producing a literal rendering.[45] His elegant Greek style helped him prepare an idiomatic translation of the Masoretic Text that sometimes displays a degree of independence and originality. Unlike Theodotion's translation, which is mainly a revision of an earlier Greek version, Symmachus appears to have prepared a fresh translation based upon these earlier works. Greenspoon describes his procedure as follows: "Symmachus generally preferred to supply his readers with translations (often, only guesses) for obscure or technical Hebrew terms that had remained untransliterated in earlier Greek versions."[46] Jerome praised Symmachus for making his translation so

intelligible—he was able to use it more than Aquila's literal translation when working on the Vulgate.[47]

Origen's Hexapla (c. 230–245)

Origen was a Christian scholar, most likely from Alexandria, Egypt, who lived about 186–253/254. He survived the persecutions of Severus (203–4) in which his father, Leonidas, died, and he traveled fairly widely before settling in Caesarea, where he succeeded his teacher, Clement, as head of the catechetical school.[48] Later in life he completed his most famous work, the Hexapla, which was one of the greatest achievements of textual criticism in the early church. This six-column work contained the following versions of the Old Testament:

1. The Hebrew text (of his day)
2. A Greek transliteration (a Hebrew text written in Greek letters)
3. Aquila's Greek version
4. Symmachus's Greek version
5. A revision of the Septuagint
6. Theodotion's Greek version (not in the Psalms or Minor Prophets)

Several portions of the Old Testament (primarily the Psalms) included additional columns known as the fifth, sixth, and seventh Greek versions,[49] all arranged so that the reader could compare the Hebrew text with the various Greek texts. Origen claims that he compiled this work primarily to equip Christians for discussions with Jews and to protect them against the charge of falsifying the biblical texts,[50] as he explains in a letter to Julius Africanus (c. 240): "I make it my endeavour not to be ignorant of their [Septuagint's] various readings, lest in my controversies with the Jews I should quote to them what is not in their copies, and that I may make some use of what is found there, even although it should not be in our Scriptures."[51] We have no copy of this priceless work, which would answer many questions, such as how the Hebrew text was pronounced during Origen's day and what the Hebrew and Greek texts of the Old Testament were like at this time.

Origen indicated with sigla or signs originally developed by Alexandrian classical scholarship (the Aristarchian symbols), how the Septuagint differed from the Hebrew text. This work was monumental, composed of about six thousand folios in fifteen volumes.[52] Ironically Origen's Hexapla was intended to confirm the accuracy of the Septuagint but later had the opposite effect, as Klein notes:

> The history of the LXX was adversely affected by Origen's Hexapla since it tended to obliterate the most original and distinctive features of the Old Greek, led to the neglect of some genuine Old Greek manuscripts, and led to the insertion into others of many non-genuine readings. Various church fathers consulted the Hexapla before its destruction in the seventh century, but the entire Hexapla, running to almost 6,500 pages, was never copied. Instead, it became customary to copy only the fifth column [Origen's compilation]. Once removed from the Hexapla, however, the asterisks and obeli of this column would be meaningless—something like footnote numbers without footnotes.[53]

Many copies of the Septuagint were corrupted because they followed the text of the Hexapla without including the asterisks and obeli, thus losing the information related to them. Copies of Origen's Hexapla written without the signs are commonly called hexaplaric, a pejorative term referring to the combined readings of the Hexapla. Fortunately a few manuscripts were not affected by hexaplaric manuscripts, such as Codex Vaticanus (B) and the Syro-Hexaplar. The latter is a copy of Origen's Hexapla translated into Syriac by Paul of Tella in the early seventh century, and it records fairly accurately the signs Origen included in his text.[54]

The Hexapla was probably housed in a library in Caesarea and was accessible to later scholars, such as Pamphilius, Eusebius, and Jerome. Presumably it was destroyed with the rest of the library during Arab invasions in the early seventh century, but several other manuscripts retain portions of the Hexapla.

The standard edition of the extant fragments of the Hexapla is F. Field's *Origenis Hexaplorum quae supersunt*, published at Oxford in 1875. The Hexapla's primary contributions to Old Testament textual criticism are its Greek translations from Aquila, Symmachus, and Theodotion and its Hebrew text from Origen's time, compiled after the standardization of the Masoretic Text.

Philo's Quotations of the Old Testament

Philo (c. 20/15 B.C.–A.D. 50), a Hellenistic Jewish philosopher, belonged to one of the wealthiest Jewish families in Alexandria, Egypt, the largest Jewish settlement outside of Palestine at this time. He received an excellent education under the Greek system of study in the areas of literature, philosophy, rhetoric, mathematics, music, and logic. He took an active part in the social life of Alexandria while maintaining loyalty to his Jewish religious heritage, making at least one pilgrimage to Jerusalem to offer prayers and sacrifices in the temple.

Philo's works can be seen in some measure as a defense of Judaism, a natural response since Alexandria was a center of anti-Jewish propaganda. His allegorical method of interpretation allowed him to present characters and events in the Pentateuch as symbols of philosophical truths (apparently in an attempt to make the Scriptures relevant to his day), but he condemned people who spiritualized the law to do away with the obligations it demanded.[55]

Philo wrote widely, but most value to Old Testament textual criticism are those treatises in which he quotes from a Greek form of the Old Testament, including *De opificio mundi* (*On the Creation of the World*); *De Abrahamo* (*On the Life of Abraham*); *De Iosepho* (*On Joseph*); *De decalogo* (*On the Decalogue*); and *Questions and Answers on Genesis and Exodus*. The Greek text of the Septuagint from which Philo quotes is very close to the Hebrew text, and he adds helpful explanations as to how it was to be interpreted. Philo may also have used other Greek texts of the Old Testament in circulation at the time since some of his readings correspond quite closely with those of the later translators, Aquila, Symmachus, and Theodotion.[56]

Aramaic Targums

History of the Targums

Following the return from the exile, the Jewish people relied more and more on Aramaic and consequently grew increasingly less familiar with Hebrew. It therefore became necessary to explain the biblical text in Aramaic, which became known as targums (possibly related to an Akkadian word, *targumannu(m)*, meaning "translator"). However, it is overly simplistic to think that the targums arose merely out of the need for Aramaic translations of the Hebrew texts[57]—targums also contain interpretations of the text. Some are a very literal translation of the Hebrew text (i.e., Targum Onqelos), while others are periphrastic (adding interpretive and explanatory material; i.e., Targum Neofiti).[58] At first these explanations were given extemporaneously by the rabbi, it being strictly forbidden to commit them to writing; the result was various oral versions existing simultaneously.[59] However, it later became obvious that to achieve standardization they would need to be written down. Some scholars have argued that these translations began very early after the return from the Babylonian exile (Neh. 8:8);[60] certainly some were written even before the time of Christ. Targums exist for every book of the Hebrew Bible except Ezra, Nehemiah, and Daniel; two targums were even found at Qumran—a targum of Job (11QtgJob) from the first century B.C. and a targum of Leviticus (4QtgLev) from the second century B.C. However, once the authoritative targums were committed to writing, earlier targums were abandoned as obsolete.

Sometime after A.D. 100, when the Hebrew text became standardized, two authoritative targums emerged: Targum Onqelos for the Pentateuch and a targum of the Prophets (Former and Latter) called the Targum of Jonathan ben Uzziel. These two targums were recorded about the fifth century but drew largely upon earlier traditional materials. The targum for the Pentateuch was the most important since the Pentateuch held a higher authority; it consisted of a literal translation of the Hebrew with extensive traditional commentary. Later other targums of unofficial status arose. The interpretive element in the targums is clear; scribes tended to paraphrase, add explanatory phrases, and reinterpret the text in order to better convey its meaning.

Two main schools emerged: a western school centered in Tiberius (Israel), which existed until the end of the third century and then revived from the eighth to tenth centuries; and an eastern school centered in Babylon at Sura, Nehardea (destroyed in 259) and later at Pumbeditha.[61] The Babylonian school produced an official version of the targum about the fifth century, but they gradually lost influence and by the tenth or eleventh century had disappeared.[62] Apparently there never was an official targum from the Palestinian schools, but fragments of seven manuscripts of Palestinian targums, dating from the eighth to tenth centuries have been found in the Cairo Genizah.[63] Only a fraction of these written Aramaic targums have survived; they are listed in table 12.1 according to the biblical books that they contain.

Importance and Use of the Targums for Textual Criticism

Technically targums are not translations or paraphrases but commentaries on the biblical books; most can be dated no earlier than the fifth century. Nevertheless they are important to textual criticism for several reasons: some contain translations of the text; they include early Jewish traditions as to the interpretation of the biblical texts; and they are written in Aramaic, which is closely related to biblical Hebrew. The quality of the translation varies greatly among the targums, but on the whole they reflect the Masoretic Text. The Palestinian targums are generally more periphrastic in nature than are the Babylonian targums, with the exception of the two Palestinian targums found at Qumran.

The targums also add greatly to our understanding of how the Jews interpreted Scripture in the first to third centuries. It is even possible that some New Testament quotations come from Jewish targums. An example from one of the targums will help the reader understand how they interpret passages and add explanations. The

Table 12.1
Aramaic Targums
Targums of the Pentateuch

Name	Date	Description
Neofiti I (Biblioteca Apostolica Vaticana, Codex Neofiti I) Has been in the Vatican Library since 1892, when it was donated as part of a collection from the Pia Domus Neophytorum in Rome.	A colophon dates this manuscript to 1504, but the text that it copied may contain traditions as old as the 3d–4th century	A nearly complete Palestinian Targum (missing only thirty verses for various reasons); the main text appears to have been written by three different scribes. Numerous glosses were added in the margins or between the lines. Its translation is not as literal as Targum Onqelos; neither is it as periphrastic as Targum Yerušalmi I.
Yerušalmi I (also called Pseudo-Jonathan because mistakenly attributed to Jonathan ben Uzziel) Prepared by Asher Forins of Venice in 1591; a copy is housed in the British Museum (Ms. Add. 27031).	Present form dated to 7th–8th century	Almost twice as long as the Masoretic Text because it combines the official Targum Onqelos with material from a variety of sources—Palestinian Targum and other later rabbinic sources.
Onqelos Represented by several manuscripts housed at the Jewish Theological Seminary of America (Mss. 131, 133a, 152, 153) and Ms. Ebr. 448 at the Vatican Library.	2d–5th century	The official Babylonian Targum of the Pentateuch; from at least the Middle Ages on, it was considered the most authoritative targum on the Pentateuch. It is also the most literal of the targums.
Fragmentary Targum (Yerušalmi II) Represented by Ebr. 440, Biblioteca Apostolica Vaticana; MS Hébr. 110, Bibliothèque Nationale, Paris; etc.	7th–15th century; somewhere between Neofiti and Yerušalmi I	Little of this work remains, but it appears to contain midrashic material from the Palestinian Targum.
Cairo Genizah Fragments At least nine fragmentary manuscripts of targums for the Pentateuch.	8th–14th century	Some of these fragments contain the full Hebrew verse, while others bear only *lemmata* (i.e., the opening words of a verse). For the most part they represent the Palestinian Targum, though there is not always agreement in places where they overlap.
Toseftot Some manuscripts that contain Toseftot are: Ms. Parma 3218; Ms. Sasson 282; Ms. Heb.c.74 (Oxford); and Ms. T-S NS 184.81 (Cambridge).	Uncertain	Some manuscripts of Targum Onqelos have additional haggadic materials (rabbinic stories that illustrate the Torah) labeled Tosefta Yerušalmi.

Table 12.1 (continued)
Targums of the Prophets

Name	Date	Description
Jonathan Represented by several Yemenite Mss. with supralinear pointing (Ms. 229, Jewish Theological Seminary of America; Mss. Or. 2210 and 2211, British Museum) and Western Ms. with Tiberian pointing (Codex Reuchlinianus).	4th–5th century	The official Babylonian Targum of the Prophets, probably translated by Rabbi Joseph ben Ḥayya (c. 270–333), head of the academy of Pumbeditha (T.B. *Baba Batra* 3b; *Yoma* 32b). Bears many similarities to Targum Onqelos; though not generally expansive, it includes a significant amount of haggadah.
Toseftot About eighty additions are found in Codex Reuchlinianus.	Uncertain	These are additions to Targum Jonathan written in the margins or in the text itself. They may be remnants of a Palestinian targum of the Prophets that the scribes desired to retain when the Babylonian Talmud began to predominate in the West.

Targum of the Writings

Name	Date	Description
Yerušalmi **(= Jerusalem)**	Uncertain	There is no official targum for the Writings, but medieval writers use the name "Targum Yerušalmi" when quoting from a targum of the Writings. Targums for each of the books are very different and often appear in more than one recension (critical revision).

following passage is from Targum Jonathan on the Prophets (Isa. 52:13–53:3):

> 52.13 Behold, my servant, *the Messiah*, shall prosper, he shall be exalted and *increase*, and shall be very *strong*. 52.14 *Just as the house of Israel hoped for him many days—their* appearances *were so dark among the peoples*, and *their aspect* beyond that of *the* sons of men—52.15 so he shall *scatter* many *peoples*; kings shall *be silent* because of him, *they shall place their hands upon* their mouth; for *things* which have not been told to them they have seen, and that which they have not heard they have understood.
> 53.1 Who has believed *this* our *report*? And to whom has *the strength of the mighty* arm of the Lord been *so* revealed? 53.2 And *the righteous shall be exalted* before him, *behold,* like *tufts which sprout*, and like *a tree which sends its* roots *by streams of waters, so holy generations will increase on the* land *which was needing him; his appearance is not a common appearance* and *his fearfulness is* not *an ordinary fearfulness,* and *his brilliance will be holy brilliance,* that *everyone who* looks at him will *consider* him. 53.3 *Then the glory of the kingdoms will be for contempt* and *cease; they will be faint and mournful, behold, as* a man of sorrows and *appointed for* sicknesses; and when *the face of the Shekhinah was taken up from us, they are* despised and not esteemed.[64]

In this targum, the Servant is clearly identified as Messiah, but all the suffering is interpreted as referring to the Israelite nation, not to the Messiah.

For Further Reading

Alexander, P. S. "Targum, Targumim." In *ABD*, 6:320–31.

———. "Jewish Aramaic Translations of the Hebrew Scriptures." In *Mikra*, ed. M. J. Mulder, 217–54. CRINT 2/1. Assen: Van Gorcum; Philadelphia: Fortress, 1988.

Barthélemy, D. *Les devanciers d'Aquila*. VTSup 10. Leiden: E. J. Brill, 1963.

Borgen, P. "Philo of Alexandria." In *Jewish Writings from the Second Temple Period*, ed. M. Stone, 233–82. CRINT 2/2. Assen: Van Gorcum; Philadelphia: Fortress, 1984.

Bowker, J. *The Targums and Rabbinic Literature: An Introduction to Jewish Interpretations of Scripture*. London: Cambridge University Press, 1969.

Jellicoe, S. *The Septuagint and Modern Study*. Oxford: Clarendon, 1968; reprint, Ann Arbor: Eisenbrauns, 1978.

McNamara, M., et al. *The Aramaic Bible*. Collegeville, MN: Michael Glazier, 1988–.

McNamara, M. *Targum and Testament: Aramaic Paraphrases of the Hebrew Bible: A Light on the New Testament*. Shannon, Ireland: Irish University Press, 1968; reprint, Grand Rapids: Eerdmans, 1972.

Mulder, M. J. "Transmission of the Biblical Text." In *Mikra*, ed. M. J. Mulder, 87–135. CRINT 2/1. Assen: Van Gorcum; Philadelphia: Fortress, 1988.

Nickelsburg, G. W. E. "The Bible Rewritten and Expanded." In *Jewish Writings of the Second Temple Period*, ed. M. E. Stone, 89–156. CRINT 2/2. Assen: Van Gorcum; Philadelphia: Fortress, 1984.

Price, I. M. *The Ancestry of Our English Bible*, 20–98. 3d ed. New York: Harper and Brothers, 1956.

Roberts, B. J. *The Old Testament Text and Versions: The Hebrew Text in Transmission and the History of the Ancient Versions*. Cardiff: University of Wales Press, 1951.

———. "The Textual Transmission of the Old Testament." In *Tradition and Interpretation*, ed. G. W. Anderson, 1–30. Oxford: Clarendon, 1979.

Strack, H. L., and G. Stemberger. *Introduction to the Talmud and Midrash*. Translated by M. Bockmuehl. Edinburgh: T & T Clark; Minneapolis: Fortress, 1991.

Swete, H. B. *An Introduction to the Old Testament in Greek*. Revised by R. R. Ottley. Cambridge: Cambridge University Press, 1914; reprint, New York: KTAV, 1968.

Trigg, J. W. "Origen." In *ABD*, 5:42–48.

Vermes, G. *Scripture and Tradition in Judaism*. SPB 4. Leiden: E. J. Brill, 1961. 2d rev. ed., 1973.

Waltke, B. K. "Samaritan Pentateuch." In *ABD*, 5:932–40.

Würthwein, E. *The Text of the Old Testament. An Introduction to the Biblia Hebraica*, 30–100. Translated by E. F. Rhodes. Grand Rapids: Eerdmans, 1979.

Young, B. H. "Targum." In *ISBE*, 4:727–33.

Transmission of the New Testament

History of the New Testament Text

While there are no autographs of the New Testament, several papyrus fragments date to the second century ($\mathfrak{P}^{32}$, $\mathfrak{P}^{46}$, $\mathfrak{P}^{52}$, $\mathfrak{P}^{64+67}$, $\mathfrak{P}^{66}$, $\mathfrak{P}^{90}$). $\mathfrak{P}^{52}$ is a fragment of the Gospel of John dated to the early second century, probably only about fifty to seventy-five years after the book was written. The autographs were probably written on papyrus, as suggested by early biblical fragments and 2 John 12, which states: "I have much to write to you, but I do not want to use paper and ink. Instead, I hope to visit you and talk with you face to face, so that our joy may be complete." The Greek word for "paper" in this verse is χάρτης (kartēs), which probably refers to a single piece of papyrus, and the word for "ink" is μέλαν (melan), meaning black. Shorter works like Jude or 2 and 3 John would require only a single piece of papyrus. Larger works like the Gospel of Luke or the Gospel of Matthew would have been written on scrolls, which were more difficult to manage and store. As Callimachus, a learned cataloger of the books in the great library of Alexandria, quipped, "A big book is a big nuisance."[1]

The loss of the autographs is not surprising given their materials and constant usage. Wide distribution of the texts required copies to be made continually. In the twentieth century the discovery of many papyrus fragments has furnished us with better insight into the earliest stages of the New Testament text.

The New Testament Text prior to 100

Some books, such as the Gospels, were originally circulated orally, whereas Paul's letters were recorded at the outset to send to their recipients. The autographs were either written by their authors or dictated to scribes (or amanuenses) who transcribed the letters (see Rom. 16:22; 2 Thess. 3:17). Once the letters were written they were delivered to the churches by scribes, by friends, or by travelers going to that destination. Tychicus, one of Paul's friends and a faithful brother, delivered Paul's letters to the Ephesians (Eph. 6:21–22), to the Colossians (Col. 4:7–9), and possibly to Titus (3:12).

Paul sometimes requested that his letters be circulated to other churches (Col. 4:16), and thus the autographs must have been copied almost immediately after they had been written. The early Christian literature is almost silent about the original manuscripts, a silence that implies that enough faithful copies were in existence that the loss of an original posed no concern. It is doubtful that the early church set apart a specific group of professional scribes for this particular purpose; scribes were more likely hired, or individuals in the church copied the letters.[2] This would explain why there are so many copies of the New Testament books and why there are more mistakes in the New Testament books than there are in the copies of the Old Testament: "In the early years of the Christian Church, marked by rapid expansion and consequent increased demand by individuals and by congregations for copies of the Scriptures, the speedy multiplication of copies, even by non-professional scribes, sometimes took precedence over strict accuracy of detail."[3]

According to the evidence from the beginning of the fourth century (shortly before the date of Codex Vaticanus) scribes were paid well for their work:

When prose works were copied, a line called a stichos, having sixteen (or sometimes fifteen) syllables, was frequently used as a measure for determining the market price of a manuscript. A price-fixing edict issued in A.D. 301 by the Emperor Diocletian set the wages of scribes at the rate of 25 denarii for 100 lines in writing of first quality, and of 20 denarii for the same number of lines in writing of the second quality (what the difference was between the qualities of writing is not mentioned) ["Concerning the Prices of Things Sold," 7.39–40 published in *Corpus Inscriptionum Latinarum*, 3.831]. According to the computation of Rendel Harris, the cost of producing one complete Bible, such as codex Sinaiticus, would have come to about 30,000 denarii—a sizeable sum notwithstanding steadily rising inflation.[4]

To help put this into perspective, Bruce Metzger goes on to say that in the preceding century under Caracalla (211–217) a legionary was paid a *stipendium* of 750 denarii per year in addition to his room and board.[5] For a church to hire a scribe to copy of one of Paul's letters or one of the Gospels would therefore have been very expensive.

The evidence suggests that all the New Testament books were written by A.D. 100. F. C. Baur, a New Testament professor from Tübingen, Germany, and his school argued that several New Testament books were falsifications from at least the latter half of the second century.[6] Evidence refuting such a view are fragments of New Testament books (dated to the second century) that are not likely to be autographs and therefore must be copies of works in existence before the second century; among these are a fragment of the Gospel of John ($\mathfrak{P}^{52}$) dated to about 125; a fragment of the Gospels ($\mathfrak{P}^{90}$) from the second century; a fragment of the Book of Titus ($\mathfrak{P}^{32}$) dated about 200; a major portion of the Pauline Epistles and Hebrews ($\mathfrak{P}^{46}$) dated about 200; a few chapters from the Gospel of Matthew ($\mathfrak{P}^{64+67}$) dated about 200; a major portion of the Gospel of John ($\mathfrak{P}^{66}$) dated about 200; a fragment of Matthew ($\mathfrak{P}^{77}$) dated to the second or third century; and a fragment of Acts (0189) from the second or third century. (See also

evidence presented in chapter 9 regarding the date of the New Testament books.)

The New Testament Text after 100

Writing Materials and Appearance of Manuscripts

Initially the New Testament books were probably written on papyrus, but from about the third century onward vellum or parchment was preferred for its better contrast to ink. But even Paul appears to have been familiar with parchment books, as 2 Timothy 4:13 implies, at a very early period. Later, manuscripts became even more elaborate—sometimes red ink was used to highlight important words such as titles, headings, or the first word of a chapter.[7] Even more ornate were manuscripts of purple vellum with silver or gold letters (e.g., Codex Perpureus Petropolitanus [sixth century; purple vellum with silver letters]; Codex Sinopensis [sixth century; purple vellum with gold letters]); many biblical manuscripts copied during the Middle Ages included elaborate decorative pictures (see fig. 13.1).

By at least the beginning of the second century, a new form of book, called a codex, was in use. It was very similar in appearance to our modern books, with leaves, or pages, bound on the left side.[8] The earliest fragment of the New Testament, $\mathfrak{P}^{52}$ (dated to the first half of the second century), is written on the front and back, which suggests that it was part of a codex and not a scroll. Early Bibles were still arranged in columns so that when they were opened their appearance was similar to scrolls. Christians may have preferred the codex since it helped to distinguish them from Jews and pagans.[9]

Extant Manuscripts Dating Later Than 100

It is surprising that any fragments of the New Testament exist, since the early church had no great libraries or sanctuaries to store its sacred books and was often persecuted. In 303 Diocletian ordered all sacred Scriptures of the Christians to be burned, but shortly afterward Emperor Constantine halted persecution of Christians when he accepted Christianity and issued the so-called Edict of Milan (313), which declared freedom of worship for citizens of the Roman Empire:

When we, Constantine Augustus and Licinius Augustus, had happily met at Milan, and were conferring about all things which concern the advantage and security of the state, we thought that amongst other things which seemed likely to profit men generally, the reverence paid to the Divinity merited our first and chief attention. Our

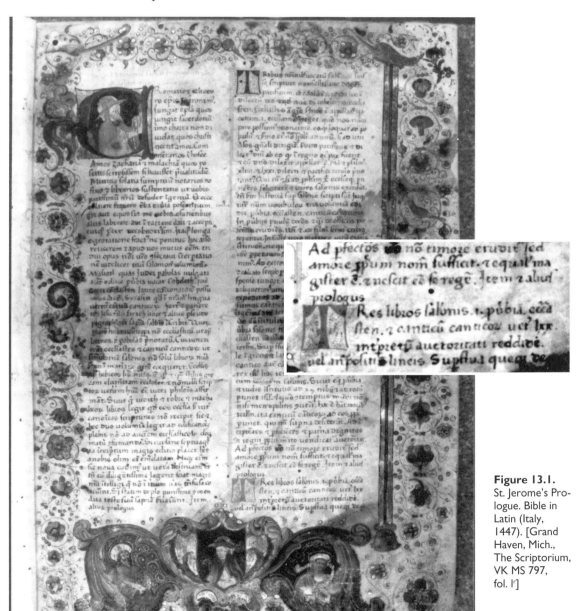

Figure 13.1. St. Jerome's Prologue. Bible in Latin (Italy, 1447). [Grand Haven, Mich., The Scriptorium, VK MS 797, fol. 1ʳ]

purpose is to grant both to the Christians and to all others full authority to follow whatever worship each man has desired; whereby whatsoever Divinity dwells in heaven may be benevolent and propitious to us, and to all who are placed under our authority.... Wherefore your Dignity should know that it is our pleasure to abolish all conditions whatever which were embodied in former orders directed to your office about the Christians, that what appeared utterly inauspicious and foreign to our Clemency should be done away and that every one of those who have a common wish to follow the religion of the Christians may from this moment freely and unconditionally proceed to observe the same without any annoyance or disquiet.[10]

During this period the Christian church grew so quickly that the emperor requested Eusebius to have fifty new copies of the Scripture copied for the churches of Constantinople.

From about the fourth century, it was primarily the work of monks to study and copy the Scriptures. About 800, Theodore the Studite, abbot of the Studium at Constantinople, which was well-known for copying Scriptures, composed the following penalties in order to maintain high standards for copying manuscripts:

A diet of bread and water was the penalty set for the scribe who became so much interested in the subject-matter of what he was copying that he neglected his task of copying. Monks had to keep their parchment leaves neat and clean, on penalty of 130 penances. If anyone should take without permission another's quaternion (that is, the ruled and folded sheets of parchment), fifty penances were prescribed. If anyone should make more glue than he could use at one time, and it should harden, he must do fifty penances. If a scribe broke his pen in a fit of temper (perhaps after having made some accidental blunder near the close of an otherwise perfectly copied sheet), he had to do thirty penances.[11]

Styles of Writing

Paleography, the study of writing, can help date New Testament manuscripts because writing styles changed over time. Four main types of Greek letters were used during the period of the New Testament's transmission.

Capital Letters (e.g., Π, Ω, Σ)

These letters, composed of straight and angular lines, were primarily used for inscriptions cut or engraved in hard substances, such as rock or metal (see fig. 13.2).

Figure 13.2. This Greek inscription in the Jewish temple courts forbade foreigners to enter the temple. [Archaeological Museum, Istanbul]

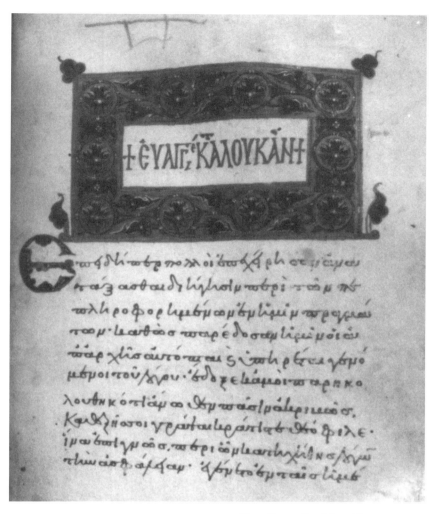

Figure 13.3.
Cursive manuscript of Luke 1. Gospels in Greek (eleventh century). [Grand Haven, Mich., The Scriptorium, VK MS 905]

Uncial Letters (e.g., Π, Ш, C)

Uncial writing (see fig. 6.14) modified the capital letters with more curves so that they could easily be inscribed with pen on common writing materials, such as papyrus, parchment, and ostracon. This Greek writing was used from the first century to about the sixth century, though it continued into the tenth and eleventh centuries, as Bruce Metzger explains: "From the fourth century B.C. till the eighth or ninth A.D. the book-hand changed very slowly and often harked back to earlier styles. During a given period more than one style of book-hand was in use, and the transition from one style to a new one always lasted at least one generation."[12]

Usually earlier New Testament manuscripts are written in uncial writing, with no breaks between words or sentences and no punctuation marks, a style of writing called *scripta continua* ("continuous script"). Difficulty in determining where to break the words sometimes leads to mistakes. For example, in Mark 10:40 Jesus says, "but to sit at my right or left is not for me to grant." In uncial manuscripts the phrase ΑΛΛΟΙΣΗΤΟΙΜΑΣΤΑΙ may be read ἀλλ᾽ οἷς ἡτοίμασται ("but [it is] for those for whom it has been prepared") or ἄλλοις ἡτοίμασται ("it has been prepared for others"). While evidence strongly supports the first reading, the example serves to show the difficulties that can arise from unclear divisions of a text. These ambigu-

Table 13.1
Common Abbreviations in Minuscule Manuscripts

Words	Meaning	Nominative Abbreviation	Genitive Abbreviation
θεός	God	θ̅ς̅	θ̅υ̅
κύριος	Lord	κ̅ς̅	κ̅υ̅
Ἰησοῦς	Jesus	ι̅ς̅	ι̅υ̅
Χριστός	Christ	χ̅ς̅	χ̅υ̅
υἱός	son	υ̅ς̅	υ̅υ̅
πνεῦμα	spirit	π̅ν̅α̅	π̅ν̅ς̅
Δαυίδ	David	δ̅α̅δ̅	
σταυρός	cross	σ̅τ̅ς̅	σ̅τ̅υ̅
μήτηρ	mother	μ̅η̅ρ̅	μ̅ρ̅ς̅
πατήρ	father	π̅η̅ρ̅	π̅ρ̅ς̅
Ἰσραήλ	Israel	ι̅η̅λ̅	
σωτήρ	savior	σ̅η̅ρ̅	σ̅ρ̅ς̅
ἄνθρωπος	man	α̅ν̅ο̅ς̅	α̅ν̅ο̅υ̅
Ἰερουσαλήμ	Jerusalem	ι̅λ̅η̅μ̅	
οὐρανός	heaven	ο̅υ̅ν̅ο̅ς̅	ο̅υ̅ν̅ο̅υ̅

ities are rare, as Metzger notes: "It must not be thought, however, that such ambiguities occur frequently. In Greek it is the rule, with very few exceptions, that native Greek words can terminate only in a vowel (or diphthong) or in one of three consonants, ν, ρ, and ς."[13]

Only about one hundred New Testament uncial manuscripts written on papyrus (dated between the early second and eighth centuries) have survived, generally in fragmented condition. There are more uncial manuscripts written on parchment (about 266), ranging from the fourth to fourteenth centuries.

Cursive Letters

Cursive or running hand followed after uncial writing and can be compared with our cursive writing. This type of writing was used from about the third to ninth centuries, and because the letters are connected it could be written more rapidly (fig. 13.3), as Metzger explains: "For daily use this way of writing [uncial script] took too much time, and at an early date cursive writing developed from the uncial and continued to be used concurrently with it. Besides being more convenient, cursive letters were often simplified as well as combined when the scribe would join two or more together without lifting the pen (ligature)."[14]

Minuscule Letters (e.g., π, ω, ς)

Eventually the minuscule style of writing predominated; it is similar to cursive, only much smaller (fig. 13.4). Metzger says, "It [uncial writing] was superseded for the writing of books by a special form of cursive letters developed at the close of the eighth or beginning of the ninth century. This minuscule script was a small book-hand that could be written more rapidly as well as more compactly, thus saving both time and parchment."[15]

At present the 2,754 New Testament minuscule manuscripts outnumber uncial manuscripts by about eight to one;[16] most date between the ninth and fifteenth centuries. In some manuscripts scribes developed a system of abbreviations for many commonly used words, probably to save space.[17] Table 13.1 indicates the most commonly abbreviated words. Abbreviations generally included the first and last letter of the word; the latter was necessary to indicate the declension, or grammatical case, of the word.

To economize, parchment and leather were also cleaned and rescraped for reuse. The resulting manuscript is called a palimpsest ("rescraped," from the two Greek words πάλιν [*palin,* "again"] and ψάω [*psaō,* "to scrape"]; fig. 13.5). About 20 percent of the New Testament manuscripts that exist are palimpsests.[18] Many that were rescraped originally bore early biblical texts; for example, Codex Ephraemi was a fifth-century manuscript of the New Testament that was erased and replaced in the twelfth century by thirty-eight sermons or treatises of Ephraem, a fourth-century Syrian church father. At points the underlying text can easily be read (for instance, between columns where the text does not cover), but elsewhere it is obliterated. Thanks to infrared technology, however, most of the original manuscript has been read; with additional aid of vidicon cameras, very faint writing can be detected, transferred to digital form, and enhanced.

At the Trullan Synod (692) the church forbade the sale of old manuscripts for reuse:

> It is unlawful for anyone to corrupt or cut up a book of the Old or New Testament or of our holy and approved preachers and teachers, or to give them up to the traders in books [βιβλιοκάπηλοι] or to those who are called perfumers [μυρεψοί], or to hand it over for destruction to any other like persons: unless to be sure it has been rendered useless either by bookworms, or by water, or in some other way.[19]

Palimpsests after this date have been found, which suggests that the edict was not entirely successful.

Helps for the Reader

Divisions of the Text

Initially the texts had no divisions or markings to aid in locating passages, but when texts were collected into a canon, it became necessary to distinguish works and sections from each other. Among the first means of determining sections were marks inserted by scribes in their own books. For instance, Codex Vaticanus (fourth century) records 170 sections within the Book of Matthew, 62 in Mark, 152 in Luke, and 50 in John. It would be a long time, however, before the insertion of chapter or verse divisions. Differing divisions appear in the various manuscripts. Archbishop Andrew of Caesarea in Cappadocia, who lived in the latter half of the sixth century, divided the Book of Revelation into twenty-four parts because of the twenty-four elders mentioned in Revelation 4:4.[20] Then, because each elder had a body, soul, and spirit, he divided the twenty-four sections into seventy-two parts. Eusebius, in the fourth century, devised a system of notations to aid in the location of parallel passages that has been found in many subsequent manuscripts.[21] Stephen Langton (1150–1228) added chapter divisions to a copy of the Latin Vulgate, and these were later added to English translations.

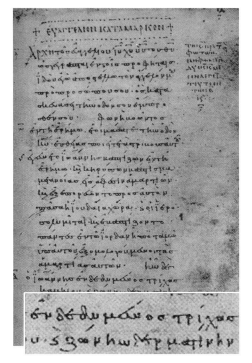

Figure 13.4. The earliest known Greek minuscule manuscript is dated to 835 and was probably written in Constantinople. It contains the four Gospels and is located in the Leningrad State Public Library (GR. 219).

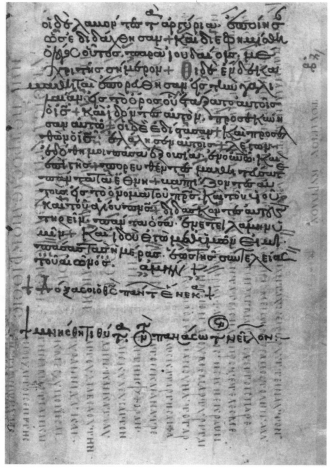

Figure 13.5.
A Greek palimpsest, Codex Zacynthius (Ξ, 040), which contains a portion of the Gospel of Luke from the seventh or eighth century that was written over in the twelfth or thirteenth century. [Cambridge University Library]

According to Stephanus's son, his father made the divisions into verse *inter equitandum* on a journey from Paris to Lyons. Although some have understood this to mean "on horseback" (and have explained inappropriate verse-divisions as originating when the horse bumped his pen into the wrong place!), the inference most natural and best supported by the evidence is that the task was accomplished while resting at inns along the road.[23]

The first English Bible to include numbered verse divisions was the Geneva Bible translated by William Whittingham in 1560. Later, difficult words that were explained in the margins or between the lines of the manuscripts became known as glosses.

Lectionaries

The church developed a lectionary system for the Old and New Testaments to enable the entire Bible to be read in the course of several years, which Metzger describes: "In order to assist the lector in finding the beginning (ἀρχή) and end (τέλος) of the lesson, several of the later uncial manuscripts were provided with the abbreviations ἀρχ and τέλ, inserted either in the margin or between the lines of the text. . . . Lection notes, indicating that a given passage is to be read on a certain day, were sometimes written in the margin with red ink."[24] These lectionaries indicated the order in which the texts were to be read, beginning with Easter; they were later written separately for the convenience of the reader. Lectionaries have become another source for determining the most accurate readings of New Testament texts.

Punctuation Marks

Few punctuation marks appear in the earliest manuscripts (e.g., 𝔓[46] and 𝔓[66], both dated to about 200, include occasional punctuation marks); more were added by scribes during the sixth and seventh centuries. The question mark, however, is rarely found in manuscripts before the ninth century.[22]

Verse Divisions and Glosses

The current verse divisions in the New Testament were added by Robert Stephanus (Estienne), who published a Greek and Latin edition of the New Testament in Geneva in 1551. The seeming arbitrariness of some of the verse divisions led to speculation about Stephanus's method. Bruce Metzger explains:

Artistic Additions

By the Byzantine period, some manuscripts bore ornamental headings and/or pictures at the beginning of the books or occasionally chapters. Pictures were often used to teach the reader the significance of specific passages or to highlight important concepts in Scripture. Manuscripts from the Middle Ages onward often contain beautiful works of art portraying Christ, the apostles, and biblical scenes. These are either multicolored original art or beautiful wood- or brass-cut prints (fig. 13.6). One way to distinguish an authentic old print is to find the watermark impression around the outside of the picture left by the wood block or brass plate pressed against the paper.

Colophons

From about the eighth century onward much of the copying process was performed in monasteries by monks who spent many hours each day standing at a desk, often in damp and poorly lit conditions. Colophons (i.e., notes at the end of a manuscript) often express the relief or joy of the scribe upon completing a copy (e.g., "the end of the book; thanks be to God").[25] Others mention difficulties encountered in the copying process; for example, in an Armenian manuscript of the Gospels one scribe says that his ink is frozen and his fingers are stiff due to the cold caused by a snowstorm.[26] Another, more graphic scribe complained that "Writing bows one's back, thrusts the ribs into one's stomach, and fosters a general debility of the body."[27] Colophons often include the name of the scribe, the date, and other information that the scribe feels is important, such as a blessing upon the one who reads the manuscript or a curse upon anyone who adds anything to it.

Colophons can help date manuscripts specifically compared with more approximate dates furnished by paleographers and carbon-14 tests or similar means. On occasion scholars can even identify specific scribes (or possibly a scribe from the same school) who copied other manuscripts.

New Testament Textual Criticism

According to Metzger, "To teach another how to become a textual critic is like teaching another how to become a poet."[28] While natural talent is certainly a factor, the skills and rules related to textual criticism can be honed and sharpened by regular interaction with and examination of the texts. One critical difference between Old and New Testament textual criticism is the vast number of extant manuscripts of the New Testament, which according to James Barr, leads text critics to different starting points:

> With a non-uniform text [the case with the NT] we may find variant readings, and textual discussion begins from the variant readings, even if all of them "make sense." With a text of high uniformity [the case with the OT], however, textual discussion will more frequently begin from the feeling that there is a "difficulty"; the procedure will be more independent of the existence of variant readings, and conjectural emendation will take a larger place in the discussion.[29]

Although Old Testament textual criticism is thus more subjective than New Testament criticism, the task of both is to evaluate which reading or variant of the text is most likely the original. Variants are not the same as errors; they are rather differences in wording among the various manuscripts.

It is important near the beginning of our discussion on New Testament textual criticism to note that the verbal agreement between various New Testament manuscripts is closer than between many English translations of the New Testament and that the actual number of variants in the New Testament is small (approximately 10 percent), none of which call into question any major doctrine.

The greatest number of variants are differences or errors in spelling. For example, the author of Codex Vaticanus spells "John" with only one *n* instead of the common spelling with two (Ἰωάννης [*Iōannēs*]). This type of variant makes no difference in the meaning of the text.

The second largest group of variants arises because of omissions of small Greek words or variations in word order. For example, in Greek a person's name may or may not be preceded by an article ("the"). And the phrase *the good man* could also be written in Greek as "the man, the good one," although in English both phrases are translated as "the good man."

Figure 13.6.
A print from
an old English
Bible.
[Paul Wegner]

These types of variants also make no difference in the meaning of the text.

It is very rare for a scribe to accidentally make nonsense out of a word or phrase when copying, but it does happen. One scribe accidentally wrote the Greek letter *pi* instead of *phi* in Luke 6:41, rendering the text, "Why do you look at the *fruit* (κάρπος [*karpos*]) in your brother's eye" instead of "Why do you look at the *speck* (κάρφος [*karphos*]) in your brother's eye." These types of errors are easily identifiable.

Brief History of New Testament Textual Criticism

New Testament textual criticism has an interesting history, beginning at least as early as Jerome, who tediously sifted through the Old Latin manuscripts to determine the correct text for the Latin Vulgate (382–390). He lamented that "there are almost as many different translations as there are manuscripts."[30] Metzger explains the process by which Jerome determined his translation: "He used a relatively good Latin text as the basis for his revision, and compared it with some old Greek manuscripts. He emphasizes that he treated the current Latin text as conservatively as possible, and changed it only where the meaning was distorted."[31] Jerome's translation, the Latin Vulgate, reigned virtually unchallenged for more than a thousand years as the New Testament text, even though in time the Vulgate's text incorporated many copying errors.

The first work to systematically collect variants was the London Polyglot Bible by Brian Walton in 1653 to 1657 (see fig. 13.7). This work includes Stephanus's Greek text from the 1550 edition and records at the bottom of the page variant readings from Codex Alexandrinus. In the sixth volume, Walton includes an appendix prepared by Archbishop Ussher of variant readings from fifteen different sources. Many works followed, noting variant readings among the Greek manuscripts. In 1675, Dr. John Fell (1625–1686), dean of Christ Church and later bishop of Oxford, edited a Greek New Testament with the Elzevir brothers'

Greek text of 1633, as well as an apparatus that he claims collates variants from one hundred manuscripts and versions. In 1707, just two weeks before he died, John Mill (1645–1707), a teaching fellow from Queen's College, Oxford, published his Greek text, which collated evidence from manuscripts, early versions, and church fathers. He claimed there were thirty thousand variants in the few New Testament manuscripts with which he was familiar. Others also collated various manuscripts and added increasingly comprehensive critical apparatuses to the Greek text in order to correct what became commonly known as the *Textus Receptus* (e.g., Edward Wells, 1709–1719; Richard Bentley, 1720; Daniel Mace, 1729).

While he was a student at Tübingen, a German scholar named Johann Bengel (1687–1752) was so disturbed by the numerous variants in the Greek manuscripts published by Mill that he devoted himself to studying the transmission of the Greek text. He collected as many editions, manuscripts, and early versions as were available and pored over them. His work showed that there were far fewer variants than originally thought, and no variant affected any article of evangelical doctrine.[32] Bengel was the first scholar to divide the manuscripts into groups and weigh them rather than assuming they were of equal value. In 1734 he published a Greek text that looked like the *Textus Receptus* but in the apparatus classified each reading into several groups (α = the original reading, with full certainty; β = a reading superior to the *Textus Receptus*, though with less than absolute certainty; γ = a reading equally as good as the one in the text; δ = a reading not as good as the one in the text; and ε = an inferior reading that was to be rejected).[33] Bengel explained the principles he developed, by which this apparatus, virtually a revision of the *Textus Receptus*, was accomplished; one of his key principles was "the difficult is to be preferred to the easy reading," which still remains a primary principle of textual criticism. His Greek text, which challenged the authority of the *Textus Receptus*, caused him to be ostracized and maligned by some, even though he was known to be a very pious man.[34]

During the 1800s the development of New Testament textual criticism experienced a great advance, beginning with Karl Lachmann (1793–1851), professor of classical philology at Berlin. He was the first to publish a Greek New Testament based entirely upon textual critical principles, abandoning the *Textus Receptus,* or in his own words: "Down with the late text of the Textus Receptus, and back to the text of the early fourth-century church!"[35] However, his editions of the Greek New Testament in 1831 and 1842–1850 did not fulfill this hope. It was left to a German Protestant theologian and textual scholar, Constantin von Tischendorf (1815–1874), who dedicated his life to preparing as many manuscripts and fragments of the New Testament as possible for publication. In a letter to his fiancée, Tischendorf states: "I am confronted with a sacred task, the struggle to regain the original form of the

Figure 13.7.
Brian Walton and two pages from Genesis 1 of the London Polyglot.
[United Library, Garrett/Seabury-Western Theological Seminaries]

New Testament."[36] During his lifetime, he discovered and published more manuscripts and fragments of the New Testament than did any other scholar. Tischendorf examined the manuscripts, versions, and writings of the church fathers available in his day; even though these sources were a fraction of what are available today, his comprehensive and accurate work paved the way for those to follow.

In the latter part of the nineteenth century two Cambridge University scholars, B. F. Westcott (1825–1901; Regius Professor of Divinity at Cambridge; later bishop of Durham) and F. J. A. Hort (1828–1892; Hulsean Professor of Divinity at Cambridge) gained renown for their comparative studies of New Testament manuscripts.

In 1881 Westcott and Hort published the text of the Greek New Testament with an introduction and appendices entitled *The New Testament in the Original Greek.* Not being interested in supplying a textual apparatus with all the various readings, they applied textual principles to determine what they believed to be the closest reading of the original Greek text. Refining the principles of earlier scholars, they classified the readings of the New Testament texts according to text types or families. Codex Vaticanus was designated the neutral text, being closest, they believed, to the original Greek text than any of the other three text families. Westcott and Hort took advantage of the ver-

Textus Receptus

This Latin phrase meaning "received text" was the name given to the Greek New Testament text published in 1633 by the Elzevir brothers in the Netherlands, though the text was essentially Erasmus's Greek text of 1535, which had been republished so often and become so popular that it was considered the standard Greek text until the nineteenth century. Thus it was "received" in the sense that it was commonly accepted by the people of that time. This phrase is also used in Old Testament textual criticism to refer to the commonly accepted Hebrew text (i.e., Masoretic Text).

Brook Foss Westcott (1825–1901)

Westcott (fig. 13.8) was born in Birmingham, England, on January 12, 1825; he attended King Edward VI's School. He was greatly influenced by the headmaster, James Prince Lee, who in Westcott's opinion was "superior . . . among the great masters of his time" (E. H. Robertson, *Makers of the English Bible* [Cambridge: Lutterworth, 1990], 136). He attended Trinity College, Cambridge, in 1844 and became a teaching fellow in 1849. Some of his own pupils were J. B. Lightfoot, E. W. Benson, and F. J. A. Hort. In 1851 he was ordained at the parish church in Prestwich by his old teacher, Lee, who was then bishop of Manchester, and the next year went to teach at Harrow School as assistant master.

Figure 13.8. B. F. Westcott (1825–1901).

In 1855, Westcott returned to Cambridge for a brief stay when he met the famous German textual critic Tischendorf, with whom he was unimpressed for his seemingly exclusive interest in "palimpsests and codices" (Ibid., 137). In 1869 Westcott was appointed as canon of Peterborough and the next year was called to Cambridge University as Regius Professor of Divinity, through the instigation of Lightfoot. He was very involved in the life of the university, both in administration and pastoral concern. He helped to found and organize the Cambridge Mission to Delhi and the Cambridge Clergy Training School (later called Westcott House). In 1875 Westcott was appointed honorary chaplain to the queen. During this time his most noted work on New Testament textual criticism progressed and in 1881 was published. In 1890, at the age of sixty-six, he was appointed to succeed Lightfoot as bishop of Durham, where he showed a deep concern for ordination candidates at Auckland Castle, as well as for the social and industrial problems in his diocese. For the next ten years, with ever failing health, he maintained his strenuous work traveling between Durham and London until his death on July 27, 1901.

Fenton John Anthony Hort (1828–1892)

Hort (fig. 13.9) was born in Dublin, Ireland, in April 1828, moved with his family to Cheltenham, England, at age nine, and then moved again at age ten to Boulogne in the north of France. There he became interested in classics. His family later returned to Cheltenham, where he finished school and entered Rugby School in October 1841. In 1846 he moved to Trinity College, Cambridge, where he became intrigued with religious things and sought out evangelicals. But they seemed to him almost careless in their forms of worship. As a result, Hort continued to vacillate between the old, stable Anglican religion that he had grown up with and the new, creative ideas that were taught at Cambridge.

Figure 13.9. F. J. A. Hort (1828–1892).

Hort graduated from Cambridge with first class honors in both moral and natural sciences and was considered one of the university's influential thinkers. Being offered a fellowship in 1852, at the same time as J. B. Lightfoot, he chose the field of New Testament. Hort was ordained in 1854 and retained his Cambridge fellowship until his marriage in 1857, when he moved to a country parish in Ippolyts-cum-Great Wymondly, near Hitchin. There he pastored for fifteen years, devoting any spare time to revising the Greek New Testament. He was finally asked to return to Cambridge in 1871 with a fellowship and lectureship in theology at Emmanuel College. In 1878 he was offered the position of Hulsean Professor of Divinity, and shortly afterward, in 1881, his work with Westcott was completed. Hort continued his work at Cambridge despite failing health until his death on November 30, 1892.

sions and New Testament quotations in ancient authors and the church fathers. Manuscripts were divided into four different groups: Syrian, Western, Alexandrian, and neutral. They considered Syrian readings to be the latest, since no distinctly Syrian readings were found in any of the church fathers of the third century, whereas they are numerous in the latter fourth century, especially in the area of Antioch (Syria). Westcott and Hort broke new ground in the study of the text of the Greek New Testament; while their classifications have been corrected and expanded, they continue in use.

Several other editions of the Greek text appeared, but Eberhard Nestle's Greek text, the *Novum Testamentum Graece*, published in 1898 by the Württemberg Bible Society, Stuttgart, Germany, dealt the final blow to the *Textus Receptus*. Kurt Aland and Barbara Aland explain the importance of the Nestle text:

> What Eberhard Nestle did was actually quite simple (a radical break-through is always simple in retrospect): he compared the texts of Tischendorf . . . and of Westcott-Hort. When the two differed he consulted a third edition for a deciding vote (at first Richard Francis Weymouth's second edition of 1892, and after 1901 Bernhard Weiss' 1894–1900 edition). This made a majority decision possible: the agreement of two editions determined the text, while the reading of the third was placed in the apparatus, and a series of symbols enabled the reader to reconstruct with accuracy the texts of the editions used (indicating even the marginal readings in Westcott-Hort's edition together with their evaluations). . . . In effect, this purely mechanical system of a majority text summarized the results of nineteenth-century textual scholarship. It eliminated the extremes of Tischendorf (due to his partiality to ℵ) and of Westcott and Hort (with their partiality to B), especially after Weiss' edition was adopted. It produced a text that not only lasted seventy years, but on the whole truly represented the state of knowledge of the time.[37]

In 1955 the American Bible Society, under the initiative of Eugene A. Nida,

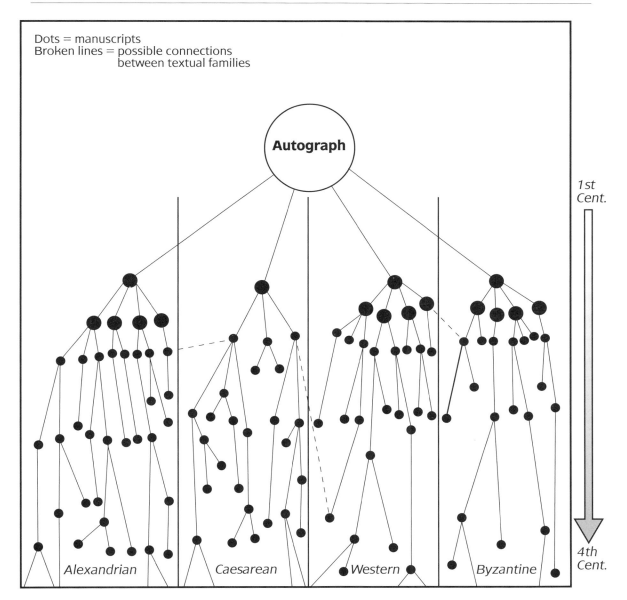

Dots = manuscripts
Broken lines = possible connections
between textual families

Autograph

1st Cent.

Alexandrian

Caesarean

Western

Byzantine

4th Cent.

called together an international group of scholars to prepare a Greek New Testament that could be used by hundreds of Bible translation committees to revise existing Bible translations or make new translations. Many missionaries, translating the New Testament into modern languages, needed an accurate and easy-to-use text of the Greek New Testament. The international team of scholars forming the editorial committee of this new Greek text were Matthew Black of St. Andrews, Scotland; Bruce Metzger of Princeton; Allen Wikgren of Chicago; and Kurt Aland of Münster, Westphalia. This was the beginning of what is commonly known as the United Bible Societies' Greek Text. At the same time, Aland was working on another Greek text that became known as the Nestle-Aland Greek Text. Aland was instrumental in both texts of the Greek New Testament (even though they seem to be competing editions), and in time the scholars agreed on enough

Figure 13.10.
Possible relationships among the major Greek textual families.

221

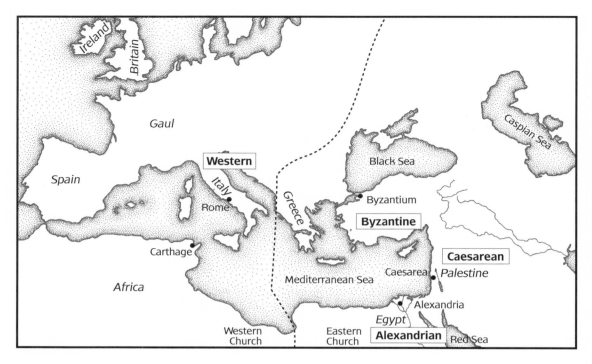

Western

Byzantium

Byzantine

Caesarean

Caesarea Palestine

Mediterranean Sea

Alexandria

Egypt

Alexandrian Red Sea

Western
Church

Eastern
Church

Map 3. Areas where the textual families developed (in bold type).

readings that they decided to use the same Greek text for both works.

Two different critical Greek texts are currently in use, namely, *The Greek New Testament* (now in the fourth revised edition, 1994) and the Nestle-Aland *Novum Testamentum Graece* (now in the twenty-seventh revised edition, 1993); the text for both is the same even though the textual apparatuses differ as follows: the textual notes of the Nestle-Aland text list more of the textual history, whereas the former lists only those that substantially affect the reading of the text; and the *Greek New Testament* (4th ed.) gives graded evaluations for each textual note so that the reader can determine how certain a variant reading is, whereas the Nestle-Aland text does not.

Figure 13.11. Two methods of textual criticism.

Textual Families

The classification of New Testament texts into textual families developed by Westcott and Hort has been expanded by New Testament textual critics. The concept of textual families is very simple: manuscripts that are copied from one another bear strong similarities to each other (fig. 13.10).

Text families were often restricted to the locality where they where copied, unless a manuscript was transported to a different region. Families are thus named for the area where they developed and can be located on map 3.

Scholars have categorized many manuscripts into related families and have evaluated them to determine which are more accurate. Once an error has been made, it

---

Eclectic Text	*Single Text*
Collects the best readings from many manuscripts	Uses the readings from a single text or textual family

generally remains within that family unless it is removed for some reason.

Scholars rate the accuracy of the various textual families in order from most to least accurate:

1. Alexandrian family
2. Caesarean family
3. "Western" family
4. Byzantine family

When manuscripts contain characteristics from more than one family, they are sometimes referred to as mixed manuscripts. Sometimes errors in certain manuscripts may be corrected by comparing that manuscript with other manuscripts outside its text family, but it is more likely that new errors will continue to be incorporated into later manuscripts in each successive copy.

Eclectic Text versus Single Text

The New Testament textual critic must decide whether one text may have been preserved more accurately than any other text and so use only that text, or whether it is better to choose the most accurate readings from all the New Testament texts and combine them into an eclectic text. The latter seems more reasonable since errors have been incorporated into every text through the transmission (or copying) process. Thus a text that combines the most plausible readings will probably read closer to the original Greek text than will any single text. An eclectic text weighs and compares the various readings, incorporating the best into one text. A single-text approach to textual criticism presumes one manuscript has superior readings. This issue is vital to the King James debate, since those who argue for the authority of the King James Bible usually do so based on the supposition that the Byzantine text is superior. However, the King James Version was translated from the combination of only about six or seven medieval manuscripts. By comparison, today we have available thousands of manuscripts, some

dating to the second century, whose early readings should at least be considered when attempting to determine the original text. (For a fuller discussion of the King James debate, see appendix 3.)

Procedure for New Testament Textual Criticism

Collecting the Evidence

The most difficult and yet the most important part of New Testament textual criticism is gathering and collecting all the available manuscripts and resources necessary to make an informed decision. The New Testament text critic must carefully study all of the evidence, both internal and external, before making this decision. There are three primary sources of external evidence: New Testament manuscripts, versions, and church Fathers (see fig. 13.12). The United Bible Societies' Greek text has already done much of this collecting.[38] Its textual apparatus includes most of the evidence for the various readings of selected passages to help the reader make an informed decision.

Evaluating the Evidence

Copyist errors in the New Testament are the same as discussed earlier for the Old Testament; tables 13.2 and 13.3 list New Testament examples of unintentional and intentional changes to the text.

Metzger observes that "scribes who thought were more dangerous than those who wished merely to be faithful in copying what lay before them."[39] Intentional errors are much harder to detect and correct since it is generally difficult to know why the changes were made. At times scribes have even reintroduced a previously corrected error into the text; Metzger cites an interesting example from Codex Vaticanus:

> In the margin of codex Vaticanus at Heb. i.3 there is a curiously indignant note by a rather recent scribe [perhaps from the thirteenth century] who restored the original reading of the

223

codex, φανερῶν, for which a corrector had substituted the usual reading, φέρων: "Fool and knave, can't you leave the old reading alone and not alter it!" (ἀμαθέστατε καὶ κακέ, ἄφες τὸν παλαιόν, μὴ μεταποίει).[40]

Errors due to intentional changes were most likely introduced when the copyist thought that there was a mistake in spelling or theology or when the text seemed to conflict with another biblical passage.

Determining the Most Plausible Reading

Determining the correct reading of a New Testament passage follows principles similar to those used in Old Testament textual criticism:

1. Manuscripts must be weighed, not counted.
2. Determine the reading that would most likely give rise to the others.
3. The more distinctive reading is usually preferable.
4. The shorter reading is generally favored.
5. Determine which reading is more appropriate in its context (examine literary context, grammatical or spelling errors, historical context).
6. Examine parallel passages for any differences and determine why they may appear.

Two types of evidence exist for various readings: internal and external. Internal evidence is that found within the text; for example the literary context, particular grammatical or spelling conventions that the author uses, and literary forms such as parallelism or chiasms. External evidence is found outside the text from other manuscripts or source documents.

External evidence. External evidence includes other New Testament manuscripts, versions, or writings of church fathers, each of which must be evaluated and ranked since some will be considerably more important than others.

Since New Testament manuscript evidence is quite extensive, it needs to be evaluated according to the criteria in table 13.4. In the evaluation process the skill of the text critic becomes very important, for each criterion cannot be weighted equally. Some sources will be weighted more heavily because they are older or come from more

Figure 13.12. Sources of textual evidence.

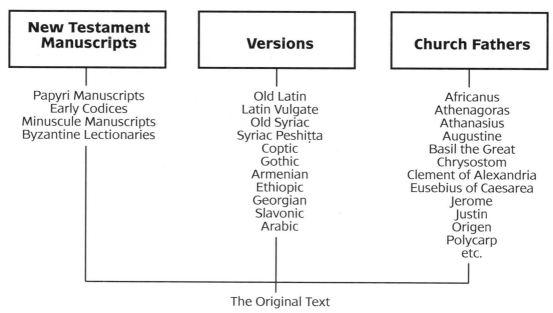

New Testament Manuscripts	Versions	Church Fathers
Papyri Manuscripts Early Codices Minuscule Manuscripts Byzantine Lectionaries	Old Latin Latin Vulgate Old Syriac Syriac Peshiṭṭa Coptic Gothic Armenian Ethiopic Georgian Slavonic Arabic	Africanus Athenagoras Athanasius Augustine Basil the Great Chrysostom Clement of Alexandria Eusebius of Caesarea Jerome Justin Origen Polycarp etc.

The Original Text

Table 13.2 Copyist Errors in New Testament Texts
Unintentional Changes

Error	Definition	Possible Examples
1. Mistaken letters	Similar-looking letters were sometimes interchanged (e.g., C, Є, Θ, and O in uncial script)	In 1 Tim. 3:16 ΟС ("who"; $\aleph$*, A*) and ΘС ("God"; $\aleph^2$, A^c) were confused in some uncial MSS.
2. Homophony	Substitution of similar-sounding words	In Rom. 5:1 similar-sounding ἔχομεν ("we have"; $\aleph^1$, B^2) and ἔχωμεν ("let us have," or "we may have"; $\aleph$*, A, B*) were confused.
3. Haplography	Omission of a letter or a word usually due to a similar letter or word in context	In John 1:13 ἐγενήθησαν (from γίνομαι; $\mathfrak{P}^{75}$, A, B*) and ἐγεννήθησαν (from γεννάω; $\mathfrak{P}^{66}$, $\aleph$, B^2) were confused. Both forms can mean "were born," but they come from different roots.
4. Dittography	A letter or word that has been written twice rather than once	In Mark 3:16 καὶ ἐποίησεν τοὺς δώδεκα ("and he appointed the twelve") may be a dittograph from Mark 3:14. In Acts 19:34 μεγάλη ἡ Ἄρτεμις Ἐφεσίων ("great is Artemis of the Ephesians") is written twice in Codex Vaticanus (B).
5. Metathesis	Reversal in order of two letters or words	In John 1:42 Ἰωάννου ("of John"; $\mathfrak{P}^{66}$, $\mathfrak{P}^{75}$, $\aleph$) and Ἰωνᾶ ("of Jonah"; A, B^2) were confused.
6. Fusion	Incorrect word division that results in two words joined as one	In Mark 10:40 ἀλλ' οἷς ("but for whom"; A, B^2) and ἄλλοις ("for others"; $\aleph$, B*) were confused.
7. Fission	Incorrect word division that results in one word written as two	In Rom. 7:14 οἴδαμεν ("we know"; B^2, D^2) and οἶδα μέν ("on the one hand I know"; 33, l 833) were confused.
8. Homoioteleuton	An omission caused by two words or phrases that end similarly	In 1 John 2:23 τὸν πατέρα ἔχει ("has the Father") appears twice, causing some copyists' eyes to skip from the first to the second and omit the intervening words ὁ ὁμολογῶν τὸν υἱὸν καί ("the one who confesses the Son also").
9. Homoioarchton	An omission caused by two words or phrases that begin similarly	In Luke 10:41–42 the similarity between Μάρθα ("Martha") and Μαριάμ ("Mary") may have caused some copyists' eyes to skip from one to the other and omit the intervening words μεριμνᾷς καὶ θορυβάζῃ περὶ πολλά, ἑνὸς δέ ἐστιν χρεία ("you are worried and troubled about many things, but there is need of one thing").

Table 13.3 Changes in New Testament Texts
Intentional Changes

Change	Possible Examples
1. Changes in grammar or spelling	In Matt. 1:7–8 Ἀσάφ ("Asaph"; 𝔓^Ivid, ℵ, B) was changed by later copyists to Ἀσά ("Asa"; L, W, Δ), the king of Judah (1 Kings 15:9–24).
2. Harmonization (modifying a passage to agree with another passage)	In Luke 23:38 words similar to John 19:20 ("it was written in Aramaic, Latin, and Greek") were added by later copyists (C³, W, D).
3. Adding natural complements or words that go together	In Matt. 6:4, 6 ἐν τῷ φανερῷ ("in the open, openly"; L, W, Θ) was added to "your Father, who sees what is done in secret, will reward you." In Matt. 27:41 καὶ Φαρισαίων ("and Pharisees"; D, W) was added to γραμματέων ("scribes").
4. Clearing up difficulties	In Mark 1:2–3 the composite quote from Mal. 3:1 and Isa. 40:3 attributed to "Isaiah the prophet" (ℵ, B) was changed to ἐν τοῖς προφήταις ("in the prophets"; A, W).
5. Conflated readings (combining two or more readings)	In Luke 24:53 some MSS read εὐλογοῦντες ("blessing"; 𝔓⁷⁵, ℵ, B), others read αἰνοῦντες ("praising"; D, some Old Latin MSS), and still others read αἰνοῦντες καὶ εὐλογοῦντες ("praising and blessing"; A, C², W).
6. Theological changes	In Luke 2:41, 43 οἱ γονεῖς αὐτοῦ ("his parents"; ℵ, B, D) was changed to "Joseph and Mary" in v. 41 (Old Latin MSS) and "Joseph and his mother" in v. 43 (A, C, Ψ), possibly to safeguard the doctrine of the virgin birth by clarifying that Joseph was not Jesus' biological father.
7. Other additions	In Luke 24:53 ἀμήν ("amen"; A, B, C²) was added at the end of the verse.

accurate text families. In general, early manuscripts take precedence over older ones since older manuscripts are further away from the originals and have probably gone through more stages of copying. Each time a text is copied errors may creep into the text. But the second criterion is also important since certain text families have fewer errors to begin with. It is at this point that manuscripts need to be arranged into groups. Those manuscripts that share peculiarities in spelling, points of grammar, or unusual errors are probably related and can be grouped into textual families. Finally it is important to consider the independence of witnesses; if two manuscripts are related or copied from the same text they should be considered as one witness

so as not to skew the evidence for that reading. It is preferable to collect evidence for specific readings from a wide geographical area to eliminate as much as possible copying from related sources. However, this criterion is sometimes difficult to evaluate, since the geographical origin of some manuscripts and people is not always known. Table 13.5 lists text families of various sources.

Versions can be evaluated by the same criteria: date, accuracy, and independence of sources. The date is fairly easy to determine, but it is difficult to know whether a version was ever modified. Accuracy can be evaluated by comparing how consistently an author translates certain terms or verb forms, now known as the author's deviation; a great deal of work has been done in this area in the last ten years. Independence of sources is a key factor among versions, as many are interrelated; for example, the Latin Vulgate, Syriac Peshiṭta, and Armenian versions are all related to the Septuagint.

It has been said that the church fathers quoted the New Testament so extensively that if all our other sources of the New Testament were to be destroyed, it could be reconstructed from the church fathers' quotations alone. Some church fathers date to a very early period and quote extensively from the New Testament; but these quotations must be used with care since the Fathers sometimes quoted from memory or modified the text to fit a given situation. The great importance of quotations from church fathers is that they help us to localize and date various readings and types of the text. Table 13.6 lists the more important church fathers.

Internal evidence. Internal evidence from a passage itself can help determine the original reading. For example, if the author of the Gospel of John always used the name "Christ" for Jesus, but then in a manuscript the name "Jesus" appears instead, this is a plausible corruption. There are many different types of clues within a passage that may help confirm a specific reading of a text (e.g., parallel units, characteristic style of an author, grammatical issues), which is why skill and familiarity with the manuscripts is useful. Some commentaries make note of internal evidence, but the most helpful work is the textual commentary on the Greek text published by the United Bible Societies.[41] This work was written by Bruce Metzger, one of the scholars who edited the United Bible Societies' Greek text. In it he explains why the committee chose specific readings and the most pertinent information that was used. There are two editions of this textual commentary, so be certain to use the one that matches your edition of the United Bible Societies' Greek text. This work can help the beginning New Testament textual

Table 13.4
Evaluating New Testament Manuscripts

Criteria	Rationale
Date	The earliest reading is closest in time to the original text, allowing less opportunity for corruption to occur.
Accuracy	Accuracy is determined by how many errors are found in a given manuscript or family.
Independence of witnesses	Witnesses that are related to each other should be considered one source since they were probably copied from each other (as in textual families).

critic understand the logic that professionals use in determining the most accurate reading of a specific passage. A later section in this chapter explains how to use the United Bible Societies' Greek text.

Emendations

An emendation is a reading of the text that is not supported by any textual evidence and, especially in the New Testament, is unlikely to be an original reading, as F. F. Bruce explains:

> It is doubtful whether there is any reading in the New Testament which requires to be conjecturally emended. The wealth of attestation is such that the true reading is almost invariably bound to be preserved by at least one of the thousands of witnesses. Sometimes what was at first put forward as a conjectural emendation has in the course of time turned up in one of our witnesses. For example, it was long suspected by a number of scholars that in John 19:29 it was not "hyssop" (Gk. *hyssōpos*) that was used to convey the sponge filled with vinegar to our Lord's mouth on the cross, but a soldier's javelin (Gk. *hyssos*). But more recently the reading "javelin," which was previously a mere conjectural emendation, has been recognised in the first hand of a rather late manuscript, and it is adopted in the text of the New English Bible; but even so it is an extremely doubtful reading.[42]

Table 13.5
Text Families and Their Sources

	Alexandrian	Caesarean	Western	Byzantine
Gospels	$\mathfrak{P}^{1}$ $\mathfrak{P}^{3}$ $\mathfrak{P}^{4}$ $\mathfrak{P}^{5}$ $\mathfrak{P}^{7}$ $\mathfrak{P}^{22}$ $\mathfrak{P}^{39}$ ($\mathfrak{P}^{66}$) $\mathfrak{P}^{75}$	$\mathfrak{P}^{37}$ $\mathfrak{P}^{45}$	$\mathfrak{P}^{25}$	
	ℵ B C L Q T W (Lk 1:1–8:12; Jn) (X) Z Δ (Mk) Ξ Ψ (exc. Mt) 054 059 060 0162	N O W (Mk 5:31ff) Θ Σ Φ	D W (Mk 1:1–5:30) 0171	A E F G H K M P S U V W (Mt; Lk 8:13ff) Υ Γ Δ (exc. Mk) Π Ω
	20 33 164 215 376 579 (exc. Mt) 718 850 892 1241 1342 (Mk)	fam¹ fam¹³ 28 157 565 700 1071 1604		most other minuscules
	Boh (Sah)	Geo Arm Pal-Syr	It (esp. e k) Sin-Syr Cur-Syr	Goth later versions
	Clem-Alex (Or) Ath Cyr-Alex	(Or) Eus Cyr-Jer	Ir Diatessaron? Clem-Alex Tert Cyp (Aug)	later fathers
Acts	$\mathfrak{P}^{8}$ $\mathfrak{P}^{45}$ ($\mathfrak{P}^{50}$)	$\mathfrak{P}^{45}$?	$\mathfrak{P}^{29}$ $\mathfrak{P}^{38}$ $\mathfrak{P}^{41}$ $\mathfrak{P}^{48}$	
	ℵ A B (C) Ψ 048 076 096	I?	D E 066	H L P S 049
	6 33 81 104 326 1175	text type not determined	257 383 440 614 913 1108 1245 1518 1611 1739 2138 2298	most other minuscules
	Boh (Sah)		It Hark-Syr^mg	Goth later versions
	Clem-Alex? (Or) Ath Cyr-Alex	Cyr-Jer?		later fathers
Pauline Epistles and Hebrews	$\mathfrak{P}^{10}$ $\mathfrak{P}^{13}$ $\mathfrak{P}^{15}$ $\mathfrak{P}^{16}$ $\mathfrak{P}^{27}$ $\mathfrak{P}^{32}$ $\mathfrak{P}^{40}$ $\mathfrak{P}^{46}$ $\mathfrak{P}^{65}$			
	ℵ A B (C) H I M P Ψ 048 081 088 0220		D E F G	K L 049
	6 33 81 104 326 424^c 1175 1739 1908	text type not determined	88 181 383 915 917 1836 1898 1912	most other minuscules
	Boh (Sah)		It	Goth later versions
				later fathers
General Epistles	$\mathfrak{P}^{20}$ $\mathfrak{P}^{23}$ $\mathfrak{P}^{72}$ $\mathfrak{P}^{74}$?		$\mathfrak{P}^{38}$	
	ℵ A B (C) P Ψ 048 056 0142 0156		D E	H K L S
	33 81 104 323 326 424^c 1175 1739 2298	text type not determined	383	42 398 most other minuscules
	Boh (Sah)		It Hark-Syr^mg	Goth later versions
	Clem-Alex? (Or) Ath Cyr-Alex		Ir Tert Cyp Eph Aug	later fathers
Revelation	$\mathfrak{P}^{18}$ $\mathfrak{P}^{24}$ ($\mathfrak{P}^{47}$)			
	(ℵ) A (C) P 0169 0207		F?	046 051 052
	61 69 94 241 254 1006 1175 1611 1841 1852 2040 2053 2344 2351	text type not determined		82 93 429 469 808 920 2048 most other minuscules
			It?	Goth later versions
				later fathers

Adapted from J. H. Greenlee, *Introduction to New Testament Textual Criticism,* rev. ed. (Peabody, MA: Hendrickson, 1995), 117–18.

The United Bible Societies' Greek Text

The following section from the current United Bible Societies' Greek text containing the textual apparatus of Ephesians 1:1 will help the reader become acquainted with how the UBS Greek text is used

¹**1 {C}** ἐν Ἐφέσῳ / Å ² A B² D F G Ψᶜ (Ψ* *illegible*) 075 0150 33 81 104 256 263 365 424* 436 459 1175 1241 1319 1573 1852 1881 1912 1962 2127 2200 2464 *Byz* [K L P] *Lect* it^ar. b, d, f, g, o, r vg syr^p, h cop ^sa. bo arm eth geo slav Ps-Ignatius Chrysostom Theodore^lat; Victorinus-Rome Ambrosiaster Jerome Pelagius //*omit* 𝔓⁴⁶ ℵ* B* 6 424ᶜ 1739 Marcion^acc. to Tertullian Origen^vid

The textual notes provide a great deal of information about the Greek text, generally in the following order.

A capital letter (A, B, C, D). This letter system was devised by the editors of the Greek text to give the reader some indication of the relative certainty of the reading. The readings are rated from A to D, depending upon the evidence. On a continuum A denotes those readings that the editors consider very certain and D the least certain. In the example from Ephesians 1:1 the footnote states that the insertion of the Greek words ἐν Ἐφέσῳ (*en Ephesō*, "in Ephesus") into the text has a C rating; that is, it is a fairly uncertain reading.

Textual evidence for the word or phrase as it appears in the Greek text. Usually the evidence is given in the order and with the abbreviations shown in table 13.7. Table 13.8 helps to decipher the

Table 13.6
Significant Church Fathers

Father	Date	Location
Justin Martyr	c. 100–165	Samaria and Rome
Tatian	c. 110–172	Syria and Rome
Marcion	c. 130–160	Pontus (Asia Minor) and Rome
Irenaeus, bishop of Lyons	c. 130–202	Lyons, France
Clement of Alexandria	c. 155–220	Alexandria, Egypt
Tertullian	c. 160–220	Carthage, North Africa
Hippolytus	c. 170–235	Rome
Origen	c. 185–253	Alexandria, Egypt, and Caesarea, Palestine
Eusebius, bishop of Caesarea	c. 265–339	Caesarea, Palestine
Athanasius, bishop of Alexandria	c. 296–373	Alexandria, Egypt
Ephraem the Syrian	c. 306–373	Edessa, Syria
Lucifer of Cagliari	c. 310–371	Cagliari, Italy
Hilary of Poitiers	c. 315–368	Poitiers, France
Epiphanius, bishop of Salamis	c. 315–403	Salamis, Cyprus
Gregory of Nazianzus	c. 330–390	Cappadocia (Asia Minor)
Gregory of Nyssa	c. 330–395	Cappadocia (Asia Minor)
Ambrose of Milan	c. 339–397	Milan, Italy
Tyrannius Rufinus	c. 345–411	Italy and Palestine
Jerome	c. 345–420	Rome and Bethlehem
John Chrysostom	c. 347–407	Constantinople, Byzantium
Theodore of Mopsuestia	c. 350–428	Cilicia (Asia Minor)
Pelagius	c. 354–after 418	Rome
Augustine, bishop of Hippo	c. 354–430	Hippo, North Africa
Isidore of Pelusium	c. 360–440	Pelusium, Egypt
Ambrosiaster (= Pseudo-Ambrose)	c. 375	Rome
Cyril of Alexandria	c. 390–444	Alexandria, Egypt

Table 13.7
Textual Evidence

Source	Description	Examples
1. Papyri	Designated by a capital P in Gothic script plus a superscript Arabic numeral	$\mathfrak{P}^{45}$, $\mathfrak{P}^{52}$, $\mathfrak{P}^{75}$
2. Uncials	Notated with capital letters in English, Hebrew, or Greek or with a number beginning with zero	A, ℵ, Ψ, 044
3. Cursives (including minuscules)	Notated with Arabic numerals	453, 984, 1574
4. Byzantine Lectionaries	The church's schedule of readings from the Old or New Testaments, notated with a lowercase l in italics plus a superscript Arabic numeral	*l*^{45}, *l*^{524}
5. Versions	Translations of the Bible in other languages	Old Latin, Old Syriac, Peshiṭta
6. Church Fathers	Quotations from the Bible in the writings of the church fathers	Augustine, Eusebius, Jerome

abbreviated information as it appears in the textual apparatus.

Several Latin abbreviations used to conserve space are listed in table 13.9.[43]

Other information about the manuscripts abbreviated in the textual apparatus, including their dates, content, and where they are currently housed, appears in a list at the beginning of the United Bible Societies' Greek text (pp. 6*–52*). Because many manuscripts do not contain the entire New Testament, some letters are reused (e.g., two D *sigla* represent two different manuscripts: the first a fifth-century Codex of the Gospels and Acts, the second a sixth-century codex of the Pauline Epistles). The abbreviations at the front of the United Bible Societies' Greek text provide this information, but one must pay close attention to the contexts of the manuscripts. When one is working in the Gospels, for instance, make sure that the manuscript *sigla* contains that part of the text:

e = Gospels

Table 13.8
Textual Apparatus

Abbreviation	Meaning
( )	Indicates that a witness supports the reading for which it is cited but deviates from it in minor details
*	The reading in the original hand of a manuscript, as distinguished from later correctors
X^{12,3,c}	Successive correctors of a manuscript (see fig. 13.13); "c" is the last corrector
?	Indicates that a witness supports a given reading, but there is some doubt
cj	Conjecture
X^{comm}	The commentary section of a manuscript where the reading differs from the accompanying Greek text
X^{gr}	The Greek text of a bilingual manuscript
X^{mg}	Textual evidence written in the margin of a manuscript
sic	Indicates an abnormality exactly reproduced from the original
X^{supp}	A portion of a manuscript supplied by a later hand where the original was missing
X^{txt}	The text of a manuscript when it differs from another reading given in the commentary section accompanying the text
X^{vid}	Indicates apparent support for a given reading in a manuscript whose state of preservation makes absolute verification impossible
X$^{v.r.}$	Indicates a variant reading specifically designated as an alternative in manuscripts or other witnesses

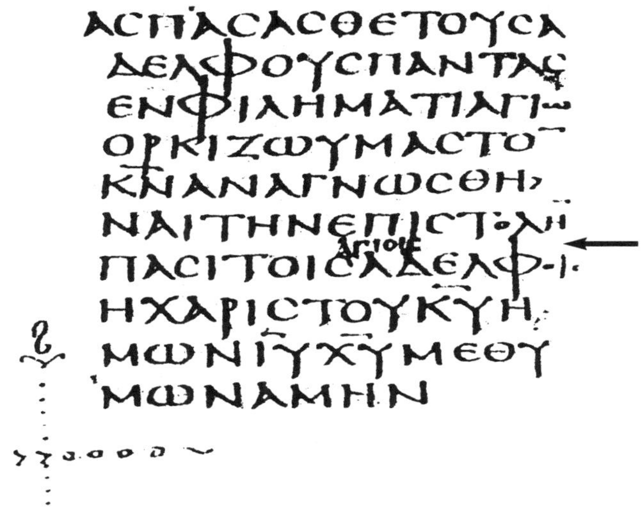

a = Acts
c = Catholic or General Epistles
p = Pauline Epistles
r = Revelation

The works are usually listed in chronological order within their categories; the century dates of the manuscripts are noted in Roman numerals (e.g., VI = sixth century).

Two slashed lines (//) indicate the end of the textual information for the first reading, after which the note for the second reading begins in the same sequence as above.

While the textual apparatus of the United Bible Societies' Greek text provides most of the information necessary to determine the most plausible original reading of a passage, a chart may prove helpful when one is collating the evidence for the various readings (see fig. 13.14).

Now we are ready to evaluate evidence found in the textual apparatus, beginning with an example from Ephesians 1:1. The information will be divided into external and internal evidence.

The first principle of textual criticism states that manuscripts must be weighed and not merely counted. If we were to rely solely on the number of manuscripts in support of a specific reading, then the phrase *in Ephesus* should be included in this verse, but a more careful examination of the evidence suggests that the original reading probably omits this phrase. The evidence to be compared is shown in table 13.10.

Earlier evidence from $\mathfrak{P}^{46}$, Codices Sinaiticus and Vaticanus, each of which is very accurate, favors omitting the phrase *in Ephesus*. Text-critical scholars have determined the texts in the Alexandrian family to be most accurate (see the discussion about textual families), which

Figure 13.13. A correction to the text of 1 Thessalonians 5:27 found in Codex Sinaiticus written in by a later copyist (see arrow). [British Library]

Table 13.9
Latin Abbreviations

Abbreviation	Definition
pc (pauci)	a few manuscripts
al (alii)	other manuscripts
pm (permulti)	a great many other manuscripts
pl (plerique)	most other manuscripts
rell (reliqui)	the remaining witnesses
vid (videtur)	as it seems, apparently
omn (omnes)	all manuscripts
codd (codices)	manuscripts of a version or church father as distinguished from an edition
ap (apud)	in the writings of, on the authority of (e.g., Papias ap Eusebius)
pt (partim)	divided evidence (e.g., Orig^pt signifies that Origen is inconsistent in his quotation of the same passage)
2/4	divided evidence (e.g., Origen 2/4 signifies that in two out of four quotations of a passage Origen supports a given reading)

Figure 13.14.
A chart for comparing textual variants.

Passage: _____

Various Readings		
Reading 1	Reading 2	Reading 3
Meaning	Meaning	Meaning
External Evidence	External Evidence	External Evidence
Which one is favored and why?		
Internal Evidence		
Conclusions		

also supports the omission of the phrase *in Ephesus.*

There is little internal evidence to help determine the correct reading, but the greeting is similar to Paul's other letters, and a location would usually be included at this point, as the grammar and other greetings indicate.

The editors of the United Bible Societies' Greek text decided that the phrase *in Ephesus* was not in the original text since it is omitted in the earliest manuscripts (𝔓⁴⁶, ℵ*, B*, Origen) and does not appear until about the fifth century (e.g., Codex Alexandrinus). From this and other evidence they argue that the document was an encyclical letter sent to various churches, the church at Ephesus being the chief, and thus the name was left out until the letter was sent to a specific church. However, by the fifth century the tradition that the letter had originally been sent to Ephesus caused the name to be placed in the letter; thus the final decision of the editors was to leave the phrase in the United Bible Societies' Greek text but to put it in square brackets. This decision is explained in detail by Bruce Metzger, one of the editors of the United Bible Societies' Greek text, in his commentary.[44]

Table 13.10
Readings of Ephesians 1:1

First Reading "in Ephesus"	Second Reading Omitting "in Ephesus"
Codex Sinaiticus (ℵ² [2d corrector]; 7th cent.; Alexandrian family)	𝔓⁴⁶ (c. A.D. 200; Alexandrian family)
Codex Alexandrinus (A; 5th cent.; Alexandrian family)	Codex Sinaiticus (ℵ* [original handwriting]; 4th cent.; Alexandrian family)
Codex Vaticanus (B² [2d corrector]; 6th–7th cent.; Alexandrian family)	Codex Vaticanus (B* [original handwriting]; 4th cent.; Alexandrian family)
Codex Claromontanus (D; 6th cent.; Western family)	Marcion (2d cent.; according to Tertullian)
33 (9th cent.; Alexandrian family)	Origenᵛⁱᵈ (d. A.D. 253; vid = Origen appears to support this reading, but the context prevents complete certainty)
81 (A.D. 1044; Alexandrian family)	
some Old Latin MSS (5th–9th cent.; Western family)	
Latin Vulgate (6th–8th cent.; Western family)	
Syriac (Byzantine family): Peshiṭta (early 5th cent.); Harclean (A.D. 616)	
Coptic versions (Alexandrian family): Sahidic (7th–9th cent.); Bohairic (12th cent.)	
Chrysostom (d. A.D. 407)	
Victorinus of Rome (4th cent.)	
Ambrosiaster (4th cent.)	
Pelagius (d. after A.D. 418)	

Overall Result of New Testament Textual Criticism

Sir Fredric Kenyon (d. August 1952), a famous New Testament text critic, summarizes the overall result of New Testament textual criticism: "[I]t is reassuring at the end to find that the general result of all these discoveries and all this study is to strengthen the proof of the authenticity of the Scriptures, and our conviction that we have in our hands, in substantial integrity, the veritable Word of God."[45]

For Further Reading

Aland, K., and B. Aland. *The Text of the New Testament: An Introduction to the Critical Editions and to the Theory and Practice of Modern Textual Criticism*. Translated by E. F. Rhodes. 2d ed. Grand Rapids: Eerdmans, 1989.

Birdsall, J. N. "The New Testament Text." In *CHB*, 1:308–77.

Black, D. A. *New Testament Textual Criticism: A Concise Guide*. Grand Rapids: Baker, 1994.

Comfort, P. W. *Early Manuscripts and Modern Translations of the New Testament*. Wheaton, IL: Tyndale, 1990; reprint, Grand Rapids: Baker, 1996.

Fee, G. D. "The Textual Criticism of the New Testament." In *The Expositor's Bible Commentary*, edited by F. E. Gaebelein, 1:419–33. 12 vols. Grand Rapids: Zondervan, 1979.

Finegan, J. *Encountering New Testament Manuscripts: A Working Introduction to Textual Criticism*. Grand Rapids: Eerdmans, 1974.

Greenlee, J. H. *Introduction to New Testament Textual Criticism*. Rev. ed. Peabody, MA: Hendrickson, 1995.

———. *Scribes, Scrolls, and Scripture: A Student's Guide to New Testament Textual Criticism*. Grand Rapids: Eerdmans, 1985.

Holmes, M. W. "Textual Criticism." In *New Testament Criticism and Interpretation*, edited by D. A. Black and D. S. Dockery, 101–36. Grand Rapids: Zondervan, 1991.

Metzger, B. M. *Chapters in the History of New Testament Textual Criticism*. New Testament Tools and Studies, vol. 4. Grand Rapids: Eerdmans, 1963.

Sources for New Testament Textual Criticism

Abundance of Extant New Testament Manuscripts

The study of New Testament manuscripts differs significantly from that of the Old Testament in that there are at least 5,400 known extant fragments or manuscripts of the New Testament text compared with about eight hundred for the Old Testament. The difficulty of Old Testament textual criticism is to find enough evidence to determine the most accurate reading of the text; New Testament textual criticism experiences the opposite problem of wading through masses of manuscripts, not to mention thousands of quotations from the early church fathers, to determine the most accurate reading. In addition there are thousands of copies of New Testament translations (e.g., Latin Vulgate, Syriac Peshiṭta, Gothic, Coptic).

Table 14.1 indicates the great abundance of New Testament materials compared with other works from antiquity.[1] The large number of New Testament manuscripts reveal to us the importance of these works for the early church.

One of the most difficult problems to emerge with the discovery of an ever-increasing number of manuscripts and other sources for the New Testament was a convenient method to record them. Initially titles and brief descriptions were assigned to each manuscript, but this proved cumbersome, and scholars often inconsistently assigned titles to the same manuscripts. A Swiss scholar, Johann Wettstein, was among the first to standardize designations in his two-volume Greek New Testament published in Amsterdam about 1751–1752. In his simple, convenient system uncial manuscripts are designated by capital letters and minus-

Table 14.1
Extant Ancient Manuscripts

Source	Date	Extant Manuscripts
Thucydides, *History of the Peloponnesian War*	c. 460–400 B.C.	Only 8 extant MSS, the earliest dating c. A.D. 900, plus a few fragments from 1st cent. A.D.
Julius Caesar, *Gallic War*	composed 58–50 B.C.	Several extant MSS, but only 9 or 10 of good quality; the oldest is about 900 years after Caesar's time
Livy, *Annals of the Roman People*	59 B.C.–A.D. 17	Only 35 of the original 142 books survived; 20 extant MSS; only 1 MS (containing fragments of bks. 3–6) is as old as the 4th cent.
Tacitus, *Histories* and *Annals*	c. A.D. 100	Only 4 and 1/2 of the original 14 books of *Histories* and 10 (with portions of 2 more) of the 16 books of *Annals* survived in 2 MSS dating from the 9th and 11th cent.

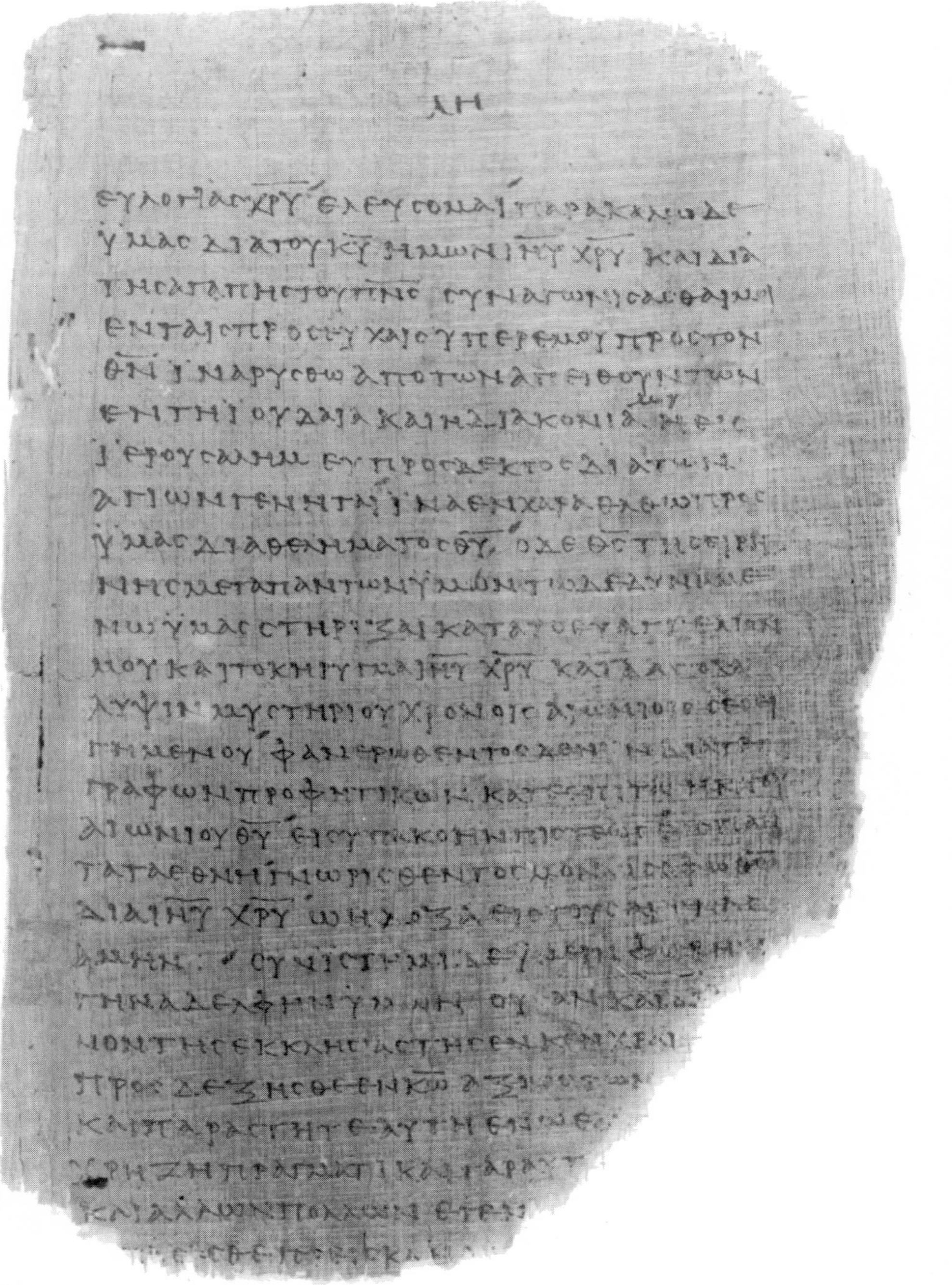

Figure 14.1.
𝔓⁴⁶, portions of which are held by the Chester Beatty Library and the University of Michigan, dates to about A.D. 200. This page is of Romans 15:29–16:3 (with the doxology of 16:25–27 placed after 15:33). [University of Michigan Library]

cules by Arabic numerals. The system was modified by Caspar René Gregory, professor at the University of Leipzig, Germany, in the latter nineteenth century, and a slightly modified form of this system is in use today. Until a few years ago, Kurt Aland, a New Testament scholar in Münster/Westphalia, Germany, was responsible for ascribing sigla to new manuscripts and fragments at the Institute for New Testament Research. This standardized system is referred to in the textual apparatus (generally at the bottom of the page) of modern printed Greek editions in cases where there are variants in the manuscripts.

New Testament Manuscripts

Of the approximately 5,400 New Testament manuscripts, about 100 are papyrus manuscripts or fragments, about 266 are uncial manuscripts, about 2,795 are minuscule manuscripts, and the others are lectionaries.

Biblical Papyri

All of the biblical papyri are fragmentary and are notated with a Gothic P followed by an Arabic numeral (e.g., $\mathfrak{P}^{32}$, $\mathfrak{P}^{52}$, $\mathfrak{P}^{74}$). A description of major collections follows.

Chester Beatty Collection

In 1931, twelve fragments of biblical manuscripts were discovered in a Coptic graveyard in Egypt. They were sold to Chester Beatty, an American living in London, but they are now housed in the Beatty Museum in Dublin, Ireland. These fragments of both Old and New Testament texts date to as early as 200 or 250; two of the more important fragments are $\mathfrak{P}^{45}$ and $\mathfrak{P}^{46}$. $\mathfrak{P}^{45}$ consists of 30 portions of leaves of a papyrus codex originally about 220 leaves in length, including all four Gospels and Acts. There are 2 leaves from the Book of Matthew, 6 from Mark, 7 from Luke, 2 from John, and 13 from Acts. $\mathfrak{P}^{46}$ contains 86 of about 104 leaves from the Pauline Epistles (see fig. 14.1). Thirty of the 86 leaves are at

the University of Michigan. Portions of several of the Epistles are lacking and may have never been included in the original work.

John Rylands Library

John Rylands Library in Manchester, England, houses many important biblical manuscripts, among them $\mathfrak{P}^{52}$ and $\mathfrak{P}^{32}$. $\mathfrak{P}^{52}$, a small papyrus fragment (2 and 1/2 inches by 3 and 1/2 inches), is one of the earliest fragments of the Gospel of John (18:31–33, 37–38); it is dated to the first part of the second century (see fig. 6.21). It was purchased by Bernard Grenfell of the John Rylands Library in 1920 but was not identified until 1934 by Colin Roberts. $\mathfrak{P}^{32}$, Rylands Greek Papyrus 5 (P. Ryl. 5), contains the text of Titus 1:11–15 and 2:3–8 and is dated to the second century.

Bodmer Collection

Martin Bodmer from Geneva, Switzerland, was founder of the Bodmer Library of World Literature at Cologny (a suburb of Geneva). In 1956 he purchased a collection of biblical papyri for the library. Among the more important biblical papyri is $\mathfrak{P}^{66}$ or Bodmer II. This manuscript contains a major portion of the Gospel of John (1:1–14:26) written about 200. The first fourteen chapters are almost complete, but the rest are fragmentary. There are 440 alterations and corrections, most of which appear in the margins or above the text; they appear to be editor's marks, probably from the copyist himself. $\mathfrak{P}^{72}$ is the earliest copy of the Book of Jude and the two Epistles of Peter (dated between 200–300).

$\mathfrak{P}^{75}$ is an early codex containing 102 leaves out of about 144 of the books of Luke and John (dated between 175 and 225). This is the earliest copy of Luke and one of the earliest for John.

Important Uncials

Codex Ephraemi (C; 04)

This fifth-century palimpsest originally bore the New Testament text and was reused during the twelfth century to copy

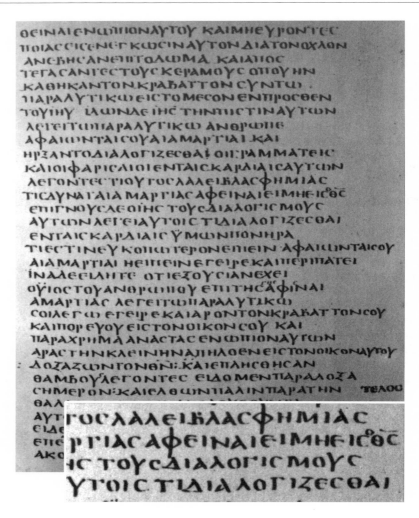

Figure 14.2. A page from Codex Bezae (fifth–sixth century) showing Luke 5:18–28. The enlarged portion shows a correction above the second line and the scribal abbreviation for "God" ($\overline{\Theta C}$ = θεός). [Cambridge University Library]

thirty-eight sermons of Ephraem, a Syrian church father. The manuscript was apparently brought first to Italy in the early sixteenth century and later to Paris by Queen Catherine dé Medici. In 1841 Constantin von Tischendorf set about the difficult task of deciphering the New Testament text, which had been partially erased. By 1843 he had completed this task, and it was published in 1845. Later, scholars treated the manuscript with chemicals and by use of improved photography were able to render the underlying New Testament text more readable. They found that Tischendorf had done admirably well with relatively few errors. Today the codex is one of the chief biblical treasures of the Bibliothèque Nationale (National Library) in Paris.

The codex is made of vellum, one column per page, with 64 leaves from the Old Testament and 145 from the New Testament out of about 238 original leaves. It contains portions of every book in the New Testament except 2 Thessalonians and 2 John.

Codex Bezae (D; 05)

In this bilingual codex, dating to the fifth or possibly sixth century, the Greek text appears on the left page (see fig. 14.2), and the Latin text on the right. It is written in sense lines, so that some sentences are short and others long depending upon the thought in the line. The first three lines of each book are written in red ink, with one column per page. The codex includes the Gospels (in Western order, i.e., Matt., John, Luke, Mark), Acts, and a short fragment of 3 John. It was found in 1562 at Lyons, France, by Théodore Bèza, successor to John Calvin at Geneva, who presented it to Cambridge University in 1581 (thus it is sometimes called Codex Cantabrigiensis). This codex should not be confused with the sixth-century Codex Claromontanus (also designated D), which contains only the Pauline Epistles and Hebrews.

Codex Bezae contains many variations from what is considered the standard New Testament text. For example, in Luke 23:53, the text says that Joseph of Arimathea, after placing Jesus' body in the new tomb, "put before the tomb a [great] stone which twenty men could scarcely roll"; and Acts 19:9 records that Paul preached in the hall of Tyrannus "from eleven o'clock to four," an unlikely time given the heat of the day.

For discussion about other important uncials, see the sections on Codex Vaticanus, Codex Sinaiticus, and Codex Alexandrinus in chapter 12.

Minuscule Manuscripts

At present approximately 2,795 minuscule texts have been recorded, as well as about 2,135 lectionaries, generally dating to a time later than the uncials. However, it does not necessarily follow that an earlier text is automatically more accurate, since a later manuscript may have been copied from a better original text. Thus a minuscule manuscript like number 33 is very accurate, even though it was copied in the ninth or tenth century. Minuscule manuscripts can be grouped into families according to their similarities.

Ferrar Family (f^{13})

In 1868 Professor William Ferrar of Dublin University identified several manuscripts belonging to the same text type or family (called the Ferrar Family, or Family 13, since the first minuscule is number 13). This family currently includes twelve manuscripts (13, 69, 124, 230, 346, 543, 788, 826, 828, 983, 1689, and 1709) dated between the eleventh and fifteenth centuries.[2] The story of the adulterous woman, which usually appears in John 7:53–8:11, is placed instead after Luke 21:38 in this family.

Lake Family (f^{1})

About 1902 Kirsopp Lake identified another text family, including manuscripts 1, 118, 131, and 209 (called the Lake Family or Family 1 after manuscript 1), all dated between the twelfth and fourteenth centuries. It is sometimes suggested that they follow a text common to Caesarea in the third and fourth centuries. Manuscript 1 was one of the manuscripts Erasmus used to prepare the first Greek New Testament.

Minuscule 33

The excellent text of this manuscript is very similar to that of Codex Vaticanus and since the time of J. G. Eichhorn in the early nineteenth century has been nicknamed the Queen of the Cursives. It includes the entire New Testament except the Book of Revelation and dates to the ninth or tenth century; currently it resides in the Bibliothèque Nationale, Paris.

Minuscule 16

This copy of the four Gospels in Greek and Latin is written in four colors: the narrative in vermilion, the words of Jesus and angels in crimson, Old Testament quotes and the words of the disciples in blue, and the words of the Pharisees, the centurion, Judas Iscariot, and the devil in black.[3] Presently the manuscript is housed in the Bibliothèque Nationale, Paris.

Ancient Versions of the New Testament

Some of the earliest translations of the New Testament were by missionaries spreading the gospel into new regions among people who spoke different languages (e.g., Coptic, Syriac, Latin, Gothic). It is always difficult to transfer the meaning from one language to another, especially between unrelated languages. Bruce Metzger highlights problems typical to translating Greek: "For example, Latin has no definite article; Syriac cannot distinguish between the Greek aorist and perfect tenses; Coptic lacks the passive voice and must use a circumlocution."[4] The problem is compounded when the translator does not have a good grasp of Greek, as was the case, according to Augustine, in the fourth century when the Hebrew and Greek texts were translated into Latin:

For the translations of the Scriptures from Hebrew into Greek can be counted, but the Latin translators are out of all number. For in the early days of the faith every man who happened to get his hands upon a Greek manuscript, and who thought he had any knowledge, were it ever so little, of the two languages, ventured upon the work of translation (Augustine *On Christian Doctrine* 2.11.16).[5]

Despite all the difficulties of translating the Bible into other languages, it was a worthy goal to provide nations with the Bible in their own language and in this way spread the gospel throughout the known world. As we shall see in the next chapter, these translations can be of great help for us today in attempting to determine the earliest text.

For Further Reading

Aland, K., and B. Aland. *The Text of the New Testament: An Introduction to the Critical Editions and to the Theory and Practice of Modern Textual Criticism.* Translated by E. F. Rhodes. 2d ed. Grand Rapids: Eerdmans, 1989.

Comfort, P. W. *Early Manuscripts and Modern Translations of the New Testament.* Wheaton, IL: Tyndale, 1990; reprint, Grand Rapids: Baker, 1996.

Finegan, J. *Encountering New Testament Manuscripts: A Working Introduction to Textual Criticism.* Grand Rapids: Eerdmans, 1974.

Greenlee, J. H. *Introduction to New Testament Textual Criticism.* Rev. ed. Peabody, MA: Hendrickson, 1995.

Hatch, W. H. P. *Facsimiles and Descriptions of Minuscule Manuscripts of the New Testament.* Cambridge, MA: Harvard University Press, 1951.

———. *The Principal Uncial Manuscripts of the New Testament.* Chicago: University of Chicago Press, 1939.

Kenyon, F. G. *Our Bible and the Ancient Manuscripts.* 5th ed. Revised by A. W. Adams. New York: Harper, 1958.

———. *The Text of the Greek Bible.* 3d ed. Revised and augmented by A. W. Adams. London: Duckworth, 1975.

Metzger, B. M. *Manuscripts of the Greek Bible: An Introduction to Greek Palaeography.* New York and Oxford: Oxford University Press, 1981.

———. *The Text of the New Testament: Its Transmission, Corruption, and Restoration.* 3d ed. New York and Oxford: Oxford University Press, 1992.

Skeat, T. C. "Early Christian Book-Production: Papyri and Manuscripts." In *CHB,* 2:54–79.

Part 4

Early Translations of the Bible

Early Versions

Wycliffe Bible translators are rendering the Bible into thousands of languages,[1] for history has shown that when persecution and heresy come, those who have the Bible in their own language are better equipped to resist it. Church history confirms that in areas such as Egypt and Syria, where the Bible was translated into the languages of the common people at an early stage, the Muslim conquest in the seventh century was not able to wipe out Christianity. But in areas where there were no translations (as with the Berber peoples in North Africa) hardly a trace of Christianity is left.

The early church realized the importance of translating the Bible into other languages; those translations that were made early on can be of great advantage to us in the history of interpretation of Scriptures and in textual criticism. Primary translations (i.e., those translated directly from the Hebrew and Greek texts) are most important, but secondary and tertiary transla-

tions have at least a limited value (see table 15.1). The most important primary translations are the Septuagint, Syriac Peshiṭta, and Latin Vulgate because they have been translated directly from some form of the Hebrew or Greek texts. Secondary translations are often helpful in determining the text that they have been translated from; for example, Old Latin texts are quite helpful in determining the text of the Septuagint since they were translated from some form of it. Tertiary translations are of much less value to textual criticism because they are quite distant from either a Greek or a Hebrew text; for instance, the Georgian version of the Old Testament appears to be a translation of the Armenian version, which is a translation of the Septuagint.

It must be noted that a few versions have greatly restricted value to textual criticism because the translators had only a limited grasp of Greek or Hebrew. Some translators may give a very loose or free translation, while others render a very lit-

Table 15.1
Types of Bible Translations

Type of Translation	Definition	Examples
Primary translation	A translation rendered directly from the Greek or Hebrew manuscripts	Septuagint, Latin Vulgate
Secondary translation	A translation of a primary translation, or a translation of a translation	Old Latin versions (translated from the Septuagint)
Tertiary translation	A translation of a secondary translation, or a translation of a translation of a translation	Georgian version (translated from the Armenian version, which was translated from the Septuagint)

243

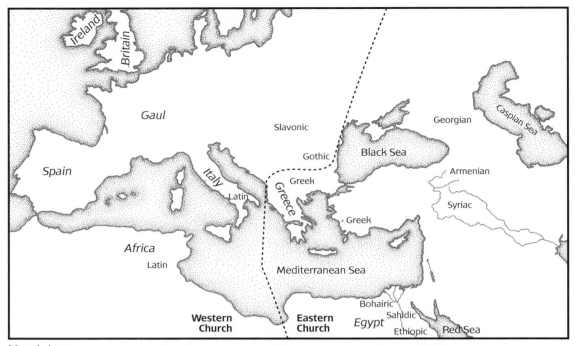

Map 4. Areas where versions of the Bible originated.

eral one; thus versions must be used with care. Nevertheless versions can be helpful in some instances for textual criticism and in fact were the earliest witnesses to the Old Testament until the Dead Sea Scrolls were found.

Early Eastern Versions of the Bible

Syriac Versions

Syriac Christianity

Some of the visitors to Jerusalem during the first Pentecost came from the other side of the Euphrates River, much of which was outside the borders of the Roman Empire (e.g., they were Parthians, Medes, and Elamites, or were from other Mesopotamian cultures, Acts 2:9; see map 4). F. F. Bruce says that there may have been as many as several million Jews in these territories by the first century,[2] and following Pentecost some of them may have been converted, bringing the gospel back

to their homeland. Another possibility is that the Christian persecution at the end of the first century brought the gospel throughout the Near Eastern area and into the upper Mesopotamian plateau. From this area the Syriac Peshitta (a translation of the Bible in the Syriac language) emerged, but whether it is of Jewish,[3] Christian, or Jewish-Christian[4] origin is still debated. Josephus offers the best historical record as to how Judaism spread into Syria (*Ant.* 20.2.1–4.3 §§17–96), which Ernst Würthwein summarizes: "During the first century the ruling house and leading circles of Adiabene (east of the Tigris) were won over to the Jewish faith for several decades (*ca.* A.D. 40–70). They needed a version of the Old Testament, especially of the Pentateuch, in their own language—Syriac. This places the beginnings of the Syriac version of the Old Testament in the middle of the first century A.D."[5]

Since Christianity originated out of Judaism, the latter may have provided the avenue for Christianity to enter Aram or Syria. Christianity spread very early into Syria, and from there the Syriac church appears to have taken the gospel as far as China. Eusebius records the following about Pantaenus, head of the catechetical school in Alexandria, who went to India as a missionary about 180:

> For indeed there were until then many evangelists of the word who had fore-thought to use inspired zeal on the apostolic model for the increase and building up of the divine word. One of these was Pantaenus, and it is said that he went to the Indians, and the tradition is that he found there that among some of those there who had known Christ the Gospel according to Matthew had preceded his coming; for Bartholomew, one of the apostles, had preached to them and had left them the writing of Matthew in Hebrew letters, which was preserved until the time mentioned. (Eusebius *HE* 5.10.2–3)[6]

Syriac, generally the name given to Christian Aramaic, is written in a distinctive variation of the Aramaic alphabet.[7]

Tatian's Diatessaron

Tatian came from Mesopotamia to Rome about 150; he was converted to Christianity and was taught by Justin Martyr. However, Tatian was later charged with heresy because of his highly ascetic beliefs. He therefore returned to Mesopotamia and founded a group of ascetic Christians called the Encratites (around 170). His major work was the earliest known harmony of the four Gospels, called the Diatessaron. The word *diatessaron* literally means "through four." That is to say, the work weaves all four Gospels into one continuous narrative. Tatian's views occasionally emerge in this work. For example, he was a vegetarian and thus in the Diatessaron John the Baptist ate "milk and honey" instead of "locusts and wild honey." Tatian's ascetic tendencies are reflected in Matthew 1:18–19, which avoids any mention of marriage when speaking of Joseph and Mary, and in John 2:10 the phrase "after the guests have had too much to drink" is removed. Eusebius briefly mentions the Diatessaron when speaking about Tatian and the Encratites, saying, "Their former leader Tatian composed in

some way a combination and collection of the gospels, and gave this the name of *The Diatessaron*, and this is still extant in some places" (*HE* 4.29.6).[8] It is unknown whether the work was originally written in Greek (the name *diatessaron* is Greek)[9] or Syriac, but it gained popularity due in large part to Ephraem, a Syrian church father from Edessa (c. 306–373), who wrote a commentary on it. Later the Diatessaron was translated into Persian, Arabic, Latin, Old Dutch, Medieval German, Old Italian, and Middle English.

Syriac Peshitta

For centuries several Syriac translations, as they circulated throughout this area, competed for superiority. Most were in Old Syriac, but around the fifth century the Syriac Peshitta emerged (see fig. 15.1), perhaps prepared by Rabbula, who was bishop of Edessa from 411 to 435. By about 400 Theodore of Mopsuestia, an early church father, wrote concerning the Syriac Peshitta: "It has been translated into the tongue of the Syrians by someone or other, for it has not been learned up to the present day who this was."[10] In the fifth century the Syriac church split into two groups—the Nestorians (East Syriac) and the Jacobites (West Syriac)—resulting in two major recensions of the Syriac Peshitta. Important resources regarding the text of the Peshitta are the writings of several early fathers of the Syriac church, such as Tatian (c. 110–172), Bardesanes (155–222), Aphraates (c. 275–345), Ephraem Syrus (c. 306–373), and Isho'dad of Merv (c. 800).

The Old Testament text appears to have been translated initially from the Hebrew but was subsequently revised at least once using the Septuagint as the basis for modification.[11] One clear example of the Septuagint's influence is the word *selah*, rendered in the Septuagint as διάψαλμα (*diapsalma*; literally, through the psalm); used mainly in the Psalms, the word may suggest a musical interlude between parts of a psalm, but the Peshitta merely transliterates this Greek word into Syriac. The Peshitta's translation of the Old Testament appears to have been made by Jewish scribes, as Paul Kahle

Early Eastern Versions

Syriac
  Tatian's Diatessaron (c. 170)
  Old Syriac (c. 3d–4th cent.)
  Peshitta (c. 5th cent.)
Coptic
  Sahidic (c. 3d cent.)
  Bohairic (c. 3d–4th cent.)
Armenian (c. 5th cent.)
Georgian (c. 5th cent.)
Ethiopic (c. 5th–6th cent.)
Arabic (c. 8th–9th cent.)

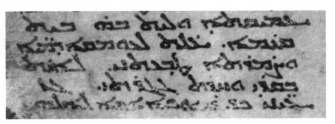

Figure 15.1.
Psalm 51.
Psalms in Syriac
(Monastery of
St. Catherine,
Mt. Sinai, seventh century).
[Grand Haven,
Mich., The Scriptorium, VK MS
631, fol. 1ʳ]

asserts: "there can be no doubt that the closest relationship existed between the Syriac Pentateuch and the old Palestinian Targum."[12] The Syriac Peshitta is important for textual criticism because it is a fairly early version of the Old Testament from a separate Jewish tradition. However, the text has been modified to bring it into closer harmony with the Septuagint.

Once Christians moved into Syria it was not long before the New Testament was translated into Syriac. The Diatessaron appeared about 170, and thus at least part of the New Testament was translated into Syriac quite early. F. F. Bruce indicates its popularity:

> Theodoretus, bishop of Cyrrhus near the Euphrates from *c*. 423 to 457, records that he collected and removed more than 200 copies from the churches in his diocese, replacing them by 'the Gospels of the Four Evangelists.' This last expression probably denotes Rabbula's revision of the Gospels. Rabbula himself seems to have taken similar steps in his neighbouring diocese of Edessa; one of his directions to his clergy ran: 'The presbyters and deacons shall see to it that in all the churches a copy of the "Gospel of the separated ones" shall be available and read'.[13]

The "Gospel of the separated ones" refers to the four Gospels, in contrast to the Diatessaron, implying that Rabbula believed the canonical Gospels superseded the Diatessaron. Modern scholars have distinguished five different Syriac versions of all or part of the New Testament: the Old Syriac, the Peshitta, the Philoxenian, the Harclean, and the Palestinian Syriac.[14] However, from the fifth century onward the standard version in Syriac was the Peshitta. The Peshitta included only twenty-two of the New Testament books, lacking four minor General Epistles (2 Peter, 2 and 3 John, and Jude)

and Revelation, but Philoxenus of Mabbug added these books in the version of the New Testament he commissioned in 507–508. More than 350 manuscripts of the New Testament of the Peshitta are known to exist. Modern scholars have sometimes overemphasized the importance of the Syriac Peshitta for New Testament studies, as Bruce explains:

> Because the Syriac Bible is written in a variant dialect of the language that Jesus spoke, extreme views are sometimes expressed about the forms in which his sayings appear in the Syriac Gospels, as though his actual words in the language in which they were uttered might be found there. The ordinary reader, for example, may readily infer from the writings of Mr. George Lamsa that the Peshitta Gospels preserve the very words of our Lord better than the Greek Gospels do. This, of course, is quite wrong; the Peshitta New Testament is simply a translation of the Greek.[15]

Coptic Versions

Christianity in Egypt

Following Pentecost the gospel spread quickly into Egypt (Acts 2:10), where papyrus fragments of the New Testament have been found dating as early as the second century. While the Greek language had significant influence on Egypt, native Egyptians would probably not have spoken Greek but rather Coptic (meaning "Egyptian"), of which there are approximately six different dialects in the Nile Valley; the two major dialects are Sahidic (Upper Egypt) and Bohairic (Lower Egypt). Since Christianity spread into Egypt by the middle of the first century, versions from this area may reflect early traditions (see map 4). Coptic is the last phase in a long history of the Egyptian language; originally the Egyptians used a hieroglyphic script, which was then superseded by a hieratic and finally a demotic script. But at least as early as the third century, Coptic was the native language of Egypt. Coptic, a combination of the common native language plus Greek loan-

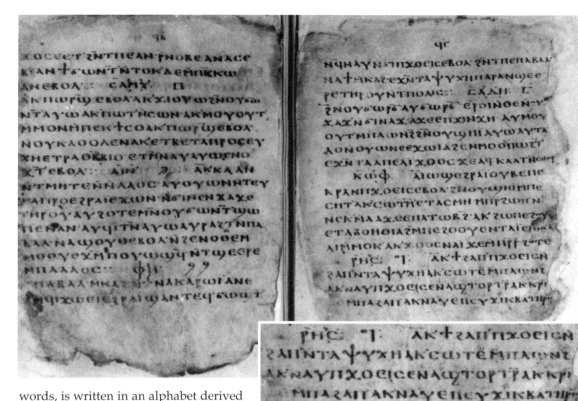

words, is written in an alphabet derived from the Greek language, with seven additional characters from Demotic (fig. 15.2).[16] Sahidic was the earlier dialect in Egypt, possibly even the official language of Alexandria long before the spread of Christianity;[17] the Bible was probably translated into this language as early as the middle of the third century. The Bohairic version was translated in the next century independently of the Sahidic version.[18] Very little is known about the history of the early church in Egypt before 180–190, even though $\mathfrak{P}^{52}$ indicates that at least part of the New Testament circulated there by about 125. Kurt Aland and Barbara Aland suggest that the reason so little is known is that Gnosticism was quite prominent in Egypt and thus the church there may not have been recognized by the official churches until later.[19]

The Sahidic Version

The Sahidic language (from Es-saʿid, the Arabic name for Upper Egypt) was spoken from Thebes, the ancient southern capital

(modern Luxor), southward. This version, probably dating to the third century, primarily agrees with the Alexandrian text-family but appears to contain western readings in the Gospels and Acts.[20] The Sahidic version has some peculiarities not found in other versions.[21] Matthew 6:13 ends with "for yours is the power and the glory forever," instead of the more common "for yours is the kingdom, and the power, and the glory forever." In the parable of the rich man and Lazarus, Luke 16:19 records the name of the rich man as Neve (Νευης, Neuēs).[22] In Acts 15 the Golden Rule is stated in the negative, namely, "do not do unto others what you would not want them to do unto you."

The Bohairic Version

Bohairic, spoken in lower Egypt in the Delta region, was the most developed dialect of the Coptic language and in time superseded all other dialects. It is still the

Figure 15.2. A page from the Book of Jeremiah in Coptic from a folio of Jeremiah, Lamentations, and Baruch (fourth century). [Grand Haven, Mich., The Scriptorium, VK MS 783, fols. 92ᵛ–93ʳ]

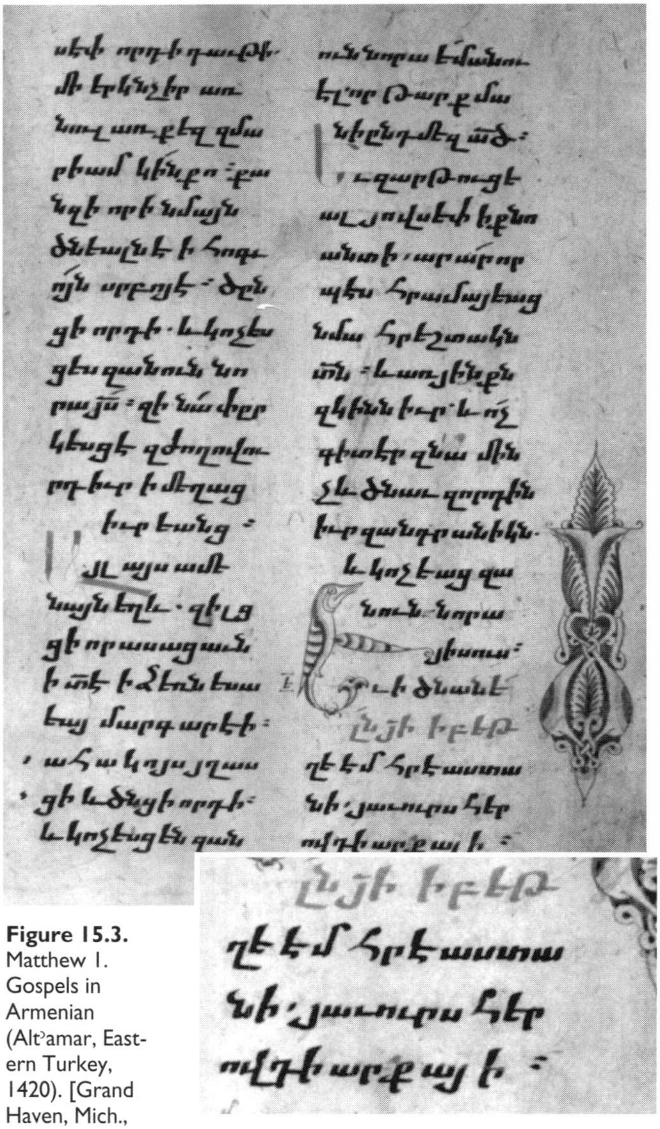

Figure 15.3.
Matthew 1.
Gospels in
Armenian
(Altʾamar, East-
ern Turkey,
1420). [Grand
Haven, Mich.,
The Scriptorium,
VK MS 781,
fol. 9ʳ]

Testament, and thus their contribution to Old Testament textual criticism is the light they can shed on the Septuagint text. However, Willem Grossouw, in *Coptic Versions of the Minor Prophets,* examined the Minor Prophets and found that the Sahidic or the Achmimic (another Coptic version), and sometimes both, agreed in two hundred instances with the Hebrew against the Septuagint.[25] This raises two questions, neither of which has been answered satisfactorily: (1) What is the relationship between these two versions and the Hebrew text? (2) How does the *Vorlage* (text from which they were copied) used for these two translations compare with the Septuagint? As regards the New Testament Coptic versions, they are a primary translation of a pure Alexandrian text and thus are quite valuable for text-critical purposes.

Armenian Version

The Armenians lived north of Mesopotamia between the Roman and Persian empires (see map 4). Armenia was the first nation to be officially declared Christian when its king, Tiridates III (c. 287–314), who had formerly persecuted the church, was converted by Gregory the Illuminator (c. 257–331) at the end of the third century. Gregory was of royal lineage and studied at Cappadocia before returning to his native land. It is possible that the apostles Thaddaeus (Matt. 10:3; Mark 3:18) and Bartholomew (Matt. 10:8; Mark 3:18; Luke 6:14; Acts 1:13) went to work among the Armenians;[26] in any case, the church existed at least by the middle of the third century, because Eusebius records that Dionysius, a bishop of Alexandria (d. c. 264) wrote "to those in Armenia, likewise On Repentance, whose bishop was Meruzanes" (*HE* 6.46.2).[27] Bruce Metzger summarizes the differing traditions as to how the first Armenian translation came into being: "According to Bishop Koriun (died *c.* 450) and the historian Lazar of Pharb (*c.* 500), it was St. Mesrop (died A.D. 439), a soldier who became a Christian missionary, who created a new alphabet and, with the help of the Catholicus Sahak (Isaac the Great, 390–439), trans-

liturgical language of the modern Coptic church centered in Cairo, Egypt,[23] and until about the eighteenth century it was the only known Coptic dialect of the New Testament.[24]

Coptic versions were the products of Egyptian Christians' missionary ventures to their non-Greek-speaking neighbors. There are a significant number of Coptic manuscripts and fragments originating from the third and fourth centuries. Both the Sahidic and Bohairic versions derive from the Septuagint's version of the Old

lated the version from the Greek text. On the other hand, Moses of Chorion, the nephew and disciple of St. Mesrop, says that Sahak made it from the Syriac text."[28]

The first version of the Armenian Bible was apparently produced in the early part of the fifth century, after the Armenian priest Mesrop Mashtotz (c. 361–439) developed the Armenian alphabet of thirty-six letters about 406. Mesrop, in the early part of the fifth century, collected manuscripts and with the help of other scholars translated the Bible into Armenian. Until this time, all books in this area had been written in either Syriac or Greek.

The Armenian version is one of the earliest translations of the Bible, and some of its readings may go back very early. The number of extant copies of this version are second only to copies of the Latin Vulgate, with more than 1,244 manuscripts in whole or in part of the New Testament alone (fig. 15.3).[29]

The Armenian version contains several books outside the biblical canon; for example, the *History of Joseph and Asenath, 4 Ezra*, and the *Testaments of the Twelve Patriarchs* appear in some manuscripts of the Old Testament, and the *Epistle of the Corinthians to Paul* and a *Third Epistle of Paul to the Corinthians* are included in some of the New Testament manuscripts.[30]

The quality of translation varies greatly from book to book in the Old Testament, so that debate continues as to which text was used for the original translation. There is little question, however, that a final, official version was dependent on the Septuagint with influence from the Peshiṭta where it does not harmonize with the Septuagint.[31] Because this version depends on the Septuagint and the Peshiṭta, in most cases it should not be considered a separate witness, but its very literal translation can be quite helpful to New Testament textual criticism.

Armenian New Testament manuscripts have some unusual characteristics; for instance, the General Epistles (Hebrews, James, 1 and 2 Peter, 1, 2, and 3 John, Jude) appear immediately after the Book of Acts. This translation also contains some interesting New Testament readings:[32]

Figure 15.4.
The New Testament in Georgian (Moscow: Andrew Johnson, 1743). [Grand Haven, Mich., The Scriptorium, VK 459, fol. 15ʳ]

1. The lame man at the pool of Bethesda in John 5:7 complains "while I drag myself, another steps in before me" instead of the more common reading "while I am coming."

2. In Mark 7:25 the normal reading of the text is that the little girl "had" an unclean spirit, whereas the Armenian version says that the girl "was pressed" or "was squeezed" by an unclean spirit.

3. Revelation 22:14 reads "those who keep his commandments" in the

Armenian version instead of "those who wash their robes."

Georgian Version

Georgia is north of Armenia in the rugged Caucasus Mountains between the Black Sea and the Caspian Sea. Today, this country is in the modern Confederation of Independent States (formerly the Soviet Union; see map 4). According to early records, Christianity was introduced into Georgia by a slave woman named Nino, who was taken captive by Bakur, the pagan king of Georgia, during the reign of the emperor Constantine.[33] Thus scholars commonly date the introduction of Christianity into Georgia about the mid-fourth century, but how or when the first copies of the Bible came into Georgia is not clear. The Georgian language is unrelated to those that surround it, so that an alphabet had to be developed before Georgians could have the Scriptures in their own language (fig. 15.4).[34] Evidence suggests that by the mid-fifth century at least the Gospels were translated,[35] but there is some disagreement as to which text was the basis for the Georgian version. Armenian tradition ascribes both the alphabet and the version to Mesrop. According to Sidney Jellicoe, it seems most likely that an original Georgian version (fifth–sixth century) was translated from the Armenian version and was then later revised by comparing it with a Greek text.[36] The oldest Georgian manuscript (Geo[1]) is the Adysh manuscript of 897, which contains the four Gospels. But fragments of at least Genesis, Deuteronomy, Judges, Proverbs, and Jeremiah are known to have existed in Armenian from between the fifth to the eighth centuries.

The Georgian version is a tertiary version from either the Syriac or Armenian versions, and thus its primary value is its corroboration of the Old Syriac versions.

Ethiopic Version

How Ethiopia (or Abyssinia, its older name; see map 4) received the gospel is not clearly known. Some early church fathers assumed that the Ethiopian official who was baptized by Philip (Acts 8:26–39) began to evangelize Ethiopia.[37] But the mention in Acts 8 that Candace was queen of Ethiopia has not, according to Metzger, been corroborated by external evidence: "Apart from other considerations, however, it is fatal to this interpretation that evidence is lacking that Ethiopia was governed at that time by a woman, whereas it is know that Candace was the title of the queens who ruled for some centuries over the kingdom of Meroë, which, lying to the north of the kingdom of Aksum, was often confused with it."[38]

Some scholars have suggested that one or more of the apostles, such as Matthew[39] or Bartholomew,[40] went to Ethiopia, but there is no solid evidence of this either. The strongest historical evidence for the spread of Christianity to Ethiopia comes from Rufinus (*HE* 1.9) and is repeated by Socrates (*HE* 1.19), Sozomen (*HE* 2.24), and Theodoret (*HE* 1.23). Metzger summarizes their accounts:

> According to Rufinus, it was during the time of Constantine the Great (about 330) that two young men, Frumentius and Ædesius, accompanied their uncle, a philosopher from Tyre named Meropius, on a voyage on the Red Sea. The ship having stopped at a port on the Ethiopian coast for provisions, the natives attacked and murdered the crew and Meropius; only Frumentius and Ædesius survived. The two youths were taken captive to Aksum, where they won confidence and honour, and eventually were allowed to preach Christianity. Some time later Ædesius returned to Tyre; Frumentius, after converting the royal family to the new faith, went to Alexandria, where he obtained mission-wonary coorkers [*sic* missionary co-workers] from Athanasius, and was himself consecrated bishop and head of the Ethiopian Church. . . .[41]

Inscriptional evidence also confirms that the Christian faith was well founded in Ethiopia by the fourth century. The inscriptions of King Ezana, dated by most scholars to the mid-fourth century, record his military victories, and in the final one he gives credit to "the Lord of the heavens who has power over all beings in heaven and earth" and to Maḥrem (i.e., Ares), to whom he had accredited earlier victories. On another stela inscription Ezana proclaims his belief in the triune God—Father, Son, and Holy Spirit—who helped him to overcome his enemies.[42] By the early sixth century Ethiopia was Christianized, at least according to the record of Cosmas Indicopleustes.[43]

By the fifth or sixth century, portions of the Bible were translated into Ethiopic (or Geʾez, as Old Ethiopic is called; see fig. 15.5), probably by monophysite monks (i.e., they held that Christ had only one nature) who fled to Ethiopia due to persecution by Byzantine rulers. It was through the influence of these monks that Coptic and Ethiopic churches came to be monophysite. At present the oldest surviving Ethiopic text is a copy of the four Gospels from the tenth century (Abba Garima, MS. 1).[44] The Ethiopic Old Testament appears to be a translation of a Greek text, though at some points it may have been modified by a Hebrew original.[45] The New Testament text is not homogeneous and largely contains readings found in the Byzantine or Western text types; however, in places a Syriac influence is displayed. Acts, the Catholic Epistles, and Revelation are most helpful since they seem to reflect some accurate, original readings. The Ethiopic New Testament also includes the two apocryphal books *1 Enoch* and *Jubilees*.

Arabic Versions

In antiquity Arabia covered the area west of Mesopotamia, south of Syria, and east of Palestine; it was about one-third the size of Europe. Very little is known about early Christian contacts with this area, but according to Eusebius, Origen was invited to attend discussions concerning the heretical teachings of Beryllus, bishop of Bostra (*HE* 6.33.1–4), and of the Helkesaites (*HE* 6.38.1). Socrates, a fourth-century historian,

Figure 15.5. Gospels in Ethiopic (eighteenth century). [Grand Haven, Mich., The Scriptorium, VK MS 205]

records that Mavia, queen of the Ishmaelites (Saracens), embraced Christianity and appointed a bishop:

All the regions of the East therefore were at that time ravaged by the Saracens: but a certain divine Providence repressed their fury in the manner I am about to describe. A person named Moses, a Saracen by birth, who led a monastic life in the desert, became exceedingly eminent for his piety, faith, and miracles. Mavia the queen of the Saracens was therefore desirous that this person should be constituted bishop over her nation, and promised on this condition to terminate the war. (*HE* 4.36)[46]

At this point Moses was installed as bishop and the war ceased. Also during this time Christians from Ethiopia probably began moving into the southern part of the Arabian peninsula.[47] Little is known about the first translation of the Bible into Arabic, but the first mention of such appears in the Midrash *Sipre* on Deuteronomy 34:3, which says that the Torah was given to

Israel in four languages: Hebrew, Greek, Arabic, and Aramaic. The spread of Islam in the seventh century forced Jews and Christians who remained in the conquered lands to adopt Arabic. Translation of the Bible into Arabic was outlawed, but Jews and Christians translated it undercover. Therefore a number of independent versions arose, some of which, as Bruce explains, reflected the influence of Docetism:

> The Scriptures do not seem to have been extant in an Arabic version before the time of Muhammad (570–632), who knew the gospel story only in oral form, and mainly from Syriac sources. These Syriac sources were marked by Docetism [the belief that Jesus had only a divine nature and only appeared to be incarnate and that the material world and thus one's body was inherently evil], which explains the statement in the Qur'an that Jesus was only apparently crucified, but did not really die.[48]

Evidence suggests that translations into Arabic were made from Greek, Old Syriac, the Syriac Peshitta, Coptic, and Latin versions. At present the oldest known manuscript of the Arabic Bible is Codex Vaticanus arabicus 13, containing a portion of the Gospels and the Pauline Epistles from the eighth or ninth century. The Arabic translation of Saadia Gaon (882–942) is usually regarded as the last ancient translation of the Old Testament and is almost identical to the Masoretic Text,[49] but most other Arabic translations are a mixture of various sources (an early Hebrew text, the Septuagint, the Peshitta, and other versions).[50] The New Testament is likewise a combined text, and an interesting saying of Jesus is included in Matthew 6:34 (see italics below), where Jesus purportedly says "Each day has enough trouble of its own, *and each hour has enough pain of its own.*"[51] Since the Arabic version was derived from a variety of sources, its greatest value to textual criticism is in the area of the history of interpretation of various texts.

Early Western Versions of the Bible

The Book of Acts also records how the gospel spread into the Western region. The Romans united the area under a single language and this paved the way for the spread of the gospel throughout the Roman Empire. Greek prevailed over Latin in most of the Roman Empire until the third century, except in southern Gaul and northern Africa, where the earliest Latin biblical texts emerged. In these two areas Latin was the official language for government and trade, but the indigenous people continued to speak their own languages. By the third century, however, Latin emerged as the major language and became extremely important to church history, as Metzger describes:

> It would be difficult to over-estimate the importance of the influence exerted by the Latin versions of the Bible, and particularly by Jerome's Latin Vulgate. Whether one considers the Vulgate from a purely secular point of view, with its pervasive influence upon the development of Latin into the Romance languages, or whether one has in view only the specifically religious influence, the extent of penetration into all areas of Western culture is well-nigh beyond calculation.[52]

Old Latin Versions

Origin of the Old Latin Versions

"Old Latin" is a collective term for the Latin versions in existence before the Latin Vulgate. Gradually the West became Latin-speaking; by 250 Latin had become the language of Christian writers and theologians, so that soon there was great need for a Latin Bible.

Latin translations probably first appeared in the Roman province of Northern Africa (covering present-day Tunisia, Algeria, and Morocco; see map 4), where Carthage had especially strong ties with the Roman culture. From about 180 an outbreak of persecution against Christians took place in Numidia (modern Tunisia); during one of the trials, a Christian named Speratus, from the town of Scillium, was asked what he carried in a box, to which he replied: "Books and letters of a just man, one Paul."[53] As a result, Metzger concludes: "Since it is not likely that the Scillitan Christians, so obviously plebeian and without culture, were able to read Greek, we are driven to conclude that they possessed at least the Epistles of Paul in a Latin version. And if the Pauline Epistles were circulating in a Latin version by A.D. 180, there is no doubt that the Gospels were likewise available in Latin."[54]

Several great biblical teachers—Tertullian of Carthage (c. 160–220), Cyprian of Carthage (c. 200–258), Augustine of Hippo (c. 354–430)—came from North Africa, but according to Aland and Aland, Cyprian was the first to use a Latin text.[55] Tertullian quotes extensively from the Scripture but apparently translated his texts directly from the Greek. Augustine, however, was not knowledgeable in Greek and must surely have used a Latin translation.[56]

Even though evidence indicates that the first Latin translation of the Bible originated in North Africa, it was undoubtedly translated elsewhere in the Roman Empire. Evidence suggests that there was not just one *Vorlage* but that a number of independent versions arose in North Africa and Southern Gaul as early as the end of the second century.[57] However, when the Vulgate gained dominance, little interest was shown in retaining the Old Latin text, so that no complete manuscripts survived. The majority of evidence concerning the Old Latin text is gleaned from quotes in the Latin fathers.

Old Latin Manuscripts

Old Latin manuscripts, commonly indicated by "it" with a small letter (e.g., it[a], it[b]), are characterized by Arthur Vööbus: "The Old Latin version is not written in the polished literary language of that time but in the didactic, vernacular idiom of the cult, often reflecting the dialect of the

common people. This colloquial flavor is colored also by the Greek idiom, seen in its transliteration of Greek terms and occasionally even in syntax."[58]

Metzger comes to a different conclusion: that the "wooden and literalistic style that characterizes many of these renderings suggests that early copies were made in the form of interlinear renderings of the Greek."[59] The Old Latin version of the New Testament is fairly well attested with just over 150 fragments—about 52 of the Gospels, 29 of Acts, 37 of the Pauline Epistles, 26 of the Catholic Epistles, and 15 of the Book of Revelation.[60] These fragments are by no means standardized and contain a variety of different readings, but they clearly reflect the Western text type. In the Old Testament fragments exist from the Pentateuch, the Psalms, and the Major and Minor Prophets; more can be gleaned from works of the church fathers.[61] The fragments were translated from a copy of the Septuagint (J. Ziegler calls it "the Septuagint in Latin clothing"),[62] though some passages seem to record a reading closer to the Hebrew text than any other.

Interesting Readings from Old Latin Versions[63]

In the parable of the barren fig tree the vineyard keeper says that he will "dig around it and fertilize it," but several Old Latin manuscripts clarify the last phrase as "I will throw on a basket of dung" (Luke 13:8). Another phrase is added to the story of Jesus' baptism which says "a great and tremendous light flashed forth from the water, so that all who were present feared" (Matt. 3:15a). In Luke 23:5 it is reported that Jesus was charged with alienating "both our sons and our wives from us, for he does not baptize as we do." In Mark 16:4 an expansion declares that Jesus, "Rose in the brightness of the living God, and at once they [the angels] ascended with Him, and immediately there was light. Then they [the women] drew near to the tomb." And when Jesus hung on the cross the bystanders exclaim, "He calls

Early Western Versions
Old Latin
(2d cent.)
Latin Vulgate
(383–405)
Gothic
(4th cent.)
Old Slavonic
(c. 9th cent.)

Helion [a pagan god]" instead of "He is calling for Elijah" (Mark 15:35).

Importance of Old Latin Versions for Textual Criticism

The Old Latin texts of the Old Testament are secondary translations, but as Würthwein notes, Old Latin is a "particularly important witness to the Septuagint text because it goes back to the period before the Septuagint recensions."[64] Passages in the Old Latin version that differ from the Septuagint should be especially noted, for they may follow readings from an alternative Septuagint tradition or other early readings. In the New Testament the Old Latin texts reflect the Western text type, but some of these texts are very early and may contain original readings. These texts of the New Testament are also important in that many are a very literal rendering of the Greek text.

The Latin Vulgate

The Latin Vulgate is important to the study of the history of the Bible on two counts. It played a dominant role in Western Europe for about one thousand years, and during the Reformation, when people needed the Bible in their own tongue, the Latin Vulgate was translated into many other languages. The Latin Vulgate was translated by Jerome during the years 383 to about 405 (fig. 15.6).

Its History

Pope Damasus I, bishop of Rome from about 366 to 384, commissioned Jerome (c. 345–420), his secretary, to revise and standardize the Old Latin version. There were so many differences among Old Latin texts in circulation within the Latin church that the people could not be certain which text to follow. Jerome, a brilliant scholar with a firm grasp of Latin, Greek, and later even Hebrew, was called upon to rectify this problem. His work, later known as the Latin Vulgate (mean-

ing "common" or "plain"), became the standard edition of the Bible for more than a thousand years. His most important contribution was probably the Latin translation of the Old Testament (390–405) which he translated from the original Hebrew text. He was the only person in the Western church qualified to make such a translation.[65]

Jerome began immediately, and in 383 the four Gospels appeared. They were followed by his first revision of the Book of Psalms from the Old Latin, which became known as the "Roman Psalter" (*Psalterium Romanum*). The rest of the New Testament may also have been revised at this time. Aland and Aland do not believe that he finished his revision of the New Testament.[66] His work was interrupted by the death of Pope Damasus at the end of 384. Jerome received a severe blow when he was passed over to replace Pope Damasus, Siricius being appointed instead. Robert Schnucker cites Jerome's ascetic views as at least one of the reasons he was overlooked:

> While in Rome he praised the ascetic life of monasticism and decried the lax moral life of the Christians in the city. He was most successful in winning the female sex to his views of ascetic living, but due to rumors about his relationship with them and the accusation that his harsh asceticism caused the death of one of them, he left Rome after the death of Pope Damasus and in 386 made his home in Bethlehem for the rest of his life.[67]

In Bethlehem, Jerome oversaw a men's monastery and also translated the Psalms from the Septuagint column of the Hexapla, including the diacritical marks; this translation was called the *Psalterium Gallicanum*. Eventually he realized the importance of translating directly from the Hebrew and so began a Latin translation of the Hebrew text; he finished that translation in 405. In general Jerome chose to translate in a sense-for-sense rather than a literal, word-for-word manner.[68] The text of the Vulgate is not uniform, either because he initially relied too heavily upon Old Latin manuscripts or perhaps because he became a better translator with practice. Some scholars have suggested that he was not the translator of much of the New Testament.[69]

Jerome realized the presumptuous nature of the job, but he undertook it as a gift of love, according to the preface he wrote to Damasus in his revision of the four Gospels:

> You urge me to revise the old Latin version, and, as it were, to sit in judgment on the copies of the Scriptures which are now scattered throughout the whole world; and, inasmuch as they differ from one another, you would have me decide which of them agree with the Greek original. The labour is one of love, but at the same time both perilous and presumptuous; for in judging others I must be content to be judged by all; and how can I dare to change the language of the world in its hoary old age, and carry it back to the early days of its infancy? Is there a man, learned or unlearned, who will not, when he takes the volume into his hands, and perceives that what he reads does not suit his settled tastes, break out immediately into violent language, and call me a forger and a profane person for having the audacity to add anything to the ancient books, or to make any changes or corrections therein?[70]

Jerome used the Hebrew text as a basis for his translation of the Old Testament, and for this he was severely criticized by the church, which claimed that the Septuagint was inspired and therefore authoritative,[71] as Bruce explains: "Jerome's dependence on the Hebrew text was thought to be a sign of Judaising, and it was thought outrageous that he should cast doubts on the divine inspiration of the Septuagint. Jerome showed little patience with his critics; in a letter to one of his friends he describes them as 'two-legged donkeys.'"[72] However, even Augustine worried that this translation would cause a division in the Western church between Greek and Latin congregations.

By the eighth or ninth century the Latin Vulgate had finally superseded the Old Latin version. The climax came on April 8, 1546, when the Council of Trent declared

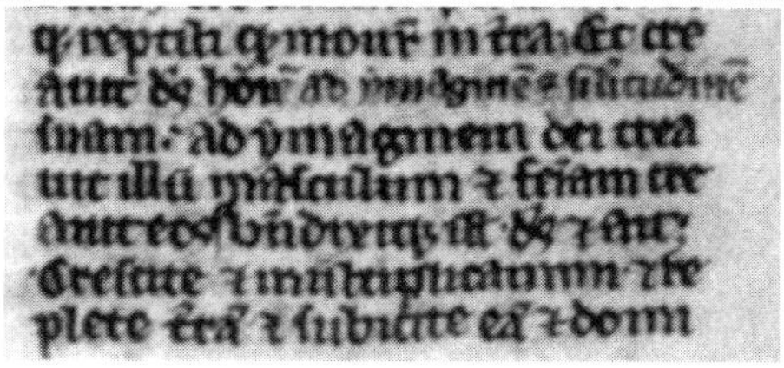

Figure 15.6.
Genesis I. Bible in Latin (Paris, thirteenth century), Vulgate Version. [Grand Haven, Mich., The Scriptorium, VK MS 649, fol. 1ʳ]

the Vulgate to be the authentic Bible of the Roman Catholic Church: "But if any one receive not, as sacred and canonical, the said books entire with all their parts, as they have been used to be read in the Catholic Church, and as they are contained in the old Latin vulgate edition; and knowingly and deliberately contemn [condemn] the traditions aforesaid; let him be anathema" [fourth session].[73] In 1592 a complete revision of the Latin Vulgate was made, called the Clementine Vulgate, published under Clement VIII (1592–1605), and it remained the authorized version of the Roman Catholic Church.

Jerome
(Sophronius Eusebius Hieronymus; c. 345–420)

Jerome was born about 346 in Stridon, on the border of Dalmatia and Pannonia (probably modern Grahovo-polje, Yugoslavia; see B. M. Metzger, *The Early Versions of the New Testament: Their Origin, Transmission, and Limitations* [Oxford: Clarendon, 1977], 331). He was the son of Christian parents of moderate means. In 363, at about the age of twelve, he went to Rome. There, under Aelius Donatus, the famous grammarian, he diligently studied the great classic writers. He then traveled extensively throughout the Roman Empire to acquire further knowledge; he apparently learned Greek in Antioch in 373–74 and Hebrew in the Syrian desert of Chalcis (374–79) and in Bethlehem (about 385). Jerome loved the Greek classics that he had been taught in Rome, but in Antioch (about 374) during a severe illness, Jerome had a dream that changed his life, as he recounts:

> Meantime preparations for my funeral went on; my body grew gradually colder, and the warmth of life lingered only in my throbbing breast. Suddenly I was caught up in the spirit and dragged before the judgment seat of the Judge; and here the light was so bright, and those who stood around were so radiant, that I cast myself upon the ground and did not dare to look up. Asked who and what I was I replied: "I am a Christian." But he who presided said: "Thou liest, thou art a follower of Cicero and not of Christ. For 'where thy treasure is, there will thy heart be also.'" Instantly I became dumb, and amid the strokes of the lash—for He had ordered me to be scourged—I was tortured more severely still by the fire of conscience, considering with myself that verse, "In the grave who shall give thee thanks?" . . . At last the bystanders, falling down before the knees of Him who presided, prayed that He would have pity on my youth, and that He would give me space to repent of my error. He might still, they urged, inflict torture on me, should I ever again read the works of Gentiles. . . . Accordingly I made oath and called upon His name, saying: "Lord, if ever again I possess worldly books, or if ever again I read such, I have denied Thee." . . . I profess that my shoulders were black and blue, that I felt the bruises long after I awoke from my sleep, and that henceforth I read the books of God with a greater zeal than I had previously given to the books of men. (*Epist.* 22.30; P. Schaff and H. Wace, eds., *Select Library of the Nicene and Post-Nicene Fathers,* 6:35–36.)

Jerome kept his oath and diligently studied the Scriptures; while in Bethlehem he was trained in Hebrew by a rabbi who came to him at night for fear that the Jews would condemn him for teaching the sacred language to a Gentile. His years of studying paid great dividends, as Metzger explains: "Although Jerome's knowledge of Hebrew was defective, it was much greater than that of Origen, Ephraem Syrus, and Epiphanius, the only other Church Fathers who knew Hebrew at all" (Metzger, *Early Versions,* 332). In 382 Jerome returned to Rome where the next year he was commissioned by Pope Damasus to begin work on a standardized version of the Latin Bible (technically not a new translation). This was a monumental task, as H. F. D. Sparks explains:

> Previous revisers had improved the version, in some cases almost beyond recognition, but the very number of revisions, the fact that they represented purely local texts and not official efforts, the natural mixture of these local texts which ensued, and the habitual carelessness of the copyists, had all combined to create such a state of confusion that there were "almost as many types of text as manuscripts" (H. F. D. Sparks, "The Latin Bible," in *The Bible in Its Ancient and English Versions,* ed. H. W. Robinson [Oxford: Clarendon, 1954], 111).

Manuscripts of the Latin Vulgate

There are more than ten thousand manuscripts of the Latin Vulgate, some of which date to the fifth or sixth centuries (Codex Sangallensis; Codex Fuldensis; Codex Foro-Juliensis). Codex Amiatinus is the earliest existing copy of the entire Latin Bible, and it was made in Northumbria, the northern part of England, in the early eighth century. A copy of the Latin Vulgate was the Bible that Wycliffe translated into English in the fourteenth century.

Importance of the Latin Vulgate for Textual Criticism

The Latin Vulgate has had a great influence on the language and thought of the Western church. Words like "justify" or "sanctify" derive from Latin, reflecting a more legalistic mindset than that of the philosophical Greeks. Because the Old Testament of the Latin Vulgate was translated directly from a Hebrew text, for text-critical analysis it may provide insight into the text at that time. Jerome's commentaries on the Minor Prophets, Isaiah, and Jeremiah (406–420) are important to the history of Old Testament exegesis, showing how he later interpreted the texts. These commentaries demonstrate that Jerome used a variety of texts according to the reading that best fit his exegesis of the passage. In the New Testament it is more

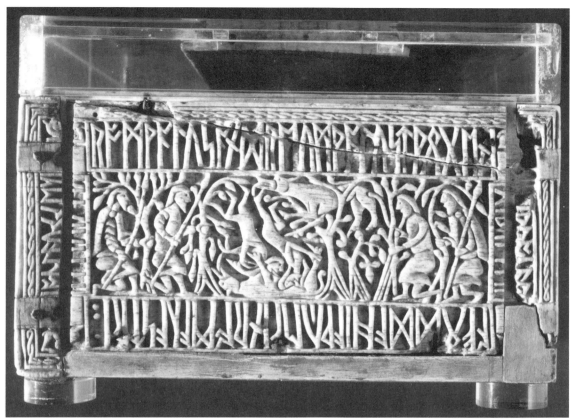

Figure 15.7.
An example of
Old German
runes on the
Franks Casket.
[British Museum]

difficult to determine the value of the Latin Vulgate to textual criticism, since the Old Latin texts significantly influenced parts of the translation, especially in the Gospels. In some passages, however, the Greek text behind the translation may precede the Byzantine text type and thus provide some very early readings of the text.

The Gothic Version

Christianization of the Goths

The ancient Goths founded an extensive empire north of the lower Danube and the Black Sea (see map 4). The empire was split into two major groups by the Dniester River—on the east lived the Ostrogoths and on the west the Visigoths. The latter heard about Christianity first and carried it to their kinsmen to the east.[74] As early as the third century, Gothic warriors occasionally made raids into the Roman Empire, and it was through Christian priests who were brought over as prisoners that the Gothic people began to hear about salvation. There was even a Gothic bishop, named Theophilus, present at the Council of Nicea in 325. At the age of only thirty, Wulfilas (or possibly Ulfilas; Gothic for Little Wolf [311–381/383]) was ordained into the episcopate by Bishop Eusebius of Nicomedia (bishop of the Gothlands). Wulfilas labored faithfully until his death and as a result has sometimes been called the "Apostle of the Goths." When Rome was sacked by the Goths in 410, Augustine was certainly relieved that they had already been Christianized, or else Rome's fate would have been much worse.[75]

Wulfilas's Translation

The Gothic version originated with Wulfilas according to the early church historian Philostorgius (c. 368–430), who wrote a fairly inaccurate and biased history of the church from about 300 through 425 (*HE* 2.5).[76] Wulfilas began his work by creating the Gothic alphabet (about two-thirds of it are Greek letters, the rest Latin characters as well as elements of Old German runes [oldest known German alphabet]; see fig. 15.7)[77] before translating the Bible into his native language.

Evidence in the Gothic translation of Nehemiah 5–7 suggests that a version of the Septuagint was followed (some scholars think it was the Lucianic text, but this is uncertain); in the New Testament a Byzantine text was used. Metzger notes that Wulfilas was an Arian or semi-Arian, which means that he denied the eternality of Christ, a heresy condemned at the Council of Nicea in 325:

> In theology Ulfilas was hospitable to Arianism (or semi-Arianism); how far his theological views may have influenced his translation of the New Testament, or whether indeed there was any influence, has been debated. Perhaps the only certain trace of the translator's dogmatic bias is found in Phil. ii.6, where reference is made to the pre-existent Christ in terms of being *galeiko guda* (= "similar to God"), whereas the Greek ἴσα θεῷ should have been rendered *ibna guda* [= "being in very nature God"].[78]

Wulfilas rendered his translation from the Septuagint for Christians who had been captured and brought into the Gothic empire during the third century. Wulfilas's translation was taken into Spain and northern Italy in the fifth century, when the Goths took over these areas, and it may have become the vernacular Bible for much of Europe.[79] According to Philostorgius, Wulfilas left out Samuel and Kings when he translated the Old Testament because he felt its war stories would encourage the warring Goths to continue to fight.[80] It is unknown whether Wulfilas finished translating the entire Bible; only a few fragmentary pieces of the Gothic Old Testament have been preserved (i.e., single words or numbers in Genesis, Psalms, and Nehemiah 5–7). This version's primary importance to textual criticism is the light it sheds on the Septuagint text. The New Testament was translated from the Greek text established at Byzantium about 350, but it is surprising how many Western readings are present in the text, many of which agree with the Old Latin version.[81] Wulfilas translated almost word for word, so that often the Greek order is retained against the common Gothic idiom, which would have been almost unintelligible to those who could not refer to the original Greek manuscripts.[82]

Manuscripts of the Gothic Version

There are only nine extant manuscripts of the Gothic version, most very fragmentary and none a complete manuscript of the whole Bible: from the Old Testament only a few words of Genesis, Psalms, and two portions of Ezra–Nehemiah survive, and from the New Testament several manuscripts of the Gospels and a portion of the Pauline Epistles. The most famous Gothic manuscript, known as Argentius (i.e., the Silver Codex), from the fifth or sixth century, contains the four Gospels arranged in Western order (Matt., John, Luke, Mark) and written in silver letters on purple vellum. The first three lines of each Gospel and the beginnings of different sections are written in gold. It is now located in the library of Uppsala University, Sweden.

Importance of the Gothic Version for Textual Criticism

The importance of this version for Old Testament textual criticism is minimal since so little remains (about fifty-five verses). However, its very literal reading of the Byzantine text from which it was translated has more value for New Testament textual criticism, though its numerous Coptic readings could indicate either that it was edited against a Coptic manuscript or that the Greek text used was already corrupted by Coptic translations. None of the extant Gothic manuscripts date before the sixth century, and they may have been modified significantly before this period.

Old Slavonic Version

Its History

During the mid-first millennium, Eastern Europe had only one Slavonic language from which all the modern dialects derive (see map 4). Much of the earliest history as to how the Slavs were evangelized is based entirely upon legend, but Metzger identifies Emperor Heraclius (c. 575–641) as the first to attempt to evangelize this area:

> In the sixth century hordes of fierce Asiatic people, the Avars, appeared prominently on the frontiers of the Roman Empire. After they had ravaged the Balkan territories of the Eastern Empire, coming up even to the very walls of Constantinople, Heraclius considered it necessary to Christianize the Croats, who then would serve as a buffer preventing further incursions and predatory raids. Consequently, according to an account given by Constantine Porphyrogenitus (905–59), Heraclius decided to bring priests from Rome, and made them an archbishop and a bishop and elders and deacons, and baptized the Croats.[83]

This account is plausible, though there is little evidence to corroborate it. More certain are the events of three hundred years later, when an attempt was made to Christianize the Moravian Empire (in modern Czech Republic), a development Bruce describes:

> About the middle of the ninth century a Moravian Empire was formed in East-Central Europe. This Empire professed Christianity, but its church dignitaries were not Slavs but Franks. The liturgy was conducted in Latin, the sermon was preached in the Germanic tongue of the Franks. But the founder of the empire, Rostislav, in order to check the growth of Frankish influence in his realm, asked, in 863, for Slavonic priests to be sent from Byzantium who should conduct the services and preach in the Slavonic language of the people.[84]

In response to Rostislav, Michael III (842–867), the eastern emperor, sent two

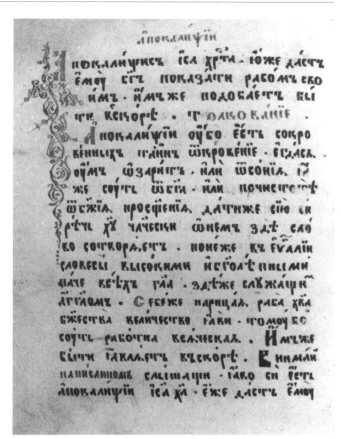

Figure 15.8. Revelation 1. Apocalypse in Old Slavonic (Russia, eighteenth century). [Grand Haven, Mich., The Scriptorium, VK MS 126, fol. 1ʳ]

brothers, Methodius (815–885) and Constantine (later called Cyril; 826/27–869), who became known as the apostles to the Slavs. The brothers preached to this Moravian group in the Slavonic language, which, according to Metzger, they had learned in Thessalonica from Slavs of Eastern Europe: "masses of Slavs had settled in the neighbourhood of Thessalonica, which was an important outpost of the empire and the second city after Constantinople, the two brothers were acquainted from childhood with the Slavic dialect spoken in the district."[85] Constantine was well educated, having completed his education at the University of Constantinople, and eventually he received a teaching position there in philosophy and theology. But about 863 he accompanied his brother to Moravia and began to train Moravians for the clergy. Very soon afterward he devised an alphabet (Glagolitic) and began translating the Greek Scriptures into Slavonic, as well as preaching in the same language. Soon after, in 864, the Byzantines evangelized the Bulgars. The Bulgars and the Slavs, now linked by both language and religion, developed Slav writing.[86] When Constantine died in 869, only the Psalms were completed from the Old Testament[87] and possibly the Gospels and Acts from the New Testament.[88] Methodius and some of his helpers finished the work by the end of the ninth century; little of the text remains except for fragments embedded in the present Slavonic Bible.[89] Metzger describes the next century: "The latter part of the tenth century, however, saw a number of setbacks to Christianity in the Balkan peninsula, and thereafter the chief creative centre of Slavic culture was in Russia, where Christianity became the state religion as a result of the baptism of the ruling prince, Vladimir, in A.D. 988."[90]

The Slavonic Translation

The earliest Slavonic manuscripts were probably written in Glagolitic script, which Metzger describes:

> It appears that Cyril [Constantine's monastic name], taking as a model the increasingly flamboyant Greek minuscule script of the ninth century, and perhaps adopting also several Latin and Hebrew (or Samaritan) signs, used his inventive powers to devise an assortment of stylized and symmetrical char-

acters made up of little quadrangles, triangles, and circles, with appendages.[91]

But there are no extant manuscripts from this earlier period, and those from the tenth or eleventh centuries (Codex Zographensis; Codex Marianus; Ostromir lectionary) already display dialectical variations of the script and language (see fig. 15.8). Constantine and Methodius are said to have translated the Gospels and Acts from Greek manuscripts. After Constantine's death, Methodius was helped by priests to translate the rest of Bible from Greek to Slavonic, omitting only the books of Maccabees. According to the *Vita Methodii (The Life of Methodius)*, the translation of the rest of the Bible into Slavonic took only eight months in 884,[92] but none of it survived. This fact is not surprising, considering the turmoil that erupted after Methodius's death. The earliest manuscripts come from the tenth or eleventh centuries.

Importance of the Old Slavonic Version for Textual Criticism

The late date of the Old Slavonic version (ninth century) means that it has little value in determining the earliest form of the text. It was probably translated from a Greek text in the Byzantine text family; however, it also has a significant number of earlier readings of the Western and Ceasarean type.[93] This translation is of more value relative to the history of interpretation and the transmission of the text in its later stages.

For Further Reading

Aland, K., and B. Aland. *The Text of the New Testament: An Introduction to the Critical Editions and to the Theory and Practice of Modern Textual Criticism,* 185–221. Translated by E. F. Rhodes. 2d ed. Grand Rapids: Eerdmans, 1989.

Bruce, F. F. *The Books and the Parchments,* 181–209. 5th ed. London: Marshall Pickering, 1991.

Jellicoe, S. *The Septuagint and Modern Study.* Oxford: Clarendon, 1968; reprint, Ann Arbor: Eisenbrauns, 1978.

Metzger, B. M. *The Early Versions of the New Testament: Their Origin, Transmission, and Limitations.* Oxford: Clarendon, 1977.

————. *The Text of the New Testament: Its Transmission, Corruption, and Restoration*, 67–86. 3d ed. New York and Oxford: Oxford University Press, 1992.

Roberts, B. J. *The Old Testament Text and Versions: The Hebrew Text in Transmission and the History of Ancient Versions.* Cardiff: University of Wales Press, 1951.

Swete, H. B. *An Introduction to the Old Testament in Greek.* Cambridge: Cambridge University Press, 1902; reprint, Peabody, MA: Hendrickson, 1989.

Vööbus, A. "Versions." In *ISBE*, 4:969–83.

Würthwein, E. *The Text of the Old Testament: An Introduction to the Biblia Hebraica.* Translated by E. F. Rhodes. Grand Rapids: Eerdmans, 1979.

The First Printed Greek Bibles

E vents and inventions in the fifteenth century, from the construction of the first printing press to the turbulent changes within the church, prepared the way for the printing of the Greek Bibles.

Major Advancements

The Development of Moveable Print

The process of printing was first developed in China with the use of carved wood block images. The first book to be printed in this fashion bears the following inscription: "Printed on May 11, 868 C.E., by Wang Chieh, for free general distribution, in order in deep reverence to perpetuate the memory of his parents."[1] Moveable print, in which individual letters are set and reset on frames to produce different printed pages, was also first used in China by Pi Shêng between 1041 and 1049, but the process was not generally adopted because of the large number of characters in the Chinese alphabet.[2] It was left to Johann Gutenberg in the West to rediscover the process of moveable type.

Gutenberg's greatest printing achievement, and the first book ever to be printed by moveable print in the West, was a magnificent two-volume copy of Jerome's Latin Vulgate, the Gutenberg Bible (fig. 16.1). It was an enormous undertaking—Gutenberg is said to have prepared about 46,000 wood blocks to set the manuscript. Approximately 120 copies were printed on paper and an additional 30 deluxe copies on parchment.[3] The expense of these works forced Guten-

Figure 16.1.
A page from the Gutenberg Bible. [British Library]

Johann Gutenberg (c. 1398–1468)

Johann Gutenberg (see fig. 16.2) was born in Mainz, Germany, about the end of the fourteenth century. Little is known about his early life except that his original name was Hans Gensfleisch, which he later changed to Gutenberg after his father's estate where he was born (D. Ewert, *From Ancient Tablets to Modern Translations: A General Introduction to the Bible* [Grand Rapids: Zondervan, 1983], 147). In his mid-thirties he moved to Strasbourg, Germany, where he purportedly constructed a printing press. About 1450, Johann Fust lent him money to continue his printing business. The story is told that one of Gutenberg's assistants accidentally dropped a woodcut page from a Bible. After severely scolding the assistant, Gutenberg pondered over the broken plate, wondering how to make it usable again. "Then it occurred to him: if these broken pieces can be put together again, why not put every page together?" (Ewert, *From Ancient Tablets to Modern Translations*, 147). Moveable print was born.

Figure 16.2. Johann Gutenberg (c. 1398–1468), who published the first Bible.

Gutenberg's first dated documents made with moveable print were letters of indulgences printed in 1454 and 1455 (*EncBrit*, "Printing," 18:499) and a Latin Psalter in 1454 (F. F. Bruce, *History of the Bible in English: From the Earliest Versions* [New York and Oxford: Oxford University Press, 1978], 24). Two years later (1456) he completed a printed copy of the Latin Vulgate, commonly called the Gutenberg Bible. It is sometimes called the Mazarin Bible because it was found in the library of Cardinal Jules Mazarin in the seventeenth century. Even with this amazing discovery, printing was an expensive business, and Gutenberg remained in debt most of his life.

berg into debt, but the Bibles sold well enough that a second edition was printed in 1457/1458.

For centuries biblical manuscripts had been hand-copied from earlier texts, a process that took many hours of painstaking effort and risked introducing new mistakes into the text. With the invention of the printing press things began to change, as Bruce Metzger notes: "Now copies of books could be reproduced more rapidly, more cheaply, and with a higher degree of accuracy than had ever been possible previously."[4]

Many Printing Presses

Within fifty years after the invention of movable print, printing houses sprang up all over Europe, and many books were printed, especially the Scriptures (fig. 16.3). During these years at least one hundred editions of the Latin Vulgate were published by various publishing houses.[5] The New Testament of the Complutensian Polyglot was completed in 1514 in Spain, and shortly afterward Erasmus's Greek New Testament (1516) was published in Basel, Switzerland. The delay in the appearance of a printed Greek text can be partially attributed to the belief that the text of the Latin Vulgate superseded that of the Greek. But technical difficulties also contributed to the delay, as Metzger explains:

the production of fonts of Greek type necessary for a book of any considerable size was both difficult and expensive. The attempt was made to reproduce in print the appearance of minuscule Greek handwriting, with its numerous alternative forms of the same letter, as well as its many combinations of two or more letters (ligatures). Instead, therefore, of producing type for merely twenty-four letters of the Greek alphabet, printers prepared about 200 different characters. (Subsequently these variant forms of the same letters were abandoned, until today there remain only the two forms of the lower-case sigma, σ and ς.)[6]

The Fall of Constantinople

On May 29, 1453, Constantinople, the capital of the Eastern church for more than a thousand years, fell to the Turkish sultan Mehmet II the Conqueror (1451–1481), and Greek scholars fled west with ancient manuscripts. According to F. G. Kenyon, this influx of ancient manuscripts gave new impetus to the study of the Greek New Testament:

> Greek, almost forgotten in Western Europe during many centuries, had always been a living language in the East, and now, journeying westwards, it met a fresh and eager spirit of inquiry, which welcomed joyfully the treasures of incomparable literature enshrined in that language. Above all, it brought to the West the knowledge of the New Testament in its original tongue; and with the general zeal for knowledge came also a much increased study of Hebrew, which was of equal value for the Old Testament.[7]

The Renaissance

At about this same time (i.e., the fourteenth to the sixteenth centuries) the Renaissance (rebirth) began in Italy and spread throughout Europe. During the Renaissance a revival of interest in knowledge and culture had many positive aspects, but among the negative consequences were the following:

> The philosophy of the Renaissance was known as Humanism. Whereas the Middle Ages in the West had put God and the transcendental at the centre of their thinking, the Renaissance focused attention on humanity and this world. The change affected scholarship: theology lost its dominant position and there was greater interest in people and nature. The study of classical texts, originally for linguistic reasons, now tacitly shifted to the study of classical values. Individualism began to replace the corporatism of the Middle Ages.[8]

Ancient Greek manuscripts brought by scholars who fled Constantinople arrived in Europe at a time when people were very interested in learning about early Greek history and language, especially as it appeared in these ancient manuscripts. This new study was fostered in England by John Colet (c. 1467–1519; appointed dean of St. Paul's in 1505), Sir Thomas More (1478–1535; chancellor and devout Roman Catholic), and the visiting scholar, Erasmus (1466–1536; lecturer at Cambridge, which became known as the center of new learning).

On the continent of Europe the historical situation was tense but exciting—many changes were taking place. In October of 1517, Martin Luther, professor of sacred theology at the University of Wittenberg, nailed his ninety-five theses to the Wittenberg church door, an act that sparked the Protestant Reformation. Number 36 epitomizes Luther's main contention with

Figure 16.3. A modern reproduction of a printing press. Also pictured (inset) is a woodcut showing a printing press in operation.

the Roman Catholic Church: "Any truly repentant Christian has a right to full remission of penalty and guilt, even without indulgence letters."[9] The Roman Catholic Church had grown very powerful and corrupt. Luther and others believed that one of the best ways to expose this corruption was to translate the Bible into the vernacular so that people could understand God's Word and see the true nature of the church for themselves. As a result many translations appeared allowing people to read the Bible in their own language:

1. Italian (two versions by 1471 and sixteen by the end of the century)
2. French (the New Testament in 1477; the entire Bible by 1487)
3. Spanish (1478)
4. Dutch (1477)
5. German (Luther's Bible in 1521, which had been preceded by nineteen other German versions)[10]

The First Printed Editions of the Greek New Testament

The stage of history was now set for the printing of the Greek New Testament, which

Figure 16.4.
Erasmus of Rotterdam (c. 1466–1536) prepared the first Greek New Testament accessible to scholars.

would spark further revolution in the church. Once the Greek text was published, it was naturally preferred by some scholars over the text of the Latin Vulgate, though the Roman Catholic Church continued to fight any nonallegiance to the Vulgate.

Complutensian Polyglot (1514–1522)

This massive four-volume work was supervised by Francisco Ximenes de Cisneros (1437–1517), cardinal and archbishop of Toledo, Spain, and regent of Castile (1506–1517). In 1502, he conceived the idea of making the first Polyglot Bible to celebrate the birth of the royal son, who grew up to become Emperor Charles V. In preparation, he collected as many manuscripts as possible and spared no expense, as Frederick Scrivener explains, "The whole outlay of Cardinal Ximenes on the Polyglot is stated to have exceeded 50,000 ducats or about £23,000, a vast sum in those days—but his yearly income as Primate was four times as great."[11] Work on the polyglot, carried out in Alcalá, Spain (called Complutum in Latin, and thus the name of the translation), involved the arrangement of Hebrew, Aramaic (various targums), Greek, and Latin texts in parallel columns. The New Testament was printed on January 10, 1514, but because it had been delayed so long by ecclesiastical authorities, Erasmus's Greek text was distributed before it. The Old Testament required another three years before completion (July 10, 1517), but it too was delayed by ecclesiastical authorities. The entire Bible finally appeared in 1522, long after the death of Cardinal Ximenes in 1517. This work was always scarce and expensive—only about six hundred copies were ever published[12]—but it was far superior to Erasmus's text, which came out six years earlier in 1516. The Greek texts used for the Complutensian Polyglot still remain unidentified, but the dedication states: "For Greek copies indeed we are indebted to your Holiness [Pope Leo X, though it was probably his predecessor, Pope Julius II], who sent us most kindly from the Apostolic Library very ancient codices, both of the Old and the New Testament; which have aided us very much in this undertaking."[13]

Erasmus's Greek New Testament (1516)

Desiderius Erasmus of Rotterdam (c. 1466–1536) is generally credited with preparing the first Greek New Testament in 1516, for his was the first one accessible to the people (fig. 16.4).

Erasmus was born in the Netherlands as the illegitimate son of a Dutch priest. Being left an orphan quite young, Erasmus was compelled to go into minor religious orders, and when he was older he entered a monastery (1492). Later, however, he was released from his vows and began studies at the Collège de Montaigu in Paris, after which he went on to Cambridge. There he met Colet and Thomas More. Scrivener describes the course of his life from this point:

> Thenceforward his was the hard life of a solitary and wandering man of letters, earning a precarious subsistence from booksellers or pupils, now learning Greek at Oxford (but αὐτοδίδακτος "taught himself"), now teaching at Cambridge (1510); losing by his reckless wit the friends his vast erudition had won; restless and unfrugal, perhaps, yet always labouring faithfully and with diligence.[14]

For a long time Erasmus had been interested in preparing a copy of the Latin Vulgate, but while he was in England a famous Swiss printer, named Froben, asked him to make a copy of the Greek New Testament. Froben needed an answer quickly, for he was well aware of the ongoing work by Cardinal Ximenes. Erasmus's training in England had impressed upon him the importance of knowing the Greek language, and thus he was very interested in such a proposal. His conviction that theology was the handmaiden of grammar forced him to conclude that knowledge of what the actual biblical text said was prerequisite to determining proper theology. He therefore agreed to prepare the Greek

New Testament and went to Basel, Switzerland, in July of 1515 to begin work.

Erasmus had hoped to find good manuscripts to send to the printer along with his Latin translation that he had been working on for some years. However, the only manuscripts available on such short notice were those requiring significant corrections before they could be sent to the printer. Preparation took longer than either had expected, so that the project was rushed to completion in about ten months. Hundreds of typographical errors appeared as a result, and in the opinion of Scrivener caused it to be "in that respect the most faulty book I know."[15] Ximenes, in the last year of his life, was shown a copy of Erasmus's edition when it appeared before his own: "When . . . his editor, Stunica, sought to depreciate it, the noble old man replied, 'would God that all the Lord's people were prophets! produce better, if thou canst; condemn not the industry of another.'"[16] The work of Stunica was indisputably better, and yet Erasmus's edition was far more popular, consisting of a thousand-page diglot (i.e., the Greek text appears on one side and Erasmus's Latin translation on the other). Erasmus had hoped to find one Greek text for the whole volume, but as this was not possible he was forced to compile numerous manuscripts: "the text of Erasmus' Greek New Testament rests upon a half-dozen minuscule manuscripts. The oldest and best of these manuscripts (codex 1, a minuscule of the tenth century, which agrees often with the earlier uncial texts) he used least, because he was afraid of its supposedly erratic text!"[17]

Erasmus later admitted that the work was "precipitated rather than edited."[18] For example, the twelfth-century manuscript of the Book of Revelation borrowed from his friend, Reuchlin, was missing the last page. Erasmus therefore translated the Latin Vulgate back into Greek for the last six verses of the book. In other places where the Greek texts were confusing, he referred to the Latin Vulgate, occasionally adding words not found in the Greek (e.g., Erasmus introduced the question "What shall I do, Lord?" in Acts 9:6 without support from Greek manuscripts, though it was present in Acts 22:10).

First Printed Editions of the Greek New Testament
Complutensian Polyglot (1514–1522)
Erasmus (1516)
Estienne [Stephanus] (1546, 1549, 1550, 1551)
Bèza (9 editions, 1565–1604)
Elzevir (1624, 1633)

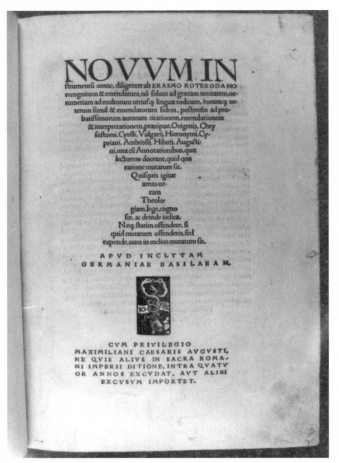

Figure 16.5.
The title page from Erasmus's Greek New Testament. Bible in Greek and Latin (Basel: Johann Froben, 1516), translated by Desiderius Erasmus, 1st edition. [Grand Haven, Mich., The Scriptorium, VK 366, title page]

the Greek texts may be older and more accurate than the Latin.

One of the most severe criticisms came from James Lopez de Stunica, an editor of the Complutensian Polyglot, because Erasmus had not included in his Greek text 1 John 5:7–8 ("the Father, the Word, and the Holy Ghost: and these three are one. And there are three that bear witness in earth" [KJV]; sometimes called the *Comma Johanneum* or Johannine clause). Erasmus was accused of removing part of God's word; his response to this charge is summarized well by Bruce Metzger:

> Erasmus replied that he had not found any Greek manuscript containing these words, though he had in the meanwhile examined several others besides those on which he relied when first preparing his text. In an unguarded moment Erasmus promised that he would insert the *Comma Johanneum*, as it is called, in further editions if a single Greek manuscript could be found that contained the passage. At length such a copy was found [now designated Greg. 61]—or was made to order! As it now appears, the Greek manuscript had probably been written in Oxford about 1520 by a Franciscan friar named Froy (or Roy), who took the disputed words from the Latin Vulgate.[20] Erasmus stood by his promise and inserted the passage in his third edition (1522), but he indicated in a lengthy footnote his suspicions that the manuscript had been prepared expressly in order to confute him. [21]

Erasmus's Greek New Testament went through five different editions (1516, 1519, 1522, 1527, and 1535; fig. 16.5). Luther used the second edition to render his German translation in 1522, and Tyndale probably used the third edition for his English translation. But the fourth edition is the definitive work, containing three parallel columns: the Greek text, the Latin Vulgate, and Erasmus's own Latin translation. Erasmus recognized the superiority of the Complutensian Polyglot and used it to modify his text (in Revelation alone he adjusted his text in about ninety places).[22] The fifth edition was primarily the same as the fourth but without the Latin Vulgate. Erasmus's text became the stan-

There were a great variety of responses to this new Greek text. Some accepted it quickly; others were skeptical or even hostile. Students at Cambridge and Oxford were forbidden to read it since some of its notes were aimed at corrupt priests. Theologians from the University of Louvain, Belgium, believed the Latin Vulgate was more accurate and sent Erasmus a letter: "What if it be contended that the sense, as rendered by the Latin version, differs indeed from the Greek text? Then, indeed, adieu [good bye] to the Greek. I adhere to the Latin because I cannot bring my mind to believe that the Greek are more correct than the Latin codices."[19] It must be remembered that by this time the Latin Vulgate had been the Bible of the western Church for a thousand years and the Greek texts had only recently reappeared. It was therefore a revolutionary idea that

dardized text for about four hundred years, even though it was clearly not the best text. Its wide circulation and popularity were due to the fact that it appeared first, was cheaper, and came in a convenient size.

Robert Estienne (1503–1559)

This famous Parisian printer, whose name is latinized as Stephanus, produced four editions of the Greek New Testament (1546, 1549, 1550, 1551). The first three, prepared in Paris for the government, were particularly beautiful editions; the last, fairly meager edition was published in Geneva after Estienne (fig. 16.6) made a profession of Protestantism. Scrivener describes Estienne: "This eminent and resolute man, 'whose Biblical work taken together had perhaps more influence than that of any other single man in the sixteenth century,' early commenced his useful career as a printer at Paris, and, having incurred the enmity of the Doctors of the Sorbonne for his editions of the Latin Vulgate, was yet protected and patronised by Francis I [d. 1547] and his son Henry II."[23] In time he was ostracized by the Roman Catholic government for having converted to Protestantism.

Estienne's first two editions of the Greek New Testament combined readings from the Complutensian Polyglot and Erasmus's editions. The third edition was the first work to include a textual apparatus with various readings from the margins of fourteen Greek manuscripts, as well as many readings from the Complutensian Polyglot and Codex Bezae. It has now become regarded by many as the standard received text, even though it has been modified significantly from Erasmus's text. The fourth edition (1551), wherein two Latin versions (the Latin Vulgate and Erasmus's translation) flank either side of the Greek text, is the first text to appear with modern verse divisions.

Théodore de Bèza (1519–1605)

Théodore de Bèza succeeded John Calvin in Geneva as the head of Reformed Protestantism. Born in Vezelay, Burgundy, he studied in Paris and Orléans, France, both in classics and the Bible. While in Paris his family wanted him to become ordained, but he had secretly married Claudine Desnoz. Later, after an illness in 1548, he renounced the Roman Catholic faith and at twenty-nine years of age went to live in Geneva, where he publicly married Claudine. Bèza was an excellent scholar known for his eloquence and learning. He published at least nine editions of the Greek New Testament in his lifetime, though several were merely small reprint editions. Annotations were included along with his own Latin translation and textual notes collating a number of Greek texts, among these Codex Bezae and Codex Claromontanus, which he owned. He appears to have used them only infrequently, since they differed significantly from the Greek text common to his day. Even though many more sources were available to him, Bèza's text was quite similar to Stephanus's fourth edition (1551).

Figure 16.6. The famous printer from Paris, Robert Estienne (1503–1559).

Bonaventure Elzevir and Abraham Elzevir

These brothers from Leiden, the Netherlands, set up a printing press renowned for elegance and correctness during much of the seventeenth century.[24] They published a small edition of the Greek text in 1624; it gained popularity because of its clear printing and convenient size, though it was primarily Bèza's text of the 1565 edition. A second edition in 1633 corrected most of the worst errors from their earlier edition. The preface claims that even the most minute mistakes had been corrected and thus this edition was "the text which is now received by all [Textum ergo habes nunc ab omnibus receptum], in which we give nothing changed or corrupted"; this advertising blurb gave rise to the name *Textus Receptus* (since the King James Version had been translated from this Greek text, it too is often called the received text).[25] This text was published so many times (by Stephanus, Bèza, and the Elzevir brothers) that people began to consider it the only authentic Greek text. It was reprinted in hundreds of subsequent editions and underlies the text of the King James Version (1611) as well as every other major Protestant translation up until 1881.[26] The next chapter will describe the progress of English Bibles up to the King James Bible, which was the English Bible for at least the next three hundred years of English history and was seriously challenged only in the twentieth century.

For Further Reading

Bruce, F. F. *The Books and the Parchments*, 166–80. 5th ed. London: Marshall Pickering, 1991.

Ewert, D. *From Ancient Tablets to Modern Translations: A General Introduction to the Bible*, 147–62. Grand Rapids: Zondervan, 1983.

Finegan, J. *Encountering New Testament Manuscripts: A Working Introduction to Textual Criticism*, 54–59. Grand Rapids: Eerdmans, 1974.

Kenyon, F. G. *Our Bible and the Ancient Manuscripts*, 155–61. 5th ed. Revised by A. W. Adams. New York: Harper, 1958.

Metzger, B. M. *The Text of the New Testament: Its Transmission, Corruption, and Restoration*, 95–106. 3d ed. New York and Oxford: Oxford University Press, 1992.

Scrivener, F. H. A. *A Plain Introduction to the Criticism of the New Testament*, 175–95. Edited by E. Miller. 4th ed. 2 vols. London: George Bell, 1894.

Wegener, G. S. *Six Thousand Years of the Bible*. Translated by M. Shenfield. New York: Harper & Row, 1963.

Part 5

English Translations
of the Bible

English Bibles prior to 1611

With the many excellent English translations available to us, it is difficult to realize that for more than nine hundred years English-speaking people did not have a Bible in their own language. Several factors were at work to delay the perceived need of an English translation. First, for approximately a thousand years the church deemed the Latin Vulgate to be the authoritative translation of the Bible. Few except the clergy could read or understand Latin, and often even the clergy themselves were poorly trained, as Geoffrey Shepherd, professor of English medieval language and literature at University of Birmingham, explains:

> The moderately educated man, usually a monk, a cleric by definition, seldom saw the Bible as a whole. Many clerics, probably most parish priests up to Wyclif's time, were unable to construe even the Latin of the Mass. Of the clergy who could read, most would still know the Bible in single books and extracts, primarily of course in the extracts of the service books. Medieval liturgies are bewildering mosaics cut and shaped for a purpose out of the Scriptures; and if this process gives a prodigious enrichment to meaning, it obscures almost completely the flow and scope of the original.[1]

Second, many of the clergy did not have the training or the time to render a translation of the Scriptures into English, even if they did believe that it was necessary (which most of them did not). King Alfred the Great, one of the first persons to translate even a portion of the Bible into English, mentions the difficulty of carving out time for translating and the skill it involves: "I began . . . amidst other diverse and manifold cares of the kingdom, to turn into English the book which is called *Cura Pastorialis* in Latin, and in English, *The Shepherd's Book*, sometimes word for word, and sometimes meaning for meaning."[2]

Third, translating the Bible was not only difficult but also dangerous. The established church was reluctant to have the Bible translated into English, sometimes even killing those who attempted to do so (e.g., William Tyndale; Matthew Rogers). To have the Bible available in English vernacular posed a threat to the established church, which feared that it would lose power over and revenue from the common people; and that commoners would misunderstand and corrupt the teachings of the Bible. On the latter point, however, the example of the Middle Ages demonstrates that keeping the Bible in a language that only educated clergy could interpret did not keep the traditions pure and free from errors.

Despite these obstacles there were those who felt the need to translate the Bible into English. The following history briefly describes the events leading up to the first English translations until the appearance of one of the most famous English Bibles, the Authorized Version of 1611, commonly known as the King James Bible.

Early British History as It Relates to the English Bible Versions

Britain was captured by the Romans in the early second century A.D., under Trajan (98–117) and Hadrian (117–38; fig. 17.1). The Roman Empire was a pagan society that worshiped many gods and even its

Trajan (98–117) Hadrian (117–138)

Figure 17.1.
Coins of Trajan and Hadrian, who incorporated England into the Roman Empire. Hadrian's Wall, built to protect the furthest border from the barbarians, can still be seen in northern England.
[Harlan J. Berk]

emperors. The early Christian church, which grew within the confines of the Roman Empire, was viewed as a threat to national religion and unity and was therefore often persecuted. One of the benefits resulting from this persecution, however, was that Christians fled to the furthest reaches of the empire. By at least the early fourth century there is significant evidence that Christianity had reached England:

> In A.D. 314 we have the record of three British bishops (those of York, London, and Lincoln) attending the Council of Arles. The earliest British writer was one of the outstanding figures in early Christian literature—Pelagius . . . , who in the first decade of the fifth century produced at Rome commentaries on the thirteen epistles of Paul. About the end of the fourth century Ninian, appointed bishop of the district now known as Galloway and Dumfries, evangelised the southern Picts [Scottish tribes north of Edinburgh], and established a monastery at Whithorn (*Ad Candidam Casam*) from which the gospel was carried farther afield, in particular to Northern Ireland.[3]

Also during the fourth century drastic changes brought about the Christianization of the Roman Empire:

> The 4th century marked the decisive turning-point. Diocletian's persecution of the Christians in 303, which was the religious aspect of his policy of restoring the Empire, was one of the most violent attacks on them but also virtually the last. In 313 the two Emperors, Constantine and Licinius, met together in Milan and recognized Christianity as one of the religions of the Empire, signalling

its definitive victory. Constantine was baptized before he died. Between 381 and 392 Theodosius banned pagan practices: temples were destroyed or turned into churches and in 393 the Olympic Games were ended. The Roman Empire had become a Christian empire.[4]

But there is no record of the Bible being translated into English at this early period; Latin was the language of the church. The Christian message at this period was best communicated by means of wood carvings or paintings, which often adorned the churches and depicted scenes from biblical stories. Stained glass windows later had a similar function.

With the coming of the Angles and Saxons from the continent in the fifth century, the Christian faith was almost obliterated. This may have been largely due to the fact that few Englishmen could read the Latin Vulgate used by earlier Roman missionaries. At the end of the sixth century the Saxons were in a state of relative peace, and in 597 Pope Gregory the Great sent a monk named Augustine to reestablish the Roman Catholic Church in England (Angleland). He converted the King of Kent and founded the bishopric of Canterbury. About the same time an Irish monk named Columba worked in Scotland and in the north of England with significant success (fig. 17.2).

Caedmon (d. c. 678)

About 670 Caedmon, a cowherder attached to the Lady Hilda monastery at Whitby on the Yorkshire coast, turned certain biblical passages into Old English poems for the people to memorize and sing. F. F. Bruce tells the story of how Caedmon first began to create these poems:

> This man Caedmon was completely ungifted in poetry and song, and one night, when his companions were enjoying themselves at a party, he stole away to the stable in case he would be asked to sing. In the stable he fell asleep, and dreamed that a man came and stood beside him and told him to sing. He replied that he could not sing, but the command was repeated. "What shall I

sing?" Caedmon asked, and he was told to sing how all things were first created. So he began to praise the Creator in words which he had never heard before:

> Now must we praise
> The Maker of the heavenly realm,
> The Creator's power and wisdom,
> The deeds of the Father of glory;
> How He, being God eternal,
> Was the Author of all wonders,
> Who first to the sons of men
> Made heaven for the roof of their abode,
> And then created the earth,
> Almighty Guardian of mankind. . . . [5]

When Caedmon woke from his dream he remembered perfectly all the words to the song. Once others realized that he had been given a gift from God, Hilda, the superior of the monastery, asked him to become a monk and live at the monastery. There he received detailed training in the Bible, which he then turned into songs. His songs contain major sections of Scripture from at least Genesis, Exodus, and Daniel; being easy to remember, they were a good source of teaching biblical doctrine to common people.

Aldhelm (d. 709)

Aldhelm, the first bishop of Sherborne in Dorset and one of the most outstanding scholars of his day, was the first to translate a portion (the Psalter) of the Latin Vulgate into Anglo-Saxon about 700. The Psalms were of particular interest to the English Christians, as Shepherd notes:

So fundamental was the Psalter to the devotional and educational system of the monasteries that it is not surprising to find that English aids to understanding were provided. Some of these aids were no more than odd glosses to hard words. But nearly fifteen psalters, some of the Roman, some of the Gallican text, survive with a continuous gloss in Old English. The best-known of these glossed psalters is the ninth-century *Vespasian Psalter* (BM Cotton MS Vespasian A.i), copied from a still earlier gloss.[6]

Bede (c. 675–735/736)

Bede, a monk of Jarrow and the father of English history, is often considered the greatest name in the history of the early English church.[7] He wrote many works of

Earliest English Translators
Caedmon (d. c. 678)
Aldhelm (d. 709)
Bede (c. 675–735/736)
Alcuin (735–804)
Alfred the Great (849–901)
Ælfric (c. 955–1020)
Orm [Ormin] (c. 12–13th cent.)

Figure 17.2. Many oratories (small chapels reserved for prayer) like the one pictured were built of limestone on the Dingle Peninsula in southwest Ireland. From the fifth century onward numerous monasteries were built throughout the British Isles.

history and exegesis in Latin, but his most famous is *Historia Ecclesiastica Gentis Anglorum* (*Church History of the English People*), tracing events beginning with Caesar's arrival in Gaul about 57 B.C. until 731. Bede also translated portions of Scripture into English out of a desire to help those with less ability to do so. He is even said to have been dictating an English translation of the Gospel of John with his dying breath, as described by Frederic Kenyon:

> On the Eve of Ascension Day, 735, the great scholar lay dying, but dictating, while his strength allowed, to his disciples; and they wrote down the translation of the Gospel as it fell from his lips, being urged by them to write quickly, since he did not know how soon his Master would call him. On Ascension morning one chapter alone remained unfinished, and the youth who had been copying hesitated to press his master further; but he would not rest. "It is easily done," he said; "take thy pen and write quickly." Failing strength and the last farewells to the brethren of the monastery prolonged the task, till at eventide the boy reminded his master: "There is yet one sentence unwritten, dear master." "Write it quickly," was the answer; and it was written at his word. "It is written now," said the boy. "You speak truth," answered the saint; "it is finished now." Then he bade them lay him on the pavement of his cell, supporting his head in their hands; and as he repeated the Gloria, with the name of the Holy Spirit on his lips, he passed quietly away.[8]

No trace of this translation exists, though other parts of his works have survived. According to Bruce, Bede had a great desire for the clergy to know at least some of the Scripture in English: "Bede himself in a letter to Egbert (who became Archbishop of York shortly before Bede died) exhorts him to take special care to see that ordinands whose Latin was weak or non-existent were conversant with the Apostle's Creed and the Lord's Prayer in the vernacular, adding that he himself 'had both these, that is, the creed and the *Pater Noster*, translated into the English tongue, for the sake of many priests, who were often unlearned.'"[9]

Alcuin (735–804)

When Egbert became bishop of York he founded a school for ministers there. One of its most famous pupils, Alcuin, recounts from his schooldays in York the following: "Sitting on his bed from sunrise until the sixth hour of the day, and often until the ninth hour, Egbert would explain the mysteries of Holy Writ to his pupils as far as they were prepared to receive them."[10] As an important and influential scholar, Alcuin was called to Charlemagne's court at Aachen (today Germany) in 782 to render a standardized text of Jerome's Latin Vulgate along with a standardized interpretation, a work that shifted the accessibility of Scripture away from common people:

> Alcuin's work initiated a scholastic approach towards the Bible which endured for centuries. From now on, Scripture was not considered to be directly accessible to an intelligent reader, nor would such a reader consider himself free to draw out of it or put into it his own associations of meaning. Each verse of the Bible became a cluster of meanings provided by tradition out of the Fathers. Any reading of the Bible implied acceptance of a huge network of orthodox associations. The Vulgate and its latinity became ever more inviolable.[11]

Alcuin effected one change for the good, however, in developing a style of handwriting called Caroline minuscule. This handwriting incorporated both small and capital letters much like our writing today and was easier to read than were earlier scripts.[12]

Alfred the Great (849–901)

In the next century, Alfred the Great, king of Wessex from 871, had the unusual distinction of being literate at a time when few monarchs viewed this as advantageous. Shepherd describes how Alfred used his literacy to promote the good of his people:

> Writing in 894 and looking back over his troubled reign of a score of years, King Alfred recalled that when he came to the

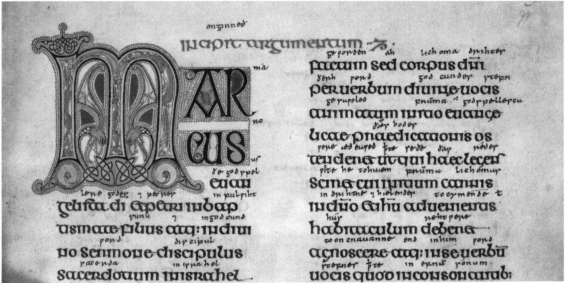

throne there were very few clergy anywhere in England who knew or could translate Latin. By the end of his reign the position had much improved. There was a body of learned clergy, and with their aid Alfred had put through a scheme of education in two phases. First, he with his helpers translated into English certain basic books of knowledge, and then the freeborn youth of England who could be maintained at schools were set to acquire at least the ability to read English. Those who were called to the priesthood were expected to stay on to learn Latin.[13]

The books chosen for translation into English were Bede's *Ecclesiastical History of the English Nation*, Orosius's *Universal History*, Pope Gregory the Great's *Pastoral Care* (a handbook for parish priests), and a portion of the Psalms. Alfred even introduced his law code with translations of the Ten Commandments and portions of Exodus 21–23 and Acts 15:23–29. While these portions may seem rather insignificant, they nevertheless opened the door for English readers to grasp the relevancy of Scripture to their situation; for example:

> The reference to buying a *Hebrew* servant in Ex. 21:2 is made more relevant to the English situation in Alfred's day; the phrase appears as "a Christian Servant"! These extracts were followed by a trans-

lation of the apostolic letter drawn up at the Council of Jerusalem (Acts 15:23–29), in a longer text which includes, at the end, the Golden Rule, in its negative form: "Whatever you would not like others to do to you, do not that to others." Thus Alfred's "dooms" (judgments) are preceded by the "dooms" of God.[14]

Interlinear Glosses

Some clergymen penned English words under their Latin counterparts, effectively producing something like interlinears for their own use. Several of these interlinear glosses are now housed at the British Museum; for example, in the Lindisfarne Gospels (c. 698; fig. 17.3), a Latin translation of the Gospels rendered by Bishop Eadfrith of Lindisfarne, a tenth-century priest named Alfred inscribed a literal translation of the Latin between the lines. In a colophon at the end of the manuscript he names the original copyists of the manuscript and that he added his translation to it.

The Bodleian Library of Oxford has a similar manuscript called the Rushworth Gospels (MS Bodley *auct.* D. 2. 19), wherein translations appear between the lines. About the same time as these interlinear versions comes the first known individual translation into Old English: the Wessex

Figure 17.3. The beginning of the Gospel of Mark from the Lindisfarne Gospels, made about 698 in the Lindisfarne monastery. The monastery is located on an island off the coast of Northumbria, England. [British Library]

Gospels, attributed to Ælfric at Bath about 1000. It is housed in the British Museum.

Ælfric (c. 955–1020)

In addition to his notable contributions to the education of rural clergy,[15] this tenth-century abbot from Eynsham, Oxfordshire, translated portions of the first seven books of the Old Testament. He also produced homilies with Old English translations of several other Old Testament passages (at least from Kings, Esther, Job, Daniel, and Maccabees), his motivation being characterized by the following statement: "Happy is he, then, who reads the Scriptures, if he convert the words into actions."[16]

Thus by the tenth century a few, sporadic Old English translations of portions of the Bible were beginning to be rendered. But it was a difficult time to attempt literary advances, as Geddes MacGregor, professor of philosophical theology at the University of Southern California, explains:

> As for the remoter parts of Europe, it should also be remembered that it was not till late in the tenth century that Christianity began to make any headway at all in the Scandinavian countries, and a long time then passed before the process might be said to be in any sense complete. The chronic disorders of the dark period brought, besides political chaos, a decline in commerce and industry so disasterous that it looked as though the world were reverting to complete savagery. The fine old Roman roads fell into disrepair. It was exceedingly dangerous to undertake even comparatively short journeys. By land one's path was beset by robbers, while pirates infested the sea. Their calling was made profitable, and their retribution rendered unlikely, by the unsettled conditions that prevailed. Towns and cities, once prosperous, decayed, dwindling in population as their impoverishment diminished their appeal.[17]

Even these small advances in the translation of the Bible into English came to a halt when the French-speaking Normans conquered England in 1066. This dealt a heavy blow to Old English culture and, according to Bruce, significantly weakened the Christian life that had existed for five hundred years previously:

> English history has sometimes been taught in schools in such a way as to suggest that the Conquest represented a cultural advance, but a comparison of William the Conqueror with Alfred the Great from this point of view points to a different conclusion. A British Museum manuscript of the Wessex Gospels, copied in the early part of the twelfth century, indicated that the Old English biblical texts continued to be read by some people at least after the Conquest. But the impact of the Conquest, carried as it was by a new ruling class speaking Norman French, brought about such radical changes in spoken English that before long the Old English versions of the tenth century must have been unintelligible to the great mass of the English people.[18]

The Norman ecclesiastical system, significantly different from the Anglo-Saxon system, used Latin exclusively, so that by the twelfth century the English language had virtually died out. At the end of the eleventh century the Crusades against Islam broke out in earnest. Pope Urban II called upon Christian knights, especially the Franks, to fight against the "infidels" and to recapture Jerusalem. For the next two centuries Christianity took on a military mode with little tolerance for opposing positions. Anyone seen to go against the established church was fighting against God. Jerusalem was taken by the Christian armies on July 15, 1099 (fig. 17.4), as the Christian historian, Raimondo d'Aguilers, recounts:

> If we told the truth about what had happened there, we should not be believed. Let us say only that in the Temple and in the porch of Solomon one had to wade in blood up to the knees and bits of horses. And it was by the just judgment of God that this place, which had so long borne insults against God, should receive the blood of His enemies. After the town was captured, it was wonderful to see the devotions of the pilgrims

before the Sepulcre of Our Lord and to hear how they showed their joy as they sang a new hymn to God. And their hearts offered to victorious and triumphant God such praises as could not be expressed in words[19]

This victory was to last only for about a century before Saladin, sultan of Egypt, recaptured Jerusalem in 1187 and returned it into the hands of the Muslims. The Crusades resumed for another hundred years when, during the sixth crusade (1228–1229) led by Frederick II, Jerusalem was again taken temporarily by the Christians. Several manuscripts arising from this period appeared in the Anglo-Norman language, but they were used more by the new ruling class than by the great mass of English people.

Early Middle English Translations

By the mid-twelfth century a new language—a mixture of Norman and English—marked the beginning of Middle English, the language of Chaucer. For more than three centuries few biblical books were translated into Middle English, except for two versions of the Psalms as well as the smaller works described below.

Orm (or Ormin)

Sometime between the twelfth and thirteenth centuries a poetic version of a harmony of the Gospels and Acts with commentary, called the *Ormulum*, was created by an Augustinian monk named Orm or Ormin, writing in the northeast Midlands. Only one copy exists today in the Bodleian Library, Oxford.

Other Works

From the middle to the end of the thirteenth century stories from Genesis and Exodus and a copy of the Psalter were put into poetry. In the first half of the next century two copies of the Psalms in prose appeared (attributed to William of Shoreham [?]; Richard Rolle of Hampole). Later in that century an obscure

Figure 17.4.
A lithograph of the Dome of the Rock showing the rock where Christians believe Abraham attempted to sacrifice Isaac and from which Muslims believe the prophet Muhammad began his ascent into heaven.

version of the New Testament Epistles was rendered into Middle English. Bruce deduces it was created for the use of monks and nuns, since the translator frequently uses the terms *brothers* and *sisters* in the introductions to various epistles.[20] Later the books of Acts and Matthew were added to this collection, and Bruce summarizes its impact: "While a version like this might freely be made for the devotional use of inmates of religious houses, there was as yet no thought of supplying ordinary layfolk with the Scriptures in the vernacular. This revolutionary idea was first entertained (so far as mediaeval English is concerned) by the Wycliffite movement. . . ."[21]

During the thirteenth and fourteenth centuries the gap between wealthy and poor widened severely, aggravating the tensions between leaders and commoners. Major works in biblical scholarship were written in Latin, and there was a clear drawing away from translating biblical texts into vernacular English, thus driving a wedge between priests and laymen. The church had claimed universal supremacy since the Gregorian reform in the eleventh century and even acquired the power to appoint the emperor. The pope stressed his direct links to God and saw himself as the champion of the universal and triumphant church.[22] But this sovereignty was shaken when England and France broke away from the rest of the Holy Roman Empire. During this Great Schism in the west (1378–1417), European Christendom was divided into two factions, each with a pope and a college of cardinals (map 5). The pope at Avignon, France, was backed by Spain, Portugal, France, the kingdom of Naples, and Scotland, while the rest of Europe supported the pope in Rome.[23] The countries of Czechoslovakia, Poland, and Bohemia later also broke away from Rome.

Even amidst all of this fighting there was a revival of interest in religion by the common people, spurred on by the horrors of the Black Death (bubonic plague and pneumonic infections) that swept across Europe from 1347 to 1351:

In the year of Our Lord 1348 almost the whole surface of the globe suffered from such mortality as has rarely been seen. The living were barely sufficient to bury the dead, or were so horrified as to avoid the task. So great a terror seized nearly everyone that no sooner had an ulcer or a swelling appeared on someone, usually in the groin or the armpit, than the victim was deprived of all help and even abandoned by his family. . . . And so, many people died owing to lack of care. . . . Many more who were thought bound . . . to die . . . were transported . . . to the grave to be buried: in this way a large number were buried alive. . . . And this plague continued . . . for two years in succession. (*Vitae Paparum Avenionensium: Clementis VI Prima vita*)[24]

When the plague reached England in 1348–1349, as much as 30 to 40 percent of

Map 5. A map of the Great Schism.

the urban population died; the plague recurred several times (1360, 1369, 1374), each time decimating much of the population (fig. 17.5). Life expectancy fell drastically in England from an average of twenty-five years in 1348 to seventeen in 1376.[25] In such a climate it was only natural that interest in religious things should increase, and as a result the desire grew for a vernacular Bible. The friars (members of certain religious orders) were the strongest opponents to an English Bible because they deemed Bible study too complicated a task to be done properly by laymen. The friars were highly educated and believed that anyone studying the Bible needed strong philological and linguistic skills as well as advanced training in exegesis and biblical theology. In their estimation the best a layperson could do was to learn under someone who had been trained in the Scriptures. From the fourth century to the fourteenth century England did not have a Bible translated into English, but John Wycliffe (c. 1330–1384) was to change all of this.

The Wycliffe Bible (NT, 1380; Entire Bible, 1382)

John Wycliffe (c. 1329–1384)

John Wycliffe (fig. 17.6) was born in Hipswell, Yorkshire, and attended Balliol College, Oxford, which was founded by his neighbors, the Balliols of Barnard Castle. He was educated at Queen's and Merton colleges of Oxford and became a teaching fellow of Merton College about 1356. Shortly afterward he was appointed master of Balliol College but resigned the post in 1361. Even though he remained a lecturer at Oxford University, he received his living from the churches to which he was subsequently appointed rector—Fillingham in Lincolnshire, then Lutterworth, fifteen miles north of Oxford.

Wycliffe was a brilliant scholar and a superb debater whose lectures were crowded with students. In time he grew greatly concerned about the corruption in the church and the papacy; the hierarchy of the church had become so wealthy and powerful that even the king of England

Figure 17.5. Drawing of a tapestry depicting the Black Plague in Tournai, France (1349).

Figure 17.6.
An etching of
John Wycliffe
(c. 1329–1384).

that the people needed the Bible in their own language for a revival to take place, a conviction for which he greatly suffered yet steadfastly maintained, stating: "it helpeth Christian men to study the Gospel in that tongue in which they know best Christ's sentence."[26]

Wycliffe is generally associated with the first translation of the entire Bible into English, but it is uncertain whether Wycliffe made the translation himself or, as is more likely, whether several of his students helped with the translation project while he oversaw the work. It matters little, for Wycliffe was responsible for the first English translation of the Scriptures, and for this he was proclaimed a heretic. Archbishop Arundel denounces Wycliffe in a letter to Pope John XXIII in 1411: "This pestilent and wretched John Wyclif, of cursed memory, that son of the old serpent . . . endeavoured by every means to attack the very faith and sacred doctrine of the Holy Church, devising—to fill up the measure of his malice—the expedient of a new translation of the Scriptures into the mother tongue."[27]

The Wycliffe Translation

Wycliffe's first version of the New Testament in Middle English was published in 1380, and a second edition appeared in 1388 after his death (fig. 17.7). The first edition was a word-for-word translation of the New Testament from the Latin Vulgate, in places following the Latin so closely that the meaning was obscured.

The Old Testament was added about 1382. Most of it was probably prepared by Nicholas of Hereford, Wycliffe's friend, before trouble broke out in Oxford in 1382 and forced him to leave. It is clear that Nicholas did not do all the work himself, since there is evidence of five different translators, each of whom used different dialectal forms.[28] In a version copied directly from Nicholas's original (Douce 309) a note in red ink after Baruch 3:20 states in Latin: "Here ends the translation of Nicholas of Hereford." This note suggests the rest was finished by someone

First English Bible Translations
Wycliffe Bible (NT, 1380; entire Bible, 1382)
Tyndale Bible (NT, 1526; OT portions, 1534)
Coverdale Bible (1535)
Matthew Bible (1537)
Great Bible (1539)
Geneva Bible (1560)
Bishops' Bible (1568)
Douay-Rheims Bible (NT, 1582; OT, 1609–10)

had to bow to their bidding. In response, Wycliffe devoted increasing time speaking and writing against this corruption, something that the papacy and the established church bitterly resented. He also opposed the requirement of an intermediary (i.e., a priest or pope) to communicate with God and the doctrine of transubstantiation (i.e., the bread and the wine of communion actually become the body and blood of Christ). The pope attempted to oust him from Oxford and from preaching, but Wycliffe had the support of John of Gaunt (Duke of Lancaster), the administration of Oxford University, and the majority of common people.

Eventually, however, the power of the Roman Catholic Church held sway, and the university officials were compelled to let Wycliffe go. Wycliffe summoned people back to a more biblical Christianity, and his views were propagated by traveling preachers, most of them his own students from Oxford, who became known as Lollards (derived from lowlanders but used in the sense of heretics). Wycliffe held

else.[29] Realizing the shortcomings of the first edition, John Purvey, a follower of Wycliffe, is credited with producing a second edition in 1388, four years after Wycliffe's death in 1384. This edition shows a much greater feeling for English idioms and was more useful to the average English layperson, even though it was still a translation of the Latin Vulgate. Purvey's edition became the predominant English Bible until the time of Tyndale about two hundred years later.

The following is the Lord's Prayer (Matt. 6:9–13) in Middle English from Wycliffe's Bible:

> Oure fadir that art in hevenes, halowid be thi name. Thi kyngdom come to. Be thi wille don in erthe as in hevene. Geve to us this day oure breed ovir othir substaunce. And forgeve to us oure dettis, as we forgeven to our dettouris. And lede us not in temptacioun, but delyver us fro yvel. Amen. (modified from the *Wycliffe Bible*, 1382)[30]

Its Reception

In his preface to the second edition Purvey prayed, "God graunte to us alle grace to kunne [understand] wel and kepe wel Holi Writ, and suffre ioiefulli [joyfully] some peyne for it at the laste."[31] The hierarchy of the church condemned the Wycliffe Bible. Both Purvey and Hereford were thrown into prison, and some of their friends were burned at the stake with Bibles tied around their necks. With the influence and support of Archbishop Arundel, a synod at Oxford in July 1408 forbade the reading of Wycliffe's Bible:

> It is a dangerous thing, . . . as witnesseth blessed St Jerome, to translate the text of the holy Scripture out of one tongue into another; for in the translation the same sense is not always easily kept, as the same St Jerome confesseth, that although *he were inspired* . . . yet oftentimes in this he erred; we therefore decree and ordain that no man hereafter by his own authority . . . translate any text of the Scripture into English or any other tongue, by way of a book, pamphlet, or treatise; and that no man read any such book, pamphlet or treatise, now lately composed in the time of John Wycliffe or since, or hereafter to be set forth in part or in whole, publicly or privately, upon pain of greater excommunication, until the said translation be approved by the ordinary of the place or, if the case so require, by the council provincial. He that shall do contrary to this shall likewise be punished as a favourer of heresy and error.[32]

People who were caught reading this Bible were liable to forfeiture of their "land, cattle, life, and goods," and yet it is also recorded that the price for borrowing a Wycliffe Bible for an hour every day for a period of time to do a course of reading was a load of hay.[33] The threat of severe penalties had the reverse effect of rousing curiosity among the people to know what

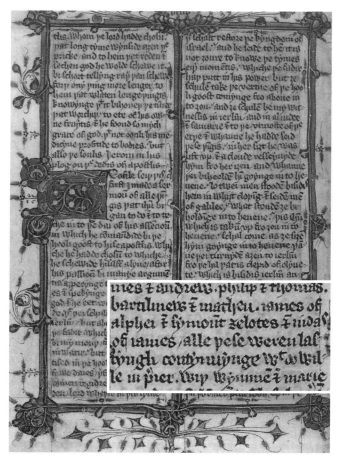

Figure 17.7.
A page from Luke 6 of the Wycliffe Bible. [Cambridge University Library]

Figure 17.8.
John Huss (1371–1415) was condemned at the Council of Constance and was burned to death on July 6, 1415.

the forbidden Bible said. Now that England had a Bible—albeit a forbidden one—people wanted to learn to read. So Wycliffe not only gave England the Word of God but also sparked a desire for literacy.

In 1415 the Council of Constance condemned John Huss (1371–1415), a reformer in Bohemia and disciple of Wycliffe, to be burned at the stake (fig. 17.8). This council also condemned Wycliffe's writings. Though Wycliffe was dead, the council ordered his bones to be dug up and burned, and his ashes were scattered in the River Swift. It is said that Wycliffe's ashes were carried out to the sea and his teachings spread to other lands, which is why Wycliffe is sometimes called "the morning star of the Reformation."

Bruce adds an interesting twist to the fate of this Bible: "[I]t is held by some, that when the citizens of London welcomed the first Elizabeth as their queen in 1558 and presented her with 'The Word of Truth', the volume which she so gratefully received was a copy of the Wycliffite Gospels. We

cannot be sure of this, but that would indeed have been a fitting climax to the history of the first English Bible."[34]

The Tyndale Bible (NT, 1526; OT Portions, 1534)

The next 150 years after the first edition of the Wycliffe Bible saw increasing unrest in Europe:

In the 15th century Europeans had suffered deep religious uneasiness, linked with famine, war and disease. The obsession with death and sin had intensified religious fervour, often tinged with superstition. There had been a growing cult of the Virgin Mary and the Saints, while to save their souls the faithful had resorted more and more to relics and indulgences for the remission of their sins.

The Church had failed to react effectively.[35]

The common people grew increasingly dissatisfied with the church, whose corrupt hierarchy lived lavishly. Cardinal Wolsey, who had almost become pope, ruled with nearly royal authority over England:

> The following year [1515] he had been made both Lord High Chancellor of England and a Roman cardinal. His revenues from these and other sources were enormous; nor did he hesitate to use them in a lavish display, living in the style of a great monarch. On special expeditions he was attended by four thousand horsemen, including nobles, prelates and knights. At home, his ordinary establishment at Hampton Court numbered about a thousand persons. Some nine or ten nobles, each with several servants, waited upon him. To attend his table there were twelve chaplains, a physician, four legal advisers, two secretaries, a herald-at-arms, and other courtiers. It is hardly surprising to learn that he disliked the Reformation.[36]

Martin Luther called for drastic reform when Pope Leo X (1475–1521) sold indulgences to finance the building of St. Peter's Basilica.

There was still strong opposition to translations in the English language since the time of Wycliffe. Nevertheless, in 1526 William Tyndale translated the New Testament into English. Three years later Sir Thomas More, who shortly afterward became Lord Chancellor of England, wrote a scathing attack on Tyndale for this. In his book More likens Tyndale to the "great arch-heretic Wycliffe," who translated the Bible into English and "purposely corrupted the holy text."[37]

William Tyndale (c. 1494–1536)

William Tyndale[38] (see fig. 17.9), born in Gloucestershire, went to Oxford University at about sixteen years of age. He received his master of arts degree in 1515 and then taught at Oxford for a year before moving to Cambridge, the center of new learning. It may have been here that Tyndale gained his proficiency in Greek from a Cambridge lecturer, Richard Croke. Tyndale remained in Cambridge until 1522, when he became the private tutor of Sir John Walsh. The Walshes lived in a large manor home in a beautiful part of the Cotswolds near Little Sodbury, Gloucestershire. The light responsibilities of his position left plenty of time for study, and Tyndale became increasingly convinced that both laity and clergy knew very little Scripture, an opinion strengthened in a heated debate with a cleric:

> Not long after, Tindall happened to be in the company of a certain divine, recounted for a learned man, and in disputing with him drave him to that issue, that the great doctor burst out into these blasphemous words: "We are better to be without God's law than the Pope's." Master Tindall, replied, "I defy the Pope and all his laws," and added that if God spared him life, ere many years he

Figure 17.9.
William Tyndale (c. 1494–1536). [British and Foreign Bible Society]

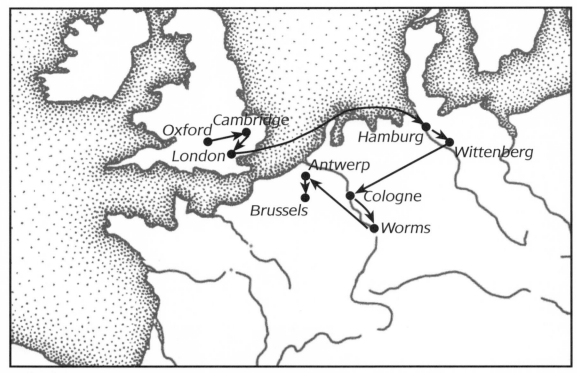

Map 6. A map of William Tyndale's travels.

would cause a boy that driveth the plough to know more of the Scripture than he did.[39]

Luther may have provided further incentive for Tyndale to produce an English translation, for Luther published his German translation in 1522. But Tyndale needed ecclesiastical permission to translate the Bible into English, as stated in the Constitutions of Oxford, so in the summer of 1523 he traveled to London to request permission from Cuthbert Tunstall (1474–1559), recently appointed bishop of London. Erasmus had spoken highly of Tunstall, who was known to be sympathetic to the newer learning, so that Tyndale hoped he would sanction an English translation and provide a place for him to perform the work. But Tunstall was not interested in the project and claimed that his palace was full.

Humphrey Monmouth, an alderman of London and a wealthy cloth merchant, housed Tyndale for six months while he began to translate the New Testament. Before long, however, Tyndale realized that England was not a safe place to do

such work, as he noted in the preface to his translation of the Pentateuch some years later (1530): "[He] vnderstode at the laste not only that there was no rowme in my lorde of londons palace to translate the new testament, but also that there was no place to do it in all englonde, as experience doth now openly declare."[40] Thus in April or May 1524, Tyndale left for Hamburg, a free city, to make his translation, though it is likely that he spent much of that year in Wittenberg, Germany, where Luther was preaching. Monmouth, the one who showed such kindness to Tyndale, was later (1528) imprisoned in the Tower of London for assisting him and other reformers.

Tyndale's First New Testament (1526)

Tyndale went to Cologne in 1525 to have his New Testament printed by Peter Quentel, but church authorities heard about it and forbade the printing. Tyndale, therefore, fled up the Rhine River to Worms, rescuing six thousand copies of Matthew 1–22 that had already been printed (map 6).

Reformation sympathies had already been aroused in Worms, providing a safer atmosphere for printing Tyndale's New Testament. The New Testament was printed in English by 1526 in two different sizes (a larger one [quarto] and a smaller [octavo]). Once printed, the Bibles were smuggled into England in cotton bales or other innocent looking containers. King Henry VIII had heard about the translations through Lee, his official distributor of alms, who was traveling on the continent, but there was little he could do.[41] When Tunstall found out about the Bibles, he was furious and gathered up as many of them as possible to be burned publicly in the presence of Cardinal Wolsey at St. Paul's Cross (fig. 17.10),[42] which he did in 1530.

Tunstall adamantly opposed Tyndale's Bible, calling it a "pestiferous and most pernicious poison."[43] He believed the translation to be infected by Lutheranism, which he strongly opposed, and was convinced that the common person could not properly interpret Scripture. Because his diocese was closest to the continent and would be most affected, Tunstall sent his merchants to buy as many Tyndale Bibles as possible in hopes of drying up the sources:

The market price was half a crown a copy. It will be recalled that in Wyclif's day the charge for borrowing a manuscript copy of the Bible over a certain period for an hour a day was a load of hay, which in Tyndale's time would have been valued at about five shillings—double the price of a printed [Tyndale] New Testament. On the other hand, in terms of wages and food prices, it was still an expensive book. It would have cost a mason, for instance, five full days' wages. Nor was a mason so badly off with his sixpence a day, for that daily wage represented the price of twelve pounds of beef or pork, or eight pounds

Figure 17.10. A picture of St. Paul's Cross, located outside St. Paul's Cathedral. [Paul Wegner]

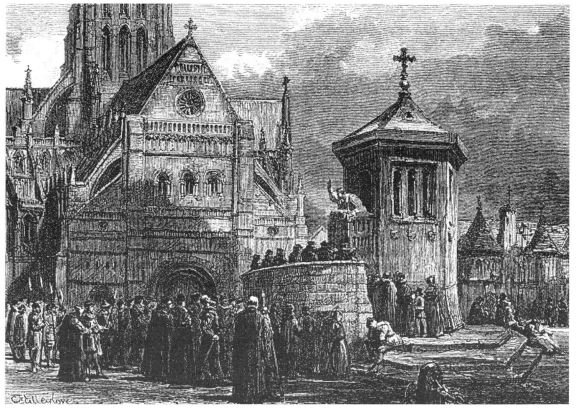

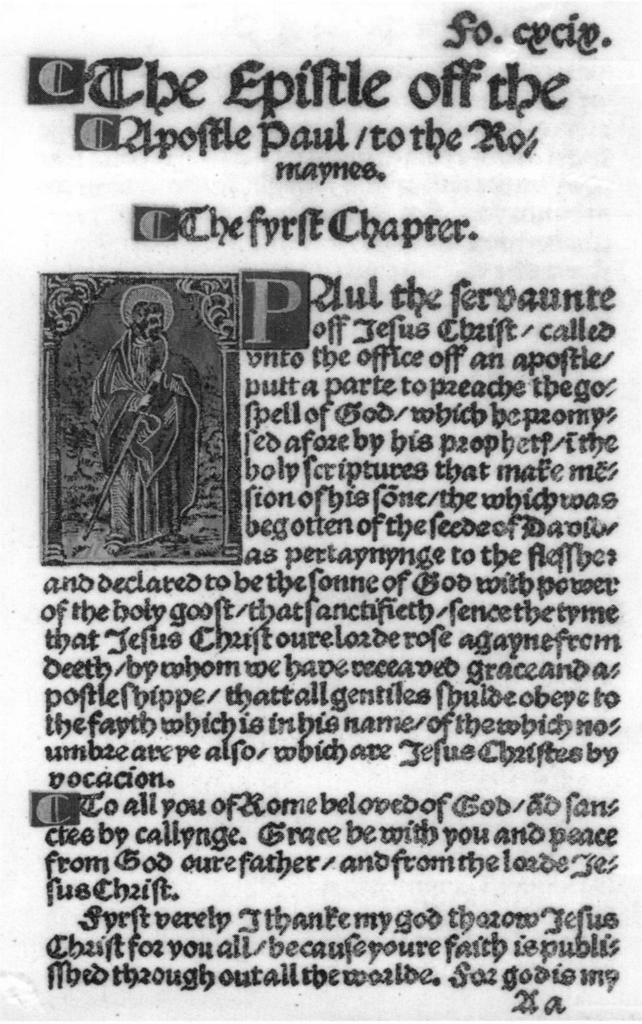
Fo. cxcix.

The Epistle off the Apostle Paul/to the Romaynes.

The fyrst Chapter.

Paul the servaunte off Jesus Christ/called unto the office off an apostle/ putt a parte to preache the gospell of God/which he promysed afore by his prophetts/in the holy scriptures that make mencion of his sonne/the which was begotten of the seede of David/ as pertaynynge to the flesshe: and declared to be the sonne of God with power of the holy goost/that sanctifieth/sence the tyme that Jesus Christ oure lorde rose agayne from deeth/by whom we have receaved grace and apostleshippe/ that all gentiles shulde obeye to the fayth which is in his name/of the which nombre are ye also/ which are Jesus Christes by vocacion.

To all you of Rome beloved of God/and sanctes by callynge. Grace be with you and peace from God oure father/ and from the lorde Jesus Christ.

Fyrst verely I thanke my god thorow Jesus Christ for you all/because youre faith is publisshed through out all the worlde. For god is my

A a

Figure 17.11. The beginning of Romans from the Tyndale Bible (1526). [Cambridge University Library]

of mutton or veal. Dutch booksellers were soon undercutting the English price: they were offering the New Testament for thirteen pence.[44]

Tunstall commissioned Augustine Packington, a London merchant in Antwerp, to buy up as many of the remaining Bibles as possible, which ironically proved to benefit the labors of Tyndale:

> The bishop, thinking that he had God by the toe, when indeed he had (as after he thought) the devil by the fist, said: "Gentle Master Packington, do your diligence and get them, and with all my heart I will pay for them, whatsoever they cost you; for the books are erroneous and naughty, and I intend surely to destroy them all, and to burn them at Paul's Cross." Augustine Packington came to William Tyndale and said: "William, I know thou art a poor man, and hast a heap of New Testaments and books by thee, for the which thou hast both endangered thy friends and beggared thyself; and I have now gotten thee a merchant, which with ready money shall dispatch thee of all that thou hast, if you think it so profitable for yourself." "Who is the merchant?" said Tyndale. "The bishop of London," said Packington. "Oh, that is because he will burn them," said Tyndale. "Yea marry," quoth Packington. "I am the gladder," said Tyndale; "for these two benefits shall come thereof: I shall get money of him for these books, to bring myself out of debt, and the whole world shall cry out upon the burning of God's word. And the overplus of the money, that shall remain to me, shall make me more studious to correct the said New Testament, and so newly to imprint the same once again; and I trust the second will much better like you than ever did the first." And so forward went the bargain: the bishop had the books, Packington had the thanks, and Tyndale had the money.[45]

While it is not entirely factual,[46] the story in general appears to be based on real events and explains how Tyndale was able to publish his second edition.

Tyndale's life was still in danger since Charles V, the Holy Roman emperor, considered him a heretic. As long as Tyndale stayed in Antwerp, a free city of Belgium, he was safe; but on May 21, 1535, Charles employed Henry Philips to kidnap Tyndale and take him outside of the city so that he could be imprisoned in the fortress of Vilvorde, near Brussels, Belguim.[47] Thomas Cromwell and possibly even Henry VIII attempted to intercede and secure his release, but Charles V was not in a bargaining mood, since Henry VIII had just divorced his aunt, Katherine of Aragon.

During the last year of his life (1535–1536), Tyndale wrote to someone in authority (perhaps the Marquis of Bergen) requesting clothing to ease his physical suffering and a copy of the Hebrew Bible:

> I believe, right worshipful, that you are not unaware of what may have been determined concerning me. Wherefore I beg your lordship, and that by the Lord Jesus, that if I am to remain here through the winter, you will request the commissary to have the kindness to send me, from the goods of mine which he has, a warmer cap, for I suffer greatly from cold in the head, and am afflicted by a perpetual catarrh [a chronic inflammation of the nasal passages], which is much increased in this cell; a warmer coat also, for this which I have is very thin; a piece of cloth, too, to patch my leggings. My overcoat is worn out; my shirts also are worn out. He has a woollen shirt, if he will be good enough to send it. I have also with him leggings of thicker cloth to put on above; he has also warmer night-caps. And I ask to be allowed to have a lamp in the evening; it is indeed wearisome sitting alone in the dark. But most of all I beg and beseech your clemency to be urgent with the commissary, that he will kindly permit me to have the Hebrew Bible, Hebrew grammar and Hebrew dictionary, that I may pass the time in that study. In return may you obtain what you most desire, so only that it be for the salvation of your soul. But if any other decision has been taken concerning me, to be carried out before winter, I will be patient, abiding the will of God, to the glory of the grace of my Lord Jesus Christ; whose Spirit (I pray) may ever direct your heart. Amen.
>
> W. TINDALUS[48]

Even under such extreme circumstances Tyndale was intent on translating the Scriptures, not having been able to finish his translation of the Old Testament. In 1530 the Pentateuch had been published and in 1531 the Book of Jonah. When Tyndale's New Testament was republished in 1534, it contained an appendix with a translation of certain Old Testament passages, but it was far from complete.

In August 1536 Tyndale was found guilty of heresy and condemned to death; within two months, on October 6, 1536, he was killed. His last words before dying at the stake were "Lord, open the King of England's eyes."[49] Little did Tyndale know

that in 1537, less than one year after his death, Henry VIII would grant permission for an English version of the Bible, which was largely Tyndale's version, to be printed in England.

Translation and Retranslation

Tyndale's First Edition (1526)

There are several major differences between Wycliffe's translation and Tyndale's:

1. Wycliffe's Bible was a translation of Jerome's Latin Vulgate, but Tyndale's went back to the original Greek and Hebrew.

2. Wycliffe's Bible was a hand-copied manuscript, whereas Tyndale's Bible was printed.

3. Wycliffe translated into Middle English, but Tyndale's version belongs to the Modern English period.

Both translations were milestones in the history of the English Bible, helping to provide the people with Scripture in their own language (see fig. 17.11).

Tyndale was a good Greek scholar who succeeded in translating Erasmus's Greek New Testament into fluent English, as this quotation of the Lord's Prayer from Tyndale's earliest edition illustrates:

> O Oure father, which arte in heven, halowed be thy name. Thy kyngdome come. Thy wyll be fulfilled, as well in erth, as it ys in heven. Geve vs thisdaye oure dayly breede. And forgeve vs oure trespases, even as we forgeve oure trespacers. And leade vs not into temptacion: but delyver vs from evell. For thyne is the kyngedome and the power, and the glorye, for ever. Amen.[50]

Tyndale's New Testament included marginal notes, about half of which were translated directly from Luther's edition, though with little of Luther's fierceness.[51] One of his more controversial footnotes regards Matthew 16:17–19:

> Peter in the greke sygnieth a stoone in englysshe. This confession is the rocke. Nowe is simon bariona, or simon ionas

Table 17.1
Translations of Ecclesiastical Terms

Common Translation	Tyndale's Translation
Church	Congregation
Priest	Senior
Penance	Repentance
Charity	Love

sonne, called Peter, because of his confession. whosoever then this wyse confesseth of Christe, the same is called Peter. nowe is this confession come too all that are true christen. Then ys every christen man & woman peter. Rede bede, austen & hierom, of the maner of lowsinge & bynding and note howe hierom checketh the presumcion of the pharises in his tyme, which yet had nott so monstrous interpretacions as oure new goddes have feyned. Rede erasmus annotations. Hyt was noot for nought that Christ badd beware of the leven of the pharises. noo thynge is so swete that they make not sowre with there tradicions. The evangelion, that ioyfull tidynges, ys nowe biterer then the olde lawe, Christes burthen is hevier then the yooke of moses, our condicion and estate ys ten tymes more grevious then was ever the iewes. The pharises have so levended Christes swete breed.[52]

The church leaders condemned Tyndale's marginal notes, claiming that they were heretical and intentionally turned people against the church; most of the notes, however, merely explained the text, and some of Tyndale's editions did not even have marginal notes. In 1531 Tyndale made the following concession: "[I]f Henry VIII would 'grant only a bare text of the scriptures to be put forth among his people . . . be it of the translation of what person soever shall please his majesty' he would 'promise never to write more.'"[53]

Thomas More, a leading humanist, attacked both Luther and Tyndale in his writings. More asserted that Tyndale's New Testament "was not worthy to be called Christ's testament, but either Tyndale's own testament or the testament of his master Antichrist."[54] He also claimed: "To study to find errors in Tyndale's book were like studying to find water in the sea."[55] The errors that More and others purportedly found can probably be attributed to differences between the Greek and Latin texts. It is interesting that More endorsed Erasmus's Greek New Testament but severely criticized Tyndale's translation. Few people could translate Erasmus's Greek New Testament, so it had little effect on the masses of people, while Tyndale's translation would change the situation in England forever. One of More's contentions with Tyndale's New Testament was over the translation of certain ecclesiastical terms (see table 17.1).

However, Tyndale's translations for these terms were very close to Erasmus's Latin translations (e.g., church was *congregatio*; *presbyteros* was *senior* or *presbyter* [and not *sacerdos*, which in the Latin Bible was traditionally reserved for priest in the Jewish or pagan sense]).[56] Apparently the problem was not so much the translation as the translator, to whom More attributed "malicious intent." In a matter of a few years (1535), however, More was executed for opposing King Henry VIII's religious reforms when Henry changed allegiance from Roman Catholicism to Protestantism.

Tyndale never finished his translation of the Bible, but by 1530 he had completed the translation of the Pentateuch, Jonah, and possibly Joshua to 2 Chronicles. His translation of the Old Testament was both bold and idiomatic, with such readings as[57]

1. The serpent says to Eve, "Tush, Ye shall not die" (Gen. 3:4).
2. Pharaoh's "jolly captains" drowned in the Dead Sea (Exod. 15:4).
3. A marginal note for Exodus 32:35, where the Israelites died because they worshiped the golden calf, asserts: "The Pope's bull slayeth more than Aaron's calf."
4. When Israel collected enough money for the temple Moses told them to stop the contributions (Exod. 36:5–7); a controversial marginal note reads, "When will the Pope say 'Hoo!' and forbid an offering for the building of St. Peter's church? . . . Never until they have it all."

Tyndale's Second Edition (1534)

Tyndale wanted to revise his translation of the New Testament for two reasons: not only was the religious climate changing in England since Henry VIII quarreled with the pope, but also Cromwell, who favored Bible reading in the vernacular, was gaining in popularity; and people were pirating Tyndale's edition, making changes to it, and then publishing it as if it were his version because of the strong demand for the Bible in English. The chief offender was George Joye, one of Tyndale's former associates, who altered Tyndale's readings considerably by comparing them to the Latin Vulgate or by inserting his own translations based upon his theological presuppositions.[58] Tyndale was rightly angered and chastened Joye in the preface to the second edition of his New Testament (1534):

> Wherefore I beseech George Joye, yea and all others too, for to translate the scripture for themselves, whether out of Greek, Latin or Hebrew. Or (if they will needs) . . . let them take my translations and labours, and change and alter, and correct and corrupt at their pleasures, and call it their own translations, and put to their own names, and not to play bo-peep after George Joye's manner.[59]

Tyndale carefully and thoroughly revised his edition in 1534, including fewer marginal notes and shorter introductions to each book. He entitled it "The Newe Testament dylygently corrected and compared with the Greke by Willyam Tindale." Bishop Westcott described it as "Tyndale's noblest monument,"[60] a judgment with which Kenyon concurs: "It is this edition of 1534, printed at Antwerp, which is the true climax of Tyndale's work on the New Testament. The text had been diligently corrected; Introductions were prefixed to each book; the marginal commentary was rewritten in a less controversial spirit; and at the end of the volume were appended certain extracts from the Old Testament which were read as 'Epistles' in the Church services for certain days of the year."[61]

Tyndale revised his translation again in 1535 but not significantly. J. Isaacs observes, "With all the tinkering to which the New Testament has been subject, Tindale's version is still the basis in phrasing, rendering, vocabulary, rhythm, and often in music as well. Nine-tenths of the Authorized New Testament is still Tindale, and the best is still his."[62] Bruce echoes this thought: "[I]n a number of places where the Authorized Version of 1611 departs from Tyndale's wording, the Revisers of 1881 return to it."[63] However, the English ecclesiastical authorities did their best to wipe out almost every trace of the Tyndale Bible, as Kenyon notes:

> The English New Testament was thus irrevocably launched upon the world;

Figure 17.12. Eberhard Zwink with a recently found copy of the Tyndale New Testament. [Eberhard Zwink]

yet so keen was the search for copies, both of then and afterwards, and so complete the destruction of them, that barely a trace of these earliest editions remains today. Of the quarto edition, begun at Cologne and ended at Worms, only one solitary fragment exists, comprising eight out of the ten leaves printed at Cologne, with the text of Matt. i.1–xxii. 12. It is now in the Grenville collection in the British Museum, . . . Of the octavo, one perfect copy exists in the library of the Baptist College at Bristol [this one has since been sold for £1,000,000], another, imperfect, in St. Paul's Cathedral. This is all that is left of the 6,000 copies which Tyndale is said to have printed in 1525 at Worms, while of all the editions that followed up to 1534 no fragment has survived.[64]

As recently as 1996 another copy of the Tyndale New Testament (1925) was found in a library in Stuttgart, Germany, by Dr. Eberhard Zwink (fig. 17.12).

Figure 17.13. A painting of Henry VIII (1491–1547) who severed ties with Rome and appointed himself head of the Anglican church. [National Portrait Gallery]

The Coverdale Bible (1535)

In 1534, shortly before the Coverdale Bible was published, a significant political event drastically changed the religious environment in England, giving rise to the Anglican church (the state Church of England). Henry VIII (fig. 17.13) had no male heir from his wife, Katherine of Aragon, so he requested that the pope nullify his marriage, freeing him to marry Anne Boleyn. When the pope refused his request, Henry severed all relationships with Rome. Thomas Cranmer, a Protestant who had been appointed Archbishop of Canterbury, suggested to Henry that he pronounce himself divorced and appoint himself head of the Church of England. This Henry did by the Act of Supremacy of 1534. He then married Anne Boleyn, who likewise was unable to provide him a male heir. When King Henry became head of the church, he distributed many of the lands of the monasteries among the nobility. He did not drastically change the doctrines of the church, but England would soon be introduced to Calvinism during Edward VI's reign (1547–1553).

Miles Coverdale (1488–1569)

Coverdale (fig. 17.14) was also an important personage in the history of the English Bible, for he not only translated the Coverdale Bible (1535) but also edited the Great Bible (1539), helped to prepare the Geneva Bible (1560), and produced several diglot (Latin and English) editions (New Testament, 1538; Psalter, 1540). Coverdale was born and grew up in York, England, and was an avid learner from childhood. In time he became an Augustinian friar[65] but was influenced so strongly by the Reformation that he eventually left his order. He continued his studies at Cambridge, where he was taught by Robert Barnes, a reputable scholar. John Bale, a Protestant writer (1495–1563), describes Coverdale at this time: "Under the mastership of Robert Barnes he drank in good learning with a burning thirst. He was a young man of friendly and upright nature and very gentle spirit, and when the church of England revived, he was one of the first to make a pure profession of Christ. Other men gave themselves in part, he gave himself wholly, to propagating the truth of Jesus Christ's gospel and manifesting his glory."[66]

In 1528 Coverdale fled to Europe for refuge from King Henry VIII, who was still sympathetic to the Roman Catholic Church and opposed to English Bible translations. In Europe Coverdale worked with Tyndale on a translation of the Pentateuch. Coverdale was not as apt a scholar as Tyndale, which he readily admits in the prologue to his translation: "Considering how excellent knowledge and learning an interpreter of scripture ought to have in the tongues, and pondering also mine own insufficiency therein, and how weak I am to perform the office of a translator, I was the more loath to meddle with this work [the Bible]."[67]

The Coverdale Translation

Jacob van Meteren, a merchant of Antwerp, apparently encouraged Coverdale to translate the Bible into English while Coverdale was in exile on the continent.[68] Since Coverdale was not proficient in the biblical languages, he consulted five different translations (Tyndale's, Luther's, the Zurich version, the Vulgate, and Pagnini's Latin version [a very literal rendering of the Old Testament]) before deciding any particular rendering. However, there was no complete English translation of the Old Testament for Coverdale to consult, since Tyndale had not yet completed his translation. Thus Coverdale's translation of the Old Testament followed Tyndale's version as far as possible (up to 2 Chronicles) before turning to a variety of other works.

Upon completion of Coverdale's translation in 1535, copies were quickly sent to England (fig. 17.15). Having heard that King Henry was now amenable to an English translation of the Bible, Coverdale took the added precaution of dedicating it to Henry VIII for being a better "Defender of the Faith" than the pope himself. When the king heard that this translation was

Figure 17.14. Miles Coverdale (1488–1569), an early translator of the English Bible. [National Portrait Gallery]

dedicated to him, he asked his counselors to look through it and advise him as to whether it should be accepted. The counselors condemned it for being saturated with problems, but when they were asked to point out even one heresy, none could be found. King Henry therefore decreed that the translation should be accepted.[69]

Bruce's rather harsh but fair evaluation is that the Coverdale Bible is "basically Tyndale's version revised in the light of the German versions, and not noticeably improved thereby."[70] On the whole the differences in wording between Tyndale's and Coverdale's versions are insignificant; the three main words that were contested in Tyndale's version (e.g., "congregation" for "church"; "elders" for "priests"; and "love" for "charity") remain unchanged. Coverdale's dependence upon the German versions surfaces in such word choices as "overbodycoat" (literal translation of *überkörpermantel*) for "ephod" in Exodus 25:7 and the term *unoutspeakable* (literal translation of *unaussprechlichem*) for "inexpressible" in Romans 8:26.[71] Nevertheless, as S. L. Greenslade argues, Coverdale's English in general and the Psalms in particular, was smooth and flowing: "His [Coverdale's] English style is commonly judged by his Psalms, where it is at its best: abounding in music, beautifully phrased. Elsewhere he is generally smoother and more melodious than Tyndale, less given to variation, missing something of his swiftness and native force, but often find-ing a better phrase."[72] The Lord's Prayer demonstrates Coverdale's fluid and smooth style:

> O oure father which art in heauen, halowed be thy name. Thy kyngdome come. Thy wyll be fulfilled vpon earth as it is in heauen. Geue vs this daye oure dayly bred. And forgeue vs oure dettes, as we also forgeue oure detters. And lede vs not in to temptacion: but delyuer vs from euell. For thyne is the kyngdome, and the power, and the glorye for euer. Amen.[73] (Matt. 6:9–13)

Coverdale's was the first English Bible to introduce chapter summaries similar to the Latin Vulgate (though longer) and to include the Apocrypha separate from the canonical books rather than scattered through the Old Testament as in the Septuagint and Latin Vulgate. A note informed the reader that the apocryphal books did not appear in the Hebrew Bible and thus were not of the same authority. Coverdale's Bible was reprinted twice in 1537 and once in 1550 and 1553, but it never became an authorized English version.

Figure 17.15. Bible in English (Cologne? or Marburg?, 1535), translated by Miles Coverdale, 1st edition. [Grand Haven, Mich., The Scriptorium, VK 106, title page]

The Matthew Bible (1537)

John Rogers

Even though Tyndale tried desperately to finish translating the Old Testament, the task was left to one of his disciples, John Rogers. Rogers was born near Birmingham about 1500 and studied at Pembroke Hall, Cambridge. After graduation, he became rector in a church in London until 1534, when he went to Antwerp as chaplain of English merchants. There he met William Tyndale, began to embrace the Reformed faith, and helped to smuggle English Bibles into England. After Tyndale's death, he took the pen name Thomas Matthew and finished editing the Bible (fig. 17.16).

In a letter dated August 4, 1537, Archbishop Cranmer appeals to Thomas Cromwell to use his influence to obtain King Henry's sanction of this translation:

You shall receive by the bringer hereof a bible in English, both of a new translation and of a new print, dedicated unto the King's majesty . . . and therefore I pray your lordship to read the same. And as for the translation, so far as I have read thereof, I like it better than any other translation heretofore made, yet not doubting but that there may and will be found some faults therein, as you know no man ever did or can do so well but it may be from time to time amended. And for as much as the book is dedicated unto the king's grace, and also great pains and labour taken in setting forth of the same, I pray you, my lord, that you will exhibit the book unto the king's highness, and to obtain of his grace, if you can, a licence that the same may be sold and read of every person, without danger of any act, proclamation or ordinance heretofore granted to the contrary, until such time that we the bishops shall set forth a better translation, which I think will not be till a day after doomsday.[74]

The Matthew Bible received royal license mainly due to Cromwell's influence, but the three-page dedication to the king was not without effect. It begins: "To the most noble and gracious prince, king Henry VIII, king of England and of France, lord of Ireland etc., defender of the faith, and under God the chief and supreme head of the church of England" and is signed by "Your grace's faithful and true subject, Thomas Matthew."[75] The Matthew Bible generated enthusiasm for owning a Bible in English; for example, other bishops followed the lead of Latimer, bishop of Worcester, who issued a series of injunctions stating that every church clerk should own a copy of the entire Bible or at least the New Testament in both Latin and English.[76] By this time there were two English Bibles with royal sanction (Coverdale's and Matthew's) giving people greater access to reading or at least hearing the Bible in English. Not everyone was excited, however, about this prospect; Edward Foxe, a theologian, complained that: "The lay people do now know the holy scripture better than many of us; and the Germans have made the text of the Bible so plain and easy by the Hebrew and Greek

tongue that now many things may be better understood without any glosses at all than by all the commentaries of the doctors."[77] Generally the English translations of the Bible were well received. Many people were able to read the Bible for the first time in England, and this fact provided incentive for the illiterate to learn to read. But when England reverted to Roman Catholicism under Mary Tudor (fig. 17.17), Rogers was one of the first people to be burned at the stake in 1555.

Figure 17.16. Genesis 1. Old Testament and Apocrypha in English (Antwerp?, 1537), Matthew's Version, 1st edition. [Grand Haven, Mich., The Scriptorium, VK 108, fol. a1ʳ]

The Matthew Bible Translation

Like Coverdale's Bible, in the Matthew Bible the Old Testament Apocrypha was grouped separately after the Old Testament. Both Matthew's and Coverdale's Bibles circulated freely in England one year after Tyndale's death, and they received royal license in 1537. Concerning the text of the Matthew Bible, Bruce observes: "Matthew's Bible was really made up of Tyndale's Pentateuch and New Testament, an unassigned version of the books from Joshua to 2 Chronicles [possibly Tyndale's which had not been published] and Coverdale's version of the books from Ezra to Malachi and of the Apocrypha."[78] Copious notes, which at times influenced the Matthew Bible's text, were included with parallel references largely borrowed from the French versions by Lefèvre and Olivetan.[79] The Lord's Prayer reads as follows in the Matthew Bible:

> Oure father which arte in heuen halowed be thy name. Let thy kingdome come. Thy will be fulfylled as well in erth as it is in heuen. Geve vs this daye oure dayly bred. And for geue vs oure treaspases euen as we forgeue oure trespacers. And leade vs not into temptacion: but delyuer vs frō euyll. For thyne is the kyngedome + the power and the glorye foreuer. Amen. (Matt. 6:9–13)

Figure 17.17. A portrait of Mary I (1516–1558). [National Portrait Gallery]

The Great Bible (1539)

Another Bible by Miles Coverdale

The Upper House of Convocation of Canterbury petitioned the king in 1534 to authorize a translation of the Bible into English.[80] Thomas Cranmer (c. 1489–1556), Archbishop of Canterbury, had probably already organized a translation program to accomplish this task, but for some reason it did not take place. Thus Thomas Cromwell, vicar-general under Henry VIII, asked Coverdale, the most prominent Bible translator at the time, to make a complete revision of the Bible, based upon the Matthew Bible. J. F. Mozley states: "He [Coverdale] was instructed—and indeed that may have been his own wish—to take the Matthew bible as his basis, and it is characteristic of his modesty that he was well content to see his own version superseded by another's."[81]

The printing of this Bible was originally commissioned to be done in Paris, a city renowned for fine printing, but at the end of 1535 the French inquisitor-general forbade the printers to continue their work. After exhaustive negotiations the print and paper were sent to England, but even then the printing process had to begin again, since the French government refused to release the sheets that had already been printed. Thus the Great Bible, as it is commonly known because its pages are so large (16 and 1/2 inches by 11 inches), was delayed for four years and did not make its appearance until April of 1539. Shortly before this Bible appeared Richard Taverner, a scholarly lawyer with no knowledge of Hebrew but a good grasp of Greek, also revised Matthew's Bible, though Taverner's version was quickly overshadowed by the Great Bible.

Copies of the Great Bible were to be placed in each church in accordance with Henry VIII's decree, but this caused two problems. First, the price of the Bible was set at 20 shillings, which was so high that many churches could not afford one; Cranmer solved this problem by forcing the printers to lower the price to 10 shillings.[82] Second, Bible reading became so popular that Bishop Bonner complained that it disrupted his services, stating: "diverse wilful and unlearned persons inconsiderately and indiscreetly read the same, especially and chiefly at the time of divine service, yea in the time of the sermon and declaration of the word of God."[83] This became such a point of irritation that in 1539 the king created the following law against reading the English Bible aloud during the service: "[No man] shall openly read the bible or New Testament in the English tongue in any churches or chapels <or elsewhere> with any loud or high voice, <and specially> during the time of divine service," but "quietly and reverently read the bible and New Testament by themselves <secretly> at all times and places convenient."[84] Obviously some people found Bible reading more interesting than listening to their parson.

The year that the Great Bible was published saw the unsettled nature of Henry VIII's government. In the years that led up to 1539 Henry had displayed Protestant leanings, probably for political advantage, but few bishops felt the same way; royal policy leaned toward Romanism in 1539 with the appearance of the Catholic Six Articles. The next year Anne of Cleves was divorced and Cromwell beheaded. The situation had become dangerous for Protestants, so Coverdale returned to Europe in 1540. He remained there until Henry VIII died in 1547; he then returned under the patronage of Edward VI, becoming bishop of Exeter in 1551. However, he was not there for long when Mary Tudor (or Bloody Mary; 1553–1558) came to power in 1553. She removed him from the position. He probably would have lost his life, as did many other Reformers, were it not for the intervention of the king of Denmark, who insisted on his release, and he returned to exile in Europe. Coverdale spent most of his time in Geneva as elder of the English church but again returned to England in 1559 after Mary's death. He stayed out of public affairs as much as possible.

Thomas Cromwell (c. 1485–1540)
In his early life Cromwell studied under Cardinal Wolsey, chaplain to Henry VIII, but in 1529 he entered Parliament (fig. 17.18). By 1535 Cromwell became vicar-general in charge of church affairs and masterminded the dissolution of the monasteries during Henry VIII's reign. He apparently approved of Luther's ideas and encouraged English translations of the Bible, a fact that angered many of the other religious leaders. However, his downfall came in 1540, when he tried to establish an alliance with certain Lutheran princes through the marriage of King Henry VIII with Anne of Cleves.

Figure 17.18. Thomas Cromwell (c. 1485–1540). [National Portrait Gallery]

Henry was not interested in this marriage or the alliance, possibly because Anne of Cleves was very unattractive (C. P. Williams, "Cromwell, Thomas," *NIDCC*, 272). This led to Cromwell's condemnation and beheading in June 1540 for heresy and treason. In the year that Cromwell died the political situation was so unsettled that nearly as many Protestants were executed as were Roman Catholics (G. MacGregor, *The Bible in the Making* [Washington, DC: University Press of America, 1982], 92).

Figure 17.19.
The title page of the Great Bible. Bible in English (London: Edward Whitchurch, 1541), Great Bible Version, 5th edition. [Grand Haven, Mich., The Scriptorium, VK 101, title page]

The Great Bible Translation

The Great Bible was the first English translation to be authorized for public use in churches. It included on the bottom of the first page the sentence, "This is the Bible apoynted to the use of the churches," and thus it fulfilled King Henry's injunction in 1538 for every parish church in England to have a Bible. An interesting woodcut, possibly by Hans Holbein, appears on its title page (fig. 17.19):

> It represents the Almighty at the top blessing Henry, who hands out copies of the Bible to [Archbishop] Cranmer and Cromwell [Secretary of State] on his right and left. Below, the archbishop and the Secretary of State, distinguished by their coats of arms beneath them, are distributing copies to the clergy and laity respectively, while the bottom of the page is filled with a crowd of people exclaiming Vivat Rex! ("Long live the King!").[85]

MacGregor adds: "Behind this devoted congregation rises the sinister outline of Newgate Prison, from the bars of which those not currently in the royal favour enjoy a view of the proceedings impeded by prison bars."[86] Surely whoever made the woodcut had a sense of humor and intended the picture to be a subtle jab at King Henry. The Great Bible was extensively revised in 1540 and five additional times by 1541; in later editions, published after 1540 when Thomas Cromwell had been executed, his arms were removed from the picture, symbolizing that he no longer supplied the Bible to the laity.

As in his earlier Bible, Coverdale was more of an editor than a translator. He brought together the best readings available in his day; thus the Great Bible was a revision of the Matthew Bible, which was a revision of Tyndale's work. The first half of the Old Testament of the Great Bible was essentially Tyndale's Bible (up to 2 Chronicles), but for the rest Coverdale apparently revised his previous version; Tyndale had not translated Ezra to Malachi, and the Matthew Bible was merely a revision of the Coverdale Bible (1535). In the New Testament, however, Coverdale appears to have used a variety of translations while still achieving a smooth translation. The Lord's Prayer (Matthew 6:9–13) from the Great Bible follows the Matthew Bible and Coverdale's earlier translation, not Tyndale's:

> Oure father which art in heuen, halowed be thy name. Let thy kingdome come. Thy will be fulfilled, as well in erth, as it is in heuen. Geue vs this daye oure dayly bred. And forgeue vs oure dettes, as we forgeue oure detters. And leade vs not into temptation: but delyuer vs from euyll. For thyne is the kyngdom and the power, and the glorye for euer. Amen.

The titles of the fourth and sixth editions (November 1540 and November 1541) were completely rewritten and authorized by Cuthbert, bishop of Durham, and Nicolas, bishop of Rochester. Ironically, Cuthbert is Cuthbert Tunstall, formerly bishop of London, who refused to give William Tyndale permission to translate the English Bible and later burned his Bibles.[87] He was surely aware that this Bible was essentially a revision of Tyndale's, but now that it had the king's authority there was little he could do.

None of the controversial notes from the Matthew Bible were included in the Great Bible, and the few marginal notes that remain clarify the readings of the text. Some of the notations direct the reader to an appendix for further information, but this appendix was never published; Bruce hypothesizes that, "even if Coverdale's 'godly annotations' were couched in the most moderate language, they could not but express his Lutheran views, which would have been objectionable to many of the clergy, not to mention the king himself."[88] There are a few other interesting characteristics of this Bible: a mistake on the title page of the Apocrypha calls them the Hagiographa (or holy writings), which is a term used exclusively for the final section of the Old Testament books;[89] and the New Testament no longer follows the order initiated by Luther (i.e., Heb., James, Jude, and Rev. placed separately at the end of the Bible). Instead it followed the order in Erasmus's Greek New Testament and the rest of the English translations (i.e., Heb.; James; 1 and 2 Pet.; 1, 2, and 3 John; Jude; and Rev.).

The Geneva Bible (1560)

Strong reaction to the Reformation arose in England toward the end of Henry VIII's reign, and in the spring of

Figure 17.20.
A portrait of Elizabeth I (1533–1603). [National Portrait Gallery]

ect, but it was never completed, much to the joy of Cranmer. When Henry VIII died on January 28, 1547, the Great Bible was still in most of the churches. With the accession of Edward VI to the throne, the trend toward restricting the use of English translations was again reversed, and all the previous versions were frequently reprinted. It is estimated that some forty editions of Tyndale's, Coverdale's, Matthew's, the Great Bible, and even Taverner's were issued in Edward's seven-year reign (1547–1553).[91] Several minor translations were also made during Edward's reign (e.g., John Cheke's version, 1550; Bishop Becke's Bible, 1551), but they were never very popular.

When Mary came to the throne in 1553, Edward's Reformation policy was reversed. Some of those responsible for making translations (e.g., John Rogers; Thomas Cranmer) were burned at the stake; others sought refuge on the continent (e.g., Coverdale), along with shiploads of Protestant refugees from England.[92] However, Queen Mary did not remove the Great Bible from the English churches even though John Standish, Coverdale's archenemy, pleaded with Parliament: "Thousands have been brought from the true meaning of God's word through the English Bible: therefore away with it; it hath killed too many souls already."[93] Bruce suggests that Mary had sympathy for the Great Bible because it included an English translation of Erasmus's paraphrase of the Gospel of John, which she had prepared in collaboration with her chaplain.[94]

When Mary died (1558), Elizabeth I (fig. 17.20) reversed the pro-Roman policies of Mary, and reading of the Great Bible was again sanctioned. Elizabeth, the daughter of Henry VIII and Anne Boleyn, became queen of a country that was severely divided. Nevertheless England flourished under her long and successful reign. One of Elizabeth's greatest victories was the sound defeat of the Spanish Armada in 1588, when Philip II of Spain, Mary's widower, attempted to retake England and return it to Roman Catholic control. P. W. Petty praises Elizabeth's abilities: "It was

1543 Parliament passed a law forbidding the lower classes to read the Tyndale Bible. The king further stated in an Act of Parliament of 1543 that "no man or woman, of what estate, condition, or degree, was . . . to receive, have, take, or keep, Tyndale's or Coverdale's New Testament."[90] Once again Bibles were ceremoniously burned in front of St. Paul's Cross in London, an effort spearheaded by the bishop of London, Edmund Bonner, who vehemently opposed the spread of the Reformation across England. Ironically the Great Bible, which the bishops had authorized, was essentially a revision of the Tyndale and Coverdale Bibles that were being burned. Realizing this inconsistency, the ecclesiastical leaders and the Upper House Convocation of Canterbury decided in 1542 that a new authorized version should be prepared, fully revised to conform to the Latin Vulgate. King Henry commanded the universities and scholars to oversee the proja remarkable achievement for one who early had lost her mother (executed by her father), and had at twenty-one been imprisoned by her sister."[95] It was also during the reign of Elizabeth I that the Geneva Bible was published.

William Whittingham

During Mary's reign, Protestant fugitives fled from England to other Protestant centers such as Geneva, the home of Calvin and Bèza. At this time Geneva was a safe haven conducive to biblical scholarship. William Whittingham, brother-in-law of John Calvin's wife and instructor at All Souls College, Oxford, was one of these Protestant fugitives. Whittingham produced an English version of the New Testament in 1557 and with some help from others undertook a revision of the entire English Bible (fig. 17.21). This Bible, now known as the Geneva Bible, was completed in 1560 and was dedicated to Queen Elizabeth I with the following prayer:

> For considering God's wonderful mercies toward you at all seasons, who hath pulled you out of the mouth of the lions, and how that from your youth you have been brought up in the holy scriptures, the hope of all men is so increased, that they cannot but look that God should bring to pass some wonderful work by your grace to the universal comfort of his Church. . . . This Lord of lords and King of kings who hath ever defended his, strengthen, comfort and preserve Your Majesty, that you may be able to build up the ruins of God's house to his glory, the discharge of your conscience, and to the comfort of all them that love the coming of Christ Jesus our Lord.[96]

The timing of the publication of the Geneva Bible was fortunate, for not only was Elizabeth, who favored Protestantism, now reigning in England, but Scotland shook off Roman Catholic domination, as MacGregor notes: "Papal jurisdiction in Scotland was soon afterwards abolished, marking the final triumph of the Reformation in that country. An Act of the Scottish Parliament made it compulsory for every householder whose income was above a specific sum to buy a copy [of the Geneva Bible], and the first generation of Scotsmen to enjoy the benefits of the Reformation were nurtured exclusively on this Bible."[97]

The Geneva Translation

Scholars editing the Geneva Bible made a thorough revision of the Great Bible in the Old Testament, especially in the books that Tyndale did not translate. These books had never been translated directly from the Hebrew, so that unclear English was often the result of underlying Hebrew idioms.

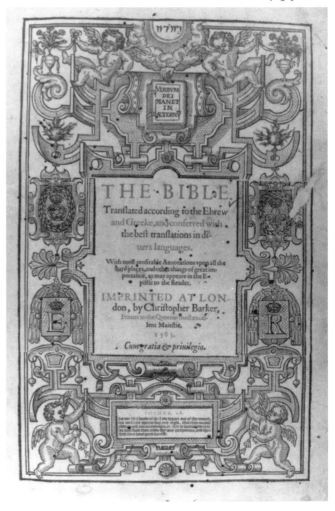

Figure 17.21. The title page of the Geneva Bible (1560). Bible in English (London: Christopher Barker, 1583), Geneva Version. [Grand Haven, Mich., The Scriptorium, VK 655, title page]

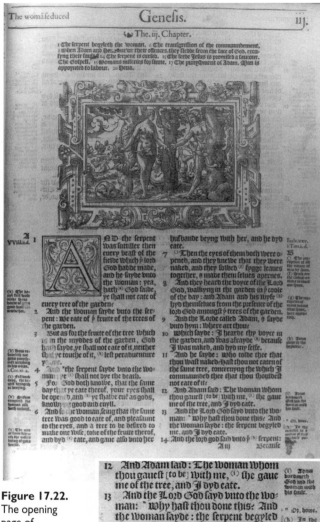

Figure 17.22.
The opening
page of
Genesis 3 from
the Bishops'
Bible (1568).
Bible in English
(London:
Richard Jugge,
1568), Bishops'
Version, 1st
edition. [Grand
Haven, Mich.,
The Scriptorium,
VK 102, fol. A3ʳ]

The New Testament was primarily Matthew's revision of Tyndale's Bible with some changes based upon the Great Bible and Bèza's Latin New Testament of 1556.[98] The smooth translation of the Lord's Prayer is almost exactly like that of the Great Bible:

> Our father which art in heauen, halowed be thy Name. Thy kingdome come. Thy wil be done euen in earth, as it is in heauen. Giue vs this day our daily bread. And forgive vs our dettes, as we also forgiue our detters. And lead vs not into

tentation, but deliuer vs frō euil: for thine is the kingdome, and the power, and the glorie for euer, Amen. (Matt. 6:9–13)

Though they were not as polemical as Tyndale's, the marginal notes of the Geneva Bible were clearly Calvinistic in doctrine, a fact that greatly irritated King James I. They also expressed anti-Roman sentiments (e.g., the beast that ascends from the pit [Rev. 11:7] is identified as "the Pope which has his power out of hell and cometh thence").[99] These notes roused the disapproval of the ecclesiastical leaders who nonetheless could not ignore this version, for it was superior to the Great Bible. The notes apparently made a strong impact upon the people of Scotland and England, where British Puritanism became a strong force. The Geneva Bible placed the Apocrypha in a separate section at the end with the following title:

> books which were not received by a common consent to be read and expounded publicly in the Church, neither yet served to prove any point of Christian religion save in so much as they had the consent of the other scriptures called canonical to confirm the same, or rather whereon they were grounded: but as books proceeding from godly men, were received to be read for the advancement and furtherance of knowledge of the history and for the instruction of godly manners.[100]

The Geneva Bible gained wide popularity in England and remained popular for many years among the English Protestants. However, it was never appointed to be read in the churches of England, but even those who disagreed with its theology recognized it as a good translation. Even Matthew Parker, the Archbishop of Canterbury, who was producing a rival translation (i.e., the Bishops' Bible) thought so highly of it that he allowed John Bodley in 1561 to have an extra twelve years of exclusive copyrights so that it could be printed.

The Bishops' Bible (1568)

Matthew Parker

Queen Elizabeth I once again enforced the previous laws allowing public Bible reading and requiring each parish church to have a copy of the English Bible. By decree the Great Bible had already been placed in the churches of England, and the bishops of England were not willing to replace the Great Bible with the superior text of the Geneva Bible because of its Calvinistic marginal notes. Recognizing the need for a new translation, Matthew Parker, the Archbishop of Canterbury, in 1563 was asked to oversee the revision of the Great Bible. Bishops were invited to have a part in the work, hence its name. The directions for the revision were fairly simple:

> they were "to follow the common English translation used in the churches [the Great Bible] and not to recede from it but where it varieth manifestly from the Hebrew or Greek original," to follow Pagninus and Münster "for the verity of the Hebrew" and "to make no bitter notes upon any text or yet to set down any determination in places of controversy." Unedifying passages should be marked "that the reader may eschew [avoid] them in his public reading," and offensive words should be altered.[101]

The Bible was completed quickly within two years (by 1568) but with varying degrees of success. Parker was an able scholar, well equipped for the work, but the translators needed more specific guidelines and directions for such a large task. Nevertheless, Queen Elizabeth and Sir William Cecil, her chief minister, were pleased with the translation, and it became the authorized version, to be placed in all the churches of England; about nineteen editions were made between 1568 and 1606.[102]

The Bishops' Bible Translation

The Bishops' Bible (fig. 17.22) followed the Geneva Bible in some of its renderings and in dividing the entire text into verses. Its few footnotes were expressly not controversial. Greenslade compares this version with the two just prior to it: "The translation was a compromise—a dignified and 'safe' version for public reading, a sign that the bishops were not unmindful of their responsibilities, in scholarship an improvement upon the Great Bible, less radical than Geneva but willing to learn from it."[103] One of its less accurate renderings in Ecclesiastes 11:1 reads "Lay thy bread upon wet faces" instead of the Great Bible's "cast thy bread upon the waters." As a whole, though, it clearly superseded the Great Bible, which was not published again after 1569 when the Bishops' Bible had gained popularity. The New Testament was clear and understandable but not as flowing as the Geneva Bible. The Lord's Prayer, however, is similar in both translations:

> Our father, which art in heauen, halowed be thy name. Let thy kyngdome come. Thy wyll be done, as well in earth, as it is in heauen. Giue vs this day our dayly breade. And forgeve vs our dettes, as we forgeve our detters. And leade vs not into temptation, but delyuer vs from euyll. For thyne is the kyngdome, and the power, and the glory, for euer. Amen. (Matt. 6:9–13)

The Geneva Bible was still much more popular than the Bishops' Bible; the former went through 120 editions while the latter merely 20.[104]

English Bible translations had progressed significantly in the sixteenth century, and Bruce summarizes well the situation at the end of this century: "It looked now as if English-speaking Protestantism was to have two versions of the Bible, representing the Anglican and Genevan standpoints respectively. The prevention of this unfortunate state of affairs stands to the credit of the version of 1611 [the Authorized Version]."[105] In addition Roman Catholics began to produce their own translations after publication of the Bishops' Bible, reflecting the great rift between the presuppositions of Protestantism and Roman Catholicism.

Douay-Rheims Bible (NT, 1582; OT, 1609–10)

William Allen and Gregory Martin

The Roman Catholic Church was driven to produce an English translation of the Bible with notes in support of its teachings; otherwise the people would read existing versions, which reflected the teachings of Calvin and other Protestants. This need was satisfied by William Allen, an Oxford fellow and devout Roman Catholic, who had left England during the reign of Elizabeth I (who favored Protestantism and was excommunicated from the Roman Catholic Church in 1570) and established an English college at Douay, France, in 1568. Allen believed that the Reformation movement was only a temporary setback, and thus he supported an unsuccessful attempt by the Spanish to conquer England and subject it to the authority of the Roman Catholic Church.[106] This attempt outraged the English people, even those who were still sympathetic toward the pope. Tensions forced Allen's college to move to Rheims in 1578 and then back to Douay in 1593. The first year that it was in Rheims, Gregory Martin, lecturer at St. John's College, Oxford, arrived at the college and began translating the Latin Vulgate into English. The New Testament was published in 1582 (at Rheims) and the Old Testament published about 1609–10 (at Douay), thus the name Douay-Rheims Bible. Martin died in 1584, and the Bible was completed by Allen and Richard Bristow, another Oxford scholar exiled in Douay. The translators acknowledge in the preface that they were compelled to make a translation to refute the many "false translations" produced by the Protestants: "To meet the Protestant challenge, priests must be ready to quote Scripture in the vulgar tongue since their adversaries have every favourable passage at their fingers' ends; they must know the passages 'correctly used by Catholics in support of our faith, or impiously misused by heretics in opposition to the Church's faith.'"[107]

The same year that the Douay-Rheims New Testament was published, Martin also wrote *A Discovery of the manifold Corruptions of the Holy Scriptures by the Heretics of our days, specially the English Sectaries.* William Fulke responded in 1589 with a masterful work wherein the Douay-Rheims and Bishops' versions appeared side by side with annotations refuting each of the doctrinal issues addressed in the marginal notes of the Douay-Rheims Bible.[108]

Table 17.2
Summary of the History of the English Bible

British Royalty		English Translations	
House of Lancaster		John Wycliffe	1380
Henry IV	1399–1413	(second edition)	1388
Henry V	1413–1422		
Henry VI	1422–1461		
House of York			
Edward IV	1461–1470		
House of Lancaster			
Henry VI	1470–1471		
House of York			
Edward IV	1471–1483		
Edward V	1483		
Richard III	1483–1485		
House of Tudor		William Tyndale	1526
		(second edition)	1534
Henry VII	1485–1509	Coverdale Bible	1535
Henry VIII	1509–1547	Matthew Bible	1537
Edward VI	1547–1553	Great Bible	1539
Lady Jane Grey	1553	(second edition)	1540
Mary I	1553–1558	Geneva Bible	1560
Elizabeth I	1558–1603	Bishops' Bible	1568
House of Stuart		Douay-Rheims Bible	1582
James I	1604–1625		
Charles I	1625–1649		
Commonwealth			
Long Parliament	1649–1653		
Protectorate			
Oliver Cromwell	1653–1658		
Richard Cromwell	1658–1659		
House of Stuart			
Charles II	1660–1685		
James II	1685–1688		
William III	1689–1702		
and Mary II	1689–1694		
Anne	1702–1714		

The Douay-Rheims Translation

This version did not match the quality of Protestant translations but provided an adequate English translation for Roman Catholics, something that the Roman church had fought against for years. The preface states that it is a translation of the Latin Vulgate, which its translators believed to be the superior text:

> It is translated from the Vulgate which possesses ecclesiastical authority and is the least partial text, "truer than the vulgar Greek itself." The translators follow it precisely, risking unfamiliar Latinisms and not presuming to mollify hard places "for fear of missing or restraining the sense of the Holy Ghost to our phantasy," whereas Protestants use "presumptuous boldness and liberty in translating."[109]

The apocryphal books are interspersed among the canonical books, as in the Latin Vulgate. Martin also consulted the Greek text, sometimes inserting Greek readings in the margin, and according to Greenslade, he even "made extensive use of the English versions which he condemned."[110] There are some noticeable improvements in wording introduced into the text that occasionally appear in the Authorized Version, but more often the literal reading of the Latin yielded a stilted translation that was hardly intelligible unless one was familiar with the Latin behind the text. For example, Psalm 57:10 reads: "Before your thorns did understand the old briar; as living so in wrath he swalloweth them" and Philippians 2:10 reads, "every knee shall bow of celestials, terrestrials and infernals." Even the Lord's Prayer evidences clear Roman Catholic overtones:

> Ovr Father which art in heauen, sanctified be thy name. Let thy Kingdom come. Thy wil be done, as in heauen, in earth also. Giue vs to day our supersubstantial bread. And forgiue vs our dettes, as we also forgiue our detters. And leade

vs not into tentation. But deliuer vs from euil. Amen. (Matt. 6:9–13)

Rigid adherence to Roman Catholic doctrines resulted in some interesting renderings: In the Lord's Prayer, "Give us today our superstantial bread" reminds the readers of the Lord's Supper when the bread was to become the body of Christ; and in Luke 10, after giving the innkeeper two pence, the Good Samaritan says, "Whatever thou shalt supererogate, I, at my return will repay thee." Readers are thus reminded of the Roman Catholic doctrine of supererogation: the act of giving more than is required by duty, obligation, or need. The translators also chose the translations "do penance" instead of "repent," and Paul and Barnabas ordained "priests" instead of "elders" in every church. Because of its great number of Latinisms, Thomas Fuller correctly calls it a "translation that needs to be translated"[111]—in fact, an index at the back defines fifty-eight of these Latinisms.

Not surprisingly the marginal notes of the Douay-Rheims version express clear Roman Catholic teachings, which Father Hugh Pope describes as "a veritable catechism of Christian doctrine."[112] Prepared by Allen and others, these notes reverted insofar as possible to St. Augustine to substantiate controversial points since they believed the Reformers looked favorably upon his opinions. Greenslade points out: "Every opportunity was taken to press the distinctive teachings of Rome against 'the intolerable ignorance and importunity of the heretics of this time . . . the false and vain glosses of Calvin and his followers.'"[113]

The text was revised in 1750 by Bishop Richard Challoner of London (1691–1781) to bring it into conformity to the authorized versions of the Latin Vulgate (i.e., the Sixtine and Clementine editions), hence the name Douay-Rheims-Challoner Bible. This Bible was not particularly popular, but some of its Latinisms appear in the King James Version, at least in the New Testament.

For Further Reading

Bruce, F. F. *History of the Bible in English: From the Earliest Versions*, 1–95. 3d ed. New York: Oxford University Press, 1978.

———. *The Books and the Parchments*, 211–19. 5th ed. London: Marshall Pickering, 1991.

Ewert, D. *From Ancient Tablets to Modern Translations: A General Introduction to the Bible*, 183–96. Grand Rapids: Zondervan, 1983.

Greenslade, S. L. "English Versions of the Bible, A.D. 1525–1611." In *CHB*, 3:141–74.

Hargreaves, H. "The Wycliffite Versions." In *CHB*, 2:387–415.

Kenyon, F. G. *Our Bible and the Ancient Manuscripts*, 265–319. Revised by A. W. Adams. New York: Harper, 1958.

Lupton, L. *The History of the Geneva Bible*. 14 vols. London: Olive Tree, 1966–82.

MacGregor, G. *The Bible in the Making*, 68–102. Washington, DC: University Press of America, 1982.

Mozley, J. F. *Coverdale and His Bibles*. London: Lutterworth, 1953.

Partridge, A. C. *English Biblical Translation*, 1–104. London: Andre Deutsch, 1973.

Price, I. M. *The Ancestry of Our English Bible*, 225–59. 3d ed. Revised by W. A. Irwin and A. P. Wikgren. New York: Harper and Row, 1956.

Robertson, E. H. *Makers of the English Bible*. Cambridge: Lutterworth, 1990.

Shepherd, G. "English Versions of the Scriptures before Wyclif." In *CHB* 2:362–87.

Westcott, B. F. *A General View of the History of the English Bible*, 1–139. London and Cambridge: Macmillan, 1868.

18

The Authorized Version of 1611 and Its Revisions

While the Bishops' Bible was an improvement over the Great Bible and the Geneva Bible was superior to both, none was universally embraced by all factions within the English church. It was left to the translators of the Authorized Version of 1611 (commonly known as the King James Version) to bridge the ever-widening gap between the translations rendered by Anglicans and those following Puritan or Reformed traditions (see table 18.1).

The Authorized Version of 1611

Historical Context

England experienced a time of great reform and growth during the reign of Queen Elizabeth I (1558–1603). A new air of toleration and freedom ensued when Elizabeth reversed the pro-Catholic policies of Mary I; England's growing political force led to the stunning defeat of the Spanish Armada in 1588. Bible translation was freely tolerated, giving rise to several new translations—the Bishops' Bible (1568), the Geneva Bible (1560), the Douay-Rheims Bible (1609–10). Rapid literary growth gave rise to such notable English figures as William Shakespeare (1564–1616), Edmund Spenser (c. 1552–1599, known in his time as the prince of poets), Philip Sidney (1554–1586, poet), Francis Bacon (1561–1626, philosopher, statesman, and essayist), Richard Hooker (1553–1600, theologian, best known for the *Laws of Ecclesiastical Polity*), Ben Jonson (1572–1637, dramatist), and Christopher Marlowe (1564–1593, the father of English tragedy). Great strides in scholarship in general were made, achieving a high standard of excellence, and it was within this historical context that the King James Version was born.

The Hampton Court Conference (1604)

Upon Queen Elizabeth I's death in 1603, James I, who from the age of one had been king of Scotland for the past thirty-six years,

Table 18.1
The King James Bible

Sponsors of the Translation	Translators	Text	Translation Techniques	Characteristics
King James and Hampton Court Conference (1604)	54 translators—most of the leading classical and oriental scholars of the day and some laymen	OT: Complutensian Polyglot; Antwerp Polyglot NT: *Textus Receptus*	Revision of Bishops' Bible (1602 ed.) Word-for-word translation	Archaic English ("thees," "thous") Sense paragraphs Marginal notes (most were literal readings of the Hebrew or Greek texts) Apocrypha Yahweh = LORD

Figure 18.1.
A portrait of
James I
(1566–1625).
[National Portrait Gallery]

any marginal notes, and only to be used in all churches of England in time of divine service."[3]

The motion for a new translation was presented by Dr. John Rainolds (1549–1607), the president of Corpus Christi College, Oxford, and a moderate Puritan leader. A good number approved of the motion, though Richard Bancroft, bishop of London (soon to be archbishop of Canterbury), opposed it and complained, "if every man's humour were followed, . . . there would be no end of translating."[4] Nevertheless, the proposal suited King James, who had been well-trained in early life as a student of the Bible and had written a paraphrase of the Book of Revelation and translated some of the Psalms.[5] One reason King James willingly took up the suggestion of a new translation was his objections to the Geneva Bible, the edition many preferred for private use. Thinking it undermined the divine right of kings, he labeled it "very partiall, untrue, seditious, and savouring too much of dangerous and traytorous conceits."[6] F. F. Bruce outlines the king's specific complaints:

Three notes which he seems to have particularly disliked were those at Exod. 1:19, 2 Kings 9:33 and 2 Chron. 15:16. The first said, with regard to the midwives' refusal to kill the boys as Pharaoh commanded: "Their disobedience herein was lawful, but their dissembling evil." The very suggestion that it could ever be lawful to disobey a king did not commend itself to James. The second declared that Jehu's command that Jezebel should be thrown down from her window was given ". . . to be a spectacle and example of Gods judgements to all tyrants." But the suggestion that violence to a royal personage could be approved by God did not consort well with James's conviction of the divine right of kings. And he suspected that some readers might think of his mother, the late Mary Queen of Scots, when they read the note anent Asa's deposition of *his* mother for idolatry: "Herein he showed that he lacked zeal, for she ought to have died . . . but he gave place to foolish pitie."[7]

succeeded to the throne (fig. 18.1). On his way to England he was presented with the Millenary Petition (so called for its thousand signatures) in which the Puritan party set out its grievances against the Church of England.[1] Although King James was from Scotland, he was not sympathetic to the Puritans as they had hoped, for they had thwarted him on several political issues. The Puritans' main contention was that "they could not with good conscience subscribe to the Communion [Prayer-] booke, since it maintained the Bible as it was there translated [in the Great Bible], which was as they said, a most corrupted translation."[2] Nevertheless King James could not ignore the Puritans' political power and convened a council at Hampton Court in 1604 to discuss the differing views of the rival parties in the Church of England. Little was resolved except "[t]hat a translation be made of the whole Bible, as consonant as can be to the original Hebrew and Greek; and this to be set out and printed, without

The new translation would be produced by university scholars, reviewed by the bishops, and ratified by the king. In order to be acceptable to all English Protestants, it was to appear without offensive marginal notes.[8]

King James was not popular among the English people, not only for the freedoms he allowed to Roman Catholics but also for his pacifist views that led to the deterioration of the English navy after Queen Elizabeth had so effectively built up its forces. Spanish fleets regained a great deal of power, and English ships were raided by pirates in the English Channel; Spain merely mocked and ignored King James's diplomatic protests.[9] King James's Bible translation project was, then, the highlight of a poor reign.

The Translation

King James took an active part in organizing the Authorized Version, appointing fifty-four men as translators (although only forty-four names are listed).[10] Most were the leading classical and Oriental scholars in England at the time, both traditional Anglican and Puritan, but some laymen were also included. The intent was to build on earlier translation work to render a translation in the vernacular that would be easy to understand yet dignified enough to be read in church. This motive is expressed in the Jacobean prose of the preface to the 1611 edition:

> Truly (good Christian Reader) we neuer thought from the beginning, that we should neede to make a new Translation, nor yet to make of a bad one a good one, . . . but to make a good one better, or out of many good ones, one principal good one, not iustly to be excepted against: that hath bene our endeauour, that our marke.[11]

The translators were arranged into six panels: two met in Oxford, two in Cambridge, and two in Westminster (London; see table 18.2). Once the panels completed their translations the work was reviewed by a smaller committee made up of two persons from each of the panels (twelve persons). The translation was then steered

The Gunpowder Plot (1605)

This event is important to the history of the English Bible, for had it succeeded the King James Bible would never have become a reality. King James's policy of attempting to pacify all of his British constituents had the reverse effect (fig. 18.2). King James showed great leniency at the beginning of his reign and relaxed restrictions against the Roman Catholics, who felt they were not being treated fairly. Those loyal to the pope even began to hope that England might once again return to the Roman Catholic faith. Protestant reaction resulted in Parliament's decision to tighten restrictions upon the Roman Catholics who in turn were infuriated.

Figure 18.2. A drawing depicting the Gunpowder Plot of 1605.

Coups-d'état had formerly taken place quite easily in early England by the removal of the king, but now it would be necessary to remove the entire Parliament. Papal loyalists rented a vault directly under the House of Lords and in March 1605 filled it with thirty-six barrels of gunpowder—a ton and a half—and then waited for the right moment. On October 26, Lord Monteagle received a letter from his brother-in-law, Francis Tresham, one of the conspirators, warning him not to appear in Parliament but to make some excuse to vacation in the country for a while. Monteagle, a loyal servant of the king, showed the letter to some of the king's ministers who, after a careful search, found the explosives merely two days before Parliament was to open. The conspirators were arrested and most were executed. For years afterward many patriotic Englishmen held in suspicion anyone supportive of the pope.

through the printing process by Dr. Miles Smith and Bishop Thomas Bilson.

The Authorized Version was guided by principles drawn up or at least authorized by King James himself:

1. The 1602 edition of the Bishops' Bible was used as the basis for the revision, but the original Greek and Hebrew texts were to be examined. ("The Preface to the Readers" cites that all the English translations, several foreign versions [Spanish, French, Italian, and Dutch], several Latin translations, the Septuagint, the targums, and the Syriac Peshitta were used in determining the best readings of the Hebrew and Greek texts.[12])

2. So that the English version did not become too stilted, a variety of words were to be used for the same Greek and Hebrew words. (In the later revisions of 1881 and 1885 this principle was reversed because it was thought that it interfered with an accurate reflection of the text.)

3. Words necessary in the English but not present in the Hebrew and Greek texts were to be set off by italics. (Sakae Kubo and Walter Specht make the following comment regarding the use of italics: "This system seems to rest on the false assumption that for every word in the original there is an equivalent in English, and that the ideal translation is a literal word-for-word rendering."[13] On a practical level italics are normally used to denote emphasis and can be dis-

tracting to the reader when they are applied in another fashion. A story is commonly told about the well-meaning preacher who thought the italics indicated emphasis and thus in his preaching he emphasized all the words that were lacking from the original texts.)

4. The names of biblical characters were to correspond as closely as possible to those in common use; however, names were not necessarily standardized (e.g., Elijah [OT], Elias [NT]; "Joshua" occurs twice as "Jesus" [Acts 7:45; Heb. 4:8]).

5. Old ecclesiastical words were to be retained: "congregation" and "washing" in the Tyndale Bible became "church" and "baptism" in the Authorized Version.

6. No marginal notes were to appear other than explanations of Greek and Hebrew words.

7. Existing chapter and verse divisions were to be retained, but new headings would be supplied.

A final stipulation was added that other specialists could be called upon to provide assistance in certain areas of difficulty, as Geddes MacGregor explains: "Every bishop in the country, moreover, was to admonish his clergy to direct all persons who might be skilled in the ancient tongues to send their particular observations to the appropriate company. It would require more than human daring to make such an invitation in our own day; but in seventeenth-century England fewer people made pretensions to liter-

Table 18.2
Translation Process for the Authorized Version

Old Testament	Apocrypha	New Testament

3 Panels
  Genesis–2 Kings
  1 Chronicles–Ecclesiastes
  Isaiah–Malachi
	1 Panel	2 Panels
		  Gospels, Acts, and Apocalypse
		  The Epistles

Headed by Lancelot Andrewes, dean of Westminster, a great scholar who mastered fifteen languages and yet was also a man of great personal piety.	Probably headed by John Bois, a brilliant, hard-working scholar from St. John's College, Cambridge.	Headed by Thomas Ravis, who later became bishop of London and archbishop of Canterbury.

acy, and those who did felt a less urgent necessity to prove them."[14] The result was a clear, fluent English translation that in time won the hearts of many English-speaking people. Its poetic rhythm and dignity is evidenced in the Lord's Prayer:

> Our father which art in heauen, hallowed be thy name.
> Thy kingdome come. Thy will be done, in earth, as it is in heauen.
> Giue vs this day our daily bread.
> And forgiue vs our debts, as we forgiue our debters.
> And lead vs not into temptation, but deliuer vs from euill: For thine is the kingdome, and the power, and the glory, for euer. Amen. (Matt. 6:9–13)

Jack P. Lewis, former professor of Bible at Harding Graduate School of Religion, notes that the sources used for the Authorized Version were significantly inferior to those available today:

> Of the five primary uncial manuscripts now received as authority for the purity of the text of the New Testament, only Codex Bezae was then available, and there is no evidence that it was used. Papyrus discoveries came three hundred years later. The King James scholars could have known fewer than twenty-five late manuscripts of the New Testament, and these were carelessly used. Today there are 5,358 known New Testament manuscripts and fragments. . . . The 1611 situation for the Old Testament was even poorer. The Complutensian Polyglot (1517) and the Antwerp Polyglot (1572) would have been the sources from which they would have known the Old Testament. Where these two differ, the KJV agrees with one or the other except in about a half-dozen places where it agrees with neither. . . . About 800 Hebrew manuscripts have now been studied.[15]

Early Editions of the Authorized Version

The Authorized Version, having taken five years to complete, first appeared in

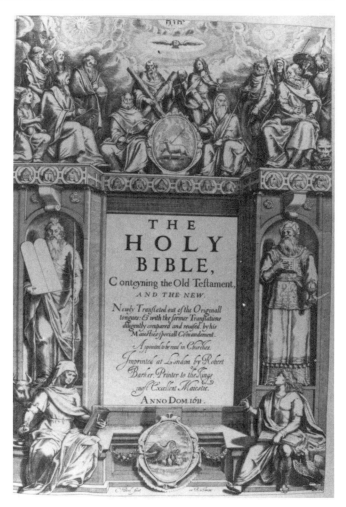

Figure 18.3.
The title page of the Authorized Version (1611). Bible in English (London: Robert Barker, 1611), King James' Version, "He" Bible, 1st edition. [Grand Haven, Mich., The Scriptorium, VK 165, title page]

1611 as a 1,500-page codex over three inches thick, each page measuring 10.5 by 16.5 inches (fig. 18.3). It was dedicated to King James and the title, in its entirety, read: *"The Holy Bible, conteyning the Old Testament and the New: Newly Translated out of the Originall tongues: & with the former Translations diligently compared and revised, by his Majestie's speciall Commandement. Appointed to be read in Churches."*

The wording of the title is somewhat surprising, since there were no decrees or laws authorizing it as a translation or requiring its usage. Its acceptance as the Authorized Version of 1611 is apparently based upon the king's influence and the reputation of its translators.

Table 18.3
Variants in Editions of the Authorized Version

Date	Title	Description
1631	The Wicked Bible	It lacked the word *not* in the seventh commandment; thus reading "thou shalt commit adultery." The king's printers were fined £300 by the archbishop for making such a blatant error.
1653	The Unrighteous Bible	It contains an error in 1 Corinthians 6:9, so that it reads "the unrighteous shall inherit the earth" instead of the "righteous."
1702	The Scribes' Bible	"Printers have persecuted me" in Psalm 119:161, which may have been true since this edition contained many printing errors, but the text should have read "Princes had persecuted me."
1717	The Vinegar Bible	This edition had many misprints, but one of the most interesting was in the chapter heading of Luke 20: "The Parable of the Vinegar" instead of "Vineyard."
1795	The Murderer's Bible	It reads in Mark 7:27 "Let the children first be killed" instead of "filled."
1805	The Steadfast Bible	This edition, published by Cambridge University Press, retained a proofreader's mark stating "to remain" included in the text, so that Galatians 4:29 reads as "him that was born after the Spirit to remain." This mistake was reprinted in the 1806 and 1819 editions.

The title page is a beautiful engraving, the symbolism of which is explained well by MacGregor:

This title forms the centre of an engraving showing the figures of Moses and Aaron to the right and to the left respectively. At the corners appear the Four Evangelists. At the top is the name of God in Hebrew, below which appears the Sacred Dove, symbol of the Holy Spirit, and again below this the Lamb, symbol of Christ. At the foot of the page is the Pelican which, "vulning" herself, that is, wounding herself with her beak to feed her young with her own blood, is a traditional symbol of Christ's redeeming work, especially in the Eucharist.[16]

There was great demand for this new translation, and in order to produce the required twenty thousand copies, two different printers were used, since no single printer could make that many copies. Concerning these two editions, MacGregor explains that they were "both standard, yet quite distinct in every leaf, and there were between them a great many, mostly minute, discrepancies."[17] These two editions are often distinguished, in fact, according to a discrepancy in Ruth 3:15 whereby one edition reads, "he measured six *measures* of barley, and laid *it* on her: and hee [Boaz]

went into the city" and the other edition reads, "she [Ruth] went into the city." These editions are consequently referred to as "the Great He Bible" and "the Great She Bible," respectively.[18] The "Great He Bible" also mistakenly reads "then cometh Judas" in Matthew 26:36 instead of "then cometh Jesus," and Mark 10:18 reads "There is no man good, but one, *that is* God" (later editions changed "no man" to the more accurate "none").[19] The "Great She Bible" was little better, for it repeated twenty words in Exodus 14:10 because of dittography.[20] In the years following its completion the Authorized Version was reprinted many times, and by the 1613 edition there were already more than three hundred variations between it and the earliest editions.[21] Several editions gained notoriety for their mistakes (see table 18.3). One error that was retained nearly until the present day was "strain *at* a gnat" instead of "strain *out* a gnat" (Matt. 23:24).

The Authorized Version of 1611, like its predecessors, included the Apocrypha, of which the Puritans strongly disapproved. It became such an issue that in 1616 Archbishop Abbot decreed that anyone who published an edition of the Authorized Version without the Apocrypha would be thrown in prison for one year. The Apocrypha continued to be fairly consistently included until about 1826 when, primarily for financial reasons, the British and Foreign Bible Society omitted it.

Reception of the Authorized Version

The Authorized Version was recognized as the standard edition of the Bible relatively quickly, but the Geneva Bible gave it competition for about fifty years, despite the fact that in about 1631 Bishop Laud ordered copies to be burned and forbade its importation from Geneva.[22] The number of editions alone of each version indicates that the vast majority accepted the Authorized Version: "Between 1611 and 1644, the *Historical Catalogue* of the British and Foreign Bible Society enumerates fifteen editions of the Geneva Bible and 182 of the Authorized."[23]

The Authorized Version was not without its detractors, however; among the most fervent were the pilgrims who brought the Geneva Bible to the New World. The Authorized Version was rejected for its emphasis on the divine right of kings.[24] Another particularly virulent detractor was Dr. Hugh Broughton, a distinguished scholar who had not been asked to serve on the translation committee, most likely because his violent temper interfered with his ability to work well with others:

> One of his contemporaries, Thomas Morton, who became Bishop of Durham, is said to have once greeted him with the request that he (Morton) be called at the outset of the conversation a dolt, a dullard, and any other such epithet that Broughton intended to bestow upon him, so that the course of the conversation itself might not be so frequently interrupted. Apparently Broughton took this in good part as a joke. But it did not improve his temper.[25]

Broughton's rejection of this new version was expected: "The late Bible . . . was sent to me to censure: which bred in me a sadness that will grieve me while I breathe, it is so ill done. Tell His Majesty that I had rather be rent in pieces with wild horses, than any such translation by my consent should be urged upon poor churches. . . . The new edition crosseth me. I require it to be burnt."[26]

Broughton himself had been working on a revision of the Geneva Bible for about thirty years, but he died in 1612 before its completion. He was not alone in his criticisms, as Luther Weigle notes:

> For eighty years after its publication in 1611, the King James version endured bitter attacks. It was denounced as theologically unsound and ecclesiastically biased, as truckling to the king and unduly deferring to his belief in witchcraft, as untrue to the Hebrew text and relying too much on the Septuagint. The personal integrity of the translators was impugned. Among other things, they were accused of "blasphemy," "most damnable corruptions," "intolerable deceit," and "vile imposture," the critic who used these epithets being careful to say that they were not "the dictates of passion, but the just resentment of a zealous mind."[27]

In time, however, criticisms died out, and according to S. L. Greenslade, the Authorized Version gained a victory so complete that "its text acquired a sanctity properly ascribable only to the unmediated voice of God; to multitudes of English-speaking Christians it has seemed little less than blasphemy to tamper with the words of the King James Version."[28] It was also to leave its mark upon the English language with such expressions as "lick the dust," "skin of his teeth," and "salt of the earth." The English language continued to develop, however, so that in time the wording of the Authorized Version would become archaic and in need of improvement. Not only that, only sixteen years after its publication Codex Alexandrinus arrived at the British Museum from Constantinople, too late to be incorporated into this version. Further work on the Authorized Version would be interrupted by two political revolutions, England's civil war (1642–1646) and the Glorious Revolution (1688).

Attempts to Improve the Authorized Version

The Bible that has become known as the Authorized Version has been a dramatic text throughout history, but today's version differs significantly from the original. Primarily the language has been modernized, but other modifications have also occurred, some authorized and others not. Broughton pointed out many flaws in the original translation requiring a major revision of the Authorized Version in 1629, and another revision was completed in 1638. Following the latter revision the text remained static for more than one hundred years. Still there were continued attempts to improve the Authorized Version, though none were very successful. In 1653 a committee to oversee the revision of the Authorized Version was appointed by the Long Parliament, which was dissolved shortly afterward, and the revision died with it. The translation stood almost unchallenged for another fifty years, when Edward Wells produced a revised edition entitled *The Common Translation Corrected* (1718–1724). Then in a short time several revisions appeared. In 1729 Daniel Mace published a Greek text with his corrected Authorized Version alongside it. William Whiston, whose translation of Josephus is famous, published an important revision called the *Primitive New Testament*, which primarily follows the Authorized Version except where it differs from older Greek texts that had recently been discovered (e.g., Codex Bezae for the Gospels and Acts). John Wesley in 1768 revised the Authorized Version with some twelve thousand changes, entitling it *The New Testament with Notes, for Plain Unlettered Men who know only their Mother Tongue*. In 1762 the Cambridge Bible of the Authorized Version, edited by Dr. Thomas Paris, was diligently corrected, spellings were modernized, and 360 marginal notes were introduced; it became the standard edition.[29] In 1768 Edward Harwood prepared a liberal translation of the Authorized Version; that is, he took great liberties with the text to render it more understandable. The Lord's Prayer is three times longer than the Greek text and reads:

> O Thou great governour and parent of universal nature—who manifestest thy glory to the blessed inhabitants of heaven—may all thy rational creatures in all the parts of thy boundless dominion be happy in the knowledge of thy existence and providence, and celebrate thy perfections in a manner most worthy thy nature and perfective of their own.[30]

Needless to say, this work was not well received. The next year (1769) Dr. Benjamin Blayney, Regius Professor of Hebrew at Oxford, once again revised the Authorized Version and introduced many modifications dealing with weights, measures, and coins.[31] E. J. Goodspeed estimated that this version differed in at least seventy-five thousand places from the Authorized Version of 1611,[32] and it became known as the Oxford standard edition with which we are familiar today.

By the early 1800s people became increasingly dissatisfied with the Authorized Edition, for reasons delineated by Herbert March, Lady Margaret Professor of Divinity at Cambridge and later bishop of Peterborough:

> It is probable . . . that our Authorized Version is as faithful a representation of the original Scriptures as *could* have been formed at *that period*. But when we consider the immense accession that has been made, both to our critical and philological apparatus; when we consider that the most important sources of intelligence for the *interpretation* of the original Scriptures were *likewise* opened after than period, we cannot possibly pretend that our Authorized Version does not require *emendment*.[33]

In addition the language had become antiquated; those who had read this Bible most of their lives were used to its oddities and archaic wording, but those new to it had a difficult time. The following phrases from the Authorized Version of 1611 illustrate the problem:[34]

Table 18.4
Changes in Word Meanings

Word	Meaning in 1611	Modern Meaning
mean man	common man	cruel man
meat	any kind of food	flesh
peculiar	that which belongs to one person	strange
cherish	to keep warm	to care about
passenger	passer by	person being transported on something
prevent	to come before	to hinder
let	prevent (some places)	to allow
wealth	welfare	money or riches
wealthy	happy	rich
forward	ready or willing	self-assertive
knit	let down	to weave
carriage	something carried	a horse-drawn vehicle

See Jack P. Lewis, *The English Bible from KJV to NIV*, 2d ed. (Grand Rapids: Baker, 1991), 55–59.

1. "And Jacob sod pottage: and Esau came from the field, and he was faint" (Gen. 25:29).
2. "And mount Sinai was altogether on a smoke" (Exod. 19:18).
3. "Dead things are formed from under the waters, and the inhabitants thereof" (Job 26:5).
4. "Thou shalt destroy them that speak leasing" (Ps. 5:6).
5. "For who can eat, or who else can hasten hereunto, more than I?" (Eccles. 2:25).
6. "I trow not" (Luke 17:9).

The meanings of some words were no longer commonly known; almug, chode, chapt, habergeon, hosen, kab, ligure, leasing, neesed, pilled, ring-saked, stacte, strake, trode, wimples, ouches, tatches, occurrent, pruit, fray, nusings, wot, trow, and sod.[35] Some words even changed in meaning (see table 18.4). Developments in biblical studies (e.g., archaeological finds, advances in comparative linguistics) and the discovery of biblical manuscripts (e.g., fourth-century Codex Vaticanus, fourth-century Codex Sinaiticus, and fifth-century Codex Alexandrinus) much earlier than the texts used for the Authorized Version led to a widely recognized need for its revision.

The Revised Version (NT, 1881; Entire Bible, 1885)

Its History

In 1870 Dr. Samuel Wilberforce, bishop of Winchester, proposed that the Authorized Version be revised, and a resolution to that effect was passed in the Upper House of Convocation of the Province of Canterbury. Sixteen scholars were appointed to supervise the project, and fifty-four people were chosen to do the translation (some say sixty-five in all[36]), many of whom were well known:

Some of the Old Testament Translators: E. H. Browne, A. B. Davidson, F. Field, C. D. Ginsburg, J. J. S. Perowne, E. H. Plumptre, N. C. Thirlwall, C. Wordsworth; chaired by Dr. E. H. Browne, the bishop of Ely

Some of the New Testament Translators: F. J. A. Hort, J. B. Lightfoot, W. Milligan, W. F. Moulton, F. H. A. Scrivener, S. P. Tregelles, B. F. Westcott; chaired by Dr. C. J. Ellicott, the bishop of Gloucester and Bristol

An additional thirty American Scholars, under Philip Schaff

With two committees set up in the United States, one for the Old Testament and one

Revisions of the Authorized Version of 1611
Revised Version (NT, 1881; entire Bible, 1885)
American Standard Version (1901)
Revised Standard Version (NT, 1946; entire Bible, 1952)
New American Standard Bible (1971)
King James II Version (1971)
New King James Version (NT, 1979; entire Bible, 1982)
New Revised Standard Version (1989)

for the New, it was hoped that one translation could be agreed upon for both England and America. However, this did not turn out to be the case. The American translators were not satisfied with the strict guidelines that their British counterparts had agreed to and wanted to remove much more of the archaic language (e.g., the Americans did not like the connotations associated with "ghost" in "Holy Ghost" and wanted to change it to "spirit"; their British counterparts did not feel free to make such a change).

The Policies of the Revisers

The translators were allowed to introduce only those readings that would render the Authorized Version closer to the original languages and would not modernize the English unduly. Each group went over the translation twice, with any subsequent changes needing a two-thirds majority. The following changes were introduced:

1. Alterations due to the adoption of a Greek text different from that used for the Authorized Version (about six thousand changes).
2. Improvements where the Authorized Version was ambiguous.
3. Correction of errors in the Authorized Version.
4. Alterations where the Authorized Version inconsistently rendered the Greek through the use of more than one English word.

5. Alterations where parallel passages were not rendered consistently.

The Translation

Although the work was carried out by eminent scholars, they were overly restricted in their ability to change the language. A. C. Partridge correctly concludes: "It was a mistaken directive, in commissioning the *Revised Version*, to limit the language of the new text to the vocabulary of Tudor and Jacobean authors. The work was faithfully carried out, but the product was an anachronism."[37] Still the wording is generally quite clear and fluent, as is demonstrated in the Lord's Prayer:

> Our Father which art in heaven, Hallowed be thy name.
> Thy kingdom come. Thy will be done, as in heaven, so on earth. Give us this day our daily bread. And forgive us our debts, as we also have forgiven our debtors. And bring us not into temptation, but deliver us from the evil *one*. (Matt. 6:9–13)

There are two specific points of interest in this translation: the wording "bring us not into temptation" seems to contradict James 1:13, which says that God does not tempt anyone; and the prayer ends after "the evil *one*" since the earliest Greek manuscripts do not include the rest of the verse as found in the Authorized Version.

Work on the New Testament faced the additional challenge of incorporating advances in textual criticism. B. F. West-

Table 18.5
The Revised Version

Sponsors of the Translation	Translators	Text	Translation Techniques	Characteristics
Anglican Church (Convocation of Canterbury)	45 well-known scholars (mostly Anglican)	OT: Masoretic Text NT: Largely Westcott and Hort's Greek text	Revision of AV Word-for-word translation	Archaic English ("thou," "art") Sense paragraphs Marginal notes (most were alternative readings) Apocrypha Yahweh = LORD

cott and F. J. A. Hort, both from the University of Cambridge, were breaking new ground in this area. At the same time as they were working on the English Revised Version they were also formulating a new text of the Greek New Testament, published five days before the English Revised Version. Bruce describes the impact of their studies on the translation committee:

> They placed their critical work at the disposal of their colleagues on the revision company, and to a very large degree their findings on the text were approved by the majority—Dr. Scrivener, it is said, being repeatedly outvoted by two-thirds of those present. While Westcott and Hort's devotion to the text of the Vatican and Sinaitic codices was excessive (as may be seen more clearly in the light of further textual study), yet at that time they did establish the Greek text of the New Testament as accurately as it could well be established on the evidence then available.[38]

The translation progressed slowly; the following quote gives some indication of the time commitment involved in translation, all of which was performed free of charge:

> The New Testament Company met . . . in Westminster Abbey. . . . They assembled at 11 a.m. Prayer was offered and any matters of business correspondence were then dealt with. These preliminaries over, the chairman read a short passage from the Authorized Version and invited textual changes. When these had been given, he then asked for proposals concerning the manner in which the revision should be rendered in the place in question. After discussion, the vote of the company was taken. The day's work continued till 6 p.m. with only an interval of half an hour. After nine days of this regime, it was found that they had been working at the rate of only seventeen verses a day. The pace quickened later on; yet it seems never to have risen above about thirty-five verses a day.[39]

This was the first major translation to make use of modern textual critical principles, frequently noting alternative readings in the margins. There were about 5,788 changes in the underlying Greek text, about one-fourth of which altered the reading of the text.[40] Equally, in many passages the well-known words of the Authorized Version were absent from the Revised Version (e.g., John 5:3–4; Acts 8:37; 1 John 5:7). Some archaisms introduced into the translation were not present in the Authorized Version (e.g., increase in words such as "howbeit," "peradventure," "holden," "aforetime," "sojourn," "must needs," "would fain," "behooved").[41] Translators of the Revised Version reversed the procedure whereby translators of the Authorized Version used a variety of words to translate repetitious Greek and Hebrew words, a policy that greatly facilitated use of an English concordance for biblical study. The Apocrypha was included, but Bruce notes that "it has been suggested that the R.V. of the Apocrypha shows signs of being the work of tired men."[42]

Its Reception

The Revised New Testament was available in England on May 17, 1881, and in America on May 20, 1881. Three million copies sold in England and America that first year, the vast majority (two million) within the first few days. In fact, the *Chicago Times* and the *Chicago Tribune* published the entire New Testament on May 22, 1881. MacGregor says, "For this Herculean achievement, ninety-two compositors and five correctors were employed by the *Tribune,* which is said to have completed its setting-up of the New Testament in twelve hours."[43] The entire Bible was completed in 1885 but did not enjoy lasting popularity since its literal rendering of the text made it less readable. As Charles Spurgeon, the most renowned preacher of his day, quipped, the new version was "strong in Greek, weak in English."[44]

An Evaluation

The Revised Version of the Old Testament text was a literal translation of the Masoretic Text (as was the Authorized

Version), from which it deviated in only a few instances. With their improved knowledge of Hebrew, scholars were able to clarify many passages. The poetic passages especially benefited, being printed as poetry and thereby improving their meaning. The New Testament did not fare as well, however, for it lacked the elegance and artistic beauty of the Authorized Version. A review of the Revised Version that appeared in *The Times* in 1935 states:

> The real trouble with the selected company of Revisers was that, while it included the most eminent authorities of the time on New Testament Greek, it included no men of letters versed in the rhythm, cadence, and euphony of good English. The Revisers began by setting before themselves a pedantic code, and for the sake of conformity with that code they cheerfully ruined many of the loveliest passages in English literature.[45]

The authors of the Revised Version attempted to render a word-for-word translation of the Greek and Hebrew texts using only one English word to represent each Greek or Hebrew word and leaving no Greek word without a corresponding English word. This principle gave rise to stilted renderings that have become known as translation English. Dr. John W. Burgon, dean of Chichester, wrote one of the most stinging criticisms of this version:

> how it happened that, with so many splendid Scholars sitting round their table, they should have produced a Translation which, for the most part, reads like a first-rate school-boy's *crib*,—tasteless, un-

lovely, harsh, unidiomatic;—servile without being really faithful,—pedantic without being really learned;—an unreadable Translation, in short; the result of a vast amount of labour indeed, but of wondrous little skill:—how all this has come about, it were utterly useless at this time of day to enquire.[46]

Even though its text was superior, the Revised Version never replaced the Authorized Version because of its deficient English style and vocabulary. Nevertheless, as MacGregor correctly states: "For all its shortcomings, the Revised Version was not only a noble achievement in itself, but one that will be found to have played a vital part in the movement to keep the Bible in a language 'understanded of the people.'"[47] This is an important point, for if the Bible had remained entrenched in the vocabulary of the King James Bible, later translations would have encountered even greater difficulty in gaining a foothold.

The American Standard Version (1901)

Its History

This version is an outgrowth of the Revised Version (1881–1885); American scholars collaborating on the Revised Version often differed with their British colleagues but had agreed not to publish a separate American version for a fourteen-year period. Until that time differing American revisions were listed in an

Table 18.6
The American Standard Version

Sponsors of the Translation	Translators	Text	Translation Techniques	Characteristics
An American committee (headed by Philip Schaff)	At least ten well-known scholars	OT: Masoretic Text NT: Largely Westcott and Hort's Greek Text	Revision of AV Word-for-word translation	Archaic English ("thou," "art") Sense paragraphs Fewer marginal notes No Apocrypha Yahweh = Jehovah

appendix to the British edition. The American committee continued work even after their British counterparts had finished. Among the more notable scholars were

William H. Green, Princeton University

George E. Day, Princeton University

Timothy Dwight, Yale University

J. H. Thayer, Harvard University

John DeWitt, University of New Brunswick

Charles M. Mead, Andover-Newton

Howard Osgood, Colgate-Rochester

Joseph Packard, Protestant Episcopal Seminary, Alexandria

Matthew B. Riddle, Hartford Seminary

Shortly before the fourteen years had passed, the university presses of Oxford and Cambridge published their own American version, which simply incorporated into the British translation the changes noted by the American committee in the appendix.[48] Undaunted, the American committee had made many more revisions to their version, which was eventually published by Thomas Nelson in 1901 and entitled the American Standard Version.

The Translation

A few of the more common changes in wording made by the American committee are detailed in table 18.7. The most severely criticized change was the use of Jehovah instead of LORD or GOD as in the Revised Version. The American Standard Version was completely reparagraphed with different titles and punctuation from the Revised Version. Marginal readings were reduced by 80 percent, and the Apocrypha was omitted. The importance of this translation is manifest in that the majority of Americans recite the Lord's Prayer beginning, "Our Father *who* art in heaven" (American Standard Version) instead of "Our Father *which* art in heaven" (Authorized Version). The rest of the Lord's Prayer reads:

Table 18.7
Changes in Wording (ASV)

British Wording	American Wording
which	who or that when referring to people
wot	know
wist	knew
LORD or GOD	Jehovah
Holy Ghost	Holy Spirit
grave, pit, or hell	Sheol
hell	Hades
charity	love
fray	frighten
seeth or sod	boil

Our Father who art in heaven, Hallowed be thy name. Thy kingdom come. Thy will be done, as in heaven, so on earth. Give us this day our daily bread. And forgive us our debts, as we also have forgiven our debtors. And bring us not into temptation, but deliver us from the evil *one*. (Matt. 6:9–13)

Its Reception

This version was much more widely accepted in America than was its British counterpart in England. Almost immediately it was adopted by the Presbyterian church to replace the King James Bible. In 1901, Clyde W. Votaw praised and highly recommended this version: "The American Standard edition is by far, and in every respect, the best English translation of the Bible in existence, both for scholars and for the people. It is the privilege, but also the duty, of every man, woman, and child in America . . . to use the best English translation of the Bible which is available to them, namely, the edition of 1901."[49]

However, every translation has its critics and this one is no exception: the Protestant Episcopal Church in 1904 rejected a proposal to use the American Standard Version, and a Methodist preacher, E. W. Alderson, objected to the uniform translation of "to baptize" for the Greek word βαπτίζω *(baptizō)*.[50] C. E. W. Dobbs complained that the Holy Spirit was referred to as "it" (Acts 8:16), while at other times as "he" (John 16:7–14).[51] This version was never as

319

popular as the Authorized Version, for two reasons especially: numerous advances in biblical archaeology and comparative semitics made the translation obsolete almost immediately; and there was a significant upsurge in interest for modern-speech versions (something this translation clearly was not).

An Evaluation

Because the text of the American Standard Version closely follows the Revised Version, it shares similar strengths and weaknesses. It was a great improvement over earlier translations because it relies heavily on Codex Sinaiticus and Codex Alexandrinus; however, since then many earlier and better papyrus fragments have been found, as Jack Lewis explains:

> The ASV had the fate of being made just before significant manuscripts were discovered of both Old and New Testament materials. This rendered it out of date before it had a fair chance to displace the KJV in popular esteem. . . . Philip Schaff stated in 1877 that there were about 1,500 manuscripts of the Greek New Testament that had been compared. Now there are 5,358 manuscripts and fragments known. . . . Though some papyri had come to light before the twentieth century, it is the age of papyrus discoveries. There are now eighty-six known papyrus portions of the New Testament.[52]

The Old Testament derives mainly from the Masoretic Text but relied on the Septuagint in passages that were unclear. Like the Revised Version, it divided the text into sense paragraphs and employed the same English word for a given Greek or Hebrew word. It attempted to render the nuance of the Greek aorist tense so that even today it is an excellent translation for those who wish to work back to the original Greek from the English.

The American Standard Version, however, also suffered from archaic wording like its counterpart, the Revised Version; for example, "blains" (Exod. 9:10), "caul" (Lev. 3:4), "maw" (Deut. 18:3), "emerods" (Deut. 28:27), "withes" (Judg. 16:7–9), "besom" (Isa. 14:23), "hosen" (Dan. 3:21), "rapine" (Nah. 3:1), and many more.[53] Quaintness of language was also the result of word order, such as "wash not" (Matt. 15:2), "defileth not" (Matt. 15:20), "they marveled all" (Luke 1:63), and "brother beloved" (Philem. 16). Antiquated numbers (e.g., "sixscore thousand" [Jonah 4:11], "thrice" [Mark 14:30], "fourscore" [Luke 2:37], "ninety and nine" [Luke 15:7]) and English coinage (e.g., "farthing" [Matt. 5:26], "shilling" [Matt. 18:28; 20:2, 9]) would not have been readily understood by early twentieth-century American readers. Lewis describes the historical setting from which this translation emerged:

> Even as late as 1901, homes were lighted by gas and kerosene lamps. Electricity was not generally available. Though the telephone had been invented, it was not yet widely used. Few people had radios, and no one had watched a television program. Trains were available, but the basic means of transportation was horse and buggy. Very few people had cars and no one had flown an airplane, not even the Wright brothers. The ocean could be crossed only by ship, and the trip took almost thirty days. Each winter many people died of pneumonia, for no one had dreamed of miracle drugs. Each summer some were crippled with dreaded polio; Salk vaccine was yet a half-century away. The ASV represented the best scholarship and biblical learning of its time. It is not, however, the final word in Bible translation. Scholarship has advanced with the passing of years, and the ASV now lags behind.[54]

The Revised Standard Version (NT, 1946; Entire Bible, 1952; Apocrypha, 1957)

Its History

In 1928 the copyright of the American Standard Bible was acquired by the Inter-

Table 18.8
The Revised Standard Version

Sponsors of the Translation	Translators	Text	Translation Techniques	Characteristics
National Council of Churches	32 well-known scholars	OT: Masoretic Text NT: Improved, eclectic Greek Text	Revision of AV Literal, but not word-for-word translation	Dignified English ("thou" when addressing God) Sense paragraphs Many emendations Apocrypha Yahweh = LORD

national Council of Religious Education (some forty-five major denominations were members and formed part of the National Council of Churches), which set up a committee to determine the feasibility and necessity of making a new revision. Because of the Great Depression in the United States, money to undertake a major revision was not available until 1937. At that time the committee recommended a thorough revision of the American Standard Version but that it should remain within the tradition established by Tyndale. The goal was to "embody the best results of modern scholarship as to the meaning of the Scriptures, and express this meaning in English diction which is designed for use in public and private worship and preserves those qualities which have given to the King James Version a supreme place in English literature."[55] Thirty-two scholars, led by Luther Weigle of Yale Divinity School, were appointed, and each served free of charge. They worked in two contingents, one for the Old Testament and the other for the New. The New Testament on its own appeared in 1946; the Bible in its entirety, entitled *The Holy Bible Revised Standard Version*, was published September 30, 1952. According to Bruce Metzger it "was launched with an unprecedented publicity campaign."[56] The Apocrypha was added in 1957 to help make it acceptable to both Roman Catholics and Protestants.

Oxford University Press published an edition of the Revised Standard Version in 1962 entitled *The Oxford Annotated Bible*, under the editorship of Herbert G. May, Old Testament professor at the Graduate School of Theology, Oberlin College, and Bruce M. Metzger, professor of New Testament at Princeton Theological Seminary. This useful edition includes brief introductions and essays by various scholars, as well as exegetical footnotes on each page. Shortly after this, in 1965, a Roman Catholic edition of the New Testament Revised Standard Version was published in Great Britain with several minor changes. In 1971 a second edition of the New Testament was produced with a few modifications based upon improvements in the Greek text, but the most notable change was the reinsertion of several passages into the text (e.g., longer ending of Mark [16:9–20]; the woman caught in adultery [John 7:53–8:11]). In 1973 an ecumenical edition appeared, entitled The Common Bible, which was accepted by Roman Catholic, Protestant, and Eastern Orthodox churches. Since it did not, however, contain the entire canon of all these denominations, on May 19, 1977 a new edition, prepared by Oxford University Press, included the rest of the deuterocanonical books (i.e., 3 and 4 Macc. and Ps. 151), making it a truly ecumenical Bible.

The Policies of the Revisers

The most significant change of the Revised Standard Version from the Authorized Version was modernization of the language. The translators attempted to retain the dignity of the language without archaism and were no longer restricted to using one English word for a given Greek or Hebrew word. Bruce offers the following favorable evaluation:

This latest revision makes full use of the most recent textual and linguistic discoveries. Archaisms have been removed, but the language is not the American idiom of the mid-twentieth century but good literary English of a quality that is acknowledged as standard on both sides of the Atlantic. It has largely superseded the American Standard Version (or British Revised Version) as a study version, and has gone a considerable way towards replacing the Authorized Version for general purposes of Bible reading.[57]

Archaisms such as "speaketh" and "seeth" were replaced by "speaks" and "sees," respectively. Similarly, "thees" and "thous" were for the most part removed except in passages addressed to God. The difficult decision was made to employ "you" for Jesus' earthly life and "thou" after the resurrection, even though critics maintained that such usage took away from Jesus' divinity while on earth. The use of "you" for both singular and plural was also found to cause confusion:

> "Ask a sign of the LORD **your** [sing.] God; let it be deep as Sheol or high as heaven." But Ahaz said, "I will not ask, and I will not put the LORD to the test." And he said, "Hear then, O house of David! Is it too little for **you** [pl.] to weary men, that **you** [pl.] weary my God also? Therefore the Lord himself will give **you** [pl.] a sign." (Isa. 7:11–14 RSV)

> "Simon, Simon, behold, Satan demanded to have **you** [pl.], that he might sift **you** [pl.] like wheat, but I have prayed for **you** [sing.] that **your** [sing.] faith may not fail; and when **you** [sing.] have turned again, strengthen **your** [sing.] brethren." (Luke 22:31–32 RSV)

The appellation LORD has been substituted for the Authorized Version's "Jehovah" (1901) to designate the one true God of Israel. Stylistic features that are often thought of as Bible English have been removed or reduced, such as the Semitic idiom *And it came to pass* as well as the conjunction *and,* which frequently links Old Testament passages. Quotation marks have been introduced, though not without having to make some difficult deci-

sions; for example the Revised Standard Version indicates in John 3 that the words of Jesus end at verse 15 and verses 16–21 are the words of the Evangelist, whereas in the New International Version all of these verses are attributed to Jesus. Other helpful accommodations in the Revised Standard Version include dividing the text into sense paragraphs and printing poetic passages in a form that highlights their structure (which, in the case of the Old Testament, amounts to about 40 percent of the text).

A noticeable characteristic of the Revised Standard Version is the increased use of emendations—more than in any previous translation. The Old Testament mainly follows the traditional Masoretic Hebrew text, except in the case of uncertain or incorrect wording. Then readings from other versions are incorporated into the text, most of which have good textual support from various ancient versions. For example, in Genesis 4:8 the insertion of the quote from Cain, "Cain said to Abel his brother, 'Let us go out to the field,'" is necessary to the sense of the text and finds support in many versions. Similarly, in Psalm 145:13 the second sentence was added to furnish the missing verse beginning with *nûn* in the alphabetic acrostic and is supported by one Hebrew manuscript, the Septuagint, and the Syriac Peshitta: "Thy kingdom is an everlasting kingdom, and thy dominion endures throughout all generations. The LORD is faithful in all his words, and gracious in all his deeds." Readings that are less certain are noted by "cn," meaning "correction" (e.g., Ps. 2:11). In Judges 16:14 the revisers included fifteen words from the Septuagint that they believe had fallen out of the Hebrew text. At the time of translation of the Revised Standard Version the Isaiah Scroll from Qumran Cave 1 was available, and thirteen of its readings were preferred (e.g., Isa. 14:30; 49:24; 51:19), although they are designated in the footnotes simply as "one ancient Ms" or similarly.

The New Testament is based upon an eclectic Greek text, described by Frederick Grant:

the New Testament translator or reviser of today is forced to adopt the eclectic principle: each variant reading must be studied on its merits, and cannot be adopted or rejected by some rule of thumb, or by adherence to such a theory as that of the "Neutral Text." It is this eclectic principle that has guided us in the present Revision. The Greek text of this Revision is not that of Westcott-Hort, or Nestle, or Souter; though the readings we have adopted will as a rule, be found either in the text or the margin of the new (17th) edition of Nestle (Stuttgart, 1941).[58]

Although the Revised Standard Version is a fairly literal translation, the English is clear, understandable, and flows well, as seen in the following example:

"You are the salt of the earth; but if salt has lost its taste, how shall its saltness be restored? It is no longer good for anything except to be thrown out and trodden under foot by men. You are the light of the world. A city set on a hill cannot be hid. Nor do men light a lamp and put it under a bushel, but on a stand, and it gives light to all in the house. Let your light so shine before men, that they may see your good works and give glory to your Father who is in heaven." (Matt. 5:13–16)

The Lord's Prayer reads:

Our Father who art in heaven,
Hallowed be thy name.
Thy kingdom come,
Thy will be done,
    On earth as it is in heaven.
Give us this day our daily bread;
And forgive us our debts,
    As we also have forgiven our
    debtors;
And lead us not into temptation
    But deliver us from evil. (Matt.
    6:9–13)

The principles for the translation of this version have been set out in two handbooks: *An Introduction to the Revised Standard Version of the New Testament* (1946) and *An Introduction to the Revised Standard Version of the Old Testament* (1952).

Its Reception

Thomas Nelson and Sons published the Revised Standard Version in 1952 and in general it enjoyed a positive reception both in the United States and England. T. W. Manson, former New Testament professor at University of Manchester, spoke highly of it in a radio broadcast: "I like the Revised Standard Version; and I like it because it is reliable and because it speaks directly to the man in the pew in language he can reasonably be expected to understand."[59] It was not without detractors, however; in a letter to Weigle someone asked: "Who is this Tom Nelson who has written a new Bible? I don't want Tom Nelson's Bible. I want the Bible the way the Apostle James wrote it." (Presumably the writer thought the King James Bible was written by James the apostle!) Criticism was also levied against the version because its copyright owner, the National Council of Churches, was considered by some to be theologically liberal. Pamphlets and books were written criticizing this translation; a more dramatic demonstration is described by Bruce:

One American preacher was reported to have burned a copy of the R.S.V. with a blowlamp in his pulpit, remarking that it was like the devil because it was hard to burn. Anything more certainly calculated to make every family in the congregation acquire a copy for itself is hard to imagine; one could almost believe that the whole incident was an ingenious publicity stunt engineered by the sponsors of the new version![60]

Some critics claimed that the Revised Standard Version denied the virgin birth because Isaiah 7:14 reads "young maiden" instead of "virgin" for the Hebrew word עַלְמָה (ʿalmâ). The former is the more accurate translation, and the intent was not to undermine this teaching. Also severely criticized was the reading in John 3:16, "For God so loved the world that he gave his only Son" and not "only begotten Son" for the Greek word μονογενής (monogenēs). The logic behind this change was that this Greek word is not used exclusively for Jesus' relationship to his father but for human relationships as well, and thus "only son" reflects its more general usage.[61] Bruce describes the balance that the Revised Standard Version successfully achieved:

> But the committee of revisers which worked on the R.S.V. was sufficiently broadly based to make it unlikely that the revision would promote any particular or sectional interest. And in fact it has found widespread acceptance in the years since its appearance in a great variety of Christian communities, theologically conservative as well as theologically liberal. No change in Christian doctrine is involved or implied in the readings and renderings of the R.S.V.; every article of the historic faith of the Church can be established as readily and as plainly from it as from the older versions in whose tradition it stands.[62]

An Evaluation

This version has become one of the most popular in America, Canada, and England and is under continual revision (1962 and 1971). It was once thought that the New English Bible would eclipse the Revised Standard Version, but this has not been the case. This version is highly rated by Bruce who estimates that "for the English-speaking world as a whole there is no modern version of the Bible which comes so near as the R.S.V. does to making the all-purpose provision which the A.V. made for so many years."[63]

New American Standard Bible (1971)

Its History

Published in 1971 by the Lockman Foundation of La Habra, California (a nonprofit Christian corporation formed in 1942 to promote Christian education, evangelism, and, above all, Bible translation in several languages),[64] this translation claims to be a revision of the American Standard Version of 1901, remedying what the editors in the preface call

> a disturbing awareness that the American Standard Version of 1901 was fast disappearing from the scene. . . . THE LOCKMAN FOUNDATION felt an urgency to rescue this noble achievement from an inevitable demise, to preserve it as a heritage for coming generations, and to do so in such a form as the demands of passing time dictate.[65]

It also proposed to take advantage of more recent advances in textual criticism and to modernize the English. Working for more than ten years, Reuben Olson served as chairman of the editorial board that supervised the work of fifty-eight anonymous translators from a wide variety of denominational backgrounds, including Presbyterian, Methodist, Southern Baptist, Church of Christ, Nazarene, American Baptist, fundamentalist, Conservative Baptist, Free Methodist, Congregational, Disciples of Christ, Evangelical Free, Independent Baptist, Independent Mennonite, Assembly of God, North American Baptist, and other

Table 18.9
New American Standard Bible

Sponsors of the Translation	Translators	Text	Translation Techniques	Characteristics
Lockman Foundation, La Habra, California	58 anonymous scholars	OT: Biblia Hebraica NT: Nestle Greek Text (1957)	Revision of ASV Word-for-word translation	Dignified English ("thou" when addressing God) Verse paragraphs Few emendations No Apocrypha Yahweh = LORD

religious groups.[66] The New American Standard Bible has sold at least sixteen million copies and in 1977 was ranked second in Bible sales next to the Living Bible by *Christian Bookseller* magazine.[67]

The Policies of the Revisers

The guidelines for making this translation are set out in its foreword:

> The Editorial Board has a two-fold purpose in making this translation: to adhere as closely as possible to the original languages of the Holy Scriptures, and to make the translation in a fluent and readable style according to current English usage. (This translation follows the principles used in the American Standard Version 1901 known as the Rock of Biblical Honesty.)[68]

According to Lewis, however, this translation differs significantly from the American Standard Version: "the gulf separating the ASV and the NASB is such that the NASB must be evaluated as a new translation. One cannot assume that it is what its title seems to imply—an update of the ASV."[69] Since the copyright on the American Standard Version had run out, the Lockman Foundation was free to use or even modify the text.

The Translation

The New American Standard Bible retains several of the characteristics of the American Standard Version, such as the use of the second-person singular form *you* instead of "thou" except when addressing divinity and italicizing words not present in the Hebrew or Greek texts but necessary to the English translation. Unlike the American Standard Version, the New American Standard Bible reverts to the principles followed in the Geneva Bible (1560) and the Authorized Version (1611) wherein each verse begins a new paragraph. "LORD" was chosen as the personal name of God because research showed that "Jehovah" (as it appears in the American Standard Version) was an incorrect rendering. Names like *Jehovah-jireh* (Gen. 22:14), *Jehovah-nissi* (Exod. 17:15), and *Jehovah-shalom* (Judg. 6:24) are therefore translated in the New American Standard Bible as "The LORD Will Provide," "The LORD is My Banner," and "The LORD is Peace," respectively. Its interesting system of capitalization is described by Lewis:

> Unlike the KJV, which capitalized the beginning of each verse, the NASB starts verses with lower-case letters when they are not the beginning of sentences. Those verses which begin a paragraph are numbered in boldface type; if a paragraph begins with a verse, the first letter of the first word is in boldface type. This indicator can easily be overlooked. I Corinthians 12:31 and the middle of Isaiah 59:15 are the beginnings of paragraphs and therefore begin with a boldface letter. The first word of each chapter is printed with all capitals. So the first word of Isaiah 4:1 is in capitals, even though Isaiah 3:16–4:1 is treated as one paragraph.[70]

Words referring to divinity are capitalized (e.g., "He" [Gen. 1:27]; "Us" [Gen. 1:26; 3:22]) as well as "Spirit" when referring to the Holy Spirit (Gen. 1:2). Similarly epithets and pronouns thought to refer to the Messiah are capitalized ("Anointed," "Son," "King" [Ps. 2:2, 6, 12]; "Holy One" [Ps. 16:10]), although the practice is not consistent ("him" [Gen. 3:15; 49:10]; "star," "scepter" [Num. 24:17]). An innovation was to print Old Testament quotations appearing in the New Testament entirely in smaller capital letters, noting parallel passages in the margins. The New American Standard Bible inserts quotation marks (the American Standard Version does not use them) and prints more material in poetic form than does the American Standard Version, even including the prophets, which are in semipoetic form.

The New American Standard Bible follows a critical text significantly different from the American Standard Version in both the Old and New Testaments. The Old Testament follows Rudolph Kittel's *Biblia Hebraica*, which was the most recent critical Masoretic Text (1949), taking into account other versions (e.g., Judg. 16:14), as well as material from the Dead Sea Scrolls (e.g., the Isaiah Scroll was used in about thirteen places [as in the Revised Standard Version]). While the editors of the New American Standard Bible claim to have followed the twenty-third edition of the Nestle Greek Text (1957), deviations can be detected in a number of cases (e.g., Matt. 6:13; 12:47; 18:11; 23:14; Mark 7:16; 9:44, 46; 11:26; 15:28; Luke 24:12; etc.). Kubo and Specht conclude that "A number of verses resting on doubtful MS authority have been reintroduced into the text from the margin."[71]

The New American Standard Bible even tries to give some indication as to verb tense, though this is a much debated topic now (e.g., the ingressive aorist denotes entrance into an act or state: "he became afraid" [Matt. 14:30]; "they all got drowsy" [Matt. 25:5]; "they became silent" [Luke 20:26]). The "historic present" noted with an asterisk in this translation is a Greek present tense form used to describe a past event; current research suggests it may have been used to describe vivid action as if it were just happening (appearing in the Gospels, especially the Gospel of Mark [approximately 151 times]).[72] Another distinctive feature of the New American Standard Bible is that it attempts to indicate questions which anticipate a negative answer: "Can this man be the Son of David?" is translated as "This *man* cannot be the Son of David, can he?" (Matt. 12:23).

Its Reception

This translation was well received among conservative evangelicals. The edi-

tors were particularly careful not to offend their conservative readership, avoiding the more controversial translations of the Revised Standard Version (1952) (e.g., in Isa. 7:14 "virgin" appears instead of "maiden," and the Greek word μονογενής [*monogenēs*] is rendered "only begotten" when referring to Jesus and simply "only" for anyone else).

An Evaluation

In general this translation is superior to many of its predecessors in its usage of ancient manuscripts and improvements in English vocabulary, as demonstrated in the translation of the Lord's Prayer:

> Our Father who art in heaven,
> Hallowed be Thy name.
> Thy kingdom come.
> Thy will be done,
> On earth as it is in heaven.
> Give us this day our daily bread.
> And forgive us our debts, as we also
>   have forgiven our debtors.
> And do not lead us into temptation,
>   but deliver us from evil. [For
>   Thine is the kingdom, and the
>   power, and the glory, forever.
>   Amen.] (Matt. 6:9–13)

The words in brackets in the last verse are a good example of Kubo and Specht's comment that wording with doubtful manuscript authority has been reintroduced into the text.

The preface of the New American Standard Bible states that one of its primary goals is to produce a translation with "fluent and readable style according to current English usage,"[73] but in many places

Table 18.10
Comparisons of Terms (ASV, NASB)

Passage	American Standard Version	New American Standard Bible
Genesis 4:1	son	manchild
Ecclesiastes 12:5	desire shall fail	caperberry is ineffective
Jeremiah 20:7	thou hast persuaded me	you deceived me
Hebrews 9:16, 17	testament for *diathēkē*	will
Luke 23:45	the sun's light failing	the sun being obscured (is not as accurate; a cloud could also obscure the light of the sun)

the translators have sacrificed English style and structure to maintain that of the Greek or Hebrew texts (e.g., "As for Hannah, she was speaking in her heart" [1 Sam. 1:13]; "The LORD, He is God" [1 Kings 18:39]; "Me and My Father" [John 15:24]). They even suggest that maintaining the order and style of the original texts achieves a more accurate translation: "Words are faithfully rendered in the New American Standard Bible even to conjunctions such as 'and' in the belief that these, too, helped mirror the writer's style and manner of expression. These are often ignored in free translation."[74] The literalness and accuracy of this translation makes it an excellent tool for those who wish to do detailed biblical study but whose understanding of Hebrew or Greek is limited. Some critics, however, have argued that this translation is merely a pony rather than a translation, arguing that a good translation transfers the content and emphasis of the Greek or Hebrew texts into accurate English idiom instead of mirroring the order and style of the original languages. There are also passages where the translators have used archaic or less accurate terminology than is found in the American Standard Version (see table 18.10).[75]

It is general policy for translations to be as theologically neutral as possible when translating passages that may be interpreted in various ways or where theological biases may affect the translation, but the *New American Standard Bible* shows a clear premillennial preference, as Lewis points out:

> The translators chose "as" in the phrase "the mountain of the house of the Lord will be established as the chief of the mountains" (Isa. 2:2; Mic. 4:1), even though the margin acknowledges that "on" is literal. The rendering, "And those who will walk by this rule, peace and mercy *be* upon them, and upon the Israel of God" (Gal. 6:16) makes it more likely that the *kai* will be taken as coordinate rather than as explanatory. In the marginal notes, "generation" regularly carries the alternate "race" (Mark 13:30; Luke 21:32). "He is near," though with a marginal note "it" (Mark 13:29), turns

the thought of the passage to the second coming. In Revelation 5:10, the Greek present tense is rendered "will reign" where the ASV had "they reign." Revelation 20:4 had "they came to life and reigned with Christ for a thousand years," which supports the contrast the premillennialist likes to make in the verse. The ASV had "they lived," which is a more literal rendering for the Greek aorist, *ezēsan*. . . . As previously noticed, the NASB carries a page heading "The Millenium" [*sic*] for the section.[76]

Whereas the prime objective of the Authorized Version was to render an impartial translation in places where the text is unclear, the Revised Version, American Standard Version, and the New American Standard Bible do not make this claim.

While the New American Standard Bible contains many passages where the translation is clearer and uses more modern terminology than do many of its predecessors, its objective of adhering to the original Greek or Hebrew word order often hinders the fluency of the English. Its theological presuppositions will probably make it unacceptable to some Christians, but Carl E. Armerding and W. Ward Gasque think that "despite its obvious limitations and idiosyncrasies, the NASB seems destined to a useful life, particularly among students in Bible schools and evangelical seminaries."[77] An updated version of this translation appeared in 1999.

King James II Version (1971)

Its History

This Bible, published by Associated Publishers and Authors, was produced by Jay Green, who claims in the preface that "it is certain that God's people do not want a new Bible! They just want the old one in a form they can read and understand and trust."[78] He asserts that the modern translations, English Revised Version (1885), the American Standard Version (1901), the Revised Standard Version (1952), and the New English Bible (1970), are slanted and

Table 18.11
King James II Version

Sponsors of the Translation	Translator	Text	Translation Techniques	Characteristics
Jay Green; published by Associated Publishers and Authors	Jay Green	Seems to be merely an updating of the Authorized Version	Revision of AV Word-for-word translation	Modern English Verse paragraphs Follows *Textus Receptus* No Apocrypha Yahweh = LORD OT quotations enclosed by quotation marks

dangerous because they use different Hebrew and Greek texts from the Authorized Version of 1611: "Having tilted the foundation in their theological direction, they then paraphrased, interpreted, deleted and added to God's words without regard to the evidencial [*sic*] facts available in all the manuscripts, the versions, and the fathers of the first centuries."[79] He further states that "A pre-study of textual criticism encompassing more than 1000 hours convinced us the best text was that used by Tyndale and the KJV scholars."[80] As we have already seen, however, Tyndale and the Authorized Version did not use the same Greek text, nor did Tyndale complete the Old Testament. This seems to matter little to Green, being convinced that the *Textus Receptus* is the most accurate text of the New Testament. Needless to say, the vast majority of modern scholars and modern translations disagree with the principles suggested here by Green.

The Policies of the Reviser

Green purports to have followed the principle of literal translation: "This Bible is translated word-for-word in an attempt to give a literal rendition of each and every one of God's words. . . . None of God's words were left out."[81] The latter statement was a not-so-subtle attack on other translations that omit phrases not found in the earliest manuscripts but are present in the *Textus Receptus*.

The Translation

Robert G. Bratcher evaluates this translation:

What does it all add up to? Not quite a bowdlerized King James, but essentially one in which archaic and obsolescent words and expressions have been replaced by current English. This is harmless enough; few would object to it. But KJII goes beyond this; in places it changes not just the wording but also the meaning of the text. In Isaiah 7:14, where the KJV faithfully translates "(a virgin) . . . shall call his name Immanuel," KJII has "they shall call His name Immanuel," in order to make it correspond exactly with the Greek text cited in Matthew 1:23.[82]

Several passages have been changed from the Authorized Version. For instance, in 1 Samuel 6:19 the King James Bible states that 50,070 men died (or literally "fiftie thousand, and threescore and tenne men"; the Hebrew says "70 men and 50,000 men") whereas the King James II Version changed it to "seventy men—fifty chief men," selecting the questionable interpretation of "chief" instead of "thousand" for the Hebrew word *ʾelep*. In Matthew 21:1–7, Green is apparently unsure whether one or two animals appear. In Zechariah 9:9 the reading of the King James Bible was changed from "upon an ass, and upon a colt" to "on an ass, even a colt"; the quote in Matthew agrees with this reading, but later in the verse the King James II Version translation reads "And they put their coats on them" (Matt. 21:7).

The language of the King James II Version is on occasion more difficult or inferior to the King James Version; for example, the baby Jesus is wrapped in a "navel-band" rather than "swaddling clothes" (Luke 2:7, 12). Or the phrase Mary "keeping them afresh in her heart" (Luke 2:19 KJII) is hardly an improvement over "pondered them in her heart" (KJV). The Lord's Prayer reads:

> Our Father, who is in Heaven, Hallowed be Your name.
> Let Your kingdom come, and let Your will be done, on earth as it is in Heaven.
> Give us today our daily bread, and forgive us our debts as we also forgive our debtors.
> And do not lead us into temptation, but deliver us from evil. For Yours is the kingdom and the power and the glory, forever, Amen. (Matt. 6:9–13)

An Evaluation

Armerding and Gasque express doubt as to whether this version would have gained an audience had it not its own distribution agency (Religious Book Discount House).[83] They further state that "it is difficult to find any particular in which this version is an improvement over what it was designed to replace."[84] For those to whom the wording of the King James Bible is preferred over newer translations, Bratcher soundly recommends "that they continue to read, use, memorize, and distribute the original, not this substitute."[85]

The New King James Version (NT, 1979; Entire Bible, 1982)

Its History

Sam Moore, president of the Thomas Nelson Corporation, which claims to be the world's leading Bible publisher, believed that the vast majority of Americans prefer the King James Bible (or Authorized Version), and thus he proposed a new revision of it. While several modern translations have gained popularity, it is still a fact that the King James Bible is favored by about one-third of America's readers of the English Bible. This version was therefore an attempt to modernize the language of the King James Bible without compromising its text or translation principles. Advertising for the New King James Version claims that it is the fifth major revision of the King James Version and the first since 1769. To arrive at this number the publishers counted only the revisions of 1629, 1638, 1762 (by Thomas Paris), and 1769 (by Benjamin Blayney) as legitimate, discounting many other revisions, namely, the Revised Version (1881–1885), American Standard Version (1901), Revised Standard Version (1952), New American Standard Bible (1971), and King James II Version (1971).

The Policies of the Revisers

More than 130 evangelical scholars are said to have worked on this translation;[86] the executive director for the New Testament was Arthur Farstad (Dallas Theological Seminary) and for the Old Tes-

Table 18.12
New King James Version

Sponsors of the Translation	Translators	Text	Translation Techniques	Characteristics
Sam Moore, president of Thomas Nelson Corporation	More than 130 evangelical scholars	OT: Biblia Hebraica Stuttgartensia (1977) NT: Revised *Textus Receptus* (1881)	Revision of AV Word-for-word translation	Updated English Sense paragraphs No Apocrypha Yahweh = LORD

tament was originally William White (author/editor) and later James D. Price (Temple Baptist Theological Seminary, Chattanooga, TN). Individual scholars worked separately, submitting completed sections to their respective executive directors. Each section was then passed to William H. McDowell, the English editor who checked grammatical accuracy, literary beauty, and effective communication. A final review was performed by a separate executive committee; any changes at this stage had to be passed by majority vote. The translators realized that the vocabulary of the King James Bible had undergone many changes throughout the years, and they saw themselves as one more step in this process. Still, it was a difficult task, as Kubo and Specht affirm:

> to produce an English Bible that retains as much of the classic KJV as possible, while at the same time bringing the English up-to-date. This is a difficult objective to achieve. It may well meet the religious needs of those Christians who sincerely believe that the KJV is *the* English Bible, but at the same time find its antiquated vocabulary and grammatical structure a handicap to understanding the message the Bible carries. Time alone can tell how well the new version will be used and accepted.[87]

The Translation

Advertisements also claimed that "the entire text of the original King James Version is included in the New King James," but the original version included the Apocrypha, which would not appeal to this version's constituents. It has become a popular translation, published in many different styles and sizes, such as New King James Version Little Hands Bible (ages 5–8), Precious Moments™ Baby Bible (for very young children), Open Bible Expanded Edition, Scofield Reference Bible, Ryrie Study Bible, Businessmen's and Businesswomen's Bibles, and Slimline New Testaments.

Like the King James Version, the New King James Version translates the name for God as LORD, and words not found in the

original text but necessary to render an understandable English translation are set off by italics (except in the 1979 printing of the New Testament). In contrast, however, the New King James Version prints each verse as a separate paragraph, uses the relative pronoun *who* when referring to persons, and prints some parts in poetic format. Pronouns are capitalized when referring to divinity, and all titles and terms are capitalized when they are applied to any member of the Trinity; for example: "Seed" (Gen. 3:15), "Him" (Gen. 49:10), "Scepter" (Num. 24:17), "Son" (Isa. 7:14), "Child" (Isa. 9:6), "Rod" and "Branch" (Isa. 11:1), "Servant" (Isa. 52:13), and "Son of Man" (Dan. 7:13).

The primary text for the Old Testament of the New King James Version was *Biblia Hebraica Stuttgartensia* (1977); texts used for comparison purposes included the Rabbinic Bible of 1516, as well as Greek, Latin, other versions, and the Dead Sea Scrolls. Significant variations from the text of the King James Version are noted in the footnotes. Text-critical differences are most noticeable in the New Testament: modern translators generally follow the modern critical editions of the New Testament, whereas translators of the New King James Version retained the *Textus Receptus*. The text chosen was prepared by F. H. A. Scrivener, published by Oxford University Press in 1881, for its editors claim this Greek text to be the closest to the King James Version as revised in 1769 by Benjamin Blayney.[88] The publishers offered four reasons for their choice of this text:

> First, to use a later text would produce something other than a KJV. Second, a growing number of scholars (obviously including the moving spirits of this N.T. revision) recognize that the Byzantine text type is older than the earliest extant Byzantine manuscripts. Third, preparers of the NKJV claim that Erasmus's few manuscripts on which the *Textus Receptus* rests are representative of all the Byzantine manuscripts. The fourth reason assumes that the true text is that represented by the KJV and asserts that the tendency of recent revisers is to remove words and verses from the text.[89]

Evidence presented earlier in this work shows these reasons to be weak; evidence overwhelmingly supports the superiority of current critical Greek texts. Harold Scanlin points out that ironically, according to the footnotes, the New King James Version lacks the support of the majority of Greek texts in about 300 passages even though it claims to use the Majority Text.[90] For example, Revelation 22:19 reads, "God shall take away his part from the Book of Life, from the holy city, and *from* the things which are written in this book," although a footnote in the New King James Version admits that the Majority Text actually reads "the tree of life" and that no Greek text reads "book of life." This reading can perhaps be traced to Erasmus's translation of the last six verses from the Latin Vulgate into Greek (in Latin *libro* [book] is very similar to *ligno* [tree]). Similarly, the *Textus Receptus* of Acts 9:5–6 includes two entire sentences not found in Greek texts but are probably attributable to a Latin manuscript. The New King James Version translates them as, "'*It is* hard for you to kick against the goads.' So he, trembling and astonished said, 'Lord, what do you want me to do?'" Scrivener himself stated that his text differs from the text followed by the King James Version of 1611 in about 160 places. Of more value in this translation are the 880 marginal notes that call attention to variant readings of the text. The most common ones make references to "N" (Nestle's twenty-sixth edition of the *Novum Testamentum Graece* [Greek New Testament, 1979]), "U" (United Bible Societies' *Greek New Testament*, 1975), and "M" (Majority Text rendered by Zane Hodges and Arthur Farstad, 1982), citing where they differ from the text of the New King James Version.[91]

The Lord's Prayer reads:

Our Father in heaven,
Hallowed be Your name.
Your kingdom come.
Your will be done
On earth as *it is* in heaven.
Give us this day our daily bread.
And forgive us our debts,
As we forgive our debtors.
And do not lead us into temptation,
But deliver us from the evil one.

For Yours is the kingdom and the
power and the glory forever.
Amen. (Matt. 6:9–13)

An Evaluation

While a great deal of vocabulary has been updated and significantly improved, the New King James Version is still encumbered with awkward phraseology and style. Sven Soderlund comments that it has "a curious mixture of Elizabethan ecclesiastical style with glosses of twentieth century vocabulary and grammar,"[92] and Heber Peacock quips "the voice is Jacob's voice, but the hands are the hands of Esau."[93] Soderlund's reference to Elizabethan style refers to such phrases as "day of his espousals" (Song 3:11), "Hew down trees" (Jer. 6:6), "purge His threshing floor" (Matt. 3:12), and "the wind *was* boisterous" (Matt. 14:30). Outdated vocabulary not readily understood by the average modern reader includes: "feigned" (1 Sam. 21:13), "winebibber(s)" (Prov. 23:20; Matt. 11:19; Luke 7:34), "eventide" (Isa. 17:14), "the matrix of My mother" (Isa. 49:1), "dandled" (Isa. 66:12), "offscouring" (Lam. 3:45; 1 Cor. 4:13), "paramours" Ezek. 23:20), and "pinions" (Job 39:13).

It is doubtful that the New King James Version will gain prominence over the King James Version, as Lewis notes: "After seven years, sales statistics from *Publishers Weekly* (1990) rank the NIV and KJV one and two in sales with NKJV (despite its impressive sales record) never more than third. . . . The bottom line is whether the drive to persuade the public that the *Textus Receptus* and the Majority Text are superior to the Critical Text will succeed. If it fails, the NKJV will be a passing phenomenon."[94]

New Revised Standard Version (1989)

Its History

The Revised Standard Version has become a very popular Bible since it was

Table 18.13
New Revised Standard Version

Sponsors of the Translation	Translators	Text	Translation Techniques	Characteristics
National Council of Churches	30 well-known scholars	OT: *Biblia Hebraica Stuttgartensia* NT: United Bible Societies' Greek Text (3rd edition, 1966; corrected 1983)	Literal as possible, as free as necessary	Modern English (no "thees" or "thous") Sense paragraphs Poetic structure Many emendations OT quotations indented

first published. In 1971 a second edition of the Revised Standard Version New Testament was published, but the Old Testament had never been revised. In 1974 the Policies Committee of the Revised Standard Version proposed that a complete revision of the Revised Standard Version be undertaken, the reasons behind which are explained by Bruce Metzger, chairman of the new revision:

> Following the publication of the RSV Old Testament in 1952, significant advances were made in the discovery and interpretation of documents in Semitic languages related to Hebrew. In addition to the information that had become available in the late 1940s from the Dead Sea texts of Isaiah and Habakkuk, subsequent acquisitions from the same area brought to light many other early copies of all the books of the Hebrew Scriptures (except Esther), though most of these copies are fragmentary. During the same period early Greek manuscript copies of books of the New Testament also became available.[95]

The translation committee for the New Revised Standard Version, still at work, is composed of thirty men and women from Protestant, Roman Catholic, Eastern Orthodox, and Jewish groups, many of whom are well-known scholars from large institutions: Joseph Blenkinsopp (Notre Dame), Paul D. Hanson (Harvard), Walter Harrelson (Vanderbilt), William Holladay (Andover-Newton), S. Dean McBride (Garrett), Patrick Miller (Union), and Marvin Pope (Yale). The group changed, however, during the fifteen years of translation work due to deaths and resignations.

The New Revised Standard Version became available in 1989, with and without the Apocrypha. On May 19, 1989, the National Council of Churches met in Louisville, Kentucky, to authorize the revision for use in the churches of its membership, and the motion was overwhelmingly approved. Even though this translation is intended to replace the Revised Standard Version, the National Council of Churches had agreed to let the Revised Standard Version continue in publication at least until 1995 (though it is still being published).

The Policies of the Translators

Unlike many of the more modern versions, which were intended to be new translations (e.g., the New English Bible, Good News Bible, New International Version), this revision was an attempt to further the line of English Bibles begun by William Tyndale in 1525 and continued through to the Revised Standard Version. Metzger explains its purpose:

> This new version seeks to preserve all that is best in the English Bible as it has been known and used through the years. It is intended for use in public reading and congregational worship, as well as in private study, instruction, and meditation. We have resisted the temptation to introduce terms and phrases that merely reflect current moods, and have tried to put the message of the Scriptures in simple, enduring words and expressions that are worthy to stand in the great tradition of the King James Bible and its predecessors.[96]

While the primary principle for this translation is "As literal as possible, as free as necessary,"[97] it is by and large a literal translation of the text. The practice of the Revised Standard Version is continued wherein masculine pronouns refer to God and Christ, but elsewhere there is a strong emphasis on inclusive gender language wherever possible; for instance, in John 12:32 the Revised Standard Version reads "men," whereas the New Revised Standard Version rendering is "all people." Another significant difference between the Revised Standard Version and the New Revised Standard Version is that the latter no longer uses the archaic second person forms when addressing God. Pronouns referring to God are not capitalized in keeping with the practice of all ancient languages as well as the King James Version.

The Translation

The text is clearly divided into paragraphs, but the addition of bold-print paragraph headings would be a great improvement. A more difficult problem, however, is that the footnote letters are almost indistinguishable from the main text.

The Old Testament

The text for the Old Testament derives from the latest version of the Hebrew text (*Biblia Hebraica Stuttgartensia*, 1977; 2d ed. emendata, 1983), though it appears to rely upon variant readings found in the ancient versions even more heavily than does the Revised Standard Version (e.g., "he began to weaken," Judg. 16:19; "Now Saul committed a very rash act," 1 Sam. 14:24; "Ishbaal," 2 Sam. 2:8).[98] Many conjectural readings of the Revised Standard Version have been continued (e.g., "with trembling kiss his feet," Ps. 2:11–12; "after his glory," Zech. 2:8), and the New Revised Standard Version notes even more passages than its predecessor where the Hebrew text is supposedly unclear (e.g., "grievous destruction," Mic. 2:10; "shatterer," Nah. 2:1; "swarms," Nah. 3:17; "healthy," Zech. 11:16).[99] The editors use the abbreviation

"cn" to indicate a "correction" in the text, as did the Revised Standard Version. In the Book of Zechariah alone the Revised Standard Version indicates that there were six corrections (4:12; 6:6; 9:1, 15; 10:11; 13:5), whereas the New Revised Standard Version notes eight (2:8; 4:12; 6:6, 10; 9:1, 15; 13:5; 14:6). One of the longest additions, appearing at the end of 1 Samuel 10, is based upon a more recently edited Qumran manuscript (4QSam^a) with additional support from Josephus *Antiquities of the Jews* (6.5.1 §§68–71)[100] and reads

> Now Nahash, king of the Ammonites, had been grievously oppressing the Gadites and the Reubenites. He would gouge out the right eye of each of them and would not grant Israel a deliverer. No one was left of the Israelites across the Jordan whose right eye Nahash, king of the Ammonites, had not gouged out. But there were seven thousand men who had escaped from the Ammonites and had entered Jabesh-gilead.

It is doubtful that there is enough textual evidence to warrant its inclusion in the text.[101]

The New Testament

The text for the New Testament comes from the United Bible Societies' Greek Text (1966; 3d ed.; corrected, 1983; also consulting the fourth edition). Metzger lists only three places where the editors believed the alternatives readings to be superior; "become" (*genesthai*, Acts 26:28, though not listed in the footnotes); "gentle" (*epioi*, 1 Thess. 2:7); and "with all the saints. Amen" (Rev. 22:21).[102] Several passages now appear in brackets in the text of the New Revised Standard Version instead of merely in footnotes as in the Revised Standard Version (Luke 22:43–44; 23:34; John 7:53–8:11); even the *Comma Johanneum* (1 John 5:7–8) is given a footnote in the New Revised Standard Version (it is not mentioned in the Revised Standard Version). The endings to the Gospel of Mark now appear in double brackets and are labeled "THE SHORTER ENDING OF MARK" or "THE LONGER ENDING OF MARK" (previously they

Table 18.14
Comparison of Terms (RSV, NRSV)

Passage	Revised Standard Version	New Revised Standard Version
Deuteronomy 13:13	base fellows	scoundrels
Proverbs 6:6, 9	sluggard	lazybones
Ecclesiastes 9:18	sinner	bungler
Mark 11:18	astonished	spellbound
Luke 18:11	unjust	rogues
Acts 7:35	judge	liberator
Acts 17:5	wicked fellows of the rabble	ruffians
Acts 24:1	spokesman	attorney

were labeled without double brackets). Another addition to the ending of the Gospel of Mark is called the "Freer Logion" and appears in a footnote in the New Revised Standard Version; it reads:

> And they excused themselves, saying, "This age of lawlessness and unbelief is under Satan, who does not allow the truth and power of God to prevail over the unclean things of the spirits. Therefore reveal your righteousness now"— thus they spoke to Christ. And Christ replied to them, "The term of years of

Satan's power has been fulfilled, but other terrible things draw near. And for those who have sinned I was handed over to death, that they may return to the truth and sin no more, that they may inherit the spiritual and imperishable glory of righteousness that is in heaven."

In an effort to make the language as accurate and clear as possible the following words from the Revised Standard Version have been changed in the New Revised Standard Version (see table 18.14). Besides removing archaic second-person forms (i.e., "thy," "thou"), the revisors have changed other antiquated wording of the Revised Standard Version (e.g., "thither," Isa. 55:10; "from thence," Isa. 52:11; Amos 6:2; "whence," Jonah 1:8; Nah. 3:7; "harken," Isa. 46:3, 12). Modern designations for time were chosen (e.g., "noon" for "sixth hour," Mark 15:33; John 19:14; "four o'clock in the afternoon" for "tenth hour," John 1:39; "nine o'clock" for "third hour of the day," Acts 2:15). Some vestiges of archaic language, however, remain (e.g., "after the manner of women," Gen. 18:11; "noontide," Isa. 38:10; "he shall work his will," Dan. 11:28) and occasionally cubits are used as measures of distances (e.g., Num. 35:5; Ezek. 41:1). The intelligible but slightly dated language of this translation is exemplified in the Lord's Prayer:

> Our Father in heaven,
>   hallowed be your name.
> Your kingdom come.
>   Your will be done,
>   on earth as it is in heaven.
>   Give us this day our daily bread.
>   And forgive us our debts,

Table 18.15
Revisions of the Authorized Version of 1611

Authorized Version
The English Revised Version (NT, 1881; entire Bible, 1885)
The American Standard Version (1901)
The Revised Standard Version (1952)
New American Standard Bible (1971)
King James II Version (1971)
New King James Version (1982)
New Revised Standard Version (1989)

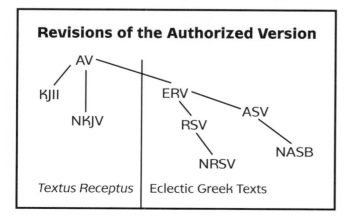

Revisions of the Authorized Version

AV
KJII
NKJV
ERV
ASV
RSV
NASB
NRSV

Textus Receptus | Eclectic Greek Texts

as we also have forgiven our
debtors.
And do not bring us to the time
of trial,
but rescue us from the evil
one. (Matt. 6:9–13)

The phrase "And do not bring us to the time of trial" is somewhat vague and differs significantly from the Revised Standard Version.

An Evaluation

The New Revised Standard Version has achieved a nice balance; it is dignified enough to be memorized and read in public yet lucid enough to be read in private. Thus it appears to have accomplished its purpose as described by Metzger:

> That message [the biblical message] must not be disguised in phrases that are no longer clear, or hidden under words that have changed or lost their meaning; it must be presented in language that is direct and plain and meaningful to people today. It is the hope and prayer of the translators that this version of the Bible may continue to hold a large place in congregational life and to speak to all readers, young and old alike, helping them to understand and believe and respond to its message.[103]

Lewis correctly states that it is unlikely to have the same "fiery reception" as its predecessor did in some circles.[104] This is not because the New Revised Standard Version has changed the more controversial readings (e.g., Isa. 7:14; John 3:16), but instead these translations have become more accepted. It still contains controversial elements especially regarding textual decisions (e.g., 1 Sam. 10:27–28; Luke 22:43–44), which are just as disputed as some of the translations of the Revised Standard Version were in their day; in this way it also carries on the tradition of the Revised Standard Version.

There is no doubt that the King James Bible has had a significant influence upon the English-speaking population, and while many people will continue to use this version due to familiarity or even because they believe the text is preferable, many newer versions are much more accurate and understandable to modern readers.

For Further Reading

Bruce, F. F. *History of the Bible in English: From the Earliest Versions*, 96–112, 135–52. 3d ed. New York: Oxford University Press, 1978.

———. *The Books and the Parchments*, 211–27. 5th ed. London: Marshall Pickering, 1991.

Cadoux, C. J. "The Revised Version and After." In *The Bible in Its Ancient and English Versions*, ed. H. W. Robinson, 235–74. Oxford: Clarendon, 1954.

Ewert, D. *From Ancient Tablets to Modern Translations: A General Introduction to the Bible*, 197–211. Grand Rapids: Zondervan, 1983.

Greenslade, S. L. "English Versions of the Bible, A.D. 1525–1611." In *CHB*, 3:141–74.

Isaacs, J. "The Sixteenth-Century English Versions." In *The Bible in Its Ancient and English Versions*, ed. H. W. Robinson, 146–95. Oxford: Clarendon, 1954.

———. "The Authorized Version and After." In *The Bible in Its Ancient and English Versions*, ed. H. W. Robinson, 196–234. Oxford: Clarendon, 1954.

Kenyon, F. G. *Our Bible and the Ancient Manuscripts*. Rev. A. W. Adams, 303–19. New York: Harper, 1958.

Kubo, S., and W. F. Specht. *So Many Versions? Twentieth-Century English Versions of the Bible*, 222–30, 273–307. Rev. ed. Grand Rapids: Zondervan, 1983.

Lewis, J. P. *The English Bible from KJV to NIV: A History and Evaluation*, 27–128, 165–97, 329–47. 2d ed. Grand Rapids: Baker, 1991.

MacGregor, G. *The Bible in the Making*, 103–64. Washington, DC: University Press of America, 1982.

Partridge, A. C. *English Biblical Translation*, 105–79. London: Andre Deutsch, 1973.

Price, I. M. *The Ancestry of Our English Bible*, 225–320. 3d ed. New York: Harper & Row, 1956.

Weigle, L. A. "English Versions since 1611." In *CHB*, 3:361–82.

Appendix 3

The King James Debate

In one sense it is amazing that a Bible translation written almost four hundred years ago continues to have such appeal; some people consider the King James Bible the only authoritative Bible translation. However, it must also be said that hesitancy to try one of the more modern translations may be overcome once it is seen how much clearer and more understandable these translations are. We live in a society where the average person changes their place of residence every five or six years, buys a different car about every four years, and changes jobs about five times during their lifetimes and yet we are reluctant to change our Bible translation.

The King James Version (Authorized Version of 1611)

This version, a good translation for the time that it was written, was based upon Erasmus's Greek New Testament, which used about six manuscripts, none earlier than the tenth century. Later Erasmus's text was improved by comparing it with the Complutensian Polyglot, but it still was based exclusively upon medieval manuscripts. Approximately twelve passages contain readings not attested by any Greek manuscripts (e.g., Acts 9:6 reads "And he trembling and astonished said, 'Lord, what wilt thou have me to do?'" [KJV]). Erasmus's Greek text was published many times in the years to follow; in time it became known as the *Textus Receptus*, which does not mean received from God but denotes the standard text of the seventeenth century.

Since the King James Bible was the standard English translation for so long, it has a significant and loyal readership. There are at least three levels of adherents to the King James Bible:[105]

1. Those who prefer its majesty and reverence, being most familiar with this Bible or having used it for much of their lives.
2. Those who believe that the text is to be preferred.
3. Those who believe that it is the only authoritative text and that it has been preserved by God through the ages.

The modern King James debate enters at level 3, wherein a few vocal evangelicals argue that the text of the King James Version preserves the original Greek text better than does any other version. By contrast, the majority of modern versions of the New Testament are based on what is called an eclectic text, which means that they are not slavishly dependent upon one text type but evaluate each specific passage and determine its reading based upon its own individual merits. Hundreds of manuscripts are examined to determine which reading is best supported by the evidence as original.

Arguments Used for the Priority of the *Textus Receptus*

Those who maintain that the *Textus Receptus* is the most accurate Greek text do so according to the following lines of argument.

Existence of Early Byzantine Texts

One of the most damaging arguments against the priority of the Byzantine text type (or the *Textus Receptus*, though these terms are not synonymous since the *Textus Receptus* is based on only about six Byzantine manuscripts) is that no manuscripts from this family date earlier than the mid-fourth century, whereas other text families have significant early manuscript evidence. Those who hold to the priority of the *Textus Receptus* argue that early manuscripts from this family did exist but either they have not yet been uncovered in any finds or have been destroyed by climate and constant use. It is surprising, however, that no early manuscripts have been found in locations where climate is not a factor (e.g., similar to what happened in the Cairo Genizah or St. Catherine's Monastery).

Incorrect Text-Critical Methods

Those who prefer the *Textus Receptus* argue that the text-critical methods used by most modern translations (initially developed by Westcott and Hort) are incorrect and that in reality the Byzantine text-type is closer to the original. Two principles of modern textual criticism are generally challenged. First, they claim that the majority of extant manuscripts support the *Textus Receptus*, and thus it must be the more correct text. It is important to remember, however, that the *Textus Receptus* first derived from only a few Greek manuscripts and that the majority of extant texts differ in many particulars from the *Textus Receptus*. Moreover, the vast majority of manuscripts are late (dating between the eighth and fifteenth centuries), allowing for the possibility of significant corruption of the texts. Second, they claim that the longer text is more correct. This is in direct opposition to the principle of textual criticism that the shorter text is preferable unless there are significant reasons to suggest that the text has been shortened (i.e.,

copyist errors, etc.). Scribes had a tendency to add words (by way of explanation or clarification) rather than subtract them, especially in cases where a text has been harmonized with another (this commonly occurs in the Gospels—the copyist attempts to make the stories in each of the Gospels agree with one another; see table 18.16).

Modern text critics believe that the Byzantine text family (and thus the *Textus Receptus*) shows much evidence of harmonization, but those who favor the *Textus Receptus* argue that other text families omitted parts of the Byzantine text to support heretical beliefs. A favorite example is the Arian heresy, which arose around Alexandria, Egypt, in the fourth century. Scribes there purportedly omitted material running counter to their denial of the deity of Christ. According to those who favor the *Textus Receptus*, the word χριστός (*Christos*, "Christ") in Romans 16:20 was removed by the Arians in support of their view. This is doubtful, however, since the word appears nine other times in the same chapter (vv. 3, 5, 7, 9, 10, 16, 18, 25, 27). Furthermore, the *Textus Receptus* is not always superior in theological passages; for in one of the most important Christological passages in the New Testament, John 1:18, the Byzantine texts read Jesus is the "only begotten son" instead of Jesus is the "only begotten God" (the latter reading appears in many texts of the Alexandrian family: $\mathfrak{P}^{66}$, $\mathfrak{P}^{75}$, $\aleph^{*,2}$, B, C*, L, 33).

Table 18.16
Textual Variations

	King James Version	New International Version
Matt. 5:44	But I say unto you, Love your enemies, bless them that curse you, do good to them that hate you, and pray for them which despitefully use you, and persecute you.	But I tell you: Love your enemies and pray for those who persecute you. (The other material comes from Luke 6:27–28.)
Matt. 17:21	Howbeit this kind goeth not out but by prayer and fasting.	(Omitted; the verse comes from Mark 9:29.)
Luke 5:38	But new wine must be put into new bottles; and both are preserved.	No, new wine must be poured into new wineskins. (The words "and both are preserved" come from Matt. 9:17b.)

The Byzantine Tradition Favored throughout Much of Church History

Those who favor the *Textus Receptus* argue that the Christian church favored the Byzantine tradition from at least the fourth to the nineteenth centuries, which suggests that God preserved this text through the church. In response, it can be argued that a large sector of the church (Roman Catholicism) favored the Latin Vulgate, prayers to saints, and praying for the dead, and that the large Eastern Orthodox Church supports the veneration of icons. Once again it should be noted that all but a small minority of scholars now reject the superiority of the *Textus Receptus*.

Arguments for the Priority of an Eclectic Greek Text

Use of a Superior Text

The *Textus Receptus* derives from manuscripts no earlier than the tenth century, whereas we now have manuscripts dating as early as the second century. While this does not guarantee a more accurate text, it is commonly acknowledged that each time a text is copied there is the possibility of introducing more errors into it. There is still no unambiguous evidence that the Byzantine text type was known before the fourth century. The scholars translating the Authorized Version of 1611 could have known of only twenty-five late manuscripts at the most for the New Testament, whereas today there are at least 5,358 New Testament manuscripts and fragments. For the Old Testament, they had only a few later Hebrew texts and one text of the Septuagint, but now about 800 manuscripts and versions are available. The following works were discovered subsequent to the translation of the Authorized Version:

1. Codex Alexandrinus
2. Codex Vaticanus
3. Codex Sinaiticus
4. All papyri fragments (discovered at least 300 years after its publication)
5. Codex Leningradensis
6. Aleppo Codex
7. British Museum Manuscript (Or 4445)
8. Qumran manuscripts

Quality More Important Than Quantity

It is commonly agreed by most modern New Testament text critics that quality is more important than quantity; not only do some of the other text families have much earlier texts, but they are thought to be more accurate as well.

Tendencies of the Scribes

It is plausible that scribes may have removed sections of Scripture because they believed them to be theologically aberrant, but it can be shown that copyists were more likely to harmonize texts. Scribes believed these works to come from God and presumably would not dare to remove part of God's sacred word. Even if, for the sake of the argument, scribes removed parts of Scripture that they thought to be flawed, that practice would surely have been more consistently carried out than it appears to be.

Which King James Version Is the Correct Edition?

It is hard to determine a standardized text of the King James Bible since even the first two editions that appeared in 1611 were significantly different. Throughout the history of the King James Bible changes continued to be incorporated, some intentionally and some not. A few of the unintentional changes are noted:

1. One of the editions of the 1611 version of the Authorized Version read

"then cometh Judas" instead of "then cometh Jesus" (Matt. 26:36).

2. Another repeated twenty words (Exod. 14:10).

3. Later printing errors of the Authorized Version resulted in some unusual readings (see table 18.3).

Unclear Wording

The wording in many passages is difficult to understand in this translation, such as:

1. "And Jacob sod pottage" (Gen. 25:29).

2. "And mount Sinai was altogether on a smoke" (Exod. 19:18).

3. "And Parbar westward, four at the causeway, and two at Parbar" (1 Chron. 26:18).

4. "Thou shalt destroy them that speak leasing" (Ps. 5:6).

5. "For who can eat, or who else can hasten hereunto, more than I?" (Eccles. 2:25).

6. "Bring forth therefore fruits meet for repentance" (Matt. 3:8).

7. "Whose fan is in his hand, and he will throughly purge his floor, and gather his wheat into the garner" (Matt. 3:12).

For Further Reading

Bridges, R., and L. A. Weigle. *The Bible Word Book, Concerning Obsolete and Archaic Words in the King James Version of the Bible.* New York: Thomas Nelson, 1960.

Bromiley, G. W. "The KJV: The Genius of Its Predecessors." *Eternity* 21 (March 1970): 30.

Bruce, F. F. *The King James Version: The First 350 Years, 1611–1961.* New York: Oxford University Press, 1960.

Carson, D. A. *The King James Version Debate: A Plea for Realism.* Grand Rapids: Baker, 1979.

Fuller, D. O. *Which Bible?* 2d ed. Grand Rapids: Grand Rapids International Publications, 1971.

Hodges, Z. C. "The Greek Text of the King James Version." *Bibliotheca Sacra* 125 (October–December 1968): 334–35.

Lewis, J. P. *The English Bible from KJV to NIV: A History and Evaluation,* esp. 17–68. 2d ed. Grand Rapids: Baker, 1991.

Meyers, R. "Will the Real King James Version Please Stand Up?" *Restoration Review* 9 (November 1967): 161–66.

Pickering, W. N. *The Identity of the New Testament Text.* Nashville: Nelson, 1977.

Weigle, L. A., ed. *Bible Words That Have Changed in Meaning.* New York: Thomas Nelson, 1955.

Modern English Bibles up to 1950

The King James Bible was recognized as the standard translation for so long that some people believed it to be the only authoritative version. So completely was it accepted that even major translations produced at the end of the nineteenth and well into the twentieth century were intended merely as revisions of this translation. People in America had grown up with the King James Bible, and it was one of the stabilizing factors in the English language. Even though much of its wording and vocabulary were archaic, people still understood it and used it when quoting Scriptures. In fact, it seemed more sacred if one cited the archaic language of this old translation. However, as the Bible became less familiar to Americans the need arose for new, modernized translations of the Bible. Table 19.7 at the end of this chapter lists the names and dates of many of these new translations; we will now turn to some of the more important ones.

The Twentieth Century New Testament (1898–1901; Revised, 1904)

Its History

In 1891, the idea was conceived by two laypeople, Mary Higgs, the wife of a Congregational minister in Oldham (near Manchester, England), and Ernest de Mérindol Malan, a signal and telegraph engineer from Hull, to translate the New Testament into "their own language." Their motivation is explained in the preface to their translation:

English-speaking people of to-day have not, until quite recently, had the opportunity of reading the Bible in the English of their own time. Though in the course of the last hundred years the Bible has been translated into the vernacular of most countries, the language of our Bible remains the English of three hundred years ago.

This translation of the New Testament is an endeavour to do for the English nation what has been done already for the people of almost all other countries—to enable Englishmen to read the most important part of their Bible in that form of their own language which they themselves use. It had its origin in the recognition of the fact that the English of the Authorized Version (closely followed in that of the Revised Version), though widely valued for its antique charm, is in many passages difficult, or even quite unintelligible to the modern reader. The retention, too, of a form of English no longer in common use is liable to give the impression that the contents of the Bible have little to do with the life of to-day. The Greek used by the New Testament writers was not the Classical Greek of some centuries earlier, but the form of the language spoken in their own day. Moreover the writers represent those whose utterances they record as using the words and phrases of every-day life.[1]

Both Higgs and Malan had a strong desire to make a new translation in modern English, but they realized that the task would be overwhelming for two people. They therefore placed an advertisement in the *Review of Reviews*, whose editor, W. T. Stead, had initially encouraged the translation project, asking for volunteers. The advertisement was very successful, with

Table 19.1
The Twentieth Century New Testament

Sponsors of the Translation	Translators	Text	Translation Techniques	Characteristics
Ernest de Mérindol Malan and Mary Higgs	About twenty English laymen and ministers	NT: Westcott and Hort's Greek text	Modern-speech translation	Modern English ("thou" when addressing God) Sense paragraphs Poetic structure Arranged in chronological order OT quotations in italics

Table 19.2
Weymouth's New Testament

Translator	Text	Translation Techniques	Characteristics
Richard Weymouth	NT: *The Resultant Greek Testament* (1862)	Modern-speech translation	Modern English ("thou" when addressing God) Sense paragraphs No poetic structure OT quotations in capitals

at least eighteen people offering to help. Most of the translators did not know each other and for most of the time communicated only by mail; yet they worked diligently on this translation for fourteen years under adverse circumstances (e.g., sickness, severe financial restrictions, and family problems). This translation, called *The Twentieth Century New Testament: A Translation into Modern English Made from the Original Greek (Westcott & Hort's Text)*, appeared in stages—the first two parts in 1898 and 1900, another in 1901, and the complete New Testament in America in 1901 and in England in 1902. Great care was taken to ensure accuracy and comprehension; it was revised for the last time in 1904. This was an unusual translation given that it was one of the earliest modern-speech versions and that it was largely the work of nonprofessionals.

The Translation

The translators followed a careful, thorough plan that greatly aided in the work's production. The first stage was to divide the original twenty translators into five groups, each person being given a section to translate. One person of good linguistic ability was designated chairperson in each of the groups. Upon completion of an individual's translation, it was given first to the other members of the group for critique, then to the other groups. All criticism and input was filtered back to the original translator, who determined what to incorporate into the translation.

In the second stage of translation each group chose a reviser to sit on a Revising Committee to which the final draft was submitted. At this stage each reviser presented the translated section of his group to the rest of the Revising Committee, and any changes had to be agreed upon by a four-fifths majority. Then the work was submitted to an English Committee to improve the quality of the English. It was then printed on slip-sheets to be distributed among the groups and outside to receive criticism from a wider audience. After all of this information had been evaluated, the translation was published in parts to gain an even broader range of criticism before its final printing. It must have been disheartening when five years after beginning the translation project the slip-sheet copy of the Gospel of Mark came back requiring so much emendation that it was necessary to print a second edition. In the end, however, the work was a great success, receiving many positive comments. Kenneth Clark, a New Testament professor from Duke University, recounts: "Yet, for all of this, when the Gospel of Mark was finished in 1896, Dr. Culross of Bristol exclaimed: 'Your Mark is a triumph.' When the first edition of Acts was printed, Weymouth pronounced it 'admirably done.'"[2]

An Evaluation

This translation opened the door for many modern-speech translations and set a high standard for those to follow. The translators decided to use the new Greek text of Westcott and Hort as the most up to date at that time. Poetry was printed as such, and the modern word *you* replaced *thou* except in prayers, speeches of God, and quotations of the Old Testament. The books are generally arranged in chronological order with brief introductions to each, and the text is laid out in paragraphs with subheadings that summarize the contexts of what follows. Quotes from the Old Testament appear in italics (following a principle similar to that in the text of Westcott and Hort, who noted them in capital Greek letters).

The clearness and simplicity of this translation is exemplified in the Lord's Prayer:

> Our Father, who art in Heaven,
> May thy name be held holy,
>   thy Kingdom come,
>   thy will be done—
>   on earth, as in Heaven.
> Give us to-day
>   the bread that we shall need;
> And forgive us our wrong-
>   doings,
>   as we have forgiven those
>   who have wronged us;
> And take us not into temptation,
>   but deliver us from Evil.
>   (Matt. 6:9–13)

The format of this translation highlights the parallel structure of the prayer.

Moody Press in Chicago reprinted this translation in 1961, presenting the books in their traditional order and omitting their introductions as well as the excellent preface by R. B. Girdlestone. About seventy-five changes were made to the text, most of which were probably intended to make it more palatable to American tastes; for example, words such as, "shilling," "pound," "farthing," and "barrister" were changed to their American equivalents.

Weymouth's New Testament (1903, 1907, 1909, 1924, 1929)

Its History

Dr. Richard F. Weymouth (1822–1902) was a distinguished classical scholar who had taught Greek most of his life either as a teaching fellow at University College, London, or as headmaster at Mill Hill School (1869–1886). He realized from his many years of teaching that a Bible in modern English was needed and decided to devote his retirement years to translating the New Testament into modern English. He used his own Greek text, entitled the *Resultant Greek Testament* (published in 1862), which was a consensus of readings from the best critical editions of his day; a critical apparatus at the bottom of each page indicated the variant readings of the Greek text. His translation, *The New Testament in Modern Speech: An Idiomatic Translation into Every-day English from the Text of the Resultant Greek Testament*, was first published in 1903, with a second edition in 1907 and a third edition in 1909. Weymouth died before the translation was published, so it was edited and guided through publication by Ernest Hampden-Cook, a Congregational minister who had worked on the *Twentieth Century New Testament* and who served as resident secretary at Mill Hill School from 1891 to 1896, where he had met Dr. Weymouth. Hampden-Cook also added notes to the trans-

Modern-Speech Translations
The Twentieth Century New Testament (1901; revised, 1904)
Weymouth's New Testament (1903, 1907, 1909, 1924, 1929)
The Moffatt Version (NT, 1913; entire Bible, 1924)
An American Translation (NT, 1923; entire Bible, 1927)

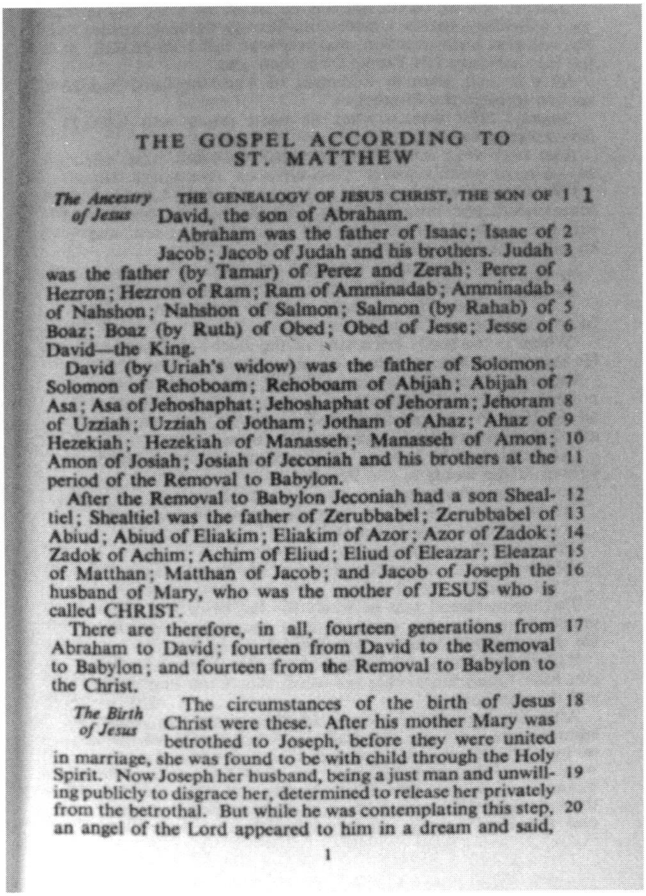
THE GOSPEL ACCORDING TO
ST. MATTHEW

The Ancestry of Jesus THE GENEALOGY OF JESUS CHRIST, THE SON OF 1 1
David, the son of Abraham.
Abraham was the father of Isaac; Isaac of 2
Jacob; Jacob of Judah and his brothers. Judah 3
was the father (by Tamar) of Perez and Zerah; Perez of
Hezron; Hezron of Ram; Ram of Amminadab; Amminadab 4
of Nahshon; Nahshon of Salmon; Salmon (by Rahab) of 5
Boaz; Boaz (by Ruth) of Obed; Obed of Jesse; Jesse of 6
David—the King.
David (by Uriah's widow) was the father of Solomon;
Solomon of Rehoboam; Rehoboam of Abijah; Abijah of 7
Asa; Asa of Jehoshaphat; Jehoshaphat of Jehoram; Jehoram 8
of Uzziah; Uzziah of Jotham; Jotham of Ahaz; Ahaz of 9
Hezekiah; Hezekiah of Manasseh; Manasseh of Amon; 10
Amon of Josiah; Josiah of Jeconiah and his brothers at the 11
period of the Removal to Babylon.
After the Removal to Babylon Jeconiah had a son Sheal- 12
tiel; Shealtiel was the father of Zerubbabel; Zerubbabel of 13
Abiud; Abiud of Eliakim; Eliakim of Azor; Azor of Zadok; 14
Zadok of Achim; Achim of Eliud; Eliud of Eleazar; Eleazar 15
of Matthan; Matthan of Jacob; and Jacob of Joseph the 16
husband of Mary, who was the mother of JESUS who is
called CHRIST.
There are therefore, in all, fourteen generations from 17
Abraham to David; fourteen from David to the Removal
to Babylon; and fourteen from the Removal to Babylon to
the Christ.
The Birth of Jesus The circumstances of the birth of Jesus 18
Christ were these. After his mother Mary was
betrothed to Joseph, before they were united
in marriage, she was found to be with child through the Holy
Spirit. Now Joseph her husband, being a just man and unwill- 19
ing publicly to disgrace her, determined to release her privately
from the betrothal. But while he was contemplating this step, 20
an angel of the Lord appeared to him in a dream and said,

1

Figure 19.1. The beginning of the Gospel of Matthew from the Weymouth New Testament (1903). Matthew 1. New Testament in English (London: Hodder and Stoughton, 1938), translated by Richard F. Weymouth. [Grand Haven, Mich., The Scriptorium, VK 242, p. 1]

lation, which were at times thought to fall short of orthodox ideas, but Weymouth appears to have had similar tendencies, as F. F. Bruce explains:

> Dr. Weymouth himself deviated from traditional orthodoxy in his views of the state of the dead and the future life. While he was a good classical scholar, he did not appreciate the Semitic idiom underlying the New Testament phrases translated "eternal life" and so forth, and used expressions like "the life of the ages" which do not convey their meaning immediately to English readers. What the expression actually meant was "the life of the age to come"—which, according to St John's writings in particular, Christ makes available here and now to those who believe in Him.[3]

The Translation

Weymouth used clear, understandable English, paying close attention to grammatical accuracy and Greek tenses without rendering a word-for-word translation (fig. 19.1). His logic was as follows:

> With a slavish literality delicate shades of meaning cannot be reproduced, nor allowance be made for the influence of interwoven thought, or of the writer's ever shifting—not to say changing—point of view. An utterly ignorant or utterly lazy man, if possessed of a little ingenuity, can with the help of a dictionary and grammar give a word-for-word rendering, whether intelligible or not, and print 'Translation' on his title-page. On the other hand it is a melancholy spectacle to see men of high ability and undoubted scholarship toil and struggle at translation under a needless restriction to literality, as in intellectual handcuffs and fetters, when they might with advantage snap the bonds and fling them away . . . more melancholy still, if they are at the same time racking their brains to exhibit the result of their labours—a splendid but idle philological *tour de force*—in what *was* English nearly 300 years before.[4]

Weymouth's intention was not to supplant the Authorized Version or the Revised Version but to provide a companion translation by which they could be more easily understood.[5] He did, however, hope that his work could be used as the basis for a version that could supersede the Authorized Version and the Revised Version.

Weymouth retained some archaic language, stating that "To be antiquated is not the same thing as to be obsolete or even obsolescent, and without at least a tinge of antiquity it is scarcely possible that there should be that dignity of style that befits the sacred themes with which the Evangelists and Apostles deal."[6] Subheadings summarizing the content appear at the beginning of each section, and quotations of Old Testament passages are printed in capital letters. He was especially attentive to the Greek forms and tenses and attempted to translate them in the most accurate rendering, but he specifically refused to make a word-for-word translation, as is indicated in his translation of the Lord's Prayer:

'Our Father who art in Heaven, may Thy name be kept holy; let Thy kingdom come; let Thy will be done, as in Heaven so on earth; give us to-day our bread for the day; and forgive us our shortcomings, as we also have forgiven those who have failed in their duty towards us; and bring us not into temptation, but rescue us from the Evil one.' (Matt. 6:9–13)

An Evaluation

Weymouth's translation is clear and generally more accurate than the *Twentieth Century New Testament*, though in some places the latter may be preferred because it indicates the poetic style better. In 1924 a major revision of Weymouth's translation removed the questionable phrase "the life of the ages," substituting instead the more common rendering "eternal life." A second, thorough revision was performed in 1929 by James Alexander Robertson of Aberdeen, which was later published in the United States in 1943.

The Moffatt Version (NT, 1913; Entire Bible, 1924)

Its History

James Moffatt (1870–1944; fig. 19.2) was recognized as a brilliant Scottish scholar

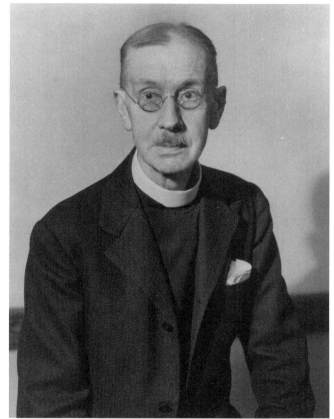

from a young age, according to Sakae Kubo and Walter Specht:

Following his ordination, he served as a minister of the United Free Church for some fifteen years. During this time he continued his scholarly pursuits. In 1901 he published The Historical New Testament, an original translation of the New Testament documents arranged in their chronological order according to the critical literary theories of his time.

Figure 19.2.
James Moffatt (1870–1944). [Union Theological Seminary Library]

Table 19.3
The Moffatt Version

Translator	Text	Translation Techniques	Characteristics
James Moffatt	OT: Hebrew Text NT: Hermann von Soden's Greek text	Modern-speech translation	Modern English ("thou" when addressing God) Sense paragraphs Poetic structure Many emendations Rearranged text OT quotations in italics

This won for him a[n honorary] Doctor of Divinity degree from St. Andrews University [Scotland], which had never previously conferred the degree on so young a man [31].[7]

He is most famous, however, for his modern-speech version of the Bible, which became the most popular such translation between the two World Wars (1914–1945). He began with a translation of the New Testament, entitled *The New Testament: A New Translation*, which appeared in 1913 when he was Yates Professor of New Testament at Mansfield College, Oxford (1911–1915). Two years later he left Oxford to teach in Glasgow, and after his departure from Oxford the university conferred on him an honorary doctor of divinity degree. The Old Testament was completed in 1924 *(The Old Testament: A New Translation)*, by which time Moffatt was professor of church history at United Free Church College, Glasgow (1915–1927). Three years later he became Washburn Professor of Church History at Union Theological Seminary, New York, where he played a major part in the preparation of the Revised Standard Version. In 1926 a one-volume edition of his translation appeared, entitled simply *A New Translation of the Bible*.

The Policies of the Translator

To ensure that his translation was genuinely new, Moffatt deliberately refrained from looking at other versions, though it was difficult at times to avoid remembering the readings of other versions. Moffatt's work was an idiomatic translation of the Greek and Hebrew texts intended to be used by both scholars and laypersons. Bruce describes Moffatt's tone:

Moffatt's translation is characterized by the freedom and vigour of his idiom. His idiom, to be sure, at times seemed to justify those who called his work the translation of the Bible into Scots; for expressions like "You may wash yourself with lye and plenty soap" (Jer. 2:22) and the parable of the dishonest "factor" (Luke 16:1ff.) sound a little exotic in English

ears. But if a translator's business is to produce on his readers the same effect as the original text produced on those who read and heard it, Moffatt succeeded wonderfully; and this is part of the secret of the popularity of his version.[8]

Moffatt's Scottish background also surfaces in the use of "barge" for Noah's ark (Gen. 6:14), the mention of "bagpipes" among the instruments played at the dedication of Nebuchadrezzar's image (Dan. 3:10), the "linen kilt" David wore while dancing before the Lord (2 Sam. 6:14), and Solomon calling together the "sheiks of Israel and all the chiefs of the clans" (2 Chron. 5:2). Some people complained that this translation is too colloquial and much less formal than the Authorized Version, but it was never intended to substitute for the latter. Its main purpose was to remove Bible English and make the text understandable to people unfamiliar with the Bible. Moffatt cited three reasons why the Authorized Version was no longer satisfactory:

1. Its archaic language.
2. Advancements in the fields of vocabulary and syntax of the New Testament since 1611.
3. New manuscript evidence.

It was nevertheless difficult for some people to accept this translation as the Word of God. Bruce tells the story of a "modern young minister in Scotland who visited an aged member of his flock and read to her a chapter from Moffatt's version. 'Well,' said she, 'that was very nice; but now, won't you just read a bittie of the Word of God before you go?'"[9]

The Translation

Moffatt was less able in the area of Old Testament scholarship than in the New. In the preface to the Old Testament he claims that the traditional text of the Old Testament was so "desperately corrupt" that he emended "nearly every page" of his translation. In passages he felt were particularly corrupt he merely inserted an ellipsis (. . .) in the translation and left it. Moffatt felt free to modify the order or wording of the Old Testament whenever he thought the text did not make sense. For example, the first few verses of Genesis begin with "This is the story of how the universe was formed," after which he inserts the first half of Genesis 2:4, "When God began to form the universe, the world was void and vacant," instead of retaining its original placement as possibly a colophon. Having thoroughly embraced the documentary hypothesis, Moffatt printed the text in either roman or italic type depending upon which source it originated from. Moffatt also commonly drew upon conjectural emendations, as Bruce notes:

> An example of Moffatt's proneness to conjectural emendation in the Old Testament may be found in I Sam. 14:11, in the story of Jonathan's attack on the Philistine garrison at Michmash. According to Moffatt, when Jonathan and his armour-bearer showed themselves to the Philistine garrison, "the Philistines said, 'Look at the mice creeping out of their hiding-holes!'" The original text does not say "mice", but "Hebrews". But in the Hebrew consonantal text the letter *k* is all that is needed to change "Hebrews" into "mice", and some editors and commentators had conjectured—baselessly—that "mice" was the original reading. [10]

Moffatt also chose the name *The Eternal* as the name of God in the Old Testament, though he admits that if the translation were for scholars *Yahweh* would have appeared instead.

The New Testament experiences similar problems, but the goal that Moffatt achieves, as stated in the preface to the New Testament (1913), was "to translate the New Testament exactly as one would render any piece of contemporary Hellenistic prose." The result is a fresh and stimulating translation. One of its defects is having been based upon the Greek text by Hermann von Soden, which later was shown to have serious weaknesses; however, most modern scholars would agree with where he chose to depart from von Soden's text (in about 130 instances). [11] Moffatt also frequently accepted readings with little or no textual support. For example, at Jesus' baptism in Luke 3:22 a voice out of heaven says, "Thou art my son, the Beloved," after which Moffatt adds "today have I become thy father," a phrase probably lifted from Psalm 2:7. In John 19:29 the text reads "so they put a sponge full of vinegar *on a spear*" rather than "on hyssop." Moffatt also felt free to modify the order of passages in the New Testament; for example, John 3:22–30 is placed between 2:12 and 2:13; John 7:15–24 appears after John 5:47; and John 12:45–50 is inserted in the middle of John 12:36. Unusual readings crop up; for example, the Gospel of John begins, "The Logos existed in the very beginning," which is merely a transliteration of the Greek word; and in Jesus' parable of the vineyard, the master summons his "bailiff" to pay the workers (Matt. 20:8).

An Evaluation

The chief criticism of Moffatt's version was its lack of dignity as compared with the Authorized Version. This was never its intention, however; Moffatt's aim was to make the text meaningful once again. A good example of the clarity and freshness of his translation is found in 1 Corinthians 13:4–8a:

> Love is very patient, very kind. Love knows no jealousy; love makes no parade, gives itself no airs, is never rude, never selfish, never irritated, *never resentful;* love is never glad when others go wrong, love is gladdened by goodness, always slow to expose, always eager to believe the best, always hopeful, always patient. Love never disappears.

Even more than eighty years later, this translation clearly expresses the meaning of the text. The Lord's Prayer also demonstrates its fresh, clear style:

> our Father in heaven,
> thy name be revered,

Table 19.4
The Holy Scriptures according to the Masoretic Text

Sponsor of the Translation	Translators	Text	Translation Techniques	Characteristics
Jewish Publication Society of America	7 Jewish scholars (Max L. Margolis, editorial chairman)	OT: Masoretic Text	Literal translation	Archaic English ("thou" when addressing God) Sense paragraphs Poetic structure Few emendations Hebrew order

thy Reign begin,
thy will be done on earth as in
   heaven!
give us to-day our bread for the
   morrow,
and forgive us our debts
as we ourselves have forgiven our
   debtors,
and lead us not into temptation
but deliver us from evil. (Matt.
   6:9–13)

It is clear by the number of copies sold that this translation filled an important void, as Bruce describes: "In spite of many criticisms that can quite justly be urged against Moffatt's version, by scholar and layman alike, it is but fair to say that to read through an Old Testament prophetical book or a New Testament epistle in his version is one of the best ways to get a grasp of the general argument."[12]

Moffatt's translation went into many editions, the last being in 1935. In the preface to this last edition he claims to have restudied almost every sentence and concluded by saying, "It is a revision as thorough as I can make it; and I mean it to be final."[13]

In addition, Moffatt also played a significant role in the preparation of the Revised Standard Version, serving as translator and, in his later years, as executive secretary of the committee. He died in 1944, just before the completion of the Revised Standard New Testament. David Ewert recounts: "He was translating the Apocrypha in 1944 and had just completed the Wisdom of Solomon 3:1, 'But the souls of the righteous are in the hand of God,

and no torment will ever touch them,' when he passed away."[14] Moffatt's sharp wit was displayed in an incident that occurred following one of the meetings of the Revised Standard Version Review Committee:

> Dr Luther A. Weigle, chairman of the revisers, tells how a proposed rendering was turned down in committee one day. The man who proposed it turned to Moffatt and said: "Do you know where I got that phrase which you just now rejected?" "No," said Moffatt. "In Moffatt's translation of the New Testament!" said the other. "Well," said Moffatt, "that phrase was right for my translation, but it will not do for this."[15]

There is no doubt that he fulfilled his goal of making the Bible "more interesting" and "less obscure."

The Holy Scriptures according to the Masoretic Text (1917)

Because of the immigration of Jews from western Europe to the United States in the late nineteenth century, the need arose for an English translation of the Hebrew Scriptures to be used in synagogues, schools, and homes. To meet this need, in 1917 the Jewish Publication Society of America published a translation of the Old Testament called *The Holy Scriptures according to the Masoretic Text*. Plans for such a translation began in 1892 by the Jewish Publication Society, only four years after its origin. Initially it was decided that Jewish scholars from Britain and America would work on parts of the translation, which would then be submitted to a critical revision by an editorial committee chaired by Dr. Marcus Jastrow. In 1901, however, it was decided that this procedure would take too long, and in 1903 Dr. Jastrow died. A few years later a new plan was developed which entailed the formation of an editorial board of six members, overseen by Max L. Margolis of Dropsie College. Dr. Margolis would prepare a draft to submit to the rest of the editorial board for critique and revision. This work was published in 1917, and was the first translation of the Hebrew Scriptures produced by Jewish scholars and arranged in the Hebrew order. The purpose for the translation is clearly stated in its preface:

> It aims to combine the spirit of Jewish tradition with the results of biblical scholarship, ancient, mediæval, and modern. It gives to the Jewish world a translation of the Scriptures done by men imbued with the Jewish consciousness, while the non-Jewish world, it is hoped, will welcome a translation that presents many passages from the Jewish traditional point of view.[16]

It was accepted immediately by English-speaking Jews all over the world. Its English idiom is dignified and fairly close to that of the Authorized Version, but for that reason it was almost obsolete the moment it was translated.

Figure 19.3. Edgar J. Goodspeed (1871–1962). [University of Chicago Library]

An American Translation (NT, 1923; Entire Bible, 1927)

Its History

Largely on account of Moffatt's and other modern-speech translations, Edgar J. Goodspeed (1871–1962), professor of New Testament at the University of Chicago (c. 1900–1937), decided to develop a translation for American readers (fig. 19.3). A well-educated man, Goodspeed had studied Greek from boyhood and attended the

Table 19.5
An American Translation

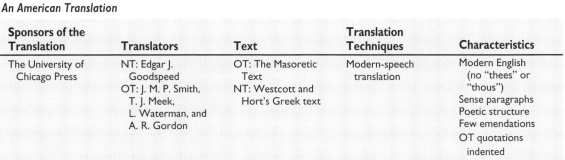

Sponsors of the Translation	Translators	Text	Translation Techniques	Characteristics
The University of Chicago Press	NT: Edgar J. Goodspeed OT: J. M. P. Smith, T. J. Meek, L. Waterman, and A. R. Gordon	OT: The Masoretic Text NT: Westcott and Hort's Greek text	Modern-speech translation	Modern English (no "thees" or "thous") Sense paragraphs Poetic structure Few emendations OT quotations indented

universities of Denison, Yale, Chicago, and Berlin. While teaching patristic Greek at the University of Chicago, he presented a paper at the university's New Testament Club on February 24, 1920, pointing out the problems with the leading modern-speech versions (i.e., *The Twentieth Century New Testament*, Weymouth's translation, and Moffatt's). In the discussion that followed, one of his colleagues, Dr. S. J. Case, suggested that if he found so many weaknesses in these translations, he should make his own. Guy M. Crippen, a representative of the University of Chicago Press, took the suggestion seriously, and shortly afterward Dr. Goodspeed was invited by the press to make a modern-speech version of the New Testament.

After a significant amount of prodding, his wife finally convinced Goodspeed to make the translation. The project took approximately three years and was published in 1923 under the name *The New Testament: An American Translation*. Goodspeed explains in the preface that "for American readers, especially, who have had to depend so long upon versions made in Great Britain, there is room for a New Testament free from expressions which, however familiar in England or Scotland, are strange in American ears."[17] Only a few weeks after publication of the New Testament, the University of Chicago Press asked him to render a translation of the Old Testament; not feeling sufficiently competent to make such a translation, he asked his colleague J. M. P. Smith to edit the Old Testament, and with the help of three other graduates of the University of Chicago (T. J. Meek, University of Toronto; L. Waterman, University of Michigan; A. R. Gordon, McGill University) the work was finished in 1927. The entire Bible appeared in 1931, entitled *The Bible: An American Translation*, and it was revised in 1935; three years later Goodspeed included the Apocrypha, the entire edition being called *The Complete Bible: An American Translation*.

The Translation

Goodspeed desired a new and fresh translation, the logic behind which is described in the preface to his New Testament translation:

> The New Testament was written not in classical Greek, nor in the "biblical" Greek of the Greek version of the Old Testament, nor even in the literary Greek of its own day, but in the common language of everyday life. This fact has been fully established by the Greek papyrus discoveries and the grammatical researches of the last twenty-five years. It follows that the most appropriate English form for the New Testament is the simple, straightforward English of everyday expression.[18]

This did not, however, prove to be an easy task for, like Moffatt before him, it was not easy to rid his memory of other translations, as Goodspeed explains:

> The most difficult thing, I found, was to forget the old translations, King James and especially the Revised Versions, English and American, which I found I knew better than I did the King James. The familiarity we all have with the English Bible was my greatest obstacle. For of course I did not wish merely to reproduce that, but to give my version something of the force and freshness that reside in the original Greek. I wanted my translation to make on the modern reader something of the impression the New Testament must have made on its earliest readers, and to invite the continuous reading of the whole book at a time. That was what I was striving for.[19]

Recognizing that originally the biblical books were intended to be read aloud, Goodspeed would read parts of his translation when speaking in chapel to see how it was received; the students seemed to appreciate the new version. His translation created quite a stir and was printed in serial form in the *Chicago Evening Post* as well as in twenty-four other papers around the United States and Canada.

Goodspeed based his translation on Westcott and Hort's Greek New Testament and departed from it in about only six places (e.g., John 19:29, "on a pike" instead of "upon hyssop"; Acts 6:9, "Libyans" for "Libertines [or freedmen]"; and 1 Pet. 3:19 included "Enoch"). Most unique to this translation was the complete omission of "thees" and "thous," which were no longer used in the English vernacular. His translation was as fresh and alive as he intended. The Lord's Prayer reads

> Our Father in heaven,
> Your name be revered!
> Your kingdom come!
> Your will be done on earth as it is
>   done in heaven!
> Give us today bread for the day,
> And forgive us our debts, as we
>   have forgiven our debtors.
> And do not subject us to temptation,
> But save us from the evil one.
> (Matt. 6:9–13)

The intention was to print the version like a modern book with quotation marks and paragraphing, leaving out paragraph headings and footnotes, so that the reader would want to read each book through to the end.

Its Reception

Like many other translators before him, Goodspeed was criticized for attempting to change the wording of Scripture, as Ewert describes:

> Although it was a very smooth translation there was considerable criticism of it at the beginning—if for no other reason that [sic] that Goodspeed taught at the University of Chicago, known for its liberal theology. The Chicago Tribune came out with the headline: "Monkeying With the Bible." The New York Times criticized him for substituting "lamp" for "candle" and "peck-measure" for "bushel," and so forth. It even suggested that if he had gone "the whole hog he would have written electric light instead of lamp." . . . The London Telegraph prayed, "Heaven preserve us from Chicago professors." The St. Louis Globe-Democrat volunteered: "It is as

much of an anachronism to put the gospels in colloquial American terms today as it would be to put pants on the twelve apostles."[20]

Goodspeed's translation was in reality much more conservative than was Moffatt's, as Geddes MacGregor notes: "This work, though exhibiting some 'advanced' features such as the use of 'you' in addressing Deity, is on the whole considerably more traditional and less free than the Moffatt Bible."[21] The final edition appeared in 1938, but Goodspeed continued work in Bible translation, serving on the translation committee of the Revised Standard Version.

The Old Testament translation followed the traditional Masoretic text, as stated by the editors: "Our guiding principle has been that the official Massoretic text must be adhered to as long as it made satisfactory sense. We have not tried to create a new text; but rather to translate the received text [the Masoretic Text] wherever translation was possible."[22] In reality, however, there are a number of significant deviations from the traditional Hebrew text. Probably the most notable improvements were made in the poetic portions of Scripture whose poetic structure and vocabulary were much easier to understand. Still the translation quality of the first edition of the Old Testament was somewhat uneven because of the variety of translators, but this was mitigated by later editing.[23]

An Evaluation

Goodspeed knew the task ahead of him was difficult, as he acknowledges in the preface to the New Testament: "It has been truly said that any translation of a masterpiece must be a failure, but if this translation can in any measure bring home the great, living messages of the New Testament a little more widely and forcibly to the life of our time, the translator will be well content."[24] When measured against Goodspeed's own goal, this translation must be considered an unequivocal success. It also provided a foundation for many English translations to

Table 19.6
The Confraternity Version/New American Bible

Sponsors of the Translation	Translators	Text	Translation Techniques	Characteristics
Bishops' Committee of the Confraternity of Christian Doctrine	59 Roman Catholic scholars	OT: The Masoretic Text (*Biblia Hebraica*, 1949) NT: Nestle-Aland's *Novum Testamentum Graece* (25th edition, 1963)	Literal translation	Modern English (no "thees" or "thous") Sense paragraphs Poetic structure Few emendations OT quotations indented

follow whose goal was to make the biblical text more understandable to the American people.

The Confraternity Version/ New American Bible (NT, 1941; Entire Bible, 1970)

Its History

The Douay-Rheims Version of 1609–1610, later revised by Bishop Richard Challoner of London in 1750, was a fairly literal translation of the Latin Vulgate. The revision of 1750 served the Roman Catholic Church for about two hundred years; however, in time the need for a revision was acknowledged. In 1941 the New Testament was revised by Roman Catholic scholars under the sponsorship of the Episcopal Committee of the Confraternity of Christian Doctrine and entitled *The New Testament of Our Lord and Saviour Jesus Christ*. This work, a substantial improvement over earlier translations, was nevertheless a translation of the Latin Vulgate. However, several improvements were incorporated based on comparison with Greek texts, and notes were added to explain when the Greek and Latin texts differed. Translation from the original Greek or Hebrew texts was not permitted by the Roman Catholic Church until the pope's encyclical [letter sent by the pope to all Roman Catholic bishops throughout the world] of 1943. Because the Old Testament was translated between 1952 and 1969, well after the time of this letter, it was not merely a revision but a completely new translation from the original languages. Publication of this new translation was completed in stages. Genesis appeared first, in 1948; volume 1 (Genesis to Ruth) in 1952; volume 3 (wisdom books) in 1955; volume 4 (prophetic books) in 1961; and volume 2 (Samuel-Maccabees) in 1969. The committee considered it unsuitable to publish a translation of the original Hebrew of the Old Testament alongside a mere revision of the Douay-Rheims-Challoner Version of the New Testament, and therefore they decided to translate the New Testament from the original Greek. The Old Testament was later revised, and the entire translation appeared in 1970, entitled *The New American Bible*. This Bible could be considered the American counterpart to the British Catholic Bible (the Jerusalem Bible, 1966) and is the first American Catholic Bible translated from the original languages.

The Policies of the Translators

The translation committee was composed of fifty-nine Roman Catholic scholars; chairman for the Old Testament was Dr. Louis Hartman, professor at the Catholic University of America, and for the New Testament Monsignor Myles Bourke of St. Joseph's Seminary, Dunwoodie, New York. For the first time in Roman Catholic translation and at the suggestion of Pope Pius XII, several well-known Protestant scholars were asked to help edit the translation:

The collaboration of scholars who are not Catholic fulfills the directive of the Second Vatican Council, not only that "correct translations be made into different languages especially from the original texts of the sacred books," but that, "with the approval of the church authority, these translations be produced in cooperation with the separated brothers" so that "all Christians may be able to use them."[25]

To assist work on the Old Testament were Frank M. Cross (Harvard University), J. A. Sanders (School of Theology at Claremont and Claremont Graduate School), and David Noel Freedman (University of Michigan and University of California, San Diego); and for the New Testament W. D. Davies (Duke University) and John Knox (Union Theological Seminary).

This was an important step forward for the Roman Catholic Church, representing an attempt to make a translation suitable to other Christian traditions as well. While the marginal notes are decidedly much less Roman Catholic than are those in the Jerusalem Bible, remnants of Roman Catholic beliefs survive; for example, the footnote to John 21:15 mentions that "The First Vatican Council cited this verse in defining that the risen Jesus gave Peter the jurisdiction of supreme shepherd and ruler over the whole flock."[26] In Mark 6:3 the footnote reads:

The question about the *brothers* of Jesus and his sisters (v 3) cannot easily be decided on linguistic grounds. Greek-speaking Semites used the terms *adelphos* and *adelphē*, not only in the ordinary sense of blood brother and sister, but also for nephew, niece, half-brother, half-sister, and cousin. The question of meaning would not have arisen but for the faith of the church in Mary's perpetual virginity.[27]

Because this version is a translation and not a paraphrase,[28] effort was made to reproduce in English the quality of Hebrew and Greek; thus, where the original text was of high literary quality or common vernacular, the goal was to match the English accordingly. An explanation of how this was achieved can be found in the introduction:

the syntactical shortcomings of Paul, his frequent lapses into anacoluthon, and the like, are rendered as they occur in his epistles rather than "smoothed out." Only thus, the translators suppose, will contemporary readers have some adequate idea of the kind of writing they have before them. When the prose of the original flows more smoothly, as in Luke, Acts, and Hebrews it is reflected in the translation.[29]

However, it is probably better to indicate the stylistic peculiarities explicitly by means of square brackets or in a footnote rather than slavishly mirroring the nuances of the Greek text. Ironically for such a literal translation, different English words are used for the same Hebrew or Greek word with the rationale that the repetition of English words would be "too displeasing to the modern ear."[30]

The Old Testament was primarily dependent upon the Masoretic Text (except in the Psalms) but was modified a significant number of times based upon evidence from Qumran or the Septuagint. The Psalms follow the Hebrew text underlying the Latin Psalter of the Catholic church (*Liber Psalmorum*—1944, 1945), which they believe is closer to the original text than the Masoretic Text. Many times the translators modified the order of the Masoretic Text, arguing that it had been disturbed during the transmission process (examples can be found in Job, Proverbs, Sirach, Isaiah, Jeremiah, Ezekiel, Hosea, Amos, Micah, Nahum, Habakkuk, and Zechariah).[31] Several more drastic rearrangements of verses occur in Ezekiel 8–11 (i.e., 8:3; 8:5–18; 9:1–11; 11:24–25; 8:1–2, 4; 10:20–22, 14–15, 9–13, 16–17, 8, 18–19; 11:22–23, 1–21). Previous to this translation, Moffatt's was the only one particularly known for rearranging the order of verses.

In 1970 this translation was revised and took the modern names for the biblical books instead of merely approximating the names in the Vulgate (e.g., Isaia to Isaiah; Malachia to Malachi). However, some weaknesses still remained in the translation, such as the unfortunate choice of the word *holocaust* for "burnt offering," which has nuances to modern readers foreign to its original meaning. Also at times the translation is unclear, as in Judges 1:28, which reads "they [the Israelites] impressed the Canaanites as laborers" incorrectly suggesting the Canaanites were impressed by the hard-working Israelites; and Judges 4:1 says that the Israelites "offended the Lord," which wrongly implies that they hurt his feelings.

The New Testament primarily follows Nestle-Aland's *Novum Testamentum Graece* (25th ed., 1963) with comparison to the text of the United Bible Society (1966). The translators chose to include "doubtful readings with some merit" within brackets (e.g., Matt. 21:44; John 7:53–8:11), which they claim can be omitted without any damage to the sense of the text. Several bold and interesting translations appear; for example, Matthew 6:7 reads, "In your prayer do not rattle on like the pagans," and Matthew 12:34 says, "The mouth speaks whatever fills the mind." But in general it is so literal that the English suffers at the hands of the Greek; for example, Matthew 6:19 reads: "Do not lay up for yourselves an earthly treasure. Moths and rust corrode; thieves break in and steal." The Lord's Prayer also reads somewhat woodenly, though the poetic structure helps to overcome some of this weakness:

> Our Father in heaven,
> hallowed be your name,
> your kingdom come,
> your will be done
> on earth as it is in heaven.
> Give us today our daily bread,
> and forgive us the wrong we have
>   done
> as we forgive those who wrong us.

> Subject us not to the trial
> but deliver us from the evil one.
>   (Matt. 6:9–13)

An Evaluation

This translation may have been a major step forward for the Roman Catholic church in several ways, but the translation still lacks greatly in English style and clarity. Yet the translators appear to have achieved their goal as described by Pope Paul VI:

> Conscious of their personal limitations for the task thus defined, those who have prepared this text cannot expect that it will be considered perfect; but they can hope that it may deepen in its readers "the right understanding of the divinely given Scriptures," and awaken in them "that piety by which it behooves us to be grateful to the God of all providence, who from the throne of his majesty has sent these books as so many personal letters to his own children" *(Divino afflante Spiritu).*[32]

Summary

More translations appeared in this brief period of time than in any other previous to it. As advancements were made in the areas of archaeology, philology, semantics, and translation principles, there was a growing awareness of the need for new translations. New interest was shown in making the Bible easier to understand for those unfamiliar with it. Table 19.7 includes most of the translations that appeared in English during this period, except those that are only small portions of the Old or New Testament.

For Further Reading

Bruce, F. F. *History of the Bible in English: From the Earliest Versions*, 79–185. 3d ed. New York: Oxford University Press, 1978.

Ewert, D. *From Ancient Tablets to Modern Translations: A General Introduction to the Bible*, 213–22. Grand Rapids: Zondervan, 1983.

Kubo, S., and W. F. Specht. *So Many Versions? Twentieth-Century English Versions of the Bible*, 17–88. Rev. ed. Grand Rapids: Zondervan, 1983.

Lewis, J. P. *The English Bible from KJV to NIV: A History and Evaluation*, 215–28. 2d ed. Grand Rapids: Baker, 1991.

MacGregor, G. *The Bible in the Making*. Washington, DC: University Press of America, 1982.

Robertson, E. H. *Makers of the English Bible*. Cambridge: Lutterworth, 1990.

Table 19.7
List of English Translations or Paraphrases (1900–1950)

1900	Hayman's Epistles, London
1901	The American Standard Version, New York
1901	Modern American Bible, New York
1901	Moffatt's Historical New Testament, Edinburgh
1901	Twentieth Century New Testament, New York
1901	Way's Epistles, London
1901	Young People's Bible, Philadelphia
1902	Rotherham's Emphasized Bible, New York
1902(?)	Godbey's New Testament, Cincinnati
1903	Fenton's Bible, London
1903	Weymouth's New Testament, London
1904	Worrell's New Testament, Louisville
1905	Lloyd's New Testament, London
1907	Moulton's Modern Reader's Bible, New York
1907	Bourne's Gospels, London
1908	Rutherford's Epistles, London
1909	The Bible in Modern English, Perkiomen, Pennsylvania
1909	Weaver New Testament, Philadelphia
1912	Improved Bible Union Version, Philadelphia
1914	Numeric New Testament, New Haven, Connecticut
1914	Cunnington's New Testament, London
1917	The Holy Scriptures according to the Masoretic Text, Philadelphia
1918	Anderson New Testament, Cincinnati
1919	The Messages of the Bible, New York
1921	Shorter Bible, New York
1922	Plainer Bible, Jersey City, New Jersey
1923	Riverside New Testament, Boston
1924	Montgomery's Centenary Translation, Philadelphia
1924	Labor Determinative Version, Jackson, Michigan
1924	Moffatt, The Old Testament, New York, London (NT, 1913)
1925	People's New Covenant, Monrovia, California
1925	Children's Bible, New York
1927	Kent's Student's Old Testament, New York
1927	The Bible: An American Translation, Chicago (NT, 1923)
1927	Christian's Bible, Strasburg, Pennsylvania
1928	Czarnomska Version, New York
1932	Chaplain Ballentine, Collegeville, Pennsylvania
1933	Torrey's Four Gospels, New York, London
1934	Royd's Epistles and Gospels, Oxford
1934	Old Testament in Colloquial English
1934	The Documents of the New Testament, London
1935	Westminster Version, London
1937	Greber's New Testament, New York
1937	Martin's New Testament, Nashville
1937	Spencer's New Testament, New York
1937	William's New Testament, Chicago
1938	Book of Books, London
1938	Clementson's New Testament, Pittsburgh
1940	Dakes's Gospels, Chicago
1941	Confraternity New Testament
1944	Wand's New Testament Letters, Brisbane, Australia
1945	Stringfellow's New Testament, Dubuque, Iowa
1945	Knox's New Testament, London
1946	Lenski's New Testament, Columbus
1946	Revised Standard Version: New Testament, New York, Toronto, Edinburgh
1947	Swann's New Testament, Louisville, Kentucky
1948	Letchworth New Testament, Letchworth, England
1948	Knox's Whole Bible, London
1949	Basic Bible, Cambridge

Modern Translations from 1950

T his chapter is selective in its presentation, having attempted to choose the translations of most importance to the reader out of many that have been published. The chief reason for so many recent versions seems to be twofold: the desire to create translations that are both accurate and expressed in modern English idiom that is intelligible and lucid. At the end of the chapter appears a list of most of the translations and paraphrases produced during the second half of this century.

Figure 20.1.
J. B. Phillips (1906–1982).

Phillips Version (1958; Revised, 1972)

Its History

John Bertram Phillips (1906–1982; fig. 20.1) was born in Barnes, a suburb in the southwest corner of London. At eighteen years old, a promising classics student and an avowed atheist, he went to Cambridge, but was won over to Christianity gradually during his first year through the influence of devout Christian members of CICCU (Cambridge Inter-Collegiate Christian Union), a Christian organ-

ization working among the university students. Concerning them he wrote, "I had never met men before to whom Christ was a living reality, as real as any human friend."[1] Being distracted by outside activities, Phillips did not do well in classics and changed to English studies in his final year. For one year after graduation he worked at Sherborne Preparatory School, returning to Ridley Hall the next year with the clear purpose of becoming an Anglican minister. During World War II Phillips was in charge of a flourishing young people's group in southeast London, to whom he would read parts of Paul's Epistles. Their inability to understand the Authorized Version, however,

Table 20.1
Phillips Version

Translator	Text	Translation Techniques	Characteristics
J. B. Phillips	NT: United Bible Societies' Greek text	Modern-speech translation	Modern English (no "thees" or "thous") Sense paragraphs Poetic structure Few emendations OT quotations in italics

led him to translate portions of the New Testament into an English vernacular they could understand. C. S. Lewis was sent some of Phillips's translation and encouraged him to continue and complete the New Testament. Phillips first published Paul's letters in 1947 as *Letters to Young Churches*. In the preface to this work Lewis writes: "It would have saved me a great deal of labour, if this book had come into my hands when I first seriously began to try to discover what Christianity was."[2]

The Policies of the Translator

Phillips chose to begin with the Epistles because he believed them to contain "the essential spiritual core of human life" and "provide that spiritual vitamin, without which human life is at best sickly, and at worst dead"[3]; his purpose was to make these passages of Scripture more meaningful. In the preface to his complete New Testament translation he cites three tests for a good translation:

> The first is simply that it must not sound like a translation at all. If it is skillfully done, and we are not previously informed, we should be quite unaware that it is a translation, even though the work we are reading is far distant from us in both time and place. . . . I would therefore make this the second test: that a translator does his work with the least possible obtrusion of his own personality. The third and final test which a good translator should be able to pass is that of being able to produce in the hearts and minds of his readers an effect equivalent to that produced by the author upon his original readers.[4]

He admits that any translation fails to meet all of these tests; nevertheless the translator must keep them in mind at all times. In the preface to his first publication, *Letters to Young Churches*, he claims to have been transformed by translating the New Testament, often feeling "like an electrician re-wiring an ancient house, without being able to 'turn the mains off.'"[5] Initially Phillips based his translation on the Greek text used in the 1881 Revised Version, but in a later revision (1972) he used the newer United Bible Societies' Greek Text in order to ensure its accuracy.

Phillips explains the technique of "imaginative sympathy" he used to bring life to the New Testament passages:

> If it is not presumptuous to say so, I attempted, as far as I could, to think myself into the heart and mind of Paul, for example, or of Mark or of John the Divine. Then I tried further to imagine myself as each of the New Testament authors writing his particular message for the people of today. No one could succeed in doing this superlatively well, if only because of the scantiness of our knowledge of the first century A.D. But this has been my ideal, and that is why consistency and meticulous accuracy have sometimes both been sacrificed in the attempt to transmit freshness and life across the centuries.[6]

The Translation

This translation is an excellent attempt at making the text come alive for the reader, being easy to read and remarkably clear. F. F. Bruce rates it highly:

> Undoubtedly, of all modern English translations of the New Testament epistles, this is one of the best—perhaps actually the best—for the ordinary reader. The reader who has never paid much attention to Paul's writings, and finds them dull and sometimes unintelligible in the older versions, would be well advised to read them through in Dr Phillips's version. He will find them (possibly to his surprise) interesting, and (more surprising still) remarkably relevant to the present day and its problems.[7]

Some people would categorize this as a paraphrase, although the distinction is not entirely clear. In any case Phillips's version is a meaning-for-meaning translation as opposed to a word-for-word translation. For example, Paul's letter to Philemon has the feeling of being a real letter to a real person:

It occurs to me that there has been a purpose in your losing him. You lost him, a slave, for a time; now you are having him back for good, not merely a slave, but as a brother Christian. He is already especially loved by me—how much more will you be able to love him, both as a man and as a fellow-Christian! You and I have so much in common, haven't we? Then do welcome him as you would welcome me. If you feel he has wronged or cheated you put it down to my account. I've written this with my own hand: I, Paul hereby promise to repay you. (Philem. 15–19a)

Phillips's translation principles, which worked exceptionally well for the Pauline Epistles, did not produce so vibrant an effect in the Gospels (published in 1952). Bruce highlights one example: "One may wonder, however, if the statement, 'At the beginning God expressed himself,' conveys even to the modern pagan the sense of the opening clause of St John's Gospel."[8] Nevertheless in general it is a clear, useful translation for people unfamiliar with the Bible, and in the Gospels the parables are particularly good. Phillips's translation of the New Testament was finally completed and published as one volume in 1958. He then turned to the Old Testament, publishing in 1963 a translation of the eighth-century prophets, Isaiah, Amos, Hosea, and Micah. Concerning the last Edwin Robertson writes, "It is impossible to find even now a more readable translation of Micah."[9]

An Evaluation

Phillips admirably achieved his goal, and his translation became one of the most popular modern-speech versions. The translation is clear and relevant to the modern reader as the following passages indicate:

"Don't pile up treasures on earth, where moth and rust can spoil them and thieves can break in and steal. But keep your treasure in Heaven where there is neither moth nor rust to spoil it and nobody can break in and steal. For wherever your treasure is, you may be certain that your heart will be there too!" (Matt. 6:19–21)

The Lord's Prayer reads

Our Heavenly Father, may your
    name be honored;
May your kingdom come, and your
    will be done on earth as it is in
    Heaven.
Give us this day the bread that we
    need,
Forgive us what we owe to you, as
    we have also forgiven those who
    owe anything to us.
Keep us clear of temptation, and
    save us from evil. (Matt. 6:9–13)

A New Translation of the Holy Scriptures according to the Masoretic Text (The Torah, 1962; The Prophets, 1978; The Writings, 1982)

Its History

This work was produced to replace the earlier one by the Jewish Publication Society of America (1917) but as a new translation and not merely a revision. As the project spanned more than two decades, the initial editor-in-chief, Harry M. Orlinsky, professor of Bible at the Hebrew Union College-Jewish Institute of Religion in New York, was later succeeded by H. L. Ginsberg, professor at the Jewish Theological Seminary of America in New York. The translation was undertaken for two reasons. First, great advances had been made in the areas of Hebrew grammar, biblical archaeology, and ancient Near Eastern languages; the preface to The Torah claims that "In accuracy alone we believe this translation has improved on the first JPS translation in literally hundreds of passages."[10] Second, modernization of the English significantly improved, being no longer restricted to a word-for-word translation and yet maintaining faithfulness to the text. As the preface

Table 20.2
A New Translation of the Holy Scriptures according to the Masoretic Text

Sponsors of the Translation	Translators	Text	Translation Techniques	Characteristics
Jewish Publication Society of America	About 14 Jewish translators	OT: The Masoretic Text	Literal translation	Modern English (no "thees" or "thous") Verse paragraphs Poetic structure Few emendations

states, "A translation which is stilted where the original is natural, heavy where the original is graceful, or obscure where the original is perfectly intelligible is the very opposite of faithful."[11]

The Translation

Initially, seven translators worked on the project: Dr. Harry M. Orlinsky, Dr. Harold L. Ginsberg, Dr. Ephraim A. Speiser, Dr. Solomon Grayzel, Rabbi Max Arzt, Rabbi Bernard J. Bamberger, and Rabbi Harry Freedman. Dr. Orlinsky began the process by making a draft translation, which was then sent to the other members for comments and suggested changes. After the changes circulated among the other members, periodic meetings were held to vote on final renderings.

The committee followed faithfully the reading of the traditional (Masoretic) Hebrew text, except where it did not make sense and appeared corrupted. In such cases other sources were examined to determine the proper reading of the text, and footnotes explained the rationale behind the translation chosen as well as any significant alternative readings. Archaic words and Hebrew idioms were avoided; the translators attempted instead to give the modern English equivalents. The goal was to prepare a translation that could convey the same message to modern-day readers as the original did to its ancient readers. Three practices in particular were used to accomplish this goal: the use of "you" for all second person forms (even when God is addressed); the Hebrew *wāw* (often translated "and"), which commonly joins sentences, was

translated as the sense demanded (e.g., "but," "however," "yet") or was left untranslated; and the common Hebrew phrase "and it came to pass" was left untranslated (e.g., Gen. 6:1; 7:10; 8:6, 13; 24:52). Chapter divisions and verse divisions were modified if they appeared to split a sentence or paragraph:

> The chapter and verse divisions found in the printed Bible are indispensable as a system of precise reference, but they do not always coincide with the organic divisions of the text. The chapter divisions, whose origin is neither ancient nor Jewish but medieval Christian, sometimes join or separate the wrong paragraphs, sentences, or even parts of sentences. The verse divisions, though considerably older and of Jewish origin, sometimes join together parts of different sentences or separate from each other parts of the same sentence.[12]

Where paragraph and sentence breaks differ from earlier translations, the previous markings are indicated. For example, when Genesis 7:24 and 8:1 are joined as a single sentence, a space appears before the former verse to indicate the new chapter division and a small number *1* in the middle of the sentence indicates where verse 1 formerly began. Quotation marks are used, and poetic material is printed in a format easy to recognize and understand. The personal name for God was never to be mentioned according to Jewish tradition, and thus it is translated "Lord," according to long-standing Jewish custom (see footnote on Exod. 6:3 in this version).

By the time of the publication of the second part of this translation (The Prophets, 1978) two members of the original translation committee had died, Dr. Speiser (1965) and Rabbi Arzt (1975). Dr. Ginsberg had become editor-in-chief and changed translation procedures so that individual members prepared an initial draft, which was then sent to the rest of the committee. The last section (The Writings, 1982) was completed by an entirely new translation committee composed of Dr. Moshe Greenberg (Hebrew University), Dr. Jonas C. Greenfield (Hebrew University), Dr. Nahum M. Sarna (Brandeis University), Rabbi Saul Leeman, Rabbi Martin Rozenberg, and Rabbi David Shapiro. In 1985 the entire translation was revised and published in a one-volume work, entitled the *TANAKH: A New Translation of the Holy Scriptures according to the Traditional Hebrew Text*. (As noted earlier in this book the word *Tanakh* is an acronym for the three parts of the Hebrew Scriptures.) This translation was the culmination of many years of Jewish scholarship and is one of the best translations of the Hebrew Bible available.

Figure 20.2.
Gerrit Verkuyl
(1872–1968).

The Berkeley Version (NT, 1945; Entire Bible, 1959)

Its History

Dr. Gerrit Verkuyl originally translated the New Testament in 1945, entitled *The Berkeley Version of the New Testament* (because the translator lived in Berkeley, California). In March 1894, at twenty-one years of age, Verkuyl came to America from the Netherlands and worked as a farm hand in California (fig. 20.2). He worked hard to learn English and get a good education. In 1904 he received a bachelor of divinity degree from Princeton Theological Seminary; subsequently, a New Testament fellowship allowed him to study in Germany where he earned his doctor of philosophy degree from the University of Leipzig in 1906, with extra study at the University of Berlin. He returned to America and began work with the Presbyterian Board of Christian Education, which work brought him into contact with children and youth all over America. It was from this interaction that

Table 20.3
The Berkeley Version

Sponsors of the Translation	Translator	Text	Translation Techniques	Characteristics
Zondervan Publishing House	NT: Gerrit Verkuyl OT: 20 scholars headed by Verkuyl	OT: Masoretic Text NT: Tischendorf's Greek text (8th edition)	Modern-speech translation	Some archaic English ("thees" and "thous") Sense paragraphs Some poetic structure Few emendations

the desire arose to make a translation in modern English. Work on the New Testament began in 1936; the complete edition was published in 1945. Five years later Zondervan Publishing House asked Verkuyl to translate the Old Testament, which took him nine years, with a staff of twenty scholars, to complete. This version was not merely a revision but a new translation (though it claims to have been compared with previous translations). The entire Bible was published in 1959 under a new name, *The Holy Bible: The Berkeley Version in Modern English*; it was revised ten years later and called *The Modern Language Bible*.

The Policies of the Translators

In the preface to his New Testament Verkuyl describes the rationale behind his translation: "As thought and action belong together so do religion and life. The language, therefore, that must serve to bring us God's thoughts and ways toward us needs to be the language in which we think and live rather than that of our ancestors who expressed themselves differently."[13]

The format is similar to that of the Revised Standard Version, and Bruce thinks that it can be considered a "more conservative counterpart to the R.S.V."[14] Like the Revised Standard Version, italics are no longer used to indicate the insertion of words necessary to render an equivalent English translation; quotation marks are added to indicate direct discourse, except that in the Berkeley Version they are not used for God or Jesus as Scripture is already considered God's word (although most readers would find it helpful to notate these with quotation marks as well); the Berkeley Version indicates poetry as in the Revised Standard Version but limits it strictly to the Psalms and Proverbs; and "you" is used for all second-person forms, except when God is being addressed. The last practice posed a particular problem for Verkuyl in Mark 4 and 5, in that he chose "you" when the disciples speak to Jesus since they are uncertain of his true identity, but "Thou" when the demons speak to him for they know (compare Mark 4:38 with 5:7).

One of the major complaints by conservatives against the Revised Standard Version was that it obscured the messianic content of many Old Testament passages (e.g., Gen. 3:15; 49:10; Num. 24:17; Ps. 45:6; Dan. 9:24–27), whereas the Berkeley Version uses capital letters to signify messianic intent in many passages. A better balance is expressed by Bruce: "It may be argued that what is ambiguous in Hebrew should have some of its ambiguity preserved in English, so that the English reader may make up his mind about the meaning, uninfluenced by capitalization."[15] This is especially true when conservative scholars disagree over the messianic content of various passages; compare the following translations of Numbers 24:17:

> Berkeley: I see Him but not now; I observe Him but not nearby. A Star shall come up out of Jacob, a Scepter shall rise out of Israel, which shall crush Moab from one end to the other and destroy all the children of Sheth.

> NASB: I see him, but not now;
> I behold him, but not near;
> A star shall come forth from Jacob,
> And a scepter shall rise from Israel,
> And shall crush through the fore-
> head of Moab,
> and tear down all the sons of Sheth.

Old Testament commentators typically view this passage as referring to King David, who would come forth from Jacob, rule over Israel, and crush the Moabites. But it is less certain whether it should also refer to the Messiah.[16] It therefore seems preferable to leave the interpretation open.

There are a number of inconsistencies in the translation of the personal name for Israel's God—"Yahweh" is usually translated "Lord" (Gen. 2:5, 7, 8; and many more), but at least once it is "Yahweh" (Hos. 12:5, "YAHWEH His name"), and several other times it is "Jehovah" (Exod. 3:15; 15:3). Equally, mistakes appear in the common designations: "Lord God" instead of "Lord God" (*'ădōnāy Yahweh*; Ezek. 2:4); "Lord God" instead of "Lord God" (*'ădōnāy Yahweh*; Amos 3:7, 8); and "Lord" instead of "Lord" (Ps. 45:11), to name only a few.[17]

The Translation

This translation was based on original Greek and Hebrew texts. Although Verkuyl never clearly indicates which text was used for the Old Testament, there is little deviation from the Masoretic Text even where other manuscript evidence would support a change (e.g., Gen. 4:8; Ps. 145:13b). Three readings are, however, incorporated from the Qumran Isaiah Scroll (Isa. 14:4; 45:8; 56:12). The New Testament is a translation of the eighth edition of Tischendorf's Greek text, compared at times with Nestle's text. Occasionally New Testament readings that are found in the Received Text but without good textual evidence, are inserted in the translation; these are usually set off with brackets and an explanatory note that the reading is not found in the majority of the most reliable manuscripts (e.g., Matt. 6:13b; 18:11; 27:35b; Mark 2:17b). In the opinion of Bruce the Old Testament is a better translation than the New,[18] especially because of such awkward readings as "Pattern after me, as I pattern after Christ" (1 Cor. 11:1) and "the left-overs will be saved" (Rom. 9:27).[19] In other passages the translation is so literal that the English is stilted: "Blessed are the hungry and thirsty for righteousness" (Matt. 5:6); "So, when you do benevolence" (Matt. 6:2); "Do not fret therefore in view of tomorrow" (Matt. 6:34); "So He embarked, crossed over and reached His own city" (Matt. 9:1); "Could not he, the opener of the blind man's eyes, have prevented this death?" (John 11:37); and "Again deeply vexed inwardly" (John 11:38). Though it is not translated as poetry, the Lord's Prayer reads well:

> Our Father who art in heaven, Thy name be kept holy. Thy kingdom come. Thy will be done on earth as in heaven.
> Give us today our daily bread. And forgive us our debts as we have forgiven our debtors. And lead us not into temptation but deliver us from the evil one. (For Thine is the kingdom and the power and the glory forever. Amen.) (Matt. 6:9–13)

While this rendering is quite similar to that in the Revised Standard Version, an additional final sentence with little textual support is inserted from the Received Text.

An Evaluation

The goal of Verkuyl's translation was to "employ our language according to its choicest current usage,"[20] but the awkward phraseology of its very literal renderings inhibited reaching that goal. This may have been due in part to the misunderstanding of the translation process itself; the preface states: "Neither is this a paraphrase, for that leads so readily to the infusion of human thought with divine revelation, to the confusion of the reader."[21] It is now recognized, however, that every translation is to some extent a paraphrase since thoughts are being transferred from one language to another; what is of greater importance is that translations strive to achieve purposeful interaction between human thought and divine revelation without diminishing either. The best translation, then, is one that so thoroughly interweds human thought with divine revelation that the text says in a different language what the original intended to say. Unless the new translation takes on the style and structure of the new language, it is not a translation but rather a mere transferal of words from one language to another.

The footnotes can also be faulted for including questionable information; for example, the footnote in Esther 1:1 says that the name *Ahasuerus* is a title instead of a name, but in fact this is the Hebrew form of the personal name;[22] and the dates in the footnotes are so greatly debated that they are of little value for the reader.

The revision of this translation, entitled the Modern Language Bible (1969), reads substantially better, much of the awkward wording having been eliminated.

The New World Translation of the Holy Scriptures (NT, 1950; Entire Bible, 1961; Revised, 1981)

This translation, so clearly flawed by its doctrinal biases, was prepared by the

Figure 20.3. A picture of Charles Taze Russell, founder of the Jehovah's Witnesses around 1918. [Billy Graham Center Museum]

for God; we have seen, however, that this is a mistaken understanding of the medieval Jewish representation of the sacred name of God as a combination of two Hebrew words (see table 11.2). Other flaws in this translation are much more serious and damaging. The Jehovah's Witnesses do not believe that Jesus is truly God but that instead he is the first created being: Jesus is "a god" but not "the God." As a result several passages of Scripture are incorrectly translated:

> In [the] beginning the Word was, and the Word was with God, and the Word was **a god**." (John 1:1 *NWT*, emphasis added)

The bold print highlights the change in this translation; the Jehovah's Witnesses argue that since no article appears with the word θεός (*theos*, God), it is intended to be understood as "a god" rather than "the God." As early as 1933 E. C. Colwell argued against such a rendering: "The absence of the article does *not* make the predicate indefinite or qualitative when it precedes the verb; it is indefinite in this position only when the context demands it. The context makes no such demand in the Gospel of John. . . ."[23]

There are two other places in the Gospel of John where theology forces similar types of translation (John 1:18; 10:33), but it is surprising that Thomas's exclamation to Jesus, "My Lord and my God" (John 20:28) is retained. The significance of this passage is delineated by Murray J. Harris, former New Testament professor at Trinity International University:

Jehovah's Witnesses and published by the Watch Tower Bible and Tract Society. The cult was founded by C. T. Russell (fig. 20.3) around 1918, but it took on the name Jehovah's Witnesses in 1931 and has approximately two million followers. We mention this translation with the purpose of signaling its deficiencies and biases so that people will not be drawn into using it unaware. First, the Jehovah's Witnesses pride themselves on using the name *Jehovah*, which they believe is the proper name

> Thomas with the exclamation, "My Lord and my God!," a confessional invocation

Table 20.4
The New World Translation of the Holy Scriptures

Sponsors of the Translation	Translators	Text	Translation Techniques	Characteristics
Jehovah's Witnesses (The Watch Tower Bible and Tract Society)	Jehovah's Witnesses scholars	OT: Masoretic text NT: unidentified Greek text	Literal translation	Modern English (no "thees" or "thous") Verse paragraphs Limited poetic structure Few emendations

that not only marks the climax (along with the accompanying beatitude) of the Thomas pericope and John 20, but also forms the culmination of the entire Gospel. . . . In uttering this confessional cry Thomas recognized the lordship of Jesus in the physical and spiritual realms as well as over his own life (ὁ κύριός μου ["my Lord"]) and the essential oneness of Jesus with the Father which made his worship of Jesus legitimate (ὁ θεός μου ["my God"]). As used in this verse, κύριος ["Lord"] and θεός ["God"] are titles, not proper names, the first implying and the second explicitly affirming the substantial deity of the risen Jesus.[24]

In other passages statements referring to Jesus' divinity are modified. For example, the phrases "while we wait for the happy hope and glorious manifestation of the great God and of our Savior Christ Jesus" (Titus 2:13 NWT) and "the righteousness of our God and [the] Savior Jesus Christ" (2 Pet. 1:1 NWT) are translated so as to give the appearance of referring to two persons instead of one. In Colossians 1:16–17 the word *other* (noted here in brackets) has been added several times even though it does not appear in the Greek text, so that these verses can be brought in line with Jehovah Witness theology: "because by means of him all [other] things were created. . . . All [other] things have been created through him. . . . Also, he is before all [other] things and by means of him all [other] things were made to exist" *(NWT).* One final example, drawn from Philippians 2:6, is compared with the Revised Standard Version (table 20.5). *The New World Translation* says that Jesus gave no con-

Table 20.5
Comparison of Philippians 2:6 (RSV, *NWT*)

Revised Standard Version	New World Translation
who, though he was in the form of God, did not count equality with God a thing to be grasped, but emptied himself,	who, although he was existing in God's form, gave no consideration to a seizure, namely, that he should be equal to God.

sideration to being equal with God; the Revised Standard Version says that Jesus did not cling to this equality but emptied himself. Two very distinct translations.

The New English Bible (NT, 1961; Entire Bible, 1970)

Its History

When the copyright of the Revised Version neared expiration in the 1930s, the university presses of Cambridge and Oxford, owners of its copyright, approached G. R. Driver, professor of Old Testament at Oxford, and J. M. Creed, professor of New Testament at Cambridge, to revise it. With the outbreak of World War II in 1939, however, plans for the revision were forced to end. After the war, in 1946, the General Assembly of the Church of Scotland adopted a proposal to make an entirely new translation of the Bible and approached the Church of England and the other major free churches (e.g., Methodist, Baptist, and Congregational churches) with the idea. All the denomi-

Table 20.6
The New English Bible

Sponsor of the Translation	Translator	Text	Translation Techniques	Characteristics
Oxford and Cambridge University Presses	About 26 British scholars	OT: *Biblia Hebraica* (1937) NT: eclectic Greek text	Dynamic equivalence Entirely new translation	Slightly archaic English ("thees" and "thous") Sense paragraphs (poor verse numeration) Poetic structure Many emendations

C. H. Dodd (1884–1973)

Charles Harold Dodd (fig. 20.4) was born in Wrexham, Wales, on April 7, 1884, to parents both trained as teachers. On June 2, 1908, he entered Mansfield College, Oxford, to train for the Congregational ministry and returned to teach New Testament (1915–1930). At university he became proficient in Greek, as well as gaining competency in Hebrew, Aramaic, and Syriac. Upon graduation, Dodd was encouraged to acquire some pastoral experience, so he accepted a call to Brook Street Congregational Church, Warwick, where he remained for about three years, greatly enjoying parish responsibilities. One parishioner described Dodd in these early days of pastoring:

> I remember Dodd as a small, spare figure of a man. Always spruce and immaculate in his dress and appearance. He had a good sense of humour and a ready laugh. A great and natural appearance of vitality always, and an easy and unconscious concentration in conversation on any subject under discussion. A wonderfully alert and logical brain (E. H. Robertson, *Makers of the English Bible* [Cambridge: Lutterworth, 1990], 196).

Figure 20.4. C. H. Dodd (1884–1973).

In 1930 Dodd was offered the chair of Rylands Professor of Biblical Criticism and Exegesis at University of Manchester as successor to A. S. Peake. He held the position until 1935, when he was offered the Norris-Hulse Professor of Divinity chair at the University of Cambridge. He was the first non-Anglican to hold a chair of divinity at the university since 1660. In 1947 he was elected as the vice chairman of the New English Bible, the duties of which occupied most of his time after his retirement in 1949 from the Cambridge professorship. Most scholars would agree that Dodd was the most influential New Testament scholar in the mid-twentieth century.

nations were enthusiastic about preparing a new English translation, and by July 1947 a joint committee was set up to oversee the project. In January 1948 additional denominations were asked to send representatives to this committee, including the Presbyterian Church of England, the Society of Friends (Quakers), the Council of Churches for Wales, the Council of Churches for Ireland, the British and Foreign Bible Societies, and the National Bible Society of Scotland. Later the Roman Catholic Church of England and Scotland was also asked to send representatives; thus this translation truly was authorized by the churches of England, more so than any translation before it. C. H. Dodd, one of the most distinguished scholars of his day, was the director of the entire project (from 1949 onward).

In 1970, when the entire Bible was published, there was some revision made to the New Testament (more than four hundred changes),[25] though the basic translation remained effectively the same. Mention should also be made of *The New English Bible with Apocrypha: Oxford Study Edition*, a helpful edition edited in the Old Testament by Dr. Samuel Sandmel, a Jewish scholar, and the New Testament by Dr. M. Jack Suggs. Thirty other scholars collaborated on this edition, which includes introductions, interpretive annotations, charts, maps, and indexes. This work is quite similar to *The New Oxford Annotated Bible*, which was based on the Revised Standard Version.

The Policies of the Translators

Three panels of translators were formed, one for the Old Testament, one for the New Testament, and one for the Apocrypha (see table 20.7; Jack Lewis remarks that it reads like a British Hall of Fame for biblical scholarship).[26]

The following translation procedures were adopted. First, each member of the translation committee was given a section to translate and prepare an initial draft. For the Old Testament the draft was sent directly to G. R. Driver, who would critique it before sending it to the other members of the panel; New Testament drafts were sent directly to the rest of the members. The drafts would be carefully discussed in meetings to follow and revised in light of these discussions. The translation was then sent to the literary advisors for critique, in order to ward off any criticism against the style and language of this new version (a charge brought against the Revised New Testament of 1881). Once the drafts had passed through these stages, they were submitted to the joint committee that had responsibility for the final translation.

The Translation

One of the main objectives of the New English Bible was to make a new translation that did not reproduce traditional biblical English. Dodd explains his perspective concerning this translation in the following memorandum:

It is to be genuinely English in idiom, such as will not awaken a sense of strangeness or remoteness. Ideally, we aim at a 'timeless' English, avoiding equally both archaisms and transient modernisms. The version should be plain enough to convey its meaning to any reasonably intelligent person (so far as verbal expression goes), yet not bald or pedestrian. It should *not* aim at preserving 'hallowed associations'; it *should* aim at conveying a sense of reality. It should be as accurate as may be with-

out pedantry. It is to be hoped that, at least occasionally, it may produce arresting and memorable readings. It should have sufficient dignity to be read aloud.[27]

In order to achieve these objectives Dodd believed that it was better to translate the original texts in a thought-for-thought rendering rather than word for word. Dodd's hope was that this translation would evoke in its readers the same response evoked in its original readers.

The Old Testament

Translators of the Old Testament used R. Kittel's *Biblia Hebraica* (1937) as the basis for translation, but there are some unusual renderings in the New English Bible (e.g., "that I may not be left picking lice," Song 1:7). Other oddities of this translation include the change in order of material (possibly as many as 136 times;[28] e.g., new orders for Gen. 26 [vv. 15, 18, 16]; Isa. 40 [40:20, 41:6–7, 40:21]; Jer. 12 [vv. 17, 14b, 15, 18]; Amos 5 [vv. 9, 7, 10]) and the removal of psalm titles and the word *selah*.

The translators chose to use LORD as the personal name for God, but in several places Jehovah is retained ("Jehovah-jireh," Gen. 22:14; "Jehovah [-nissi]," Exod. 3:15; 6:3; 17:15–16; "Jehovah-shalom," Judg. 6:23–24; "Jehovah-shammah," Ezek. 48:35). The rationale was that it has become customary to use the name *Jehovah*. Bruce raises the counterargument that "if the New English Bible had ventured to break

Table 20.7
Translators of the New English Bible

Old Testament Translators	New Testament Translators	Apocrypha Translators
G. R. Driver (Cambridge), chairman	C. H. Dodd (Cambridge), chairman	W. D. McHardy (Oxford), chairman
W. D. McHardy (Oxford)	G. S. Duncan (St. Andrews)	W. Barclay (Glasgow)
J. A. Emerton (Cambridge)	R. V. G. Tasker (London)	W. H. Cadman (Oxford)
A. R. Johnson (Cardiff, Wales)	C. F. D. Moule (Cambridge)	G. B. Caird (Oxford)
N. W. Porteous (Edinburgh)	G. D. Kilpatrick (Oxford)	C. F. D. Moule (Cambridge)
B. J. Roberts (Bangor, Wales)	J. A. T. Robinson (Bishop of Woolwich)	J. R. Porter (Exeter)
N. H. Snaith (Leeds)	G. M. Styler (Cambridge)	G. M. Styler (Cambridge)
L. H. Brockington (Oxford)	T. W. Manson (Manchester)	
T. H. Robinson (Cardiff)	W. F. Howard (Birmingham)	
H. Danby (Oxford)	E. G. Selwyn (Dean of Winchester)	
H. H. Rowley (Manchester)		
C. A. Simpson (Oxford)		

with tradition here, the process of naturalization might have been expedited."[29] On about fifty occasions (many more than the Revised Standard Version), readings of the Isaiah Scroll from Qumran have been accepted (e.g., Isa. 41:27, "advocate"; Isa. 53:3, "we despised him"; Isa. 53:11, "light"). In an attempt to make the text more understandable, there are considerably more conjectural emendations in the Old Testament translation of the New English Bible than in the Revised Standard Version; however, they should be used with caution as being mere guesses as to the meaning of the text.

Two of the more interesting readings from the Old Testament appear in Genesis 1:1, where the first line is taken as a title ("In the Beginning of Creation"), and in verse 2, where the phrase *rûaḥ ʾelōhîm* is translated as "a mighty wind" instead of "the Spirit of God" or the like.

The New Testament

The translators did not use any set form of the Greek text available at the time, choosing instead an eclectic text combining the best readings in each passage. Dodd explains their rationale for doing so in the introduction to the New Testament:

> There is not at present any critical text which would command the same degree of general acceptance as the Reviser's [Revised Version of 1881] text did in its day. Nor has the time come, in the judgement of most scholars, to construct such a text, since new material constantly comes to light, and the debate continues. The present translators therefore could do no other than consider variant readings on their merits, and, having weighed the evidence for themselves, select for translation in each passage the reading which to the best of their judgement seemed most likely to represent what the author wrote. Where other readings seemed to deserve serious consideration they have been recorded in footnotes.[30]

Dodd's statement is surprising since in 1960 (just shortly before this translation was started), the Nestle's Greek text was in its twenty-fourth revision, and in 1970, when the whole translation finally appeared, there were two major eclectic Greek texts that the translators could have used for comparison purposes (Nestle's and United Bible Societies'). These two Greek texts differ significantly from that compiled by the translators of the New English Bible, even though they claim to have employed the same principles to determine the Greek text. A simple way to see this is to compare some of the different readings of the Revised Standard Version with the New English Bible. Each uses an eclectic Greek text.[31] It is apparent that the editors of the New English Bible relied more strongly on the ancient versions, such as Old Latin, Latin Vulgate, Syriac, Coptic, and Georgian, than did the translators of the Revised Standard Version, choosing at times readings with weak textual support.

The New English Bible New Testament contains only one conjectural reading, that of John 19:29, which reads, "A jar stood there full of sour wine; so they soaked a sponge with wine, fixed it on a **javelin,** and held it up to his lips." A footnote reads "So one witness; the others read majoram." "Majoram" (or "hyssop"), a small bushy plant which could not hold a sponge, is not parallel to "reed" found in both Mark and Matthew. Several scholars therefore suggested changing "hyssop" (ὕσσωπος, *hyssōpos*) to "spear" or "javelin" (ὑσσός, *hyssos*), and the editors of the New English Bible followed their lead.[32] More recently one medieval manuscript was found to contain this reading, so that it can no longer technically be considered a conjectural reading. While this reading seems logical, several scholars argue that its textual basis is weak.[33]

Since no specific Greek text for the New English Bible was used, footnotes should have provided more textual information than merely "some witnesses read." This problem was partially remedied in 1964, when R. V. G. Tasker published *The Greek New Testament, Being the Text Translated in the New English Bible 1961* (Oxford and Cambridge: The University Presses, 1964), which provided the rationale behind readings of the New English Bible that vary from the standard text; few laypeople, however, would be likely to purchase a separate book to accompany their *New English Bible.*

In most cases the style and vocabulary of the English can be commended, as is illustrated in the following passages:

> Therefore I bid you put away anxious thoughts about food and drink to keep you alive, and clothes to cover your body. Surely life is more than food, the body more than clothes. Look at the birds of the air; they do not sow and reap and store in barns, yet your heavenly Father feeds them. You are worth more than the birds! (Matt. 6:25–26)

> Our Father in heaven,
> Thy name be hallowed;
> Thy kingdom come,

> Thy will be done,
> On earth as in heaven.
> Give us today our daily bread.
> Forgive us the wrong we have done,
> As we have forgiven those who
> have wronged us.
> And do not bring us to the test,
> But save us from the evil one.
>   (Matt. 6:9–13)

The poetic structure highlighted in the New English Bible facilitates understanding, but the phrase "And do not bring us to the test" is translated more clearly in the New Living Translation as "And don't let us yield to temptation."

There are occasions, however, where more difficult vocabulary could be improved; for example, "widow's weeds" = "garments" (Gen. 38:14), "stooks" =

Table 20.8
Comparison of Revised Standard Version and New English Bible Texts

Passage	Revised Standard Version	New English Bible	Textual Evidence for NEB
Matt. 1:18	Now the birth of Jesus Christ took place in this way.	This is the story of the birth of the Messiah.	Old Latin MSS, Vulgate, Syriac, Irenaeus (Latin MSS), etc.
Matt. 9:34	But the Pharisees said, "He casts out demons by the prince of the demons."	[verse omitted]	D, some Old Latin MSS, Sinaitic Syriac, etc.
Matt. 10:3	Thaddaeus	Lebbaeus	D, some Old Latin MSS, Origen (Latin MSS), etc.
Matt. 27:16–17	Barabbas	Jesus Bar-Abbas	Θ, f^1, 700*, some Syriac MSS, Armenian, Georgian, etc.
Mark 1:41	moved with pity	in warm indignation	D, some Old Latin MSS, (Diatessaron)
Mark 8:26	Do not even enter the village	Do not tell anyone in the village	two Old Latin MSS (but combined readings are common)
Mark 8:38	For whoever is ashamed of me and of my words	If anyone is ashamed of me and mine [i.e., my followers?]	$\mathfrak{P}^{45vid}$, W, one Old Latin MS, Sahidic Coptic
Luke 12:27	Consider the lilies, how they grow; they neither toil nor spin	Think of the lilies: they neither spin nor weave	D, Old Syriac, two Old Latin MSS, Ethiopic, etc.
John 13:10	He who has bathed does not need to wash, except for his feet	A man who has bathed needs no further washing	$\aleph$, 579, Old Latin, Vulgate, Origen, Tertullian, etc.
Acts 1:26	he was enrolled with the eleven apostles	who was then assigned a place among the twelve apostles	D, Old Latin MSS
Acts 3:21	by the mouth of his holy prophets from of old	by his holy prophets	D, four Old Latin MSS, Armenian, Georgian, etc.

"stocks" (Judg. 15:5), "panniers" = "baskets" (Job 5:5), "in spate" = "being flooded" (Job 6:17), "reck" = "to pay heed" (Job 9:21), "ague" = "shivering fits (flu?)" (Job 33:19), and "gaff" = "barbed fishing spear" (Job 41:1). Special difficulties in wording, spelling, and coinage for Americans surface: "cairn" = "memorial" (Gen. 31:46–53); "calumny" = "false accusations" (Matt. 5:11); "Whitsuntide" = "Pentecost" (1 Cor. 16:8); "midge" = "gnat" (Matt. 23:24); and "fortnight" = "two weeks" (Gal. 1:18); even the spellings take a little getting used to: "plough" = "plow" (Deut. 22:10); "mouldy" = "moldy" (Josh. 9:5, 12); "gaoler" = "jailer" (Isa. 10:4); and coinage is suited to the British and not the American public ("twopence," Luke 12:6; "farthing," Mark 12:42; "pounds," Mark 6:37). An unwittingly humorous translation from the New English Bible is 1 Corinthians 5:9: "you must have nothing to do with loose livers."

One translation that gave rise to great debate appears in 2 Timothy 3:16: "Every inspired scripture has its use for teaching" instead of the common "All Scripture is God-breathed and is useful." The first translation may be used to argue that only parts of Scripture are God-breathed and therefore useful, which is clearly against what was originally intended in the passage.[34]

Its Reception

The New Testament was completed on March 14, 1961; within twelve months about four million copies were sold, and in nine years the total was about seven million. Every translation has its detractors; some of the criticism the New English Bible received is noted by Bruce:

> "It's quite good," a little girl is said to have remarked, "but it's not so *holy* as the old one, is it?" This absence of a hieractic quality from its diction was noted also by Mr Robert Graves, who is credited with the judgment that the new version lacked *baraka* [blessing] and that he would not feel that an oath sworn on it was so binding as one sworn on the A.V.

... But, so far as its style was concerned, the severest criticism came from T. S. Eliot. "So long as the *New English Bible* was used only for private reading," he wrote, "it would be merely a symptom of the decay of the English language in the middle of the twentieth century. But the more it is adopted for religious services the more it will become an active agent of decadence." (*The Sunday Telegraph*, Dec. 16, 1962)[35]

One of the most important criticisms was leveled by N. A. E. Earle. In a pamphlet entitled *Spiritual Losses in the New English Bible* he notes that the translators of the New English Bible have made no distinction between δαιμόνιον (*daimonion*; or δαίμων, *daimōn*, demon) and διάβολος (*diabolos*, devil), though New Testament teaching makes it very clear that there are many demons but only one devil.

An Evaluation

The New English Bible was the first British Bible to be commissioned as a cooperative effort and took longer (twenty-four years) and cost more to produce than did any earlier Bible. It was produced by capable scholars and contains some fresh and lively translations, though American readers (and even British readers at times) will need a British dictionary to understand certain passages (esp. in Job). However, it also suffers some notable weaknesses: it is sometimes more paraphrastic than a translation, occasionally wandering somewhat from the meaning of the text (e.g., John 1:1; Gal. 5:12; 2 Tim. 3:16; James 1:2–8); at times the editors include readings in the translation that have little textual support; and the dubious translation of 2 Timothy 3:16.

The Jerusalem Bible (1966)

Its History

This is the first complete Roman Catholic Bible translated from the original languages into English (prior to the papal encyclical of 1943, translations were required to be based on the Latin Vulgate). Father Roland DeVaux's French edition, *La Bible de Jérusalem,* based upon the original languages, appeared in 1956; Roman Catholic scholars led by Alexander Jones of Christ's College, Liverpool, then translated it into English (the Jerusalem Bible, 1966). Realizing that it would not be nearly as accurate if it were merely translated from the French, they translated first from Greek and Hebrew manuscripts, comparing the result closely to the French translation. Many scholars worked on this translation, but probably the most famous was J. R. R. Tolkien. The character of this edition is described in the editor's foreword:

> The form and nature of this edition of the Holy Bible have been determined by two of the principal dangers facing the Christian religion today. The first is the reduction of Christianity to the status of a relic—affectionately regarded, it is true, but considered irrelevant to our times. The second is its rejection as a mythology, born and cherished in emotion with nothing at all to say to the mind.[36]

The Translation

The apocryphal books (or as the Roman Catholics entitle them "the deuterocanonical books") are interspersed among the rest of the Old Testament books in the Jerusalem Bible. The footnotes have a clear Roman Catholic flavor; for example, Jesus' brothers in Matthew 12:46 are described as "Not Mary's children but near relations, cousins perhaps," and the footnote to

Matthew 1:25 reads, "The text is not concerned with the period that followed and, taken by itself, does not assert Mary's perpetual virginity which, however, the gospels elsewhere suppose and which the Tradition of the Church affirms." Second person forms are consistently rendered "you," and the personal name for Israel's God is "Yahweh." The English is readily understandable but not homogeneous, some parts being freer or tending more toward paraphrase than others. The following passages illustrate the pleasing flow of this English translation:

> Be careful not to parade your good deeds before men to attract their notice; by doing this you will lose all reward from your Father in heaven. So when you give alms, do not have it trumpeted before you; this is what the hypocrites do in the synagogues and in the streets to win men's admiration. I tell you solemnly, they have had their reward. (Matt. 6:1–2)

> Our Father in heaven,
> may your name be held holy,
> your kingdom come,
> your will be done,
> on earth as in heaven.
> Give us today our daily bread.
> And forgive us our debts,
> as we have forgiven those who
>   are in debt to us.
> And do not put us to the test,
> but save us from the evil one.
>   (Matt. 6:9–13)

The structure of the Lord's Prayer is helpful, but the phrase "may your name be held holy" would have been better translated as "may your name be honored" or

Table 20.9
The Jerusalem Bible

Sponsors of the Translation	Translators	Text	Translation Techniques	Characteristics
Catholic Church of the United Kingdom	27 Roman Catholic scholars led by A. Jones	OT: Masoretic Text NT: eclectic Greek text	Literal translation Roman Catholic footnotes	Modern English (no "thees" or "thous") Sense paragraphs Poetic structure Few emendations OT quotations in italics

the like, and the phrase "put to the test" is somewhat awkward.

An Evaluation

By and large the translation is clear and understandable, except for a few passages where archaic wording is retained: "My enemies whet their eyes on me" (Job 16:9); "Sleeplessness, biliousness and gripe are what the glutton has to endure" (Sir. 31:20b). The footnotes are quite useful in explaining the meaning of several passages as long as the reader is aware of their bias. This translation was revised in 1985 and is called *The New Jerusalem Bible*.

The Living Bible (NT, 1967; Entire Bible, 1971)

Its History

Events leading to Kenneth N. Taylor's (fig. 20.5) preparation of a popular, simplified paraphrase called *The Living Bible* were very similar to those surrounding the Phillips translation about ten years earlier. Taylor first realized the need for a Bible in modern English from his travels in America and Canada as a speaker for InterVarsity; but later, when he had ten

children of his own, he encountered firsthand the difficulty they had in understanding the King James Bible.

As Taylor retold these Bible stories in clear and simple modern English to his own children, he came to the realization that others could also benefit from his labors. His first systematic attempt at translating Scripture began in 1956 when, as the director of the Moody Literature Mission of the Moody Press, he determined to use commuting time on the train to produce his translation. His work appeared in stages: in 1962 he published the *Living Letters*, in 1965 the *Living Prophecies*, in 1966 the *Living Gospels*, and in 1967 the entire New Testament. Almost immediately afterward he began work on the *Living Psalms*, which were published in 1967 and were followed by the *Living Lessons of Life and Love* in 1968. Next appeared the *Living History of Israel* in 1970, and in 1971 the entire Bible was published, entitled *The Living Bible*. His translation was so well received that he established his own publishing company (which he called Tyndale House after William Tyndale, the father of English translations) to promote and publish the paraphrase.

Since this translation was originally prepared for Taylor's children, not surprisingly it has proven to be very popular among young people throughout the English-speaking world. In 1965 Wheaton College awarded Taylor an honorary doctor of literature for his work in Bible translation. The English version has been published a number of different ways under a variety of titles (e.g., *Reach Out* [1969]; *The Way* [1972]; *The Way: Catholic Version* [1973]; *Soul Food* [1973]), and a program was launched called Living Bible International for the production of similar types of paraphrases in other languages. Jack P. Lewis describes the popularity of the Living Bible:

> Though moving slowly at first, once Taylor's material had received the endorsement of Billy Graham in 1963 and was offered on Graham's television program, its sales became fantastic. Over nine million copies of Living Letters were sold. The LB was the best-selling book in the United States in 1972, and the royalties

for the year amounted to four million dollars. Royalties for 1973 were eight million dollars. By 1974 it accounted for 46 percent of the sales of Bibles in the United States, and the paraphrase had produced royalties in excess of twenty million dollars. For the month of September 1977 the *Christian Bookseller's Magazine* 13 (September 1977): 10 listed it as leading all other Bibles in sales. The profits support the Tyndale House Foundation, which sponsors translators working in forty-two countries.[37]

The Policies of the Translator

The word *paraphrase* means "a restatement of an author's thoughts, using different words than he did."[38] Taylor's goal was to paraphrase the American Standard Version of 1901 into simple, modern English. He admitted that he was not proficient enough in the languages to render a paraphrase directly from the originals. In the Old Testament, Taylor followed the text of the American Standard Version fairly closely. Genesis 4:8 is one exception, where the Living Bible reads, "One day Cain suggested to his brother, 'Let's go out into the fields.'" The latter phrase, not found in the American Standard Version, has good textual support from the Samaritan Pentateuch, the Septuagint, and the Syriac Peshiṭta (though these versions read "field," not "fields"), but the change is not noted in the footnotes to the Living Bible. In 1 Samuel 13:1 the Living Bible rejects the American Standard Version's conjectural reading of "thirty years," following instead the incorrect King James Version reading of "reigned for one year." In the New Testament the American Standard Version was a vast improvement over the

Textus Receptus of the King James Version but was well behind advancements since 1881, when this text was produced. More frequently in the New Testament Taylor did not adhere to the text of the American Standard Version, with the result that some of the passages of doubtful authenticity, which had been removed from the American Standard Version and placed in footnotes, were reintroduced into the Living Bible with a footnote mentioning that they were omitted in many of the ancient manuscripts (e.g., Matt. 17:21; 18:11; Mark 15:28; John 5:3b–5a; Acts 8:37; 24:6b–8a [no note]; Rom. 16:24 [no note]).

Taylor claims that his translation was carefully scrutinized by a team of Greek and Hebrew experts for content and English scholars for form and style, though he admits that none were entirely satisfied with the results; it therefore remains a "tentative edition."[39]

The Translation

One of the greatest assets of the Living Bible is its simple and vivid language:

> "Again, the law of Moses says, 'You shall not break your vows to God, but must fulfill them all.' But I say: Don't make any vows! And even to say 'By heavens!' is a sacred vow to God, for the heavens are God's throne. And if you say 'By the earth!' it is a sacred vow, for the earth is his footstool. And don't swear 'By Jerusalem!' for Jerusalem is the capital of the great King. Don't even swear 'By my head!' for you can't turn one hair white or black. Say just a simple 'Yes, I will' or 'No, I won't.' Your word is enough. To strengthen your

Table 20.10
The Living Bible

Translator	Text	Translation Techniques	Characteristics
Kenneth N. Taylor	American Standard Version of 1901	Paraphrase	Modern English (no "thees" or "thous") Sense paragraphs Poetic structure OT quotations in italics

promise with a vow shows that something is wrong." (Matt. 5:33–37)

The Lord's Prayer reads:

Our Father in heaven, we honor your holy name. We ask that your kingdom will come now. May your will be done here on earth, just as it is in heaven. Give us our food again today, as usual, and forgive us our sins, just as we have forgiven those who have sinned against us. Don't bring us into temptation, but deliver us from the Evil One. Amen. (Matt. 6:9–13)

The language is clear and easy to understand, but it is unfortunate that poetry is never indicated in the Living Bible. Another weakness is that the text is often expanded by what Sakae Kubo and Walter Specht label "imaginative details for which there is no warrant in the original."[40] Table 20.11 compares several passages in the American Standard Version and the Living Bible.

The expansions are often dubious, and occasionally the original literary masterpiece is lost in the simple insertions of the text (e.g., Ps. 119:7–9). At least twice the Living Bible misses the point of the text. Isaiah 40:26 reads, "Look up to the heavens! Who created all these stars? As a shepherd leads his sheep, calling each by its pet name, and counts them to see that none

are lost or strayed, so God does with stars and planets!" The idea here is not of a loving shepherd as found in the Living Bible, but the majestic sovereign of the universe who summons the stars as a general would his armies. A second more serious problem, however, arises in the Gospels, where Jesus often claims to be the "Messiah" in the Living Bible. In fact Jesus was reticent to be called the Messiah, preferring instead to use other less political terms like "the son of Man" (e.g., Mark 8:38; 9:11, 13).

Taylor acknowledges in the preface the problems facing a paraphrase:

For whenever the author's exact words are not translated from the original languages, there is a possibility that the translator, however honest, may be giving the English reader something that the original writer did not mean to say. This is because a paraphrase is guided not only by the translator's skill in simplifying but also by the clarity of his understanding of what the author meant and by his theology. For when the Greek or Hebrew is not clear, then the theology of the translator is his guide along with his sense of logic. . . . The theological lodestar in this book has been a rigid evangelical position.[41]

Kubo and Specht are correct in their evaluation that "Taylor cannot be faulted for

Table 20.11

Comparison of American Standard Version and Living Bible Texts

American Standard Version (1901)	Living Bible
Amos 1:1–2 The words of Amos, who was among the herdsmen of Tekoa, which he saw concerning Israel in the days of Uzziah king of Judah, and in the days of Jeroboam the son of Joash king of Israel, two years before the earthquake. And he said, Jehovah will roar from Zion, and utter his voice from Jerusalem; and the pastures of the shepherds shall mourn, and the top of Carmel shall wither.	Amos was a herdsman living in the village of Tekoa. All day long he sat on the hillsides watching the sheep, keeping them from straying. 　　One day, in a vision, God told him some of the things that were going to happen to his nation, Israel. This vision came to him at the time Uzziah was king of Judah, and while Jeroboam (son of Joash) was king of Israel—two years before the earthquake. 　　This is his report of what he saw and heard: The Lord roared—like a ferocious lion from his lair—from his Temple on Mount Zion. And suddenly the lush pastures of Mount Carmel withered and dried, and all the shepherds mourned.
Mark 12:27 "He is not the God of the dead, but of the living: ye do greatly err."	"God was telling Moses that these men, though dead for hundreds of years, were still very much alive; for he would not have said, 'I *am* the God' of those who don't exist! You have made a serious error."

his simple, direct rewording of the ASV into everyday English. But when he assumes the role of a commentator, and freely interprets or reinterprets a passage, his fidelity to the original is often subject to question."[42]

An Evaluation

The Living Bible is exactly that; the language is vivid, easy to understand, at times even shocking—Saul's response to Jonathan in 1 Samuel 20:30 reads "You son of a bitch!" While this is an accurate rendering of the verse, the Revised Standard Version maintains the sharp tone (e.g., "You son of a perverse, rebellious woman") without resorting to colloquialism that is unnecessarily inappropriate for children. It is unfortunate, as well, that Taylor was compelled to use the American Standard Version as the basis for his paraphrase instead of working from the original languages. To remedy this problem, the New Living Translation (1996) was produced by more than one hundred evangelical scholars from the original languages.

Taylor must be commended for achieving a paraphrase of the Bible that can be grasped easily by someone who finds Bible English generally unintelligible. In the preface to the Living Bible, Taylor states his goal: "If this paraphrase helps to simplify the deep and often complex thoughts of the Word of God, and if it makes the Bible easier to understand and follow, deepening the Christian lives of its readers and making it easier for them to follow their Lord, then it has achieved its goal."[43] There is no doubt that this paraphrase has aroused interest in reading the Bible, and for this it cannot be faulted, but one of its major drawbacks is that it frequently sacrifices accuracy in the process of making the Bible understandable. It should be remembered that this is a paraphrase and be used as such, as Taylor himself makes note of: "For study purposes, a paraphrase should be checked against a rigid [literal?] translation."[44]

Good News Bible/Today's English Version (NT, 1966; Entire Bible, 1976)

Its History

On September 15, 1966, the American Bible Society published a new, modern-speech version entitled *Good News for Modern Man: The New Testament in Today's English Version.* Dr. Robert G. Bratcher, who had previously translated for the American Bible Society the Gospel of Mark, entitled *The Right Time*, was asked to oversee completion of the entire New Testament, a project that took about two and one-half years. This translation first sold for twenty-five cents, but the price was later raised to sixty cents to cover the cost of publication. By 1976 the American Bible Society had already sold fifty-two million copies of this New Testament under two different titles (*Today's English Version* and *Good News for Modern Man*).[45]

Table 20.12
Good News Bible

Sponsors of the Translation	Translator	Text	Translation Techniques	Characteristics
American Bible Society	Robert G. Bratcher (editor-in-chief)	OT: *Biblia Hebraica* (1937) NT: United Bible Societies' Greek text (1975)	Dynamic equivalence	Modern English (no "thees" or "thous") Sense paragraphs Poetic structure Few emendations OT quotations enclosed by quotation marks

Table 20.13
Comparison of Traditional and Good News Bible Expressions

Expression	Good News Bible's Translation
Antichrist	enemy of Christ (1 John 2:18, 22)
bishops	church leaders (Phil. 1:1; 1 Tim. 3:2)
Caesar	Emperor or Roman Emperor (Luke 2:1; 3:1)
centurion	army officer (Matt. 27:54)
captain of the temple	officer in charge of the temple guards (Acts 4:1; 5:24, 26)
deacons	church helpers (Phil. 1:1; 1 Tim. 3:8)
publicans	tax collectors (Matt. 5:46)
Sanhedrin	Council (Matt. 26:59; John 11:47)

It was so popular that it went through a second and third edition (1967 and 1971, respectively), each time incorporating further improvements in faithfulness, style, and English. In 1976 the Old Testament was completed and published together with a fourth edition of the New Testament called the *Good News Bible*. The American Bible Society now prefers the designation Good News Bible for the complete work, but in this book we will refer to earlier editions of the New Testament as the Today's English Version.

The Policies of the Translators

The goal of this translation was to achieve an accurate, understandable translation of the original texts, as the preface to the Good News Bible states:

> The primary concern of the translators has been to provide a faithful translation of the meaning of the Hebrew, Aramaic, and Greek texts.... After ascertaining as accurately as possible the meaning of the original, the translators' next task was to express that meaning in a matter and form easily understood by the readers. Since this translation is intended for all who use English as a means of communication, the translators have tried to avoid words and forms not in current or widespread use; but no artificial limit has been set to the range of the vocabulary employed. Every effort has been made to use language that is natural, clear, simple, and unambiguous.[46]

This translation is not a paraphrase, since it is not merely an attempt to reword the original texts; it uses the translation principle known as dynamic equivalence in which the translator attempts to produce the same effect as the original had on its readers.[47] The foreword of the Good News Bible states it a little differently: "The aim of this Bible is to give today's readers maximum understanding of the content of the original texts."[48] There is, therefore, equally strong emphases upon faithfulness to the message and on making it understandable to English readers in all walks of life. While no strict limitations were imposed as to which words could be used, R. C. Fuller, one of the translators, indicated that the language of the Good News Bible is generally at an elementary-school reading level to ensure that it can be understood.[49]

The Translation

Because the principle of dynamic equivalence puts more weight on clarity of meaning than on literary form, questions are often simplified into statements; for example, "Do not even the tax collectors do the same?" (Matt. 5:46 RSV) becomes "Even the tax collectors do that!"; or "For what can a man give in return for his life?" (Mark 8:37 RSV) becomes "There is nothing he can give to regain his life." Technical vocabulary is also avoided; table 20.13 lists some examples.

Slang and regional variations that would not be understood by many English-speaking people have been avoided, although some phrases are borderline, such as "until it comes out of your ears" (Num. 11:20); "You smart aleck, you!" (1 Sam. 17:28); and "smashed ... to bits" (2 Kings 23:12). A few phrases would not be considered "current English idiom"; for example, an American may say "be courageous," but never simply "Courage!" as found in Mark 6:50.

For the benefit of readers unfamiliar with the Bible, there are introductions to each of the biblical books, maps, and a dictionary of more difficult words. The books are divided into sense paragraphs with titles highlighted in bold print. The personal name for Israel's God is translated "LORD" and the title "Adonai (Lord) Yahweh" is rendered "Sovereign LORD." Distinctive to this translation are the line drawings by Annie Vallotton, a Swiss artist living in Paris (fig. 20.6).

The Old Testament

Bratcher served as chairman over six Old Testament specialists, most of whom had foreign missionary experience, chosen to make this translation: Roger A. Bullard (Atlantic Christian College), Keith R. Crim (Virginia Commonwealth University), Herbert G. Grether, Barclay A. Newman (United Bible Society), Heber F. Peacock (United Bible Society), and John A. Thompson (American Bible Society). In 1971 a British consultant, Brynmor F. Price, joined the translation team. The third edition of Kittel's *Biblia Hebraica* (1937) was used for the Old Testament, which was completed in 1975. On the few occasions where this translation departs from the traditional Hebrew readings it follows those of the versions (e.g., Septuagint, Vulgate, Syriac Peshiṭta, etc.); for example, in Genesis 4:8b the phrase "Let's go out in the field" is included from the versions, and in Psalm 145:13b the phrase "The Lord is faithful to his promises, and he is merciful in all his acts" is added from the Septuagint. Only rarely do the translators resort to emendations (e.g., Amos 6:12b; Ps. 2:11–12).

Each of the translators was responsible for preparing a preliminary translation with detailed notes of an Old Testament section. These were sent to the rest of the committee, whose written suggestions as to how the translation could be improved were then incorporated into a revised draft.

This draft was read aloud, allowing the members to make further changes, before it was sent to approximately two hundred consultants in various parts of the world for criticism. Next a special panel of eight people, including biblical scholars, linguists, and church laypeople, discussed and critiqued the translation. The draft was then reviewed for stylistic and English quality. Lastly, it was submitted to the Translation Committee of the American Bible Society for final approval.

One of the most serious criticisms leveled against the Good News Bible Old Testament translation concerns poetry, as Bruce notes: "the poetical literature of the Old Testament . . . has been turned into the same kind of pedestrian prose as the narrative and didactic parts of the Bible, whereas a more elevated style would be necessary if the same effect were to be produced today as in antiquity."[50] Poetic structure is crucial to achieving the translation goal of this version, even more so than for the translators of the King James Version, who succeeded in producing very fine poetry. It is also somewhat surprising that the psalm titles were removed, though they are included in the footnotes because they appear in *Biblia Hebraica*. Unfortunately *Biblia Hebraica Stuttgartensia* (1966–1977) was not finished in time to be used for this translation, but it appears that the translators incorporated most of the major changes into the Good News Bible (e.g., Isa. 14:4; 56:12).

Figure 20.6.
Illustration from Mark 14, Good News Bible. [American Bible Society]

"*This is my body.*" (14.22)

Several interesting readings surface; for example, Genesis 1:2 says that "the power of God was moving over the water," and Isaiah 7:14 reads that "a young woman who is pregnant will have a son" (though both passages list a number of optional readings in the footnotes). In one respect Kubo and Specht believe that the translators were perhaps too thorough in making the translation smooth and understandable: "There can be no question that the translation given by the GNB is simple, clear, and unambiguous. The OT is clear even when the Hebrew is uncertain or ambiguous. This raises the possibility that the translation may not always give the correct interpretation."[51] However, one could make the same criticism when the text is not nearly so smooth and clear.

The New Testament

The translators of the Good News Bible revised the earlier Today's English Version in light of the third edition of the Greek New Testament by the United Bible Societies (1975) (each of the previous editions of Today's English Version had used the most up-to-date edition of the Greek New Testament). The third edition of the Today's English Version did not indicate variant readings in the footnotes but included them instead in a four-page appendix at the end; in the fourth edition they were included in the preferred footnote position. About 135 footnotes explain textual variants; brackets indicate where material is added to the text with a footnote indicating supporting evidence (e.g., Matt. 12:47; 16:2b–3; Mark 10:7b; 14:68c; Luke 11:33b; John 3:25). The longer ending of Mark 16 is placed in square brackets with the heading "AN OLD ENDING TO THE GOSPEL"; the shorter ending then appears with the title "ANOTHER OLD ENDING." Modern equivalents were attempted for expressions of time (e.g., "between three and six o'clock in the morning," Matt. 14:25), distances (e.g., "half a mile away," Acts 1:12), capacity (e.g., "twenty and thirty gallons," John 2:6), and money (e.g., "millions of dollars," Matt. 18:24),

though the last sometimes represents only very general guesses as to meaning. More important is the fact that simple words were chosen to express great biblical concepts; for example, "repent" reads "turn away from your sins" (e.g., Matt. 3:2; Mark 1:15) and "justify" is expressed as "to put right with God" (e.g., Rom. 2:13; 5:1). Two famous New Testament textual changes appear in the Good News Bible: John 7:53–8:11 is bracketed with a footnote to the effect that it is not found in many early manuscripts and that early versions often include it after John 21:24; and the *Comma Johanneum* in 1 John 5:7 is omitted without comment.

Figures of speech and Semitisms are some of the most difficult things for translators to bring into modern speech, but according to the principle of dynamic equivalence they would not necessarily need to be carried over since they are part of the Greek or Hebrew language. An idiom like "the finger of God" therefore becomes "God's power" (Luke 11:20), and "cut to the heart" becomes "deeply troubled" (Acts 2:37). Semitic concepts like "Son of peace" becomes "a peace-loving man" (Luke 10:6), and "Father of glory" becomes "glorious Father" (Eph. 1:17). One unfortunate change appears in Ecclesiastes 1:1, where the Preacher becomes the Philosopher. Nevertheless, the text is simple and understandable:

You have heard that it was said, "Love your friends, hate your enemies." But now I tell you: love your enemies and pray for those who persecute you, so that you may become the sons of your Father in heaven. For he makes his sun to shine on bad and good people alike, and gives rain to those who do good and to those who do evil. Why should God reward you if you love only the people who love you? Even the tax collectors do that! (Matt. 5:43)

Our Father in heaven:
May your holy name be honored;
may your Kingdom come;
may your will be done on earth
as it is in heaven.
Give us today the food we need.

Forgive us the wrongs we have
done,
as we forgive the wrongs that
others have done to us.
Do not bring us to hard testing,
but keep us safe from the Evil
One. (Matt. 6:9–13)

In response to the rendering "Do not bring us to hard testing," W. F. Stinespring of Duke University, points out: "Temptation or hard testing is inevitable in this world. What we need is help from God to withstand the temptation. It seems to me that the Syriac versions may be translated: 'Let us not succumb to temptation but deliver us from the evil one.'"[52] Stinespring's rendering appears to capture the meaning of the text better than does the Good News Bible.

At the same time as the American edition, a British edition also appeared, which included various British idioms, spellings, and metric weights and measures. The Apocrypha was sponsored by a British company (William Collins Sons and Co.) and was included in a publication of the Bible in 1979. The Good News Bible has become so popular that it is being translated into other languages as well.

An Evaluation

The Good News Bible has effectively achieved a simple, straightforward style that makes even the most difficult passages understandable, a goal expressed in the foreword: "The aim of this Bible is to give today's readers maximum understanding from the content of the original texts." In practice this aim was not achieved by adding more words (as in the Living Bible) but by simplifying the words used. While readers may not always agree with their interpretation (e.g., Gen. 6:1–4), at least one traditional rendering of the text is provided in the footnotes. The translation was produced with the utmost care and contains far fewer mistakes than does the Living Bible.

New International Version (NT, 1973; Entire Bible, 1978)

Its History

This work arose from dissatisfaction among evangelicals with existing translations.[53] In 1965 a Committee on Bible Translation (fifteen scholars from many religious denominations) met to consider making a new modern-speech translation. The translation project, backed by the Christian Reformed Church and the National Association of Evangelicals, began in 1965 but received new impetus in 1967 when the New York International Bible Society agreed to sponsor it financially. Dr. Edwin H. Palmer served as executive secretary until his death in 1980; then Kenneth Barker, secretary of the Committee for Bible translation of the New York International Bible Society, assumed the position. The translation, entitled *The Holy Bible: New International Version*, was appropriate not only because it was produced by more than 110 evangelical translators from many English-speaking countries, including America, Canada, England, Australia, and New Zealand, but also because it used English that is internationally recognized. This objective was apparently successful since a British version published in 1974 had few changes in the vocabulary of the text (though British spellings and punctuation were used). Isaiah and Daniel were published in 1976 in order to obtain the reaction of the general reading population; Proverbs and Ecclesiastes appeared in 1977. By the time the entire Old Testament was published on October 27, 1978, advance sales had risen to almost 1,200,000 copies. Theological and denominational biases in this translation are minimal since the translators come from a wide variety of denominations (about thirty-four), including Anglican, Assemblies of God, Baptist, Brethren, Christian Reformed, Church of Christ, Episcopalian, Evangelical Free Church, Lutheran, Mennonite, Methodist, Nazarene, Presbyterian, and Wesleyan Methodist. Among the distinguished scholars who helped on this translation were Gleason L. Archer (Trinity International University), Ralph Earle (Nazarene Theological Seminary), R. Laird Harris (Covenant Theological Seminary), Roland K. Harrison (University of Toronto), Walter C. Kaiser (Gordon-Conwell), Meredith G. Kline (Gordon-Conwell), William Lane (Western Kentucky University), Richard N. Longenecker (MacMaster's Divinity School), A. R. Millard (University of Liverpool), Leon Morris (Ridley College, Sidney), Martin H. Woudstra (Calvin Theological Seminary), and Donald J. Wiseman (University of London).

The Policies of the Translators

The translators were divided into twenty teams composed of a translator, cotranslator, two consultants, and an English stylist appointed to each team. Initial work was performed by the translation team, which then submitted its work to an intermediate editorial committee for review, after which a general editorial committee of critics from all walks of life evaluated it. A fifteen-member executive committee then reviewed and revised the text before a final reading by literary consultants. In the opinion of Kubo and Specht the process was highly effective:

> At each stage of the process there has been a careful wrestling of various minds with the sacred text and an honest attempt to say in simple, clear English what the Bible writers express in the originals. It is difficult to conceive a plan that could have better checks and bal-

ances than the one used. Along with this, attention has been given to the literary quality of the English and an attempt has been made to achieve a version worthy of memorization.[54]

The New International Version has attempted to bridge the gap between word-for-word and dynamic-equivalence translations. They have sought not only accuracy and clarity but a degree of formality as well. The preface to the New International Version provides a helpful summary of the translation principles employed:

> The first concern of the translators has been accuracy of the translation and its fidelity to the thought of the biblical writers. They have weighed the significance of the lexical and grammatical details of the Hebrew, Aramaic and Greek texts. At the same time, they have striven for more than a word-for-word translation. Because thought patterns and syntax differ from language to language, faithful communication of the meaning of the writers of the Bible demands frequent modifications in sentence structure and constant regard for the contextual meanings of words.[55]

In an attempt to steer this middle course in translation, renderings are quite literal without using the same English word for a specific Greek or Hebrew word. For example, the traditional idea of "God repenting" is translated variously as "relent(s)" (Jer. 18:8; 26:3, 13, 19; Amos 7:3, 6; Joel 2:13); "turn back" (Jer. 4:28); "change his mind" (1 Sam. 15:29); "is (was) grieved" (Gen. 6:6; 1 Sam. 15:11, 35); "have compassion" (Ps. 90:13; Isa. 49:13; 51:3), but

Table 20.14
New International Version

Sponsors of the Translation	Translators	Text	Translation Techniques	Characteristics
New York International Bible Society	About 110 evangelical translators	OT: *Biblia Hebraica Stuttgartensia* NT: eclectic Greek text (Nestle-Aland and United Bible Societies Greek text)	Literal/dynamic equivalence	Modern English (no "thees" or "thous") Sense paragraphs Poetic structure Few emendations OT quotations enclosed in quotation marks

never as "repenting." Again, the Hebrew word זֶרַע (zeraʿ, "seed") is translated as "offspring" (Gen. 12:7; 13:16), "descendant" (Lev. 21:21; Num. 16:40), and "descendants" (2 Sam. 22:51; Ps. 18:50). Poetic structures are noted in the New International Version, and the parallelism and rhythm of the original poetry are approximated. However, the translators do not go as far as the Knox Version, which even reflects alphabetic acrostics in the English wording of the Psalms.

The Translation

The goal was to achieve an English translation that would "have clarity and literary quality and so prove suitable for public and private reading, teaching, preaching, memorizing and liturgical use."[56] Thus the language of the New International Version was to be both dignified and simple. Some people would question whether one translation can achieve both goals; for instance, the New International Version uses many contractions, which tend to be less formal, and yet discreet wording was chosen where some translations have been less so (e.g., 1 Sam. 25:22 reads "May God deal with David, be it ever so severely, if by morning I leave alive one male of all who belong to him!" [NIV], but the very literal reading of the Authorized Version of 1611 is "if I leave of all that pertain to him by the morning light, any that pisseth against the wall").

The New International Version removes many Hebrew idioms; for instance, "and it came to pass" is omitted (Gen. 6:1; Luke 2:1); "to lift up the voice and weep" becomes "to weep aloud" (Gen. 27:38; 29:11); and "uncircumcised lips" becomes "faltering lips" (Exod. 6:12, 30). Anthropomorphic language, which is common in the Hebrew Bible, is still present in the New International Version (e.g., "the eyes of the LORD your God are continually on it," Deut. 11:12; "Surely the arm of the LORD is not too short to save, nor his ear too dull to hear," Isa. 59:1). Archaic forms of the second-person pronouns do not appear anywhere in the New International

Version for two reasons: they are no longer contemporary English, and the original languages did not use special forms when addressing God. Standard practice is followed for rendering the tetragrammaton (YHWH) as "LORD" and Adonai YHWH as "Sovereign LORD." Passages are divided into thought paragraphs with titles in bold print. Thoughts interrupting the main flow of the passage are indicated in parentheses (e.g., Gen. 23:2; 2 Sam. 4:4; 9:10; 11:4; Rev. 20:5), though surprisingly none are found in Isaiah 7:8. Half-brackets indicate words that are not in the original text but are included for translation or clarification, although their usage is inconsistent (e.g., Gen. 4:1 "with the help of" is inserted in the text without brackets whereas in Nah. 1:8–14 "Nineveh" has been added in brackets to vv. 8, 11, 14).

The New International Version has more than 3,350 footnotes indicating textual variations, other translations, parallel Scripture quotations, and explanatory notes. Nouns (but not pronouns) that refer to divinity or the Messiah are capitalized (e.g., "Shepherd," Gen. 48:15; "Name," Exod. 23:21; "Anointed One," Ps. 2:2; "Branch," Isa. 11:1), except for some New Testament terms for Messiah (e.g., "prophet," Deut. 18:15, 18; "priest," Ps. 110:4; "servant," Isa. 52:13); some footnotes to passages offer alternative capitalization (e.g., "son," Ps. 2:7, 12 and "Anointed One," Dan. 9:26). Lewis notes, however, that "It does not go to the extremes seen in some translations in which every appearance of the angel of the Lord is said in a note to be that of the Messiah."[57] Other scholars would argue that there are far too many capitalizations[58] and that it is better to let the reader determine whether or not the references are to the Messiah.

The Old Testament

The preface to the New International Version states that the translation was made from "the latest editions of *Biblia Hebraica*," occasionally following readings from ancient versions (Gen. 4:8; Ps. 145:13b), Qumran manuscripts (Isa. 33:8 "witnesses" [עֵדִים, ʿēdîm] instead of "cities" [עָרִים, ʿārîm]; Isa. 53:11 "he will see the light" instead of simply "he will see"), or emendations (2 Kings 10:25; Ps. 40:2; Isa. 2:6); the last tend to be less frequent, however, than those found in the Revised Standard Version (cf. Ps. 2:11–12; Amos 6:12).

The New Testament

The preface says that an "eclectic" Greek text was used and that the translators chose the "best current printed texts of the Greek New Testament," which were for the most part the critical Greek texts of Nestle-Aland and the United Bible Societies' Greek text. Eighteen passages in the New International Version are footnoted to the effect that they are omitted from manuscripts; of these eighteen passages the New International Version agrees with the Revised Standard Version in all but six. Other passages are left in the text even though they have weak textual support (e.g., Matt. 21:44; Luke 24:6a). Mark 16:9–20 is set off by lines separating the sections with a footnote stating that these verses are not included in the most reliable manuscripts. The footnote to John 7:53–8:11, however, does not mention that these verses are sometimes found at the end of John or after Luke 21:38.

The New International Version, while clear and understandable, is not as fresh and striking as the Phillips translation; nevertheless it achieves a nice balance of language that is accurate and dignified:

Do not think that I have come to abolish the Law or the Prophets; I have not come to abolish them but to fulfill them. I tell you the truth, until heaven and earth disappear, not the smallest letter, not the least stroke of a pen, will by any means disappear from the Law until everything is accomplished. (Matt. 5:17–18)

Our Father in heaven,
hallowed be your name,
your kingdom come,
your will be done
    on earth as it is in heaven.
Give us today our daily bread.
Forgive us our debts,
    as we also have forgiven our
    debtors.
And lead us not into temptation,
    but deliver us from the evil one.
                        (Matt. 6:9–13)

The New International Version is somewhat inconsistent in its terminology for money, times, measures, and distances. For example, "talent(s)" (Matt. 18:24; 25:14–30), "denarius" (Matt. 20:2; Mark 12:15) and "mina(s)" (Luke 19:11–27) appear frequently, but in John 12:5 the perfume is said to be worth "a year's wage" with a footnote that indicates a value of "300 denarii;" similarly, John 6:7 reads "eight months wages would not buy enough bread for each one to have a bite!" and the footnote states "200 denarii." Roman time keeping

Table 20.15
Comparison of Interpretations

NIV	RSV	NASB	NEB
1 Samuel 20:30 son of a perverse and rebellious woman	son of a perverse, rebellious woman	son of a perverse, rebellious woman	son of a crooked and unfaithful mother
Isaiah 7:14 the virgin will be with child	a young woman shall conceive	a virgin will be with child	a young woman is with child
Matthew 5:3 Blessed are the poor in spirit	Blessed are the poor in spirit	Blessed are the poor in spirit	How blest are those who know their need of God
John 1:1 and the Word was God	and the Word was God	and the Word was God	and what God was, the Word was

is cited (e.g., "the sixth hour until the ninth hour" [Matt. 27:45] without a footnote to offer the present-day equivalent (cf. Luke 24:13; John 1:39; 4:52; 6:19), and yet modern designations are also used (e.g., "three in the afternoon" [Acts 10:3]; "about noon" [Acts 10:9]). As far as distances are concerned, both "stadia" (Rev. 14:20; 21:16) and "miles" (Luke 24:13; John 6:19; 11:18) are used, as well as "cubits" (Rev. 21:17) and "yards" (John 21:8). Even the name *Peter*, which is the more common rendering (e.g., 1 Cor. 15:5; Gal. 1:18; 2:8, 9, 11, 14), sometimes appears as "Cephas" (1 Cor. 1:12; 3:22; 9:5).

Though the New International Version is a new translation, it is interesting how many passages retain traditional interpretations (see table 20.15).

An Evaluation

Kubo and Specht highly commend the New International Version: "It is a monument of Christian scholarship at its best. It does not have the color or striking characteristics of PHILLIPS or the NEB, but is dependable and straightforward. It is more modern than the RSV, less free than the NEB, and more literary than the GNB."[59] While the New International Version still has areas where it could be improved, it nevertheless has been well received; according to *CBA Marketplace*, it was the top-selling Bible version of 1999.[60] Bratcher, best known for his work on the Good News Bible, states: "The NIV bids fair to establish itself as the Bible for evangelicals. Its reception has been nothing short of spectacular . . . and it seems reasonable to

assume that in time this translation will replace the King James Bible in private and church usage among evangelical conservatives."[61]

The Revised English Bible (1989)

Its History

After the New English Bible was published in 1970, the New Testament underwent slight revisions when it was republished in 1972, but the Old Testament had never been revised. As a result, in 1974 the decision was made to perform a major revision of the New English Bible under the directorship of Professor W. D. McHardy, who had been deputy director of the New English Bible. His intent was to carry on the tradition begun by the New English Bible, the reasoning for which is stated in the preface to the Revised English Bible:

> It was right that The New English Bible in its original form, like any other version, should be subject to critical examination and discussion, and especially the Old Testament, which had not had the advantage of even a limited general revision. From the beginning helpful suggestions and criticisms had come in from many quarters. Moreover the widespread enthusiasm for The New English Bible had resulted in its being frequently used for reading aloud in public worship, the implications of which had not been fully anticipated by the translators.[62]

Table 20.16
The Revised English Bible

Sponsors of the Translation	Translators	Text	Translation Techniques	Characteristics
Oxford and Cambridge University Presses	About 26 British scholars (some the same for NEB)	OT: *Biblia Hebraica Stuttgartensia* NT: Nestle-Aland Greek text (26th edition, 1979)	Literal translation	Modern English (no "thees" or "thous") Sense paragraphs Poetic structure Many emendations OT quotations indented

Table 20.17
Comparison of New English Bible and Revised English Bible Texts

Passage	New English Bible	Revised English Bible
Genesis 1:1	In the beginning of creation, when God made the heaven and earth	In the beginning God created the heavens and the earth
Genesis 1:2	and a mighty wind that swept over the surface of the waters	and the spirit of God hovered over the surface of the waters
Genesis 5:1	This is the record of the descendants of Adam	This is the list of Adam's descendants
Psalm 1:1	Happy is the man who does not take the wicked for his guide	Happy is the one who does not take the counsel of the wicked for a guide
Isaiah 53:11	After all his pains he shall be bathed in light, after his disgrace he shall be fully vindicated	By his humiliation my servant will justify the many; after his suffering he will see light and be satisfied
John 1:1	When all things began, the Word already was. The Word dwelt with God, and what God was, the Word was.	In the beginning the Word already was. The Word was in God's presence, and what God was, the Word was.
1 Timothy 2:11	A woman must be a learner, listening quietly and with due submission	Their role is to learn, listening quietly and with due submission
2 Timothy 3:16	Every inspired scripture has its use for teaching the truth and refuting error	All inspired scripture has its use for teaching the truth and refuting error

Two primary features that were addressed were its archaic speech and the need for gender-inclusive language.

The Policies of the Translators

As with the New English Bible, a committee was made up of members from many denominations who examined the drafts of each of the books and in many cases gave detailed comments and criticism for the consideration of the director and the revisers. The translators worked for five years on this revision, which was published on September 28, 1989. Donald Coggan, chairman of the joint committee, describes their guidelines:

> Care has been taken to ensure that the style of English used is fluent and of appropriate dignity for liturgical use, while maintaining intelligibility for worshippers of a wide range of ages and backgrounds. The revisers have sought to avoid complex or technical terms where possible, and to provide sentence

structure and word order, especially in the Psalms, which would facilitate congregational reading but will not misrepresent the meaning of the original texts. As the "you"-form of address to God is now commonly used, the "thou"-form which was preserved in the language of prayer in The New English Bible has been abandoned. The use of male-oriented language, in passages of traditional versions of the Bible which evidently apply to both genders, has become a sensitive issue in recent years; the revisers have preferred more inclusive gender reference where that has been possible without compromising scholarly integrity or English style.[63]

The Translation

The revisers went through the New English Bible verse by verse to incorporate current scholarship and to improve the English fluency of the text. It was reviewed by both scholars and poets in an attempt to bring out the "fullness of the

English language."[64] Table 20.17 indicates some of the changes.

Many of the more unique renderings of the Old Testament were changed to follow more traditional renderings; there has been much less change, however, in the New Testament. Lewis states: "The language which in the original text refer to Deity in masculine terms remains unchanged, but 'person,' 'mankind,' 'mortals,' 'human beings,' or 'one' may be used where 'man' occurs in the KJV."[65] Two helpful stylistic changes were introduced: verse numbers have been incorporated into the text instead of in the margins so that it is much easier to determine where verses begin and end; and there are many more section headings than in the New English Bible, although bold print would help to distinguish them from the text. Another change between the New English Bible and the Revised English Bible is that the latter retains the numbering system of the King James Version, so that when verses originally appearing in the King James Version are omitted because of insufficient textual support the verse number is skipped and placed in a footnote (see Matt. 23:14).

The Old Testament

The Revised English Bible uses the most recent Masoretic Text, the *Biblia Hebraica Stuttgartensia* (1966–1977); where there were questions, passages were checked against the versions, patristic quotations, and other relevant manuscripts. In this way several of the conjectural readings of the New English Bible have been removed (e.g., "how can they raise themselves?" [Isa. 2:9]; "and buffaloes" [Isa. 34:7]). The Revised English Bible continues to rearrange a number of passages (e.g., Gen. 26:18 is after 26:15; 1 Sam. 24:4–7 is arranged as vv. 4a, 6, 7a, 4b, 5, 7b), though not as many as the New English Bible (e.g., Job 12:25 and then 22; Job 14:22, 21). The Revised English Bible also differs from the New English Bible by including psalm titles and the word *selah*. The fairytale-like beginning to Genesis 11:1, "Once upon a time" (NEB), now reads "There was a time when" (REB).

The New Testament

The Nestle-Aland Greek text (*Novum Testamentum Graece*, 26th ed. 1979) was used for the revision, though it is modified in several passages (e.g., the Revised English Bible reads "Thaddaeus" instead of "Lebbaeus" in Matt. 10:3, and "hyssop" instead of "javelin" in John 19:29). Another significant improvement over the New English Bible is that the revisers made a distinction in the New Testament between "demons" and the "devil" (e.g., the Revised English Bible reads "demons" in Matt. 8:16, 28, 31 instead of "devils"), although mistakes still crop up (e.g., Matt. 12:24–28 should read "demons"). It is unfortunate that the revisers chose to retain the New English Bible's translation of the first part of 2 Timothy 3:16, which reads "All inspired scripture has its use for teaching the truth and refuting error"; instead of the reading found in almost every other version, "All scripture is God-breathed." The former allows for the possibility of uninspired parts of Scripture.

The Revised English Bible in general is clear and understandable, though it still contains some of the colloquialisms of the New English Bible (e.g., "double-dealer," Prov. 14:2; "took to their heels," Matt. 8:33; 7:54) with the addition of new ones (e.g., "turned tail," Ps. 78:9; "tight-fisted," Prov. 11:24; "play the grandee," Prov. 12:9; "fritter them away," Prov. 21:20; "spiked themselves on many a painful thorn," 1 Tim. 6:10). Improvements in the wording of the Revised English Bible have made it more acceptable than the New English Bible, but the former still requires that the reader possess an extensive vocabulary (e.g., "vitiligo" = "dull white leprosy" [Lev. 13:39]; "connivance" = "full knowledge" [Prov. 6:35]; "canker in his bones" = "rot" [Prov. 12:4]; "decanted" = "emptied" [Jer. 48:11]; "calumnies" = "false accusations" [Matt. 5:11]). The Lord's Prayer reads

Our father in heaven,
may your name be hallowed;
your kingdom come,
your will be done,
on earth as in heaven.
Give us today our daily bread.
Forgive us the wrong we have done,

Figure 20.7.
Eugene H.
Peterson
(1932–).

in the New English Bible to "and do not put us to the test," which seems to contradict James 1:13–15 even more. It would probably have been better to translate it literally "and do not lead us into temptation," which some scholars suggest reflects a permissive force (i.e., "Do not let us fall victim") to temptation.[66]

An Evaluation

The Revised English Bible is a significant improvement over the New English Bible, especially in passages that return to traditional renderings, but it is doubtful that it will replace other translations already on the market. Lewis is correct in his judgment that "it is not likely to become the translation chiefly used by those who want to know in the nearest English equivalent the specific details of exactly what the original texts say."[67]

The Message (NT, 1993; OT Wisdom Books, 1997)

Its History

The Message attempts for the 1990s what the Living Bible did for the 1970s. It is a fresh rendering of the Greek (and soon Hebrew) texts into contemporary language by Eugene H. Peterson (fig. 20.7), professor emeritus of spiritual theology at Regent College, Vancouver. While he was a pastor for twenty-nine years at Christ Our King Presbyterian Church in Bel Air, Maryland, Peterson began trans-

as we have forgiven those who have wronged us.
And do not put us to the test,
but save us from the evil one. (Matt. 6:9–13)

The revisers have chosen to modify the phrase "and do not bring us to the test"

Table 20.18
The Message

Sponsors of the Translation	Translator	Text	Translation Techniques	Characteristics
NavPress	Eugene H. Peterson	NT: United Bible Societies' Greek text (4th edition, 1993)	Paraphrase	Modern English Sense paragraphs Poetic structure Few emendations OT quotations indented

lating the Scripture into the idiom of today's generation. At present the New Testament, Psalms, Proverbs, Job, Ecclesiastes, and Song of Songs have been published, and the rest of the Old Testament is soon to appear.

The Policies of the Translator

The Message is a paraphrase translation whose aim is "to convert the tone, the rhythm, the events, the ideas, into the way we actually think and speak."[68] It is interesting to see how Peterson views his work:

> In the midst of doing this work, I realized that this is exactly what I have been doing all my vocational life. For thirty-five years as a pastor I stood at the border between two languages, biblical Greek and everyday English, acting as a translator, providing the right phrases, getting the right words so that the men and women to whom I was pastor could find their way around and get along in this world where God has spoken so decisively and clearly in Jesus. I did it from the pulpit and in the kitchen, in hospitals and restaurants, on parking lots and at picnics, always looking for an English way to make the biblical text relevant to the conditions of the people.[69]

Several consultants critiqued Peterson's work in the New Testament and suggested changes: William W. Klein, Denver Seminary; Darrell L. Bock, Dallas Theological Seminary; Donald A. Hagner, Fuller Theological Seminary; Moisés Silva, Gordon-Conwell; Rodney A. Whiteacre, Trinity Episcopal School for Ministry.

The Translation

The aim of *The Message* is to render the meaning of the Greek and Hebrew texts into clear, modern English idiom; Peterson explains his rationale:

> A striking feature in all this writing (i.e., the New Testament) is that it was done in the street language of the day, the idiom of the playground and marketplace. In the Greek-speaking world of

that day, there were two levels of language: formal and informal. Formal language was used to write philosophy and history, government decrees and epic poetry. If someone were to sit down and consciously write for posterity, it would of course be written in this formal language with its learned vocabulary and precise diction. But if the writing was routine—shopping lists, family letters, bills and receipts—it was written in the common, informal idiom of everyday speech, street language.

> This is the language used throughout the New Testament.[70]

While Peterson attempts to produce an informal translation, his primary goal is not to choose simple English words (for instance, he chooses such words as "chagrined," "embryonic," "consummate," and "curt") but words that forcefully convey meaning to the reader. Thus the renderings of *The Message* are often fresh and vivid, which can be illustrated by comparing *The Message* to the New Living Translation (see table 20.19).

The Message is much freer in translation than is the New Living Translation, but its renderings are more novel and stimulating than the latter translation. These striking translations flesh out the meaning of the text and are a fairly accurate reflection of what is being said. There is, however, the use of paraphrase to grab one's attention.

The Message follows *The Greek New Testament* (United Bible Societies' Greek Text, fourth edition, 1993), even including passages placed in brackets in the Greek text but without indicating the brackets (e.g., Luke 23:34; John 7:53–8:11; Eph. 1:1; Mark 16:9–21). It is divided into thought paragraphs, with headings beginning each section, but unfortunately it has no verse divisions.

The Message presents the New Testament in fresh, contemporary English idiom with vivid word pictures and flowing style:

> Let me tell you why you are here. You're here to be salt-seasoning that brings out the God-flavors of this earth. If you lose your saltiness, how will people taste

Table 20.19
Comparison of *The Message* and New Living Translation

The Message	New Living Translation
Matthew 7:7–11 "Don't bargain with God. Be direct. Ask for what you need. This isn't a cat-and-mouse, hide-and-seek game we're in. If your child asks for bread, do you trick him with sawdust? If he asks for fish, do you scare him with a live snake on his plate? As bad as you are, you wouldn't think of such a thing. You're at least decent to your own children. So don't you think the God who conceived you in love will be even better?"	"Keep on asking, and you will be given what you ask for. Keep on looking, and you will find. Keep on knocking, and the door will be opened. For anyone who asks, receives. Everyone who seeks, finds. And the door is opened to everyone who knocks. You parents—if your children ask for a loaf of bread, do you give them a stone instead? Or if they ask for a fish, do you give them a snake? Of course not! If you sinful people know how to give good gifts to your children, how much more will your heavenly Father give good gifts to those who ask him."
Mark 9:38–40 John spoke up, "Teacher, we saw a man using your name to expel demons and we stopped him because he wasn't in our group." Jesus wasn't pleased. "Don't stop him. No one can use my name to do something good and powerful, and in the next breath cut me down. If he's not an enemy, he's an ally. Why, anyone by just giving you a cup of water in my name is on our side. Count on it that God will notice."	John said to Jesus, "Teacher, a man was using your name to cast out demons, but we told him to stop because he isn't one of our group." "Don't stop him!" Jesus said. "No one who performs miracles in my name will soon be able to speak evil against me. Anyone who is not against us is for us. If anyone gives you even a cup of water because you belong to the Messiah, I assure you, that person will be rewarded."
Luke 1:1–4 So many others have tried their hand at putting together a story of the wonderful harvest of Scripture and history that took place among us, using reports handed down by the original eyewitnesses who served this word with their very lives. Since I have investigated all the reports in close detail, starting from the story's beginning, I decided to write it all out for you, most honorable Theophilus, so you can know beyond the shadow of a doubt the reliability of what you were taught.	Most honorable Theophilus: Many people have written accounts about the events that took place among us. They used as their source material the reports circulating among us from the early disciples and other eyewitnesses of what God has done in fulfillment of his promises. Having carefully investigated all of these accounts from the beginning, I have decided to write a careful summary for you, to reassure you of the truth of all you were taught.
Romans 9:30–32 How can we sum this up? All those people who didn't seem interested in what God was doing actually *embraced* what God was doing as he straightened out their lives. And Israel, who seemed so interested in reading and talking about what God was doing, missed it. How could they miss it? Because instead of trusting God, *they* took over. They were absorbed in what they themselves were doing. They were so absorbed in their "God projects" that they didn't notice God right in front of them, like a huge rock in the middle of the road.	Well then, what shall we say about these things? Just this: The Gentiles have been made right with God by faith, even though they were not seeking him. But the Jews, who tried so hard to get right with God by keeping the law, never succeeded. Why not? Because they were trying to get right with God by keeping the law and being good instead of by depending on faith. They stumbled over the great rock in their path.
Galatians 1:1–2 I, Paul, and my companions in faith here, send greetings to the Galatian churches. My authority for writing to you does not come from any popular vote of the people, nor does it come through the appointment of some human higher-up. It comes directly from Jesus the Messiah and God the Father, who raised him from the dead.	This letter is from Paul, an apostle. I was not appointed by any group or by human authority. My call is from Jesus Christ himself and from God the Father, who raised Jesus from the dead. All the brothers and sisters here join me in sending greetings to the churches of Galatia.

godliness? You've lost your usefulness and will end up in the garbage.

Here's another way to put it: You're here to be light, bringing out the God-colors in the world. God is not a secret to be kept. We're going public with this, as public as a city on a hill. If I make you light-bearers, you don't think I'm going to hide you under a bucket, do you? I'm putting you on a light stand. Now that I've put you there on a hilltop, on a light stand—shine! (Matt. 5:13)

Our Father in heaven,
Reveal who you are.
Set the world right;
Do what's best—as above, so below.
Keep us alive with three square
    meals.
Keep us forgiven with you and for-
    giving others.
Keep us safe from ourselves and the
    Devil.
You're in charge!
You can do anything you want!
You're ablaze in beauty!
Yes. Yes. Yes. (Matt. 6:9–13)

The renderings of both passages are fresh and meaningful, but their paraphrastic nature is obvious, and the Lord's Prayer follows the longer ending not found in the earliest manuscripts.

An Evaluation

Peterson should be commended for creating a fresh, new translation that is clearly in the idiom of the 1990s but often crosses over into paraphrase. It will undoubtedly meet the needs of some readers for personal reading and study, especially when it is used alongside another translation. It

was ranked sixth among best-selling Bible versions of 1999.[71]

New Living Translation (1996)

Its History

With forty million copies sold, the Living Bible has helped to satisfy the need for a simple, understandable English translation of the Bible. Nevertheless, because it was more than twenty years old, its publishers decided in 1989 to submit it to a revision. The result, entitled the *Holy Bible, New Living Translation* (1996), is a thorough revision of the Living Bible, translated from the original languages using a completely different translation technique (i.e., dynamic equivalence). These changes have given rise to significant differences in readings between the two translations (see table 20.21).

This revision was the work of ninety biblical scholars over a seven-year period. The New Living Translation is still backed and funded by Kenneth N. Taylor and is published, as is the Living Bible, by Tyndale House Publishers, Inc., of Wheaton, Illinois. It can be purchased in several formats (e.g., Life Application Study Bible, Touch Point-Topical Reference System, New Believers, and Deluxe Text Edition), and a concordance is being produced by John R. Kohlenberger III.

The Policies of the Translators

In order to guard against biases, qualified evangelical scholars were chosen from

Table 20.20
New Living Translation

Sponsors of the Translation	Translators	Text	Translation Techniques	Characteristics
Kenneth N. Taylor and Tyndale House Publishers, Inc.	About 90 evangelical scholars	OT: *Biblia Hebraica Stuttgartensia* NT: United Bible Societies' Greek text (4th Edition, 1993)	Dynamic equivalence	Modern English Sense paragraphs Some poetic structure Few emendations OT quotations indented

a wide variety of denominations and theological backgrounds. A complete list of translators appears in the introduction to the New Living Translation and includes Daniel I. Block (Southern Baptist Theological Seminary); Craig Blomberg (Denver Conservative Baptist Seminary); Frederic W. Bush (Fuller Theological Seminary); D. A. Carson (Trinity Evangelical Divinity School); Donald A. Hagner (Fuller); Tremper Longman III (Westminster Theological Seminary); Scot McKnight (North Park College); Douglas J. Moo (Trinity); Moisés Silva (Gordon-Conwell Theological Seminary); Klyne Snodgrass (North Park Theological Seminary); Hugh G. M. Williamson (Oxford University); and Al Wolters (Redeemer College). A general reviewer was appointed to oversee work on each of the six major sections of Scripture—Pentateuch, Historical Books, Poetry, Prophets, Gospels and Acts, Letters and Revelation. Each major section was subdivided into five smaller sections, each of which was assigned to three different scholars who usually had developed expertise in that part of Scripture. Each

Table 20.21
Comparison of the Living Bible and the New Living Translation

Living Bible	New Living Translation
Genesis 1:1–2 When God began creating the heavens and the earth, the earth was at first a shapeless, chaotic mass, with the Spirit of God brooding over the dark vapors.	In the beginning God created the heavens and the earth. The earth was empty, a formless mass cloaked in darkness. And the Spirit of God was hovering over its surface.

Genesis 49:10
The scepter shall not depart from Judah until Shiloh comes, whom all people shall obey.
	The scepter will not depart from Judah,
	    nor the ruler's staff from his descendants,
	until the coming of the one to whom it belongs,
	    the one whom all nations will obey.

Exodus 3:14–15 "'The Sovereign God,'" was the reply. "Just say, 'I Am has sent me!' Yes, tell them, 'Jehovah, the God of your ancestors Abraham, Isaac, and Jacob, has sent me to you.' (This is my eternal name, to be used throughout all generations.)"	God replied, "I AM THE ONE WHO ALWAYS IS. Just tell them, 'I AM has sent me to you.'" God also said, "Tell them, 'The LORD, the God of your ancestors—the God of Abraham, the God of Isaac, and the God of Jacob—has sent me to you.'"
1 Samuel 20:30 Saul boiled with rage. "You son of a bitch!" he yelled at him. "Do you think I don't know that you want this son of a nobody to be king in your place, shaming yourself and your mother?"	Saul boiled with rage at Jonathan. "You stupid son of a whore!" he swore at him. "Do you think I don't know that you want David to be king in your place, shaming yourself and your mother?"
Psalm 145:13b [omitted]	The LORD is faithful in all he says; he is gracious in all he does.
Matthew 6:13 'Don't bring us into temptation, but deliver us from the Evil One. Amen.'	"And don't let us yield to temptation, but deliver us from the evil one."
Matthew 23:14 "And you pretend to be holy, with all your long, public prayers in the streets, while you are evicting widows from their homes. Hypocrites!"	[verse omitted]
Mark 16:9–20 [Appears in the text with a footnote indicating that it is not in the earliest manuscripts.]	[Set off from the text by the titles "Shorter Ending of Mark" and "Longer Ending of Mark."]

scholar made a thorough study of the assigned section and submitted a list of suggested revisions to the respective general reviewer, who in turn critiqued potential revisions and prepared from them a first draft. This draft was then further revised by other biblical scholars and by English stylists. Lastly, the Bible Translation Committee reviewed the translation verse by verse to prepare a final revision.

The Translation

One of the major differences between the Living Bible and the New Living Translation is that the latter uses dynamic equivalence rather than paraphrase. The twofold goal of reliability and readability is set forth in the introduction to the New Living Translation:

> In making a thought-for-thought translation, the translators must do their best to enter the thought patterns of the ancient authors and to present the same ideas, connotations, and effects in the receptor language. In order to guard against personal biases and to ensure the accuracy of the message, a thought-for-thought translation should be created by a group of scholars who employ the best exegetical tools and who also understand the receptor language very well.[72]

A dynamic-equivalence translation may use a variety of different English words to capture the meaning of a Hebrew, Aramaic, or Greek word; for example, the Hebrew word _hesed_ may be translated "love," "mercy," "grace," or "faithfulness," depending upon the context.

The second noteworthy difference between the Living Bible and the New Living Translation is that the latter is translated from the original languages, vastly improving its accuracy. Because the translators were experts in the portions of Scripture assigned to them, they were able to bring out nuances of meaning.

The Old Testament

The most recent version of the Hebrew Masoretic Text, the _Biblia Hebraica Stuttgartensia_ (1977), was used as the basis for translation. On those occasions when the translators chose to deviate from the Masoretic Text, the text is compared with other ancient sources, such as the Qumran manuscripts (e.g., 1 Sam. 1:24; 2 Sam. 22:36; Isa. 21:8; 33:8; 45:2) and versions (e.g., Num. 26:17, 39, 40; Judg. 9:29; 14:15; 1 Sam. 8:16), to assure the most accurate reading of the text. Deviations were more frequent than in the New International Version (e.g., 1 Sam. 2:33; Isa. 15:9; 49:12) but not as many as in the New Revised

Table 20.22
Comparison of the New Living Translation and the New International Version

New Living Translation	New International Version
Genesis 25:18b The clans descended from Ishmael camped close to one another.	And they lived in hostility toward all their brothers.
Genesis 37:3b So one day he gave Joseph a special gift—a beautiful robe.	and he made a richly ornamented robe for him
Genesis 48:22a And I give you an extra portion	I give the ridge of land
1 Chronicles 17:17b You speak as though I were someone very great	you have spoken about the future of the house of your servant
Psalm 58:7b Make their weapons useless in their hands.	when they draw the bow, let their arrows be blunted

Standard Version (e.g., 1 Sam. 1:11, 22; 2:1, 33). At times the New Living Translation follows emendations (e.g., 2 Kings 10:25; Ps. 40:2), but much less frequently than does the New Revised Standard Version (cf. Ps. 2:11–12; Amos 6:12). Where footnotes indicate that the Hebrew is uncertain, the New Living Translation differs greatly from other translations, as comparison with the New International Version illustrates (see table 20.22).

The New Testament

This translation is based upon the most recent eclectic editions of the New

Table 20.23
Further Comparison of Translations

New Living Translation	New International Version
Genesis 1:1–2 In the beginning God created the heavens and the earth. The earth was empty, a formless mass cloaked in darkness. And the Spirit of God was hovering over its surface.	In the beginning God created the heavens and the earth. Now the earth was formless and empty, darkness was over the surface of the deep, and the Spirit of God was hovering over the waters.
Genesis 6:1–3 When the human population began to grow rapidly on the earth, the sons of God saw the beautiful women of the human race and took any they wanted as their wives. Then the Lord said, "My Spirit will not put up with humans for such a long time, for they are only mortal flesh. In the future, they will live no more than 120 years."	When men began to increase in number on the earth and daughters were born to them, the sons of God saw that the daughters of men were beautiful, and they married any of them they chose. Then the Lord said, "My Spirit will not contend with man forever, for he is mortal; his days will be a hundred and twenty years."

Psalm 1:1
Oh, the joys of those
    who do not follow the advice of the wicked,
    or stand around with sinners,
    or join in with scoffers.
	Blessed is the man
	    who does not walk in the counsel of the wicked
	or stand in the way of sinners
	    or sit in the seat of mockers.

Psalm 2:11–12a
Serve the Lord with reverent fear,
    and rejoice with trembling.
Submit to God's royal son,
    or he will become angry . . .
	Serve the Lord with fear
	    and rejoice with trembling.
	Kiss the Son, lest he be angry
	    and you be destroyed in your way . . .

Ecclesiastes 1:1–2
These are the words of the Teacher, King David's son, who ruled in Jerusalem.
    "Everything is meaningless," says the Teacher, "utterly meaningless!"
	The words of the Teacher, son of David, king in Jerusalem:
	"Meaningless! Meaningless!"
	    says the Teacher.
	"Utterly meaningless!
	    Everything is meaningless."

John 1:1 In the beginning the Word already existed. He was with God, and he was God.	In the beginning was the Word, and the Word was with God, and the Word was God.
John 3:16 For God so loved the world that he gave his only Son, so that everyone who believes in him will not perish but have eternal life.	For God so loved the world that he gave his one and only Son, that whoever believes in him shall not perish but have eternal life.
2 Timothy 3:16 All Scripture is inspired by God and is useful to teach us what is true and to make us realize what is wrong in our lives. It straightens us out and teaches us to do what is right.	All Scripture is God-breathed and is useful for teaching, rebuking, correcting and training in righteousness.

Testament—*The Greek New Testament* (United Bible Societies' fourth revised edition, 1993) and *Novum Testamentum Graece* (Nestle and Aland's 27th edition, 1993), with very few variations (e.g., 1 Thess. 2:7 reads "gentle" [*ēpioi*] instead of "babes" [*nēpioi*]). It even includes passages that are placed in double brackets in these Greek texts (e.g., Luke 22:43–44; 23:34, and John 7:53–8:11) with footnotes indicating that they are not found in the earliest Greek manuscripts.

The language of the New Living Translation is clear and intelligible, with sensitivity to inclusive gender wording; its vastly improved accuracy over the Living Bible can be credited to the fine team of translators. Nevertheless, to effectively render the intent of some passages, exegetical decisions were made that are not agreed upon by all scholars. An important improvement is a strong emphasis on producing a translation suitable for public reading; the rationale is that "It is still the case today that more people will hear the Bible read aloud in church than are likely to read it for themselves. Therefore, a new translation must communicate with clarity and power when it is read aloud."[73] The more dignified wording of the New Living Translation can be seen in the following excerpts.

Table 20.24
Most Popular Recent Translations

Translation	Date	Translating Principle, Sponsor, and Translators	Comments
RSV	1952	Word for word (National Council of Churches; 32 distinguished scholars)	Excellent literal revision of the ASV; "Thou" for divinity; frequent emendations of the text
NEB	1970	Word for word (Oxford and Cambridge Presses; distinguished British scholars)	New literal translation; "Thou" for divinity; frequent emendations of the text
NASB	1971	Word for word (Lockman Foundation; 58 evangelical scholars)	Excellent literal revision of the ASV; "Thou" for divinity; few emendations of the text; capitals for divinity (or Messiah)
GNB	1976	Dynamic equivalence (American Bible Society)	Clear and simple new translation; emphasis on comprehension; about elementary grade reading level
NIV	1978	Between word for word and dynamic equivalence (New York International Bible Society; more than 110 international evangelical scholars)	Excellent new translation; updated language; few emendations of the text; moderate use of capitals for divinity (or Messiah)
NKJV	1982	Word for word (Thomas Nelson; more than 130 distinguished evangelical scholars)	Literal translation of the MT and *Textus Receptus*; generally modern language; capitals for divinity (or Messiah)
NRSV	1989	Word for word (National Council of Churches; about 30 distinguished scholars)	Excellent literal revision of the RSV; updated language; gender inclusive; frequent emendations of the text
REB	1989	Word for word (Oxford and Cambridge Presses; distinguished British scholars)	Literal revision of NEB; updated language; gender inclusive; frequent emendations of the text
The Message	1993	Dynamic equivalence (NavPress; Eugene Peterson)	Clear and simple new translation; emphasis on comprehension; gender inclusive; about junior high reading level
NLT	1996	Dynamic equivalence (Tyndale House; about 90 distinguished evangelical scholars)	Clear and simple new translation; emphasis on intelligibility; gender inclusive; about elementary grade reading level

Table 20.25
Twentieth-Century English Translations or Paraphrases (1950–)

1951	Authentic Version, Plattsburg, Missouri
1952	New Testament in Plain English, London
1952	Revised Standard Version: Old Testament, New York, Toronto, Edinburgh
1952	Rieu's Penguin Bible, London
1954	Kleist and Lilly's New Testament, Milwaukee, Wisconsin
1954	Moore's New Testament, Chevy Chase, Maryland
1955	Knox Bible, London
1955	Schonfield's Authentic New Testament, London
1956	Laubach's Inspired Letters, New York
1957	Concordant Version, Los Angeles
1957	Lamsa, The Holy Bible from Ancient Eastern Manuscripts, Philadelphia
1958	Hudson, London
1958	Meissner's Gospels, Portland, Oregon
1958	Phillips's New Testament, New York
1958	Tomanek's New Testament, Pocatello, Idaho
1959	Modern Language Bible (Berkeley), Grand Rapids, Michigan
1960	The Children's "King James," Evansville, Indiana
1961	New World Translation—Jehovah's Witnesses, Brooklyn, New York
1961	Noli's Greek Orthodox New Testament, Boston
1961	One Way: The Jesus People New Testament, Pasadena, California
1961	Simplified New Testament, Grand Rapids, Michigan
1961	Wuest's Expanded New Testament, Grand Rapids, Michigan
1962	Children's Version, New York
1963	Beck's New Testament, St. Louis, Missouri
1963	The Holy Name Bible, Irvington, New Jersey
1964	Anchor Bible, Garden City, New York
1965	Amplified Bible, Grand Rapids, Michigan
1965	Bruce's Expanded Paraphrase, Exeter
1966	The Bible in Simplified English, Collegeville, Minnesota
1966	Jerusalem Bible, London, New York
1966	Living Scriptures, New York
1967	Dale's New World, London
1967	Liverpool Vernacular Gospels, London
1968	Cotton Patch Version, New York
1968	Restoration of the Original Name New Testament, Junction City, Oregon

(continued on next page)

Don't misunderstand why I have come. I did not come to abolish the law of Moses or the writings of the prophets. No, I came to fulfill them. I assure you, until heaven and earth disappear, even the smallest detail of God's law will remain until its purpose is achieved. So if you break the smallest commandment and teach others to do the same, you will be the least in the Kingdom of Heaven. But anyone who obeys God's laws and teaches them will be great in the Kingdom of Heaven. (Matt. 5:17–19)

Our Father in heaven,
    may your name be honored.
May your kingdom come soon.
May your will be done here on earth,
    just as it is in heaven.
Give us our food for today,
and forgive us our sins,
    just as we have forgiven those
    who have sinned against us.
And don't let us yield to temptation,
    but deliver us from the evil one.
                          (Matt. 6:9–13)

The difficult phrase in verse 13, "And don't let us yield to temptation," is probably the best rendering among the current translations.

A page from the Internet indicates that the English of the New Living Translation is rated at about grade 6.3, which means that "it can be read with adequate understanding by the average person who has reached the third month of the sixth grade."[74] By comparison, according to this same scale the King James Version is rated

Table 20.25 (continued)
Twentieth-Century English Translations or Paraphrases

1969	Barclay's New Testament, London/Cleveland
1969	Children's New Testament, Waco, Texas
1970	The Mercier New Testament, Cork, U.K.
1970	New American Bible, New York
1970	New English Bible, Oxford and Cambridge
1971	King James II New Testament, Byron Center, Michigan
1971	Living Bible, Wheaton, Illinois
1971	New American Standard Bible, Carol Stream, Illinois
1972	The Bible in Living English, New York
1973	The Common Bible, New York
1973	A Child's Bible, New York/London
1973	New International Version: New Testament, Grand Rapids, Michigan
1973	The Better Version of the New Testament, Muscle Shoals, Alabama
1973	The Translator's New Testament, London
1974	Klingensmith New Testament, Fargo, North Dakota
1975	The Word Made Fresh, Atlanta
1976	Good News Bible, New York (Today's English Version NT, 1966)
1976	Beck's: An American Translation, Nashville
1976	Renaissance New Testament, Bowling Green, Kentucky
1976	New Life Testament, Canby, Oregon
1977	The Gospels in Scouse, London
1977	The Holy Bible for Children, St. Louis
1977	Christian Counselor's New Testament, Grand Rapids, Michigan
1978	The Holy Name Bible, Brandywine, Maryland
1978	The New International Version (entire Bible), Grand Rapids,Michigan
1978	The New Jewish Version: The Prophets, Philadelphia
1978	New Testament for the Deaf, Grand Rapids, Michigan
1979	The New King James Bible: New Testament, Nashville
1982	The New Jewish Version: The Writings, Philadelphia (Torah, 1962; Prophets, 1978)
1982	The New King James Version (entire Bible), Nashville
1982	The Reader's Digest Bible, Pleasantville, New York
1989	The Revised English Bible, Cambridge and Oxford
1989	The New Revised Standard Version, New York and Oxford
1993	The Message, Colorado Springs, Colorado
1996	New English Translation Study Bible: The Net Bible, Spokane, Washington
1996	New Living Translation, Wheaton, Illinois

12.0, the New American Standard Bible 10.0, the Living Bible 8.3, and the New International Version 7.3; the average adult reading level is between 6.0 and 9.0.

The text is also laid out in thought paragraphs with new headings in italics and chapter divisions in bold print. Unlike the Living Bible, the Psalms are indicated clearly as poetry, although it would have been helpful to do so for poetic sections in Proverbs and the Prophets. Parentheses indicate parenthetical material (except, surprisingly, for 1 Kings 8:42, 46; and Isa. 7:8). Most footnotes contain helps for the readers to better understand various words or even entire passages.

It is interesting to compare how similar the New Living Translation can be to the New International Version even though different translation principles were used (see table 20.23). This table also indicates how important the translation principles are in rendering specific passages; for example, inclusive language can be readily seen in Genesis 6:1–3 and Psalm 1:1 of the New Living Translation.

An Evaluation

The goal of the New Living Translation is stated well in its introduction:

We pray that the New Living Translation will overcome some of the barriers of history, culture, and language that have kept people from reading and understanding

Table 20.26
The Greek Text behind Modern Versions

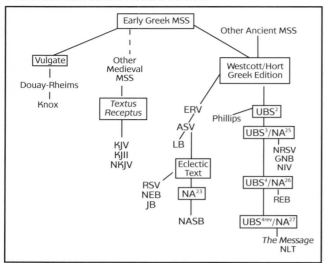

among best-selling Bible versions of 1999.[76] While the text is clear and readable, its wording does not always provide readers who are well versed in Scripture "a fresh perspective," as the Living Bible did for those reading it in the 1970s. Similarly, this translation was not always able to capture the meaning of the biblical texts better than does the New International Version, which claims to be a balance between the word-for-word and dynamic-equivalence translation principles.

God's Word. We hope that readers unfamiliar with the Bible will find the words clear and easy to understand, and that readers well versed in the Scriptures will gain a fresh perspective. We pray that readers will gain insight and wisdom for living, but most of all that they will meet the God of the Bible and be forever changed by knowing him.[75]

According to *CBA Marketplace*, the New Living Translation was ranked third

Summary

The many new translations in the past half century have striven to achieve accuracy balanced with intelligibility. Translation principles have made great strides, proceeding from word-for-word to paraphrase, dynamic equivalence, and combinations of word-for-word and dynamic equivalence translations. Experimentation and practice continue to guide the translations of particular passages of Scripture, and we hope future efforts will improve them even more. New versions are continuing to be made, and at present work is being done on a Bible translation on the Internet.[77]

Net Bible, The New English Translation

The New Testament of the Net Bible appeared in 1998, and it is claimed that the rest will be finished by the year 2000. The Internet allows this translation to have several very nice features that have not been available for Bible translations in the past. First, one of the major problems with most translations is that the moment they are printed they begin traveling down the road toward obsolescence; however, the Internet has solved this difficulty and allows for immediate updating and improvement. Second, most Bibles have to be very brief with footnotes for they escalate the cost of publishing the translation, but the

Internet can allow the translator space to provide more thorough explanations of the word choices, in-depth discussions about textual variations, or commentary on the reasons for certain translations. In fact, the Net Bible has 16,025 translators' notes in the New Testament alone, which averages about two notes per verse, and yet they do not interfere with the reading of the translation, for they are on pop-up menus and only need to be examined if an issue arises demanding such information. Third, the Net Bible is easily accessible for anyone who has access to the Internet—no matter where one lives

in the world. This may prove valuable for Bible translators and missionaries serving around the world.

There is also a weakness with the Net Bible. Its fluidity will make it difficult to critique the translation, since its text is in constant flux.

All in all, the Net Bible was inevitable and will provide a helpful resource for many people. The Internet is a convenient method for anyone with Internet access to have a Bible translation with a great deal of scholarly research concerning the text.

For Further Reading

Bailey, L. R., ed. *The Word of God: A Guide to English Versions of the Bible*. Atlanta: John Knox, 1982.

Bruce, F. F. *History of the Bible in English: From the Earliest Versions*. 3d ed. New York: Oxford University Press, 1978.

———. *The Books and the Parchments*, 231–54. 5th ed. London: Marshall Pickering, 1991.

Comfort, P. W. *Early Manuscripts and Modern Translations of the New Testament*. Wheaton, IL: Tyndale, 1990; reprint, Grand Rapids: Baker, 1996.

Ewert, D. *From Ancient Tablets to Modern Translations: A General Introduction to the Bible*, 223–51. Grand Rapids: Zondervan, 1983.

Kubo, S., and W. F. Specht. *So Many Versions? Twentieth-Century English Versions of the Bible*. Rev. ed. Grand Rapids: Zondervan, 1983.

Lewis, J. P. *The English Bible from KJV to NIV: A History and Evaluation*. 2d ed. Grand Rapids: Baker, 1991.

MacGregor, G. *The Bible in the Making*. Washington, DC: University Press of America, 1982.

Why So Many Translations?

I t is hard to believe that just a little over a century ago there was essentially one English translation of the Bible. Translations have multiplied to the extent that choosing a Bible can be quite confusing. Each translation attempts to fulfill a need that, as Frederick C. Grant states, "is an endless process, as languages change, as additional copies of ancient manuscripts continue to turn up, and as scholars come to know and understand the ancient languages better."[1] This chapter will review the principles behind various translations, pointing out their strengths and weaknesses. Suggested criteria as to how to choose a Bible version are also discussed. Choosing a Bible is an important decision, as its message is intended to affect the life of the reader.

Preliminary Principles of a Translation

Which Greek and Hebrew Texts Does It Use?

It is important to note that not all translators use the same Hebrew and Greek texts, and these texts are fundamental to determining the meaning of specific passages. Most of the recent versions use some form of an eclectic Greek text (e.g., the United Bible Societies' Greek text or Nestle-Aland Greek text) for the New Testament and the Masoretic Hebrew text (e.g., *Biblica Hebraica Stuttgartensia*) for the Old Testament. However, some scholars still

argue that the *Textus Receptus* (the text of the King James Bible) is most accurate and therefore choose translations based upon the Byzantine family.

Preferred Texts

Current scholarship favors an eclectic text for the New Testament (e.g., United Bible Societies' text or Nestle-Aland) and a diplomatic Masoretic Text for the Old Testament (e.g., *Biblia Hebraica Stuttgartensia*), primarily because of the differences in the ways each testament was transmitted. (For a more thorough discussion of the eclectic versus single-text debate, see chapters 11 and 18).

Choosing the New Testament Text

Eclectic Text	Single Text
Collects the best readings from many manuscripts	Single text used for the entire translation
Examples:	**Examples:**
RSV	KJV
NASB	KJII
NRSV	NKJV
NEB	
NIV	
GNB	
REB	
The Message	
NLT	

Translation Principles

It is always difficult to translate from one language to another because the structures of languages differ. Thus a high degree of skill is necessary to translate the Bible. The problem is enhanced when different translating principles are used. Translation may be depicted as a continuum, and translations may be placed at any point along it; for example, the New International Version attempts both, but others that are either strongly literal trans-

Word-for-Word Translation	Combination	Dynamic Equivalence Translation
ASV	NIV	NEB
RSV		GNB
NASB		*The Message*
NRSV		NLT

lations or are dynamic-equivalence translations will be placed on the outer edges.

Literal Translation

Some scholars believe that it is preferable to reflect the sentence structure, verbal nuances, and idioms of the original languages in order to assure accuracy in emphasis and style. This is primarily the logic behind italicizing words that are not in the original text but are needed for the English translation.

Dynamic Equivalence

Other scholars believe that it is not crucial to carry over the style, structure, and idioms of the host language but to use the style, structure, and idioms of the new language. Thus, for example, there is an attempt to choose English idioms that most closely mirror the original intent of the Hebrew or Greek idioms.

Combination

It may be possible to achieve a delicate balance between these two translation policies to provide even greater accuracy. For instance, dynamic equivalency is especially useful in poetic passages to bring across the original meaning and intent of the host language. However, it may be preferable to use some aspects of a literal translation to convey specific types of poetry (e.g., so far only the Knox Version has attempted to represent alphabetic acrostics).

Some scholars believe that it is the job of the translator to emend the text to make it as smooth and intelligible as possible, while others make emendations only when the text is obviously corrupted. The two approaches can be highlighted when comparing the translation of Psalm 2:11–12a in the Revised Standard Version or New Revised Standard Version to the New American Standard Bible or New International Version; the former rely upon emendation to modify a difficult text, while the latter attempt to render an intelligible translation of the extant text. An emendation by definition is modification to a translation without textual support and by nature is a risky practice. Sometimes an error can be made on the opposite extreme when a scholar retains traditional readings even though more recent evidence suggests that new translations are preferable (e.g., Revised Standard Version's interpretation of μονογενής [*monogenēs*] as "only son" is preferable to New American Standard Bible's translation "only begotten son").

Qualifications of the Translators

Theological and Denominational Biases

It is generally best to choose a translation that has been made by a committee of translators from a variety of denominations so that specific theological or denominational peculiarities will have been worked out. Nevertheless, it cannot guarantee that a translation will be guarded from serious theological faults; for example, the New English Bible and the Revised English Bible were made by committees of translators and yet they translated 2 Timothy 3:16 as "Every inspired scripture has its use for teaching" instead of "All scripture is inspired and useful for teaching" as does every other translation. Is it possible that theological presuppositions are showing? The wording of the former could reflect theological presuppositions that allow for the possibility that some parts of Scripture are not inspired by God, whereas the grammar of the Greek argues against this interpretation.[2]

Skill in Biblical Languages

In the past century scholars have learned a great deal about the biblical languages in the areas of grammar, syntax (the way words are related to each other), and lexicography (study of word meanings). Thus it is extremely important that translators are up to date regarding current scholarship in these areas. Again it is important that a translation be the work of a committee, since no single scholar can keep abreast of the information in each of these areas. Knowing the credentials of the translators of a version can help determine the credibility of their work.

A thorough knowledge of the historical, cultural, and sociological background of the biblical text can also aid in producing an accurate translation, as exemplified in the following two passages:

1. Amos 4:6 warns that God will give Israel "cleanness of teeth" (NASB); this is not a comment on dental hygiene but rather that God will send famine upon the land.
2. The phrase "Upon Edom will I toss my sandal" (Ps. 60:8) is not an expression of anger but ownership—God is claiming Edom as his own.

Style of English

The English language is living and fluid. Words change in meaning, new words are created, old words drop from usage, even the way things are stated is sometimes modified. William Barclay reckons that "there is a sense in which a translation begins to go out of date on the day when it is completed, for language is never static, but always on the move."[3] A translation must be understood for it to make a difference in the life of a person, but the more colloquial the English, the sooner it will be out of date.

Purpose for the Translation

The purpose of a translation can greatly influence its readings. The following questions should therefore be considered when choosing translations:

1. Is this translation a revision of an existing version or a new translation?
2. Is the aim of the translation to be as literal as possible or as meaningful as possible?
3. For whom is the translation written? The following examples may help determine the proper translation for the reader.

   The New English Bible—sophisticated modern English

   Good News Bible—someone whose first language is not necessarily English

   New International Version—international English

   The Living Bible—originally intended for children
4. What will be the main use of the translation—Bible study, devotional reading, public reading?
5. Who will be using the Bible—child, seminary professor, pastor?

Special Translation Problems

The Proper Name for God

The problem of translating the biblical names for God is further complicated by the sensitivities of Jews and Jewish Christians, many of whom have been taught never to say God's name. Most translations render YHWH as "Lord," and "Adonai" as "the Lord," to distinguish between them. The name *Jehovah* is now known to be an artificial form and generally is no longer used.

Punctuation

Punctuation makes a significant difference in the translation of several passages:

Psalm 121:1
KJV: "I will lift up mine eyes unto the hills, from whence cometh my help."

NIV: "I lift up my eyes to the hills—where does my help come from?"

Ephesians 4:11–12

NASB: "And He gave some as apostles, and some as prophets, and some as evangelists, and some as pastors and teachers, for the equipping of the saints for the work of service, to the building up of the body of Christ. . . ."

KJV: ". . . For the perfecting of the saints, for the work of the ministry, for the edifying of the body of Christ. . . ."

In the case of punctuation, however, each passage must be dealt with individually, and therefore it is best merely to choose one of the more recent translations that has relied upon modern interpretations for the punctuation.

Monetary Terms

Monetary terms are either transliterated (denarius, drachma) or rendered in modern-day equivalent terms. The latter option conveys the most meaning to modern readers but must be considered only roughly equivalent.

Table 21.1
Principles for Choosing a Bible

I. Who Is Using the Bible?
A. Children (LB)
B. Older person used to KJV (RSV)
C. Person with fine literary tastes (NEB, Phillips)
D. English is a second language (GNB)
E. Unchurched person (GNB or Phillips, which avoid Bible English)

II. What Is the Intended Use?
A. A study Bible (ASV, NASB)
B. Easy to memorize or designed for public worship (RSV, NIV)
C. Devotional reading (LB, GNB, Phillips)
D. For Roman Catholics (NAB, JB)
E. For Jews *(The Tanakh)*

III. Which Format Is Preferred?
A. People with poor eyesight may prefer large print.
B. Some versions begin each verse as a new paragraph, while others use logical thought paragraphs.
C. Some versions offer helpful footnotes, marginal references, maps, and charts. (Care should be taken not to become too dependent upon the marginal notes and footnotes since they reflect merely the editor's point of view.)

IV. In Which Country Will It Be Used?
Some foreign editions may contain words unfamiliar to the American reader, but at times these editions may prove interesting and stimulating (Knox, Phillips, JB, NEB). The GNB and NIV attempt to employ international English so that they can be understood wherever English is spoken.

V. How Accurate Is the Translation?
A. The translation must use the most accurate original texts possible, but versions vary as to how literal the renderings are or whether they tend toward dynamic equivalence.
B. Since translating always includes a certain amount of interpretation, a Bible that was translated by a team (NASB, RSV, NEB, NIV, GNB) rather than by an individual (Moffatt, Goodspeed, Knox, Phillips, LB) is more likely to be accurate.

For Further Reading

Arichea, D. C. "Taking Theology Seriously in the Translation Task." *BT* 33. 3 (1982): 309–16.

Bruce, F. F. *History of the Bible in English: From the Earliest Versions.* 3d ed. New York: Oxford University Press, 1978.

Duthie, A. S. *How to Choose Your Bible Wisely.* 2d ed. Carlisle: Paternoster, 1995.

Ewert, D. *From Ancient Tablets to Modern Translations: A General Introduction to the Bible,* 253–66. Grand Rapids: Zondervan, 1983.

Fee, G. E., and D. Stuart. *How to Read the Bible for All Its Worth.* 2d ed. Grand Rapids: Zondervan, 1993.

Glassman, E. H. *The Translation Debate: What Makes a Bible Translation Good?* Downers Grove, IL: InterVarsity, 1981.

Kubo, S., and W. F. Specht. *So Many Versions? Twentieth-Century English Versions of the Bible,* 336–44. Rev. ed. Grand Rapids: Zondervan, 1983.

Nida, E. "Quality in Translation." *BT* 33.3 (1982): 329–32.

———. "Why So Many Bible Translations?" In *The Word of God: A Guide to English Versions of the Bible,* ed. L. R. Bailey, 13–27. Atlanta: John Knox, 1982.

Notes ••

Preface

1. G. L. Archer, *A Survey of Old Testament Introduction*, updated and revised ed. (Chicago: Moody, 1994); R. B. Dillard and T. Longman, *An Introduction to the Old Testament* (Grand Rapids: Zondervan, 1994); R. K. Harrison, *Introduction to the Old Testament* (Grand Rapids: Eerdmans, 1969); A. E. Hill and J. H. Walton, *A Survey of the Old Testament* (Grand Rapids: Zondervan, 1991); W. S. LaSor, D. A. Hubbard, and F. W. Bush, *Old Testament Survey: The Message, Form, and Background of the Old Testament*, 2d ed. (Grand Rapids: Eerdmans, 1996).
2. D. A. Carson, D. J. Moo, and L. Morris, *An Introduction to the New Testament* (Grand Rapids: Zondervan, 1992); R. H. Gundry, *A Survey of the New Testament*, 3d ed. (Grand Rapids: Zondervan, 1994); D. Guthrie, *New Testament Introduction* (Downers Grove, IL: InterVarsity, 1990); E. F. Harrison, *Introduction to the New Testament*, rev. ed. (Grand Rapids: Eerdmans, 1974); W. G. Kümmel, *Introduction to the New Testament*, trans. H. C. Kee, rev. ed. (Nashville: Abingdon, 1975).

Chapter 1: *The Bible as the Word of God*

1. P. Hicks, "A Very Special Book," in *The Complete Bible Study Tool Kit*, ed. J. F. Balchin, D. H. Field, and T. Longman (Downers Grove, IL: InterVarsity, 1991), 236.
2. J. H. Hayes, *Introduction to the Bible* (Philadelphia: Westminster, 1971), 3.
3. *Foxe's Book of Martyrs*, ed. and abridged by G. A. Williamson (Boston: Little, Brown, 1965), 130.
4. H. G. Wood, "Bible," *EncBrit*, 3:499.
5. The text reads: "quanquam et in Vetere Novum lateat, et in Novo Vetus pateat" (Augustine *Quaestiones in Exodum* 73).
6. Wood, "Bible," 3:499.
7. W. W. Klein, C. L. Blomberg, and R. L. Hubbard, *Introduction to Biblical Interpretation* (Dallas: Word, 1993), 16; G. D. Fee and D. Stuart, *How to Read the Bible for All Its Worth* (Grand Rapids: Zondervan, 1982), 19.
8. The word *Islam* comes from the Arabic word for "submission" to the will of God.
9. Hicks, "A Very Special Book," 237.
10. H. W. Attridge, *The Epistle to the Hebrews*, Hermeneia (Philadelphia: Fortress, 1989), 39; D. Guthrie, *The Letter to the Hebrews: An Introduction and Commentary*, TNTC (Grand Rapids: Eerdmans, 1983), 64; P. E. Hughes, *A Commentary on the Epistle to the Hebrews* (Grand Rapids: Eerdmans, 1977), 36; W. L. Lane, *Hebrews 1–8*, WBC 47A (Dallas: Word, 1991), 11.
11. J. B. Phillips, *Letters to Young Churches: A Translation of the New Testament Epistles* (New York: Macmillan, 1947), xii.

Chapter 2: *Description of the Bible*

1. J.-P. Migne, *Hieronymi: Opera Omnia* (Paris: Vrayet, 1845–1846), 18, 2.683, para. 915.
2. G. I. Williamson, *The Westminster Confession of Faith for Study Classes* (Philadelphia: Presbyterian and Reformed Publishing, 1964), 1.
3. A. J. Hoover, "God, Arguments for the Existence of," in *Evangelical Dictionary of Theology*, ed. W. A. Elwell (Grand Rapids: Baker, 1984), 449.

4. Ibid.

5. Colossians 1:26 and 2:2 contain anacolutha (a change of construction in the course of a sentence leading to a grammatical breach in continuity). See M. J. Harris, *Colossians and Philemon*, Exegetical Guide to the Greek New Testament (Grand Rapids: Eerdmans, 1991), 69, 80.

6. M. Green, *The Second Epistle General of Peter and the General Epistle of Jude: An Introduction and Commentary*, 2d ed., TNTC (Grand Rapids: Eerdmans, 1987), 102–3.

7. J. Daane, "Infallibility," *ISBE*, 2:820.

8. The form *biblion* (little book) is a diminutive of *biblos* (book), but later in the New Testament it lost its diminutive sense and simply meant scroll or book. The word *biblaridion* is used in the New Testament for "little book" (Rev. 10:9).

9. D. Ewert, *From Ancient Tablets to Modern Translations: A General Introduction to the Bible* (Grand Rapids: Zondervan, 1983), 21.

10. C. H. Roberts and T. C. Skeat underscore the importance of the codex's convenience: "The most momentous development in the history of the book until the invention of printing was the replacement of the roll by the codex...." (*The Birth of the Codex* [London: Oxford University Press, 1983], 1).

11. D. J. Wiseman, K. A. Kitchen, and A. R. Millard, "Writing," *IBD*, 3:1664; C. H. Roberts, "Books in the Graeco-Roman World and in the New Testament," in *CHB*, 1:56–60; E. Sellin, *Introduction to the Old Testament*, rev. G. Fohrer, trans. D. E. Green (Nashville: Abingdon, 1968), 492.

12. The precise reading of the Greek in Dan. 9:2 is ἐν ταῖς βίβλοις (*en tais biblois*, in the books) and in 1 Macc. 12:9 is τὰ βιβλία τὰ ἅγια (*ta biblia ta hagia*, the holy books).

13. W. L. Holladay, *Jeremiah 2: A Commentary on the Book of the Prophet Jeremiah, Chapters 26–52*, ed. P. D. Hanson, Hermeneia (Minneapolis: Fortress, 1989), 140.

14. R. K. Harrison, *Introduction to the Old Testament* (Grand Rapids: Eerdmans, 1969), 266; J. J. Collins, *Daniel: A Commentary on the Book of Daniel*, Hermeneia (Minneapolis: Fortress, 1993), 348.

15. F. F. Bruce, *The Books and the Parchments*, 5th ed. (London: Marshall Pickering, 1991), 3.

16. K. Lake, *The Apostolic Fathers*, LCL (Cambridge, MA: Harvard University Press, 1935), 1:151.

17. Ibid., 4; G. D. Fee, *1 and 2 Timothy, Titus*, NIBC (Peabody, MA: Hendrickson, 1988), 295; T. D. Lea and H. P. Griffin, *1, 2 Timothy Titus*, NAC 34 (Nashville: Broadman, 1992), 254. However, M. Dibelius and H. Conzelmann point out that the usual writing material for New Testament books at this time was still papyrus (*The Pastoral Epistles*, trans. P. Buttoloph and A. Yarbro, Hermeneia [Philadelphia: Fortress, 1972], 123).

18. *Webster's New Collegiate Dictionary* (Springfield, MA: Merriam, 1973), 1205.

19. W. L. Holladay, *A Concise Hebrew and Aramaic Lexicon of the Old Testament* (Grand Rapids: Eerdmans, 1971), 48–49; L. Koehler and W. Baumgartner, *The Hebrew and Aramaic Lexicon of the Old Testament*, trans. and ed. M. E. J. Richardson (Leiden and New York: E. J. Brill, 1994), 1:157–59; E. B. Smick, בְּרִית *bᵉrit* covenant, *TWOT*, 1:128–30.

20. Greek has another word signifying "covenant" (συνθήκη [*synthēkē*] H. G. Liddell and R. Scott, *A Greek-English Lexicon*, rev. and augmented by H. S. Jones [Oxford: Clarendon, 1996], 1717), but it generally refers to a covenant between equals, which does not accord well with the relationship between God and man.

21. Ewert, *From Ancient Tablets to Modern Translations*, 21.

22. A. von Harnack, *Marcion: The Gospel of the Alien God*, trans. J. E. Steely and L. D. Bierma (Durham, NC: Labyrinth, 1990), 134.

23. Representative works include P. C. Craigie, *The Problem of War in the Old Testament* (Grand Rapids: Eerdmans, 1978); J. L. Crenshaw, *A Whirlpool of Torment: Israelite Traditions of God as an Oppressive Presence*, OBT (Philadelphia: Fortress, 1984); J. L. Crenshaw and J. T. Willis, *Essays in Old Testament Ethics* (New York: KTAV, 1974); W. Harrelson, *The Ten Commandments and Human Rights*, OBT (Philadelphia: Fortress, 1980); J. H.

Yoder, *The Politics of Jesus: Vicit Agnus Noster,* 2d ed. (Grand Rapids: Eerdmans, 1994).

24. Bruce, *The Books and the Parchments,* 72.

25. D. A. Carson, "Matthew," vol. 8 in *The Expositor's Bible Commentary,* ed. F. E. Gaebelein, 12 vols. (Grand Rapids: Zondervan, 1984), 141–44.

26. L. I. Rabinowitz, "Bible," *EncJud,* 4:917.

27. Ibid. See also G. F. Moore, *Judaism in the First Centuries of the Christian Era: The Age of the Tannaim,* 3 vols. (Cambridge, MA: Harvard University Press, 1927–30), 1:239.

28. Moore, *Judaism,* 1:251–54.

29. A. E. Hill and J. H. Walton, *A Survey of the Old Testament* (Grand Rapids: Zondervan, 1991), 435.

Chapter 3: *The Old Testament*

1. R. L. Braun, *1 Chronicles,* WBC 14 (Waco: Word, 1986), 54; J. M. Myers, *I Chronicles: Introduction, Transmission, and Notes,* AB (Garden City, NY: Doubleday, 1965), 20–21.

2. G. F. Hasel, "Chronicles, Books of," *ISBE,* 1:670.

3. R. Beckwith, *The Old Testament Canon of the New Testament Church and Its Background in Early Judaism* (Grand Rapids: Eerdmans, 1985), 111–15.

4. Origen *Commentarii in evangelium Joannis* 5.6.1.5; 13.26.154.2; Origen *Comm. Matt.* 11.10.5; Origen *Selecta in Genesim* 12.140.31.

5. R. K. Harrison, *Introduction to the Old Testament* (Grand Rapids: Eerdmans, 1969), 495.

6. E. E. Carpenter, "Pentateuch," *ISBE,* 3:740.

7. Technically other books also are written in poetic form, such as Ecclesiastes, Song of Songs, and Lamentations, as well as many portions of the prophetic books.

8. Harrison, *Introduction to the Old Testament,* 965.

9. N. H. Ridderbos and H. M. Wolf, "Poetry, Hebrew," *ISBE,* 3:891.

10. Harrison, *Introduction to the Old Testament,* 272–73.

11. Beckwith, *Old Testament Canon,* 181–82.

12. See T.B. *Baba Batra* 14b, which states, "Who wrote the Scriptures?—Moses wrote his own book and the portion of Balaam and Job."

13. I. Epstein, *The Babylonian Talmud* (London: Soncino, 1935), *Seder Nezikin* 2:7.

14. W. Barclay, *The Making of the Bible* (New York: Abingdon, 1961), 31–32; D. Ewert, *From Ancient Tablets to Modern Translations: A General Introduction to the Bible* (Grand Rapids: Zondervan, 1983), 33.

15. F. F. Bruce, *The Books and the Parchments,* 5th ed. (London: Marshall Pickering, 1991), 81–82.

16. J. Bright, *Jeremiah: A New Translation with Introduction and Commentary,* 2d ed., AB 21 (Garden City, NY: Doubleday, 1978), cxii–cxxiv; P. C. Craigie, P. H. Kelly, and J. F. Drinkard, *Jeremiah 1–25,* WBC 26 (Dallas: Word, 1991), xlii–xlv; W. L. Holladay, *Jeremiah 2: A Commentary on the Book of the Prophet Jeremiah, Chapters 26–52,* ed. P. D. Hanson, Hermeneia (Minneapolis: Fortress, 1989), 2–8.

Chapter 4: *The New Testament*

1. The exact date of Galatians, like that of most ancient documents, is disputed. The date of this book hinges primarily upon whether it was written before or after the Jerusalem council (A.D. 49), which covered similar issues but is not mentioned in the book. See R. N. Longenecker, *Galatians,* WBC 41 (Dallas: Word, 1990), lxxii–lxxxviii; J. D. G. Dunn, *The Epistle to the Galatians,* Black's New Testament Commentary (Peabody, MA: Hendrickson, 1993), 7–8.

2. D. Ewert, *From Ancient Tablets to Modern Translations: A General Introduction to the Bible* (Grand Rapids: Zondervan, 1983), 35.

3. P. Beasley-Murray, "The Letters," in *The Complete Bible Study Tool Kit,* ed. J. F. Balchin, D. H. Field, and T. Longman (Downers Grove, IL: InterVarsity, 1991), 202.

4. Ibid.

5. W. M. Ramsay, *The Westminster Guide to the Books of the Bible* (Louisville, KY: Westminster/John Knox, 1994), 292–93. For a more detailed discussion see A. C. Bou-

quet, *Everyday Life in New Testament Times* (New York: Scribner's Sons, 1954).

6. R. Marcus, *Josephus, with an English Translation*, LCL (Cambridge, MA: Harvard University Press, 1976), 7:127–31.

7. J. J. Collins, *Daniel: A Commentary on the Book of Daniel*, Hermeneia (Minneapolis: Fortress, 1993), 357–58; J. E. Goldingay, *Daniel*, WBC 30 (Dallas: Word, 1989), 267–68; L. F. Hartman and A. A. Di Lella, *The Book of Daniel: A New Translation with Notes and Commentary*, AB 23 (New York: Doubleday, 1978), 252–53.

8. Bouquet, *Everyday Life*, 41.

9. E. Schürer, *The History of the Jewish People in the Age of Jesus Christ (175 B.C.–A.D. 135)*, rev. and ed. G. Vermes and F. Millar (Edinburgh: T & T Clark, 1973), 1:148–49.

10. Ramsay, *Westminster Guide*, 294.

11. L. L. Grabbe, *Judaism from Cyrus to Hadrian*, vol. 2, *The Roman Period* (Minneapolis: Fortress, 1992), 419.

12. Ramsay, *Westminster Guide*, 295.

13. Grabbe, *The Roman Period*, 420.

14. M. Hengel, *Acts and the History of Early Christianity*, trans. J. Bowden (Philadelphia: Fortress, 1979), 41–42.

15. G. N. Stanton, *The Gospels and Jesus*, OBS (Oxford: Oxford University Press, 1989), 69–70.

16. R. A. Cole, "Mark, Gospel of," *IBD*, 2:950–51.

17. Ibid., 2:948–51.

18. P. J. Achtemeier, "Mark, Gospel of," *ABD*, 4:542–43.

19. Stanton, *The Gospels and Jesus*, 82.

20. For a further explanation of these see Ramsay, *Westminster Guide*, 522–23.

21. R. H. Gundry, *A Survey of the New Testament*, 3d ed. (Grand Rapids: Zondervan, 1994), 254.

22. Gundry, *Survey of the New Testament*, 297. For a thorough examination of this topic see C. J. Hemer, *The Book of Acts in the Setting of Hellenistic History*, ed. C. H. Gempf (Winona Lake, IN: Eisenbrauns, 1990) and the series of books entitled The Book of Acts in Its First-Century Setting (Grand Rapids: Eerdmans, 1993–).

23. Much of this information comes from F. F. Bruce, *Paul: Apostle of the Heart Set Free* (Grand Rapids: Eerdmans, 1977), 475.

24. Bruce, *Paul*, 389–99; other scholars suggest it may be Ephesus or Caesarea (see arguments in D. Guthrie, *New Testament Introduction*, 3d ed. [Downers Grove, IL: InterVarsity, 1970], 472–78).

25. R. V. G. Tasker, "Catholic Epistles," *IBD*, 1:254.

26. K. Lake and J. E. L. Oulton, *Eusebius: The Ecclesiastical History*, LCL (Cambridge, MA: Harvard University Press, 1926–32), 2:79.

27. Lake and Oulton, *Eusebius*, 1:235.

28. Ewert, *From Ancient Tablets to Modern Translations*, 37.

29. F. F. Bruce, *The Book of Acts*, NICNT (Grand Rapids: Eerdmans, 1988), 5.

30. B. M. Metzger, *The Text of the New Testament*, 3d ed. (New York: Oxford University Press, 1992), 205.

31. Titles to New Testament books of Codex Sinaiticus (fourth century) were apparently added later.

32. Scholars note varying numbers of verses that overlap between the Gospels; this diagram is based on information collected from F. F. Bruce, "Gospels," *IBD*, 2:582.

33. R. H. Stein, "Synoptic Problem," in *Dictionary of Jesus and the Gospels*, ed. J. B. Green and S. McKnight (Downers Grove, IL: InterVarsity, 1992), 786.

34. C. M. Tuckett, "Synoptic Problem," *ABD*, 6:263.

Chapter 5: *The Unity of the Two Covenants*

1. F. F. Bruce says that it has become "finally incarnated in Christ" ("Bible," *IBD*, 1:197).

2. J. Orr, "Bible," *ISBE*, 1:491.

3. J. Bright, *The Kingdom of God: The Biblical Concept and Its Meaning for the Church* (New York and Nashville: Abingdon, 1953), 7.

4. G. von Rad, *Old Testament Theology*, trans. D. M. G. Stalker, 2 vols. (Edinburgh and London: Oliver and Boyd, 1962–65).

5. O. Cullmann, *Salvation in History*, trans. S. G. Sowers, NTL (London: SCM, 1967), 54.

6. G. E. Wright, *God Who Acts: Biblical Theology as Recital*, SBT 8 (London: SCM, 1952), esp. 11–14.

7. O. P. Robertson, *The Christ of the Covenants* (Phillipsburg, NJ: Presbyterian & Reformed, 1980). See also T. E. McComiskey, *The Covenants of Promise: A Theology of the Old Testament Covenants* (Grand Rapids: Baker, 1985).

8. W. C. Kaiser, *Toward an Old Testament Theology* (Grand Rapids: Zondervan, 1978).

9. See E. C. Blackman, *Marcion and His Influence* (London: SPCK, 1948).

10. W. M. Ramsay, *The Westminster Guide to the Books of the Bible* (Louisville, KY: Westminster/John Knox, 1994), 11.

11. R. N. Soulen, *Handbook of Biblical Criticism*, 2d ed. (Atlanta: John Knox, 1981), 15.

12. See R. M. Grant, *A Short History of the Interpretations of the Bible* (New York: Macmillan, 1972), 89.

13. J. F. Balchin, "How to Interpret the Bible," in *The Complete Bible Study Tool Kit*, ed. J. F. Balchin, D. H. Field, and T. Longman (Downers Grove, IL: InterVarsity, 1991), 59.

14. See Grant, *Short History*, 89.

15. R. N. Soulen, *Handbook of Biblical Criticism*, 206. See also R. B. Laurin, "Typological Interpretation of the Old Testament" in *Hermeneutics*, ed. B. L. Ramm (Grand Rapids: Baker, 1987), 118.

16. Leon Morris explains it this way: "Adam is spoken of as *a pattern* (or 'type') *of the one to come.* He was the first man and thus the head of the race. . . . Christ initiated the new race, the race of the redeemed, just as Adam was the head of the old race, the race of sinners" (*The Epistle to the Romans* [Grand Rapids: Eerdmans, 1988], 234).

17. F. F. Bruce, *The New Testament Development of Old Testament Themes* (Grand Rapids: Eerdmans, 1968).

18. F. F. Bruce, "Promise and Fulfilment in Paul's Presentation of Jesus," in *Promise and Fulfilment: Essays Presented to S. H. Hooke* (Edinburgh: T & T Clark, 1963), 36–50; F. F. Bruce, "Bible," *IBD*, 1:196; C. H. Dodd, *The Authority of the Bible* (London: Fontana, 1960); H. H. Rowley, *The Unity of the Bible* (New York: Meridian, 1957); B. F. Westcott, *The Epistle to the Hebrews: The Greek Text with Notes and Essays*, 3d ed. (London: Macmillan, 1920), esp. 471–97; W. Zimmerli, "Promise and Fulfilment," *Int* 15 (1961): 310–38.

19. B. S. Childs, *Introduction to the Old Testament as Scripture* (Philadelphia: Fortress, 1979), 671.

20. J. Barr, *Holy Scriptures: Canon, Authority, Criticism* (Oxford: Oxford University Press, 1983), 152.

Chapter 6: *Prerequisites to the Bible*

1. H. Ewald, *The History of Israel*, 3d ed. (London: Longman, Green, 1876), 1:47–48; H. Gunkel, *The Legends of Genesis: The Biblical Saga and History*, trans. W. H. Carruth (New York: Schocken, 1964), 1–4; H. Schultz, *Old Testament Theology*, trans. S. A. Paterson (Edinburgh: T & T Clark, 1895), 1:25–26; J. Wellhausen, *Prolegomena to the History of Israel*, trans. J. S. Black and A. Menzies (Edinburgh: Adam and Charles Black, 1885), 392–410.

2. R. K. Harrison, *Introduction to the Old Testament* (Grand Rapids: Eerdmans, 1969), 201.

3. K. N. Schoville, *Biblical Archaeology in Focus* (Grand Rapids: Baker, 1978), 129.

4. C. B. F. Walker, *Cuneiform*, Reading the Past (London: British Museum, 1987), 7.

5. Walker, *Cuneiform*, 7.

6. Ibid., 11.

7. Schoville, *Biblical Archaeology*, 131–34.

8. Ibid., 139.

9. I. J. Gelb argues that West Semitic languages (e.g., Phoenician, Hebrew, Aramaic) are not the purest form of an alphabet since each sign represents a consonant and a vowel (or vowel zero). Nevertheless, while Hebrew and other West Semitic languages are not as highly developed as Greek, they still represent alphabetic forms of writing since there are a limited number of fixed letters that make up the words (*A Study of Writing*, rev. ed. [Chicago: University of Chicago Press, 1963], 166–89; see also J. Naveh, *Origins of the Alphabet* [Jerusalem: Palphot, 1994], 17).

10. Naveh, *Origins of the Alphabet*, 8–11.
11. A. H. Gardiner, "The Egyptian Origin of the Semitic Alphabet," *JEA* 3 (1916): 1–16.
12. Schoville, *Biblical Archaeology*, 142.
13. F. Rosenthal, *A Grammar of Biblical Aramaic*, Porta Linguarum Orientalium (Wiesbaden: Otto Horrassowitz, 1974), 5–6.
14. F. F. Bruce, *The Books and the Parchments*, 5th ed. (London: Marshall Pickering, 1991), 24.
15. Ibid., 24.
16. M. Kochavi, "An Ostracon of the Period of the Judges from ʿIzbet Ṣarṭah," *Tel Aviv* 4 (1977): 1–13; A. Demsky, "A Proto-Canaanite Abecedary Dating from the Period of the Judges and Its Implications for the History of the Alphabet," *Tel Aviv* 4 (1977): 14–27; A. Demsky and M. Kochavi, "An Alphabet from the Days of the Judges," *BAR* 4 (September/October 1978): 23–30.
17. See B. K. Waltke and M. O'Connor, *An Introduction to Biblical Hebrew Syntax* (Winona Lake, IN: Eisenbrauns, 1990), 3–4.
18. W. F. Albright, *The Archaeology of Palestine*, rev. ed. (Harmondsworth, Middlesex: Penguin, 1960), 149–50.
19. F. M. Cross, "The Oldest Manuscripts from Qumran," *JBL* 74 (1955): 147–72, reprinted in *Qumran and the History of the Biblical Text*, ed. F. M. Cross and S. Talmon (Cambridge, MA: Harvard University Press, 1975), 147–76; F. M. Cross, "The Development of the Jewish Scripts," in *The Bible and the Ancient Near East; Essays in Honor of William Foxwell Albright*, ed. G. E. Wright (Garden City, NY: Doubleday, 1961), 133–202.
20. E. Würthwein, *The Text of the Old Testament* (Grand Rapids: Eerdmans, 1979), 4.
21. T. W. Manson, *The Teaching of Jesus*, 2d ed. (Cambridge: Cambridge University Press, 1951), 45–50.
22. W. S. LaSor, "Aramaic," *ISBE*, 1:229.
23. *The New York Times*, Friday, August 6, 1993; A. Biran and J. Naveh, "An Aramaic Stele Fragment from Tel Dan," *IEJ* 43 (1993): 81–98; A. Biran, "David Found at Dan," *BAR* 20 (March/April 1992): 26–39; see also A. R. Millard and P. Bordreuil, "A Statue from Syria with Assyrian and Aramaic Inscriptions," *BA* 45 (1982): 135–41.
24. Additional Aramaic words are scattered in the Old and New Testaments (e.g., Ps. 2:12; Mark 5:41; 7:34; 1 Cor. 16:22).
25. See B. T. Arnold for a plausible reason why these passages are written in Aramaic ("The Use of Aramaic in the Hebrew Bible: Another Look at Bilingualism in Ezra and Daniel," *JNSL* 22 [1996]: 1–16).
26. J. C. de Moor, "Systems of Writing and Nonbiblical Languages," in *The World of the Bible*, vol. 1 of *Bible Handbook*, ed. A. S. Van der Woude (Grand Rapids: Eerdmans, 1986), 113; LaSor, "Aramaic," 1:229.
27. See Bruce, *The Books and the Parchments*, 12–13.
28. Ibid., 13.
29. Ibid.
30. Richard Rothe, a German theologian, called Koine Greek a language of the Holy Ghost; *Zur Dogmatik*, 3 vols. (Heidelberg: Mohr, 1863), 1:238.
31. A. Deissmann, *Light from the Ancient East*, trans. L. R. M. Strachan, 4th ed. (London: Hodder and Stoughton, 1927), esp. 62–145.
32. Determined from evidence found in G. L. Archer and G. Chirichigno, *Old Testament Quotations in the New Testament* (Chicago: Moody, 1983), xi–xxxii.
33. Bruce, *The Books and the Parchments*, 61–62.
34. Ibid., 52.
35. Ibid., 4; D. Ewert, *From Ancient Tablets to Modern Translations: A General Introduction to the Bible* (Grand Rapids: Zondervan, 1983), 20.
36. E. J. Goodspeed and I. A. Sparks, "Papyrus," *ISBE*, 3:651; A. Lemaire, "Writing and Writing Materials," *ABD*, 6:1003.
37. Herodotus 5.58 states: "Thus also the Ionians have from ancient times called papyrus-sheets skins, because formerly for lack of papyrus they used the skins of sheep and goats; and even to this day there are many foreigners who write on such skins" (A. D. Godley, ed. *Herodotus*, 4 vols., LCL [Cambridge, MA: Harvard University Press, 1922–38], 3:65).

38. F. G. Kenyon, *Our Bible and the Ancient Manuscripts* (New York: Harper, 1958), 40.
39. Bruce, *The Books and the Parchments*, 6.
40. Kenyon, *Our Bible and the Ancient Manuscripts*, 37.
41. R. J. H. Shutt, "Letter of Aristeas," in *The Old Testament Pseudepigrapha*, ed. J. H. Charlesworth (Garden City, NY: Doubleday, 1983–85), 2:24.
42. B. M. Metzger, *Manuscripts of the Greek Bible: An Introduction to Greek Palaeography* (New York and Oxford: Oxford University Press, 1981), 14.
43. C. G. Kühn, ed., *Claudii Galeni: Opera Omnia* (Hildesheim: Olms, 1964), 3.776; 18.630.
44. Lemaire, "Writing and Writing Materials," 6:1003.
45. Metzger, *Manuscripts of the Greek Bible*, 17.
46. D. J. Wiseman, "Assyrian Writing Boards," *Iraq* 17 (1955): 3–13.
47. Lemaire, "Writing and Writing Materials," 6:1002.
48. Deissmann, *Light from the Ancient East*, 50–61.
49. *The Daily Telegraph* (London newspaper), Friday, June 20, 1986; G. Barkay, *Ketef Hinnom: A Treasure Facing Jerusalem's Walls* (Jerusalem: Israel Museum, 1986), 29–34.
50. Metzger, *Manuscripts of the Greek Bible*, 17.
51. Lemaire, "Writing and Writing Materials," 6:1004.
52. Ibid., 6:1005.
53. A. R. Millard, "An Assessment of the Evidence for Writing in Ancient Israel," in *Biblical Archaeology Today*, Proceedings of the International Congress on Biblical Archaeology, Jerusalem, April 1984 (Jerusalem: Israel Exploration Society, 1985), 308.
54. Walker, *Cuneiform*, 34.
55. Metzger, *Manuscripts of the Greek Bible*, 4.

Chapter 7: *Canonization of the Old Testament*

1. R. K. Harrison, *Introduction to the Old Testament* (Grand Rapids: Eerdmans, 1969), 260.

2. F. F. Bruce, *The Books and the Parchments*, 5th ed. (London: Marshall Pickering, 1991), 86–87.
3. R. N. Soulen, *Handbook of Biblical Criticism*, 2d ed. (Atlanta: John Knox, 1981), 37.
4. Bruce, *The Books and the Parchments*, 86; D. Ewert, *From Ancient Tablets to Modern Translations: A General Introduction to the Bible* (Grand Rapids: Zondervan, 1983), 65.
5. *The Fathers of the Church: A New Translation*, vol. 89, *Origen: Commentary on the Gospel according to John, Books 13–22*, trans. R. E. Heine (Washington, DC: Catholic University of America Press, 1993), 88. See also Bruce, *The Books and the Parchments*, 86; Origen *Comm. Matt.* 2.46.
6. P. Schaff and H. Wace, eds., *A Select Library of the Nicene and Post-Nicene Fathers of the Christian Church*, vol. 4, *St. Athanasius: Select Works and Letters*, 2d series, 14 vols. (Grand Rapids: Eerdmans, 1991), 161–62 (italics added). See also R. P. C. Hanson, "Origen's Doctrine of Tradition," *JTS* 49 (1948): 23; Harrison, *Introduction to the Old Testament*, 260–61.
7. G. C. Aalders, *Oud-Testamentische Kanoniek* (Kampen: Kok, 1952), 56–57.
8. A. A. Di Lella, "Wisdom of Ben-Sira," *ABD*, 6:932.
9. "The holy scriptures," τὰ ἱερὰ γράμματα (Philo *Spec.* 2.28 §159; 2.43 §238; Philo *Contempl.* 3 §28; 10 §§75, 78); "the (most) holy writings," αἱ ἱεραὶ (ἱερώταται) γραφαί (Philo *Decal.* 1 §8; 10 §37; Philo *Spec.* 1.39 §214; 2.21 §104; 2.25 §134).
10. H. St. J. Thackeray et al., *Josephus with an English Translation*, 10 vols., LCL (Cambridge, MA: Harvard University Press; London: Heinemann, 1926–65), 1:174–75.
11. W. L. Holladay, *Jeremiah 2: A Commentary on the Book of the Prophet Jeremiah, Chapters 26–52*, ed. P. D. Hanson, Hermeneia (Minneapolis: Fortress, 1989), 140.
12. Harrison states: "If the reference in Daniel 9:2 to the books is to a collection of prophetic writings, as seems most probable, it would imply that these works were regarded as having divine authority, and were thus akin to the Pentateuchal compositions" (*Introduction to the Old Testament*, 266); J. J. Collins,

Daniel: A Commentary on the Book of Daniel, Hermeneia (Minneapolis: Fortress, 1993), 348.

13. J. A. Sanders, *Torah and Canon* (Philadelphia: Fortress, 1972), 6.

14. I. Epstein, ed., *The Babylonian Talmud*, 12:46 (London: Soncino, 1935), *Seder Nezikin*, 3:46.

15. R. Beckwith, *The Old Testament Canon of the New Testament Church and Its Background in Early Judaism* (Grand Rapids: Eerdmans, 1985), 370.

16. Ibid.

17. Epstein, ed., *Babylonian Talmud*, 4:94, *Seder Moʿed*, 3:94.

18. Ibid., 11:59, *Seder Nezikin*, 2:59.

19. Harrison, *Introduction to the Old Testament*, 287.

20. F. F. Bruce, "Dead Sea Scrolls," *IBD*, 1:373.

21. H. F. D. Sparks, "Jerome as Biblical Scholar," in *CHB*, 1:534.

22. P. Schaff, *The Creeds of Christendom, with a History and Critical Notes*, vol. 2, *The Greek and Latin Creeds, with Translations* (New York: Harper and Brothers, 1882), 80–82.

23. W. Whitaker, *A Disputation on Holy Scripture against the Papists* (Cambridge: Parker Society Translation, 1849), 51–52: "This is what Augustine says of the books of Maccabees: 'the Jews do not esteem this scripture as the Law and the Prophets, to which the Lord bears testimony as his witnesses.'"

24. F. K. Movers, *Loci Quidam Historiae Canonis Veteris Testamenti Illustrati* (Breslau: Hirt, 1842), 1–32.

25. H. H. Graetz, *Kohélet oder der Salomonische Prediger* (Leipzig: Winter, 1871), 160–63.

26. H. E. Ryle, *The Canon of the Old Testament* (London: Macmillan, 1892; 2d ed. in 1895).

27. Beckwith, *Old Testament Canon*, 4.

28. A. C. Sundberg, *The Old Testament of the Early Church*, HTS 20 (Cambridge, MA: Harvard University Press, 1964).

29. J. P. Lewis, "What Do We Mean by Jabneh?" *The Journal of Bible and Religion* 32 (1964): 125–32.

30. S. Z. Leiman, *The Canonization of Hebrew Scripture: The Talmudic and Midrashic Evidence*, Transactions of the Connecticut Academy of Arts and Sciences 47 (Hamden, CT: Archon, 1976), 29–30; Beckwith, *Old Testament Canon*, 164–66.

31. M. K. H. Peters, "Septuagint," *ABD*, 5:1094.

32. Beckwith, *Old Testament Canon*, 384–86.

33. Ibid., 389.

34. Bruce, *The Books and the Parchments*, 96.

35. Beckwith, *Old Testament Canon*, 112.

36. F. H. Colson, *Philo, with an English Translation*, 10 vols., LCL (Cambridge, MA: Harvard University Press, 1949–62), 9:127.

37. P. E. Kahle, *The Cairo Geniza*, 2d ed. (Oxford: Basil Blackwell, 1959), 88–89.

38. Beckwith, *Old Testament Canon*, 385–86.

39. Thackeray et al., *Josephus*, 1:176–79.

40. K. Lake and J. E. L. Oulton, *Eusebius: The Ecclesiastical History*, 2 vols., LCL (Cambridge, MA: Harvard University Press, 1926–32), 1:393.

41. Bruce, *The Books and the Parchments*, 91. See also G. F. Moore, *Judaism in the First Centuries of the Christian Era: The Age of the Tannaim*, 3 vols. (Cambridge, MA: Harvard University Press, 1927–30), 1:238, 244–45.

42. Bruce, *The Books and the Parchments*, 91–92. See also J. P. Audet, "A Hebrew-Aramaic List of Books of the Old Testament in Greek Transcription," *JTS* n.s. 1 (1950): 135–54.

43. Lake and Oulton, *Eusebius*, 2:72–75.

44. Schaff and Wace, *Library of Nicene and Post-Nicene Fathers*, 4:551–52.

45. P. Schaff and H. Wace, eds., *A Select Library of Nicene and Post-Nicene Fathers of the Christian Church*, vol. 6, *St. Jerome: Letters and Select Works*, 2d series, 14 vols. (Grand Rapids: Eerdmans, 1983), 493.

46. Ibid., 6:489–90.

47. P. Schaff and H. Wace, eds., *A Select Library of Nicene and Post-Nicene Fathers of the Christian Church*, vol. 3, *Theodoret, Jerome, Gennadius, Rufinus: Historical Writings, Etc.*, 2d series, 14 vols. (Grand Rapids: Eerdmans, 1979), 557–58.

48. Epstein, ed., *Babylonian Talmud*, 11:70–71, *Seder Nezikin*, 2:70–71.

49. H. H. Graetz, *Kohélet*, קֹהֶלֶת; oder, *Der Salomonische Prediger: übers. und Kritische erl. von H. Graetz* (Leipzig and Heidelberg: Winters, 1871), 155–56.

50. H. H. Rowley, *The Growth of the Old Testament* (London: Hutchinson's University Library, 1953), 170.

51. J. P. Lewis, "Jamnia (Jabneh), Council of," *ABD*, 3:634.
52. Epstein, ed., *Babylonian Talmud*, 2:55, *Seder Moʿed*, 1:55.
53. Beckwith, *Old Testament Canon*, 318.
54. Epstein, ed., *Babylonian Talmud*, 2:137, *Seder Moʿed*, 1:137.
55. Ibid.
56. Ibid., 12:137, *Seder Nezikin*, 3:137.
57. Beckwith, *Old Testament Canon*, 292.
58. Ibid., 284.
59. Epstein, ed., *Babylonian Talmud*, 13:32, *Seder Nezikin*, 4:32.
60. Beckwith, *Old Testament Canon*, 276.
61. Ewert, *From Ancient Tablets to Modern Translations*, 72; R. P. Lawson, *Origen: The Song of Songs. Commentary and Homilies*, ACW 26 (Westminster, MA: Newman; London: Longman, Green, 1957); R. A. Greer, *Origen*, The Classics of Western Spirituality (New York: Ramsey; Toronto: Paulist, 1979), 217–44.
62. B. Bayer, "Song of Songs," *EncJud*, 15:147.
63. Ibid.
64. R. E. Murphy, *The Song of Songs: A Commentary on the Book of Canticles or The Song of Songs*, Hermeneia (Minneapolis: Fortress, 1990), 16–28; M. H. Pope, *Song of Songs: A New Translation with Introduction and Commentary*, AB 7C (Garden City, NY: Doubleday, 1977), 112–32.
65. Bruce, *The Books and the Parchments*, 88.
66. Beckwith, *Old Testament Canon*, 30–31.
67. Ibid., 385.
68. Bruce, *The Books and the Parchments*, 93.
69. Thackeray et al., *Josephus*, 1:177–81 (emphasis added).

Chapter 8: *Old Testament Extracanonical Books*

1. G. W. Anderson, "Canonical and Non-Canonical," in *CHB*, 1:145.
2. Euripides *Hercules Furens* 1070; Xenophon *Memorabilia* 3.5, 14.
3. Dan. 2:22; 11:43 (Theodotion); Sir. 14:21; 39:3, 7; 42:19; 43:32; 48:25.
4. Mark 4:22 par. Luke 8:17; Col. 2:3 (ἀπόκρυφοι, treasure of Christ *hidden*).
5. P. Schaff and H. Wace, eds. *A Select Library of Nicene and Post-Nicene Fathers of the Christian Church*, vol. 6, *St. Jerome: Letters and Select Works*, 2d series, 14 vols. (Grand Rapids: Eerdmans, 1983), 194.
6. F. F. Bruce, *The Books and the Parchments*, 5th ed. (London: Marshall Pickering, 1991), 164.
7. R. Beckwith, *The Old Testament Canon of the New Testament Church and Its Background in Early Judaism* (Grand Rapids: Eerdmans, 1985), 388.
8. Eusebius *HE* 6.25.1–2.
9. Ibid., 5.8.7 (cf. Irenaeus *Haer.* 2.28.9).
10. R. J. Bauckham, *Jude, 2 Peter*, WBC 50 (Waco: Word, 1983), 96; S. J. Kistemaker, *Exposition of the Epistles of Peter and the Epistle of Jude*, New Testament Commentary (Grand Rapids: Baker, 1987), 395.
11. E. Isaac, "1 (Ethiopic Apocalypse of) Enoch," in *The Old Testament Pseudepigrapha*, ed. J. H. Charlesworth, 2 vols. (Garden City, NY: Doubleday, 1983–85), 1:6–7.
12. N. Hillyer, *1 and 2 Peter, Jude*, NIBC (Peabody, MA: Hendrickson, 1992), 257.
13. J. N. D. Kelly, *A Commentary on the Epistles of Peter and of Jude*, Harper's New Testament Commentaries (New York: Harper & Row, 1969), 277; M. Green, *The Second Epistle General of Peter and the General Epistle of Jude: An Introduction and Commentary*, TNTC (Grand Rapids: Eerdmans, 1994), 192–93.
14. Bauckham, *Jude, 2 Peter*, 96.
15. C. F. Hornemann remarks that there is a "profound silence of Philo about all the apocryphal books" and that he quotes more distinctly from the Greek philosophers (*Observationes ad Illustrationem Doctrinae de Canone Veteris Testamenti ex Philone* [prefixed to his *Specimen Secundum*] [Copenhagen: Martinum Hallagerum, 1776], 28–33).
16. Beckwith, *Old Testament Canon*, 351.
17. J. H. Charlesworth, "Pseudepigrapha, OT," *ABD*, 5:539.
18. Beckwith, *Old Testament Canon*, 354.
19. Ibid., 351–54.
20. J. H. Charlesworth, "Introduction for the General Reader," in *Old Testament Pseudepigrapha*, 1:xxv.
21. Charlesworth, "Pseudepigrapha, OT," *ABD*, 5:537.

22. O. S. Wintermute, "Jubilees," in *Old Testament Pseudepigrapha*, 2:43–44; H. C. Kee, "Testaments of the Twelve Patriarchs," in *Old Testament Pseudepigrapha*, 1:777–78; Isaac, "1 (Ethiopic Apocalypse of) Enoch," in *Old Testament Pseudepigrapha*, 1:6–7.

23. Charlesworth, *Old Testament Pseudepigrapha*.

Chapter 9: *Canonization of the New Testament*

1. C. F. Evans, "The New Testament in the Making," in *CHB*, 1:232.

2. D. Ewert, *From Ancient Tablets to Modern Translations: A General Introduction to the Bible* (Grand Rapids: Zondervan, 1983), 125.

3. F. V. Filson, *A New Testament History: The Story of the Emerging Church* (Philadelphia: Westminster, 1964), 390.

4. F. F. Bruce, *Jesus and Christian Origins outside the New Testament*, Knowing Christianity (London: Hodder and Stoughton, 1974), 15.

5. For more examples see Bruce, *Jesus and Christian Origins*.

6. Quote from J. Jackson, *Tacitus: The Annals, with an English Translation*, LCL (Cambridge, MA: Harvard University Press, 1962), 4:283.

7. L. H. Feldman, *Josephus with an English Translation*, 10 vols., LCL (Cambridge, MA: Harvard University Press, 1965), 9:49–51.

8. G. C. Richards and R. J. H. Stutt, "Critical Notes on Josephus' Antiquities," *Classical Quarterly* 31 (1937): 176; G. C. Richards, "The *Testimonium* of Josephus," *JTS* 42 (1941): 70–71.

9. Bruce, *Jesus and Christian Origins*, 38.

10. Ibid., 37–41.

11. Ibid., 40–41.

12. I. Epstein, ed., *The Babylonian Talmud*, 12:281–82 (London: Soncino, 1935), *Seder Neziḳin*, 3:281–82.

13. K. Lake and J. E. L. Oulton, *Eusebius: The Ecclesiastical History, with an English Translation*, 2 vols., LCL (Cambridge, MA: Harvard University Press, 1926–32), 1:293.

14. Ewert, *From Ancient Tablets to Modern Translations*, 114.

15. Epstein, ed., *Babylonian Talmud*, 13:18, *Seder Neziḳin*, 4:18.

16. F. F. Bruce, *New Testament History* (Garden City, NY: Doubleday, 1980), 415.

17. E. A. Judge, "Greece," *IBD*, 2:592.

18. Lake and Oulton, *Eusebius*, 2:256–59.

19. J. Stevenson, ed., *The New Eusebius: Documents Illustrating the History of the Church to A.D. 337*; rev. W. H. C. Frend (London: SPCK, 1975), 285–89.

20. Ewert, *From Ancient Tablets to Modern Translations*, 135.

21. See information in *The New Testament in the Apostolic Fathers*, a Committee of the Oxford Society of Historical Theology (Oxford: Clarendon, 1905).

22. W. Barclay, *The Making of the Bible* (New York: Abingdon, 1961), 65.

23. K. Lake, *The Apostolic Fathers, with an English Translation*, 2 vols., LCL (Cambridge, MA: Harvard University Press, 1977), 1:89.

24. *The New Testament in the Apostolic Fathers*, 67.

25. Ignatius *To the Ephesians* 12.2.

26. Polycarp *To the Philippians* 3.2. The plural is probably a "rhetorical plural" (A. Souter, *The Text and Canon of the New Testament*, rev. C. S. C. Williams [London: Duckworth, 1965], 151).

27. B. Dehandschutter, "Polycarp's Epistle to the Philippians an Early Example of 'Reception,'" in *The New Testament in Early Christianity*, ed. J. M. Sevrin BETL 86 (Leuven: Leuven University Press, 1989), 281; *New Testament in Apostolic Fathers*, 85–98.

28. A. Roberts and J. Donaldson, eds., *Ante-Nicene Fathers: Translations of the Writings of the Fathers Down to A.D. 325* (Grand Rapids: Eerdmans, 1991), 1:35.

29. E. F. Harrison, *Introduction to the New Testament*, rev. ed. (Grand Rapids: Eerdmans, 1971), 101–2.

30. Quoted from Lake, *Apostolic Fathers*, 1:321. Souter states that "in three other passages 'the Gospel' (singular) is referred to, and clearly means 'the (written) Gospel'" (*Text and Canon*, 147–48).

31. Lake, *Apostolic Fathers*, 1:247.

32. W. R. Schoedel, *The Apostolic Fathers: A New Translation and Commentary*, vol. 5, *Polycarp, Martyrdom of Polycarp, Fragments*

of Papias (London: Thomas Nelson, 1967), 5:91.

33. Roberts and Donaldson, *Ante-Nicene Fathers*, 1:573.

34. F. F. Bruce, *The Books and the Parchments*, 5th ed. (London: Marshall Pickering, 1991), 99.

35. A. von Harnack, *The Origin of the New Testament and the Most Important Consequences of the New Creation*, trans. J. R. Wilkinson, New Testament Studies 6 (London: Williams and Norgate, 1925), 64–65.

36. F. F. Bruce, *The Acts of the Apostles: The Greek Text with Introduction and Commentary*, 3d ed. (Grand Rapids: Eerdmans, 1990), 1–2.

37. E. Ferguson, "Canon Muratori: Date and Provenance," *Studia Patristica* 18.2 (1982): 677–83.

38. D. Guthrie, *New Testament Introduction* (Leicester, England: Apollos; Downers Grove, IL: InterVarsity, 1990), 940; G. E. Ladd, *A Commentary on the Revelation of John* (Grand Rapids: Eerdmans, 1972), 7–8; L. Morris, *The Revelation of St. John*, TNTC, rev. ed. (Grand Rapids: Eerdmans, 1987), 40.

39. D. A. Carson, D. J. Moo, and L. Morris, *An Introduction to the New Testament* (Grand Rapids: Zondervan, 1992), 471; J. R. Michaels, *Interpreting the Book of Revelation*, Guides to New Testament Exegesis (Grand Rapids: Baker, 1992), 85–94.

40. Filson, *New Testament History*, 392.

41. R. H. Charles, *A Critical and Exegetical Commentary on the Revelation of St. John*, 2 vols., ICC (Edinburgh: T & T Clark, 1920), 1:xcviii.

42. Eusebius *HE* 3.3.4–5.

43. W. L. Lane, *Hebrews 1–8*, WBC 47A (Dallas: Word, 1991), lxii.

44. Ibid., cliii.

45. R. J. Bauckham, *Jude, 2 Peter*, WBC 50 (Waco: Word, 1983), 17.

46. Dehandschutter, "Polycarp's Epistle," 283.

47. *New Testament in the Apostolic Fathers*, 37–62.

48. Ibid., 63–83.

49. Ibid., 67.

50. See Stevenson, *New Eusebius*, 18–26.

51. Dehandschutter, "Polycarp's Epistle," 281–91.

52. Souter, *Text and Canon*, 154. See also Justin Martyr *Dial.* 81.3.

53. Souter, *Text and Canon*, 12. See also Tertullian and Epiphanius.

54. Roberts and Donaldson, *Ante-Nicene Fathers*, 3:262.

55. See quotes from Eusebius *HE* 5.8.1–8 and Irenaeus *Against Heresies*, in Roberts and Donaldson, *Ante-Nicene Fathers*, vol. 1: Acts, 495; Rom. and Gal., 454; 1 Cor., 446; 2 Cor., 498; Eph., 446, 548; Col. and Phil., 538; 1 Thess., 532; 2 Thess., 554; 1 Tim., 315; 2 Tim., 438; Tit., 341, 416; Heb., 406, 574; James, 478, 481; 1 Pet., 482; 2 Pet., 551, 557; 1 and 2 Jn., 443; Jude(?), 574, 516. See also Bruce, *The Books and the Parchments*, 100.

56. According to Eusebius *HE* 5.8.7.

57. Souter, *Text and Canon*, 164.

58. Filson, *New Testament History*, 394. See also R. M. Grant, "The New Testament Canon," in *CHB*, 1:308.

59. Stevenson, *New Eusebius*, 144–47.

60. B. F. Westcott, *A General Survey of the History of the Canon of the New Testament*, 7th ed. (London and New York: Macmillan, 1896), 223–24.

61. Souter, *Text and Canon*, 163–66; J. K. Elliott, *The Apocryphal New Testament: A Collection of Apocryphal Christian Literature in an English Translation* (Oxford: Clarendon, 1993), 350, 390, 593.

62. Clement of Alexandria, *Stromateis: Books One to Three*, trans. J. Ferguson, Fathers of the Church (Washington, DC: Catholic University of America Press, 1991), 314.

63. Souter, *Text and Canon*, 151–52, 159.

64. Ibid., 165.

65. Ewert, *From Ancient Tablets to Modern Translations*, 126.

66. Elliott, *Apocryphal New Testament*, 350.

67. Souter, *Text and Canon*, 164, 167–68. See also Eusebius *HE* 6.25.3–14.

68. Lake and Oulton, *Eusebius*, 1:257.

69. Souter, *Text and Canon*, 170.

70. P. Schaff and H. Wace, eds., *A Select Library of Nicene and Post-Nicene Fathers of the Christian Church*, 2d series, 14 vols. (Grand Rapids: Eerdmans; Edinburgh: T & T Clark, 1991), 4:552.

71. E. F. Harrison, *Introduction to the New Testament* (Grand Rapids: Eerdmans, 1971), 107.

72. Bruce, *The Books and the Parchments*, 102.

73. Souter, *Text and Canon*, 173.

74. W. G. Kümmel, *Introduction to the New Testament*, trans. H. C. Kee, rev. ed. (Nashville: Abingdon, 1975), 497.

75. Schaff and Wace, *Nicene and Post-Nicene Fathers*, 4:552.

76. Kümmel, *Introduction*, 504.

77. Ewert, *From Ancient Tablets to Modern Translations*, 128–29. See also E. J. Goodspeed, *The Formation of the New Testament Canon* (Chicago: University of Chicago Press, 1926), 120.

78. Souter, *Text and Canon*, 168.

79. Stevenson, *New Eusebius*, 144–46 (bold added).

80. Lake, *Apostolic Fathers*, 1:79–81.

81. Roberts and Donaldson, *Ante-Nicene Fathers*, 1:416.

82. Lake, *Apostolic Fathers*, 1:231.

83. Ewert, *From Ancient Tablets to Modern Translations*, 130.

84. Ibid. See Eusebius *HE* 6.12.1–6.

85. J. B. Adamson, *The Epistle of James*, NICNT (Grand Rapids: Eerdmans, 1976), 132–33; F. F. Bruce, *The Letter of Paul to the Romans: An Introduction and Commentary*, 2d ed., TNTC (Grand Rapids: Eerdmans, 1989), 103; B. Byrne, *Romans*, Sacra Pagina 6 (Collegeville, MN: Liturgical Press, 1996), 137; M. Dibelius, *James: A Commentary on the Epistle of James*, trans. M. A. Williams, rev. H. Greeven (Philadelphia: Fortress, 1976), 177–80; D. Moo, *Romans 1–8*, Wycliffe Exegetical Commentary (Chicago: Moody, 1991), 253–54.

86. Bruce, *The Books and the Parchments*, 104.

87. H. E. W. Turner, *The Pattern of Christian Truth: A Study in the Relations between Orthodoxy and Heresy in the Early Church*, Bampton Lectures 1954 (London: Mowbray, 1954), 250.

88. Bruce, *The Books and the Parchments*, 97.

Chapter 10: *New Testament Extracanonical Literature*

1. S. J. Patterson, "Apocrypha," *ABD*, 1:294.

2. Some have suggested that these are oral traditions of Synoptic sayings; see C. L. Blomberg, *1 Corinthians*, NIVAC (Grand Rapids: Zondervan, 1994), 138, and G. D. Fee, *The First Epistle to the Corinthians*, NICNT (Grand Rapids: Eerdmans, 1987), 292.

3. J. K. Elliott, *The Apocryphal New Testament: A Collection of Apocryphal Christian Literature in an English Translation* (Oxford: Clarendon, 1993), 28. See also E. F. Harrison, *Introduction to the New Testament*, rev. ed. (Grand Rapids: Eerdmans, 1971), 131; J. Jeremias, *Unknown Sayings of Jesus*, trans. R. H. Fuller (New York: Macmillan, 1957), 49–54.

4. Elliott, *Apocryphal New Testament*, 29.

5. Ibid., 28–29.

6. Ibid., 29–30.

7. Ibid., 30.

8. Ibid.

9. Ibid.

10. Jeremias, *Unknown Sayings*, 57.

11. Elliott, *Apocryphal New Testament*, 11.

12. Ibid.

13. Jeremias, *Unknown Sayings*, 35–36.

14. Ibid., 17–18.

15. Elliott, *Apocryphal New Testament*, 33–34.

16. Ibid., 31; Jeremias, *Unknown Sayings*, 36–49.

17. Elliott, *Apocryphal New Testament*, 139; Jeremias, *Unknown Sayings*, 13.

18. Elliott, *Apocryphal New Testament*, 139; Jeremias, *Unknown Sayings*, 69.

19. Elliott, *Apocryphal New Testament*, 139–40; Jeremias, *Unknown Sayings*, 95.

20. Elliott, *Apocryphal New Testament*, 135.

21. F. F. Bruce, *The Books and the Parchments*, 5th ed. (London: Marshall Pickering, 1991), 262.

22. Elliott, *Apocryphal New Testament*, 677.

23. J. M. Robinson, ed., *The Nag Hammadi Library in English* (San Francisco: Harper & Row, 1988), 249–50.

24. Elliott, *Apocryphal New Testament*, 75–76.

25. J. D. Crossan, *The Historical Jesus: The Life of a Mediterranean Jewish Peasant* (San Francisco: HarperCollins, 1991).

26. J. P. Meier, *A Marginal Jew: Rethinking the Historical Jesus*, ABRL (Garden City, NY: Doubleday, 1991).

27. Ibid., 140–41.

28. O. Hofius, "Unknown Sayings of Jesus," in *The Gospel and the Gospels*, ed. P. Stuhlmacher (Grand Rapids: Eerdmans, 1991), 357.

29. Ibid., 355–57.

30. Harrison, *Introduction to the New Testament*, 121–22.

31. Bruce, *The Books and the Parchments*, 261.

32. Origen *First Homily on Luke*, commenting on 1:1; quoted from Harrison, *Introduction to the New Testament*, 122.

33. This list is adapted from Patterson, "Apocrypha," *ABD*, 1:295–96.

34. Ibid., 1:296.

35. See J. D. Crossan, *The Cross That Spoke: The Origins of the Passion Narrative* (San Francisco: Harper & Row, 1988).

36. Harrison, *Introduction to the New Testament*, 122–23.

37. Bruce, *The Books and the Parchments*, 260–61.

38. Patterson, "Apocrypha," *ABD*, 1:296.

Chapter 11: *Transmission of the Old Testament*

1. For a good description of common writing materials, see E. Würthwein, *The Text of the Old Testament*, trans. E. F. Rhodes (Grand Rapids: Eerdmans, 1979), 6–11.

2. E. Würthwein offers another plausible reason as to why there are so few older manuscripts: "Jewish accounts in the Mishna and the Babylonian Talmud imply that although manuscripts of the Bible in the old script were still circulating in the first two centuries of the Christian era, they were ascribed an inferior degree of holiness—they did not 'defile the hands' levitically as did scrolls written in the square script" (*The Text of the Old Testament*, 5).

3. Ibid., 4.

4. W. F. Albright, *The Archaeology of Palestine*, rev. ed. (Harmondsworth, Middlesex: Penguin, 1960), 149–50; F. M. Cross, "The Oldest Manuscripts from Qumran," *JBL* 74 (1955): 147–72 reprinted in *QHBT*, 147–76; F. M. Cross, "The Development of the Jewish Scripts," in *BANE*, 133–202.

5. F. F. Bruce claims that the background of this example is "an old moral tale of an infidel father who had the inscription '*God is Nowhere*' hung in his house and invited his little daughter to read it; she spelt it out, '*God is Now Here*.'" *The Books and the Parchments*, 5th ed. (London: Marshall Pickering, 1991), 167.

6. See וַיִּשְׁפְּכֵם (*wayyišp̄ᵉkēm*, "and he poured them out," Amos 5:8); וְלֹא־תֵשְׁבוּ בָם (*wᵉlōʾ-tēšᵉbû bām*, "but you will not live in *them*," Amos 5:11); כֻּלָּם (*kullām*, "all of *them*," Amos 9:1).

7. F. I. Andersen and D. N. Freedman, *Amos: A New Translation with Introduction and Commentary*, AB 24A (New York: Doubleday, 1989), 577–78; J. L. Mays, *Amos: A Commentary*, OTL (Philadelphia: Westminster, 1969), 120–21; S. M. Paul, *Amos: A Commentary on the Book of Amos*, Hermeneia (Minneapolis: Fortress, 1991), 218–19.

8. E. Tov, "The Text of the Old Testament," in *The World of the Bible*, ed. A. S. van der Woude, trans. S. Woudstra (Grand Rapids: Eerdmans, 1986), 160. See also Sir. 38:24–39:15.

9. I. Epstein, ed., *The Babylonian Talmud* (London: Soncino, 1935), *Seder Nashim*, 4:144.

10. E. Sellin, *Introduction to the Old Testament* (Nashville: Abingdon, 1968), 492.

11. Bruce, *The Books and the Parchments*, 5.

12. P. de Lagarde, *Anmerkungen zur griechischen Übersetzung der Proverbien* (Leipzig: Brockhaus, 1863), 3–4.

13. P. Kahle, "Untersuchungen zur Geschichte des Pentateuchtextes," *Theologische Studien und Kritiken* 38 (1915): 399–439.

14. W. F. Albright, "New Light on Early Recensions of the Hebrew Bible," *BASOR* 140 (1955): 27–33; F. M. Cross, *The Ancient Library of Qumran and Modern Biblical Studies*, rev. ed. (reprint, Grand Rapids: Baker, 1980), 188–94; F. M. Cross, "The History of the Biblical Text in the Light of Discoveries in the Judean Desert," *HTR* 57 (1964): 218–99; F. M. Cross, "The Contribution of the Qumran Discoveries to the Study of the Biblical Text," *IEJ* 16 (1966): 81–95.

15. Cross, "Contribution of the Qumran Discoveries," 81–95, reprinted in *QHBT*, 278–92.

16. B. K. Waltke, *Prolegomena to the Samaritan Pentateuch* (Ph.D. diss., Harvard University, 1965); S. Talmon, "The Textual Study of the Bible—A New Outlook," in *Qumran and the History of the Biblical Text*, ed. F. M. Cross and S. Talmon (Cam-

bridge, MA: Harvard University Press, 1975), 321–400; E. Tov, *The Text-Critical Use of the Septuagint in Biblical Research* (Jerusalem: Simor, 1981); E. Tov, "A Modern Textual Outlook Based on the Qumran Scrolls," *HUCA* 53 (1982): 11–27.

17. Tov, *Text-Critical Use of the Septuagint*, 274.

18. E. Tov, *Groups of Biblical Texts Found at Qumran*, forthcoming; E. Tov, *Textual Criticism of the Hebrew Bible* (Minneapolis: Fortress; Assen/Maastricht: Van Gorcum, 1992), 114.

19. See F. M. Cross and D. N. Freedman, *Early Hebrew Orthography: A Study of the Epigraphic Evidence*, AOS 36 (New Haven, CT: American Oriental Society, 1952), 45–60, 65–70.

20. To date, the earliest manuscript containing full vocalization is the Cairo Manuscript of the Prophets, dated to A.D. 895.

21. D. N. Freedman, "The Massoretic Text and the Qumran Scrolls: A Study in Orthography," *Textus* 2 (1962): 87–102, reprinted in *QHBT*, 196–211.

22. Even as late as Codex Reuchlinianus (A.D. 1105) another pointing system (not Tiberian) was used. Scholars disagree as to whether it was pre-Masoretic (A. Sperber, *Codex Reuchlinianus with a General Introduction: Masoretic Hebrew* [Corpus Hebraicorum Medii Aevi, 2/1; Copenhagen: E. Munksgaard, 1956], Introduction), post-Masoretic (S. Morag, "The Vocalization of Codex Reuchlinianus: Is the 'Pre-Masoretic' Bible Pre-Masoretic?" *JSS* 4 [1959]: 229, 237), or a Tiberian pointing system not accepted by the Masoretes (M. H. Goshen-Gottstein, "The Rise of the Tiberian Bible Text," in *Biblical and Other Studies*, ed. A. Altmann [Cambridge: Harvard University Press, 1963], 113–14; Würthwein, *Text of the Old Testament*, 25 n. 36).

23. See F. G. Kenyon, *Our Bible and the Ancient Manuscripts*, rev. A. W. Adams (New York: Harper & Brothers, 1958), 78–79; S. Davidson, *Introduction to the Old Testament* (Edinburgh: T & T Clark, 1856), 89.

24. See T.B. *Masseketot Sopherim* (mid-eighth-century tractate of the Talmud), which gives detailed instructions for copying biblical manuscripts (A. Cohen, ed., *The Minor Tractates of the Talmud*, 2 vols. [London: Soncino, 1965], 1:211–324).

25. Würthwein, *Text of the Old Testament*, 21.

26. H. W. Robinson, "The Hebrew Bible," in *The Bible in Its Ancient and English Versions*, 2d ed. (London: Oxford University Press, 1954), 29.

27. S. Grayzel, *History of the Jews*, rev. ed. (Philadelphia: Jewish Publication Society, 1968), 248–49; M. L. Margolis and A. Marx, *A History of the Jewish People* (Philadelphia: Jewish Publication Society of America, 1934), 266.

28. M. H. Goshen-Gottstein, "The Rise of the Tiberian Bible Text," in *Biblical and Other Studies*, ed. A. Altmann (Cambridge, MA: Harvard University Press, 1963), 112. Würthwein notes: "This close relationship is also attested by Mishael, who mentions more than four hundred instances where Ben Asher and Ben Naphtali stand in agreement, apparently against other Masoretes" (*Text of the Old Testament*, 25).

29. E. Würthwein, *Text of the Old Testament*, 24; I. Yeivin, *Introduction to the Tiberian Masorah*, trans. and ed. E. J. Revell, SBLMasS 5 (Missoula, MT: Scholars Press, 1980), 142–43.

30. Ten in the Pentateuch: Gen. 16:5; 18:9; 19:33; 33:4; 37:12; Num. 3:39; 9:10; 21:30; 29:15; Deut. 29:28. Four in the Prophets: 2 Sam. 19:20; Isa. 44:9; Ezek. 41:20; 46:22. One in the Writings: Ps. 27:13. See Tov, "Text of the Old Testament," 161; Würthwein, *Text of the Old Testament*, 17; R. Butin, *The Ten Nequdoth of the Torah* (New York: KTAV, 1969); Yeivin, *Masorah*, 44–46.

31. C. D. Ginsburg, *Introduction to the Massoretico-Critical Edition of the Hebrew Bible* (reprint, New York: KTAV, 1966), 318–21; S. Lieberman, *Hellenism in Jewish Palestine*, 2d ed. (New York: Jewish Theological Seminary of America, 1962), 43–46.

32. Yeivin, *Masorah*, 45.

33. Ibid., 46.

34. The great Jewish expositor Rashi (1040–1105) argued: "Because of the honour of Moses was the *Nun* written so as to alter the name. The *Nun*, however, is suspended to tell thee that it is not Manasseh,

but Moses" (Ginsburg, *Introduction*, 336). See also Yeivin, *Masorah*, 47; Würthwein, *Text of the Old Testament*, 20; Tov, *Textual Criticism*, 57; T.B. *Baba Batra* 109b.

35. As often as 848 to 1,566 times depending on the manuscript. See Tov, *Textual Criticism*, 60–63; Tov, "Text of the Old Testament," 162; Yeivin, *Masorah*, 52–59; Würthwein, *Text of the Old Testament*, 17–18.

36. S. Jellicoe, *The Septuagint and Modern Study* (Oxford: Clarendon, 1968), 131, 272.

37. I. Hilberg, *Sancti Eusebii Hieronymi Epistulae*, Part 1: Epistles 1–70 (Leipzig: Tempsky, 1910), 219.

38. G. I. Williamson, *The Westminster Confession of Faith for Study Classes* (Grand Rapids: Baker, 1964), 174.

39. Robinson, "The Hebrew Bible," 29.

40. Würthwein, *Text of the Old Testament*, 39.

41. E. R. Brotzman, *Old Testament Textual Criticism* (Grand Rapids: Baker, 1994), 47; Ginsburg, *Introduction*, 25.

42. For a good explanation of this development see S. Talmon, "The Old Testament Text," in *CHB*, 1:159–99; and B. K. Waltke, "The Textual Criticism of the Old Testament," in *Biblical Criticism: Historical, Literary, and Textual*, by R. K. Harrison et al. (Grand Rapids: Zondervan, 1978), 48–59.

43. P. K. McCarter, *Textual Criticism: Recovering the Text of the Hebrew Bible*, OTG (Philadelphia: Fortress, 1986), 18.

44. B. K. Waltke, "Old Testament Textual Criticism," in *Foundations for Biblical Interpretation*, ed. D. S. Dockery, K. A. Matthews, and R. Sloan (Nashville: Broadman, 1994), 157.

45. Talmon, "The Old Testament Text," in *CHB*, 1:162.

46. Sometimes versification in the Hebrew text differs from the English translation; these differences are indicated as ET.

47. McCarter, *Textual Criticism*, 72.

48. See McCarter for an example of this principle (*Textual Criticism*, 65).

Chapter 12: *Sources for Old Testament Textual Criticism*

1. *The Daily Telegraph*, Friday, June 20, 1986; G. Barkay, *Ketef Hinnom: A Treasure Facing Jerusalem's Walls* (Jerusalem: Israel Museum, 1986), 29–34.

2. See 2 Kings 17 and Josephus (*Ant.* 9.14.3 §§288–91; 11.7.2 §§302–3).

3. J. MacDonald, *Theology of the Samaritans* (Philadelphia: Westminster, 1964), 15-21; R. T. Anderson, "Samaritans," *ISBE*, 4:307.

4. R. T. Anderson argues that the Samaritans were already separated as early as the fifth century B.C. since a letter among the Elephantine Papyri requests help for the building of a temple from both the Samaritan and the Jewish priests (CAP, 30) ("Samaritan Pentateuch," *ABD*, 5:941). F. M. Cross argues that the final break took place in the Hasmonean period (169–37 B.C.) because he believes that the Samaritan script was derived from the archaizing of the Old Hebrew script of the Hasmonean period (*The Ancient Library of Qumran and Modern Biblical Studies*, 2d ed. [Grand Rapids: Baker, 1961], 34).

5. R. W. Klein claims about sixteen hundred correlations (*Textual Criticism of the Old Testament: The Septuagint after Qumran*, GBS, OTG [Philadelphia: Fortress, 1974], 17), whereas E. Würthwein counts approximately nineteen hundred (*The Text of the Old Testament: An Introduction to the Biblia Hebraica*, trans. E. F. Rhodes [Grand Rapids: Eerdmans, 1979], 43).

6. In the Masoretic Text, Exodus 20:8 begins with זָכוֹר (*zākôr*, "to remember") and Deuteronomy 5:12 with שָׁמוֹר (*šāmôr*, "to observe" or "to keep"), whereas the Samaritan Pentateuch reads שָׁמוֹר *(šāmôr)* in both places. It is also common for the Samaritan Pentateuch to include conflated readings in the case of parallel passages; e.g., in Exodus 18:24 the parallel verses from Deuteronomy 1:9–18 are included.

7. W. F. Albright, "A Biblical Fragment from the Maccabaean Age: The Nash Papyrus," *JBL* 56 (1937): 145–76.

8. P. Kahle, *Die hebräischen Handschriften aus der Höhle* (Stuttgart: Kohlhammer, 1951), 5–6.

9. M. Greenberg, "The Stabilization of the Text of the Hebrew Bible Revised in the Light of the Biblical Materials from the Judean Desert," *JAOS* 76 (1956): 157–67; reprinted in *Canon and Masorah of the Hebrew Bible: An Introductory Reader*, ed. S. Z. Leiman, The Library of Biblical

Studies (New York: KTAV, 1974), 198–326.

10. See "Masada," *Baker Encyclopedia of the Bible,* ed. W.A. Elwell (Grand Rapids: Baker, 1988), 2:1412–14.

11. Y. Aharoni, "Expedition B," *IEJ* 11 (1961): 11–24 (esp. pp. 22–23 and plate 11); *Illustrated London News,* February 20, 1960, p. 230 (photograph); *The Times* (London) February 16, 1960 (= two phylactery fragments, Exod. 13:2–10, 11–16).

12. For an interesting history of the Cairo Geniza, see P. Kahle, *The Cairo Geniza,* 2d ed. (New York: Praeger, 1960), 3–13.

13. Ibid., 4.

14. Ibid., 13.

15. Würthwein, *Text of the Old Testament,* 34.

16. C. D. Ginsburg dates this manuscript much earlier, about 820–850 (*Introduction to the Massoretico-Critical Edition of the Hebrew Bible* [New York: KTAV, 1966], 469).

17. The colophon states: "This codex, the whole of the Holy Scriptures, was written and completed with pointing and Masora and carefully corrected in the Metropolis of Egypt [Cairo]. It was completed (a) in the month of Siwan of the year 4770 of the Creation of the world. (b) This is the year 1444 of the Exile of King Jehoiakin [*sic*]. (c) This is the year (1)319 of the Greek Reign, according to the reckoning of the Seleucid era and the Cessation of Prophecy. (d) This is the year 940 after the destruction of the second Temple. (e) This is the year 399 of the Reign of the Small Horn [cf. Dan. 8:9; Islam is intended]." (Würthwein, *Text of the Old Testament,* 168.)

18. Ibid.

19. B. K. Waltke, "The Textual Criticism of the Old Testament," in R. K. Harrison, *Biblical Criticism: Historical, Literary, and Textual* (Grand Rapids: Zondervan, 1978), 47–65.

20. S. Jellicoe, *The Septuagint and Modern Study* (Oxford: Clarendon, 1968), 29–58; S. Jellicoe, ed., *Studies in the Septuagint: Origins, Recensions, and Interpretations* (New York: KTAV Publishing House, 1974), esp. 158–224; R. J. H. Shutt, "Letter of Aristeas," in *The Old Testament Pseudepigrapha,* ed. J. H. Charlesworth, 2 vols.

(Garden City, NY: Doubleday, 1983–85), 2:7–34.

21. F. F. Bruce, *The Books and the Parchments,* 5th ed. (London: Marshall Pickering, 1991), 136.

22. Klein, *Textual Criticism,* 1–2.

23. B. M. Metzger, ed., *The Apocrypha of the Old Testament: Revised Standard Version, The Oxford Annotated Apocrypha* (New York: Oxford University Press, 1965), 129.

24. Bruce, *The Books and the Parchments,* 137.

25. Würthwein, *Text of the Old Testament,* 49.

26. R. N. Soulen, *Handbook of Biblical Criticism,* 2d ed. (Atlanta: John Knox, 1981), 208.

27. F. G. Kenyon, *Handbook to the Textual Criticism of the New Testament,* 2d ed. (London Macmillan, 1912), 77. See also J. H. Ropes, *The Text of Acts,* vol. 3 of *The Beginnings of Christianity,* part 1, *The Acts of the Apostles,* ed. F. J. Foakes Jackson and K. Lake (London: Macmillan, 1926), xxxi.

28. For the specific passages see H. B. Swete, *An Introduction to the Old Testament in Greek* (New York: KTAV, 1968), 129–30.

29. F. G. Kenyon, *Our Bible and the Ancient Manuscripts,* 5th ed., rev. A. W. Adams (New York: Harper, 1958), 192.

30. Ropes, *Text of Acts,* xlviii.

31. See D. Barthélemy, "Les devanciers d'Aquila," *VTSup* 10 (1963): 130.

32. See Jellicoe, *Septuagint and Modern Study,* 81, and Klein, *Textual Criticism,* 6.

33. Jellicoe, *Septuagint and Modern Study,* 77.

34. Klein, *Textual Criticism,* 6.

35. See J. Reider, *An Index to Aquila,* completed and revised by N. Turner, *VTSup* 12 (Leiden: E. J. Brill, 1966).

36. Jellicoe, *Septuagint and Modern Study,* 79.

37. Irenaeus *Haer.* 3.21.i, according to Eusebius, *HE* 5.8, 10. Jerome claims that he was an Ebionite (a Jewish-Christian sect) (*De viris illustribus* 54). Jellicoe further explains: "It is more probable that he was a Jew of the Dispersion who for a time became loosely attached to Christianity (hence the origin of the Ebionite tradition) but whose Jewish nurture and training, too strong to be permanently overcome, finally brought him back to his native faith" (*Septuagint and Modern Study,* 83–84).

38. Bruce, *The Books and the Parchments,* 143.

39. F. Field quotes over one hundred, most of which are technical terms (*Origenis Hexaplorum quae supersunt; sive Veterum Interpretum Graecorum in totum Vetus Testamentum Fragmenta* [Oxford: Clarendon, 1875], Prolegomena, xl–xli).

40. Kahle, *Cairo Geniza*, 254.

41. L. J. Greenspoon, "Theodotion, Theodotion's Version," *ABD*, 6:448.

42. The original Septuagint form of Daniel appears in only two manuscripts: Cursive 87 in the Chigi Library in Rome (ninth or eleventh century) and one papyrus codex in the Chester Beatty collection (third century).

43. L. J. Greenspoon, "Symmachus, Symmachus's Version," *ABD*, 6:251.

44. Jerome, *De viris illustribus* 54; *Commentariorum in Habacuc libri II* 3.13; *Praefatio in Job*; Eusebius *HE* 6.17. See H. J. Schoeps, *Ausfrühchristlicher Zeit: Religionsgeschichtliche Untersuchungen* (Tübingen: Mohr, 1950), 82–119. According to Epiphanius, Symmachus was a Samaritan converted to Judaism (*De mensuris et Ponderibus* 16–17).

45. Jerome *Praefatio in Amos* 3.11. See Swete, *Introduction*, 50–51.

46. Greenspoon, "Symmachus, Symmachus's Version," 6:251.

47. Jellicoe, *Septuagint and Modern Study*, 99; Klein, *Textual Criticism*, 6.

48. Jellicoe, *Septuagint and Modern Study*, 100.

49. Bruce, *The Books and the Parchments*, 145.

50. S. P. Brock, "Origen's Aims as a Text Critic of the Old Testament," *Studia Patristica* 10 (1970): 215–18; Würthwein, *Text of the Old Testament*, 55. Origen recognized that the Hebrew text he used disagreed with the common Jewish text but attributed these differences to deteriorization caused by the carelessness of the copyists. He said in his commentary on Matthew: "Great differences have arisen in the transcripts, from the carelessness of some of the scribes, or from the recklessness of some persons, or from those who made additions to the text or omissions from it, as they thought fit. With God's help we were able to repair the disagreement in the copies of the Old Testament on the basis of the other versions. We judged what was doubtful in the Septuagint (on account of disagreement of the codices) according to the rest of the versions, and retained what was in agreement with them" (Kahle, *Cairo Geniza*, 240).

51. Origen, *Origen to Africanus* 5 (quoted from F. Crombie, "The Writings of Origen," in *Ante-Nicene Christian Library: Translations of the Writings of the Fathers down to A.D. 325*, ed. A. Roberts and J. Donaldson [Grand Rapids: Eerdmans, 1991], 4:387); see also D. C. Parker, "Hexapla of Origen, The," *ABD*, 3:188–89.

52. Würthwein, *Text of the Old Testament*, 57; Parker, "Hexapla of Origen," 3:189.

53. Klein, *Textual Criticism*, 8.

54. See W. Baars, *New Syro-Hexaplaric Texts Edited, Commented upon and Compared with the Septuagint* (Leiden: E. J. Brill, 1968).

55. Philo *De Migratione Abrahami* 16 §§89–90; see also: R. M. Wilson, "Philo Judaeus," *ISBE*, 3:847–49.

56. Kahle, *Cairo Geniza*, 248–49; P. Katz, *Philo's Bible: The Aberrant Text of Bible Quotations in Some Philonic Writings and Its Place in the Textual History of the Greek Bible* (Cambridge: Cambridge University Press, 1950), 95–121.

57. B. H. Young, "Targum," *ISBE*, 4:728; D. M. Golomb, *Grammar of Targum Neofiti* (Chico, CA: Scholars Press, 1985), 5, 8.

58. For a good example of this see Young, "Targum," 4:731–32.

59. J. C. de Moor, "Systems of Writing and Nonbiblical Languages," in *Bible Handbook*, vol. 1, *The World of the Bible*, ed. A. S. van der Woude, trans. S. Woudstra (Grand Rapids: Eerdmans, 1986), 116. Würthwein suggests that the Aramaic translation was to be made orally in a worship service to separate it from the sacred text (*Text of the Old Testament*, 75).

60. K. Hruby, "La survivance de la langue hébraïque pendant la période post-exilienne," *Ecole des Langues Orientales Anciennes de l'Institut Catholique de Paris: Mémorial du Cinquantenaire 1914–1964*, Travaux de l'Institut Catholique de Paris 10 (Paris: Bloud and Gay, 1964), 109–20. The rabbis appear to understand this phrase as the first reference to the targums (see T.B. *Meg.* 18b; *Genesis Rabbah* 36.8).

61. Würthwein, *Text of the Old Testament*, 14.

62. Ibid.

421

63. P. Kahle, *Masoreten des Westens II* (Stuttgart: Kohlhammer, 1930), 3.

64. M. McNamara, ed., *The Aramaic Bible*, vol. 11, *The Isaiah Targum: Introduction, Transmission, Apparatus and Notes* (Wilmington, DE: Michael Glazier, 1987), 103–4.

Chapter 13: *Transmission of the New Testament*

1. B. M. Metzger, *The Text of the New Testament: Its Transmission, Corruption, and Restoration*, 3d enlarged ed. (New York and Oxford: Oxford University Press, 1992), 5 n. 2.

2. Compare Augustine's complaint (*On Christian Doctrine* 2.11.16) about overzealous translators of the Bible into Latin: "For in the early days of the faith every man who happened to get his hands upon a Greek manuscript, and who thought he had any knowledge, were it ever so little, of the two languages, ventured upon the work of translation" (P. Schaff, ed., *A Select Library of the Nicene and Post-Nicene Fathers of the Christian Church*, vol. 2, *St. Augustin's City of God and Christian Doctrine*, 1st series [Grand Rapids: Eerdmans; Edinburgh: T & T Clark, 1988], 540).

3. B. M. Metzger, *Manuscripts of the Greek Bible: An Introduction to Greek Palaeography* (New York and Oxford: Oxford University Press, 1981), 21.

4. Metzger, *Text of the New Testament*, 15. See also J. R. Harris, *New Testament Autographs*, Supplement to the *American Journal of Philology*, no. 12 (Baltimore: Isaac Friedenwald, 1882), 23.

5. Metzger, *Text of the New Testament*, 15 n. 2.

6. W. G. Kümmel, *Introduction to the New Testament*, trans. H. C. Kee, rev. ed. (Nashville: Abingdon), 30–31; D. A. Carson, D. J. Moo, and L. Morris, *An Introduction to the New Testament* (Grand Rapids: Zondervan, 1992), 191, 202, 250.

7. J. Finegan, *Encountering New Testament Manuscripts: A Working Introduction to Textual Criticism* (Grand Rapids: Eerdmans, 1974), 31.

8. C. H. Roberts and T. C. Skeat, *The Birth of the Codex* (London: Oxford University Press, 1983), 61.

9. P. Katz, "The Early Christians' Use of Codices Instead of Rolls," *JTS* 44 (1945): 63–65; Roberts and Skeat, *The Birth of the Codex*, 60.

10. J. Stevenson, *A New Eusebius. Documents Illustrating the History of the Church to A.D. 337*, rev. ed., rev. W. H. C. Frend (London: SPCK, 1987), 284–85.

11. Metzger, *Text of the New Testament*, 19. These rules appear in J.-P. Migne, PG 99:1739–40.

12. Metzger, *Manuscripts of the Greek Bible*, 24.

13. Ibid., 31.

14. Ibid., 24.

15. Ibid., 25.

16. Ibid., 25–26.

17. Ibid., 36–37.

18. Metzger, *Text of the New Testament*, 12.

19. P. Schaff and H. Wace, eds., *A Select Library of Nicene and Post-Nicene Fathers of the Christian Church*, vol. 14, *The Seven Ecumenical Councils*, 2d series, 14 vols. (Grand Rapids: Eerdmans; Edinburgh: T & T Clark, 1988), 396.

20. Metzger, *Text of the New Testament*, 23.

21. See the description of these notations in ibid., 24–25.

22. Ibid., 27.

23. Metzger, *Manuscripts of the Greek Bible*, 41 n. 106.

24. Metzger, *Text of the New Testament*, 30–31.

25. For these and other examples of colophons, see Metzger, *Manuscripts of the Greek Bible*, 20.

26. Metzger, *Text of the New Testament*, 18.

27. Ibid., 17–18.

28. Ibid., 211.

29. James Barr, *Comparative Philology and the Text of the Old Testament: With Additions and Corrections* (Winona Lake, IN: Eisenbrauns, 1987), 4.

30. Quoted in K. Aland and B. Aland, *The Text of the New Testament: An Introduction to the Critical Editions and to the Theory and Practice of Modern Textual Criticism*, trans. E. F. Rhodes (Grand Rapids: Eerdmans; Leiden: E. J. Brill, 1987), 187.

31. Metzger, *Text of the New Testament*, 76.

32. Ibid., 112.

33. Aland and Aland, *Text of the New Testament*, 9; Metzger, *Text of the New Testament*, 113.

34. Metzger, *Text of the New Testament*, 113.
35. Quoted in Aland and Aland, *Text of the New Testament*, 11.
36. Metzger, *Text of the New Testament*, 126.
37. Aland and Aland, *Text of the New Testament*, 19–20.
38. A more comprehensive collection of textual variants can be found in Nestle-Aland, *Novum Testamentum Graece*, 27th edition (NA[27]) than in the United Bible Societies' *Greek New Testament*, 4th edition (UBS[4]). The UBS edition presents only the most important textual variants but cites more supporting evidence for the variants it does present, and it indicates by letters A–D the editors' degree of certainty about the chosen reading. For an exhaustive collection of textual variants, see the volumes of the International Greek New Testament Project (IGNTP), only some of which have been published to date.
39. Metzger, *Text of the New Testament*, 195.
40. Ibid., 195–96.
41. B. M. Metzger, *A Textual Commentary on the Greek New Testament*, 2d ed. (Stuttgart: Deutsche Bibelgesellschaft, 1994).
42. F. F. Bruce, *The Books and the Parchments*, 5th ed. (London: Marshall Pickering, 1991), 169–70.
43. From Metzger, *Text of the New Testament*, 220.
44. Metzger, *Textual Commentary*, 532.
45. F. G. Kenyon, *The Story of the Bible*, 2d ed. (Grand Rapids: Eerdmans, 1967), 113.

Chapter 14: *Sources for New Testament Textual Criticism*

1. F. F. Bruce, *The New Testament Documents: Are They Reliable*, 7th ed. (London: Inter-Varsity, 1983), 16–17. The popular apologist Josh McDowell offers a useful summary of more sources in *Evidence That Demands a Verdict*, rev. ed. (San Bernardino, CA: Here's Life Publishers, 1979), 41–44.
2. B. M. Metzger, *The Text of the New Testament: Its Transmission, Corruption, and Restoration*, 3d ed. (New York and Oxford: Oxford University Press, 1992), 61.
3. See Metzger, *The Text of the New Testament*, 66.
4. Ibid., 68.

5. Quoted from P. Schaff, ed., *A Select Library of the Nicene and Post-Nicene Fathers of the Christian Church*, vol. 2, *St. Augustin's City of God and Christian Doctrine*, 1st series (Grand Rapids: Eerdmans; Edinburgh: T & T Clark, 1988), 540.

Chapter 15: *Early Versions*

1. As of May 1996, Wycliffe Bible translators were at work on or actively involved with 2,445 translations. (My thanks to Marilyn Henne from the Summer Institute of Linguistics, a branch of Wycliffe Bible Translators.)
2. F. F. Bruce, *The Books and the Parchments*, 5th ed. (London: Marshall Pickering, 1991), 181.
3. A. Vööbus, *Peschitta und Targumim des Pentateuchs: Neues Licht zur Frage der Herkunft der Peschitta aus dem altpalästinischen Targum* (Stockholm: Estonian Theological Society in Exile, 1958); L. Delekat, "Die syrolukianische Übersetzung des Buches Jesaja und das Postulat einer alttestamentlichen Vetus Syra," *ZAW* 69 (1957): 21–54; L. Delekat, "Die Peschitta zu Jesaja zwischen Targum und Septuaginta," *Bib* 38 (1957): 185–99, 321–35.
4. Cf. A. Vööbus, "Syriac Versions," *IDB-Sup*, 849.
5. E. Würthwein, *The Text of the Old Testament*, trans. E. F. Rhodes (Grand Rapids: Eerdmans, 1979), 80–81. See also P. Kahle, *The Cairo Geniza*, 2d ed. (Oxford: Basil Blackwell, 1959), 270–72.
6. K. Lake and J. E. L. Oulton, *Eusebius: The Ecclesiastical History*, 2 vols., LCL (Cambridge, MA: Harvard University Press, 1926–32), 1:463.
7. Bruce, *The Books and the Parchments*, 183.
8. Lake and Oulton, *Eusebius: Ecclesiastical History*, 1:397.
9. A third-century fragment of the Greek text of the Diatessaron was discovered in 1933 at a Roman fort at Dura-Europos on the Euphrates River.
10. Bruce, *The Books and the Parchments*, 183.
11. Würthwein, *The Text of the Old Testament*, 81. L. Delekat has argued that the Peshiṭta is based upon "oral traditions" that were first included in the Septuagint and later

became part of the Peshiṭta and targums ("Ein Septuagintatargum," *VT* 8 [1958]: 225–52).

12. Kahle, *Cairo Geniza*, 272.

13. Bruce, *The Books and the Parchments*, 185.

14. B. M. Metzger, *The Text of the New Testament: Its Transmission, Corruption, and Restoration*, 3d ed. (New York and Oxford: Oxford University Press, 1992), 68.

15. Bruce, *The Books and the Parchments*, 190.

16. Würthwein, *Text of the Old Testament*, 96; Metzger, *Text of the New Testament*, 79.

17. B. M. Metzger, *The Early Versions of the New Testament: Their Origin, Transmission, and Limitations* (Oxford: Clarendon, 1977), 106.

18. Würthwein, *Text of the Old Testament*, 96; B. J. Roberts, *The Old Testament Text and Versions: The Hebrew Text in Transmission and the History of Ancient Versions* (Cardiff: University of Wales Press, 1951), 235.

19. K. Aland and B. Aland, *The Text of the New Testament: An Introduction to the Critical Editions and to the Theory and Practice of Modern Textual Criticism*, trans. E. F. Rhodes, 2d ed. (Grand Rapids: Eerdmans, 1989), 200.

20. Metzger, *Text of the New Testament*, 79.

21. D. Ewert, *From Ancient Tablets to Modern Translations: A General Introduction to the Bible* (Grand Rapids: Zondervan, 1983), 169; Metzger, *Early Versions*, 135–36.

22. See Metzger, *Text of the New Testament*, 41–42.

23. Metzger, *Early Versions*, 121.

24. Ibid., 109; F. G. Kenyon, *Our Bible and the Ancient Manuscripts*, rev. A. W. Adams, 5th ed. (New York: Harper; London: Eyre & Spottiswoode, 1958), 234.

25. W. Grossouw, *The Coptic Versions of the Minor Prophets: A Contribution to the Study of the Septuagint*, Monumenta Biblica et Ecclesiastica 3 (Rome: Pontifical Biblical Institute, 1938), 111–12.

26. Metzger, *Early Versions*, 153; S. C. Malan, *Life and Times of S. Gregory the Illuminator; the Founder and Patron Saint of the Armenian Church* (London, Oxford, and Cambridge: Rivington, 1868), 66–103.

27. Lake and Oulton, *Eusebius: Ecclesiastical History*, 2:129.

28. Metzger, *Text of the New Testament*, 82–83.

29. Ibid., 82. J. M. Alexanian says that there are over 2,500 Armenian biblical manuscripts ("Versions, Ancient [Armenian]," *ABD*, 6:807).

30. Metzger, *Early Versions*, 161.

31. Würthwein, *Text of the Old Testament*, 99.

32. Ewert, *Ancient Tablets*, 170; Metzger, *Early Versions*, 162–64.

33. Metzger, *Early Versions*, 182.

34. J. N. Birdsall, "Versions, Ancient (Georgian)," *ABD*, 6:811.

35. Metzger, *Early Versions*, 184.

36. S. Jellicoe, *The Septuagint and Modern Study* (Oxford: Clarendon, 1968; reprint, Ann Arbor: Eisenbrauns, 1978), 261. See also R. P. Blake, "Georgian Theological Literature," *JTS* 26 (1924–25): 50–64.

37. Irenaeus *Haer.* 4.23.2 and Eusebius *HE* 2.1.13.

38. Metzger, *Early Versions*, 217. See also C. K. Barrett, *A Critical and Exegetical Commentary on the Acts of the Apostles*, 2 vols., ICC (T & T Clark, 1994), 424–25; I. H. Marshall, *The Acts of the Apostles: An Introduction and Commentary*, TNTC (Leicester, England: Inter-Varsity, 1980), 162; J. Munck, *The Acts of the Apostles: Introduction, Translation, and Notes*, AB (Garden City, NY: Doubleday, 1967), 78.

39. Rufinus *HE* 10.9; Socrates *HE* 1.19.

40. Gelasios of Cyzicus *HE* 3.9.

41. Metzger, *Early Versions*, 218.

42. F. Anfray, A. Caquot, and P. Nautin, "Une nouvelle inscription grècque d'Ézana, roi d'Axoum," *Journal des savants* (1970): 260–73.

43. *Topographia Christiana* 3 (J.-P. Migne, PG 88, col. 169).

44. Metzger, *Early Versions*, 224–25.

45. Jellicoe, *Septuagint and Modern Study*, 264–66; A. Vööbus, "Versions," *ISBE*, 4:981; Bruce, *The Books and the Parchments*, 206.

46. P. Schaff and H. Wace, eds., *A Select Library of Nicene and Post-Nicene Fathers of the Christian Church*, vol. 2, *Socrates, Sozomenus: Church Histories*, 2d series, 14 vols. (Grand Rapids: Eerdmans, 1957), 116.

47. Metzger, *Early Versions*, 258.

48. Bruce, *The Books and the Parchments*, 206–7.

49. E. Tov, "The Text of the Old Testament," in *The World of the Bible*, ed. A. S. van der

Woude (Grand Rapids: Eerdmans, 1986), 181.

50. B. J. Roberts, *The Old Testament Text and Versions: The Hebrew Text in Transition and the History of Ancient Versions* (Cardiff: University of Wales Press, 1957), 269.

51. Metzger, *Early Versions*, 267.

52. Ibid., 285.

53. Ibid., 289. See also *Acts of Scillitan Martyrs*, ed. J. A. Robinson (Cambridge: Cambridge University Press, 1891).

54. Metzger, *Early Versions*, 289. See also A. Vööbus, *Early Versions of the New Testament: Manuscript Studies* (Stockholm: Estonian Theological Society in Exile, 1954), 35–37.

55. Aland and Aland, *Text of the New Testament*, 186–87.

56. D. F. Wright, "Augustine of Hippo," *NIDCC*, 86.

57. Jellicoe, *Septuagint and Modern Study*, 249.

58. Vööbus, "Versions," *ISBE*, 4:970.

59. Metzger, *Text of the New Testament*, 72.

60. Metzger, *Early Versions*, 294, 461–64.

61. For more information on Old Latin manuscripts, see Würthwein, *Text of the Old Testament*, 87–90.

62. J. Ziegler, *Antike und moderne lateinische Psalmenübersetzungen*, SBAW 3 (1960): 5.

63. Ewert, *Ancient Tablets*, 176; Metzger, *Early Versions*, 315–16, 324–26.

64. Würthwein, *The Text of the Old Testament*, 87.

65. Ibid., 92. See also J. Barr, "St. Jerome's Appreciation of Hebrew," *BJRL* 49 (1966–67): 281–302.

66. Aland and Aland, *Text of the New Testament*, 191–92.

67. R. Schnucker, "Jerome," *NIDCC*, 528.

68. H. F. D. Sparks, "Jerome as Biblical Scholar," in *CHB*, 1:523.

69. Aland and Aland, *Text of the New Testament*, 192.

70. P. Schaff and H. Wace, eds., *A Select Library of Nicene and Post-Nicene Fathers of the Christian Church*, vol. 6, *St. Jerome: Letters and Select Works*, 2d series, 14 vols. (Grand Rapids: Eerdmans, 1983), 487–88.

71. Augustine, who represented a majority of people at the time, claimed that the Septuagint was inspired (*De civitate Dei* 18.43), but Jerome questioned its inspiration (*Praefatio in Pentateuchum, Biblia Sacra iuxta Latinam Vulgatam Versionem*, ed. A. Gasquet [Rome: Typis Polyglottis Vaticanis, 1926], 1.67; see also W. Schwarz, *Principles and Problems of Biblical Translation* [Cambridge: Cambridge University Press, 1955], 26–30).

72. Bruce, *The Books and the Parchments*, 196.

73. P. Schaff, *The Creeds of Christendom with a History and Critical Notes*, 6th ed., 3 vols. (Grand Rapids: Baker, 1931), 2:82.

74. Metzger, *Early Versions*, 375.

75. Bruce, *The Books and the Parchments*, 207.

76. D. C. Scavone, "Philostorgius," *NIDCC*, 778.

77. Metzger, *Early Versions*, 376.

78. Ibid., 376–77.

79. Ibid., 377.

80. H. B. Swete, *An Introduction to the Old Testament in Greek* (Cambridge: Cambridge University Press, 1902; reprint, Peabody, MA: Hendrickson, 1989), 117.

81. Vööbus, "Versions," *ISBE*, 4:982.

82. Ibid.

83. Metzger, *Early Versions*, 394.

84. Bruce, *The Books and the Parchments*, 208.

85. Metzger, *Early Versions*, 397.

86. Frédéric Delouche, ed., *Illustrated History of Europe: A Unique Portrait of Europe's Common History* (London: Weidenfeld and Nicolson, 1992), 107.

87. Jellicoe, *Septuagint and Modern Study*, 262.

88. Metzger, *Early Versions*, 403.

89. Swete, *Introduction*, 121; Jellicoe, *Septuagint and Modern Study*, 262.

90. Metzger, *Early Versions*, 401.

91. Ibid., 402.

92. Ibid., 403.

93. Metzger, *Text of the New Testament*, 85.

Chapter 16: *The First Printed Greek Bibles*

1. *EncBrit*, s.v. "Printing," 18:499.

2. Ibid.

3. D. Ewert claims that about one hundred and seventy calves were slaughtered to supply enough parchment (*From Ancient Tablets to Modern Translations: A General Introduction to the Bible* [Grand Rapids: Zondervan, 1983], 148).

4. B. M. Metzger, *The Text of the New Testament: Its Transmission, Corruption, and*

Restoration, 3d ed. (New York and Oxford: Oxford University Press, 1992), 95.

5. Ibid.

6. Ibid., 95–96.

7. F. G. Kenyon, *Our Bible and the Ancient Manuscripts*, 5th ed., rev. A. W. Adams (New York: Harper, 1958), 282.

8. Frédéric Delouche, ed., *Illustrated History of Europe: A Unique Portrait of Europe's Common History* (London: Weidenfeld and Nicolson, 1992), 185.

9. *Luther's Works*, vol. 31, *Career of the Reformer I*, ed. H. J. Grimm (Philadelphia: Muhlenberg, 1957), 28.

10. G. MacGregor, *The Bible in the Making* (Washington, DC: University Press of America, 1982), 111.

11. F. H. A. Scrivener, *A Plain Introduction to the Criticism of the New Testament*, ed. E. Miller, 4th ed., 2 vols. (London: George Bell, 1894), 2:176.

12. Ibid., 2:177.

13. Metzger, *Text of the New Testament*, 98.

14. Scrivener, *A Plain Introduction*, 2:182.

15. Ibid., 2:185.

16. Ibid., 2:184.

17. Metzger, *Text of the New Testament*, 102.

18. Ibid., 99.

19. Quoted from H. G. G. Herklost, *How Our Bible Came to Us* (New York: Oxford University Press, 1954), 24.

20. See J. R. Harris, *The Origin of the Leicester Codex of the New Testament* (London: C. J. Clay, 1887), 46–53; and C. H. Turner, *The Early Printed Editions of the Greek Testament* (Oxford: Clarendon, 1924), 23–24.

21. Metzger, *Text of the New Testament*, 101.

22. Ibid., 102.

23. Scrivener, *A Plain Introduction*, 2:188.

24. Ibid., 2:193–94.

25. J. Finegan, *Encountering New Testament Manuscripts: A Working Introduction to Textual Criticism* (Grand Rapids: Eerdmans, 1974), 58.

26. Metzger, *Text of the New Testament*, 106.

Chapter 17: *English Bibles prior to 1611*

1. G. Shepherd, "English Versions of the Scriptures before Wyclif," in *CHB*, 2:363.

2. F. F. Bruce, *History of the Bible in English: From the Earliest Versions*, 3d ed. (New York: Oxford University Press, 1978), x.

3. F. F. Bruce, *The Books and the Parchments*, 5th ed. (London: Marshall Pickering, 1991), 211.

4. Frédéric Delouche, ed., *Illustrated History of Europe: A Unique Portrait of Europe's Common History* (London: Weidenfeld and Nicolson, 1992), 88.

5. Bruce, *History of the Bible in English*, 2–3.

6. Shepherd, "English Versions" 2:370.

7. F. G. Kenyon, *Our Bible and the Ancient Manuscripts*, 5th ed. rev. A. W. Adams (New York: Harper, 1958), 266.

8. Ibid., 267.

9. Bruce, *History of the Bible in English*, 6. See also Shepherd, "English Versions," 2:372.

10. Shepherd, "English Versions," 2:371.

11. Ibid., 2:372.

12. R. G. Clouse, "Alcuin of York," *NIDCC*, 23.

13. Shepherd, "English Versions," 2:373.

14. Bruce, *History of the Bible in English*, 7.

15. J. Tiller, "Aelfric," *NIDCC*, 15.

16. J. I. Mombert, *English Versions of the Bible* (London: Samuel Bagster, 1907), 17.

17. G. MacGregor, *The Bible in the Making* (Washington, DC: University Press of America, 1982), 69.

18. Bruce, *History of the Bible in English*, 9.

19. Delouche, *Illustrated History of Europe*, 149.

20. Bruce, *History of the Bible in English*, 10.

21. Ibid., 11.

22. Delouche, *Illustrated History of Europe*, 172.

23. Ibid.

24. Ibid., 168.

25. Ibid.

26. W. A. Craigie, "The English Versions (to Wyclif)," in *The Bible in Its Ancient and English Versions*, ed. H. W. Robinson (Oxford: Clarendon, 1940), 138.

27. H. Hargreaves, "The Wycliffite Versions," in *CHB*, 2:388.

28. Kenyon, *Our Bible*, 275.

29. Ibid.

30. A. C. Partridge, *English Biblical Translation* (London: Andre Deutsch, 1973), 25.

31. Kenyon, *Our Bible*, 279.

32. B. F. Westcott, *A General View of the History of the English Bible*, 3d ed., rev. W. A. Wright (London and Cambridge: Macmillan, 1905), 22–23.

33. MacGregor, *The Bible in the Making*, 85.
34. Bruce, *History of the Bible in English*, 23.
35. Delouche, *Illustrated History of Europe*, 232.
36. MacGregor, *The Bible in the Making*, 83.
37. Bruce, *History of the Bible in English*, 22–23.
38. He sometimes used the alternate family name of Hutchins (ibid., 28).
39. *Foxe's Book of Martyrs*, ed. and abr. G. A. Williamson (London: Secker and Warburg, 1965), 121.
40. Bruce, *History of the Bible in English*, 30.
41. Lee's letter, written from Bordeaux on December 2, 1525, states: "Please your highness moreover to understand that I am certainly informed, as I passed in this country, that an Englishman your subject, at the solicitation and instance of Luther, with whom he is, hath translated the New Testament into English, and within a few days intendeth to arrive with the same imprinted in England. I need not to advertise your grace what infection and danger may ensue hereby if it be not withstanded. This is the next way to fulfil your realm with Lutherans. . . . All our forefathers, governors of the Church of England, hath with all diligence forbid and eschewed publication of English Bibles, as appeareth in constitutions provincial of the Church of England" (Westcott, *A General View of the History of the English Bible*, 34).
42. This cross was destroyed in 1643 by the Long Parliament, but today a plaque indicates where it once stood in the courtyard behind St. Paul's Cathedral, London.
43. MacGregor, *The Bible in the Making*, 85.
44. Ibid.
45. Bruce, *History of the Bible in English*, 38.
46. See J. F. Mozley, *William Tyndale* (Westport, CT: Greenwood, 1971), 147–50.
47. Bruce, *History of the Bible in English*, 50–52.
48. Bruce, *The Books and the Parchments*, 1.
49. *Foxe's Book of Martyrs*, 130.
50. N. H. Wallis, *The New Testament Translated by William Tyndale 1534* (Cambridge: Cambridge University Press, 1938), 34.
51. Bruce, *History of the Bible in English*, 34.
52. Ibid., 34–35.
53. S. L. Greenslade, "English Versions of the Bible, A.D. 1525–1611," in *CHB*, 3:146.
54. Bruce, *History of the Bible in English*, 40.
55. Bruce, *The Books and the Parchments*, 216.
56. Bruce, *History of the Bible in English*, 41.
57. D. Ewert, *From Ancient Tablets to Modern Translations: A General Introduction to the Bible* (Grand Rapids: Zondervan, 1983), 188–89.
58. Kenyon, *Our Bible*, 288.
59. Bruce, *History of the Bible in English*, 43.
60. Ibid., 44.
61. Kenyon, *Our Bible*, 288.
62. J. Isaacs, "The Sixteenth-Century English Versions," in *The Bible in Its Ancient and English Versions*, ed. H. W. Robinson (Oxford: Clarendon, 1940), 160.
63. Bruce, *History of the Bible in English*, 44.
64. Kenyon, *Our Bible*, 286.
65. J. F. Mozley, *Coverdale and His Bibles* (London: Lutterworth, 1953), 1–2.
66. Ibid., 3.
67. Bruce, *History of the Bible in English*, 57.
68. Mozley, *Coverdale and His Bibles*, 72.
69. Bruce, *History of the Bible in English*, 55–56.
70. Ibid., 59.
71. Ibid.
72. Greenslade, "English Versions of the Bible, 1525–1611," in *CHB*, 3:149.
73. Bruce, *History of the Bible in English*, 62.
74. Mozley, *Coverdale and His Bibles*, 125.
75. Ibid., 143.
76. Ibid., 167.
77. Greenslade, "English Versions of the Bible, 1525–1611," in *CHB*, 3:149–50.
78. Bruce, *The Books and the Parchments*, 216.
79. Bruce, *History of the Bible in English*, 66.
80. Kenyon, *Our Bible*, 290.
81. Mozley, *Coverdale and His Bibles*, 201.
82. Ibid., 262.
83. Kenyon, *Our Bible*, 295.
84. Mozley, *Coverdale and His Bibles*, 177.
85. Kenyon, *Our Bible*, 294.
86. G. MacGregor, *The Bible in the Making*, 93.
87. Bruce, *History of the Bible in English*, 71–72.
88. Ibid., 78.
89. Ibid.
90. Ibid., 79.
91. Kenyon, *Our Bible*, 298.
92. MacGregor, *The Bible in the Making*, 97.
93. Mozley, *Coverdale and His Bibles*, 293. See also Greenslade, "English Versions of the Bible, 1525–1611," in *CHB*, 3:153.
94. Bruce, *History of the Bible in English*, 84–85.
95. P. W. Petty, "Elizabeth I," *NIDCC*, 338.
96. Bruce, *History of the Bible in English*, 87.
97. MacGregor, *The Bible in the Making*, 98.

98. Bruce, *History of the Bible in English*, 86.
99. Ibid., 90.
100. Ibid., 89–90.
101. Greenslade, "English Versions of the Bible, 1525–1611," in *CHB*, 3:159–60.
102. Bruce, *History of the Bible in English*, 94.
103. Greenslade, "English Versions of the Bible, 1525–1611," in *CHB*, 3:160.
104. Kenyon, *Our Bible*, 301.
105. Bruce, *The Books and the Parchments*, 218.
106. MacGregor, *The Bible in the Making*, 101.
107. Greenslade, "English Versions of the Bible, 1525–1611," in *CHB*, 3:161.
108. W. Fulke, *The Text of the New Testament . . . translated out of the vulgar Latine by the Papists of the . . . Seminarie at Rhemes. . . .* (London: C. Barker, 1589).
109. Greenslade, "English Versions of the English Bible, 1525–1611," in *CHB*, 3:162.
110. Ibid.
111. Thomas Fuller, *The Church History of Britain*, ed. J. S. Brewer (Oxford: Oxford University Press, 1845), 5:76.
112. H. Pope, *English Versions of the Bible* (St. Louis and London: Herder, 1952), 301.
113. Greenslade, "English Versions of the English Bible, 1525–1611," in *CHB*, 3:162.

Chapter 18: *The Authorized Version of 1611 and Its Revisions*

1. G. MacGregor, *The Bible in the Making* (Washington, DC: University Press of America, 1982), 108; A. C. Partridge, *English Biblical Translation* (London: Andre Deutsch, 1973), 105.
2. Adapted from E. F. Rhodes and L. Lupas, eds., *The Translators to the Reader: The Original Preface to the King James Version of 1611 Revisited* (New York: American Bible Society, 1997), 16.
3. F. F. Bruce, *History of the Bible in English: From the Earliest Versions*, 3d ed. (New York: Oxford University Press, 1978), 96.
4. S. L. Greenslade, "English Versions of the Bible, A.D. 1525–1611," in *CHB*, 3:164; Bruce, *History of the Bible in English*, 96.
5. I. M. Price, *The Ancestry of Our English Bible*, 3d ed. (New York: Harper & Row, 1956), 268. His teacher, George Buchanan, "endeavoured to inculcate into his royal pupil, to whom he also imparted a taste, then unusual in princes, for languages, literature and theology" (G. MacGregor, *The Bible in the Making* [Washington, DC: University Press of America, 1982], 105).
6. F. F. Bruce, *The Books and the Parchments*, 5th ed. (London: Marshall Pickering, 1991), 219.
7. Ibid., 219–20.
8. E.g., the note for Exodus 32:28 in the Tyndale version (Protestant) claims, "The Pope's bull slayeth more than Aaron's calf." The heading to Acts 8 in the Douay-Rheims version (Roman Catholic) reads, "Simon Magnus more religious than the Protestants."
9. MacGregor, *The Bible in the Making*, 115.
10. Price, *The Ancestry of Our English Bible*, 270.
11. Rhodes and Lupas, *Translators to the Reader*, 18.
12. Ibid., 19; Bruce, *The Books and the Parchments*, 221.
13. S. Kubo and W. F. Specht, *So Many Versions? Twentieth-Century English Versions of the Bible*, rev. ed. (Grand Rapids: Zondervan, 1983), 302.
14. MacGregor, *The Bible in the Making*, 121.
15. J. P. Lewis, *The English Bible from KJV to NIV: A History and Evaluation*, 2d ed. (Grand Rapids: Baker, 1991), 41–42.
16. MacGregor, *The Bible in the Making*, 135.
17. Ibid., 136–37.
18. Ibid., 137.
19. Bruce, *History of the Bible in English*, 108.
20. Lewis, *The English Bible*, 37.
21. MacGregor, *The Bible in the Making*, 137.
22. L. Lupton, *History of the Geneva Bible*, 14 vols. (London: Olive Tree, 1966–82), 7:203, 211.
23. Kenyon, *Our Bible*, 305.
24. Nevertheless the first Bible printed in America (1782) was the text of the Authorized Version (C. Anderson, *The Annals of the English Bible*, abr. S. I. Prime [New York: Robert Carter and Bros., 1849], 486).
25. MacGregor, *The Bible in the Making*, 134.
26. Bruce, *History of the Bible in English*, 107.
27. L. A. Weigle, "English Versions since 1611," in *CHB*, 3:361.
28. Greenslade, "English Versions of the Bible, 1525–1611," in *CHB*, 3:168.
29. T. H. Darlow and H. F. Moule, *Historical Catalogue of Printed Editions of the English*

Bible, 1525–1961, ed. A. S. Herbert (London: The British and Foreign Bible Society, 1968), 1142.

30. Bruce, *History of the Bible in English*, 130.
31. Price, *Ancestry of Our English Bible*, 275–76.
32. Kubo and Specht, *So Many Versions*, 274.
33. MacGregor, *The Bible in the Making*, 151.
34. Lewis, *English Bible*, 53–54.
35. Ibid., 55.
36. Weigle, "English Versions since 1611," in *CHB*, 3:371.
37. A. C. Partridge, *English Biblical Translations* (London: Andre Deutsch, 1973), 173.
38. Bruce, *History of the Bible in English*, 139.
39. MacGregor, *The Bible in the Making*, 158–59.
40. Lewis, *English Bible*, 69–70; Kenyon, *Our Bible*, 313.
41. Weigle, "English Versions since 1611," in *CHB*, 3:372.
42. Bruce, *History of the Bible in English*, 148.
43. MacGregor, *The Bible in the Making*, 161.
44. Ibid., 162.
45. *The Times*, May 14, 1935.
46. J. W. Burgon, *The Revision Revised* (London: John Murray, 1883), 238.
47. MacGregor, *The Bible in the Making*, 164.
48. I. M. Price, *Ancestry of Our English Bible*, 304. See also Weigle, "English Versions since 1611," in *CHB*, 3:374.
49. C. W. Votaw, "The American Standard Edition of the Revised Bible," *The Biblical World* 17 (October 1901): 267.
50. Lewis, *English Bible*, 78.
51. C. E. W. Dobbs, "The Preferences of the American Revisers," *Homiletical Review* 25 (February 1893): 182.
52. Lewis, *English Bible*, 86.
53. See ibid., 96–104.
54. Ibid., 105.
55. H. G. May and B. M. Metzger, eds., *The Oxford Annotated Bible: Revised Standard Version* (New York: Oxford University Press, 1962), x.
56. B. M. Metzger, "The Revised Standard Version," in *The Word of God: A Guide to English Translations of the Bible*, ed. L. R. Bailey (Atlanta: John Knox, 1982), 33.
57. Bruce, *The Books and the Parchments*, 230.
58. F. C. Grant, "The Greek Text of the New Testament," in *An Introduction to the Revised Standard Version of the New Testament*, by Members of the Revision Committee, L. A. Weigle, Chairman (New York: Charles Nelson and Sons, 1946), 41.
59. Bruce, *History of the Bible in English*, 187.
60. Ibid., 196.
61. R. E. Brown, *The Gospel According to John (i–xii). Introduction, Translation, and Notes* (Garden City, NY: Doubleday, 1966), 13–14; D. A. Carson, *Exegetical Fallacies*, 2d ed. (Grand Rapids: Baker, 1996), 31; D. Moody, "The Translation of John 3:16 in the Revised Standard Version," *JBL* 72 (1953): 213–19; G. R. Beasley-Murray, *John*, WBC 36 (Waco: Word, 1987), 14.
62. Bruce, *History of the Bible in English*, 200.
63. Ibid., 203.
64. Kubo and Specht, *So Many Versions*, 222.
65. *New American Standard Bible* (Chicago: Moody Press, 1973), vi–vii.
66. "*New American Standard Bible*: Translation and Format Facts" (La Habra, CA: The Lockman Foundation, n.d.), 7.
67. Lewis, *English Bible*, 165.
68. *New American Standard Bible*, iii.
69. Lewis, *English Bible*, 167.
70. Ibid.
71. Kubo and Specht, *So Many Versions*, 230.
72. Ibid., 224.
73. *New American Standard Bible*, iii.
74. "Translation and Format Facts," 6.
75. See Lewis, *English Bible*, 183–85.
76. Ibid., 180–81.
77. C. E. Armerding and W. W. Gasque, "Some Significant Books of 1971: Part 1: The Bible as a Whole," *Christianity Today* 16 (February 18, 1972): 8.
78. *King James II Version of the Bible*, ed. J. Green (Byron Center, MI: Associated Publishers and Authors, 1971), x.
79. Ibid., ix.
80. Ibid., x.
81. Ibid.
82. R. G. Bratcher, "Old Wine in New Bottles," *Christianity Today* (October 8, 1971), 16.
83. Armerding and Gasque, "Some Significant Books of 1971," 9.
84. Ibid., 8.
85. Bratcher, "Old Wine in New Bottles," 16.
86. For a list of the translators see the advertisement in *Christianity Today* 26 (September 3, 1982): 60–61.
87. Kubo and Specht, *So Many Versions*, 307.
88. Lewis, *English Bible*, 333.
89. Ibid.

90. H. P. Scanlin, "The Majority Text Debate: Recent Developments," *The Bible Translator* 36 (January 1985): 136–40.

91. Luke 17:36 and John 16:16 include words not found in N and/or U, but the New King James Version inadvertently fails to note them.

92. S. K. Soderlund, "Review of *The New King James Bible: New Testament*," *Crux* 16 (June 1980): 32.

93. H. F. Peacock, "Review of *The New King James Bible New Testament*," *The Bible Translator* 31 (July 1980): 339.

94. Lewis, *English Bible*, 347.

95. *The Holy Bible Containing the Old and New Testaments: New Revised Standard Version* (Grand Rapids: Zondervan, 1990), x.

96. Ibid., xii.

97. Ibid., xi.

98. Lewis, *English Bible*, 380.

99. Ibid., 382.

100. P. K. McCarter, *1 Samuel: A New Translation with Introduction, Notes and Commentary*, AB 8 (New York: Doubleday, 1980), 199.

101. McCarter argues that this cannot be a secondary addition since it introduces completely new material; however, 1 Samuel 11:2 provides sufficient reason for this explanation to be added to the passage.

102. B. M. Metzger, "Some Comments on the New RSV Bible," in *Scribes and Scripture: New Testament Essays in Honor of J. Harold Greenlee*, ed. D. A. Black (Winona Lake, IN: Eisenbrauns, 1991), 112.

103. *New Revised Standard Version*, xii.

104. Lewis, *English Bible*, 406.

105. Personal communication with J. H. Walton.

Chapter 19: *Modern English Bibles up to 1950*

1. *The Twentieth Century New Testament: A Translation into Modern English* (New York and Chicago: Revell, 1904), iii.

2. K. W. Clark, "The Making of the Twentieth Century New Testament," *BJRL* 38 (1955–56): 71.

3. F. F. Bruce, *History of the Bible in English: From the Earliest Versions*, 3d ed. (New York: Oxford University Press, 1978), 156.

4. R. F. Weymouth, *The New Testament in Modern Speech*, 3d ed. (London: James Clarke; Boston: Pilgrim, 1909), vi.

5. Ibid., vii.

6. Ibid., vi.

7. S. Kubo and W. F. Specht, *So Many Versions? Twentieth-Century English Versions of the Bible*, rev. ed. (Grand Rapids: Zondervan, 1983), 35.

8. Bruce, *History of the Bible in English*, 167–68.

9. Ibid., 168.

10. Ibid., 170.

11. Kubo and Specht, *So Many Versions*, 35.

12. Bruce, *History of the Bible in English*, 171.

13. J. Moffatt, *A New Translation of the Bible, Containing the Old and New Testaments* (New York: Harper & Row, 1935), vi.

14. D. Ewert, *From Ancient Tablets to Modern Translations: A General Introduction to the Bible* (Grand Rapids: Zondervan, 1983), 217.

15. Bruce, *History of the Bible in English*, 171–72.

16. *The Holy Scriptures according to the Masoretic Text: A New Translation* (Philadelphia: Jewish Publication Society, 1917), vii.

17. E. J. Goodspeed, *The New Testament: An American Translation* (Chicago: University of Chicago Press, 1923), vi.

18. Goodspeed, *The New Testament*, v.

19. E. J. Goodspeed, *As I Remember* (New York: Harper, 1953), 162.

20. Ewert, *From Ancient Tablets to Modern Translations*, 218.

21. G. MacGregor, *The Bible in the Making* (Washington, DC: University Press of America, 1982), 172.

22. *The Old Testament: An American Translation* (Chicago: University of Chicago Press, 1927), v.

23. MacGregor, *The Bible in the Making*, 172.

24. Goodspeed, *The New Testament: An American Translation*, vii.

25. *The New American Bible: Translated from the Original Languages with Critical Use of All the Ancient Sources* (New York: Benziger, 1970), v.

26. Ibid., 169.

27. Ibid., 57.

28. Ibid., vi.

29. Ibid.

30. Ibid., vi.

31. Ibid.

32. Ibid., vii.

Chapter 20: *Modern Translations from 1950*

1. E. H. Robertson, *Makers of the English Bible* (Cambridge: Lutterworth, 1990), 206.
2. J. B. Phillips, *Letters to Young Churches: A Translation of the New Testament Epistles* (New York: Macmillan, 1953), ix.
3. Ibid., xii.
4. J. B. Phillips, *The New Testament in Modern English* (New York: Macmillan, 1958), vii.
5. Phillips, *Letters*, xii.
6. Phillips, *The New Testament*, xii.
7. F. F. Bruce, *History of the Bible in English: From the Earliest Versions*, 3d ed. (New York: Oxford University Press, 1978), 223.
8. Ibid., 225.
9. Robertson, *Makers of the English Bible*, 212.
10. *A New Translation of the Holy Scriptures according to the Masoretic Text: The Torah* (Philadelphia: Jewish Publication Society of America, 1962), i.
11. *The Torah*, i.
12. Ibid., iii.
13. G. Verkuyl, *The Berkeley Version of the New Testament* (Berkeley, CA: James J. Gillick, 1945), iii.
14. Bruce, *History of the Bible in English*, 229.
15. Ibid., 231.
16. T. R. Ashley, *The Book of Numbers*, NICOT (Grand Rapids: Eerdmans, 1993), 502–3; P. J. Budd, *Numbers*, WBC 5 (Waco: Word, 1984), 270; E. W. Davies, *Numbers*, NCBC (London: Marshall Pickering; Grand Rapids: Eerdmans, 1995), 272–74; M. Noth, *Numbers: A Commentary*, OTL (Philadelphia: Westminster, 1968), 192–93; G. J. Wenham, *Numbers: An Introduction and Commentary* (Leicester, England; Downers Grove, IL: InterVarsity, 1981), 178–79.
17. Bruce, *History of the Bible in English*, 231.
18. Ibid., 231–32.
19. These readings were changed in later revisions.
20. *The Holy Bible: The Berkeley Version in Modern English*, ed. G. Verkuyl (Grand Rapids: Zondervan, 1959), v.
21. Ibid.
22. C. A. Moore, *Esther: Introduction, Translation, and Notes*, AB 7B (New York: Doubleday, 1971), 3–4.
23. E. C. Colwell, "A Definite Rule for the Use of the Article in the Greek New Testament," *JBL* 52 (1933): 21.
24. M. J. Harris, *Jesus as God: The New Testament Use of Theos in Reference to Jesus* (Grand Rapids: Baker, 1992), 129.
25. A. A. MacIntosh, G. Stanton, and D. L. Frost, "The New English Bible Reviewed," *Theology* 74 (April 1971): 154–66.
26. J. P. Lewis, *The English Bible from KJV to NIV: A History and Evaluation*, 2d ed. (Grand Rapids: Baker, 1991), 130.
27. T. H. Robinson, "A New Translation of the English Bible," *The Bible Translator* 2 (1951): 168.
28. Lewis, *English Bible*, 134.
29. Bruce, *History of the Bible in English*, 251.
30. *The New English Bible* (Oxford: Oxford University Press; Cambridge: Cambridge University Press, 1970), v.
31. See also F. W. Danker, "The New English Bible," *Concordia Theological Monthly* 31 (1962): 324.
32. R. F. Bailey, *The Gospel of S. John. An Introductory Commentary* (London: Student Christian Movement Press, 1940), 217; C. H. Dodd, *Historical Tradition in the Fourth Gospel* (Cambridge: Cambridge University Press, 1963), 123–24 n. 2; F. C. Fenton, *The Gospel according to John in the Revised Standard Version: With Introduction and Commentary*, NCB (Oxford: Clarendon, 1970), 196–97.
33. R. E. Brown, *The Gospel according to John (xii–xxi): Introduction, Translation, and Notes*, AB 29A (Garden City, NY: Doubleday, 1970), 909–10; Bruce, *History of the Bible in English*, 241; G. D. Kilpatrick, "The Transmission of the New Testament and Its Reliability," *Journal of Transactions of the Victoria Institute* 89 (1957): 98–99; B. Lindars, *The Gospel of John*, NCB (London: Oliphants, 1972), 581–82.
34. G. D. Fee, *1 and 2 Timothy, Titus*, NIBC (Peabody, MA: Hendrickson, 1988), 279–82; D. Guthrie, *The Pastoral Epistles*, rev. ed., TNTC (Leicester: InterVarsity; Grand Rapids: Eerdmans, 1990), 175–76; A. T. Hanson, *The Pastoral Epistles* (Grand Rapids: Eerdmans; London: Marshall, Morgan & Scott, 1982), 151–52; W. Hendriksen, *I & II Timothy and Titus*, NTC (London: Banner of Truth Trust, 1972), 301–4.
35. Bruce, *History of the Bible in English*, 239.

36. *The Jerusalem Bible*, ed. A. Jones (Garden City, NY: Doubleday, 1966), v.
37. Lewis, *English Bible*, 238.
38. *The Living Bible* (Wheaton: Tyndale House, 1971), preface.
39. Ibid.
40. S. Kubo and W. F. Specht, *So Many Versions? Twentieth-Century English Versions of the Bible*, rev. ed. (Grand Rapids: Zondervan, 1983), 233.
41. *Living Bible*, preface.
42. Kubo and Specht, *So Many Versions*, 235.
43. *Living Bible*, preface.
44. Kubo and Specht, *So Many Versions*, 242.
45. G. E. Jones, "Another 'Readable' Bible, But Is It Any Better?" *U.S. News & World Report* 81 (December 20, 1976): 54; E. A. Nida, *Good News for Everyone* (Waco: Word, 1977), 115.
46. *Good News Bible* (New York: American Bible Society, 1976), preface.
47. Nida, of the American Bible Society, describes this translation principle as the "quality of a translation in which the message of the original text has been so transported into the receptor language that the RESPONSE of the RECEPTOR is essentially like that of the original receptors." (E. A. Nida and C. R. Taber, *The Theory and Practice of Translation* [Helps for Translators, vol. 8; Leiden: E. J. Brill, 1974], 200).
48. *Good News Bible*, foreword.
49. R. C. Fuller, "Today's Bible," *Scripture Bulletin* 7 (winter 1976–1977): 27–28.
50. F. F. Bruce, *The Books and the Parchments*, 5th ed. (London: Marshall Pickering, 1991), 249.
51. Kubo and Specht, *So Many Versions*, 191.
52. W. F. Stinespring, in *The Word of God: A Guide to English Versions of the Bible*, ed. L. R. Bailey (Atlanta: John Knox, 1982), 131.
53. Stanley E. Harwick and R. Laird Harris, "Do Evangelicals Need a New Translation?" *Christianity Today* 12 (September 27, 1968): 10–15; C. J. Youngblood, "The *New International Version* Translation Project: Its Conception and Implementation," *JETS* 21 (September 1978): 239–41.
54. Kubo and Specht, *So Many Versions*, 245.
55. *The Holy Bible: New International Version* (Grand Rapids: Zondervan, 1978), viii.
56. Ibid.
57. Lewis, *English Bible*, 324.
58. See argument by R. G. Bratcher on Ps. 16:10 in *The Word of God: A Guide to English Versions of the Bible*, ed. L. R. Bailey (Atlanta: John Knox, 1982), 155.
59. Kubo and Specht, *So Many Versions*, 272.
60. According to information found on the Internet: http://www.cbaonline.org/voice/a_bibles.htm.
61. Bratcher, in *The Word of God*, 152.
62. *The Revised English Bible* (Oxford: Oxford University Press; Cambridge: Cambridge University Press, 1989), vii.
63. Ibid., viii-ix.
64. Lewis, *English Bible*, 350.
65. Ibid., 351.
66. W. D. Davies and D. C. Allison, *A Critical and Exegetical Commentary on the Gospel according to Saint Matthew*, 3 vols., ICC (Edinburgh: T & T Clark, 1988), 1:613. See also U. Luz, *Matthew 1–7: A Commentary*, trans. W. C. Linss (Minneapolis: Augsburg/Fortress, 1989), 384–85.
67. Lewis, *English Bible*, 376.
68. E. H. Peterson, *The Message: The New Testament in Contemporary Language* (Colorado Springs, CO: NavPress, 1993), 7.
69. Ibid., 7.
70. Ibid., 6–7.
71. According to *CBA Marketplace*, http://www.cbaonline.org/voice/a_bibles.htm.
72. *Holy Bible: New Living Translation* (Wheaton, IL: Tyndale House, 1996), xli.
73. Ibid., xlii.
74. http://www.tyndale.com/nlt/faq/faq7.html.
75. *New Living Translation*, xlvi.
76. According to information found on the Internet: http://www.cbaonline.org/voice/a_bibles.htm.
77. *New English Translation Study Bible: The Net Bible* (Spokane, WA: Biblical Studies Press, 1996).

Chapter 21: Why So Many Translations?

1. F. C. Grant, *Translating the Bible* (Grenwich, CT: Seabury, 1961), 97.
2. See chap. 2, under "Special Revelation."
3. W. Barclay, *The New Testament: A New Translation*, vol. 1, *The Gospels and the Acts of the Apostles* (London and New York: Collins, 1968), 308.

General Index ....

Scripture Index ·························

Old Testament

Credits ······································

Every effort has been made to obtain permission for the use of illustrative material and to give proper attribution. Please notify the publisher of any inaccuracies so that the error can be corrected in subsequent printings.

Paul D. Wegner (Ph.D., King's College, University of London) is professor of Bible at Moody Bible Institute, Chicago, Illinois.